CHALLENGES
FACING
SPECIAL EDUCATION

Edited by

Edward L. Meyen, *University of Kansas*
Glenn A. Vergason, *Georgia State University*
Richard J. Whelan, *University of Kansas*

D1404933

LOVE PUBLISHING COMPANY®
Denver, Colorado 80222

Library of Congress Catalog Card Number 92-74810

Copyright © 1993 Love Publishing Company
Printed in the U.S.A.
ISBN 0-89108-229-8

Contents

Preface

THIS BOOK represents some exciting efforts in special education today. Compiled by the editorial board of *Focus on Exceptional Children*, the two sections consist of recent issues of *Focus*, carefully selected to meet the test of current relevance. These articles illustrate present and emerging challenges facing the special education profession now and in the future. The decisions we make in special education today clearly will influence special education in the future. We are not making future decisions in special education now; we are making current decisions that will have a profound impact upon future practices in special and general education.

All of the articles in the first section address major policy issues influencing special education practices today. They run the gamut from early childhood challenges to rethinking secondary school programs for students with mild disabilities. They include three articles about the importance of consultation and collaboration among special and general educators in providing special education and related services to students with disabilities. The challenges posed in bringing general and special education together again after so many years of being apart are great. Success is predicated upon including students with special needs in the new educational reform movements sweeping the country today and assessing instructional outcomes in terms of the efficacy of the process of achieving them. Students in special education must not be excluded from the exciting developments in the educational reform movement.

Ironically, upon examining the content of the major reforms in general education, it does not take a leap of intellect to find that most, if not all, of what is being described as new developments are rooted in special education practices from the past and the present. Because special educators developed these practices, we must not allow students with disabilities to be pushed aside under the guise that the reforms should be applied only to students without disabilities or those who are not at risk.

The articles in the second section are important as the profession moves into the next century of educating students in need of special education and related services. The article by Tom Skrtic, for example, questions the adequacy of the theoretical grounding of 20th-century special education practices. If the field is to respond adequately to the challenges of the 21st century, he argues, it must do more than change its practices; it must change the theoretical assumptions upon which traditional practices have been premised.

The article by Shinn and Hubbard addresses a knowledge and skill area that all teachers must have if they are going to function effectively within the education reform movement. How is one to determine if a student has achieved a specific outcome unless one can measure the student's performance in the curriculum provided as an instructional activity to achieve that outcome?

An emerging challenge is society's recognition that children at risk come in many varieties. Some students in our classrooms do not pay attention to teacher instructions or to the important events related to the learning going on around them. This inability to attend has a profound effect upon the student because of the knowledge and skills that are not learned and practiced. Clearly, a way has to be found in general and special education to accommodate students who have attention deficit problems.

Another group of students who have long been with us and now are finally receiving the attention they deserved for many years are those who come back into the educational setting after suffering traumatic brain injury. These students are puzzling in the sense that they often bear no physical marks of their injury but their learning styles and capacity to assimilate information have been affected dramatically by injury to the cerebral cortex. They do not fit the typical and well known categories of special education. They have different instructional problems requiring creative solutions. Their problems in learning do not stop when they leave the hospital setting. They present to school personnel different students educationally than they were before the injury occurred.

Other articles in this section review the challenges of educating students with severe and multiple disabilities within the local school setting and the home community, as contrasted to special schools that may be some distance from where a family resides. This challenge, of course, relates to including all children with disabilities in settings that accommodate students without disabilities. Within this group of students are increasing numbers with complex health problems. These children, described as medically fragile, need a full array of comprehensive services to maintain them in instructional environments. Services may include intermittent catheterization, availability of oxygen, and special methods for feeding. Their education must involve a team of professionals who will also address their health care needs. These children require a truly interdisciplinary approach as mandated by the individualized education program (IEP).

Another article in this section addresses depression in children and adolescents. Educators have assumed that children's aggression in classrooms reflects intentional violation of rules and attempts to challenge people in authority. We have failed to recognize that all too often this outward aggression masks severe depression and signals that the students are in need of professional help, often beyond that which special education personnel can provide. Again, serving these children requires an interdisciplinary team of special educators and mental health professionals.

Finally, professional educators are recognizing that students who have the potential to perform at the gifted level do not survive on their own in all instances. The concluding article points out that they need assistance and recognition of their needs from well trained special educators. We disregard these students at the expense of our society's future. They are indeed a challenge to be met by special and general educators.

We hope this book will stimulate ongoing program planning by our colleagues in special and general education. Special education today faces many challenges and will continue to do so. Over time we have recognized that students present to educators many complex needs. The simplicity of bygone days when special educators served only students with obvious disabilities is long past. Now we must become ever more proficient in recognizing new needs and more effective in responding to them.

Introduction

THROUGHOUT its history special education has shown a remarkable ability to meet challenges. In many ways the development of special education as a profession mirrors the mission of the field: to help individuals with disabilities overcome personal limitations. A major early challenge was in attaining professional status despite few trained professionals and, in some cases, no knowledge base for the proposed assessment strategies, interventions, and curricular or even organizational structures. In reflecting on the early history of the field, one gains the impression that special educators were risk-takers in two major areas: first, by believing that children and youth with disabilities, who at the time were prevented from benefiting from schooling as a matter of practice if not policy, could actually learn; and second, by strongly aspiring to gain a professional presence.

Initially public education decision-makers had to be convinced that the abilities of students with disabilities could be assessed and that interventions could be designed to enhance their progress toward effective citizenship. Then came the challenge of shaping public policy at the state and federal levels of government and, ultimately, the focus on equity in all aspects of life. Today the challenges largely involve achieving conditions essential to the quality of life all people deserve. No longer are special educators alone in their quest to bring about full citizenship for individuals with disabilities. Over the years, they have been joined by many advocacy groups. Some are dedicated to groups focusing on a specific disability, others have broader commitments, and some groups have missions that had not previously included the disability community.

Today the most important people are those with disabilities who are strong self-advocates. In meeting these challenges and thereby bringing about dramatic changes in the field, education and many other human service professions have matured in carrying out their responsibilities to the disability community.

Notwithstanding major strides, challenges remain. Some pertain to the needs of special populations, in particular children who until recently were seen only rarely in the school. Examples are children with AIDS, children of mothers who are prey to substance abuse, and infants and toddlers requiring special interventions.

For the most part, however, the challenges of today are coming from within the profession. Some of these relate to looking at what the profession has been espousing and offering new directions. Others involve resolving conflicts within the profession. Finally, major challenges stem from the dynamics of educational reform.

This book provides special educators a resource on contemporary and emerging challenges. Though the practices and programs discussed are generally considered sound and deserving of attention, the best way to implement these initiatives remains unclear. Also, some challenges are left over from previous decades, in need of today's technology and general knowledge base to be successful.

The selections have been grouped into two categories: contemporary challenges and emerging challenges. This sample of readings will help readers gain a perspective on the challenges confronting special education. As the field continues to mature, more internal challenges of current practices will arise as past practices are called into question. An indicator of a mature profession is its capacity for self-analysis and its ability to tolerate diverse views and challenges to what represents its core. Among the many views of the topics identified as challenges, we have chosen what we consider to be the most descriptive and representative.

CONTEMPORARY CHALLENGES

Public education in the United States is undergoing serious change. Many current reform initiatives are not directed specifically at restructuring, but most policymakers, media representatives, and the public in general believe schools must be restructured to result in a more efficient and effective system, a better product.

From the perspective of business, the outcome means more sophisticated workers who are better prepared to meet the demands placed on our workforce as it strives to position American businesses in international markets. Specifically, this means workers who have strong problem-solving skills, are able to apply higher-order thinking skills, have behaviors conducive to teamwork, and have strong work ethics. The overall assumption is that today's high school graduates fall short of these attributes and that school restructuring will make the difference.

Even though many educators take exception to the accusation that the declining performance of American students is related primarily to the organizational structure of the schools, most recognize that the traditional structure has to be reexamined. What the most appropriate form of restructuring is, or even how to go about it, is not clear. As a result, the process is occurring piecemeal and, like the general reform movement, is guided by the view that restructuring will produce a more able product.

Most of the reform initiatives are represented as benefiting all students. In reality, however, little attention is directed to the needs of students with disability, and these proposals are rarely challenged. Obviously, the promised reforms would be good for all students, assuming the necessary investment is forthcoming. For example, reducing dropout rates, ensuring that all students learn higher-order thinking skills, and preparing all students to meet world-class standards in math, science, English, history and geography would benefit all students, including students with disabilities.

Reference to *all* students, however, is made too often without proper consideration of the wide range of abilities *all* students demonstrate. As a result, special educators need to take seriously the references to *all* students, seek clarification, and work to obtain a commitment. Left unchecked, many reform initiatives will gain support on the pretense that they will benefit all students, without full disclosure of the additional costs involved in applying them beyond the most talented of students.

The major challenge is to ensure that efforts to restructure public education take into consideration the needs of students with disabilities. Historically, special education has used the organizational structure of the schools at the state and local levels to create the conditions necessary to offer and maintain special education programs. Without the involvement of special educators in the restructuring process, the conditions necessary to protect the rights of students with disabilities and to achieve equity on their behalf may wane. This is particularly likely to happen because many members of the profession are challenging the way the structure currently serves students with special needs. New conceptual models resulting from these efforts will not necessarily be part of the larger restructuring movement, as they tend to be generated through the special education community and communicated with the special education literature. Therefore, we must examine how these new conceptual changes may be integrated into the restructuring that is occurring in regular education. The challenge for the special education profession is twofold: first, to engage the profession in the discourse that will lead to the needed re-examination of how special education has been accommodated in the current structure of American education; and second, to interact more closely with those providing leadership in restructuring regular education.

Surrounding the challenge of restructuring are a number of other challenges familiar to special educators. These include several issues centering on infants and toddlers with disabilities and, to some extent, programming for children with disabilities in the early childhood range. Comprehensive programs for infants and toddlers with disabilities are still rare, even though the advantages of early intervention are now well known. This area of concern is shared with one of the goals of the America 2000 program: that all children come to school ready to learn. Most likely, however, this goal was generated without considering the implications for infants and toddlers with disabilities, for whom services currently are a patchwork at best. The challenge is to ensure the availability of comprehensive services for all young children with special needs so all children will in fact arrive at school ready to learn.

A complementary challenge, central to other challenges facing special education today *and* supported by the reform movement in regular education, is the need to prepare and involve parents as teachers. To date, evidence has shown that investing in parent education and providing the support necessary to assist parents in implementing and maintaining programs designed to enhance their child's development is fruitful. The costs associated with these programs represent an investment in the future. The challenge consists of convincing policymakers of the value of investing in programs that are developmental and preventive.

Past practices that require rethinking include programs at the secondary level. Historically, special education intervention approaches have been more successful at the elementary level than at grade levels for older students. Whether this is a consequence of the way middle and secondary schools are organized, the more recent nature of these programs, or merely a lack of attention is not clear. What is clear, however, is that developing effective special education programs at the secondary level, particularly those for students with mild disabilities, represents a major challenge.

Collaboration is evolving as a potentially effective approach to serving exceptional children. As such, it warrants the attention of regular and special educators alike. To yield maximum benefits, collaboration requires considerable training and a serious level of commitment by all participants.

EMERGING CHALLENGES

The complex challenges facing the field of special education for some time are compounded by a set of emerging challenges, the extent of which remains to be determined. Perhaps the greatest challenge facing the field is to respond adequately to changes in thought and belief that are taking place in the academic disciplines of the social sciences. As noted in the first article in this section, an unprecedented reconceptualization of the very nature of knowledge over the past thirty years has called the validity of social scientific knowledge into question. This has important implications for all professional fields, including special education, because the knowledge, skills, and practices of the professions are grounded in the theoretical knowledge of the social sciences.

Another emerging challenge facing the field is the fact that the outcomes-based accreditation policies being established in most states are in many ways underdeveloped for special education. They tend to emphasize exit outcomes for high-achieving students. Similarly, the indicators used are for the most part inappropriate for assessing programs for students with disabilities or their performance. The problem is not that the concept of outcomes is inappropriate for special education students. Rather, only limited attention has been directed to applying outcomes to accreditation practices that ensure quality programs for students with disabilities. The most significant challenge is being able to relate failure to attain specified outcomes to identified indicators so corrections can be made.

Although special education has a long history of employing the principles of outcomes-based education, outcomes-based accreditation is a new concept for special education as well as regular education. In view of this history, special educators need to be more involved in state-level efforts to establish outcomes-based accreditation systems to ensure appropriateness for *all* students.

Attention deficit disorder and traumatic brain injury have been with us a long time. Unfortunately, however, educators and other human service professionals have been slow to meet the needs of young people with these conditions. Because the number is relatively small compared to other types of disabilities, students with these disorders have been less visible and, therefore, have caused less concern to the profession. The prevalence of these conditions seems to be increasing, however, and effective advocacy by families of these children has resulted in more attention to development of proper interventions. For this population of students, the challenge is more than the design of interventions. It is also one of ensuring coordination with other agencies serving the students and the family and of providing effective transitional programs if the individual needs continued service after leaving formal education.

Schools have made progress in developing programs for students with severe disabilities, but the need for similar efforts in the home and the community represents a major challenge. Much of what has been learned from implementation and refinement of educational strategies can be translated into initiatives that will work in other settings. The challenge, in part, is determining who will provide the necessary leadership in non-school settings.

A related challenge is that of meeting the needs of students with complex health care problems, who are becoming increasingly common in the schools. In many cases, these children's health problems do not affect their cognitive abilities except that their access to education on a regular basis is often limited. The challenge becomes one of effectively accommodating the health condition while also providing an educational program that allows these students to achieve their potential.

Two other challenges that are emerging, yet have been present for some time, relate to students with depression and gifted students who are also disadvantaged. The only similarities between these groups is that their needs often go unattended and both groups probably are much larger than currently estimated. The challenge is to be more sensitive to their presence and increase efforts to meet their needs.

Special education as a profession set out to meet challenges. As the field encountered success, it created more challenges. For example, new groups of children emerged, requiring special consideration to assure access to quality education. Old practices failed to meet the demands of changing conditions. Continuing to change, regular education has altered the circumstances under which students with disabilities are served. Most important, changes in public attitudes and expectations have necessitated rethinking how to bring equity to education and to society in general for individuals with disabilities.

We have attempted in this book to distinguish between challenges that have been with the field and remain as contemporary challenges and those that, while known, are viewed as emerging challenges. In the future, the major challenge for special education may well be to determine if the field has a future as a separate professional entity. Although it is too early to speculate on the validity of this assertion, it is not too early to think about how the needs of all students can best be met rather than how a particular profession can best meet the needs of students with disabilities.

Some articles in *Challenges Facing Special Education* reflect the recent changes in the titles of the federal laws; others do not. However, the substance and intent of federal policies and laws have not been altered, and the included articles remain up-to-date and highly relevant.

Part One:
Contemporary Challenges

IN THIS SECTION of the book, we identify three central themes that reflect current challenges facing special and general educators:

1. The importance of identifying and providing services to preschool-aged children. Within the preschool designation, we include articles on transitions in early childhood education, the Missouri Project using parents as teachers, and policy implications of the infant and toddler legislation under Public Law 99–457.
2. Significant developments in the relationship between general and special educators within our school system. This theme addresses the importance of collaboration and consultation among colleagues in providing special education and related services for students with disabilities.
3. Programs that serve all school ages. This includes the significant manuscript by Zigmond on secondary school programs for students with learning disabilities.

Clearly, the profession has gone beyond past notions of finding permanent cures for students at risk because of disability. In many instances, the students' disabilities are lifelong conditions that will require accommodations not only through the formal education years but also through the years devoted to the world of work and indeed to retirement. In saying this, we do not imply that special education and related support services should be forever time-intensive and constant. Certainly, as students progress through the educational system, their needs will change both in terms of intensity and in the type of services required for them to adjust to and progress in learning experiences.

Many challenges face special educators today. These challenges, largely reflected in the articles included in this section, extend also to other challenges often expressed in terms of questions or issues. For example, has special education become such a parallel instructional service organization apart from general education that there is little communication in policy planning between the two? If the answer to this question is yes, the students served by each system obviously will become more and more isolated from one another. This challenge should require review of some of the key conceptual issues and perspectives involving special education, including a look at our history and the common foundations supporting general and special education. This reflective study

1

should take into account what has happened historically to children with disabilities in our public education system. One will find that these children have largely been excluded or, if allowed to remain in general education, have had to fend for themselves in regard to performance when exposed to a fixed curriculum and a fixed time in which to master it. So, to respond to contemporary challenges, one must recognize that the origin of these challenges is in past practices as well as ever-changing needs in response to society's expectations of the educational system.

Other ongoing concerns include the continuous, and often not too enlightening, debates and arguments regarding definitions of children with disabilities. Unfortunately, in these debates, professionals in our field have not really gone to the heart of the challenge. The definitions included in the federal law, and regulations in support of them, have printed criteria on the basis of which students are entered on a database contingent upon a specific label or category of disability. Congress clearly intended these categories to be used for demographic purposes in terms of reporting numbers of students needing services and for allocating funds to the states equitably based upon head counts served within each state.

Unfortunately, we have missed the true definition of special education described in the federal regulations. That definition of special education requires specially designed instruction to meet the unique needs of each student with a disability. The presence of a disability, especially if it adversely affects educational performance in a general education setting and curriculum, requires specially designed instruction to meet a student's unique needs that are functionally grounded in the presence or impact of the disability itself.

The key part of this somewhat circular description of students eligible for special education and related services is the emphasis professionals have placed on the two elements of the criteria that affect eligibility. We have long ignored the specially designed instruction component of the definitional process. For example, a child with a disability whose educational performance is not affected adversely by its presence does not need specially designed instruction. Hence, the student is not eligible for special education and related services. The other side of the challenge is that a student may need specially designed instruction to meet unique needs but may not have the characteristics associated with one of the disability categories allowed under special education law and regulations.

Therefore, the challenge as to who is to serve the student with special needs—special education professionals or professionals who serve children at risk (meaning children from low-income families and environments that often preclude readiness to succeed in school)—must be addressed to avoid costly duplication of service. Clearly, special educators have become bogged down in the definitional and identification swamps of our own making. In so doing, we have not paid sufficient attention to the instructional planning required for students with disabilities and otherwise at risk for accomplishing academic, social, and affective outcomes during their school years.

Although the manuscripts in this section cannot respond to all of the current challenges confronting special education professionals, they do provide a direction. For instance, early intervention has proved again and again to be effective both in cost and, more important, in making life better in general for children and their families. Also, if we are to get beyond the dysfunctional categorization of students (i.e., Chapter I or special education), we need to increase situations of collaboration among special and general educators in our schools. By concentrating on designing special instructional experiences to meet the needs of all students, professional educators can tear down the barriers that until now have artificially limited cooperative, team-based program planning.

Within the challenges reflected in the articles, then, are other challenges of a contemporary nature affecting special educators today. We have described some, but they also include challenges in assessment, instruction, the place of special education in the general education reform movement, and problems and issues associated with prevention and early intervention. We hope the articles included in this section will stimulate our colleagues to look further into the challenges associated with special education today.

The author points out that transition must occur even in early childhood programs and identifies three places where this must occur. Wolery offers a variety of suggestions for evaluating and assessing the effectiveness of transitions, including ways to assist parents and students in the process.

Transitions in Early Childhood Special Education: Issues and Procedures

Mark Wolery

Providing adequate early intervention programs requires consideration of many questions. These questions are related to the philosophy of the program, service delivery model, assessment of needs, and development of intervention plans. In addition, program leaders must ask, "How can we facilitate the transition of infants and preschoolers from one program to another?" This question, issues that surround it, and procedures for planning transitions are described in this article. Initially, the term *transition* and related terms are defined, and the relevant types of transitions that occur during early childhood are discussed. Then the rationale for studying and planning transitions is explored, and particular transitions are discussed.

DEFINITION AND TYPES OF TRANSITIONS

In the past decade, considerable emphasis has been placed on facilitating transitions from school-based programs to adult service programs (Ianacone & Stodden, 1987; Pueschel, 1988). *Transition* is defined as "passage from one state, stage, subject, or place to another . . . a movement, a development, or evolution from one form, stage, or style to another (*Webster's Ninth New Collegiate Dictionary*, 1988, p. 1254). Will (1984) defined transitions as a process that is "a bridge between the security and structure offered by the present program and the opportunities and risks of a subsequent least restrictive environment" (p. 4). The procedures used to construct this bridge, known as *transition practices*, have been defined by Hutinger (1981) as "strategies and procedures that are planned and employed to insure the smooth placement and subsequent adjustment of the child as he or she moves from one program into another" (p. 8). Noonan and Kilgo (1987) maintain that these definitions indicate that transition is: (a) a longitudinal *plan*; (b) a *goal* of smooth/efficient movement from one program to the next; (c) a *process* including preparation, implementation, and follow up; and (d) a *philosophy* that movement to the next program implies movement to a program that is less restrictive than the previous program (p. 26).

In addition to defining transitions, definition of related terms is necessary. In this article the term *infant program* refers to an intervention program serving infants and toddlers and their families who are eligible under the Education of the Handicapped Amendments of 1986 (PL 99-457), now called the Individuals with Disabilities Education Act. This designation is used regardless of the administrative agency responsible for providing those programs. Likewise, *preschool program* refers to an early intervention program serving children from 3 to 5 years of age who are eligible under PL 99-457, regardless of whether the services are provided directly by the local education agency (LEA) or through contracts with the LEA. Using Hutinger's (1981) lead, the program from which the infant/child is moving is referred to as the "sending" program, and the program to which the infant/child is moving is called the "receiving" program.

Using a broad conceptualization of transition, at least three types of transitions may occur in early childhood special education programs, and each deserves attention by early interventionists. The first type of transition might be called *developmental transitions*. These are sequential transitions that are frequently age-based and are the type frequently thought of when discussing transitions. Developmental transitions include movement from extended hospitalization to home and infant programs, movement from infant programs to preschool programs, and movement from preschool programs to school-age programs. Developmental transitions also include movement from one class in a center-based program to another class in that program. Most infants and preschoolers with disabilities will experience developmental transitions.

The second type of transition can be termed *nondevelopmental transitions* and occur within each age group. Usually they involve movement from one program to another that varies on the dimension of restrictiveness and possibly the extent of contact with typical peers. For example, a preschooler might move from a program that enrolls only preschoolers with disabilities to a less restrictive preschool program designed primarily for typical children. Not all infants and preschoolers experience nondevelopmental transitions; however, when they occur, planning is necessary.

The third type of transition can be called *within-class transitions*. These transitions occur in center-based programs and focus on movement from one activity to another. This article deals with developmental and nondevelopmental transitions; within-class transitions are not addressed. Other sources describe designing schedules for preschool classrooms (Bailey & Wolery, 1992; Carta, Sainato, & Greenwood, 1988), reducing within-class transition times (Sainato, Strain, Lefebvre, & Rapp, 1987; Goetz, Ayala, Hatfield, Marshall, & Etzel, 1983), and teaching during within-class transitions (Wolery, Doyle, Gast, Ault, & Simpson, in press).

RATIONALE FOR STUDYING AND PLANNING TRANSITIONS

At least four rationales can be identified for studying and planning transitions:

1. To ensure continuity of services (Flynn & McCollum, 1989; Noonan & Kilgo, 1987).
2. To minimize disruptions to the family system by facilitating adaptation to change (Diamond, Spiegel-McGill, & Hanrahan, 1988; Fowler, Chandler, Johnson, & Stella, 1988).
3. To ensure that children are prepared to function in the receiving program (Fowler, 1982; Noonan & Kilgo, 1987).
4. To fulfill, in some cases, the legal requirements of PL 99-457.

The relative emphasis of each of these rationales varies for different types of transitions.

Continuity of services refers to the extent to which the services needed and provided in the sending program are continued in the receiving program. Continuity has two primary elements: (a) the needed services, and (b) the provided services. Almost by definition, transitions imply changes in needs. If no change in needs exists, a transition may not be necessary. Because different programs have different missions, they undoubtedly are designed to meet different needs, or at least to place different emphasis on given needs.

For example, the primary mission of an intensive care nursery is to ensure infants' survivability and promote health. But the primary mission of most infant programs is to promote adequate parent-infant interactions, facilitate the infant's development and independence, and enhance the family's capability to promote the infant's development and meet individually defined goals within the family. Thus, transition from intensive care nurseries to a community-based infant programs may constitute a dramatic shift in which needs are addressed.

Different needs or different emphases on continuing needs imply that different services will be provided. These shifts may result in some needs not being addressed or being given less emphasis in the receiving program. Thus, it is imperative that the needs and services that were given priority in the sending program not be ignored in the receiving program. For example, attention to the infant's survivability and health should continue in the infant program after his or her leaving the intensive care nursery.

In relation to ensuring continuity, it is important to focus on the perception of needs as well as the reality of need. For example, an infant may leave the hospital quite healthy, but because of the history of extended hospitalization and life-threatening events, the family may continue to perceive this as the primary focus of intervention rather than recognize the need to provide a responsive, development-producing environment. Thus, to ensure continuity of services, the transition from one program to the other should be planned.

Transitions cause change in the family system that may be related to increases in reported stress (Fowler et al., 1988). Diamond et al. (1988) suggest that Bronfenbrenner's (1986) ecological-developmental model is useful in conceptualizing changes in the family system as a result of a transition. This model adopts a systems perspective of the family, meaning that each member and the unit as a whole have needs, roles, and functions (Dunst, 1985; Dunst, Trivette, & Deal, 1988; Simeonsson, 1988b). The infant/child and family are seen as functioning in several environments called *microsystems* (e.g., home environment, program environment, community environments such as church or neighborhood, support systems such as medical or respite programs). These microsystems, which are related to and influence one another, constitute the *mesosystem*. Events that occur in one microsystem can influence performance in another; therefore, changes such as transition from one microsystem to another can influence the entire mesosystem.

A systems view of families also assumes that it changes with time; families progress through a sequence of events or stages (Simeonsson, 1988b). These events, called *critical events*, have been divided into two categories: normative events and non-normative events (Bailey, 1988). *Normative events* include getting married, having children, rearing children during early childhood, providing independence during adolescence, and adapting to life as children leave home. *Non-normative events* include things such as job loss, divorce, death of a family member, and serious illness. The presence in the family of an infant or child with disabilities also influences development of the family.

Bailey (1988b) reviewed information from a number of authors who identified stressful events related to rearing a child with disabilities; these are summarized in Table 1. As noted in this listing of critical events, each of these authors viewed entry into public school programs and program transitions as stressful events in the lives of families (Hanline, 1988). This reported stress may occur for many reasons. For example, the sending and receiving programs may differ in terms of location of services, schedule, transportation system, staff members involved, manner and frequency with which communication with families occurs, contact with social support such as other families, cost of services, expectations for family participation, and many others. Further, the receiving program may hold many unknowns for the family. Thus, to minimize disruption to the family system and to minimize the stress involved in the potential changes, transitions should be planned carefully.

In addition to ensuring continuity of services and minimizing disruptions to the family system, transitions should be planned to ensure that children can perform the skills needed in the receiving program (Fowler, 1982). Because one goal of early intervention is to prepare infants and preschoolers to function in current and future environments, some of the instructional activities should be designed to prepare infants and preschoolers for the next most probable placement (Vincent et al., 1980). The intent of these activities is to promote maintenance and generalization of skills acquired in the sending program, to facilitate performance of idiosyncratic skills needed in the next program, to ensure that the child's behavior falls within the norm of children in the receiving program, and to identify adaptations and supports needed in the receiving program. Thus, to ensure that infants and children are ready for the next placement, careful planning of the transition is necessary.

TABLE 1   *Critical Events Related To Rearing a Family Member with Disabilities*

Author(s)	Issue of Concern	Specific Events of Concern
MacKeith (1973)	Major crisis points in family development	Family becomes aware that child is handicapped Family must decide on educational placement Disabled family member leaves school as young adult Family realizes parents can no longer care for disabled family member
Bray, Coleman, & Bracken (1981)	Events causing stress for family in parenting disabled family member	Family learns of diagnosis Family must deal with medical management Family receives incomplete or inaccurate diagnostic information Family deals with prognosis for disabled family member Family must decide on educational placement and services
Wickler (1981)	Critical events that are stressful for families	Age child should have begun to walk Age child should have begun to talk Beginning public school Onset of puberty Child's 21st birthday Initial and subsequent diagnoses Younger typical child equals or exceeds abilities of disabled family member Consideration of placements outside of home Excessive inappropriate behaviors, seizures, health problems Consideration of guardianship and long-term care
Bailey et al. (1986)	Events to be assessed	Family recently learned of diagnosis Typical sibling is matching or beginning to exceed abilities of handicapped child Program transition will occur in next few months Medical procedure (e.g., operation) will occur in next few months Child reached age of walking but is not Child reached age of independent feeding but is not Child reached age of talking but is not Child reached age of being toilet trained but is not

Finally, transitions should be planned and studied because this type of planning is required by PL 99-457. The Individualized Family Service Plan (IFSP) must include a statement of the infant's present levels of functioning, statement of family priorities and concerns, statement of outcomes, statement of services needed, projected dates of services, name of case manager, and "steps to be taken supporting the transition of the handicapped toddler to services provided under part B to the extent that such services are considered appropriate" (sec. 677, p. 6).

Thus, transition planning is a requirement of the IFSP process for toddlers who are leaving infant programs. In addition, one of the primary provisions of The Education for All Handicapped Children Act (PL 94-142) is that children be educated in the least restrictive appropriate environment. Thus, when children move from a more restrictive to a less restrictive placement, planning may be necessary.

TRANSITION ISSUES AND PROCEDURES

The transition from hospital neonatal intensive care units (NICU) to home and infant programs is described separately from other developmental and nondevelopmental transitions because of its uniqueness. Following this discussion, issues and procedures related to other transitions are addressed.

Facilitating Transitions from NICU To Home and Infant Programs

Not all infants with disabilities experience extended hospitalizations in an NICU, and not all infants who have extended hospitalizations will need infant intervention programs. Many infants with disabilities, however, will spend from a few days to several weeks or months in an NICU. Transition from the NICU to home and infant programs should begin prior to the discharge of the infant from the hospital (Lang, Behle, & Ballard, 1988). Communication with the family concerning the infant's status, progress, and prognosis is important.

In addition, parents should be encouraged and allowed to visit the infant frequently and at different times of the day. These visits can assist the family in becoming acquainted with the infant, the infant's response patterns, and the use of specialized treatments (Lang et al., 1988). Actual discharge from the hospital requires planning several issues including assessment of the (a) medical and developmental status of the infant, (b) needs and strengths of the family, (c) home environment, and (d) resources in the community (Katz, Pokorni, & Long, 1988).

Medical and Developmental Status

The neonatologist and nursing staff are responsible for monitoring and assessing the infant's medical status to identify when transition to the home is warranted (Katz et al., 1988). In addition to ongoing monitoring, these professionals should ensure that all appropriate information and medical procedures needed prior to discharge are accomplished, specialized screening is completed (e.g., of sensory functioning), and a thorough discharge examination is executed (Lang et al., 1988). The medical status also should include assessment of "the level of respiratory support that the infant needs; the feeding method and rate of weight gain; the infant's autonomic regulation including respiration, heart rate and body temperature, and medical needs" (Katz et al., 1988, p. 43).

These assessments assist in determining when discharge is appropriate, what growth patterns are expected, and what equipment and assistance families will need in the home. Assessment of the developmental status will assist the NICU staff in determining whether support from an infant intervention program is necessary (Katz et al., 1988).

Family Needs and Strengths

When planning the transition from the NICU to the home, family needs and strengths should be assessed and considered. As noted, families ideally would visit the infant frequently during the hospitalization. In addition, attendance in parent support groups may assist the family in adapting to having an infant with disabilities (Lang et al., 1988).

Assessment of family needs in terms of transition to the home should involve several areas. Family members' understanding of the infant's condition, medical status, prognosis, and their ability to explain this information to others are important issues (Bailey, 1988b). The family's willingness to care for the infant at home should be assessed through ongoing interviews and contacts during the hospitalization. Once families have decided to care for the child at home, NICU staff members must assess their knowledge and competence in providing routine care for the child. Prior to discharge, the family should be competent in bathing, feeding, diapering, and handling the infant (Harrison, 1983; Katz et al., 1988).

Further, the ability of families to provide specialized care and detect problems should be assessed (Harrison, 1983; Katz et al., 1988). To assist in assessment, several checklists have been developed. Katz et al. (1988) present a checklist to assess caregivers' competence with infants who have been tracheostomized or are ventilator assisted. It includes documentation of competence in (a) assessing breathing and other signs and symptoms of distress; (b) implementing procedures such as suctioning, trach care, and emergency care (e.g., CPR); (c) using, checking, and caring for specialized equipment such as apnea monitors, ventilators, humidity systems, suction machines, and trach collars; (d) administering medications; and (e) documenting activity levels, respiratory distress, and nursing procedures. This checklist also includes a section for assessing individualized skills families may need.

Platzker et al. (1988) also present guidelines and lists of equipment related to home care of infants with chronic lung diseases. This includes a checklist for home care, description of medications, listing of equipment for infants with chronic lung disease, instructions for bronchodilator aerosol treatments, equipment needed for infants with tracheostomy, criteria for discharge of ventilator-assisted infant, and a listing of equipment needed for the infant. Howell (1988) presents descriptions of supplies and procedures for ostomy care for infants and young children. Lang et al. (1988) and Katz et al. (1988) recommend that the family stay overnight at the NICU to ensure that they are acquainted with the procedures for providing 24-hour care for the infant.

Assessment of family needs in other areas is also important. Katz et al. (1988) present a 43-item checklist for assessing home care needs, focusing on a number of relevant areas. Examples include response to emergencies (who to call, procedures for getting the child out of the house in the case of fire), availability of respite or alternative caregiving, training of alternative caregivers, availability of adequate transportation, identification of support personnel (e.g., pediatrician, nursing services), need for specialized therapists (e.g., occupational therapy, physical therapy), use of equipment, need for social services, and child care supplies (e.g., diapers, clothing). A number of scales and checklists that assess family needs but are not designed specifically for hospital-to-home transitions also are available (cf. Bailey & Simeonsson, 1988; Dunst et al., 1988; Seligman & Darling, 1989).

Finally, as the transition is planned, parents should be encouraged to ask questions related to taking the infant home. During the final discharge meeting, opportunities should be afforded parents to ask questions (Lang et al., 1988). Harrison (1983) lists 20 questions that families should ask of the NICU staff. These questions deal with organization of the home, feeding, sleeping patterns, immunizations, response to crying, the infant's current sensory status, and many others. Interventionists who will be serving the infant in the program also should assist parents in asking questions.

Home Environment

Assessment of the home environment should address two major areas: adequacy of the physical characteristics of the home, and adequacy of the home in promoting the infant's/child's development. In the transition from the NICU to the home, physical characteristics are of primary importance. This assessment should identify the need to adapt the physical environment, whether space is adequate, whether the electrical supply allows for medical equipment, and access to telephone and alarms for smoke and potential power failures. Katz et al. (1988) present a checklist for evaluating the physical facilities of a home. Families should be informed of and assisted in making the necessary adaptations. Simeonsson (1988a) presents information on assessing adequacy of the home in facilitating the infant's development. This assessment and resulting intervention should be part of the infant intervention program.

Community Resources

Identification and assessment of the needed community resources are important to the hospital-to-home transition plan. During the hospitalization, the community pediatrician or family physician must be notified and informed of the infant's condition, progress, care, and medical needs (Lang et al., 1988). If possible, these physicians should participate in the discharge meeting; however, if they are not present, the NICU staff should directly contact them soon after discharge (Lang et al., 1988).

The discharge should not signal an end to communication between the NICU staff and the family. Families should be encouraged to contact the NICU if they need certain information or face new problems related to the infant's medical care. Likewise, follow-up telephone contacts or home visits from the NICU staff can ease the transition (Katz et al., 1988; Lang et al., 1988). These contacts can ensure that the family has been linked to needed resources.

Other resources the family may need, such as social services and intervention services, should be identified, and contact with those programs should occur prior to discharge. Ideally, families would be encouraged to avail themselves of the informal as well as formal support systems (Dunst et al., 1988). Informal support may come from the extended family members, church, neighbors, and other individuals. A number of scales and interview formats exist for identifying needed resources (cf. Bailey & Simeonsson, 1988; Dunst et al., 1988). Still, referral to and contact with an infant intervention program are necessary to ensure that the family is not lost to the established service system (Flynn & McCullom, in press).

In sum, transition from the NICU requires attention to a number of areas including the infant's medical and developmental status, needs of the family, adequacy of the home environment, and identification and availability of community resources. Much of the preparation for transition activities should focus on (a) the family's ability to care for the infant in the home, and (b) the linkage with resources (formal and informal) that will ensure continued development of the infant. Although much of this will be conducted by social workers, nurses, or others in the NICU, the infant intervention program staff also can play a role in identifying community services and supporting the family as they bring the child home.

Other Developmental and Nondevelopmental Transitions

Both developmental transitions (e.g., from an infant program to a preschool program and from preschool programs to school-age programs) and nondevelopmental transitions (from one infant program to another and from one preschool program to another) are addressed in this section. Smooth, systematic transitions have at least four dimensions: (a) assessment of, and attention to, the needs of both the infant/child and the family; (b) open communication and information exchange between family members and staff members of the sending and receiving programs; (c) joint decision making between professionals and families; and (d) communication and information exchange between the personnel of the sending and receiving programs (Fowler, Schwartz, & Atwater, 1991; Hains, Fowler, & Chandler, 1988; Johnson, Chandler, Kerns, & Fowler, 1986). The issues and procedures for implementing transitions are discussed in the following section. This section is organized by family, child, and interagency issues and procedures.

Family Issues and Procedures

The general goals for family participation in transitions are to ensure smooth movement of the child and family to the receiving program and to reduce family stress and disruption during the transition. In accomplishing this, the staff of the sending program in collaboration with the family should (a) identify and address parents' information and skill needs related specifically to transitions, (b) establish parents' roles and responsibilities during the transition, (c) determine and deal with parents' concerns and fears about transitions, and (d) establish appropriate communication between parents and relevant professionals in the sending and receiving programs (Hains et al., 1988; Hanline & Knowlton, 1988).

As noted earlier, families should be assessed to identify their general needs related to enhancing the infant's/child's development (Bailey & Simeonsson, 1988; Dunst et al., 1988). Although this is required for parents of infants and toddlers, the intent of PL 99-457 (as specified in the Congressional Report on the act, Report 99-860, Education of the Handicapped Act Amendments of 1986, p. 20) is that it applies to the parents of preschoolers as well. Thus, infant and preschool programs should be continuously engaged in assessing and meeting the needs of families. Part of that assessment and intervention should focus on transition planning, including assessment of their needs for information, skills, and support.

Family information needs may include (a) parent and child rights and due process procedures; (b) referral and assessment procedures; (c) eligibility criteria including criteria for related services; (d) roles of parents and professionals during transition; (e) procedures related to IEP development, parents' roles and input into the IEP process, and the manner in which the IEP meeting will be conducted; (f) placement options including the curriculum, teaching practices, opportunities for interactions with typical children, procedures for observing each program, procedures for evaluating the adequacy of those programs, expectations for parents, and teacher and therapist experience in each option; (g) procedures for facilitating their infant's/child's transition; (h) strategies for providing input and influencing transition decisions; and (i) community services that may be available. Clearly, not all parents will need information in each of these areas, but many parents will. Procedures for assessing these information needs frequently involve interviews and program-developed checklists.

Fowler et al. (1988) described a two-step interview process in which parents are interviewed in the fall of their infant's/child's final year in the program and again in the spring of that year. The first interview focuses on "general transition information, sources of information regarding new programs, the parents' participation level, and sources of information on their child's progress" (Fowler et al., 1988, p. 210). Each of these areas has 7 to 13 items, rated from "not applicable" to "very important." Parents then are asked to rank the three most important items, and these are considered priorities in planning for the transition. Several open-ended questions are also included to stimulate communication and information exchange about transition. The second interview deals with choosing the best program and includes items focused on:

> . . . general description of the receiving (new) programs, ways to obtain information about the program, the parent's participation in making decisions about the new program, specific features of the receiving programs, a description of teacher characteristics, a description of classroom characteristics, a description of other children in the classroom, and criteria for selecting the receiving program. (Fowler et al., 1988, p. 210)

Each of these areas contained a number of items, and three open-ended items. Based on the results, parents were given a list that summarized the information they had rated as most important. They were encouraged to use this list in their contacts with potential receiving programs. This two-step interview process facilitated discussions of information about transitions, allowed some parents to add transition goals to the child's IEP, and assisted them in reviewing potential receiving programs.

Hanline and Knowlton (1988) also present a parent transition preparation checklist. It includes 12 items that can be used as an initial assessment of parents' preparedness for transition. After parents complete the checklist, it can be reviewed with a professional and specific information needs can be identified. Winton, Turnbull, and Blacher (1984) suggest that parents consider what various programs can provide for them and for their child. Variables they suggest that parents use to evaluate programs' provisions for parents include the cost, convenience, availability of day care services, amount of contact with other parents, and several others. In regard to what programs provide for children, they suggest evaluating whether the program promotes independence, helps the child feel good about himself or herself, facilitates children getting along with one another, and other issues.

To meet information needs, a number of strategies can be applied. Many programs have developed manuals designed specifically for parents in transition (see Hanline & Knowlton, 1988; Noonan & Stodden, 1986). Group meetings frequently are used; these include presentations by sending and receiving program staff members, videotapes of potential programs, group discussions, and question-and-answer sessions (Hanline & Knowlton, 1988; Noonan & Kilgo, 1987). Individual conversations with staff members from sending and receiving programs comprise another major source of information. Observation of the potential options and discussion with persons in those programs also are rich sources of information. Conversations with parents who have experienced transition and whose children are in the receiving programs offer a viable means of providing information to parents. A number of published and commercially available sources also exist; examples are presented in Table 2.

A variety of parent skill needs also may be identified and addressed. These include skills in teaching their infants/children behaviors needed in the receiving programs, decision-making strategies, and strategies for participating in IEP meetings. These probably are best assessed through direct observation and interviews. A well-established method for teaching parents to teach their children involves describing the teaching procedure, demonstrating it for parents, observing the parents use the procedure, and providing them with feedback. Role playing and didactic instruction can be used for teaching decision making and IEP participation strategies.

For assessing needs for support, a number of scales exist (Bailey & Simeonsson, 1988; Dunst et al., 1988). Moreover, program personnel should assume that most parents will need some social support during transitions. As shown in Table 1, parents frequently report that school entry or program transitions are stressful events. Use of the Critical Events Checklist (Bailey et al., 1986) allows program personnel to determine whether other stressful events are occurring simultaneously with transition. If so, the need for social support may be increased. In meeting social support needs, programs frequently opt for linking parents with other parents, providing them with professionals to contact about the transition process, and checking frequently on progress of the transition. As Dunst

TABLE 2 *Commercially Available Parent Resources in Transition*

Title	Author(s)	Source/Publisher
An Education Handbook for Parents of Handicapped Children	S.I. Mopsik & J.A. Agard	Brookline Books, Cambridge, MA
Children's Psychological Testing: A Guide	D.L. Wodrich	Paul Brookes, Baltimore, MD
Getting Your Child Ready for School	L. Murphy & S.D. Corte	*Special Parent-Special Child* Sept./Oct., 1985
Just How Special Should a Preschool Be?	P. Winton & A. Turnbull	*Ways*, Jan., 1986
One Miracle at a Time: How To Get Help for Your Disabled Child	I. Dickman with S. Gordon	Simon & Schuster, New York, NY
PL 94-142, Section 504, and PL 99-457: Understanding What They Are and Are Not	J. Ballard, B. Ramirez, & K. Zantal-Wiener	Council for Exceptional Children, Reston, VA
Related Services for Handicapped Children	M.E. Esterson & L.F. Bluth	College-Hill Press, Boston, MA
Selecting a Preschool: A Guide for Parents of Handicapped Children	P.J. Winton, A.P. Turnbull, & J. Blacher	Pro-Ed, Austin, TX
Some Practical Suggestions for the IEP	K. Marafino	*Down Syndrome News*, Nov., 1986
Unraveling the Special Education Maze: An Action Guide for Parents	B.C. Cutler	Research Press, Champaign, IL

Source: From "A Collaborative Model for Providing Support to Parents During Their Child's Transition from Infant Intervention to Preschool Special Education Public School Programs" by M.F. Hanline and A. Knowlton, 1988, *Journal of the Division for Early Childhood, 12,* 121. Reprinted by permission.

et al. (1988) indicate, however, use of existing support systems such as extended family members and neighbors is advisable.

A number of roles have been suggested for parents during transitions. Parents can serve as teachers, information providers, decision makers, advocates, and transition coordinators (Hains et al., 1988; Noonan & Kilgo, 1987).

As teachers, they would instruct their infant or child on skills that will increase the probability of success in the receiving programs. This may consist of teaching new skills that are needed, or assisting in establishing generalization of skills taught by others. In home-based or clinic/parent-consultation models, parents may have to assume a more active role as teacher in the transition process than parents whose infants/children are being served in center-based programs.

As information providers, parents supply information to transition planners about the infant's/child's skills and needs, effective instructional strategies, family needs related to transition, and other relevant information (Diamond et al., 1988). Also, as information providers they can participate in meetings related to the transition.

As decision makers, parents may be asked to participate in deciding which placement best fits their infant or child, what behaviors and skills should be taught to him or her, what services the infant or child needs, what services other family members need during transition and from the receiving program, and when transition should occur.

As advocates, they must understand their rights and the rights of their children, ensure that due process procedures are implemented, identify instances when the best interests of their child and the family are not being met, and initiate appropriate action when their child is not being served appropriately. Also, as advocates, they can provide their support for programs and services, assist other parents in obtaining appropriate services, and lobby local, state, and national government officials for services for individuals with disabilities and their families.

As transition coordinators for their infant/child, parents assume the responsibilities for initial transition planning, implementing actual transition events, and providing follow-up information on the transition (Noonan & Kilgo, 1987). Noonan and Kilgo provide three rationales for parents serving as transition coordinators. First, many parents will face several transitions during the life of their child. Thus, learning how to negotiate transitions smoothly may empower them to be more independent of professionals and deal with less than ideal situations where transitions are needed. Second, as members of teams and as transition coordinators, parents are in a powerful position to advocate for the services and placements that are most appropriate for their offspring. Third, assuming the role of transition coordinators provides parents with more control of the process, which in turn may reduce the stress related to transition.

Smooth, successful transitions probably are most likely when parents serve multiple roles. Nevertheless, program personnel must recognize that not all parents can or desire to serve multiple roles in the transition process. Assuming particular roles probably is predicated on having the skills to function adequately in those roles. For example, parents who do not have good teaching skills will need to learn those skills before their efforts in the teacher role will benefit the child during transitions. Similarly, parents will need certain information before they can adequately serve some roles. Making decisions about services and placement options requires information about what is needed and what is available. Serving as an advocate for their child requires information about their rights and how to exercise those rights. Serving as a transition coordinator requires knowledge of the transition process, available options, procedures related to transition, and many other issues. It also requires skill in soliciting, analyzing, and acting on information. Finally, serving as a transition coordinator requires considerable time during the day to devote to the transition process.

To expect that all parents will have the skills, resources, and desire to serve as the transition coordinators for their children is undoubtedly unrealistic. Therefore, program personnel must engage in helping behaviors that promote as much independence as possible on the part of parents and at the same time provide them with the support they need to accomplish the roles they have chosen (see Dunst et al., 1988, for characteristics of helping behaviors).

Clearly, some parents frequently fear the transition process or have important concerns about it. Consider the following statements by parents:

- "I saw making the transition to a preschool program in the school district as an extremely traumatic experience, second only to learning of Amy's diagnosis." (Hanline & Knowlton, 1988, p. 116)
- "Getting on the bus for the first time was the biggest shock." (Johnson et al., 1986, p. 15)
- "I was scared to have him go to public school. I worry about him a lot . . . If I had it my way, I'd never send him to school." (Johnson et al., 1986, p. 15)

These comments and the unpublished comments of many other parents indicate that transition from one program to the next is filled with uncertainty. Five statements about these fears and concerns are pertinent. First, being fearful or having concerns about the transition process is a realistic emotion. Many parents of typical children can recall their uneasiness about their child's first days at school. Second, the intensity and amount of fear parents experience varies from family to family and from time to time. As a result, program personnel should provide families with frequent opportunities to express their concerns. Assessment of fears and concerns can occur through formal and informal interviews (Johnson et al., 1986) and perhaps through scales and checklists. Third, failure to identify and address fears and concerns may interfere with the transition process and may increase transition-related stress for families. Fourth, some fears and concerns may require ongoing monitoring. In many cases, fears and concerns may originate from lack of information, but contact with the receiving program and provision of information may cause the fears or concerns to diminish. In other cases, however, the fears and concerns may be less easily dispelled. For example, a family may fear that a child's educational needs will not be appropriately addressed in a particular kindergarten class. In such cases, monitoring the appropriateness of that class should occur after the child is enrolled. If the child's needs are not met, then changes in the operation of the class or a transition to another more appropriate placement is warranted.

Fifth, several standard procedures exist for dealing with many fears and concerns. These include having a clearly defined transition process (cf. Diamond et al., 1988; Hanline & Knowlton, 1988); providing needed information (Hains et al., 1988; Hanline, 1988); providing needed family services (Hanline, 1988); providing informal, personal, and frequent contact and communication between families and the staff of the sending and receiving programs (Diamond et al., 1988); allowing parents to visit potential placement sites and teachers prior to transition (Johnson et al., 1986); and identifying one person in the receiving program who can deal with questions and concerns about transition (Hanline, 1988).

To increase the smoothness of transitions and reduce family stress, communication between the family and sending and receiving programs must be established (Diamond et al., 1988). The communication must occur at several different levels. First, all programs providing services to families should have some system for formally and informally communicating with families (cf. Winton, 1988). If frequent communication exists between the program and families, communication related to transitions is simply an extension of previous exchanges. In addition to communication between the sending program and families, communication has to be established between the receiving program and families. Parents appear to prefer to have one person from the receiving program with whom to communicate (Hanline, 1988). This person should be knowledgeable about the transition process, placement options, and availability of related services. In large systems this may be unrealistic, but individuals to contact clearly should be identified to parents. In many cases, someone in the administration of programs can serve that role. But, once a placement has been identified, the parents should have contact and communication with the direct service staff.

"The most effective way to enhance communication and interrelationships between settings is by providing opportunities for frequent, personal, and informal contact between these settings" (Diamond et al., 1988, p. 246). These contacts may include having the receiving program provide information about available services directly to parents well before the transition, inviting parents to social events at the receiving program in the months preceding the actual transition, allowing families to visit the receiving program and observe the program in operation, encouraging visits by the receiving staff to the sending program or the family's home, and allowing visits by the child and parents to the receiving program.

In summary, meeting the goal of a smooth, unstressful transition for families requires attention to several issues. Their information and service needs must be assessed and addressed. The various roles parents may play in the transition should be described to parents, and they should be supported in the roles they assume. Parents should be given opportunities to express their fears and concerns about the transition, and those fears and concerns should be addressed. Finally, communication between the sending and receiving programs and the parents should be established and monitored.

Child Issues and Procedures

The goals of transition for infants and children are to provide them with a program that meets their needs more effectively and efficiently and to minimize the adjustment difficulties during transition. To accomplish these goals, the sending program must (a) define its exit criteria, (b) determine the infant's/child's current abilities and needs, (c) identify the skills and performance levels needed in potential receiving programs, (d) develop and implement a transition plan that maximizes the infant's/child's probability for success in the receiving program, and (e) implement follow-up procedures to determine whether the transition was successful and to identify and correct problems that arise.

Transition implicitly suggests that the sending program has met its objectives with the child or that the program can no longer adequately meet the child's needs. Recent investigations suggest, however, that this frequently is not the case (Thurlow, Lehr, & Ysseldyke, 1987; Thurlow, Ysseldyke, & Weiss, 1988). In reality, children usually leave programs because of their age.

Two disadvantages exist when exit decisions are based on age. First, children who are ready to exit from programs frequently are not allowed to leave them; second, children are moved to the next program without adequate preparation (Thurlow et al., 1988). To solve these difficulties, programs should allow for determination of whether their exit criteria are based on age only, progress only, or some combination of age and progress. They also should have provisions for assessing a variety of alternative placements and for modifying those programs to ensure that adequate services are provided to program graduates. Parents should be involved in exit/transition decisions, and timelines for determining progress should be defined and implemented (Thurlow et al., 1988).

Transition procedures, if based on age alone or on some combination with progress, should involve adequate assessment of the infant or child. This should include an interdisciplinary assessment and should address all relevant developmental domains and therapy needs. Conducting curriculum-based assessments involves the use of direct testing, direct observation, and interviews with relevant persons (Bailey & Wolery, 1989). This information should be passed on to the receiving program.

In addition to an adequate curriculum-based assessment, the student should be assessed to identify the skills and performance levels needed in potential receiving programs. Developmental assessments usually do not provide this information. It must come from the demands of the receiving program (Noonan & Kilgo, 1987) and can be obtained by conducting ecological inventories of those programs.

The steps for conducting ecological inventories are: (a) identify curricular domains needed by the child, (b) identify and survey the receiving program, (c) divide the receiving program into subenvironments, (d) identify all relevant activities and routines used in each subenvironment, (e) identify the specific skills needed to perform the relevant activities and routines, and (f) assess the child against the skills needed in the activities and routines (Brown et al., 1979; see also Snell & Grigg, 1987).

In addition to determining whether children have acquired the skills needed in the receiving program, determining whether the child can perform the skills fluently and within the range of children in that program is important. This can be accomplished through the use of discrepancy analysis (Wolery, Bailey, & Sugal, 1988).

The steps for conducting a discrepancy analysis are: (a) identify children who are competent performers of the target behaviors in the receiving classroom, (b) identify the situations and setting where the target behaviors will be needed, (c) select a measurement system, (d) collect data on the competent performers doing the target behaviors in needed situations over 2 to 4 sessions, and (e) analyze the data by computing the mean and range for the competent performers. The performance of the child who is being prepared for transition then is compared to the mean and range of the competent performers.

Fowler (1982) recommends analyzing the differences in the sending and receiving programs to identify skills to teach the preschooler and ways to modify the sending program to prepare the child for transition. She suggests that these programs may differ in terms of classroom composition, teacher attention and reinforcement, physical arrangement, daily schedule, classroom rules and routines, academics, self-care skills, and support systems. Questions for assessing each of these potential differences are listed.

An alternative is to assess the child using developed checklists of "survival skills" in kindergarten and primary special education programs. Examples of behaviors from such checklists are shown in Table 3. Although limited evidence exists suggesting that the behaviors listed in Table 3 promote greater success in receiving programs, some of these behaviors clearly are helpful. Skills in initiating interactions, staying on task when not interacting; complying with classroom rules and routines (thereby reducing teacher management time), and performing task requirements of the classroom appear to be important for succeeding in integrated kindergarten (Walter & Vincent, 1982).

Once a receiving program has been targeted and an assessment of the demands of that program has been completed, the team should develop and implement an individualized transition plan. This may be a part of the child's IEP, or it can be a separate document. Intervention procedures used to prepare children for the receiving program involve (a) teaching the behaviors needed in that program (Wolery, 1987; Wolery et al., 1988; Wolery, Ault, & Doyle, 1992); (b) using contingencies and behavior management systems found in that program (Fowler, 1982); (c) modifying the sending classroom design and operation to match that of the receiving program (Byrd, 1987; Fowler, 1982); and (d) using procedures to facilitate maintenance and generalization of needed skills (Wolery, 1987; Wolery et al., 1992). As with any instructional program, the plan should be monitored and adjusted as needed (Byrd, 1987).

Once intervention has occurred, follow-up is important (Fowler, 1982; Hanline, 1988; Diamond et al., 1988). The sending program can use follow-up information to modify its transition procedures, to identify and assist in correcting problems, to assess appropriateness of the placement, and to identify skills that should be taught to other students (Fowler, 1982; Vincent et al., 1980). Follow-up information can be collected by interviews and informal contacts with the receiving program staff members, interviews with families, and observation of the transition child.

In summary, the goals of transition procedures with children are to prepare them to function in the receiving program and to ensure a smooth adjustment to that program. Defining exit criteria, assessing children for developmental performance and for the skills needed in the receiving program, implementing a transition plan, and following up on the success of that plan and placement are appropriate activities.

Interagency Issues and Procedures

Developing and implementing transition procedures are seen as primary functions of early intervention program administrators (Shearer & Mori, 1987). Communication between programs is a necessary prerequisite for smooth transitions of infants/children and families. This communication is best established through frequent, informal contacts between the relevant parties (Diamond et al., 1988). In addition to communication, the sending and receiving programs must establish coordinated transition guidelines and procedures. This involves establishing what information is needed by the receiving agency, securing the release of confidential information, identifying persons to whom information should flow, determining what assessment information is needed and can be used, scheduling the events of the transitions (e.g., assessment dates, IEP planning meetings),

TABLE 3   Skills on Checklists for Assessing Entry into School-Age Programs

Source/Skill Area	Selected Examples of Specific Skills
Polloway (1987)	
Self-Related Skills	Accepts consequences for own behavior Has self-care/hygiene abilities
Task-Related Skills	Completes task within time allotted Demonstrates task persistence
Interpersonal Skills	Shows respect for others' feelings and property Greets others
Environmental Awareness	Moves appropriately about the classroom Locates and replaces materials
Byrd (1987)	
Classroom Rules	Waits quietly in line Replaces materials, cleans up own work place
Work Skills	Stops activity when given direction "stop" Completes tasks given developmentally appropriate material
Communication Skills	Comes to adult when signaled Attends to peers or adult who is talking to a group
Social Behavior Skills	Modifies behavior when provided with verbal direction Is willing to try something new
Self-Management Skills	Eats lunch or snack with minimal assistance Is aware of obvious dangers and avoids them
McCormick & Kawate (1982)	
Independent Task Work	Stays on task without extra teacher directions Completes task at criterion
Group Attending/Participation	Sits appropriately Does not disrupt peers
Follows Class Routine	Locates own possessions and returns them to appropriate locations Makes transitions from one activity to the next with general group verbal cues
Appropriate Classroom Behavior	Waits appropriately Uses time between activities appropriately
Self-Care	Washes hands without supervision Takes care of own toileting needs without supervision
Direction Following	Complies with simple directions provided by adult to child Follows two-step directions
Social/Play Skills	Spontaneously begins play activities during play time Interacts verbally with peers
Functional Communication	Asks for information States needs

Source: Adapted from "Transition Services for Early Age Individuals with Mild Mental Retardation" by E.A. Polloway, 1987, in R.N. Iancone and R.A. Stodden (Eds.), *Transition Issues and Directions* (pp. 11–24), Reston, VA: Council for Exceptional Children, Division on Mental Retardation; *Project STEPS: Helpful Entry Level Skills and Instructional Strategies* by R. Byrd, 1987, Lexington, KY: Child Development Centers of the Bluegrass; "Kindergarten Survival Skills. New Directions for Preschool Special Education" by L. McCormick and J. Kawate, 1987, *Education & Training of the Mentally Retarded, 17,* 247–252.

and negotiating difficulties that arise. To ensure smooth transitions, the procedures should be reviewed yearly, and new staff in both programs should receive orientation and training related to those procedures.

Several models exist for establishing interagency transition procedures. These include the Skidmore College Center for Child Study model (Diamond et al., 1988), the Supported Transition to Integrated Preschools model in San Francisco (Hanline & Knowlton, 1988), and the Sequenced Transition to Education in the Public Schools (STEPS) in Lexington, Kentucky (Byrd, 1987; Weiner & Koppelman, 1987).

SUMMARY

Transitions involve movement from one program to another. They should be studied and planned to ensure continuity of services, minimize disruptions to families, and prepare the infant/child for the next placement. Also, such planning is required, in part, by PL 99-457. Smooth transitions are accomplished by assessing and addressing the needs of infants/children and families, establishing communication between families and sending and receiving programs, including families in decision making, and ensuring information exchange and coordinated procedures between the sending and receiving programs.

REFERENCES

Bailey, D.B. (1988a). Assessing critical events. In D.B. Bailey & R.J. Simeonsson (Eds.), *Family assessment in early intervention* (pp. 119–138). Columbus, OH: Charles Merrill.

Bailey, D.B. (1988b). Assessing family stress and needs. In D.B. Bailey & R.J. Simeonsson (Eds.), *Family assessment in early intervention* (pp. 95–118). Columbus, OH: Charles Merrill.

Bailey, D.B., & Simeonsson, R.J. (1988). *Family assessment in early intervention*. Columbus, OH: Charles Merrill.

Bailey, D.B., Simeonsson, R.J., Winton, P.J., Huntington, G.S., Comfort, M., Isbell, P., O'Donnell, K.J., & Helm, J.M. (1986). Family-focused intervention: A functional model for planning, implementing, and evaluating individualized family services in early intervention. *Journal of the Division for Early Childhood, 10,* 156–171.

Bailey, D.B., & Wolery, M. (1992). *Teaching infants and preschoolers with disabilities* (2nd ed.). Columbus, OH: Merrill.

Bailey, D.B., & Wolery, M. (1989). *Assessing infants and preschoolers with handicaps*. Columbus, OH: Merrill.

Bray, N.M., Coleman, J.M., & Bracken, M.B. (1981). Critical events in parenting handicapped children. *Journal of the Division for Early Childhood, 3,* 26–33.

Bronfenbrenner, U. (1986). Ecology of the family as a context for human development: Research perspectives. *Developmental Psychology, 22,* 723–742.

Brown, L., Branston, M.B., Hamre-Nietupski, S., Pumpian, I., Certo, N., & Gruenwald, L.A. (1979). A strategy for developing chronological age appropriate and functional curricular content for severely handicapped adolescents and young adults. *Journal of Special Education, 13,* 81–90.

Byrd, R. (1987). *Project STEPS: Helpful entry level skills and instructional strategies*. Lexington, KY: Child Development Centers of the Bluegrass.

Carta, J.J., Sainato, D.M., & Greenwood, C.R. (1988). Advances in the ecological assessment of classroom instruction for young children with handicaps. In S.L. Odom & M.B. Karnes (Eds.), *Early intervention for infants and children with handicaps: An empirical base* (pp. 217–239). Baltimore: Paul Brookes.

Diamond, K.E., Spiegel-McGill, P., & Hanrahan, P. (1988). Planning for school transition: An ecological-developmental approach. *Journal of the Division for Early Childhood, 12,* 245–252.

Dunst, C.J. (1985). Rethinking early intervention. *Analysis & Intervention in Developmental Disabilities, 5,* 165–201.

Dunst, C.J., Trivette, C., & Deal, A. (1988). *Enabling and empowering families: Principles and guidelines for practice.* Cambridge, MA: Brookline Books.

Flynn, L.L., & McCollum, J. (1989). Support systems: Strategies and implications for hospitalized newborns and families. *Journal of Early Intervention, 13,* 173–182.

Fowler, S.A. (1982). Transition from preschool to kindergarten for children with special needs. In K.E. Allen & E.M. Goetz (Eds.), *Early childhood education: Special problems, special solutions* (pp. 309–334). Rockville, MD: Aspen.

Fowler, S.A., Chandler, L.K., Johnson, T.E., & Stella, M.E. (1988). Individualizing family involvement in school transitions: Gathering information and choosing the next program. *Journal of the Division for Early Childhood, 12,* 208–216.

Fowler, S.A., Schwartz, I., & Atwater, J. (1991). Perspectives on the transition from preschool to kindergarten for children with disabilities and their families. *Exceptional Children, 58,* 136–145.

Goetz, E.M., Ayala, J.M., Hatfield, V.L., Marshall, A.M., & Etzel, B.C. (1983). Training independence in preschoolers with an auditory stimulus management technique. *Education & Treatment of Children, 6,* 251–261.

Hains, A.H., Fowler, S.A., & Chandler, L.K. (1988). Planning school transitions: Family and professional collaboration. *Journal of the Division for Early Childhood, 12,* 108–115.

Hanline, M.F. (1988). Making the transition to preschool: Identification of parent needs. *Journal of the Division for Early Childhood, 12,* 98–107.

Hanline, M.F., & Knowlton, A. (1988). A collaborative model for providing support to parents during their child's transition from infant intervention to preschool special education public school programs. *Journal of the Division for Early Childhood, 12,* 116–125.

Harrison, H. (1983). *The premature baby book: A parents' guide to coping and caring in the first years.* New York: St. Martin's Press.

Howell, L.J. (1988). Home ostomy care. In R.A. Ballard (Ed.), *Pediatric care of the ICN graduate* (pp. 306–316). Philadelphia: W.B. Saunders.

Hutinger, P.L. (1981). Transition practices for handicapped young children: What the experts say. *Journal of the Division for Early Childhood, 2,* 8–14.

Iancone, R.N., & Stodden, R.A. (1987). *Transition issues and directions.* Reston, VA: Council for Exceptional Children, Division on Mental Retardation.

Johnson, T.E., Chandler, L.K., Kerns, G.M., & Fowler, S.A. (1986). What are parents saying about family involvement in school transitions? A retrospective transition interview. *Journal of the Division for Early Childhood, 11,* 10–17.

Katz, K.S., Pokorni, J.L., & Long, T.M. (1988). *Project CIII: Chronically ill infant intervention project, continuity in intervention from hospital to home.* Washington, DC: Georgetown University, Child Development Center.

Lang, M.D., Behle, M.B., & Ballard, R.A. (1988). The transition from hospital to home. In R.A. Ballard (Ed.), *Pediatric care of the ICN graduate* (pp. 12–16). Philadelphia: W.B. Saunders.

MacKeith, R. (1973). The feelings and behavior of parents of handicapped children. *Developmental Medicine and Child Neurology, 15,* 524–527.

Noonan, M.J., & Kilgo, J.L. (1987). Transition services for early age individuals with severe mental retardation. In R.N. Iancone & R.A. Stodden (Eds.), *Transition issues and directions* (pp. 25–37). Reston, VA: Council for Exceptional Children, Division on Mental Retardation.

Noonan, M.J., & Stodden, R.A. (1986). *The preschool preparation and transition model: Preparing handicapped infants for least restrictive preschool environments.* (Technical Proposal, U.S. Office of Special Education Project No. 024RH60073). Honolulu: University of Hawaii, Dept. of Special Education.

Platzker, A.C.G., Lew, C.D., Cohen, S.R., Thompson, J., Ward, S.L.D., & Keens, T.G. (1988). Home care of infants with chronic lung disease. In R.A. Ballard (Ed.), *Pediatric care of the ICN graduate* (pp. 289–294). Philadelphia: W.B. Saunders.

Pueschel, S.M. (1988). *The young person with Down syndrome: Transition from adolescent to adulthood.* Baltimore: Paul Brookes.

Sainato, D.M., Strain, P.S., Lefebvre, D., & Rapp, N. (1987). Facilitating transition times with handicapped preschool children: A comparison between peer-mediated and antecedent prompt procedures. *Journal of Applied Behavior Analysis, 20,* 285–291.

Seligman, M., & Darling, B.R. (1989). *Ordinary families, special children: A systems approach to childhood disability.* New York: Guilford Press.

Shearer, M.S., & Mori, A.A. (1987). Administration of preschool special education programs: Strategies for effectiveness. *Journal of the Division for Early Childhood, 11,* 161–170.

Simeonsson, R.J. (1988a). Assessing family environments. In D.B. Bailey and R.J. Simeonsson (Eds.), *Family assessment in early intervention* (pp. 167–183). Columbus, OH: Charles Merrill.

Simeonsson, R.J. (1988b). Unique characteristics of families with young handicapped children. In D.B. Bailey & R.J. Simeonsson (Eds.), *Family assessment in early intervention* (pp. 27–43). Columbus, OH: Charles Merrill.

Snell, M.E., & Grigg, N.C. (1987). Instructional assessment and curriculum development. In M.E. Snell (Ed.), *Systematic instruction of persons with severe handicaps* (3rd ed., pp. 64–109). Columbus, OH: Charles Merrill.

Thurlow, M.L., Lehr, C.A., & Ysseldyke, J.E. (1987). Exit criteria in early childhood programs for handicapped children. *Journal of the Division for Early Childhood, 11,* 118–123.

Thurlow, M.L., Ysseldyke, J.E., & Weiss, J.A. (1988). Early childhood special education exit decisions: How are they made? How are they evaluated? *Journal of the Division for Early Childhood, 12,* 253–262.

Vincent, L.J., Salisbury, C., Walter, G., Brown, P., Gruenwald, L.J., & Powers, M. (1980). Program evaluation and curriculum development in early childhood special education: Criteria of the next environment. In W. Sailor, B. Wilcox, & L. Brown (Eds.), *Methods of instruction for severely handicapped students* (pp. 303–328). Baltimore: Paul Brookes.

Walter, G., & Vincent, L. (1982). The handicapped child in the regular kindergarten classroom. *Journal of the Division for Early Childhood, 6,* 84–95.

Webster's Ninth New Collegiate Dictionary. (1988). Springfield, MA: Merriam-Webster.

Weiner, R., & Koppelman, J. (1987). *From birth to five: Serving the youngest handicapped children.* Alexandria, VA: Capitol Publications.

Wickler, L. (1981). Chronic stresses of families of mentally retarded children. *Family Relations, 30,* 281–288.

Will, M. (1984). *OSERS programming for the transition of youth with disabilities: Bridges from school to working life.* Washington, DC: U.S. Department of Education, Office of Special Education & Rehabilitative Services.

Winton, P.J. (1988). Effective communication between parents and professionals. In D.B. Bailey & R.J. Simeonsson (Eds.), *Family assessment in early intervention* (pp. 207–228). Columbus, OH: Charles Merrill.

Winton, P.J., Turnbull, A.P., & Blacher, J. (1984). *Selecting a preschool: A guide for parents of handicapped children.* Austin, TX: Pro-Ed.

Wolery, M. (1987). Overview of instructional issues. In R. Byrd (Ed.), *Project STEPS: Helpful entry level skills and instructional strategies.* Lexington, KY: Child Development Centers of the Bluegrass.

Wolery, M., Ault, M.J., & Doyle, P.M. (1992). *Teaching students with moderate and severe disabilities: Use of response prompting strategies.* White Plains, NY: Longman.

Wolery, M., Bailey, D.B., & Sugal, G.M. (1988). *Effective teaching: Principles and procedures of applied behavior analysis with exceptional students.* Boston: Allyn & Bacon.

Wolery, M., Doyle, P.M., Gast, D.L., Ault, M.J., & Simpson, S.L. (in press). Comparison of progressive time delay and transition-based teaching with preschoolers who display developmental delays. *Journal of Early Intervention.*

Mark Wolery is a senior research scientist in the Early Childhood Intervention Program at Allegheny-Singer Research Institute, Pittsburgh.

○ 2 ○

As we enter the 1990s, the emphasis on infant and early childhood programs cannot be ignored. In this article, the authors review legislation enabling each state to have these programs. The article covers all the necessary regulations and considerations for program implementation.

Implementing Services for Infants and Toddlers with Developmental Delays

Ron P. Colarusso and Thomas G. Kana

The U.S. Congress enacted the Education of the Handicapped Act Amendments of 1986, Public Law 99–457, with the intent of providing comprehensive services to preschool handicapped children and their families. Public Law 99–457 was updated in the Individuals with Disabilities Education Act of 1990, Public Law 101–476. On October 7, 1991, President George Bush signed the reauthorization legislation for Part H of the Individuals with Disabilities Education Act (IDEA), the program for Infants and Toddlers with Disabilities and their Families.

The contents and requirements of the Individuals with Disabilities Education Act of 1991 (PL 102–119) hold great opportunity and great challenge for a variety of professionals. In establishing a national policy for early intervention, this law provides incentives and assistance to states that extend existing special education services from school age to birth. This law breaks new ground in its recognition of the critical importance of the family in its impact upon development. It also requires the application of a variety of models other than traditional education models, employing a team of multidisciplinary professionals to serve young children with disabilities and their families. As of 1991, all states agreed to provide educational services for every child with a developmental disability from birth.

IDEA divides the preschool population into two groups: infants/toddlers (birth to age 3) and preschoolers (ages 3 to 6). Title I (Part H), for infants and toddlers with disabilities from birth to age 3, and Title II (Part B), for preschool children with disabilities, ages 3 to 6, under PL 102–119, The Individuals with Disabilities Education Act of 1991. Following a brief description of Part B, the remainder of this article addresses the implications and issues unique to Part H.

PROVISIONS OF PART B

A brief discussion of Part B is warranted because of the interrelation of parts B and H. Part B adds a mandate to the previously permissive section of PL 94–142, now requiring that each state provide a free, appropriate public education and related services to all eligible children with handicaps aged 3 through 5.

Part B extends the existing provisions for school-age children—the individualized education program (IEP), due process, confidentiality, and placement in the least restrictive environment—to these younger children. Part B services, under Part B, were to be in place by the 1991–1992 school year. If not, all federal funds for services to children birth to age 6, as well as funding for related programs (research, personnel development, demonstration projects) would be lost to states that are not in compliance.

The state education agency (SEA), working through local education agencies (LEAs) or other contracted service agencies, is responsible for implementing Part B. Federal funding is provided on a per-child basis according to those currently receiving services and to those identified as not presently receiving services but who will be served (each new school year). Appropriate service delivery models are left up to individual states. Services may be direct or indirect to the child. For example, a family may be recognized for its importance in the child's development and therefore may receive the only services considered necessary for the good of the child, while the child receives no direct service. Although services might be the more traditional school-based, the lead agency has the right to provide appropriate services through home-based models or by contracting with other government or private service providers such as day-care centers.

PROVISIONS OF PART H

Part H is a completely new section of the Education of the Handicapped Act. Congress declared, "There is an urgent and substantial need to enhance development, reduce potential future special education costs, maximize the potential for future independence, and to enhance a family's capacity to meet their infant/toddler's needs" [Title I, Part H, § 671(a) 1,2,3,4]. Financial assistance to states is provided to "develop and implement a statewide, comprehensive, coordinated, multidisciplinary, interagency program of early intervention services for handicapped infants and toddlers and their families" [Title I, Part H, § 671(b) 1]. The federal requirements are broad, giving individual states considerable autonomy as to who will be served, what state agencies will be charged with the responsibility to ensure services, and what type of delivery systems are appropriate.

A COMPREHENSIVE SYSTEM FOR PART H

A comprehensive, statewide early intervention system must include the following 14 points in the infant and toddler program:

1. A state definition of the term *developmentally delayed*.
2. A timetable to ensure services by the start of the fifth year. In years one and two, the state shall designate a lead agency and the governor of each state must name an Interagency Coordinating Council (ICC). In years three and four, the state must adopt a public policy containing all components for statewide early intervention and demonstrate that it is in effect. Some latitude is permitted in the timeline; the law allows exceptions for making "good faith effort" or "assurances" for appropriate programming.
3. A comprehensive, multidisciplinary evaluation for the infant/toddler and family.
4. An individualized family service plan (IFSP) for each infant/toddler and family, developed by a multidisciplinary team including the parent/guardian, and reviewed in at least 6-month intervals. Each IFSP must include present levels of functioning, a statement of family strengths and needs, expected outcomes, specific services provided, projected dates of initiation and duration of services, and name of the service manager, and steps to support the transition to the preschool program.
5. A comprehensive child find system and a system for referral.
6. A public awareness program focusing on early identification.
7. A state central directory of services, resources, experts, and demonstration projects.
8. A single line of responsibility, in a designated lead agency, for general administration, supervision and monitoring of programs and activities, and promotion of interagency agreements.
9. A comprehensive system of personnel development.
10. A policy pertaining to contracting with service providers.
11. Procedures for timely reimbursement from agencies responsible for payment.
12. Procedural safeguards with respect to programs, infants/toddlers, and parents/guardians.
13. Standards to ensure appropriately trained, prepared, and qualified personnel.
14. A data collection system showing numbers served and types of services provided.

Administrative Responsibilities

IDEA requires interagency cooperation and flexibility, especially for Part H, as the provision calls for "identification and coordination of all available resources within the state from federal, state, local, and private sources" [Title I, Part H, § 676 (b)9(B)]. State agencies must become adept at identifying these resources and working in concert rather than in adversarial positions. The goal of cooperative activities must be improved unduplicated services and better use of limited financial resources. Private insurance is a largely untapped potential resource (Fox, Freedman, & Klepper, 1989). Administration of Part H is the responsibility of each state's designated lead agency and Interagency Coordinating Council (ICC).

Lead Agency

To participate in Part H, each state must designate a lead agency responsible for developing the state's plan, coordinating the interagency services, and implementing the services. Because of the range of services needed from the health and social services areas, many states have chosen lead agencies other than education. The majority of states (twenty-eight) chose health, mental health, mental retardation, human services, or developmental disabilities lead agencies, and twenty-one states chose their education agency. Three states, Maine, Rhode Island, and Texas designated the State ICC as the lead agency, and Maryland chose its Office of Children and Youth. The lead agency for Part H in each state and territory are identified in Table 1.

Interagency Coordination

To ensure cooperation between the various agencies that provide needed services, the law requires coordination of services at the local, state, and federal levels. The lead agency is responsible for entering into formal interagency agreements designating each agency's responsibility for providing and paying for early intervention services. These formal agree-

TABLE 1   Lead Agencies for Part H Services

Agency	States/Territories
Department of Education	Alabama, Colorado, Connecticut, Delaware, Florida, Guam, Illinois, Iowa, Louisiana, Maryland, Michigan, Minnesota, Missouri, Nebraska, New Hampshire, New Jersey, Oklahoma, Palau, South Dakota, Tennessee, Mariana Islands, Vermont
Department of Health	American Samoa, Alaska, Hawaii, Idaho, Kansas, Massachusetts, Mississippi, New Mexico, New York, Ohio, Puerto Rico, South Carolina, Utah, Virgin Islands, Washington, West Virginia, Wisconsin, Wyoming
Department of Mental Health/ Mental Retardation/DD	Arizona, California, Indiana, Montana, Oregon, Virginia
Department of Human Services/ Human Resources	Arkansas, Washington, DC, Georgia, Kentucky, Nevada, North Carolina, North Dakota
Department of Public Welfare	Pennsylvania
Interagency Coordination Council	Maine, Rhode Island, Texas

Source: "An Introduction to PL 99-457 and the National Policy Agenda for Serving Young Children with Special Needs and Their Families" by P. L. Trohanis, 1989, in J. J. Gallagher, P. L. Trohanis, and R. M. Clifford (Eds.), *Policy Implementation and PL 99-457* (pp. 1–18), Baltimore: Paul H. Brookes.

ments must be completed to qualify for fourth-year funding. A policy for contracting with public or private service providers also is required, along with procedures for resolving disputes about payments and other matters. Not only does this ensure services, but it also requires that each agency provide financial support, when appropriate, and maintain any services it provided before the law was enacted. Regardless of the agency involved, however, the lead agency is responsible for ensuring that services are provided. The components of Part H that have shown least progress across states are interagency agreements and those addressing financial responsibilities (Harbin, Gallagher, Lille, and Eckland, 1990).

An important provision in Part H is the "payor of last resort" [Title I, Part H, § 681 (a,b)]. Identification and use of alternative public and private funds are needed for success in financing services to infants/toddlers and their families. Various financing options may exist depending upon an individual's situation and the state's specifications. Families may be called upon to share the cost of services on a "schedule of sliding fees" that match their ability to contribute at the appropriate level. Private insurance may be used to help defray costs. Medicaid also may be used for qualifying families. Agencies that have been providing needed services to eligible infants/toddlers must continue to do so, as part H is not designed to supplant funding in these cases. Thus, a combination of sources might be needed. Interagency participation and cooperation is crucial to the successful delivery of services to eligible infants/toddlers and their families.

Federal Interagency Coordination

In implementing the Handicapped Infants and Toddlers Program, Congress required that the Secretary of Education and the Secretary of Health and Human Services facilitate interagency coordination to assure maximum funding of services from all agencies, and also to ensure that funds are not being withdrawn or reduced in programs not directly under the Education of the Handicapped Act. Therefore, a Federal Interagency Coordinating Council (FICC) was established to coordinate Part H services at the federal level. In a joint study, the U.S. Department of Education and the U.S. Department of Health and Human Services (1989) identified sixteen programs they administer that should contribute resources to the program:

1. *Handicapped Infants and Toddlers Program.* Education of the Handicapped (Part H).
2. *Chapter 1 Handicapped Program.* Education Consolidation and Improvement Act (Chapter 1).
3. *Assistance for Education of All Handicapped Children.* Education of the Handicapped Act (Part B).
4. *Head Start Program.* Head Start Act.
5. *Medicaid.* Social Security Act (Medicaid).
6. *Maternal and Child Health Block Grants.* Social Security Act (MCH Block Grant).
7. *Child Welfare Services Program.* Social Security Act (Child Welfare).
8. *Developmental Disabilities Basic State Grants Program.* Developmental Disabilities Assistance and Bill of Rights Act (ADD Basic State Grants).

9. *Alcohol, Drug Abuse and Mental Health Block Grant Program.* Public Health Service Act (Mental Health Block Grant).
10. *Community Health Service Program.* Public Health Service Act (Community Health).
11. *Indian Health Service Program.* Indian Health Care Improvement Act (Indian Health).
12. *Migrant Health Services Program.* Public Health Service Act (Migrant Health).
13. *Preventive Health and Health Services Block Grant.* Public Health Service Act (Health Block Grant).
14. *Health Care for the Homeless Program.* Homeless Assistance Act (Health for Homeless).
15. *Social Services Block Grant.* Social Security Act (Social Services Block Grant).

These sixteen programs differ in eligible age groups and allow for discretion at the state level in prioritizing services emphases. Nevertheless, they all have the potential to use federal funds to provide services to infants and toddlers with disabilities. Figure 1 presents the organizational location of each program.

State Interagency Coordination

A State Interagency Coordinating Council (ICC), with a minimum of 15 members, appointed by the governor of each state, has the responsibility to "advise and assist" the lead agency in performing its responsibilities. The ICC is responsible for:

—identifying various sources of fiscal and other support services,
—assigning financial responsibility to appropriate agencies,
—promoting interagency agreements and preparing federal applications.

The ICC also is responsible for preparing and submitting an annual status report to the governor.

State ICC members must "reasonably" represent the population of the state and be composed of, at least, three parents, three public providers of early intervention services, one representative of the state legislature, one person involved in personnel preparation, and other representatives of appropriate agencies.

Some confusion exists in relation to the terms *advise* and *assist* as ICC responsibilities. Therefore, the range of authority of each state's ICC varies from a reactive/advisory role to a proactive policy-making authority (Harbin & Van Horn, 1990).

The Executive Office of the Division for Early Childhood (DEC) of the Council for Exceptional Children (1991) has recommended that the ICC be responsible for planning the entire system, encompassing ages birth through 5. This is in response to the possibly fragmented system that may exist when two different agencies are responsible for parts H and B. If the ICC were to be entrusted with these additional responsibilities at this time, state education agencies currently planning and implementing part B programs might significantly change the manner in which they conduct their overall systems.

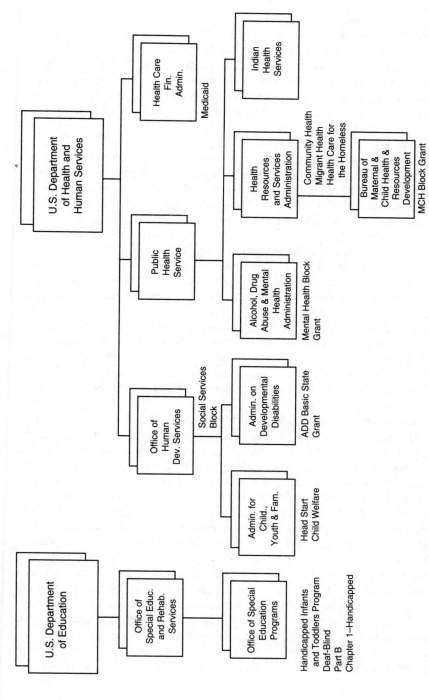

Source: Department of Education and Department of Health and Human Services, 1989.

FIGURE 1   *Organizational Location of Programs Providing at Least One Intervention Service*

Local Interagency Coordination

Because of the miltidisciplinary approach required in providing services under Part H, local interagency agreements are essential in delivering comprehensive services. Assessment of the infant and family requires a multidisciplinary team. The intervention plan in most cases specifies services from several disciplines. Therefore, interagency coordination and formal agreements are essential because a number of agencies and private service providers are involved in extending the direct services specified in the law.

Transition of Services

The transition from Part H to Part B services creates a major difficulty in the continuum of services and requires interagency cooperation and planning, especially when the Part H lead agency is not education. Noneducation Part H lead agencies, which do not follow a traditional education model, provide services to the third birthday. In contrast, the traditional education model determines eligibility by age at the beginning of the school year and does not provide for new students during the school year based on age. Therefore, some children could be without services for nearly a year.

To clarify the issue of continued services, the Office of Special Education Programs (Schrag, 1990, p. 1) has stated, "Under the statutory and regulatory provisions, children with handicapping conditions are eligible for a free appropriate public education upon their third birthday." This clearly places the responsibility under Part B at the child's third birthday, regardless of when it is. If agreed, however, the child could continue to receive the same services from the same service providers for the remainder of the school year. The 1991 amendments of PL 102–199 have proposed a new provision that permits a state to use funds under Part H to provide a free, appropriate public education in accordance with Part B to children with disabilities from their third birthday to the beginning of the following school year.

Another confounding variable in the transition between Part H and Part B is the eligibility definition. Two different definitions, especially when the Part B is more restrictive, could leave a child who is eligible for Part H ineligible at the third birthday. The greatest concern is in states that have included "at-risk" in their definition of developmental delay. A state education agency is allowed to adopt Part H eligibility criteria in determining eligibility for Part B except for the at-risk children who could not receive services funded by Part B and be counted in the 3–5-year-old program (Tucker, 1990). The 1991 amendments of PL 102–119 recognize the need to enhance services for minority, low-income, inner-city, and rural populations, which may force the use of an at-risk category.

The service delivery model for the two programs may differ to the extent that services to the child or family could change radically. The Individual Family Service Plan (IFSP) of Part H might focus more specifically on services to the parents, such as parent training and counseling, which may not be included in an individualized education program (IEP) under Part B. Again, state education agencies may use IFSPs in place of IEPs under Part B as long as they meet all the requirements specified for an IEP. Regardless, they may include parent counseling and training as a related service in the IEP (Tucker, 1990).

Eligible Population

Within Part H, the term "handicapped infants/toddlers" covers the age range of birth up to age 3. As one of the 14 required components, states have been given individual responsibility in developing a definition for developmental delay. Federal guidelines require that the identified population must be having "developmental delays," as measured by appropriate diagnostic instruments and procedures, in a minimum of one of five areas: cognitive development, physical development including vision and hearing, communication development, social and emotional development, adaptive development. Also included are those whose diagnosed physical/mental condition has a "high probability" of resulting in developmental delays. At the state's discretion, those who would be "at risk" for developmental delays without special services may be included as well.

Determining the population to be served under Part H is challenging for a number of reasons. One addresses the state of the art (or science) in the ability to identify handicapped infants and toddlers correctly. Designating the type of handicapping condition present is necessary to be eligible for services. Medical professionals can identify with some reliability, at an early age, medical conditions highly related to developmental delays, but reliable and valid assessment instruments that identify delays in developmental areas are not available. Infants and toddlers who do not have medical syndromes challenge educators because of the false positives and negatives associated with available assessment instruments. Developmental assessment of infants/toddlers requires teams of professionals who are highly skilled in both development and formal assessment—and they are in short supply.

Harbin, Terry, and Daguio (1989) noted several difficulties in identification:

- Detection, because of the complexity of developmental patterns.
- Lack of predictive ability of assessment instruments.
- Scant professional literature identifying what risk factors will likely result in disability or delay.
- Possible "contradictory policies from other federally mandated programs."

Harbin and Terry (1990) further noted the lack of reliable and valid instruments for this age population, as well as the failure of traditional instruments to detect some delays and disabilities.

Including infants born with medical or environmental conditions that may be associated with handicapping conditions further complicates the issue. If an individual state decides to include the "at risk" in developmental delay definition, that decision impacts both programming and funding. In addition to the "biologically at risk," Part H eligibility also may include the "environmentally at risk." States are now struggling to decide whether to include this "at risk" population in their definitions. If the environmentally at-risk are included, will special education be open to the same criticism received in the 1970s associated with mislabeling minorities, and will funding be available for a much larger population than originally projected? The transition issue discussed earlier also must be considered because "at-risk" is not a qualifying criterion for Part B. Therefore, services to children and their families might end abruptly on the child's third birthday.

The system of classification, left open to the discretion of each state, might best be described as noncategorical, and definitely a departure from the traditional school-age definitions of handicap. Harbin et al. (1989) analyzed the draft definitions from 28 states and found large variations in the criteria for eligibility. States were similar in that most relied on traditional test instruments for determining eligibility. Developmental delay was determined by specified departures from the norm in either standard deviations or in percentages of delay. These ranged from 15% to 50% differences and differences of one to two standard deviations depending upon the individual state. Differences also were found in eligibility requirements in the number of areas in which delay must be present, one or two. States "tended to ignore" the problems engendered by the inability to find valid instruments to measure developmental areas of these young children.

When included, the "at risk" definitions showed even wider variation. For example, 36 different terms were used in the area of environmentally "at risk." These terms sometimes were used singularly as a requirement for eligibility rather than as part of a more professionally valid multiple-risk scheme. The varied definitions will create problems when mobile American families lose eligibility as they move to states that have stricter criteria.

A population that will have a significant effect on Part H consists of children exposed to cocaine (and other substances) in utero. They exemplify the complexity involved in defining and serving this population. Depending on the professional source, the disabilities associated with substance abuse include poor feeding patterns, increased tremulousness and startles, decreased muscle tone, and poor state control (Schneider, Griffith, & Chasnoff, 1989). These infants require immediate attention. They will likely qualify for Part H services if a state's eligibility criteria include the biologically "at risk." Substance abuse population studies have involved mostly lower socioeconomic mothers. Therefore, many of these infants would meet eligibility criteria in states that include the environmentally at-risk. Current professional literature, being primarily medical, addresses the infant exclusively. The potential long-term effects of interuturinal exposure to substances is uncertain, but speculation is that the disabilities may continue into the school years and may require long-term treatment.

Only time and research can answer the questions of how long this population should be served and, if so, under what eligibility criteria services will be provided. Again, these children may meet criteria for Part H services but be ineligible for Part B programs, presenting a difficulty with transition.

Another issue related to the specified population is the service delivery model required by the myriad of exceptionalities. How will all children and families determined as eligible for services receive them? Once defined, diverse types of trained personnel will be required to dispense services. Families are to be included throughout the process. Family assessment and intervention, however, may become intrusive. Professionals' resistance to family wishes, which conceivably could become reality under these assessment and intervention requirements, goes against the spirit of the law. Although some questions raised are not targeted exclusively at operationalizing the definition, they do show that determination of the definition affects the other 13 required components.

Service Delivery

Intervention services specified as primary Part H services for infants/toddlers and their families are:

—family training and counseling.
—home visits.
—special instruction.
—speech pathology and audiology.
—occupational and physical therapy.
—assistive technology devices.
—transportation.
—psychological services.
—service coordination services (mandatory).
—diagnostic and evaluative medical services.
—early identification screening and assessment services.
—health services necessary to enable the infant/toddler to benefit from the other early intervention services.

These services are to be provided by qualified personnel. Many of these primary services are completely new to the traditional special education model. Others are considered related services for older exceptional children.

Each state has autonomy in determining its own service delivery model. Although the lead agency is responsible for assuring that services are provided, it may not be responsible as the direct provider of services. Other public and private agencies may be the direct service provider to the child and family. The method and location of the service depends on individual needs, as determined by the multidisciplinary team and specified in the IFSP. The 1991 Amendments to PL 102–119, however, add a requirement that early intervention services be provided to the maximum extent possible in "natural" environments, including the home and community settings in which children without disabilities participate. Natural environments are settings that are normal for the child's age.

In that services to the infant/toddler and family vary as a result of the diverse needs of this population, a continuum of service delivery models must be cost-effective as well as professionally sound. Because children and families vary in their resources and needs, no one type of program is best. Appropriate IFSPs dictate the most effective interventions based upon child and family needs. Figure 2 presents a continuum of the main components needed for a comprehensive service delivery plan.

Evaluation and Assessment

From the time of referral, an evaluation of the referred child (including the family assessment) must be completed to allow enough time for the initial IFSP meeting to occur within 45 days. Reassessment must be done at least once a year but may be more frequent when appropriate. *Evaluation* refers to the procedure to determine a child's initial and continued eligibility. *Assessment* denotes an ongoing process to identify the eligible child's needs for program planning for the child and family. Evaluation and assessment

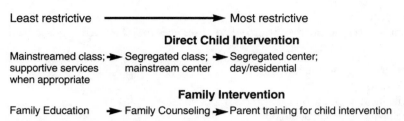

FIGURE 2   Services for Part H Intervention

must be both comprehensive and multidiciplinary. *Multidisciplinary* describes the team of professionals from the appropriate disciplines who have specialized training and expertise in the appropriate methods and procedures. *Comprehensive* means that, as a minimum, the child's level of functioning must be determined in each of the following developmental areas:

—cognitive development.
—physical development, including vision and hearing.
—communication development.
—social or emotional development.
—adaptive development.

Information related to the child's current health status and medical history also must be reviewed and included when appropriate. A family assessment (voluntary) must be designed to determine the familys strengths and needs related to enhancing the child's development.

Individualized Family Service Plan (IFSP)

As mentioned, the initial IFSP meeting must take place within 45 days after the eligible child has been referred for evaluation. Part H is novel in its view of the family as crucially important in its impact upon development (Trohanis, 1989). This is evident with the IFSP. Each infant/toddler and family will have and IFSP, developed by a multidisciplinary team including the parent/guardian. It is to be reviewed in a meeting or by other means in at least 6-month intervals, because of rapid changes in such young children. In addition, an annual meeting must be conducted to evaluate the IFSP for the child and family. To remain useful and practical, IFSPs should allow for ease in changes coinciding with changes in child and family needs.

Each IFSP must include

—present levels of functioning.
—a statement of family strengths and needs.
—expected outcomes.
—specific services provided.

—projected dates of initiation and duration of services.
—name of the service coordinator.
—steps taken to support the transition to the preschool program.

The IFSP includes the required early intervention services as well as other services not required or covered under Part H, the latter of which are intended to provide a comprehensive picture of the child's total service needs (Tucker, 1990).

Appropriate IFSPs allow for the most effective interventions based upon child and family needs. These plans enable close monitoring of the child's developmental changes and changes in family needs to maintain appropriate intervention services. Service delivery models are expected to depart from the traditional single-setting and school-based models. Combinations of school- and home-based models, consultative models to parents, and the involvement of multiple agencies and programs will be incorporated to provide complete services (National Early Childhood Technical Assistance System, 1990). PL 102–119 adds assistive technology devices, physical therapy, transportation, and vision services to the list of early intervention services. Physicians, pediatricians, orientation and mobility specialists, and family therapists are added to the list of qualified personnel. This might especially affect local education agencies in that they will be providing services under a relatively new model.

Family input into the IFSP is a primary consideration. Traditionally, the school IEP process places the child receiving services at the forefront. Under Part H, family members other than the child with a disability may receive services including assessment. Sometimes these services may even be exclusive to family members other than the child having the disability, if those services are deemed critical to the development of the child with a disability.

Professionals and parents too often are at odds with each other. Values and priorities for goals and services frequently differ. The changing nature of today's family (e.g., cultural and economic issues, more single and working parents) further complicates the relationship (Vincent & Salisbury, 1988). Professionals and parents at times disagree about goals of intervention, methods to achieve goals, priorities for treatment, and values related to treatment. Bailey (1987) suggested collaborative goal setting, including selecting intervention strategies, to attain the specified goals. Parents then have a stake in the decision and may participate more actively in attaining those goals. If the child's needs are included and integrated into normal family activities and rituals, the possibility for normalization also increases (National Early Childhood Technical Assistance System, 1990).

Dunst (1988) is a strong advocate for parents' need to become empowered to make decisions, advocate for themselves, and solve their own problems. This entails aiding the family to access its own support to avoid possible isolation as a unit (National Early Childhood Technical Assistance System, 1990). To be effective in collaborative goal setting, professionals must view families as systems and be able to assess family needs, interview effectively, negotiate joint solutions, and be able to match needs to available resources.

Gallagher, Harbin, Thomas, Clifford, and Wenger (1988) noted the difficulties inherent in developing an all-encompassing policy that covers the diverse needs of such a heterogeneous group of families. They suggested that the single common denominator in the group—the family having a child with a handicap or at-risk for a handicapping condition—"brings only a limited amount of communality to the group." Differences in variables such as socioeconomic status, marital status, cultural background, geographical location, family values, attitudes, interests, desires, and coping strategies for dealing with this potentially stressful situation leave policymakers the potential to design rules that are applicable and appropriate for some families and not others.

Procedural Safeguards

Procedural safeguards for Part H correspond to previously developed safeguards for PL 94–142. Although safeguard regulations such as notification, native language, and timelines are straightforward, some safeguards are more controversial. For example, obtaining parental consent is required before conducting the initial evaluation and assessment, as well as providing services for the first time. Although the parent has the right to refuse these services, override procedures are available to the Part H agency. A Part H agency may initiate a hearing to override parental refusal for initial evaluation and assessment. If an impartial reviewer rules in favor of the Part H provider agency, the Part H provider agency may initiate the evaluation process without parental consent. The parent may appeal this decision to a court of competent jurisdiction.

The IFSP requires assessment of a family's needs and resources as related to the enhanced development of the child with a disability. A statement of the family's strengths and needs is to be one of the components. This "virtually assures that the professionals involved will be collecting sensitive information about intrafamily relationships and special family problems" (Gallagher et al., 1988). Family assessment has the potential of becoming intrusive. Disclosure needed for appropriate assessment may be difficult to obtain. A family might gain an unwanted label in order to receive services. This may infringe upon a family's rights to confidentiality, mandated by procedural safeguards within the law. Gallagher et al. (1988) further noted that multiple agency involvement (e.g., records passing between more hands and service agencies) complicates this right to confidentiality.

Parents also have the right to "examine records related to assessment, screening, eligibility determination and the development of the IFSP" (Gallagher et al., 1988). Thus, records must be completed in a clear and understandable manner.

Coordination of services to eligible children and families is necessary because of the variety of agencies and professionals involved in service delivery. A service coordinator must be assigned to each child and family to ensure that the appropriate services are coordinated. The service coordinator is to be assigned from the profession most immediately relevant to the infant's/toddler's or family's needs.

Although support for single responsibility for coordinating services is strong, the term *case management*, as written in the original law, has been criticized for its connotation that families are "cases to be managed." The Division for Early Childhood (DEC) of the Council for Exceptional Children (1990) successfully recommended that the terms be changed to *service coordination* and *service coordinator*.

The concept of least restrictive environment (LRE) must remain true to its "scientific" purposes (Smith & Strain, 1988). In providing a continuum of services, the team must consider if, when, and how much integration will be of appropriate benefit to he infant/toddler and family. Services should be provided in the context of a family's community when it is deemed in the best interest of both the child and family (National Early Childhood Technical Assistance System, 1990). Placement in a mainstreamed setting without trained personnel and planned integrative activities, however, is inappropriate. Once a system of programming has been activated, continuing quality assurances and checks must remain in place.

Personnel Preparation and Standards

Another of the 14 requirements of Part H requires a comprehensive system of personnel development. The law further mandates that appropriate personnel provide services that may include family training and counseling, home visits, special instruction, speech pathology and audiology, occupational and physical therapy, assistive technology devices, transportation, psychological services, service coordination services (mandatory), diagnostic and evaluative medical services, early identification screening and assessment services, and health services necessary to enable the infant/toddler to benefit from the other early intervention services (not including general treatment or surgery).

These services are to be provided by qualified personnel including special educators, speech/language pathologists, occupational/physical therapists, orientation and mobility specialists, family therapists, psychologists, social workers, pediatricians and other physicians, nurses, and nutritionists. Interventions will involve a multidisciplinary approach in which the interventionists work together as a team. The law requires professionals to have the highest entry-level academic degree needed for any state-approved or recognized certification, licensing, registration, or other comparable requirements that apply to that profession or discipline. This requirement has generated confusion surrounding its meaning of "highest level of certification or licensing." It does not mean the standards of the profession or the highest level of standards. It denotes the highest entry-level standards for employment in a profession or discipline enacted by a state legislature or an authorized state agency.

The law does not designate specifically who should serve as service coordinator from specific groups of professionals. This raises questions as to what specific qualifications might be required of a service coordinator. Bailey (1989) specified certain issues for professionals who work with young children with disabilities and unique to the requirements of Part H: the special professional competence and knowledge necessary to work with this age population, the possible varied contexts in which the child may be receiving services, multiagency involvement in service delivery, and the number and types of professionals who may be providing services. Also unique is the level of family involvement as both program contributors and receivers.

Once a system of programming has been put into place, continuing quality assurances and checks must remain. Within the 14 points, one point specifically calls for establishment and maintenance of standards for personnel so they remain appropriately and adequately trained. This includes establishment of state-approved licenses, registration, or other approved requirements. Effective service providers are needed. Personnel shortages, certification standards, and the quality of training programs are all essential features to be addressed for programming to be effective (Burke, McLaughlin, & Valdivieso, 1988).

Each discipline involved has its own formal education track, its own certification requirements, and its own professional organizations. As Bailey (1989) noted, little is done in preparation for working with young children who are disabled (along with their families) in these separate professions. For example, an adequately licensed physical therapist may have little or no training or experience working with infants. Requirements must assure that personnel are trained adequately for this young population.

Compounding the potential difficulty in setting standards is the probable difficulty in filling positions. In a study reported by Meisels, Harbin, Modigliani, and Olsen (1988), personnel shortages nationally were recognized as a "serious policy issue" that all states will face in providing services. More than 68% of states reported lacking in necessary personnel preparation programs, more than 80% reported too few trained early intervention personnel, and almost 100% reported shortages in therapists.

Standards alone will not assure quality staff. Burke, McLaughlin, and Valdivieso (1988) reported on the shortage of well-trained personnel. Although training programs exist in all but seven states, for those who will work with infants and young children, existing programs are unlikely to be able to handle the immediate demands of PL 102–119. Faced with increased demand, along with potential personnel shortages, states may be tempted to lower or alter standards for certification. Programs provided at institutions of higher learning and state certification standards must remain true to the intent of the law. Inservice training can provide necessary skills to professionals already in the field who may wish to work with this population. The same threats to quality service, however, remain.

SUMMARY/CONCLUSION

The opportunity for change has been extended. Part H of Public Law 102–119, the Individuals with Disabilities Education Act, is in place. The importance of families in their children's development has been acknowledged. The degree of cooperation needed between and among the various groups charged with implementation and provision of service is to an extent never previously attempted. Professionals must remember who the law is intended to serve and do their utmost to assure that these services become reality.

REFERENCES

Bailey, D. B. (1987). Collaborative goal-setting with families: Resolving differences in values and priorities for services. *Topics in Early Childhood Special Education*, 7(2), 59–71.

Bailey, D. B. (1989). Issues and directions in preparing professionals to work with young handicapped children and their families. In J. J. Gallagher, P. L. Trohanis, & R. M. Clifford (Eds.), *Policy Implementation and PL 99–457* (pp. 97–132). Baltimore: Paul H. Brookes.

Burke, P. J., McLaughlin, M. J., & Valdivieso, C. H. (1988). Preparing professionals to educate handicapped infants and young children: Some policy considerations. *Topics in Early Childhood Special Education, 8*(1), 73–80.

Division for Early Childhood, Council for Exceptional Children. (1990). *Statement of the International Division for Early Childhood of the Council for Exceptional Children to the Congress of the United States with respect to reauthorization of Part H and amendments to Part B of the Education of the Handicapped Act regarding services to children from birth to age six years.* Pittsburgh: Author.

Division for Early Childhood, Council for Exceptional Children. (1991). *DEC recommendations for reauthorization of Part H and amendments to Part B of the Individuals with Disabilities Act.* Pittsburgh: Author.

Dunst C. J. (1988). Resources, social support, and family functioning. In C. J. Dunst (Ed.), *Enabling and empowering families.* Cambridge, MA: Brookline Books.

Fox, H. B., Freedman, S. A., & Klepper B. R. (1989). Financing programs for young children with handicaps. In J. J. Gallagher, P. L. Trohanis, & R. M. Clifford (Eds.), *Policy implementation and PL 99-457* (pp. 169–182). Baltimore: Paul H. Brookes.

Gallagher, J. J., Harbin, G., Thomas, D., Clifford, R., & Wenger, M. (1988). *Major policy issues in implementing Part H, PL 99–457, infants and toddlers.* Chapel Hill, NC: Carolina Institute for Child & Family Policy.

Harbin, G. L., Gallagher, J. J., Lillie, T., & Eckland, J. (1990). *Executive summary: Status of states' progress in implementing Part H of PL 99–457* (Rep. No. 2). Chapel Hill, NC: Carolina Institute for Child & Family Policy.

Harbin, G. L., & Terry, D. (1990). *Definition of developmentally delayed and at-risk infants and toddlers.* Chapel Hill, NC: Carolina Policy Studies Program.

Harbin, G. L., Terry, D., & Daguio, C. (1989). *Status of the states' progress toward developing a definition for developmentally delayed as required by PL 99-457, Part H.* Chapel Hill, NC: Carolina Policy Studies Program.

Harbin, G. L., & Van Horn, J. (1990). *Interagency coordinating council roles and responsibilities.* Chapel Hill, NC: Carolina Policy Studies Program.

Meisels, S. J., Harbin, G., Modigliani, K., & Olson, K. (1988). Formulating optimal state early childhood intervention policies. *Exceptional Children, 55,* 159–165.

National Early Childhood Technical Assistance System. (1990). *Least restrictive environment for infants, toddlers, and preschoolers.* Chapel Hill, NC: Frank Porter Graham Child Development Center.

Schneider, J. W., Griffith, D. R., & Chasnoff, I. J. (1989). Infants exposed to cocaine in utero: Implications for developmental assessment and intervention. *Infants and Young Children, 2*(1), 25–36.

Schrag, J. A. (1990). *Age of eligibility for a free appropriate public education for preschool-aged children with handicaps under the Education of the Handicapped Act, as amended by PL 99–457.* Washington, DC: U.S. Department of Education, Office of Rehabilitative Services.

Smith, J. S., & Strain, P. S. (1988). Early childhood special education in the next decade: Implementing and expanding PL 99–457. *Topics in Early Childhood Special Education, 8*(1), 37–47.

Trohanis, P. L. (1989). An introduction to PL 99–457 and the national policy agenda for serving young children with special needs and their families. In J. J. Gallagher, P. L. Trohanis, & R. M. Clifford (Eds.), *Policy implementation and PL 99-457* (pp. 1–18). Baltimore: Paul H. Brookes.

Tucker, J. A. (1990). *Response to Pennsylvania questions on implementing a birth through five early intervention program.* Washington DC: U.S. Department of Education, Office of Special Education & Rehabilitative Services.

U.S. Department of Education and Department of Health and Human Services. (1989). *Meeting the needs of infants and toddlers with handicaps: Federal resources, services, and coordination efforts in the Departments of Education and Health and Human Services.* Washington, DC: U.S. Government Printing Office.

Vincent, L. J., & Salisbury, C. L. (1988). Changing economic and social influences on family involvement. *Topics in Early Childhood Special Education, 8*(1), 48–59.

Ron Colarusso is a professor in the Department of Special Education and coordinator of the Early Childhood/Special Education program at Georgia State University. Thomas Kana is a Ph.D. candidate at Georgia State University and currently is working as a project associate on Project SAMS, a model curricular process for persons with profound disabilities.

3

Missouri was the first state to mandate parent education and family support. This article describes how it was done and offers a model that other states might want to emulate. It includes evidence of the effectiveness of the model with younger children and the success in training parents as the first teachers of their children.

The Challenge of Effective Programming for the Missouri Project— Parents As Teachers

Vicki L. Ehlers and Micca Ruffin

Parents As Teachers (PAT) is based on the premise that:

- Parents are the first and most important teachers of their children.
- The home is the child's first schoolhouse.
- Children will learn more during the early years than at any other time in life.
- All parents want to be good parents and care about their child's development.

The Parents As Teachers program is designed to serve *all* families. Parents who have access to early childhood developmental information in a timely manner can use it to enhance the teaching that naturally resides in the role of parenting. How a child grows and learns during these early years, beginning at birth, will affect later development and lay the foundation for future school success.

HISTORICAL PERSPECTIVE

In 1984 Missouri became the first state in the nation to mandate parent education and family support services, beginning at the child's birth, in every school district. The origin of this mandate dates back to 1972, when the State Board of Education adopted a position paper on early childhood education, defining the role and responsibility of the public education system during the years when home is the child's school.

The State Board's position was rooted in research of the 1950s and 1960s indicating the critical nature of the first three years of life in terms of development of major abilities. This period is also the time when parents are forming and cementing their approaches to child rearing. Studies of early intervention programs initiated in the 1960s showed parent involvement in their child's learning to be the key to the child's success. Findings of the Harvard University Preschool Project, begun in 1965, indicated that the degree of a child's development in language, cognitive intelligence, and social skills at school entry could be predicted at age 3, with few exceptions.

A series of events, orchestrated by the Missouri Department of Elementary and Secondary Education beginning in 1972, led to passage of the Early Childhood Development Act by the Missouri General Assembly in 1984. The legislation mandated statewide parent-child early education.

In 1975 the Department of Education convened its first Conference for Decision Makers on early childhood education and parenting education. Participants included decision makers from the Departments of Health, Education, Social Services, Mental Health, and Corrections. Presenters laid out the benefits of a solid educational foundation in the first years of life and the damaging effects to children of poor parenting. Missouri's governor subsequently designated early education and parenting education as one of five areas of study at the 1976 Governor's Conference on Education.

During the 1977 legislative session legislators who had served on the Governor's Conference Committee on Early Childhood/Parenting Education introduced a bill proposing state funding for developmental screening and follow-up services for children 3 to 5 years of age. The intent was to establish awareness of the improved chances for healthy development of children through early childhood/parent education.

In 1981 the Department again convened a statewide Conference for Decision Makers to consider the importance of supportive services to children even younger than 3. From the research on prevention presented at the conference came the conceptual framework for a Parents As Teachers program for families with children birth to age 3.

PILOT PROJECT STUDY

The foundation for statewide implementation of parent education had begun. With funds from the Department of Education, the Danforth Foundation of St. Louis, and four local school districts, the pilot project was launched in 1981. At the same time, the Commissioner's Committee on Parents As Teachers was formed to promote parents' involvement in their children's education statewide.

The funds enabled establishment of four pilot projects to include 380 families who were expecting their first child December 1981–September 1982. Care was taken to ensure that all socioeconomic strata, parental ages, and family configurations were represented.

Beginning in the third trimester of pregnancy and continuing until children reached age 3, Parents As Teachers pilot project participants received the following services:

- Information and guidance before the baby was born, to help expectant parents psychologically prepare for the important job of parenting.
- Timely information about what to look for and expect as the child grew and developed, plus guidance in fostering the child's language, cognitive, social, and motor skill development.
- Periodic screening of the child's educational, hearing, visual, and motor development to detect possible problems or handicaps. If problems were discovered, families were linked with other agencies or professionals for help.
- Monthly personal visits in the home by professionally trained parent educators to individualize the program for each family.
- Monthly group meetings for parents to share experiences and discuss topics appropriate to their children's stage of development. Group meetings were held at Parent Resource Centers in the schools.

PILOT PROJECT EVALUATION

The PAT pilot project had specified seven goals or expected outcomes:

1. Increased knowledge of child development by participating parents.
2. Improved confidence in child rearing by participating parents.
3. Better cognitive and language development of participating children as compared to a comparison group or norm.
4. Better social development of participating children as compared to a comparison group or norm.
5. Fewer undetected incidences of handicapping conditions, particularly hearing and vision, in participating children as compared to a comparison group or norm.
6. Positive feelings about the program's usefulness by participating parents.
7. Positive attitudes toward the school district by participating parents.

Parents' responses to periodic questionnaires and telephone interviews by an independent evaluator indicated that families highly valued the services they were receiving and were proud of their children's accomplishments. The best evidence of parents' satisfaction may well have been the low attrition rate.

Research and Training Associates of Overland Park, Kansas, conducted an independent evaluation of the project in 1985, under contract with the Missouri Department of Elementary and Secondary Education. The program's effectiveness was determined by a treatment/comparison group design, using posttests of children's abilities and assessments of parents' knowledge and perceptions. Evaluators randomly selected 75 project children, and from the same communities 75 comparison children whose parents had not received Parents As Teachers services. Traditional ANCOVE and LISREL analyses of covariance were used to adjust for difference between the two samples. All children were evaluated within 2 weeks of their 3rd birthday at sites equally unfamiliar to the treatment and comparison groups. Examiners did not know the identifying groups of the individual children.

Evaluators used the Kaufman Assessment Battery for Children (KABC) to measure cognitive levels. Zimmerman's Preschool Language Scale (PLS) was selected to assess children's understanding and use of language. Parents rated their children's social development using selected and adapted items from the "personal-social" domain of the Battelle Developmental Inventory. In addition, psychometrists rated selected aspects of the children's social development at the time of testing. A parent knowledge questionnaire was given to all parents to determine their understanding of child development and appropriate child-rearing practices.

Results of the evaluation confirmed the benefits of the pilot project. At age 3, project children were:

- Significantly more advanced than comparison group children in language development.
- Significantly ahead of their peers in problem solving and other intellectual abilities.
- Significantly advanced over comparison group children in demonstrating coping skills and positive relationships with adults.

Traditional characteristics of "risk" (e.g., parents' age, educational achievement, income, and single-parent status) bore no correlation with project children's achievement. Participation in the project positively affected parents' perceptions of themselves and of their school district. These findings played an important role in stimulating statewide interest in the project. They also lent valuable credibility to pilot project staff members who subsequently trained parent educators and administrators for statewide implementation of the model.

ENABLING LEGISLATION

During 1983 the Governor called together the heads of principal state agencies serving young children and their families—public health, social services, education, mental health, and corrections—and asked them for statements to present to the legislature in support of early childhood family education. He asked for written estimates of savings that could accrue to their agencies through such a program.

The Health Department, for example, detailed how a program of parent education and developmental screening could be instrumental in reestablishing contact with families of children needing health care who had dropped out of their tracking system. In like manner, the Department of Corrections pointed to the high incidence of abuse and neglect in early childhood reported by the prison population. The Education Department spoke to the cost of remedial and special education services for children who lacked a stimulating, supportive home environment in the formative early years.

The basis for statewide implementation of parent education had been formed. Financing from the Danforth Foundation and the Department of Elementary and Secondary Education followed shortly thereafter. At the same time, the Commissioner's Committee on Parents As Teachers was established to promote parents' involvement in their children's education statewide.

Enabling legislation came in 1984 with passage of the Early Childhood Development Act (Senate Bill 658). A legislative appropriation of $2.8 million in 1985–86 allowed for statewide implementation to begin, providing services to 10 percent of the families with children under age 3. School districts were mandated to provide the programs, and parental participation was voluntary. The impressive results of the independent evaluation of the Parents As Teachers pilot project led to designation of this approach as the state's model of parent education for families with children birth to age 3.

Widespread acceptance of the program has led to a steady increase in funding to allow for manageable growth. The 1987–88 school year brought statewide implementation and reimbursement of the Screening for Children Ages Three and Four Program and the Parent Education for Families with Children Ages Three and Four Program.

Adding the program for families with children ages 3 and 4 enabled school districts to offer a continuum of services from the last trimester of pregnancy until the child's entrance into kindergarten (see Figure 1). This would include some 5-year-old children who have not yet entered formal schooling. The same components of service are recommended in the program for 3- and 4-year-old children as that of the birth to 3-year-old program. Personal visits with families, group meetings, and early childhood screenings are offered through a school district and within guidelines set forth by the Department of Elementary and Secondary Education. Age-appropriate early childhood material is given to parents to further enhance parents' role as teacher of their children.

The goal of the entire early childhood effort in Missouri is to help children develop to their fullest potential, whatever that might be, and to create the role of parent as teacher by understanding the developmental timeline through which all children move to become well-rounded 5-year-olds. The program is not intended to teach academics to children, but it does enable parents to teach the joy of learning through appropriate and positive developmental opportunities and the development of self-esteem, and by helping parents become good observers of their children.

Funds have been made available to school districts that wish to apply for implementing activities and strategies targeted at the hard-to-reach/hard-to-engage population, as defined by the districts. Districts using these supportive funds have realized successful recruitment and retention. Of 543 school districts in the 1987–88 and 1988–89 school years, 339 and 391, respectively, chose to access the funds. An estimated 11,590 families in 1987–88 and 22,059 families in 1988–89 were served through the parent education programs in the participating school districts.

Families for whom the funds were used were divided into the following categories:

Low Income	Geographically Isolated
Teen Parents	Two Working Parents
Single Parents	English as Second Language
Abusive/Neglectful	Low Functioning Parents
Migrant	Special Needs Children
Transient	Institutionalized Parents

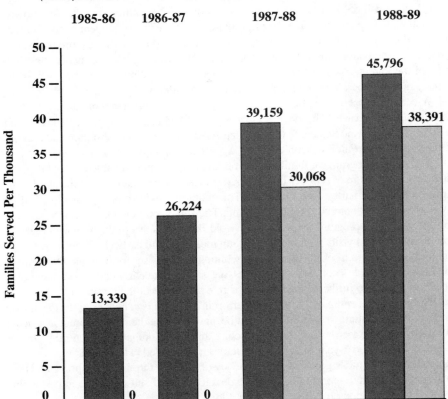

(As Reported to the Missouri Department of Elementary and Secondary Education)

FIGURE 1   *Missouri Families Served Through Early Childhood Development Act of 1984 Parent Education Programs*

An example of effective strategies one school district employed in providing services for hard-to-reach families, as reported to Missouri's Department of Elementary and Secondary Education, reads as follows:

Two of the hard-to-reach families served had special needs children, in addition to other factors which designated them as "hard-to-reach." One of the families has a child with neurological impairment which is manifesting itself in language, speech, motor, and cognitive delays. A second family has a 3-year-old with gross motor and language delays as well as vision concern. Both parents are developmentally disabled. One-year-old twins in the family have gross motor delays, hearing impairment, and diagnosed epilepsy with grand mal seizures.

Because of the mentioned conditions, the strategy that was most effective for our hard-to-reach families was more frequent home visits. Many more hours were involved in working with these families, as we attempted to help connect their needs with available agency services. Contacts were made with DFS [Department of Family Services], Community Action, Franklin County Board for the Handicapped, Cardinal Glennon Hospital, Head Start, and our Cooperative for Special Education. The empowerment concept has worked in these instances, as the families seem better able to assume their roles as teachers and advocates for their children as they follow through on suggestions and referrals.

During 1988–89, appropriations allowed for 30% of eligible families with children ages birth to 3 to participate. Since 1987–88, additional funds have been provided for parent education and screening for families with 3- and 4-year-old children. The state provides local school districts a base payment for each participating family. Many districts voluntarily enroll more than their state-funded quota of families. Reimbursement has been made available to districts for "hard-to-reach" families.

Statewide expansion has challenged the program to demonstrate its effectiveness in the inner cities, with the rural poor, with adolescent parents, and with other special populations. The Missouri experience has shown that the need for support and assistance in the parenting role crosses all socioeconomic and educational levels. "High-risk" families are attracted to this nontargeted program because it does not imply their inadequacy or incompetence as parents. Their special needs are met through intensified service provided by the local school district.

Although it is delivered by the public schools, PAT has been a public/private partnership from the outset. Its widespread support can be attributed to its many benefits. Health care providers see it as improving children's physical well-being. Mental health, social services, and corrections personnel view it as preventing and reducing abuse and neglect. Churches endorse it as strengthening family life. Businesses see its potential for reducing stress and improving the quality of life for employees. Schools realize the benefits of reducing the need for special and remedial education and of forming a positive relationship with families from early on. Representatives from multiple agencies and organizations serving families of young children sit on each district's PAT Advisory Committee. They are, therefore, in a position to refer families to the program and to serve as referral resources for parents in need of help that is beyond the scope of the PAT program.

PARENTS AS TEACHERS PERSONNEL TRAINING

Each school district selects personnel for training to serve as parent educators in the PAT program offered throughout the state. Qualification for the parent educator position is a background in early childhood education/development, nursing, or social work involving young children and their families. Initial training for state certification occurs after trainees have successfully completed an intensive 30-hour training institute, provided by the Parents As Teachers National Center. Certification follows the final approval of the district's implementation plan for its Parent Education for Families with Children Ages Birth to Three program.

After initial certification, parent educators are credentialed annually, based upon completion of incremented inservice training hours correlated with the number of years a parent educator has served in the program. Ongoing inservice sessions are offered through a comprehensive training program. Bimonthly inservice sessions are held in five designated regions across the state.

Onsite consultations are offered to every school district. Continually updated and newly developed resource materials and assistance opportunities are made available annually to all parent educators. Individual parent educators may request onsite consultations to provide personal training in different program categories. Known as Individualized Inservice Training, a state trainer goes onsite with a parent educator to provide training by:

- Participating in a personal visit conducted by the parent educator and providing follow-up consultation.
- Assisting in conducting a personal visit with a family for whom a specific concern is identified.
- Administering or providing consultation on screening instruments.
- Providing consultation on parent meetings.
- Providing consultation on program organization and operation.
- Providing consultation to a group of parent educators from the same or neighboring districts.
- Consulting with a group specifically in the area of special education.

In 1989 the Early Childhood Special Education Section of the Missouri Department of Elementary and Secondary Education set aside funding to implement special education inservice training for parent educators. Issues and topics addressed during the year encompassed handicapping conditions of children, the scope of needs of families with a handicapped child, and enhancing parents' understanding of diagnostic evaluations.

NATIONAL DISSEMINATION AND PROGRAM REPLICATION

Widespread interest in the Parents As Teachers program is substantiated by the thousands of inquiries that have come from around the world. Professionals from more than 30 states, Canada, Great Britain, and Saudi Arabia have come to Missouri for training in the model. Educators and government officials from as far away as Japan, Australia, and New Zealand have come to Missouri for consultation and observation of the program in operation. Extensive media coverage and awards, including the prestigious Innovations in State and Local Government Award from the Ford Foundation and Harvard University John F. Kennedy School of Government in 1987, and the Council of State Governments Award in 1988, have increased the program's national visibility.

Representatives from the Harvard University Family Research Project visited Missouri in June, 1989, to review operation of the PAT program and the role it plays within the community and the state. The Missouri Parents As Teachers program was one of five family support programs the Harvard team researched throughout the United States. Dr. Richard Harris, senior research analyst from the Harvard Family Research Team, spent time with local programs and with representatives from the Missouri Department of Elementary and Secondary Education. Indicating that a national movement for family support seems to be appearing at all levels of government and that strengthening parents' educations often helps to strengthen the family, Dr. Harris said:

> We are looking at these pioneer programs to help show other states what can be done to support the family. The information we're gathering will be useful to policy makers in other states and on the national level. We've seen that the Parents As Teachers program is a successful one, and one that receives a lot of support at the local level as well as at the state level. I'm impressed with how much it has grown in a short period of time.
>
> The Missouri program often informally helps parents find help and assistance where they need it. It is beginning to diffuse into other agencies, and that is important with any family help group. At the local level, there seems to be a lot of collaboration with other agencies, especially the public health departments. It's very innovative, because it departs dramatically from the classical form of school, and it involves the parents much more than any other school program. With the parents becoming involved so early, it is expected they will carry their interest in their child into the school years.

The number and scope of requests for information, consultation, and training suggested the appropriateness of developing a center for national dissemination and program expansion. Early in 1987, the Missouri Department of Education established the Parents As Teachers National Center in cooperation with the University of Missouri - St. Louis. The center provides the following services for personnel in Missouri and for professionals from other states and nations:

- PAT institutes on program implementation.
- Inservice workshops and seminars, as well as advanced training in summer.
- Consultation by center staff and program observation and consultation in local school districts.
- Customized training programs outside Missouri by special arrangement.
- Program and materials development and adaptation.
- Research and evaluation activities to further study program effectiveness and to document program adaptations for diverse populations.

In 1988 the National Center designated five regional coordinators to implement regional inservice sessions throughout each region. Regional coordinators and regional training teams, composed of parent educators identified as regional trainers, provided onsite individual inservice training as requested by individual parent educators or school districts.

Outside funding from foundations makes possible the research and national dissemination activities of the National Center. A National Advisory Board, appointed by the Missouri Commissioner of Education, lends direction and support to the center. The Board includes leading educators and child development specialists from across the nation.

FOLLOW-UP EVALUATION

The Parents As Teachers National Center, in cooperation with the Missouri Department of Education, initiated three evaluation research projects following the 1985 pilot project evaluation. The Danforth, Ford, Mailman, and Smith-Richardson Foundations contributed funding for these studies.

The Second Wave Evaluation Study, begun in 1986–87, was designated to investigate the impact of PAT on different types of families enrolled in 37 diverse school districts. A randomly selected sample of 400 families from the 37 districts includes families varying in residence, marital status, income level, education, and ethnicity. The study looks at parent and child outcomes in a manner similar to the 1985 study. It also examines the impact of different levels of service and parents' participation on the development of children and parents. The evaluation report is to be completed in December 1990.

An 18-month case study of PAT adaptations for disadvantaged urban families in St. Louis was initiated in January 1988. It is anticipated that this report will provide valuable information on program operation in the inner city.

The NPAT Longitudinal Study, begun in 1988–89, tracks the achievement of pilot- and comparison-group children in public and private schools in the state. Teachers are asked to complete questionnaires focusing on children's classroom behavior, attendance, achievement, and involvement of parents in the school. Parents are asked to complete questionnaires on their children's feelings about school and their own involvement in their child's schooling and their child's learning at home.

REFLECTIONS ON THE PAST AND FUTURE

The Missouri experience has shown an ongoing need for the kind of coalition building and marketing that resulted in legislation and state funding for the PAT program. To maintain their advocacy and support, decision makers at local and state levels are informed and involved. As a new initiative, the program documents its benefits and sustains high public visibility.

Offering PAT through the public schools communicates to families that participation will enhance their child's future school achievement. It behooves schools to maintain contact with families and prepare educators to welcome parents as partners in their children's education.

Looking ahead, funds are being sought to conduct qualitative studies addressing the question of program adaptation for distinct populations, including teen parents, bilingual families, and families in poverty, in both urban and rural areas. The challenge of adding new dimensions to curriculum, training, and service delivery, while maintaining the model's integrity, is ever present.

Finally, efforts are under way to strengthen the Parents As Teachers National Center's capacity to respond to requests for information and consultation on shaping public policy for family support and education in the early childhood years.

DEVELOPMENTAL SCREENING

The Early Childhood Development Act of 1984 provides each family with children ages 1 through kindergarten entry and opportunity to participate in developmental screenings offered through each school district. The goals of the screening programs are to review a child's development, to identify possible delays, physical problems, and advanced abilities, and to give parents information and guidance regarding their child's development. The areas screened at each age level are: language, personal-social development, fine and gross motor skills, hearing, vision, and health and physical development. The screenings can be administered in the home as a component of the home visit for PAT families, through scheduled appointments, or through large-scale screenings. District service delivery options are illustrated in Table 1.

Criteria for the selection of the screening instruments are detailed for school districts. The instruments chosen and administered must be:

1. Reliable.
2. Valid.
3. Easily administered.
4. Approved by the Missouri Department of Elementary and Secondary Education.

TABLE 1   Screening Delivery Options as Reported by School Districts Implementing Missouri's Early Childhood Development Act of 1984

(as reported to Missouri Department of Elementary and Secondary Education)

	Delivery System	1986–87	1987–88	1988–89
Screening Program for Children Ages 1 and 2	Large-scale screening	206	229	270
	Scheduled appointments	212	213	248
	As a component of parent education program	272	295	352
	Other	7	8	20
Screening Program for Children Ages 3 and 4	Large-scale screening	—	275	323
	Scheduled appointments	—	229	275
	Other	—	27	35

Screening instruments are administered by parent educators who have received training in the instruments, along with educators, psychologists, speech/language clinicians, and school nurses or other health care professionals. After the screening, parents immediately receive the results and interpretations of the screening findings. At the conference with parents, the results are explained, any suspected problems or delays are identified, and the child's hearing and vision tests are discussed. Parents of children ages 3 and 4 also are apprised of possible advanced abilities in a child. The screener offers suggestions for activities or materials parents may wish to use at home to encourage appropriate development. Referrals are offered, when warranted, as the screener is a representative of the educational system and works in collaboration with many professionals to provide services for families and children that best meet their needs as indicated by the screening results.

Screening information is kept at the district level as part of the child's cumulative school records until the child reaches the third grade. Districts report to the Department of Elementary and Secondary Education at the end of each program year. Results from those yearly reports are shown in Table 2. Identification of children for early intervention increases their potential for enhanced academic achievement in later school years.

SERVICE DELIVERY

As a parent educator delivers services to a family, several basic assumptions about families are taken into consideration. Recognizing that all parents want to be good parents and that all parents need support based upon the family's needs, support programs increase families' abilities to cope rather than provide a system upon which families become dependent. The basic assumptions are:

- Information on child development assists parents in their parenting role.
- Support in the first years of life serves a prevention function.
- Availability of social networks, mutual aid, and peer groups is essential to the family's ability to enhance the child's development.
- The family is part of the community; therefore, support is provided through links with community resources.
- Support enables parents to build the confidence required to manage their lives.
- Families will be involved if the support makes sense to them.
- Families will be involved if they participate in decision making and get good feedback.
- Families will feel best when the support is specific and they can see direct application.

The PAT program offered to eligible families across Missouri consists of a minimum of four private visits and four group meetings. Parent educators provide information on child development and help parents become informed observers of their children. Parents' concerns and questions are responded to in a timely fashion. Information and materials pertinent to the child's developmental stages are provided to the parents.

TABLE 2 Developmental Screening Programs Through Missouri's Early Childhood Development Act of 1984

(as reported to Missouri Department of
Elementary and Secondary Education)

		Possible Language Delays	Possible Motor Delays	Possible Vision Problems	Possible Hearing Problems	Possible Physical Delays	Possible Advanced Abilities	Total # of Children Served
Screening Program for Children Ages 1 and 2	1988-89	2,436	904	696	3,000	1,343	—	36,617
	1987-88	2,031	939	628	2,789	1,332	—	31,216
	1986-87	1,522	674	445	2,431	811	—	22,746
	1985-86	1,448	—	432	1,837	695	—	14,229
Screening Program for Children Ages 3 and 4	1988-89	7,558	6,232	2,862	5,840	2,164	4,952	62,148
	1987-88	6,077	4,759	1,918	4,781	1,419	2,988	45,852
	1986-87	—	—	—	—	—	—	—
	1985-86	—	—	—	—	—	—	—

The personal visit or home visit is a key component of Parents As Teachers. Observing the parent and child in their natural setting enables the professional to personalize the input to the family. The purpose and content of the personal visit varies throughout the time a family participates in the program.

Developmental information that the parent educators deliver to parents is specific and easily observable. The activities suggested can be done easily in the context of everyday living experiences and do not require expensive or elaborate materials. The interactions supported should be fun, comfortable, and applicable to the daily interactions between parents and their children. The materials and advice adopted by the parent educators are those that best meet the needs, concerns, and beliefs of each family and are based on the child's developmental stage. Parents are valued as their child's first and most important teachers.

Following each personal visit, the parent educator completes a brief report of the visit, covering the content of the visit, issues the parents brought up, and general comments and plans for the next personal visit.

In evaluations mailed to parents at the end of each program year, parents have rated the personal visit as their favorite segment of the PAT program, often citing the time spent with their parent educator and the support given them in their parenting skills as the reason. When questioned, "What are the benefits of the Parents As Teachers program?" these parents responded:

Gene: "Peace of mind. I found a support group who shares the same situations I do. Parent educators give professional advice, ways to make our child's life safe, emotionally happy, and intellectually stimulating. Parenting is the most important thing we do. There is no training. Belonging to Parents As Teachers is the best thing parents can do for themselves and for their child." (Gene and his wife are parents of children age 3 years and age 5 months.)

Sharon: "I'm able to communicate with someone who lets me know the reasons why Janelle is doing what she does at different stages. I've learned safety tips and good nutrition for my child. I needed to know that. This helps me get in contact with people in (my district). When Janelle is ready to start school, I have someone who knows me personally and will help me." (Sharon and her husband are the parents of a child age 11 months.)

Nancy: "I can't say enough good about it. It made me aware of different things to look for developmentally, things I might not have noticed. It helped me to know my frustrations are shared by other parents. Group meetings offer encouragement and support, but my favorite part is the home visit. My parent educator has become a good friend. She has made me more confident. Parenting is more fun." (Nancy and her husband are the parents of children age 3 years and age 3 months.)

Group meetings are arranged so that parents meet with other parents who have children in the same age grouping (e.g., all parents of children ages 24–36 months meet together). Programs are offered to further inform and enhance the developmental information used in the home visit. Guest speakers, parent-child interactive programs, community resource individuals, make-and-take workshops, and parent-led discussions are some of the formats used in the group meetings. Child care usually is provided, and a portion of each group meeting is devoted to observing interactions of the children in the child care area.

At the group meetings parents meet other parents with children who are at similar developmental stages. Parents find that they are not alone, that behaviors described by other parents are the same as their own experiences, and that open communication exists between home and school. Records maintained on group meetings include attendance, content covered, issues parents raise, and a general appraisal of how the lecture, audiovisual presentation, or printed materials were received.

Participation in the personal visits, the group meetings, and the early childhood screenings creates a strong bond between the parent educator and the family. When the time arrives for the family to exit the programs to begin formal education in a private or public school, this bond translates into a partnership with the school, a desire to be actively involved in their child's educational process. Parents will have become accustomed to communicating with an educator and in actively teaching their children. Educational institutions can anticipate strong interest in parents participating in educational decisions involving their child.

PARENTS AS TEACHERS TELECONFERENCE

On May 25, 1989, Parents As Teachers sponsored and presented a $2\frac{1}{2}$-hour teleconference, "Working with Families of Infants with At-Risk and Handicapping Conditions." Working with the Missouri School Board Association Education Satellite Network (ESN), a Midlands Consortium Star Schools Project, a committee was formed consisting of media experts representing the Missouri Department of Elementary and Secondary Education and ESN, as well as representatives from the Parents As Teachers National Center, a Parents As Teachers program, the Special Learning Center, Early Childhood Special Education, and the Region C Coordinator of Parents As Teachers. The goal of this committee was to present, as a first-time effort, a statewide teleconference primarily for parent educators in Missouri, disseminating information in the area of special education that would inform parent educators and enhance parent educators' abilities in delivering services to families with children having at-risk and handicapping conditions.

It was decided to air the teleconference from the Missouri Department of Elementary and Secondary Education's audiovisual studio and link up with 26 satellite sites throughout the state of Missouri. Regional coordinators and specified parent educators served as site facilitators together with site technical coordinators provided by ESN. Sites were selected in various areas of the state to eliminate the need to travel long distances to view the teleconference. The format consisted of one hour featuring a keynote speaker, with time to call in questions directed to the keynote speaker, and one hour featuring a panel of parents of special needs children, with time to call in questions directed to those parents. In addition to the 26 Missouri sites, approximately 10 states accessed the program for viewing and call-in questions. A moderator expedited the program.

Descriptions of the Parents As Teachers and the First Steps programs opened the telecast. In 1988, Missouri introduced the First Steps program to serve families with infants considered to be at-risk at birth. Currently in its pilot stages, the First Steps program identifies children born in selected birthing hospitals and links the family to a case manager who coordinates the agencies available to provide the services these children and their families need. The Parents As Teachers program works closely with the First Steps program and its case managers to offer and provide services to these families. The First Steps case manager and PAT program coordinators make periodic follow-up contacts to assure that families are being contacted and offered services from the PAT programs.

Working with families of premature infants presents special challenges for the parent educator. The birth of any baby is an anticipated event, and as the pregnancy progresses, thoughts and ideas of this new little person begin to formulate, especially in the expectant mother. Typically parents look forward to a normal baby, perhaps not unlike the image of the "Gerber" baby. When something causes the baby to be born earlier than planned, everything changes and the parents are shocked. If the baby is admitted to a neonatal unit, many adjustments are ahead for the parents. Parent educators begin working with families in the last trimester of pregnancy and the need to be supportive at this time is critical.

Sessions Cole, Director of Newborn Medicine Services, St. Louis Children's Hospital, and Associate Professor of Pediatrics and Cell Biology, Washington University School of Medicine, St. Louis, served as keynote speaker for the teleconference. In discussing the role of a parent educator serving a family with an at-risk infant, Dr. Cole stated:

> There is no promise of perfection around any child, and that's especially dramatized around children who have been through neonatal intensive care. However, the medical literature

has now identified the fact through several studies that interventions like those carried out by Parents As Teachers can be extremely influential in improving, for example, communication skills and mother-infant interaction within families, and specifically improving Bayley Mental scores, which is an infant kind of intelligence quotient score, as well as home environment ratings and infant temperament scores. Therefore, your [parent educators'] interventions are at least as important as the things that we do around the time that the babies are born, in optimizing their long-term outcome and outcomes of their families.

The parent educator helping the family of a premature infant uses the same techniques as with any other family. Parent educators especially recognize three specific basics around which to build interactions with this family:

1. The parent educator works hard at being a good listener.
2. The parent educator counsels with the family and serves as a support system for the family, especially reassuring the parents that their feelings are valid.
3. The parent educator redirects family observations into the baby's positive actions, no matter how small the positive point may be. By doing so, the family and the parent educator identify and align themselves with the baby's positive accomplishments.

The parent educator may help families understand their responses to the situation that presents itself. Helping the family recognize the commonality of responses to their situation tells them that their response is normal. Being patient with the family as it moves through the stages of acceptance of the premature baby affords the parent educator many opportunities to help the family.

Sandy McCurdy, the mother of a son with Cornelia De Lange syndrome, observed that parents need to learn to accept children for what they are and what they come with. Parents repeatedly experience grief and guilt as they move through the cycles of development in anticipation of where the child will be when they (the parents) are no longer here or that this child will never experience typical milestones such as high school graduation, marriage, or leaving home. Therefore, the parent educator must be sensitive to parents' ongoing need to process these feelings of guilt and grief.

When asked how they became involved in Parents As Teachers, Mrs. McCurdy replied, "Our daughter was already in the Parents As Teachers program, so we signed him up before birth, so we were able to have the support from the beginning." When asked how her parent educator adapts the home visit to meet the needs of this child, her reply was:

> One of the main ways is she tries to suggest things that will help stimulate his vision and hearing and just ways that we might deal with problems. Right now we're dealing with head banging a lot, and so the last time I talked with [our parent educator] she offered some suggestions about that. It sort of depends on where we are and what our needs are. I think that's important for any parent educator to realize—that parents need help in understanding where their kids are developmentally, oftentimes, and for them to be able to recommend stimulation that is appropriate for that level of development is very, very important.

When administering screening instruments, the parent educator adjusts the developmental timeline for each premature child. Each child is evaluated from the original expected birth date instead of the actual birth date. For Carol Strong, mother of a 4-year-old son with spina bifida, the Parents As Teachers screening was especially helpful. When asked about how PAT screening has helped her son, Mrs. Strong responded:

> We've been going to Parents As Teachers since he was about a year old. He's been screened at least once or twice a year through Parents As Teachers, and last year during the screening they [parent educators] decided that there might be a chance that he had a visual impairment. So we took him to see a doctor, and they [Parents As Teachers] were very accurate and he did need glasses. He has come leaps and bounds since he got his glasses in the past year. He has learned to write his name—do all sorts of things. We thought he was going to be slow from the beginning because he was not interested in doing those things and as it turns out, a lot of it was just because he was sight-impaired.

Participants' evaluations of the teleconference revealed a strong interest in PAT from states that accessed the program and strong praise from the Missouri sites for providing this kind of training to parent educators. School administrators, First Steps case managers, staff from regional diagnostic centers, and hospital and clinic personnel viewed the program, in addition to the parent educators. As a result of the success of this first-time effort, future teleconferences may be planned.

SUMMARY

Missouri's early childhood parent education and screening programs have made available continuing services from birth until the child enters formal schooling. These nontargeted programs are designed to support all families through services, resources, and referrals based upon individual family needs. Home visits, group meetings, and early childhood developmental screenings make up three components of Missouri's Early Childhood Development Act of 1984 (Senate Bill 658).

The success of Missouri's project, Parents As Teachers, is grounded in the belief that parents are the first and most important teachers of children and that children will learn more during the early years than at any other time in life. Missouri is committed to the future of Early Childhood and of Parents As Teachers. In October 1989, strong support emerged in the final report of the Governor's Advisory Council on Literacy. Entitled "Jobs Without People: The Coming Crisis for Missouri's Workforce," the report focused on three recommendations, for the early years, the school years, and the adult years. The recommendations are supported by 30 specific action plans, three of which identify areas specifically noted in this article. The Early Years focus identified:

- Expanding the Parents As Teachers program and involving families in education.
- Better efforts for prenatal care and identification of young children at risk.
- Expanding the First Steps program.

Educators in Missouri's schools may anticipate greater interaction with parents who have participated in the PAT program. Educators need to be prepared to enjoy the partnership in education that is now developing from the positive exposure parents are experiencing through empowerment of families as designers of their child's world, from the support that parent educators as representatives of the public schools give to these families, and from successful teaching by parents of their own children.

RESOURCES

"Capitol Kids." *Jefferson City News Tribune*, Spring 1989.

Central Missouri Focus—Parents As Teachers. KMOS-TV, Warrensburg, Spring 1989. (Video)

Evaluation Report: New Parents As Teachers Project. Missouri Department of Elementary and Secondary Education, Jefferson City, 1985.

Final Report, Governor's Advisory Council on Literacy. Secretary of State's Office, Jefferson City, October 13, 1989.

"Parents As Teachers' Focus on Families." *Jefferson City News Tribune*, July 2, 1989.

"Parents As Teachers Makes Difference." *St. Louis Post-Dispatch*, October 23, 1989.

Parents As Teachers National Center.

Parents As Teachers Program Planning and Implementation Guide, revised edition, 1989. Missouri Department of Elementary and Secondary Education, Jefferson City.

Parents As Teachers Teleconference. Missouri Department of Elementary and Secondary Education, Jefferson City, May 25, 1989. (Video)

Parent Evaluations of Jefferson City, Missouri's Parents As Teachers Program.

White, B. L. 1974. *Reassessing Our Educational Priorities.* Speech presented to Education Commission of the State, Early Childhood Education Symposium, Boston, August 3–4.

The authors wish to thank the staff at the Parents As Teachers National Center for their support of and contributions to this article.

For further information on Missouri's parent education and screening programs contact:
Department of Elementary and Secondary Education
Early Childhood Section
P.O. Box 480
Jefferson City, Missouri 65102

Parents As Teachers National Center
Marillac Hall, University of Missouri–St. Louis
8001 Natural Bridge Road
St. Louis, Missouri 63121-4499

Vicki Ehlers is a family education consultant in College Station, Texas. Micca Ruffin is the Region C Coordinator for Parents As Teachers, the director of Early Childhood/Parents As Teachers for Jefferson City Public Schools, and a parent educator.

4

This article describes a model by which special educators can offer support for general education through collaboration in regular classrooms. Central to the model are the development of flexible departmentalization, program ownership, identification and development of supportive attitudes, student assessment to determine effectiveness, and classroom modifications to support mainstreaming. The authors discuss these program concerns and offer suggestions based on the success they have had in developing such programs.

General Education Collaboration: A Model for Successful Mainstreaming

Richard L. Simpson and Brenda Smith Myles

The Education for All Handicapped Children Act (EHA) was designed to improve the quality of education received by children and youth with exceptionalities, including provisions for an appropriate education in the least restrictive environment. Thus, EHA requirements stipulate that students be removed from general education programs only when the nature or severity of their exceptionality is such that education in regular classrooms, even with the use of supplementary aids or services, cannot be conducted satisfactorily (Office of the Federal Register, 1987). For many children and youth with mild disabilities, this requirement has been translated to mean education in resource room and other pull-out programs (U.S. Department of Education, 1987).

Critics argue that service provision outside the regular classroom has led to discontinuity in instruction (Wang, Reynolds, & Walberg, 1986), reduction of curricular options for students with exceptionalities (Stainback & Stainback, 1984), and education with a limited scope. As a result, children and youth with disabilities are prevented from gaining skills that would facilitate their full-time reentry into regular classrooms (Dunn, 1968). Alleged byproducts of pull-out and other segregated programs include lower self-concept and self-esteem for students with disabilities than for nonhandicapped peers (Rogers

& Saklofske, 1985); less than adequate social skills (Madden & Slavin, 1983); and lack of preparation for adulthood, manifested by a high rate of unemployment among people with exceptionalities (Will, 1984).

The present educational system also has proven inadequate for students without labeled exceptionalities (Reynolds, Wang, & Walberg, 1987). Specifically, at least 20% of nonlabeled children and youth experience difficulty in regular classrooms. "These children are commonly described as slow learners, students who exhibit social, conduct, and behavior difficulties; possess low self-esteem; or have problems in understanding or using language (Will, 1986, p. 413).

Prompted by these issues, educators, policy makers, researchers, and theorists have called for a variety of educational reforms, all designed to serve more effectively and efficiently mildly handicapped and at-risk students in general education programs. Although specific methodologies vary, reform procedures consistently identify general and special education collaboration and shared decision making as essential ingredients for success. Yet, in spite of general acceptance of a need for greater cooperation and involvement between regular and special education, few models for achieving such collaboration have been presented. In particular, conceptual and procedural models that offer a broad perspective (i.e., focus on educational practices, environmental factors, and personnel considerations) are needed. In response, we offer the General Education Collaboration Model, designed to support general educators through collaboration with special educators.

GENERAL EDUCATION COLLABORATION MODEL

The General Education Collaboration Model, illustrated in Figure 1, is designed to support general educators working with exceptional children by means of collaboration with special educators or having special educators in the classroom. Based on shared input, shared responsibility, and shared decision making (AASA/NAESP/NAASP School-Based Management Task Force, 1988; Bauwens, Hourcade, & Friend, 1989; Crisci & Tutela, 1990), the model facilitates integration of students with mild-to-moderate learning and behavior difficulties into general classrooms; at the same time, it provides assistance that allows students to be successful. The model emphasizes both instructional variables and learner behaviors, based on the rationale that instructional variables and learner behaviors cannot be separated from instructional settings (Salend, 1990).

The following four major assumptions underlie the General Education Collaboration Model:

- The general educator assumes primary responsibility for teaching; the special educator's role is to provide support and resources to enhance student success.
- Social and academic interactions in the general education classroom are beneficial for all students, including those with disabilities.
- Students, parents, and school personnel prefer education in the general education classroom to pull-out and other segregated programs.

- Contingent upon appropriate support and resources, most general education teachers and administrators are willing and capable to serve students with mild-to-moderate disabilities in general classrooms.

COMPONENTS OF THE MODEL

The General Education Collaboration Model is based on five essential elements:

1. Flexible departmentalization (Jones, Gottlieb, Guskin, & Yoshida, 1978; Lawrence & Lorsch, 1967; Margolis & McGettigan, 1988).
2. Program ownership (Roubinek, 1978).
3. Identification and development of supportive attitudes (Heller & Schilit, 1987; Hersh & Walker, 1983).
4. Student assessment as a measure of program effectiveness (Jones et al., 1978; Rogers & Saklofske, 1985).
5. Classroom modifications that support mainstreaming (Myles & Simpson, 1989, 1990; Simpson & Myles, 1989).

Although each model component is presented as a discrete item, in actuality components are interwoven; each component significantly affects the others and cannot operate effectively in isolation. In fact, for school reform and mainstreaming to be effective, all components of the model must be in place.

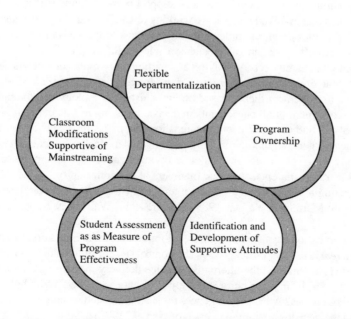

FIGURE 1 Essential Elements of General Education Collaboration Model

Flexible Departmentalization

Departmentalization recognizes that individuals within a school organization each have unique job functions. In fact, their roles often are designed such that educators are able to function independently. To provide an optimal education for *all* students, however, departmentalization must allow for coordination, communication, and control.

Coordination here refers to the orchestration of defined roles for service delivery personnel. In recognition of this need, Judy Schrag (1990), Director of the U.S. Office of Special Education Programs, observed that:

> Special education program enhancements include better coordination across special programs and general education, increased roles of the building principals, continued exploration of the circumstances under which students with special needs can be educated in the regular classrooms and exploration of refinements in our assessment and classification procedures. (p. 7)

Coordination of special and general education programs requires that individuals be aware of their own responsibilities, as well as the responsibilities of others. Thus, much of the teacher discontent concerning mainstreaming programs stems from a lack of orchestration (e.g., role duplication or conflict) of school personnel responsibilities (McCoy & Prehm, 1987).

As it relates to departmentalization, *communication* serves as the basis for developing a collaborative relationship. Hence the need to involve all school organization members, including administrators, parents, teachers, support personnel, and students. Communication ensures that involved persons are working toward the same purpose and that each individual provides program implementation feedback. Improved communication is the *sine qua non* of effective general-special education collaboration.

The need for shared decision making and participatory management has been recognized for some time. In his book, *Eupsychian Management: A Journal*, Maslow (1962) presented a management theory based on humanistic psychology and the premise that optimal involvement of all participants in decision making results in (a) the well-being of all involved, and (b) an efficient organization that meets the needs of the individual. As in society in general, schools are not operating under Maslow's ideal; moreover, they likely never will. Yet, the advantages of involving a variety of participants (e.g., teachers, administrators, parents, students, members of the community) in decision making and in creating a supportive environment are increasingly being recognized (Clune & White, 1988; Mertens & Yarger, 1988; Sickler, 1988; Walberg & Lane, 1989; White, 1989).

In the context of departmentalization, adoption and implementation of an effective *control system* is another critical issue. The control system should address the following questions: How long will the alternative service delivery model (e.g., mainstreaming, support services) be in place before efficacy issues are addressed? Who holds responsibility for those issues? Are there assurances for shared decision making? What criteria will be used in the decision-making process (Jones et al., 1978)?

Program Ownership

Historically, issues related to mainstreaming have been the domain of special education (McIntosh, 1979). Thus, special educators have assumed responsibility for determining if and when special needs students can be served appropriately in general education settings, which general education programs and instructors will best meet mainstreamed students' needs, and how mainstreaming may best be accomplished. This system, in combination with other ill-considered mainstreaming activities, has retarded general educators' participation in and embracement of mainstreaming practices. Knoff (1985), for instance, reported that many general educators feel imposed on by mainstreaming, consider themselves unprepared to teach students with disabilities, and are put upon by mainstreaming practices.

Significant improvements in the mainstreaming system can be expected only with the support of and close working relationship between general and special educators (Roubinek, 1978). In this regard, the General Education Collaboration Model stresses shared responsibility by general and special educators for students with disabilities. Accordingly, general educators must accept responsibility for mainstreamed students placed in regular education programs. In return, general educators can expect full participation in the decision-making processes associated with mainstreaming along with appropriate support (e.g., training, consultation). The importance of shared ownership and ownership clarification cannot be underestimated (Heller & Schilit, 1987; Hersh & Walker, 1983).

Identification and Development of Supportive Attitudes

The advantages of placing students with disabilities in general education classes have been well established. Thus, pursuing what the National Association of Retarded Citizens (1973) referred to as "an existence as close to normal as possible" (p. 72) for persons with disabilities, parents and professionals have increasingly endorsed both the least restrictive environment concept and mainstreaming. At one time mainstreaming was considered radical. Today, however, it is estimated that most students with disabilities receive part of their education in regular class settings (U.S. Department of Education, 1987). Moreover, many educators have accepted the philosophy of mainstreaming students with mild handicaps in regular classes, a recognition that bodes well for a continuation of this trend. Yet, in spite of this backing, limited attention has been given to preparing general classroom settings to accommodate students with disabilities.

In particular, selecting teachers, school staff, and students who are aware and supportive of students with disabilities is a basic requirement for successful mainstreaming (Hersh & Walker, 1983). As Martin (1974) cautioned, unless educators develop strategies for creating an accepting environment for students with disabilities, "we will be painfully naive, and I fear we will subject many children to a painful and frustrating educational experience in the name of progress" (p. 150). Reister and Bessette (1986) also contended that integration programs can be successful only to the extent that they create an educational environment in which children and youth with disabilities thrive, develop, and experience acceptance. Such a supportive environment requires strategies that assure not only that appropriate instructional materials and procedures are used, but that social, emotional, and attitudinal concerns receive proper attention.

The overall atmosphere within a school determines the extent to which the General Education Collaboration Model or any alternative mainstreaming strategy will be accepted and employed (Gersten & Woodward, 1990). Hence, attitudes of administrators, teachers, parents, and students must be assessed to determine to what extent these essential people are prepared and willing to accommodate students with disabilities in regular class settings.

With regard to *administrator* attitudes, O'Rourke (1980) found a significant relationship between teaching personnel and building principals' attitudes toward students with exceptionalities. Hence, principals' positive attitudes, as well as administrative support for working with all students (including those with exceptionalities), must exist if mainstreamed students are to receive optimal educational benefits (Heller & Schilit, 1987; McIntosh, 1979). Indeed, we recommend that administrative personnel should be selected, partly, on the basis of their integration attitude and their willingness to accommodate both disabled and normally developing students. Administrator attitudes toward students with disabilities can be modified (Donaldson, 1980); however, it is more efficient to select for educational leadership positions individuals who demonstrate positive attitudes toward mainstreaming and students with special needs and who are, thus, able to establish a positive school atmosphere.

Positive *teacher* attitudes are also essential determinants of mainstreaming success. Research on teacher attitudes toward mainstreaming has shown that general education teachers generally perceive themselves to be ill equipped to deal with students with disabilities (Miller, 1990). Yet, they agree that mainstreaming is a positive educational practice, contingent on appropriate teacher support and training (Knoff, 1985; Moore & Fine, 1978; Reynolds, Martin-Reynolds, & Mark, 1982; Stephens & Benjamin, 1981; Williams & Algozzine, 1979). Myles and Simpson (1989) reported that 86% of general educators surveyed were willing to accept an exceptional child in their classrooms on a full-time basis, given appropriate support and training. Without support and training less than 33% of the respondents were willing to accept mainstreamed students in their general classrooms.

Mainstreaming success also hinges on the leadership and involvement of *parents*, both those with exceptional and with normally developing children (Heller & Schilit, 1987). Indeed, the activities and lobbying of parent groups led to the largest special education system reform in history (i.e., PL 94-142).

Many parents of children with disabilities report that they are willing to place their children in general classrooms, contingent on appropriate support and individualization (Myles & Simpson, 1990; Simpson & Myles, 1989). Of the parents of children with learning disabilities surveyed by Abramson, Wilson, Yoshida, and Hagerty (1983), 72% responded that educating handicapped and nonhandicapped children together would improve the handicapped children's academic achievement. In a related study, 79% of parents surveyed by Abelson and Weiss (1984) agreed that handicapped and nonhandi-capped children could learn in the same classroom, but 40% of the participating parents stated that handicapped children's educational gains would come at the expense of the quality of other students' education. As noted, most parents whose children have had mainstreaming experiences appear to support those programs, contingent on appropriate services and attitudes.

Recognizing the importance of *student* attitudes, Simpson (1987) observed that a note-worthy factor in the success or failure of mainstreaming is whether normally develop-ing students accept, understand, and interact with peers with exceptionalities. Clearly, mainstreaming programs must include methods and procedures that facilitate normally achieving students' awareness and acceptance of exceptional students in the mainstream (Sasso, Simpson, & Novak, 1985). In the absence of this component, students with ex-ceptionalities will fail to become fully integrated in mainstreamed settings.

As we suggested, *individuals with whom children and youth with disabilities will in-teract in general education settings* must be maximally supportive. Relative to the Gen-eral Education Collaboration Model, therefore, teachers, administrators, and other adult staff members (e.g., custodians, cafeteria workers) must receive information about indi-viduals with disabilities along with facts on the rationale and advantages of integration and mainstreaming. As a part of this process, adults need opportunities to discuss their mainstreaming roles and their attitudes and feelings regarding mainstreaming. Thus, a supportive general educational environment for students with disabilities is best developed by combining information with discussion opportunities.

Procedures for positively modifying the *attitudes and behavior of normally develop-ing children and youth* toward their disabled peers is also a basic element of the General Education Collaboration Model. Nonhandicapped students require information and ex-periences designed to (a) familiarize them with the characteristics and needs of children and youth with disabilities, (b) foster more accepting attitudes toward individuals with dis-abilities, and (c) promote better interactions between handicapped and nonhandicapped students. Positive attitudes toward students with disabilities do not occur automatically; hence, this frequently overlooked mainstreaming element must be planned.

Use of *curricula and procedures* designed to facilitate better understanding and sen-sitivity toward students with disabilities has proven significant in integration programs (Fiedler & Simpson, 1987). Accordingly, the time and resource investment required to work with classmates of children and youth with disabilities appears to be cost-efficient and utilitarian.

Not all students are candidates for mainstreaming. Thus, selection of students most acceptable for integration must be based on both objective and subjective criteria. Ob-jective criteria may include aptitude and achievement eligibility levels. Subjective crite-ria may include student motivation, social responsibility, and behavior. Although stu-dent mainstreaming criteria will vary from setting to setting, exceptional students must be assigned to general education classes to possess the basic skills necessary to allow them to be successful and accepted.

Student Assessment as a Measure of Program Effectiveness

Assessment is a key component of any program serving students with exceptionalities and acts as an ongoing part of the instructional strategy (Carroll, 1974). In fact, evaluation is a key component of PL 94–142. To facilitate successful mainstreaming, assessment must be comprehensive, encompassing student achievement, self-concept, and social integration.

Decisions pertaining to *student achievement* include types of assessment measures (or specific instruments) as well as the frequency with which they are used. Because norm-referenced standardized tests may be unacceptable for students with exceptionalities, many educators prefer curriculum-based assessment methods. As noted by Marston, Fuchs, and Deno (1986), curriculum-based assessment measures allow for (a) reliability, (b) curricula compatibility, (c) validity with respect to criterion achievement measures, (d) ease and repetition of administration, and (e) sensitivity to student growth. Thus, curriculum-based assessment methods allow for consistent validation of instructional effectiveness and student growth.

Self-concept is a construct that correlates with school achievement and social adjustment. Thus this variable must be monitored and, if necessary, addressed through social skills instruction and other intervention programs. Results of investigations of the self-concept of students with mild exceptionalities have been conflicting; some report that the self-concept of students with mild handicaps does not differ from that of nonhandicapped peers (Coleman, 1984; Stone, 1984; Yauman, 1983); others note a marked discrepancy between the self-concepts of handicapped and nonhandicapped students (Ribner, 1978). At least in part, researchers attribute these equivocal research results to service delivery model differences. That is, resource room students who use normally achieving peers as a reference group appear to have lower self-concepts than resource room students who compare themselves with exceptional peers. But students with learning disabilities who use exceptional peers as a reference group appear to have self-concepts commensurate with those of nonhandicapped students (Coleman, 1984; Yauman, 1983). Preliminary studies of self-concept of students served in an alternative service delivery model revealed no differences between the self-concept of normally achieving and exceptional students (Hudson & Myles, 1989; Wang & Birch, 1984). To be conclusive, however, these results must be submitted to further investigation.

Social integration refers to the relationships between students. With respect to mainstreaming, social integration involves relationships between students with exceptionalities and normally achieving peers in terms of physical proximity, interactive behavior, assimilation, and acceptance (Kaufman, Gottlieb, Agard, & Kukic, 1975). Positive and accepting relationships between children with disabilities and their normally achieving peers are crucial to successful mainstreaming to the extent that exceptional students' rejection by or isolation from nonhandicapped peers could doom for failure an otherwise successful mainstreaming program (Reister & Bessette, 1986).

As suggested earlier, general education students must be made aware of the needs and characteristics of their exceptional classmates. Traditionally, little has been done to prepare general education students to interact with exceptional peers. Thus, significant change can and must occur via specific curricula and teaching strategies that facilitate normally developing students' interactions with persons with exceptionalities (Newman & Simpson, 1983).

Recognizing the importance of mainstreamed student success, we contend that ongoing assessment in a variety of areas is crucial to the success of the General Education Collaboration Model. Such assessment should be multifaceted, taking into account the "whole" child in terms of both self-concept and social integration.

Classroom Modifications Supportive of Mainstreaming

Researchers have demonstrated interest in classroom modifications that influence the educational process. In addition, the National Education Association (NEA) has taken a leadership role in this area. Harris (1974), NEA president, challenged schools to initiate reform to foster educational improvement, recommending, for example, that schools reduce class size and obtain the services of more specialists. A myriad of other modifications designed to enhance mainstreaming has also been suggested (Hersh & Walker, 1983).

Class Size

In his call to improve schools, Harris (1974) indicated that the educational system could improve if the average class size were reduced to 10 students. Harris's recommendation was supported by the results of an NEA survey (Teacher Opinion Poll, 1975a). When asked to state the importance of class size to (a) academic achievement, (b) social and personal development of pupils, and (c) teacher job satisfaction, 80% of teachers surveyed responded that small class size is extremely important. In a related study, 78% of general educators surveyed stated that class size is an important issue in mainstreaming. This group of teachers indicated that a maximum class size of 15 to 19 students is required to accept and accommodate one mainstreamed exceptional student (Myles & Simpson, 1989).

Although challenged (Robinson, 1990), a body of empirical data supports reduced class size. According to McKenna and Olson (1975), for example, a class size of 25 or fewer students would lead to: (a) wider variety of instructional methods, (b) better classroom management and fewer discipline problems, (c) improved teacher attitudes, and (d) improved student attitudes. Smith and Glass (1980) reported similar findings when class size was reduced to fewer than 15 to 20 students.

Thus, small class size seems to contribute to the academic achievement of mainstreamed students as well as to positive teacher and student attitudes. Therefore, the General Education Collaboration Model suggests that classes be small enough to allow teachers to meet the individual needs of students and to provide successful mainstreaming experiences.

Consultation

According to Idol and West (1987), school consultation in special education has flourished. At least 26 states currently have policies that mandate consultation (West & Brown,

1987). In addition, consultation appears to have general educator support. Approximately half of the educators surveyed by Myles and Kasselman (1990) reported that they used collaborative consultation, although a formalized consultation program was not in place in their schools. Further, 95% stated that they would use collaborative consultation for exceptional and at-risk students if it were available in their schools. When asked to select modifications needed to mainstream an exceptional student, 65% of the 100 teachers polled by Myles and Simpson (1989) selected consultation.

In a data-based analysis of consultation, Miller and Sabatino (1978) compared student academic performance in a resource room with performance in a consultation model. Results showed that student academic performance gains were equivalent for both models. According to Miller and Sabatino:

> One could argue that the consultation model was surprisingly effective, since academic gains were on par with the direct service approach. That is, regular teachers seemingly became as effective in delivering instruction to special children within their classes as resource teachers were in intensive, "out of mainstream" classes. (p. 89)

Concurring with the position taken by Miller and Sabatino, we contend that consultation between general and special educators is necessary to the success of the General Education Collaboration Model. This vehicle provides general education with information and support regarding the characteristics and needs of students with exceptionalities.

Inservice Programs

Inservice has been viewed as contributing to program change. Although the efficacy of traditional inservice programs has been challenged (Fullan, 1985), it appears that effective inservice may assist teachers in mainstreaming students with exceptionalities. In a 1975 nationwide NEA survey, teachers were asked which classroom modifications would result in improved education (Teacher Opinion Poll, 1975b, p. 14). Opinions were diverse, totaling more than 16 different suggestions, including additional inservice programming.

According to a number of studies, teacher inservices may be desirable in implementing mainstreaming programs. For example, Myles and Simpson (1989, 1990) and Simpson and Myles (1991) found that parents of exceptional children, support service staff, and general educators favor inservice programs as a vehicle to enhance mainstreaming of students with mild handicaps. Approximately half of those surveyed selected this mainstreaming option.

The General Education Collaboration Model supports continued inservice programs as a means of enhancing the knowledge base of general educators through both group and individual training. Group inservice is well suited for providing a general body of information regarding student characteristics and needs, and individual training can give general educators specific information and feedback opportunities.

Paraprofessionals

Paraprofessionals play an important role in special education, as evidenced by the large number of people employed in this role. As of 1980, more than 80,000 paraprofessionals worked in special education public schools (Pickett, 1980). Research suggests that special educators are aware of the contributions that aides make in the classroom. Paraprofessionals are far less widespread in general education programs, though, suggesting that they are perceived to play a minor role in supporting mainstreamed students.

Regardless of the current use of paraprofessionals in general education programs, the General Education Collaboration Model is based on the premise that paraprofessionals are needed, to varying degrees, to support the mainstreamed students. Karagianis and Nesbit (1983) agreed with this assessment, noting that teachers' aides are "a necessary adjunct to the regular classroom where the teacher has a defined responsibility for handicapped children" (p. 19). General educators appear to concur; 65% of those surveyed by Myles and Simpson (1989) saw paraprofessionals as necessary facilitators of mainstreaming.

Paraprofessionals should be available to general education teachers who serve children and youth with disabilities. Specifically, paraprofessionals may assist teachers with a variety of tasks, including (a) reinforcing previously instructed concepts, (b) documenting student progress, and (c) assisting with daily planning. Paraprofessionals also can perform time-consuming tasks such as toilet training and modifying written materials (Kargianis & Nesbit, 1983; McKenzie & Houk, 1986).

Planning Time

Additional planning time was another frequently selected modification among general educators in the 1975 NEA poll (Teacher Opinion Poll, 1975b). Respondents selecting this modification suggested that increased planning time would improve teacher efficacy. With regard to mainstreaming, planning time takes on even greater importance. According to approximately half of the general educators and ancillary staff surveyed, additional planning would be required if one student with an exceptionality were to be placed full time in a mainstreamed setting. The majority of respondents indicated that they would prefer one hour daily planning time (Myles & Simpson, 1989; Simpson & Myles, 1991). Parents did not view this mainstreaming option to be as important as school personnel did (only one-quarter indicated that one hour of daily planning was a necessary mainstreaming modification) (Myles & Simpson, 1990).

Teachers need adequate planning to be able to individualize academic tasks and plan optional or additional activities that can enhance the performance of students with exceptionalities. This time also is needed to allow general education personnel to consult with other education personnel or work with a paraprofessional. Hence, the General Education Collaboration Model incorporates adequate planning time as essential for general education teachers assigned to work with exceptional students. Additionally, the school day should be organized such that general and special educators share common blocks of time for planning.

Support Services

Availability of support service personnel has been seen to facilitate mainstreaming. Thus, the majority of general educators surveyed by Hudson, Graham, and Warner (1979) reported that although support service personnel were not generally available, they were needed to provide mainstreaming assistance.

Results similar to those of Hudson et al. (1979) were reached by Larrivee and Cook (1979), Moore and Fine (1978), and Knoff (1984). Those authors found that the availability of support services impacted teacher attitudes positively. Specifically, teacher attitudes toward mainstreaming seemed more positive when support services were available. In fact, in one study general educators indicated that, without assistance from resource personnel, they would not generally support full-time mainstreaming for students with learning disabilities or mental retardation (Knoff, 1984).

Further, both parents and support service personnel agree that support services play an important role in mainstreaming. Over half of the parents surveyed (Myles & Simpson, 1990) and three-fourths of ancillary staff surveyed (Simpson & Myles, 1991) responded that support staff availability was necessary to mainstreaming. Based on these findings, teachers are generally accepting of mainstreaming and having special students in their classes if they can rely on personnel for necessary support (Larrivee & Cook, 1979). Thus, based on sound professional practice, the General Education Collaboration Model maintains that these resources are essential for successful maintenance of students with disabilities in regular classrooms.

CONCLUSIONS

The myriad needs of children, youth, and their families and the ever-changing needs of society demand new ways of providing an appropriate education to children and youth with behavior and learning problems. Schrag (1990) reminded us that "the students we serve in special education today are not the students that we served five years ago. There is an increase in the number of students with learning and behavior problems because of poverty, child abuse, ethnic and language diversity, teen pregnancy, and drug dependence" (p. 2). Hence, legislators, educators, and the general public are increasingly demanding change, observing that education will either need to evolve or dissolve.

Students with special needs will continue to pose a special challenge to schools. Thus, educational change must include a methodology for more effectively serving these children and youth. The increasing reliance on general educators to assume responsibility for high-risk and disabled students demands an efficacious support system. A multifaceted system that takes into consideration shared input, responsibility, and decision making between general and special educators is needed to ensure an appropriate education for all. The General Education Collaboration Model, with its emphasis on meeting student, parent, teacher, and administrator needs, is a valuable contribution to this undertaking.

REFERENCES

AASA/NAESP/NAASP School-Based Management Task Force. (1988). *School-based management: A strategy for better learning.* Arlington, VA: American Association of School Administrators.

Abelson, A. G., & Weiss, R. (1984). Mainstreaming the handicapped: The views of parents of nonhandicapped pupils. *Spectrum, 2*, 27–29.

Abramson, M., Wilson, V., Yoshida, R. K., & Hagerty, G. (1983). Parents' perceptions of their learning disabled child's educational performance. *Learning Disability Quarterly, 6*, 184–194.

Bauwens, J., Hourcade, J., & Friend, M. (1989). Cooperative teaching: A model for general and special education integration. *Remedial & Special Education, 10*(2), 17–22.

Carroll, A. W. (1974). The classroom as an ecosystem. *Focus on Exceptional Children, 6*, 1–12.

Clune, W. H., & White, P. A. (1988). *School-based management: Institutional variation, implementation, and issues for further research.* New Brunswick, NJ: Rutgers University Center for Policy Research in Education.

Coleman, J. M. (1984). Handicapped labels and instructional segregation: Influences on children's self-concepts versus the perceptions of others. *Learning Disability Quarterly, 6*, 3–11.

Crisci, P. E., & Tutela, A. D. (1990). Preparation of educational administrators for urban settings. *Urban Education, 11*(4), 414–430.

Donaldson, J. (1980). Changing attitudes toward handicapped persons: A review and analysis of research. *Exceptional Children, 43*, 504–516.

Dunn, L. (1968). Special education for the mildly retarded—Is much of it justifiable? *Exceptional Children, 35*, 5–22.

Fiedler, C., & Simpson, R. L. (1987). Modifying the attitudes of nonhandicapped high school students toward handicapped peers. *Exceptional Children, 53*(4), 342–351.

Fullan, M. (1985). Change processes and strategies at the local level. *Elementary School Journal, 85*(5), 391–421.

Gersten, R., & Woodward, J. (1990). Rethinking the regular education initiative: Focus on the classroom teacher. *Remedial & Special Education, 11*(3), 7–16.

Harris, J. A. (1974). Drastic proposals for educational improvement. *Today's Education, 63*(4), 5.

Heller, H., & Schilit, J. (1987). The regular education initiative: A concerned response. *Focus on Exceptional Children, 20*, 1–6.

Hersh, R., & Walker, H. M. (1983). Great expectations: Making school effective for all students. *Policy Review Studies, 2*, 147–188.

Hudson, F., Graham, S., & Warner, M. (1979). Mainstreaming: An examination of the attitudes and needs of regular classroom teachers. *Learning Disability Quarterly, 3*(2), 558–562.

Hudson, F. G., & Myles, B. S. (1989). *An evaluation of the adaptive behavior, problem behavior and self-concept of students with mild-to-moderate learning disabilities in an alternative service delivery model: Class within a class.* Unpublished manuscript, University of Kansas, Lawrence.

Idol, L., & West, J. F. (1987). Consultation in special education (Part 2): Training and practice. *Journal of Learning Disabilities, 20*(8), 474–494.

Jones, R. L., Gottlieb, J., Guskin, S., & Yoshida, R. K. (1978). Evaluating mainstreaming programs: Models, caveats, considerations, and guidelines. *Exceptional Children, 44*, 588–601.

Karagianis, L., & Nesbit, W. (1983). Support services: The neglected ingredient in the integration recipe. *Special Education in Canada, 53*(3), 18–19.

Kaufman, M. J., Gottlieb, J., Agard, J. A., & Kukic, M. B. (1975). Mainstreaming: Toward an explication of the construct. *Focus on Exceptional Children, 7*, 1–12.

Knoff, H. M. (1984). Mainstreaming attitudes and special placement knowledge in labeling versus nonlabeling states. *Remedial & Special Education, 5*(6), 7–14.

Knoff, H. M. (1985). Attitudes toward mainstreaming: A status report and comparison of regular and special educators in New York and Massachusetts. *Psychology in the Schools, 22*, 410–418.

Larrivee, B., & Cook, L. (1979). Mainstreaming: A study on the variables affecting teacher attitude. *Journal of Special Education, 13*(3), 315–324.

Lawrence, P. R., & Lorsch, J. W. (1967). *Organization and environment.* Boston: Harvard Business Press.

Madden, N. A., & Slavin, R. E. (1983). Mainstreaming students with mild handicaps: Academic and social outcomes. *Review of Educational Research, 53*, 519–569.

Margolis, H., & McGettigan, J. (1988). Managing resistance to instructional modifications in mainstreamed environments. *Remedial & Special Education, 9*, 15–21.

Marston, D., Fuchs, L., & Deno, S. (1986). A comparison of standardized achievement tests and direct measurement techniques in measuring pupil progress. *Diagnostique, 11*, 77–90.

Martin, E. (1974). Some thoughts on mainstreaming. *Exceptional Children, 41*, 150–153.

Maslow, A. S. (1962). *Eupsychian management: A journal.* Homewood, IL: Richard D. Irwin Publishers.

McCoy, K. M., & Prehm, H. J. (1987). *Teaching mainstreamed students: Methods and techniques.* Denver: Love Publishing.

McIntosh, D. K. (1979). Mainstreaming: Too often a myth, too rarely a reality. *Academic Therapy, 15*, 53–59.

McKenna, B. H., & Olson, M. N. (1975). Class size revisited. *Today's Education, 64*, 29.

McKenzie, R. G., & Houk, C. S. (1986). Use of paraprofessionals in the resource room. *Exceptional Children, 53*(1), 41–45.

Mertens, S., & Yarger, S. J. (1988). Teaching as a profession: Leadership, empowerment, and involvement. *Journal of Teacher Education, 39*(1), 32–37.

Miller, L. (1990). The regular education initiative and school reform: Lessons from the mainstream. *Remedial & Special Education, 11*(3), 17–22.

Miller, T. L., & Sabatino, D. A. (1978). An evaluation of the teacher consultant model as an approach to mainstreaming. *Exceptional Children, 44*(1), 86–91.

Moore, J., & Fine, M. J. (1978). Regular and special class teachers' perceptions of normal and exceptional children and their attitudes toward mainstreaming. *Psychology in the Schools, 15*, 253–259.

Myles, B. S., & Kasselman, C. J. (1990). *Collaborative consultation: The regular educator's view.* Manuscript submitted for publication.

Myles, B. S., & Simpson, R. L. (1989). Regular educators' modification preferences for mainstreaming mildly handicapped children. *Journal of Special Education, 22*(4), 479–492.

Myles, B. S., & Simpson, R. L. (1990). Mainstreaming modification preferences of parents of elementary-age children with learning disabilities. *Journal of Learning Disabilities, 23*(4), 234–239.

National Association for Retarded Citizens. (1973). *The right to choose.* Arlington, TX: Author.

Newman, R. K., & Simpson, R. L. (1983). Modifying the least restrictive environment to facilitate the integration of severely emotionally disturbed children and youth. *Behavioral Disorders, 8*(2), 103–112.

Office of the Federal Register, National Archives and Records Administration. (1987). *Code of federal regulations: Education.* Washington, DC: U. S. Government Printing Office.

O'Rourke, A. P. (1980). A comparison of principal and teacher attitudes toward handicapped students and the relationship between those attitudes and school morale of handicapped students. *Dissertation Abstracts International, 40*(7-A), 3954.

Reister, A. E., & Bessette, K. M. (1986). Preparing the peer group for mainstreaming exceptional children. *Pointer, 31*, 12–20.

Reynolds, B. J., Martin-Reynolds, J., & Mark, F. D. (1982). Elementary teachers' attitudes toward mainstreaming educable retarded students. *Education & Training of the Mentally Retarded, 17*, 171–176.

Reynolds, M. C., Wang, M. C., & Walberg, H. J. (1987). The necessary restructuring of special and regular education. *Exceptional Children, 53*, 391–398.

Ribner, S. (1978). The effects of special class placement on the self-concept of exceptional children. *Journal of Learning Disabilities, 11*, 60–64.

Robinson, G. E. (1990). Synthesis of research on the effects of class size. *Educational Leadership, 47*(7), 80–90.

Rogers, H., & Saklofske, D. H. (1985). Self-concepts, locus of control and performance expectations of learning disabled children. *Journal of Learning Disabilities, 18*, 273–278.

Roubinek, D. (1978). Will mainstreaming fit? *Educational Leadership, 35*, 410–411.

Salend, S. J. (1990). *Effective mainstreaming.* New York: Macmillan.

Sasso, G. M., Simpson, R. L., & Novak, C. G. (1985). Procedures for facilitating integration of autistic children in public school settings. *Analysis & Intervention in Developmental Disabilities, 5*, 233–246.

Schrag, J. (1990). Charting the course for the 1990's. In L. M. Bullock & R. L. Simpson (Eds.), *Monograph on critical issues in special education: Implications for personnel preparation* (pp. 2–8). Denton: University of North Texas.

Sickler, J. L. (1988). Teachers in charge: Empowering the professionals. *Phi Delta Kappan, 375*, 354–356.

Simpson, R. L. (1987). Social interactions of behaviorally disordered children: Where are we and where do we need to go? *Behavioral Disorders, 12*, 292–298.

Simpson, R. L., & Myles, B. S. (1989). Parents' mainstreaming modification preferences for children with educable mental handicaps, behavior disorders and learning disabilities. *Psychology in the Schools, 26*, 292–301.

Simpson, R. L., & Myles, B. S. (1991). Ancillary staff members' mainstreaming recommendations for students with exceptionalities. *Psychology in the Schools, 28*(1), 26–32.

Smith, M. L., & Glass, G. V. (1980). Meta-analysis of research on class size and its relationship to attitudes and instruction. *American Educational Research Journal, 17*(4), 419–433.

Stainback, W., & Stainback, S. (1984). A rationale for the merger of regular and special education. *Exceptional Children, 51*(2), 102–111.

Stephens, T. M., & Benjamin, L. B. (1981). Measures of general classroom teachers' attitudes toward handicapped children. *Exceptional Children, 46*, 292–297.

Stone, B. (1984). Ecological view of self-concept. *Remedial & Special Education, 5*, 43–44.

Teacher opinion poll: Class size. (1975a). *Today's Education, 64*, 109.

Teacher opinion poll: Professional satisfaction. (1975b). *Today's Education, 64*, 14.

U. S. Department of Education. (1987). *Ninth annual report to Congress on the implementation of the Education of the Handicapped Act.* Washington, DC: Author.

Walberg, H. J., & Lane, J. J. (1989). *Organizing for learning: Toward the 21st century.* Reston, VA: National Association of Secondary School Principals.

Wang, M. C., & Birch, J. W. (1984). Comparison of a full-time mainstreaming program and a resource room approach. *Exceptional Children, 51*, 33–40.

Wang, M. C., Reynolds, M. C., & Walberg, H. J. (1986). Rethinking special education. *Educational Leadership, 44*, 26–31.

West, J. F., & Brown, P. A. (1987). State departments of education policies on consultation in special education: The state of the states. *Remedial & Special Education, 8*(3), 45–51.

White, P. A. (1989, September). An overview of school-based management: What does the research say? *NASSP Bulletin*, 1–8.

Will, M. (1984). Let us pause and reflect—But not for long. *Exceptional Children, 51*, 11–16.

Will, M. (1986). Educating children with learning problems: A shared responsibility. *Exceptional Children, 52*, 411–416.

Williams, R. J., & Algozzine, B. (1979). Teachers' attitudes toward mainstreaming. *Elementary School Journal, 80*, 63–67.

Yauman, B. E. (1983). Special educational placement and the self-concepts of elementary school age children. *Learning Disability Quarterly, 3*, 30–35.

Richard Simpson and Brenda Smith Myles are with the Department of Special Education at the University of Kansas.

○ 5 ○

This article recognizes the new role of special education personnel as they increase their work with and in general education classes. Moving from the resource room to a new role with the regular classroom teacher will require additional training and skills on the part of regular and special education personnel alike. The authors review potential problems and pitfalls and offer suggestions for improving working relations.

Rethinking the Relationship Between Consultation and Collaborative Problem Solving

Marleen C. Pugach and Lawrence J. Johnson

Professionals in the field of special education have responded to the challenge of how best to meet the needs of students with mild learning and behavior problems by introducing a variety of informal service delivery options that have come to be known as *prereferral interventions*. These procedures are designed to provide intervention assistance quickly and informally to general educators. The intent is to enhance communication between special and general education teachers and to prevent the need for lengthy and costly student evaluations and placement in special education by remediating student difficulties in a timely, efficient manner within the general education environment. As a result, general educators should become more independent in their abilities to solve problems and be less likely to access the special education system unnecessarily.

Prereferral interventions grew out of an increasing recognition of the restrictive nature of procedures by which students become eligible to receive special education services. They represent an attempt to place a greater proportion of special education's resources into more informal, immediate service delivery approaches and a lesser proportion into diagnosis, prescription, and formal staffing procedures and meetings.

Among the major forms of prereferral service delivery is consultation on the part of special education teachers (Fox et al., 1973; Fuchs & Fuchs, 1988; Idol, Paolucci-Whitcomb, & Nevin, 1986). The purpose of special education consultation is to have special education teachers work directly with general educators to develop specific instructional and management interventions for students with learning and behavior problems. With programs of consultation in place, general educators receive immediate help in problem identification, intervention, and monitoring of student behavior. Consultation services such as these are not delivered by special education teachers alone; school psychologists also have promoted their use (Graden, Casey, & Christenson, 1985; Shapiro, 1987) and have been successful in implementing similar consultation services at the school level (Ponti, Zins, & Graden, 1988).

As it is mostly commonly practiced, consultation is a one-to-one relationship based on the belief that as general educators are able to utilize data-based approaches through consultation with a specialist, their students will enjoy greater success in school. Although the specifics of consultation services may differ from program to program, typically they are based on a triadic model of interaction between the student as the target of concern, the general educator as mediator of the change, and the specialist as the consultant (Tharp & Wetzel, 1969). General educators, under the guidance of specialists, are encouraged to use data-based techniques to identify problem behaviors and monitor progress once interventions are started. Interventions are developed jointly and implemented for the target student or students by general educators. As a consequence, general educators are afforded the input of a specialist who helps the teacher use more systematic approaches with students who have difficulty finding success in school.

Consultation between adult professionals in the schools is an extremely important value for educators to promote. Through joint problem-solving, teachers are able to focus expertise on particular problems of teaching practice; collegial interaction encourages pairs of teachers and consultants to develop strong working relationships from which both can benefit by receiving mutual reinforcement. Further, with the introduction of consultation, special educators engage in greater interaction with general education around problematic situations, modeling among adults at a different but no less important level what integration is meant to do for handicapped and nonhandicapped students. Also, by supporting the development of consultation, special education professionals express their awareness that change is needed in the way special education services now are obtained. Equally important, consultation as a value appears to be consistent with educational reform efforts that stress increased responsibility for decision-making on the part of teaching professionals.

In principle, then, consultation is a collaborative endeavor, one that is meant to share expertise in developing new teaching skills on the part of general educators, who in turn can become more self-sufficient and less dependent upon support from special education. As often occurs when a new model is implemented, however, the practice of consultation may not be consistent with the intent of its underlying principles. At this point in its development, consultation is not yet well accepted despite its apparent value; in comparison to other activities, special educators actually spend little time consulting (see Evans, 1980; Idol-Maestas & Ritter, 1985; Sargeant, 1981).

PROBLEMS IN THE PRACTICE OF CONSULTATION

Elsewhere we have argued that existing conceptual and pragmatic barriers seriously inhibit the potential of consultation as a collaborative mode of professional interaction (Johnson, Pugach, & Hammitte, 1988). Germane to this discussion are five practices, described in detail later in this article, stemming from the common presupposition that the expertise belonging to those trained in special education or school psychology puts these particular professionals in the position of being most well suited to take on the consulting role. As a result of this hierarchical orientation on the part of support services specialists who practice consultation, the joint and collaborative intent of consultation is diminished. Instead, a top-down approach exists, in which general educators typically are characterized as needing assistance and specialists as typically being sources of assistance.

Recognizing the potential problem inherent in this kind of relationship, Idol et al. (1986) have attempted to break away from an expert model of consultation, proposing instead a variation of the triadic model of consultation called collaborative consultation. This form of consultation is described as *a reciprocal arrangement between individuals with diverse expertise to define problems and develop solutions mutually.*

As defined in the collaborative consultation model, general educators, special educators, speech therapists, principals, parents, or others might serve in the role of consultant. In practice, however, special educators typically function as the consultant—retaining the implication that their discrete expertise qualifies them best to fulfill that role (see, for example, Friend, 1985; Idol et al., 1986; Idol-Maestas & Ritter, 1985). This underlying belief—that special educators are in the best position to help general educators solve classroom problems—inhibits the relationship between general and special educators and contributes to the following problems of practice.

The *first* problem with consultation is that a lack of congruence may exist between suggestions for classroom interventions made by consultants and general educators' understanding of those suggestions (Abidin, 1975; Gans, 1985). The training and experience of special education teachers generally is geared to individualized instructional settings, which are very different from the demands and pressures of the typical general education classroom.

This problem is compounded when the special educator in an intervention capacity is asked to consult with teachers regarding students who typically would not qualify for special education services. Special educators have limited experiences with these students. In such situations the consultant is likely to have little familiarity with both the students and the environments for which they are being asked to consult and provide suggestions regarding alternative approaches. It is in the context of this problem that we may hear classroom teachers reporting that consultants often make unrealistic suggestions.

Second, research from cognitive psychology would suggest that individuals may have difficulty attempting new strategies with which they have little prior experience. Vygotsky's "zone of proximal development" (see, for example, Wertsch, 1984) is a concept describing the relationship between independent problem-solving and one's existing level of development. With collegial guidance, one can reach new levels of development proximal to the existing ones—but one would not likely leap to an entirely new mode of functioning. Similarly, Rosenfield (1985) cites the notion of teachers' "working knowledge," reminding us that new and diverse information and skills are not assimilated easily. She states: "Teachers favor sources of knowledge and expertise that tend to be close by and within the same guild" (p. 156).

For special education consultants, the behavioral model is likely to be the preferred approach. Although other methodologies in general education have been developed as a means of accommodating diverse learners (e.g., Wang, 1987; Wang, Reynolds, & Walberg, 1986), behavioral techniques that are less likely to be in the repertoire of classroom teachers continue to be suggested as alternatives. As a result, the interventions that special education consultants are most likely to propose are those that general educators may be least likely to use easily or accept.

Third, although special educators are beginning to receive training at the preservice level in concepts and issues associated with consultation, this is not commonly the case with students prepared in general programs of teacher education. Differential training underscores the preparedness of special educators to engage in consultation and the absence of preparedness of general educators to do so. Thus, a system has been created to support the assumption that the special educator is the one person appropriately trained to be a consultant. Not only are the skills of behavioral intervention deemed as the specialist's area of expertise but so also are the skills of consultation and collaboration themselves.

A *fourth* issue that inhibits the collaborative nature of consultation involves the attitudes that general and special educators hold regarding each other's abilities. Because of differences in training, general educators may question the ability of special education consultants to make suggestions that are realistic for implementation in the general classroom (Spodek, 1982). On the other hand, serious concern has been raised regarding general educators' abilities to modify their classroom structures to accommodate the needs of students with handicapping conditions (Aloia & Aloia, 1982; Furey & Strauch, 1983; Leyser & Abrams, 1984; Johnson & Johnson, 1980; Ringlaben & Price, 1981).

Although general educators question the ability of special educators to make useful suggestions and may have greater faith in their own abilities to teach mildly handicapped students, special educators conversely question the abilities of general educators to identify and implement appropriate accommodations and have greater confidence in their own abilities to address the needs of handicapped students (Furey & Strauch, 1983). This dissonance is a serious problem when consultation models of service delivery are initiated.

Finally, we must recognize that traditionally the provision of services to children with handicapping conditions simply has not been a shared partnership with general educators. General educators often have been ignored in the referral-to-identification process originally legislated in Public Law 94-142 and have played a secondary role in developing instructional plans for students with handicapping conditions, even situations in which the student's primary placement is the general education classroom. As the structure is now configured, the value of input from general educators is limited presumably because of their lack of knowledge and expertise with students who deviate from the norm. These attitudes on the part of special educators no doubt contribute to the tension that exists between special and general educators.

Before progress can be made toward developing an educational system that more equitably and efficiently addresses the needs of all students, we must recognize that both special and general education have contributed to less than ideal mutual relationships. In the special education literature, much has been written about general education's contribution to these problems. Now it is time to give careful and equal consideration to special education's contribution and to overcome the tendency toward a singularly hierarchical interpretation of consultation in which general educators are perceived to have less expertise and knowledge. If we continue to communicate this message in the practice of consultation, its success as an effective alternative to alleviate burdens now placed on the educational system will continue to be limited.

CONSULTATION AS COLLABORATION: ALTERNATIVE CONSIDERATIONS

To overcome these limitations so that consultation occurs in schools as a truly collaborative undertaking, its practice has to be reconceptualized along the following four dimensions:

1. Consultation should be a reciprocal, mutual activity among all professionals in a school.
2. Consultation should facilitate independent problem-solving skills on the part of general educators.
3. Consultation should be a routine part of interprofessional interaction and daily functioning.
4. The language used to discuss consultation should reflect its centrality in the school as a whole and not only its relationship to special education.

Consultation as a Mutual and Reciprocal Schoolwide Activity

To correct the assumption that only specialists are considered to be sources of consultation, consultation should be practiced as a mutual, reciprocal form of interaction. Certainly the deliberate expertise of those trained in special education is needed at times to resolve challenging learning and behavior problems. Likewise, however, general educators often possess crucial knowledge in specific subject areas, grouping for instruction, and knowledge of student performance within a group context—knowledge that may have particular import when students are making the transition from more segregated to more integrated settings. In current interpretations of consultation, the general educator is the recipient of expert advice from either a special education teacher or a school psychologist; rarely are general educators considered to possess expertise useful to special educators or school psychologists.

With consultation practiced as a reciprocal and mutual form of interaction, all professionals in a building would have the potential to be considered consultants in their areas of expertise. Consultation as a process would not belong solely to those who are not directly involved in general classroom education. In fact, the idea of the career or lead teacher, as conceptualized by the Holmes Group (1986) and the Carnegie Forum (1986) reform proposals, respectively, is consistent with the development of various kinds of expertise among the teaching staff in a particular school.

Consultation as a Facilitative Process

Consultation should facilitate independent problem-solving for teaching professionals as well as be a source of direct information. Teachers are used to approaching their colleagues for advice, and they typically receive a set of ideas tried previously by those colleagues, regardless of whether the advice is coming from a peer in general education or from a specialist. When this type of advice-giving comes from other classroom teachers, it is highly informal and impromptu, occurring often in the hallways or during teachers' brief lunch breaks. It most often is unsystematic, based on the assumption that others' experience is adequate as a central source of solutions to problems in school. In the specific case of special education consultation, general educators receive more formal advice regarding how to identify the problem, what kinds of interventions might be best to try, and how to keep track of those interventions.

The suggestions and prescriptions teachers and consultants offer to their colleagues during these interactions are well meaning, made in a spirit of helpfulness and sharing. In the short-term, they may be a source of useful ideas. But the long-term outcome of this kind of prescriptive, external advice-giving as the major mode of assistance is likely to work against teachers' gaining independence in solving classroom problems. Efficiency in the short-term, represented by existing conceptions of consultation, does not logically result in providing teachers with the means for increasing their own skills to serve their students better.

It is as if consultation is at cross-purposes with its intent. Although the overriding purpose is to create greater self-sufficiency on the part of general educators, consultation attempts to achieve this end by creating a dependent relationship between general and special education teachers. This is not to say that special education expertise is never needed; rather, it should be reserved for cases in which the issue or problem under consideration is clearly outside the general educator's expertise.

To reach this goal of long-term independence, the concept of consultation can be redefined to include not only prescriptive, advice-giving interaction, but interaction that facilitates independent problem-solving as well. We choose to call this form of consultation "facilitative consultation" as a way of defining its unique purpose: facilitating teachers' abilities to acquire specific problem-solving strategies themselves. In the facilitative mode, the consultant's job is to assist small groups or pairs of teachers in developing the necessary skills to reach their own solutions to classroom problems. The facilitative consultant displays trust in teachers' capabilities to own their own problems while also respecting their existing levels of expertise as problem solvers.

Consistent with the notion of the zone of proximal development, facilitative consultation requires great restraint on the part of the consultant from "giving" advice or solutions. Rather, teachers learn to guide each other to progressively more complex levels of problem solving. This approach to consultation also entails a letting go of control that may not be easy given the historical role of special educators in the schools.

One facilitative strategy the authors have been investigating with success is a highly structured dialogue known as *peer collaboration* (Pugach & Johnson, 1988a, 1988b). In this process, pairs of general educators learn to use a series of specific strategies as a problem-solving technique based on the development of metacognitive thinking. The purpose is to encourage professionals encountering a problem to develop independent problem-solving skills under the guidance of a peer. In contrast to advice-giving, peer collaboration guides partners as they help peers develop their own solutions to problems through strategies such as clarification, self-questioning, and predicting outcomes of various solutions.

Facilitative consultants can learn to provide training to pairs of general education teachers in processes such as peer collaboration, and monitor their acquisition until teachers feel comfortable and skilled using them independently. With the capability to utilize a facilitative set of skills as the primary mode of consultation, accompanied by a set of prescriptive skills as needed, consultants can begin to differentiate, with greater confidence, problems requiring their specific knowledge and those for which solutions can be reached among general educators themselves.

Consultation as a Routine Professional Role

Finding time for consultation is a major challenge. Given the need for consultation to take place often and between all professionals in schools, work conditions must support its occurrence on a regular basis. Currently professionals have little, if any, time in which to confer and consult. Planning time is not the norm, nor is using existing meeting times for group meetings focusing on problem resolution. In attempts to implement existing models of special education consultation, identifying and reserving time for it to take place has been one of the major obstacles identified by advocates (Idol-Maestas & Ritter, 1985). There is no reason to think this will not continue to be a problem with truly collaborative forms of consultation as well.

For the value of consultation to be operationalized in schools, time for interaction has to be built into the school day. Should more widespread, facilitative norms of consultation be enacted, however, that time cannot be associated only with special education and its attendant regulations. Reorganizing schooling to provide time for teachers to interact professionally is likewise one of the hallmarks of reform proposals (Carnegie Forum 1986; Holmes Group, 1986).

Major reorganization and differentiation of staffing to provide teachers with clerical and routine assistance for noninstructional tasks is essential in targeting time for professional interaction. In the interim, some more immediate ways of providing time may be workable. For instance, schoolwide schedules could be organized so the time of various content-area specialists (music, art, physical education, etc.) regularly would allow a subgroup of teachers (for example, grade-level teachers) to meet specifically for purposes of problem solving. Special and general educators might team-teach to provide more options for various configurations of professionals to interact. Regularly scheduled planning time then could be devoted to facilitative consultation.

Also, principals could reserve faculty meetings for consultation purposes on a regular basis (for example, every third faculty meeting) and deal with procedural issues in less time-consuming ways; small groups of teachers could be formed early in the year as teams to work at these meetings. These are only a few examples of ways to begin rethinking the problem of time needed for consultation that would reorient consultation as a regular schoolwide activity among all professionals.

The Language of Consultation

The final issue has to do with the language we use to describe and locate consultation in the operation of schooling. Because the term "consultation" typically has been applied to services deriving from special education and school psychology, it retains its association with carefully delimited expertise and with a professional hierarchy in schools. In more meetings than we care to remember involving the relationship between special and general education, we hear general educators describe themselves as "just regular teachers," and learn of the failures of consultation because of its singularly one-way meaning as expert-to-novice delivery of information.

Issues of language are paramount because language is the medium through which the norms of consultation are introduced and maintained. Whether consultation is presented and implemented as a function solely of special education or of education in general is dependent largely upon both explicit and assumed meanings ascribed to the term and its practice. Professionals within a particular specialization usually have difficulty recognizing the impact on their peers of the specialized terminology they routinely use. Special care and a measure of objectivity both are necessary in choosing terminology to describe new approaches and practices such as consultation.

A troublesome, timely example of a language problem is the unfortunate use of the term "regular education initiative" to denote special education's concern with the relationship between itself and general education. The way in which the REI movement is being framed continues to set up special and general education as two parallel systems rather than special education being a subspecialty within general education. Because of this, the very problems the REI is attempting to overcome are intensified rather than reduced.

Further, notwithstanding the fact that the relationship between special and general education requires redefinition, special educators should not be surprised that more "regular" educators are not interested in or knowledgeable about REI. After all, even though reforms in special education are part of the REI, it is essentially a term that special educators developed to describe, in large part, their view of what should change in "regular" education. Even so, all too frequently special educators wonder why more general educators are not involved in discussions of REI. Realistically, how would we as special educators react if we were to learn of a movement developed in general education that had as a major component the need to reform special education?

It is critical that we understand the inhibiting or facilitating power of connotations associated with new reforms and movements for which we advocate, and the responsibility for the effect of the terms used should lie with the professionals promoting their use. Consider how quickly the term REI has become integrated into the vocabulary of special education. It is now part of our jargon with little consideration for its meaning and the assumptions it embraces.

In the case of consultation, the term typically is introduced as a new form of special education service delivery or as a new role for school psychologists. Although teachers are likely to welcome more efficient and informal modes of assistance, they may at the same time understand that consultation is necessary because of their own shortcomings as teachers. As a function of specialized services, consultation may seem proper only as a professional activity within special education: Consultation is what you do when you have a student who is going to require special education. In some districts consultation is being proposed as a requirement, a step that must be taken before the referral process occurs. It may even be listed on a referral form as a prior service required before a referral can be processed.

Clearly, consultation prior to referral is not in itself problematic; in fact, it should occur regularly. The difficulty comes in isolating consultation as a step in the special education continuum of services rather than as a building-wide norm for problem-solving. It is not even essential to use the term "consultant" or "consulting teacher," thereby reserving this practice for specialists. Consultation can be presented as one of the goals of professional interaction that can be expected to take place in a particular building.

It is just as imperative that consultation not be defined as, or limited to, solving problems associated with student deficits. Teachers face many problems that are unrelated to student deficits. For example, accommodating the needs of students with outstanding ability can be a highly perplexing problem. Developing alternative instructional approaches in general, or identifying schoolwide needs for curriculum change, are issues that might require a consultative approach. Consultation has the potential to serve as a tool that will make the classroom and the school itself a more enriching and growth-producing environment for all students—but only if it is cut loose from its singular association with special services.

We also must examine the use of terms such as *prereferral* and *preplacement*. "Pre" implies that this is something we must do while we wait for special education services. Or, more troublesome, it suggests that we engage in developing alternative strategies in the classroom only when we already are considering special education as a possibility. This orientation prevents growth by creating a system that reacts to problems rather than initiates innovations.

One might argue that good teacher consultants would not let such things happen, and that districts implementing consultation as a collaborative concept would plan carefully to avoid such difficulties. The danger, however, lies in the rapid spread of practices associated with prereferral by districts and states as they attempt to institutionalize less formal, more efficient distribution of special education services. Even the best intentioned mandated practice can all too quickly take on the form of rule-driven behavior at the implementation stage. In the case of special education services, the regulatory nature of its practices is perhaps its most salient feature (Lilly, 1988), and the way to which the field is heavily accustomed. Relying on the language of expertise to introduce consultation is likely to result in its lukewarm reception. What to special educators may appear to be a flexible mode of service delivery might be interpreted among general educators as greater institutionalization of its practice. Although issues of language are more easily workable that the fundamental end of having teachers work collaboratively in schools, they reflect the philosophical environment in which consultation is introduced and thus deserve focused consideration at the planning stages.

CONCLUSIONS

In closing, consultation is an important activity for education professionals, and its practice should be encouraged. If it is implemented well, consultation has the potential to enhance the educational environment significantly and is supported in the intent of the education reform movement. As it is now practiced, however, consultation is predicated on the faulty presupposition that special educators and school psychologists are singularly able to provide expertise in the consulting role. This one-way notion greatly impedes the success of consultation and prevents it from being a collaborative form of interaction.

Potential problems associated with the implementation of schoolwide collaboration through consultation are not insurmountable. But preventing implementation problems will take great changes on the part of specialists regarding their roles and relationships. The following guidelines should be considered when implementing new consultation programs:

- Planning for consultation has to be a joint process, including both special and general education personnel.
- The skills of all professionals in a building have to be identified to clarify sources of expertise in various areas, of which special education is but one.
- The language associated with the introduction of consultation has to reflect its role as a schoolwide professional activity, not a special education-related activity alone.
- Consultation should not be identified simply as a requirement to be completed before special education referrals are made.
- Consultants need the skills to provide facilitative assistance as well as prescriptive advice.

The term "consultation" has at least two meanings: One is to give professional advice, and the other is to deliberate together. The purpose of the analysis offered here is to encourage districts and district personnel to err on the side of the second definition when implementing programs of consultation. Only in the context of *joint deliberation* does consultation have the potential to change the way adults interact in schools. In our opinion, consultation will never be successful as long as it represents special education's answers to the problems of general education. We must develop a partnership in which problems and solutions are shared equally. With joint deliberation as the guiding principle toward development of such a partnership, the goal of collaboration—which places special education as a lateral, not a vertical, source of assistance—is surely within our grasp.

REFERENCES

Abidin, R.R. (1975). Negative effect of behavioral consultations: "I know I ought to, but it hurts too much." *Journal of School Psychology, 13*, 51-57.

Aloia, G.F., & Aloia, S.D. (1982). Variations in expectations of the mainstreamed handicapped child by regular and special education teachers. *Journal of Special Educators, 19*(1), 13-19.

Carnegie Forum on Education and the Economy. (1986, May). *A nation prepared: Teachers for the 21st century.* New York: Carnegie Corp.

Evans, S. (1980). The consultant role of the resource teacher. *Exceptional Children, 46*, 402-404.

Fox, W.L., Egner, A.N., Paolucci, R.E., Perelman, P.F., McKenzie, H.S., & Garvin, J.S. (1973). An introduction to a regular classroom approach to special education. In E.L. Deno (Ed.), *Instructional alternatives for exceptional children.* Reston, VA: Council for Exceptional Children.

Friend, M. (1985). Training special educators to be consultants. *Teacher Education & Special Education, 8*(3), 115-120.

Fuchs, D., & Fuchs, L.S. (1988). Mainstream assistance teams to accommodate difficult-to-teach students in general education. In J.L. Graden, J.E. Zins, & M.J. Curtis (Eds.), *Alternative educational delivery systems: Enhancing instructional options for all students (pp. 49–70).* Washington, DC: National Association of School Psychologists.

Furey, E.M., & Strauch, J.D. (1983). The perceptions of teacher skills and knowledge by regular and special educators of mildly handicapped students. *Teacher Education & Special Education, 6*(1), 46-50.

Gans, K.D. (1985). Regular and special educators. *Teacher Education & Special Education, 8*(4), 188-189.

Graden, J.L., Casey, A., & Christenson, S.L. (1985). Implementing a prereferral intervention system: Part I. The model. *Exceptional Children, 51*, 377-384.

Holmes Group. (1986). *Tomorrow's teachers: A report of the Holmes Group.* East Lansing, MI: Author.

Idol, L., Paolucci-Whitcomb, P., & Nevin, A. (1986). *Collaborative consultation.* Rockville: MD: Aspen.

Idol-Maestas, L. (1986). Setting the stage for successful school consultation. In C.L. Warger & L.E. Aldinger (Eds.), *Preparing special educators for teacher consultation.* Toledo, OH: University of Toledo.

Idol-Maestas, L., & Ritter, S. (1985). A follow-up study of resource/consulting teachers. *Teacher Education & Special Education, 8*(3), 121-131.

Johnson, D.W., & Johnson, R.T. (1980). Integrating handicapped students into the mainstream. *Exceptional Children, 47*, 90-98.

Johnson, L.J., Pugach, M., & Hammitte, D. (1988). Barriers to special education consultation. *Remedial & Special Education, 9*(6), 41–47.

Leyser, Y. & Abrams, P.D. (1984). Changing attitudes of classroom teachers toward mainstreaming through in-service training. *Clearing House, 57*, 250-255.

Lilly, M.S. (1988, April). *The regular education initiative: A force for change in general and special education.* Paper presented at the CEC Conference on Mental Retardation, Honolulu, HI.

Ponti, C.R., Zins, J.E., & Graden, J.L. (1988). Implementing a consultation-based service delivery system to decrease referrals for special education: A case study of organizational considerations. *School Psychology Review, 17*, 89-100.

Pugach, M., & Johnson, L.J. (1988a). Peer collaboration: Helping teachers help themselves. *Teaching Exceptional Children, 20* (3), 75-77.

Pugach, M., & Johnson, L.J. (1988b). *Peer collaboration: Enhancing teacher problem-solving capabilities for students at risk.* Paper presented at the Annual Meeting, American Educational Research Association, New Orleans. (ERIC Document No. SP 030114)

Ringlaben, R.P., & Price, J. (1981). Regular classroom teachers' perceptions of mainstreaming effects. *Exceptional Children, 47*, 302-304.

Rosenfield, S. (1985). Teacher acceptance of behavioral principles. *Teacher Education & Special Education*, *8*, 153-158.

Sargeant, L.R. (1981). Resource teacher time utilization: An observational study. *Exceptional Children, 47*, 420-425.

Shapiro, E.S. (1987). *Behavioral assessment in school psychology*. Hillsdale, NJ: Lawrence Erlbaum.

Spodek, B. (1982). What special educators need to know about regular classrooms. *Educational Forum, 46*, 295-307.

Tharp, R.G., & Wetzel, R.J. (1969). *Behavior modification in the natural environment*. New York: Academic Press.

Wang, M.C. (1987). Toward achieving educational excellence for all students: Program design and student outcomes. *Remedial and Special Education, 8*(3), 25–34.

Wang, M.C., Reynolds, M.C., & Walberg, H.J. (1986). Rethinking special education. *Educational Leadership, 44*, 26-31.

Wertsch, J.V. (1984). The zone of proximal development: Some conceptual issues. In B. Rogoff & J. Wertsch (Eds.), *Children's learning in the ZPD* (pp. 7-18). San Francisco, CA: Jossey-Bass.

Marleen Pugach is an associate professor in the Department of Curriculum and Instruction at the University of Wisconsin, Milwaukee. Lawrence Johnson is an associate professor and head of the Department of Early Childhood and Special Education at the University of Cincinnati.

6

Criticism of resource rooms and greater pressure from advocates have resulted in a need for modifications in service delivery. Some have advocated collaboration or special educators' working with regular class teachers. This article describes successful programs in which students with disabilities and regular class students make up a joint class, with a special educator and the regular class teacher both conducting the instruction. The article points out the necessary administrative and inservices necessary to accomplish successful programs.

A Collaborative Model for Students with Mild Disabilities in Middle Schools

Alan E. White and Lynda L. White

The Individuals with Disabilities Education Act of 1990 (PL 101-476) and implementing regulations are responsible for shifting students with disabilities from one educational setting to another. Earlier efforts had been aimed at serving students with disabilities in special programs as a part of the public schools but not necessarily with general education students. This was followed by a movement to establish all programs for special students on the general education campus. Educators also identified and classified more students with mild disabilities and moved them from regular classes into special education resource classrooms. Approximately 15 years elapsed before Americans came to understand that what is really needed for many students with disabilities is to place them back into a more normalized regular classroom setting and educate them with their nondisabled peers.

This movement is not that unusual. The simple recognition of a need to help students with disabilities in school has always been an underlying theme of special education, and no one could argue with that idea. It seems, however, that we have been quite guilty of trying to educate those with disabilities by moving them away from the regular curriculum via a separate special education track. In doing so, we have succeeded in isolating the students physically and socially and have severely limited their opportunity for exposure to the established regular education curriculum. This is especially true for students with mild learning disabilities, behavior/emotional disorders, and intellectual disabilities.

BACKGROUND

Over many years, the pull-out delivery of service was the mainstay of school programs for the majority of students with disabilities. Large numbers of programs for the gifted, remedial, and non-English speaking students also employed this model. This delivery system has come under scrutiny as a result of policy, litigation, and research in special education. Wang and Baker (1986) and Wang and Zollers (1990), for example, demonstrated the educational benefit of participation in regular classes. The investigations of Stainback and Stainback (1989, 1990) also provide clear indicators for inclusive educational approaches.

The efficacy of interaction with nondisabled peers in a regular class setting is now fortified by a more practical need for comparable instruction in curriculum content for students with disabilities. Likewise, attention to learning styles, behavioral strategies, augmentive communication, and motivational techniques are examples of special education instruction that can take place in the regular education classroom.

Designing and implementing an instructional model for integrating students with disabilities into the regular classroom setting is a process of defining and redefining the requirements of the least restrictive environment under the Individuals with Disabilities Education Act (IDEA). Models that broadly fall into this concept are those of collaborative teaching, team teaching, inclusion, pull-in, and similar terminology used to describe integrated instructional procedures. The emphasis on joint efforts by general and special education is found more often at the secondary level but is becoming increasingly accepted as appropriate for middle and elementary age groups as well.

Many states and local school systems have developed required curriculum content for middle school students, designed to meet the unique learning needs of students in grades six through eight. The delivery of services for special education students in these grades, however, has not been modified at the same pace as the changing national emphasis on the middle school learner. In many instances, the traditional pull-out program of elementary school special education continues into the middle school program. Nevertheless, the middle school team approach by grade level and the instructional design for each specific grade level form a ready foundation for implementing the collaborative or team-teaching efforts of regular and special education students.

The purpose of this article is not to try to convince educators of the need of instructing students with disabilities in regular classes. A significant body of information already exists in research, law, and policy, plus common sense, that not only supports but actually demands that we offer similar educational opportunity to disabled and nondisabled students alike. Rather, we present a systematic approach for implementing a middle school collaborative model for the delivery of service to students with mild disabilities.

AN OVERVIEW

Various terms have been used to describe a combined instructional model for general and special education. In this article, collaboration refers to a single classroom combining disabled and nondisabled students, with instruction by one special education teacher and one general education teacher. The model for collaborative special and regular educational instruction is applicable to the high school and elementary levels, but the discussion here is directed specifically to the middle school level.

Students entering the sixth through eighth grades are well suited for the collaborative teaching model. The separation of students by grade and, more important, the emphasis on instructional teaming at the middle school level provide a ready avenue for collaborative teaching.

COMPONENTS OF THE MODEL

Major components of the model are denoted in Figure 1.

Program Design

Some school systems may not begin the collaborative teaching effort without a systemwide adoption of instructional philosophy for all special education programs. Decisions should be made with regard to the issues of inclusion and the regular education initiative positions, such as those expressed by Will (1986), Lilly (1986), or of Hallahan, Keller, McKinney, Lloyd, and Bryan (1988). Villa and Thousand (1990) provide strategies to promote a system philosophy for including special education students in the regular education mainstream. It is recommended that systems first demonstrate success of the program by establishing one or more pilot projects.

However the system chooses to approach initial implementation, the program philosophy and program design must be the result of joint regular and special education decision making. Special education staff cannot hope to implement a collaborative teach-

FIGURE 1   *Major Components of the Collaborative Teaching Model*

ing model together with regular education instruction without advance planning, discussion, and agreement with system-level curriculum personnel.

Pilot Program Selection

Prior to implementing a model for delivery of services to students with mild disabilities, school districts may choose to identify a pilot site. School districts with small student enrollments might target one class or one grade in a school. Larger districts with several middle schools may select more than one school for participation during the initial implementation year. We do suggest that the number of pilot sites be limited because of the significant impact of staff training and data collection. Working through problems on a small scale during the first year allows orderly expansion later on.

Site Pre-Selection Activities

Prior to selecting the site, information should be gathered and reviewed to determine potential success of the model in a specific school. Types of information to be considered may include:

1. Local school administrative support
    —Does the school principal support the concept of collaborative teaching?
    —Will the model receive the necessary attention during development of the school's master schedule?
    —Can the regular and special education teachers have common planning time?
    —Will the model have support of parents and the community?
    —Will the principal support the school's selection as a pilot site?

2. Local school teacher support
    —Do special and regular education teachers support the philosophy of collaboration?
    —Are both groups willing to plan, provide instruction, and evaluate student performance collectively?
    —Is there potential for a positive "match" of regular and special education teachers?
    —Are both groups open to change as it relates to the instructional process?
    —Are there teachers with similar classroom behavior management strategies?
    —Are there teachers who have demonstrated the ability to share teaching responsibilities and to work together effectively?
    —Can teachers collectively plan for positive parent involvement?
    —Will teachers be returning to the school the following year?
    —Does the school have more than one special education teacher?
    —Are there teachers who are willing to participate in data collection activities?

3. Special education student information
    —What data are available on special education students by area of disability and by grade level?

A data grid such as that presented in Figure 2 may assist school staff in gathering information regarding the number of students and periods per day of service as required in the students' IEPs. The maximum number of students served during each instructional period may be restricted by state or local regulations. The format of the grid, however, may be useful in identifying a group of students with common disabilities and grade levels. An appropriate number of students with the same grade placement and similar IEP goals and objectives could constitute a potential group for collaborative teaching.

Data collected might reflect, for example, that eight learning disabled students in the seventh grade have IEP goals and objectives focusing on the broad areas of reading comprehension and written expression skills. If the IEPs of these same students recommend two periods per day in special education, the eight special education students could be scheduled into a regular class for the determined curricula area. In addition, if collaborative opportunities exist, IEPs can be modified according to due process to allow more participation of special education students in a general education classroom.

Pilot Site Selection

Once data on potential sites have been collected, a review by special and regular education administration is recommended. Sites are rated as to potential effectiveness for a pilot program, followed by a final determination of sites. The local schools are officially contacted and their willingness to participate is confirmed.

Pre-Implementation Activities

Teacher Selection

After pilot sites have been selected, the participating teachers should be identified. According to Stalvey, Dye, and Goldblatt (1985), the most critical factor for pilot success is the selection and match of teachers involved. White, Spurgeon, Jackson, and Green-Folks (1991) suggest that selection criteria be based on:

—common interest and willingness to participate in collaborative teaching.
—established relationships between regular and special educators in the school.
—similar behavior management strategies.

	No. of Students/No. of Periods		
	6th Grade	7th Grade	8th Grade
Learning Disabilities	/	/	/
Emotional/Behavior Disorders	/	/	/
Mild Intellectual Disabilities	/	/	/

FIGURE 2   Site Selection Data Grid

—ability to share responsibilities of planning, presenting instruction, and evaluating students.
—demonstration of a plan for positive parent involvement.

Actual selection of a teacher team may occur formally or informally. A formal method suggested in Figure 3 by White et al. (1991) may utilize a teacher survey to assess attitudes toward collaborative teaching. Several other inventories are available for assessment, such as the *Learning Styles Inventory* (Silver & Hanson, 1980). The informal method, more feasible in most instances, consists of a meeting of interested teachers to discuss possibilities, interest in the model, and their ability to work together as a team. Even though formal instruments and inventories are useful, the most crucial issue is the willingness and commitment of teachers to work together in teams. Determination of teachers' characteristics, whether by formal or by informal means, is necessary to insure success. The pilot site should begin with one selected team for initial implementation.

Student Selection and Scheduling

Information on number of students, categories of disability, periods of service, and IEP goals and objectives should be available from data gathered during the site selection stage. The co-teaching team reviews the data and identifies the largest group of students in the same grade and with similar IEP goals and objectives. Table 1 presents data on a middle school that serves 60 resource students with mild disabilities through special education.

Teacher _____	Date _____		
A collaborative teacher will:	Agree	Disagree	No Opinion
1. Provide increased effective interaction among regular and special education teachers.			
2. Work to improve student self-esteem.			
3. Increase teacher/student awareness of individual differences.			
4. Provide lower teacher/pupil ratios.			
5. Provide for intensive interdisciplinary common planning.			
6. Allow for students to problem-solve and improve self-management skills.			
7. Allow for more flexibility in scheduling.			
8. Provide for generalization and transfer of learning strategies.			
9. Provide for cooperative learning experiences.			
10. Provide exposure to an increased awareness of regular education curriculum.			

Source: From Cobb County School District, Cobb County, Georgia.

FIGURE 3 Collaborative Teaching Survey

TABLE 1   Example Middle School Data

Area of disability	6th	7th	8th
Learning Disabled	10	12	12
Emotional/Behavioral	5	7	7
Mild Intellectual	3	2	2

In this scenario, review of the data may reveal that of the sixth-grade LD students, eight have IEP goals in the language arts area and two students have goals for math. Then a sixth-grade language arts group could be considered for co-teaching. Selection of the students might be limited to the grade level taught by teachers participating in the pilot. If an eighth-grade language arts teacher is a willing participant, the co-teaching team would review and select appropriate eighth-grade students.

When selecting students, other considerations are:

1. Prior success in a regular education setting.
2. Student success in other cooperative learning situations
3. Consideration of class content and student IEP objectives.
4. The degree of student behavior management required.

Students who do not meet these criteria may not be selected and thus continue to receive services through the traditional resource model. When all considerations have been applied to individual students, the team can determine the final group for inclusion in the collaborative teaching class. The school schedule then should include this group of students in the class. In many instances the pilot group is scheduled first to avoid difficult and often unpopular schedule changes later.

Parent Notification

Parents of students participating in the pilot should be included in the planning process. This may be done through an announced group meeting of parents with students who are considered for the model. Also, IEP meetings can be used—or may be required if the amount of time in special education or goals and objectives are to be modified. If the amount of time or goals and objectives remain the same, a less formal meeting or discussion may be held with the parents.

The special education administrators should review local due process procedures to assure that all requirements of the system are maintained. Regardless of the procedure, parents should be informed of the background, philosophy, and procedures to be used in the collaborative model. The increased participation with nondisabled students should be approached in a positive manner. Hanline and Halvorsen (1989) indicate that parental involvement during this transitional process is important to success.

Staff Training

Teachers participating in the collaborative model also must be assisted in adjusting to the change, because implementing the model is an ongoing process that is not limited to a single event. Staff training for co-teachers must occur prior to implementation of the model. Even though training activities often focus on routine tasks such as timelines, data collection, and the like, a significant amount of time in the initial training session should center on changing certain mindsets or paradigms (". . . because that's the way it's always been done") and stressing the importance of sharing and working together.

If more than one school is involved, all participating teachers and administrators can be trained at the same time, although teacher teams should participate in activities together. Bonding activities and simulations proved successful in districts such as the Cobb County School District, Georgia, where collaborative models are in place. Communication is the key to successful collaborative teaching and activities that build rapport and strengthen communication are critical, during initial implementation as well as throughout the entire pilot phase. Initial training should provide teachers with a repertoire of communication strategies that will help them get started as a team and serve as a resource if communication issues develop later.

Implementation

The Instructional Process

The goal of instruction is student performance and achievement.

In a two-year study by the National Association of State Boards of Education, Roach (1991) reported:

> States are exploring "outcome-based" education. They are shifting the focus away from processes and "input" measures such as the number of textbooks in a school and types of courses offered. Instead, there is an interest in performance, achievement, and "outcome" measures such as student knowledge and skills, student participation in social experiences, student participation in community and school life, and student satisfaction.
>
> The "model" chosen for instruction should address all these areas. In the collaborative teaching model, the regular and special education teachers share responsibility of the instructional process by jointly planning, presenting and evaluating the instruction.

Planning Phase

Planning for instruction is vital to instructional effectiveness. Common planning time should be scheduled for both teachers in the collaborative model. Administrative support is required to allow for this planning time in the schedule. During the planning phase, the general education teacher responsible for content pinpoints the concepts and material to be taught. The special education teacher suggests various modes and forms of presenting the information (Stalvey et al., 1985). Special educators bring to the team specialized skills in the areas of diagnosis and assessment, individualized instruction, and classroom management. The general educator's knowledge of course content for middle school curricular areas provides the foundation for instruction. Planning emphasizes not only what is to be taught in content but also how it is to be taught employing various methodologies.

Included in the planning phase is joint decision making by both teachers regarding the method for evaluating instructional lessons. Among various evaluative considerations are completion of assignments, earning daily points, turning in homework, class projects, and participation in cooperative learning activities. For example, both teachers may agree on the use of an assignment notebook to address the improvement of organizational skills. The planning encompasses the needs of all disabled and nondisabled students.

Planning time also provides the opportunity to review daily, weekly, or other results of student performance. The development, scoring, and weighting of tests and other assessment measures should be agreed upon jointly as part of the district's required grading procedures. Consideration and completion of final grades is a shared effort for all students in the class.

Instructional Phase

Lesson presentation is a responsibility of both teachers. This process has to be shared to prevent one teacher from becoming subordinate to the other. Students should not be given the impression that one assumes the role of "teacher" and one of "helper." Shifting of leadership in lesson presentation prevents negative role patterns from developing.

Lesson presentation can be shared using techniques such as the following.

1. The general education teacher presents new information to the class. The special education teacher writes notes on the chalkboard for students to copy. At the conclusion of the presentation, the special education teacher reviews the main points of the lesson from the chalkboard and leads class discussion.
2. The special education teacher organizes students into cooperative learning groups and presents an activity or assignment for each group to complete. Both teachers move about the room and answer questions, providing assistance to the groups as they work. When work is complete, groups share their work with the class as both teachers provide feedback.
3. Both teachers, prior to a test, have planned and developed questions for a competition as a study session, using a *Jeopardy* format. The special education teacher serves as the moderator, covers the rules, and conducts the game. The general education teacher serves as time-and-score keeper and conducts a summary review at the end of the game.
4. Both teachers assist students in developing organizational skills through the use of individual student notebooks. Both teachers direct disabled and nondisabled students through a process that may include: maintaining weekly logs by outlining daily required topics or issues and properly placing them in an appropriate section. Teachers share in a weekly notebook check of all students to maintain current and useful study guides.

Classroom management is the responsibility of both teachers. Each teacher shares the responsibility for modeling behavior, intervening in situations of inappropriate behavior, and planning strategies to assure a team approach in maintaining an orderly classroom. Again, advance planning and agreement on behavioral approaches is necessary to create a positive learning environment.

Presentation of facts to be learned does not assure mastery by all students. Presentation of concepts accompanied by study sheets, highlighted textbooks, color coding, clear directions, tips on how to identify main ideas, and multimodality approaches make the content meaningful. Although each of these methods may be found in a classroom, it is essential to select methodology that matches *what* students are to learn with *how* they learn. The excitement of learning will be maintained in this model as teachers identify their own individual talents, talents of the teaching team, and talents of individual students in the class.

Instructionally, collaborative teaching involves planning, presenting, and evaluating by both teachers. The interaction of curriculum content and specialized methodology presented in Figure 4 is the significant characteristic that makes this model unique. The strengths of both regular and special education are shared during a common classroom period to produce what can be a more effective instructional opportunity through collaborative teaching.

Evaluation and Data Collection

School districts implementing the collaborative teaching model should evaluate its effectiveness in a number of areas. The main focus should be on student outcomes, but additional feedback from teachers, administrators, and parents should be considered as well. Progress in academic areas should be assessed by reviewing mastery of IEP goals and objectives and final reported grades. Homework, class participation, organization skills, and other areas also should be included in the review of progress for all students in the program. Additional data should be assessed for student attitudes toward participation in the pilot.

Individualized Education Program

For students with disabilities, objectives mastered should be reviewed at the end of the pilot or during the routine annual IEP review. A data collection form should be kept for

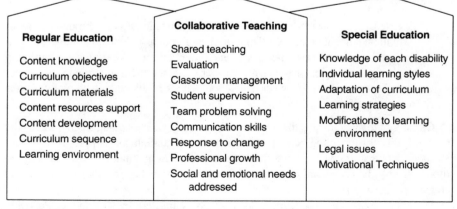

FIGURE 4   *Content and Methodology Interaction*

each student, reflecting the IEP objectives. These data can be summarized at the conclusion of the pilot. Prior to beginning the pilot program, the IEP committee should establish an expected percentage of mastery of goals by students with disabilities.

Report Cards

Data from report cards should be reviewed for each student in the pilot and should not be limited to a single grade in the pilot class. Each of the academic, social, organizational skills, and other areas should be included for review and comparison. The kind and type of data available on report cards may differ between school systems, and identification and selection of data to be reviewed should be decided prior to implementation.

Student Attitudes

Pre- and post-assessment of student attitudes should be included as a data collection component. An initial student survey should be administered during the first two weeks and again during the final two weeks of the pilot term. Survey topics might include student attitudes toward having two teachers in one classroom, interest in the subject area, preference toward being in a regular, resource, or collaborative classroom, opinion of school, desire to participate in class, and willingness to work with other students. Topics should be assessed for both the disabled and nondisabled students in the class. A summary of the survey should be reviewed for the entire class and by each subgroup.

Teacher Attitudes

Attitudes of the teachers involved should be recorded throughout the pilot period. The pilot coordinator or other appropriate staff member should record responses to questions during the informal discussion and feedback sessions. Classroom observations and discussions should be maintained for review. The assessment of teacher attitudes might include opinions of perceived success or failure in providing curriculum content, increased learning for all students involved, student discipline, team efforts, and grading procedures, for example.

Administrator Attitudes

The school principal and other building administrators should be interviewed to assess the leadership perception of the collaborative model pilot. Central office administrators in both regular and special education also should observe the class and be interviewed. Administrative staff members should give their opinion of the program's strengths and weaknesses, along with specific suggestions and comments. The pilot coordinator should summarize all the information gained from the administrative assessment.

Parent Survey

One of the most important data collection aspects is the perception of parents regarding success of the pilot program. Their feedback is necessary to indicate if their child's IEP needs are being met through collaborative teaching and whether they have observed changes in their child's behavior. In some cases, parents are able to compare the child's attitude toward school, the pilot class, and instruction between team teaching and the traditional resource or pull-out model. The parent questionnaire provided in Figure 5 may be used to summarize parental opinion as part of the data collection effort.

The pilot program coordinator and other involved administrators should analyze all of the data collected to determine the effectiveness of the collaborative teaching class. Review of the data should be a group process designed to arrive at specific implications and decision making for continuation and modification of the collaborative approach.

Pilot Replication

Decisions regarding the success of a pilot class may result in consideration to expand or replicate the pilot at additional sites. The data collection process and decision making regarding the data should lead to the replication decision. Systems typically add one or two programs at a time, depending on the overall size of the district. Expansion of the program should be made through the step-by-step procedure used in the pilot.

SUMMARY

The collaborative teaching model was designed as an alternative to the traditional resource, or pull-out, model for serving students with mild disabilities. Development of a middle school model should include consideration of opinions and concerns of teachers, administrators, parents, and students. The message seems clear that we can maintain instructional integrity for students with and without disabilities through a model that teaches both groups at the same time, in the same room. A collaborative teaching model also should be considered for other age groups of disabled students and, because the model's instructional planning and strategies may be appropriate, it can be applied to at-risk populations as well.

Collaborative teaching should be viewed as an arrangement between specialists in content and methodology that delivers the strengths of both special and general education within a single instructional setting. Stalvey et al. (1985) described a ripple effect as an incidental advantage of co-teaching. One teacher's strategy is observed by another, who uses it in a different setting, where it is observed by another teacher, and so on. A similar effect has been noted in students, who experience success from observing a learning strategy from another student, who uses it later, and so on. This exchange happens again and again because teachers and students take advantage of learning events that work in producing success.

Finally, we recognize that the collaborative model should not be considered as the best and only way to provide instruction. Some students will continue to be best served through a pull-out model to meet their individual learning needs. We are suggesting, however, that using the collaborative model at the middle school level significantly expands learning opportunities for many different types of students when they are educated together.

Parent Name ———————————————————————— School ——————

Student Name ———————————————————————— Date ——————

Please circle your response:

1. My child's participation in the collaborative teaching project:
   a. had a positive effect on my child.
   b. was not a positive experience for my child.
   c. did not seem to be very different from previous years.

2. Do you think the collaborative teaching project helped your child to be more successful in other subjects?
   a. Yes, it helped in other subjects.
   b. No, it did not help.
   c. I am not sure if it made a difference.

3. How do you think your child responded to the collaborative teaching project?
   a. preferred having the special education teacher come into the regular classroom.
   b. preferred leaving the regular classroom to go into the special education resource room.
   c. does not seem to have a preference.

4. Academically, I believe my child has:
   a. made more progress this year.
   b. made less progress this year.
   c. made about the same progress as in previous years.

5. Behaviorally, I believe my child has:
   a. made more progress this year.
   b. made less progress this year.
   c. made about the same progress as in previous years.

6. Please complete the following statements:
   a. My child would rather be in a collaborative teaching class because

   ————————————————————————————————

   ————————————————————————————————

   ————————————————————————————————

   b. My child would rather be in a special resource class because

   ————————————————————————————————

   ————————————————————————————————

   ————————————————————————————————

   c. I also would like to comment or suggest that:

   ————————————————————————————————

   ————————————————————————————————

   ————————————————————————————————

FIGURE 5 *Parent Questionnaire*

REFERENCES

Hallahan, D. P., Keller, C. E., McKinney, J. D., Lloyd, J. W., & Bryan, T. (1988). Examining the research base of the regular education initiative: Efficacy studies and the adaptive learning environments model. *Journal of Learning Disabilities, 21,* 29-34.

Hanline, M. R., & Halvorsen, A. (1989). Parent perceptions of the integration transition process: Overcoming artificial barriers. *Exceptional Children, 55,* 487–492.

Lilly, M. S. (1986). The relationship between general and special education: A new face on an old issue. *Counterpoint, 6,* 10.

Roach, V. (1991). Special education: New questions in an era of reform. *Issues in Brief* (National Association of State Boards of Education) *11,* 1–7.

Silver, H. F., & Hanson, J. R. (1980). *The TLC learning style inventory.* Moorestown, NY: Hanson Silver & Associates.

Stainback, S., & Stainback, W. (Eds.). (1990). *Support networks for inclusive schooling—Interdependent integrated education.* Baltimore: Paul H. Brookes.

Stainback, S., Stainback, W., & Forest, M. (Eds.). (1989). *Educating all students in the mainstream of regular education.* Baltimore: Paul H. Brookes.

Stalvey, K., Dye, B., & Goldblatt, J. (1985). *Team teaching: A resource guide.* Cobb County, GA: Cobb County School District.

Villa, R., & Thousand, J. (1990). Administrative supports to promote inclusive schooling. In S. Stainback & W. Stainback (Eds.), *Support networks for inclusive schooling—Interdependent integrated education* (pp. 201–218). Baltimore: Paul H. Brookes.

Wang, M. C. & Baker, E. T. (1986). Mainstreaming programs: Design features and effects. *Journal of Special Education, 19,* 503–521.

Wang, M. C. & Zollers, N. (1990). Adaptive instruction: An alternative service delivery approach. *Remedial & Special Education, 11,* 7–21.

White, L., Spurgeon, J., Jackson, P., & Green-Folks, N. (Eds.). (1991). Cobb County School System Special Education Department procedures manual—collaborative teaching model—middle school pilot, 1991–92. Cobb County, GA: Cobb County School District.

Will, M. C. (1986). Educating children with learning problems: A shared responsibility. *Exceptional Children, 52,* 411–415.

Alan White is the director of Special Services for the Marietta City School District, Marietta, Georgia. Lynda White is a supervisor in the Special Education Department for the Cobb County School District, Marietta, Georgia.

7

Zigmond examines the research on the effectiveness of programs for students with learning disabilities. She concludes that we have much reason to question the effectiveness of our present programs. As opposed to many other special educators, Zigmond does not believe special programs should be abandoned. In fact, she believes the lack of structure and intensive instruction in mainstream classrooms is part of the problem. She recommends programs with even more restrictive environments and supports her contentions with an effective research base.

Rethinking Secondary School Programs for Students with Learning Disabilities

Naomi Zigmond

Nearly 15 years have passed since enactment of the Education for All Handicapped Children Act (PL 94-142) and the federal government's assurance of a free and appropriate public education for students with handicaps. During that time the numbers of students served in special education programs has grown to nearly 4.5 million, an increase of 21% over 1976 –77 counts.

Nowhere has the change in size and scope of special education services been more astounding than in the field of learning disabilities (LD). In the 15 years just passed, the number of students identified and served in programs for students with learning disabilities has increased by more than 145%. Every state in the nation has seen an increase in service rates in learning disabilities, with the service rates for students of secondary school age accounting for the greatest change. According to the *Eleventh Annual Report to Congress* (U.S. Department of Education, 1989) 1,025,010 students 12 to 17 years old have been diagnosed as LD and are receiving special education services.

Before passage of PL 94-142, only a small body of literature specifically addressed the characteristics and needs of adolescents with learning disabilities. It is not that learning disabilities were not thought to exist in adolescents and young adults. Indeed, early descriptions of students with dyslexia and related learning disabilities often included case studies of students in the age range of 12 to 21 years (see Critchley, 1964, pp. ix–xi; Johnson & Myklebust, 1967, pp. 229–232). But secondary school-aged students with learning disabilities were not considered a distinct population with distinct characteristics and programming needs.

The tide certainly has turned in the past decade and a half. Since 1975, there has been an enormous expansion of concern for, programming with, research on, and literature about students with learning disabilities in high school, and in the process of moving from school to work or further education. After reviewing past service delivery models and efficacy data, two models of services are proposed here. These models incorporate four components that I believe have potential for meeting the goals of a meaningful high school education and a smooth transition to life beyond school, each with important implications for staffing and teacher preparation as well as for general school policy and administration.

EARLY SERVICE DELIVERY MODELS: THE CSDC EXPERIMENTS

In the mid-1970s, special education programs for students with learning disabilities at the elementary level were commonplace, but few school districts provided programs for students with learning disabilities in secondary schools. After PL 94-142 was passed in 1975, schools were legally mandated to provide appropriate services for students with learning disabilities until graduation from high school or until age 21 (or age 25 in some states) and school districts undertook widespread efforts to develop secondary-level special education programs.

Of course, school authorities were not only responding to the mandate; parents and educators had a growing realization that, despite the emphasis on, and the optimism associated with, early intervention efforts, the learning difficulties of students with learning disabilities were not being ameliorated in the elementary grades. Many of these youngsters were leaving elementary school special education programs poorly equipped in the academic skills necessary for success in high school. Furthermore, many students were being identified as learning disabled in the intermediate and middle school grades and were entering high school having had no opportunity for early intervention.

Most of the new approaches to secondary school services for students with learning disabilities grew out of the network of Child Service Demonstration Centers (CSDCs) funded by the Bureau of Education for the Handicapped (BEH) between 1975 and 1977. These included:

1. The Parallel Alternate Curriculum for Secondary Classrooms, developed in Arizona.
2. Strategies to Increase Learning Efficiency Among LD Adolescents, developed in Kansas.
3. The Model Resource Room Project, developed in Michigan.
4. The Oklahoma Child Service Demonstration Center.

5. The Synergistic Education Model: A Comprehensive Plan for Learning Disabled, developed in Texas.
6. The Pittsburgh Child Service Demonstration Center (see Riegel & Mathey, 1980).

These CSDC models had in common a commitment to the concept of mainstreaming, consideration of the students' learning and behavioral characteristics, a focus on students with mild to moderate learning disabilities, attention to characteristics of the high school settings in which the students operated, design of specific, replicable methodologies of instruction, incorporation of motivational strategies, and attention to the importance of generalization and maintenance of skills.

But the CSDC models also differed on a number of important dimensions. For example, in the Kansas model, the primary focus for change was the student; in the Arizona model, it was the school environment; in the remaining models, both the students and the environment were targets for change efforts. A fundamental philosophy of the Kansas model was that students with learning disabilities must and can learn to become autonomously successful in academic and social environments, even if those environments often seem hostile and resistant. In contrast, developers of the Arizona model believed that students' academic and behavioral deficiencies could not be ameliorated and that students with learning disabilities would be successful in high school only if mainstream content demands (i.e., the environment and curriculum) could be modified to accommodate the disabilities and deficiencies of the students. The Oklahoma, Michigan, Texas, and Pittsburgh models incorporated strategies to promote change both in student behaviors and in mainstream curricular and instructional processes.

Another dimension upon which the CSDC models varied was the setting in which primary interventions were designed to take place. For example, in the Kansas model, primary interventions were designed for the resource room setting. In the Arizona model, mainstream content subject classes were the target sites for intervention. In the Oklahoma, Michigan, Texas, and Pittsburgh models, interventions were designed for both resource room and mainstream class settings.

Some of the CSDC models emphasized direct services to students, whether by the special education resource room teacher (Kansas) or by the mainstream teacher (Arizona). Others featured a combination of direct and *indirect* services to students through consultation to mainstream teachers (Oklahoma, Michigan, Texas, and Pittsburgh).

The CSDC models also varied significantly with regard to instructional emphasis. The Kansas model emphasized instruction in a wide range of learning strategies (i.e., techniques, principles and rules that would enable the student to learn independently and to solve problems) in lieu of basic skills instruction. The Oklahoma model combined remediation of academic skill deficiencies with training in compensatory strategies. The Texas model combined reading remediation to promote comprehension and vocabulary development with a social-behavioral program to build stronger self-concepts, develop communication skills, foster self-responsibility, and teach problem-solving strategies. The Pittsburgh model provided for basic skills remediation in reading or mathematics along with instruction in nonacademic skills (self-management, social, organizational, and study skills) that the developers believed were necessary for survival both within and outside the school setting.

Federal funding for the CSDC network ended within 2 years, although pressures on school districts to provide secondary school programs intensified. Forced to move quickly, school districts developed a plethora of hastily conceived adaptations of the CSDC models without the funding for technical support that might have ensured adequate implementation. By 1979 the most common service delivery model for secondary school-aged students with learning disabilities was simply an adaptation of the elementary school resource room—primary placement in mainstream classes with part-time instruction provided by special education personnel (Deshler, Lowrey, & Alley, 1979).

Most of these resource room programs continued the elementary school emphasis on remediation of basic skills (reading, writing and mathematics); the goal was competence in basic literacy and numeracy. But many resource room teachers also provided instruction to students with LD designed to help them achieve better grades in mainstream content subject classes, assisted students in completing regular class assignments, offered drill exercises to prepare students for an upcoming test in a mainstream class, arranged with mainstream content subject teachers to allow for administration of chapter tests or final exams by the resource teacher in the resource room (thus permitting more time for oral presentation of test items), and arranged for students to tape mainstream class lectures in lieu of taking notes. For many LD teachers and their students these additional "tutorial" activities gradually consumed all of the resource room time, and little time was left for remedial instruction, or for the other curricular elements introduced in the CSDCs, such as social or survival skills or learning strategies.

EVIDENCE OF PROGRAM EFFECTIVENESS

Dropout Rate

Special education programs are supposed to be nurturing, sustaining, and personalized, somewhere in the school system where students with handicaps can find special education teachers who care, who explain the importance of sustaining an interest in high school, who make learning relevant and accessible, and who help students to succeed. These are the very elements that have also been associated with successful dropout prevention programs (see Wehlage, Rutter, Smith, Lesko, & Fernandez, 1989)—attention to individual student needs, small student-teacher ratios, more opportunities for personal counseling, and utilization of individualized and diversified instructional strategies. So, if high school programs for students with learning disabilities are implemented appropriately, we should expect students with LD to be staying in school.

My colleagues and I spent 6 years working with special education and mainstream administrators, supervisors, and teachers in a large urban school district, to refine implementation of the Pittsburgh CSDC model of secondary school services for students with learning disabilities. By 1981 the model program had been in place long enough so that 52 students who had entered high school in 1977–78 as ninth graders and had been placed in the LD program should have been in 12th grade. We set out to document the progress of these 52 adolescents (see Levin, Zigmond, & Birch, 1985). We expected to find the students in 11th or 12th grade, some fully mainstreamed, some still being served in special education resource rooms, all showing improved basic skills and getting ready for the world of work. Instead, as far as we could determine, 47% of the students with LD had dropped out of school, a rate far in excess of the 36% dropout rate for nonhandicapped students reported by the host school district for the same time period.

The Levin et al. (1985) sample was very small, but the findings deeply troubled us. We had worked hard with the school district to develop a secondary school LD program that was sensible and meaningful. We had taught teachers how to help students make it in their mainstream classes. We had trained one special education teacher to function in a consulting teacher role to help students with learning disabilities and their mainstream teachers alike. We had data to indicate that a large percentage of the students with learning disabilities who came to school were earning passing grades (Zigmond, Levin, & Laurie, 1985). Disappointed to discover that students for whom we had designed this "special" education were abandoning it, we embarked on a second study to verify our original dropout findings.

Zigmond and Thornton (1985) located and interviewed students with LD from the same urban school district who should have been in the graduating class of 1982, and a control sample of non-learning disabled students from the same high schools. Students were part of the LD or non-LD groups based on their status as ninth graders in the 1978–79 school year. Of the 60 LD participants in the study, 28 had completed high school and 32 had left school before graduation, a 53% dropout rate among high school students with LD. In sharp contrast, the dropout rate for non-LD participants was 27%.

A third follow-up study of the 1983 graduating class confirmed the finding again: 39% of students with LD who entered ninth grade in the 1979–80 school year dropped out before graduating from high school, as compared with 22% of nonhandicapped peers (Thornton & Zigmond, 1988). The picture that was emerging was that students with learning disabilities in this urban area seemed to be leaving high school at nearly twice the rate of nonhandicapped classmates. And follow-up studies in a neighboring blue-collar community (Morrow, Thornton, & Zigmond, 1988) and in rural Virginia (deBettencourt, Zigmond, & Thornton, 1989) showed that the phenomenon was not limited to the urban school.

Nor were we the only researchers to be reporting alarmingly high dropout rates among students served in special education programs in secondary schools. In Vermont, Hasazi and her colleagues reported that 34% of public school youth with mild disabilities were not completing a high school education (Hasazi, Gordon, & Roe, 1985). The reported dropout rate of youth with LD in several school districts in Florida was pegged at 31% (Fardig, Algozzine, Schwartz, Hensel, & Westling, 1985). In a large Alabama county school district, Cobb and Crump (1984) reported a dropout rate of 42% among students with learning disabilities. In a middle class suburban school district in the Midwest, White, Schumaker, Warner, Alley, and Deshler (1980) found that 26% of the youth with learning disabilities had dropped out.

In its *Tenth Annual Report to Congress* (U.S. Department of Education, 1988), the Office of Special Education Programs (OSEP) reported that in the 1985–86 school year,

26,644 students with learning disabilities, aged 16 through 21, dropped out of high school before completing their education, an average of 148 students each school day. This figure, which OSEP believed to be an underestimate, represented about 26% of all students with learning disabilities who left school that year and was nearly double the dropout rate reported by the National Center for Educational Statistics for the general school-aged population (see Rumberger, 1987). Data reported for the subsequent year (U.S. Department of Education, 1989), and data from the National Longitudinal Transition Study being carried out at SRI International under contract from OSEP confirm the finding (see U.S. Department of Education, 1989, p. 70).

My colleagues and I consider the dropout rate to be indirect evidence of the efficacy of secondary school programs for students with learning disabilities, and we find these dropout data compelling and disturbing. Surely if school programs were meeting students' needs, high school students with learning disabilities would not be leaving school! The dropout rates alone force a rethinking of special education services at the secondary school level.

But does it matter that students with learning disabilities are dropping out? Are those who leave school early just as well off in terms of employment and post-school adjustment as their counterparts who stay? Do the dropouts get a "jump on the job market?" Do they get some practical experience out there on the streets that is even better for them than what they get in school? A series of studies on the employment and post-school adjustment of graduates and dropouts over the past few years has provided the data to answer these questions: There is a significant differential in employment patterns and post-school adjustment of youth with LD who are dropouts and graduates.

In 1985, we reported that among urban youth, 75% of graduates with LD were employed at the time of follow-up, 18 to 28 months after graduation (see Zigmond & Thornton, 1985). This contrasted sharply with the employment figures for high school dropouts; only 47% of dropouts with LD were employed. High school leavers who returned to complete their GED were not much better off than those who did not; only 37.5% of youth with LD who had GEDs were holding jobs at the time of the follow-up interviews.

In some communities, of course, the job market is extremely good and *everyone* (graduates and dropouts, disabled and nondisabled) can find a job; such was the case in a rural Virginia Study (see deBettencourt et al., 1989). In other communities the job market is extremely poor and *no one* can find a job, not graduates or dropouts, disabled or nondisabled; such was the case in the blue collar community studied by Morrow et al. (1988). But in most of our work, and in the work of others across the nation, in terms of the transition from school to work, it pays for students with learning disabilities to stay in high school and graduate. Nevertheless, special education programs for these students seem to have minimal holding power, and many students with learning disabilities drop out of school to face uncertain, grim futures on the streets.

Achievement

Many researchers have reported academic achievement levels in reading and mathematics among adolescents with learning disabilities that are consistently low, 3 to 5 years behind actual grade placement at entrance to ninth grade (see Cobb & Crump, 1984;

Levin et al., 1985; Norman & Zigmond, 1980; Schalock et al., 1986; Thornton & Zigmond, 1987a; Warner, Alley, Schumaker, Deshler, & Clark, 1980; Zigmond & Thornton, 1985). Unfortunately, students with learning disabilities do not seem to recoup these basic skill deficiencies during their years of attending secondary school resource room programs (Zigmond & Thornton, 1985; Gregory, Shanahan, & Walberg, 1986) and, in fact, the gap between achievement scores and grade expectancy level actually seems to widen as students with learning disabilities progress through high school (Norman & Zigmond, 1980; Warner et al., 1980).

The follow-up studies we completed speak to this point as well. We have had the opportunity to assess basic skill levels among dropouts, who in general completed only 1 or 2 years of a high school LD program, and graduates, who had at least 4 years. Their achievement levels are essentially the same. Data taken from Zigmond and Thornton (1985), Thornton and Zigmond (1987b) and deBettencourt et al. (1989) illustrate a persistent finding: Special education programs at the high school level fail in their attempts to improve the basic skills of adolescents with LD. Many students with learning disabilities enter ninth grade barely literate and leave high school after 1, 2, 3, or 4 years, with literacy skills virtually unchanged.

COMPONENTS OF AN EFFECTIVE HIGH SCHOOL PROGRAM FOR STUDENTS WITH LD

Over the past decade, several researchers have attempted to delineate factors associated with low achievement and premature school leaving. The results have implicated environmental and family background factors including low socioeconomic level, large family size, established patterns of dropping out in parents and siblings, and nonintact families (Bachman, 1972; Tseng, 1972; Kowalski & Cangemi, 1974; Lloyd, 1976; Hewitt & Johnson, 1979; Hill, 1979; Mare, 1980), individual student characteristics including race, gender, IQ, and achievement level (Cervantes, 1965; Combs & Cooley, 1968; Kowalski & Cangemi, 1974; Lloyd, 1976; Kaplan & Luck, 1977; Hammontree, 1978; Stoughton & Grady, 1978; Hill, 1979; Howell & Frese, 1982; Rumberger, 1983), and grade retentions and high absence rates (Schreiber, 1962; Curley, 1971; Dean, 1973; Kowalski & Cangemi, 1974; Kaplan & Luck, 1977; Mahood, 1981).

Implicit in much of this research is the assumption that a better understanding of the characteristics of low achievers and dropouts and of their families and communities will lead to the development of school policies and programs that will reduce the number of adolescents who fail to graduate. The intent is noble, but the results have been negligible because the focus on social, family, and personal characteristics does not carry any obvious implications for reshaping school policies and practices.

We share the view of Wehlage and Rutter (1986) that to increase the effectiveness and the holding power of schools, *alterable* school conditions must be identified. So, in our research and writing over the past decade, instead of focusing on environmental and family background factors or immutable student characteristics, we have concentrated on school program variables—the curriculum and student schedules—and on student *behaviors* in and around school—behaviors that students can control and that schools can teach. These also have been shown to contribute to low achievement and dropping out, and they can be reshaped and redirected.

Four components appear to be essential to more effective secondary school programming for students with learning disabilities: intensive instruction in reading and mathematics; explicit instruction in "survival" skills; successful completion of courses required for high school graduation; and explicit planning for life after high school.

Intensive Instruction in Basic Skills

Our own research has shown that many high school graduates of secondary school LD programs score at poorer than eighth-grade proficiency on a basic skills assessment in reading. Operationally, as the writing sample in Figure 1 illustrates, this means they are barely literate and unable to make functional use of written communications. They also are incapable of meeting the increasingly high demands for literacy that are present in today's reform-minded mainstream high school. As our recent data have shown (see Donahoe &

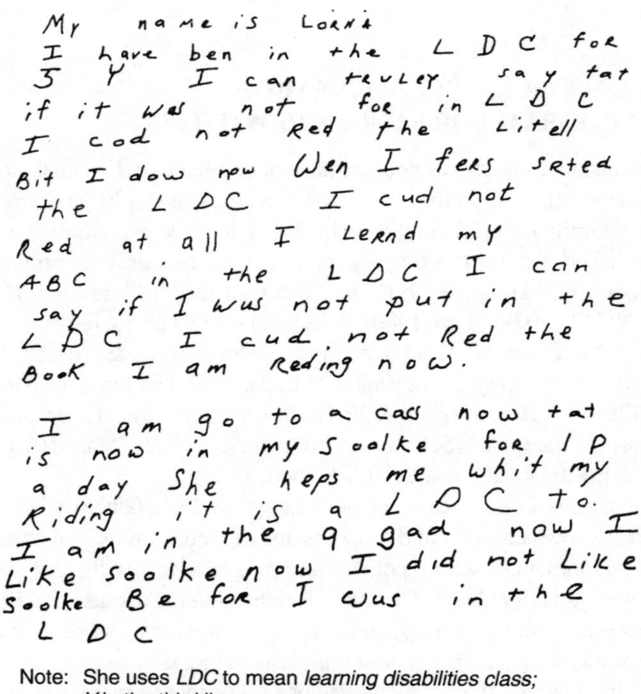

My name is Lorna
I have ben in the LDC for
3 Y I can trulcy say tat
if it was not foe in LDC
I cod not Red the Litell
Bit I dow now Wen I fers srted
the LDC I cud not
Red at all I Lernd my
ABC in the LDC I can
say if I wus not put in the
LDC I cud not Red the
Book I am Reding now.

I am go to a cass now tat
is now in my soolke for 1p
a day She heps me whit my
Riding it is a LDC to.
I am in the 9 gad now I
Like soolke now I did not Like
Soolke Be for I wus in the
LDC

Note: She uses *LDC* to mean *learning disabilities class*;
Y in the third line means *years*;
1p in the second paragraph means *1 period*.

FIGURE 1   Composition Written by a Ninth-Grade Girl with Learning Disabilities

Zigmond, 1990), many students with learning disabilities are now earning failing grades in mainstream courses such as social studies, which place heavy demands on reading and writing, and even in less academically oriented courses such as health.

Some would say that the problem lies within the student; by adolescence, ability to learn basic skills plateaus and further progress in reading proficiency cannot be expected (see Alley & Deshler, 1979). Nevertheless, our observational studies of instruction in LD resource rooms at the secondary school level would assign the culprit elsewhere.

Figures 2, 3 and 4 summarize data gathered from four 42-minute observations in each of eight LD resource rooms in high schools in a large urban school district. Using a time-sample protocol (described fully in Zigmond, 1988), observers coded three dimensions of the classroom experience: the activity structure of the class, the behaviors of the students with LD being observed, and the nature of the instructional interactions between teacher and students. Activity structure meant how the teacher arranged the class and the assignments. Observers coded activity structures as lecture or large-group question/answer format, small-group lessons, independent seatwork, or transition (when no activity was assigned to students). Figure 2 shows that students spent more than 85% of their resource room time assigned to independent seatwork and no time assigned to small group instruction.

Student behaviors were coded into one of three categories: on-task, off-task, or transition (no task to be done). Figure 3 shows that students in these LD resource rooms were on-task more than three fourths of the time.

Instructional interactions characterized how the teachers spent their time during each 42-minute period. Teachers could be instructing, listening (to student questions or student answers), managing the flow of academic activities (giving directions for an assignment, telling students to find materials or worksheets or a particular page in a book), socializing with students, or not engaged in any sort of interaction at all with students. Figure 4 shows that LD resource room teachers spent, on the average, slightly less than 40% of each class period in instructional interactions (instructing and listening), most of these one-to-one interactions with students as they completed worksheets at their desks. Teachers spent about 28% of class periods telling students what to do but not teaching them how to do it, and another 23% of class time not interacting with students at all. These data suggest that high school students with learning disabilities may not be making progress in basic skills because they are receiving so little teaching!

Literacy

We have all heard and read about the crisis of adult illiteracy in the United States. Depending upon the definition of literacy used, the figures on adult illiteracy range from 23 to 78 million Americans (Kozol, 1985), or a minimum of one in five adults who are totally or functionally illiterate. And numbers alone do not adequately portray the complexity of the problem. A disproportionate number of the individuals included in the figures are unemployed, poor, and disadvantaged minorities (Nickerson, 1985).

Students with learning disabilities who leave high school unable to read join this swelling mass of adult illiterates. High school programs for students with learning dis-

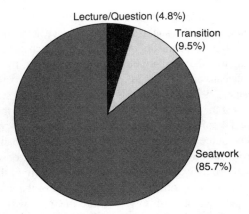

FIGURE 2   *Activity Structures in Eight LD Resource Rooms*

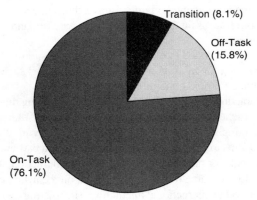

FIGURE 3   *Student Behaviors in Eight LD Resource Rooms*

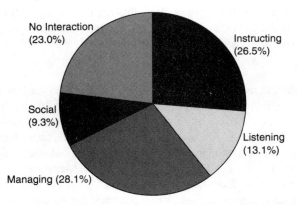

FIGURE 4   *Instructional Interactions in Eight LD Resource Rooms*

abilities *must* provide intensive, relentless instruction in basic literacy skills to prepare students with LD for independence, employment flexibility, and job security.

Reading Instruction

Instruction in reading at the secondary school level has to be interesting and imaginative. Goals of the reading instruction are to make students independent, fluent readers, confident enough in decoding skills to be willing to attack unfamiliar text in a popular magazine, a novel, a technical manual, or a mainstream textbook. Reading instruction should be individualized but should not be delivered as predominantly one-to-one instruction. Assignments should be based on an analysis of the entering skills of each student, but instruction should be directed to the group, because this arrangement affords *all* students assigned to the special education teacher during a particular class period more opportunities for teacher-directed instruction and less time on independent seatwork.

Under no circumstances should high school students with learning disabilities simply be placed in a basal reading text series and taught a developmental reading program. Instead, reading lessons should be organized around a three-part curriculum: decoding; vocabulary, comprehension, and fluency; and writing. Time is short, and careful attention must be paid not only to teaching the most critically needed literacy skills but also to building students' self-confidence as readers.

Phonics Review and Decoding

Each year, students probably will need an intensive phonics review emphasizing word parts and word families, not individual sound-symbol associations (see Bradley & Bryant, 1985; Fayne & Bryant, 1981; Williams, 1980; Graham & Johnson, 1989). Decoding strategies such as those emphasized in the Glass analysis techniques also should be reviewed (Glass, 1978). Rapid drill and practice of words in isolation might be suitable for the early part of the school year, but soon after that, decoding strategies should be practiced in continuous narrative and expository text.

Vocabulary Development

Although skills are important, the major part of each reading period should be devoted to text-based activities for developing vocabulary, comprehension, and fluency. Text materials should include short stories or novels from a variety of genres (mysteries, real-life adventures, science fiction), selected for high interest and motivation. Most students with learning disabilities have never had the experience of not being able to put down a book, of wanting to read to the end to find out how it all turns out. Few students with LD think of themselves as readers competent enough to read for entertainment or distraction. Class time, as well as homework, could be devoted to reading a whole book, although the teacher could read parts of the book aloud, to move the action along. Requiring repeated readings (see O'Shea, Sindelar, & O'Shea, 1987) might help students get through particularly difficult or dense sections of the book and also are useful for developing fluency and enhancing comprehension.

During text reading, opportunities should be afforded to review decoding strategies for words in context and to develop vocabulary through semantic mapping and group discussion (see Calfee, 1976; McKeown & Beck, 1988). Teachers also should teach students strategies for understanding the structure of narrative text and engage students in plot and character analyses using graphic organizers such as those depicted in Figures 5 and 6. But mostly, with narrative texts, students should be encouraged to read for the pleasure of reading.

Work on narrative text should be alternated (in 4- to 6-week cycles, perhaps) with work on expository text. Now, popular magazines, newspapers, or science, social studies, or health textbooks can be used as vehicles for developing strategies to cope with exposition. Strategies involving summarization, mental imagery, self-questioning, ques-

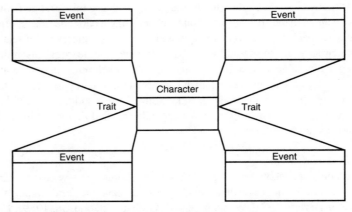

FIGURE 5   Graphic Organizer for Character Analysis

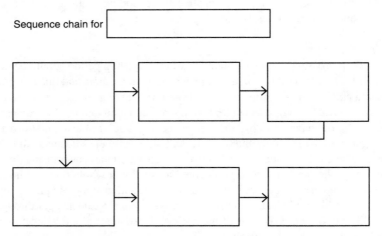

FIGURE 6   Graphic Organizer for Plot Analysis

tion answering, and so forth, reviewed by Graham and Johnson (1989), should be taught and practiced. Of particular use might be the reciprocal teaching strategy introduced by Palinscar and Brown (1984), which involves summarization, questioning, clarifying, and predicting, or the self-monitoring strategies reviewed by Wong (1986). Opportunities for vocabulary development should not be overlooked in expository text reading, again using semantic mapping and graphic organizers to help students see relationships among word meanings and concepts.

Writing

Finally, some part of each week of reading instruction must be devoted to writing. Writing activities should be an extension of the reading comprehension lessons and should build on the semantic maps and graphic organizers used in discussions of text. Strategies for improving the quality and technical adequacy of student writing, discussed extensively by Deshler (Alley & Deshler, 1979) and Graham and Harris (1989a, 1989b), should be incorporated into the writing part of the reading curriculum as well.

Measuring Learning

At regular intervals, perhaps as frequently as twice per week, curriculum-based measures (CBM) should be taken with students who are reading well below the eighth-grade level, to determine whether they are profiting from instruction. Students may be asked to complete 1-minute oral readings from grade-appropriate text material (see Deno & Mirkin, 1977) or to complete maze tasks delivered via computer (see Fuchs, Hamlett, Fuchs, Stecker, & Ferguson, 1988). Performance data then should be graphed and analyzed for trend. These CBM data provide a global indicator of reading fluency, a measure that is sensitive to improvements in reading performance over time.

If CBM data show a student making steady improvements (see Figure 7), the teacher can feel confident that the reading program is working. If a student's CBM data indicate a level or downward trend (see Figure 8), the teacher is informed that a change in the instructional program is warranted, that "business as usual" is no longer appropriate for this student. The change may involve tutoring the student in a strategy the rest of the class has mastered, changing the intensity and frequency of teacher feedback to the student during reading instruction, changing the nature of the assignments during independent seatwork, changing the incentives for student performance (see Howell & Morehead, 1987). Whatever the change, continual monitoring of CBM data will inform the teacher of the success of the new approach or of the need to continue to adjust instruction.

Math Skills

Intensive instruction in basic skills is not, of course, limited to reading and writing domains. Math skills of high school students with LD also demand considerable attention. Many students have not acquired fluency in basic math facts by the time they enter ninth grade. More important, they don't understand or feel comfortable using mathematics in everyday life—in shopping, measuring, estimating prices, solving problems.

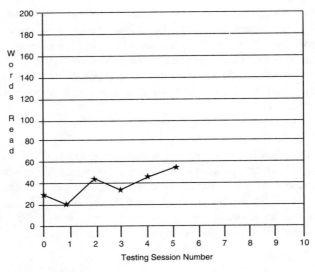

FIGURE 7   J.B.'s CBM Scores

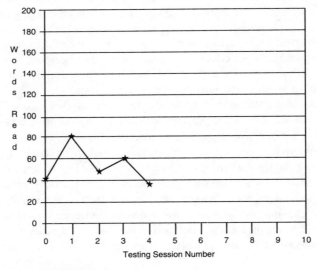

FIGURE 8   C.A.'s CBM Scores

A functional math curriculum should teach students basic algorithms up through simple algebra but emphasize problem solving and practical applications of math concepts.
Lloyd and Keller (1989) provide excellent suggestions for effective math instruction for
students with LD, which could be used at the secondary school level. Problem-solving
strategies being explored by Cawley and his colleagues (see Cawley, Fitzmaurice, Shaw,

Kahn, & Bates, 1978, 1979a, 1979b; Cawley, Fitzmaurice-Hayes, & Shaw, 1988) also are particularly relevant in teaching mathematics to students with LD in secondary school.

Explicit Instruction in Survival Skills

Several years ago we introduced readers of *Focus on Exceptional Children* to a curriculum for teaching coping skills to adolescents with learning disabilities (Silverman, Zigmond, & Sansone, 1981). We have not changed our minds about the importance of these survival skills to the successful functioning of high school students with learning disabilities, nor about the need to teach these skills explicitly. A survival skills curriculum would have three strands: behavior control, teacher-pleasing behaviors, and study skills/test-taking strategies. Descriptions of the objectives of each of these strands and sample activities were provided in Silverman et al. (1981). Some extensions of these ideas are provided next.

Behavior Control Activities

Behavior control activities are designed to help students who are always getting into trouble, who consistently do the wrong things, and who often are suspended or punished. These students do not seem to understand the role they play in creating the conflicts in which they are continually involved. In behavior control activities, the goal is to help students alter their locus of control from external ("I'm not at fault; someone else made these things happen to me") to internal ("I behaved in a certain way so these things happened; if I behave differently, different things might happen"). Students learn to take responsibility for their actions. They learn alternative ways of responding to situations that arise in the everyday course of school. They learn that they can change their school lives because they can change their own behaviors.

As is the case in all three strands of the school survival skills curriculum, teaching behavior control relies heavily upon simulations and role playing to help students learn to recognize what they and others do in school situations, the impact of one's behavior on other people, alternative ways of responding to specific situations, and the consequences of behaving one way or another. Early experiences in teaching behavior control in secondary schools have taught us that students with learning disabilities cannot use simulations or role playing effectively without explicit instruction in how to observe and document. So we spend time, initially, teaching students to use a graphic to organize their observations and record their feelings and impressions. An example of one such graphic is presented in Figure 9.

Once students are good observers, efforts can be concentrated on the content rather than on the process of the simulation or role play. Now we introduce a problem-solving strategy to help students become analytic about their experiences in school and their personal responsibility for events and consequences. The graphic displayed in Figure 10 becomes the basis for a group discussion on alternative ways of responding to situations such as the following:

> As you are walking down the hall with a few of your friends, you see someone you know way down at the other end of the building. You call to him. Right at that moment, a teacher

Role Players

1. _____(_____)   2. _____(_____)   3. _____(_____)
         Role   Initials   Role   Initials   Role   Initials

Situation _____

Directions: Place an "X" on each line below to describe the role players' behaviors. Focus on the role or behaviors rather than on the individual playing it.

Verbal Behaviors
What I Heard

Role
Player

                    (Loudness)

Comfortably   1 _____   Not Comfortably
Heard   2 _____   Heard
               3 _____

                  (Rate of Speech)

Easy to   1 _____   Difficult to
Follow   2 _____   Follow
               3 _____

                  (Tone of Voice)

Pleasant   1 _____   Unpleasant
               2 _____
               3 _____

Nonverbal Behaviors
What I Saw

Role
Player

                  (Eye Contact)

Engaged in   1 _____   Avoided Eye
Eye Contact   2 _____   Contact
               3 _____

                 (Body Proximity)

Comfortable   1 _____   Uncomfortable
Distance   2 _____   Distance
               3 _____

            (Body Positions/Movement)

Open and   1 _____   Closed and
Accepting   2 _____   Rejecting
               3 _____

Feelings
How I Reacted

Role
Player

Calm/   1 _____   Uneasy/
Comfortable   2 _____   Uncomfortable
               3 _____

FIGURE 9   *Graphic to Teach Students to Observe and Analyze Role Playing*

steps out of her classroom. She is very upset that you have disturbed her class while they are taking an important test.

You are standing in line at the cafeteria. As you are waiting, two students attempt to cut in front of you. You have been waiting patiently for some time, and you think this is unfair.

Students analyze the situation, discuss alternative ways of behaving, act out the various ways, and analyze the probable consequences of each scenario. Some role playing is videotaped so that the action can be replayed, observed, and stopped for extended discussion. Then, after practicing alternative behaviors within the safe environment of the resource room, students are encouraged to try new behaviors in their interactions around the school. They also are encouraged to keep track of the extent to which using behavior control strategies changes the rate at which they are assigned suspensions, detentions, demerits, and so forth.

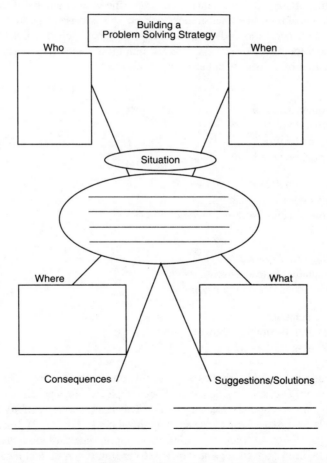

FIGURE 10   Graphic for Development of Problem-Solving Skills

Teacher-Pleasing Behaviors

Teacher-pleasing behaviors focus on the behaviors students use to cope with rules and demands within their classes. This part of the curriculum helps students acquire behavior patterns that usually lead teachers to consider students more positively. Most students learn, in an incidental fashion, that certain behaviors ingratiate students with the teacher. These students learn to make eye contact, look interested in the lesson, volunteer responses in class, look busy. Many students with learning disabilities do not learn these behavior patterns, and their failure to display teacher-pleasing behaviors puts off the teacher.

The student with LD often needs to be taught, explicitly, how to act like a "good" student. Since writing the *Focus on Exceptional Children* article in 1981, my colleagues and I have developed scripts for 20 lessons on teacher-pleasing behaviors (see Zigmond, Kerr, Schaeffer, Farra, & Brown, 1986). During one of the earliest lessons, students complete a School Survival Skills Scale, a self-assessment of school-appropriate behaviors. Then each student compares the self-generated profile with one derived from a Scale completed by one of his or her mainstream teachers. The exercise helps students become aware of their own behaviors and of differences in how they view themselves in regular classes and how mainstream teachers view them in these same classes. The remaining lessons cover four basic aspects of behavior, as follows:

Attendance
- Coming to school
- Coming to class
- Coming on time
- Coming prepared

Assignment Completion
- Keeping track of assignments
- Turning in classwork/homework

Attentiveness
- Being more "on-task"
- Responding to teacher requests
- Asking questions/making comments

Compliance behavior
- Reducing disruptive behavior
- Talking more "appropriately"

Instructional formats and activities vary considerably from lesson to lesson to maintain student interest and active participation. For example, we use a pencil-and-paper task for an activity on remembering (see Figure 11). This remembering activity comes just before a simulation task on how to use an assignment book (Figure 12). In contrast, we use a Q-sort-like task to get students to think about appropriate classroom behavior. The statements in Figure 13 are each printed on a 4x6 card, and each student receives an entire deck of 16 cards. Students silently read the statements on the cards and sort the cards

Name _____

Date _____

Directions: Put a check in the appropriate box.

Have you ever forgotten:

	Often	Some-times	Almost never
1. to bring in a field trip permission slip?			
2. to study for a test?			
3. to bring in your homework?			
4. to find a newspaper or magazine article?			
5. to attend chorus or football practice?			
6. to hand in a book report?			
7. to bring in something you did for extra credit?			
8. to bring your just-washed gym clothes from home?			
9. to bring lunch or lunch money?			
10. to bring in an excuse for being absent?			

FIGURE 11   *School Survival Skills Curriculum: Task on Remembering*

into two piles representing "cool" and "not cool" classroom behaviors. Then the students engage in a group discussion of the cards in each pile.

An important aid in teaching students to use new teacher-pleasing behaviors involves self-monitoring strategies. Students contract to perform first one, then more and more of the target behaviors. Students daily record whether they performed these behaviors, on self-monitoring forms checked by the special education teacher at regular intervals. The number of skills that students self-monitor increases gradually until students are recording their performance on as many as seven or eight skills. Figure 14 is a sample of a self-monitoring form used in the School Survival Skills Curriculum (Zigmond et al., 1986), on which students are recording behaviors of coming to class; arriving on time; bringing notebook, paper, and text; staying on task; following directions; asking questions; answering questions; and entering assignments in an assignment book for one mainstream class for one week of school. Figure 14 shows this self-monitoring form.

Study Skills and Test-Taking Strategies
Study skills and test-taking strategies help students with LD organize their time, approach a textbook, take notes from a lecture or a text, organize information, study for tests, and take tests. The goals of the study skills component of the school survival skills curriculum is to teach students strategies for gathering and retaining information that they will use in completing assignments and fulfilling the requirements of content subject courses. Students are taught systematic methods for approaching classroom tasks and for compensating for deficiencies in basic skills. The activities of this component draw heavily on the work of Deshler and his colleagues (see Alley & Deshler, 1979) as well as on time-honored study skills such as SQ3R (see Alexander, 1985; Schumaker, Deshler, Alley, Warner, & Denton, 1982).

"WHAT IF . . . ?" WORKSHEET

What if you are monitoring yourself and keeping track of assignments in your English class, and . . .

1. Today is Monday of Week 1
    . . . you have an essay to write, which is due in English class on Tuesday. What do you write in your Assignment Book?

2. Today is Tuesday of Week 1
    . . . you have a test on Friday in math class. What do you write in your Assignment Book?

3. Today is Wednesday of Week 1
    . . . you are supposed to read pages 192–241 in your English Literature book for Thursday. What do you write in your Assignment Book?

4. Today is Thursday of Week 1
    . . . your English teacher says, "Do the assignment on page 42. I will collect it at the end of class today." What do you write in your Assignment Book?

5. Today is Friday of Week1
    . . . your social studies teacher tells you that term projects are due the next Friday. What do you write in your Assignment Book?

TURN TO NEXT PAGE
WE ARE STARTING A NEW WEEK NOW.

6. Today is Monday of Week 2
    . . . you have to write another essay for English class on Wednesday. What do you write in your Assignment Book?

7. Today is Tuesday of Week 2
    . . . your English assignment (an essay), which was due on Wednesday, has been postponed until Thursday. What do you write in your Assignment Book?

8. Today is Wednesday of Week 2
    . . . your science teacher tells you that Friday you have to make up the unit test that you missed when you were absent last week. What do you write in your Assignment Book?

9. Today is Thursday of Week 2
    . . . you didn't have an English assignment on Wednesday because there was an assembly and you did not have English class. What did you write in your Assignment Book?

FIGURE 12   Practice Task to Learn to Use an Assignment Book

Successful Completion of Courses Required for Graduation

When students with learning disabilities are assigned to resource room programs, they take most of the courses they need in order to graduate from high school in the mainstream. Our research shows that students with LD in these courses cut class frequently and are often late to the classes they do attend (Zigmond, Kerr, Brown, & Harris, 1984). They arrive without a writing implement, notepaper or textbook at least 30% of the time (Zigmond et al., 1984). Their mainstream teachers characterize them as being poor at organizing themselves and their time, taking notes, identifying main ideas in lectures or texts, following directions, and completing and turning in assignments (Barrett, 1986; Zigmond, Kerr, & Schaeffer, 1988).

Card Number

1. Even if I'm daydreaming, I keep my eyes open and look at the teacher.
2. When the teacher asks a question, I raise my hand even if I'm not sure of the answer. If she calls on me, I'll ask her, politely, to repeat the question.
3. It is O.K. for me to correct the teacher during the lecture if he or she makes a mistake.
4. It is O.K. to sharpen my pencil while the teacher is talking.
5. During a class discussion I take the opportunity to comb my hair.
6. During English class I am doing my homework for math class.
7. When I need help with my work, I raise my hand and wait for the teacher to come.
8. I don't bring my text to class so that I don't have to do the work assigned.
9. Sometimes I use the dictionary during class time.
10. It is O.K. to talk to my friends during class if I whisper.
11. I don't understand the assignment sheet, so I ask for help.
12. If someone gets in trouble during class, I stop what I am doing to see what's going on.
13. I copy from the chalkboard only the words that make sense to me.
14. If I think I can't do an assignment, I just put it down.
15. I never participate in class discussions.
16. Classtime is a good chance for me to read a magazine or the paper.

FIGURE 13   "Cool" and "Not Cool" Classroom Behaviors

Date Given_____

Name _____

Due Date _____

Directions: Put a check (✔) if you did each step.
Put an "X" if you did not.

Period	Class	Room	Monday Date	Tuesday Date	Wednesday Date	Thursday Date	Friday Date
			Went to class ____ Got there on time ____	Went to class ____ Got there on time ____	Went to class ____ Got there on time ____	Went to class ____ Got there on time ____	Went to class ____ Got there on time ____
REMEMBER TO USE YOUR ASSIGNMENT BOOK!			Brought to class pen/pencil____ paper/ notebook ____ text ____	Brought to class pen/pencil____ paper/ notebook ____ text ____	Brought to class pen/pencil____ paper/ notebook ____ text ____	Brought to class pen/pencil____ paper/ notebook ____ text ____	Brought to class pen/pencil____ paper/ notebook ____ text ____
			Be on task/ working/ following directions ____	Be on task/ working/ following directions ____	Be on task/ working/ following directions ____	Be on task/ working/ following directions ____	Be on task/ working/ following directions ____
			Asked questions____	Asked questions ____	Asked questions____	Asked questions ____	Asked questions ____
			Answered questions____	Answered questions____	Answered questions____	Answered questions____	Answered questions ____

FIGURE 14   Self-Monitoring Form H from the School Survival Skills Curriculum

Despite these deficiencies, some students with learning disabilities do not fare too badly. Zigmond et al. (1985) found that only 20% of secondary school students with LD in a large urban school district failed more mainstream courses than they passed. Overall passing grades were obtained in approximately 75% of courses, and more than 30% of the students passed everything they took. But Donahoe and Zigmond (1990) found that 5 years later in this same school district, although approximately 75% of ninth graders with LD passed mainstream health courses, only 60% passed science and less than 50% earned passing grades in social studies.

Students with learning disabilities who are successful in high school participate actively and efficiently in the educational process. They can describe the skills that are important for making it in high school, and their behavior is consistent with their rhetoric (Brown, Kerr, Zigmond, & Harris, 1984). In contrast, the unsuccessful high school students seem to function in a more passive, less efficient manner, and their behavior is not consistent with their apparent knowledge of school rules and expectations (Kerr, Zigmond, Schaeffer, & Brown, 1986; Zigmond et al., 1988; Zigmond et al., 1984). Consistently, across studies and research teams, students with learning disabilities who fail mainstream courses can be differentiated from those who pass on the basis of class attendance behaviors (failing students have significantly higher absence rates) and proficiency in learning strategies and organizational skills (Alley & Deshler, 1979; Barrett, 1986; Donahoe & Zigmond, 1990; Warner et al., 1980; Zigmond et al., 1988).

In designing a secondary school program for students with LD, something must be done about these failure rates because the consequences of failing courses needed for graduation are serious. Our data (Thornton & Zigmond, 1986) show that students who fail to accumulate sufficient numbers of required credits to pass ninth grade inevitably drop out of high school before graduation. Passing ninth grade does not guarantee successfully completing high school, but failing ninth grade is devastating to students with learning disabilities.

Three approaches can be taken to this problem:

1. School survival skills and strategies training may make the student more capable of coping with the demands of the mainstream.
2. A consulting teacher may be able to influence mainstream teachers to alter the demands of the mainstream environment to accommodate students' learning difficulties (Miller, Leinhardt, & Zigmond, 1988).
3. Students could be placed in less demanding courses to meet graduation requirements (Hartwell, Wiseman, & Van Reusen, 1979).

Explicit Planning for Life After High School

More and more educators have begun to recognize the need to provide adolescents who are learning disabled with opportunities to prepare them for a successful transition to life after high school. Several studies, our own included, indicate that a small proportion of students with learning disabilities (12%–30%) continue on to 2- and 4-year colleges after graduating from high school (see White et al., 1980; Cobb & Crump, 1984; Association for Children and Adults with Learning Disabilities, 1982; Zigmond & Thornton, 1988; Hoffman et al., 1987). These students need help in selecting appropriate higher education institutions, in arranging for adapted versions of college entrance examinations, and in completing the applications for admission.

The non-college-bound students need help in planning what they will do with their lives, what occupations might be satisfying, and what training might be needed both in high school and after it. As part of transition planning, many students with learning disabilities are being counseled into a vocational education high school track, but placement in vocational education does not guarantee a successful transition. In fact, Zigmond and Thornton (1985) found no basis for assuming that mainstream vocational education programs better prepared students with LD for the world of work than the more traditional academic curriculum. In their first follow-up sample, the post-high school employment picture was no better for the 10 students with learning disabilities who were vocational education graduates than for the 16 students with LD who were graduates of a regular high school curriculum.

Thornton (1987) further explored the relationship between completing an intensive mainstream skill-centered vocational training program in high school and post-school employment patterns. She interviewed a sample of young adults with learning disabilities who had graduated from high school nearly 2 years prior to follow-up. Thornton hypothesized that the skills acquired in vocational training experiences would give vocational education graduates with LD an advantage in the post-school employment market over graduates with LD who had not taken vocational education courses. Again, the hypothesis was not confirmed. The two groups showed no differences on several measures of post-school adjustment, including employment rates (approximately 61% in both groups) and percentage of time employed since graduating from high school (approximately 50% for both groups). Furthermore, only 35% of the vocational education graduates were in post-school employment or training that even remotely related to their high school vocational education curriculum.

A second measure of the benefits of vocational education for students with LD relates to the assumption among vocational educators that enrollment in vocational training classes in high school tends to hold in school students who otherwise might drop out (Weber & Silvani-Lacey, 1983). Thornton and Zigmond (1987b) examined the holding power of mainstream vocational education for adolescents with LD by analyzing the risk status of those enrolled in vocational programs in a large urban school district. We assigned a dropout risk status to all students on the basis of their ninth-grade attendance and course completion. We found that the holding power of vocational education for students with LD at greatest risk for dropping out was minimal, at best, because the majority of high-risk students with LD left school before entering their third year of high school (i.e., before they could access their first skill-centered mainstream vocational training courses).

Students with LD who persisted in school long enough to enroll in the vocational education track were actually low-risk in terms of school dropout (based on ninth-grade attendance and course completion data) and were expected to finish high school regardless of their course choices. Furthermore, the few high-risk students with LD who persisted in school long enough to access vocational training courses still left school before graduation.

Many students with LD want to learn practical skills during their years in high school. Figure 15 is an indication of one student's desire to do this. Nevertheless, school personnel charged with developing appropriate transition planning opportunities for students with LD must recognize that enrollment in vocational education programs in the junior and senior years may not be the only answer.

TWO MODELS OF SERVICE DELIVERY

A comprehensive high school program for students with learning disabilities must contain the four components just discussed: intensive instruction in basic skills, explicit instruction in survival skills, successful completion of courses required for graduation from high school, and explicit planning for post high school life. The challenge for schools is to construct an efficient and affordable service delivery model with the appropriate combination of special and mainstream educational experiences to address these components, and at the same time to develop an appealing and motivating educational program that holds students in school.

The best model will accomplish little if students abandon it early in their high school careers. I propose two ways in which the four components can be organized into a comprehensive high school program for students with learning disabilities. The models differ in the extent to which they rely on direct services from special education personnel and in their emphasis on preparation for work as contrasted with postsecondary education or training.

I do not like school, when I leave I will be so glad. The reson I do not like is because you have (r)ight. I think that I would like to go too a school were I could learn somthing I would like to learn, but I know that you have to learn how to count read and so on.

I think that it would be nice if I could do something I like in school like training in a field that I would be very pleace to do something like that when I get out of school. I would like to all read know how to do these thing.

FIGURE 15   Composition Written by a Ninth-Grade Boy with Learning Disabilities

Model One: Less but Very Special Special Education

The first model for special education services at the secondary school level could be sub-titled "Back to the Future" because it looks much like the model of services first proposed in our 1975 CSDC (see Zigmond, 1978). In this model, special education personnel are responsible for educating students with LD for three periods per day in ninth grade and two periods per day in the remaining years of high school. The mainstream high school program is offered to the students for the remainder of the school day. Model One utilizes the special education resource room as the service delivery setting and has five features:

1. *Students with LD are assigned to mainstream classes for math, content subjects required for graduation, and elective courses.* Students with LD are scheduled to take basic math courses with nonhandicapped students who likewise are not proficient in math. Basic, applied math courses offered in the mainstream are used to meet the math requirements for graduation. Students also are scheduled into mainstream science, social studies, and health classes so as to profit from learning these subjects from a content specialist.

2. *One special education teacher is assigned as a support or consulting teacher to work with mainstream teachers in whose classes students with LD are placed.* Many students with LD do not have the skills to manage the setting demands of the mainstream. In contrast to the individualized instruction in secondary school resource rooms, the majority of student time in mainstream academic classes is spent in teacher-directed, large-group instruction (Zigmond et al., 1984) with the instructional configuration most likely to be individualistic and competitive (Johnson & Johnson, 1978). Regular class teachers spend a great deal of time lecturing and at a speed that often makes note taking difficult (Moran, 1980).

    Mainstream content subject teachers offer few opportunities for student involvement in discussion and rarely present advanced organizers to help students listen more effectively or check on student comprehension of the content delivered by asking students to paraphrase what they have heard. Mainstream teachers typically evaluate competence through written products and infrequently provide direct oral feedback and reinforcement (Moran, 1980). Few regular class teachers spend time teaching test-taking skills (Cuthbertson, 1978). Teachers assume that students are capable of gaining knowledge of the material to be tested from reading textbooks or from absorbing information presented in lectures and class discussions. Few teachers offer students in a mainstream class the opportunity to retake a test on which they have performed poorly.

    A special education teacher in the role of support or consulting teacher will work with mainstream faculty to change their attitudes, expectations, and teaching and testing styles. The support or consulting teacher role has been shown repeatedly to facilitate successful integration of students with LD into mainstream academic courses (see Graden, Casey, & Bonstrom, 1985; Polsgrove & McNeil, 1989; West & Idol, 1987; Laurie, Buchwach, Silverman, & Zigmond, 1978), although to be effective, the role of consulting or support teacher in a high school must be considered a full-time indirect service special education job, not an activity tacked onto the job of a direct service resource room teacher.

3. *Additional special education teachers are responsible for yearly English/reading courses, one survival skills class, and a supervised study hall, which students with LD are scheduled to take each year of high school.* The curriculum of the English/reading courses over the four years of high school would follow the pattern outlined earlier in this article. It would include attention to decoding, vocabulary, comprehension and fluency, and writing. It would emphasize text-based instruction, make heavy use of graphic organizers in developing vocabulary and concepts, teach strategies for coping with narrative and expository text, and use curriculum-based measurement in reading to monitor student progress and signal needed changes in the instructional program.

   The survival skills course would be offered to all ninth-grade students with learning disabilities, and to any student assigned to the LD program after ninth grade or transferring into the high school after ninth grade. Attention would be paid to teaching behavior control, teacher-pleasing behaviors, and study skills.

   Each year, students would be scheduled for a study hall supervised by an LD teacher. This study hall would provide an opportunity for the students to receive guidance on homework assignments, to be coached to use reading comprehension strategies, learning strategies, and study skills that they have been taught in the English/reading and survival skills courses, and to receive tutoring, if necessary.

4. *From the start of ninth grade, students with LD interact regularly with a counselor for transition planning.* A counselor who is knowledgeable about the needs of students with handicaps is assigned to counsel students with LD on transition planning beginning early in ninth grade. Outcomes of these discussions are reflected in the selection of elective courses over the 4-year period so that students develop a growing sense of direction and purpose. The counselor helps students who are college-bound in the application process as early as the end of the sophomore year, when it may be appropriate to begin taking college entrance examinations.

5. *Courses required for graduation are spaced evenly throughout the four years to reduce academic pressures, particularly in ninth grade.* Students never take a full load of courses, because each year includes a study hall. In addition, one required course traditionally scheduled for ninth grade is slipped to eleventh grade to increase the likelihood that students will pass required courses in ninth grade and beyond and persist in school.

Figure 16 provides a 4-year schedule of courses for students in Model One. The schedule is designed to meet graduation requirements in the Commonwealth of Pennsylvania and assumes that, for their elective courses, students will be guided to take the two courses in arts or humanities that round out the requirements. The schedule also assumes that students carry seven classes at a time and are scheduled for each of them 5 days per week. The program of study outline in Figure 16 contains all four of the essential components of an effective LD program: intensive instruction in basic literacy skills (delivered by a special education teacher) and functional math skills (delivered in the mainstream); explicit instruction in survival skills (available as a course to be taken in ninth grade); opportunities for success in courses required for graduation (through the availability of a full-time consulting teacher, a shift in the scheduling of required courses, and a reduced schedule that incorporates a study hall supervised by a special education teacher); and explicit planning for post-school life (through counseling and judicious scheduling of six elective courses).

Model One is, however, appropriate only for certain students with learning disabilities. Students who are college-bound should be exposed to subject matter taught by mainstream content subject specialists, and they have to test themselves in a context larger than special education. Model One provides these college-bound students with that opportunity. In addition, students who are uncertain about their plans beyond high school and who do not want to limit their postsecondary education or training options would be well served in Model One, if they have sufficiently developed language and social skills to cope with mainstream content demands.

One advantage of Model One is that most special education teachers currently in the field feel comfortable teaching English/reading, although most of these teachers will

Year 1	Year 2	Year 3	Year 4
English/ Reading*	English/ Reading*	English/ Reading*	English/ Reading*
Math	Math	Math	
Social Studies		Social Studies	Social Studies
	Science	Science	Science
Survival Skills*			
Study Hall*	Study Hall*	Study Hall*	Study Hall*
PE/Health	PE	PE/Health	PE
Elective**	Elective**	Elective**	Elective**
	Elective**		Elective**

* Course taught by special education teacher.

** Electives selected with advice from counselor to meet distribution requirements for graduation, college entrance requirements for students considering post-secondary education, and/or student's vocational interests.

Note: This schedule meets Pennsylvania requirements for graduation.

FIGURE 16   Four-Year Course Schedule for Students with Learning Disabilities in Model One

need considerable inservice training to help them change the direction and emphasis of the curriculum. They also will need training in how to teach survival skills. Furthermore, in implementing this model, special education teachers will have to be enjoined against drifting into tutoring in content subjects during English/reading and survival skills instruction.

In implementing Model One, administrators will face at least two challenges. One will be to develop a school climate that promotes accommodation to students with learning differences in the mainstream. Principals play a key role in setting the tone of a school building, and their support will be critical to accomplishing changes in mainstream attitudes and instructional styles needed if students with learning disabilities are to be accommodated successfully. The second challenge facing administrators will be to support the role of a full-time consulting teacher, troubleshooting with teachers and students across the school. Teachers who do not have direct service responsibilities are uncommon in secondary schools, yet this role will be critical to successfully implementing Model One.

Model One, the *resource room model*, is consistent with the mandate of PL 94-142 for education of students with handicaps in the least restrictive environment. It combines opportunities for special instruction with opportunities to accumulate mainstream academic credits to meet high school graduation and college entrance requirements. But the Model One service delivery alternative is not for everyone.

Model Two: More Special Education

Restructuring, the rising tide of the school reform movement, is part of the response of the education community to criticisms originating in the *A Nation At Risk* report (National Commission on Excellence in Education, 1983). The basic agenda of the restructuring movement has been to increase the academic pressure on the schools, to increase achievement in core skills, to increase student competence in higher-order thinking skills, to produce a high school graduate who is better prepared to enter the workforce so that America can compete successfully with Europe and the Pacific Rim countries. Restructuring at the high school level has meant tougher, more uniform standards; increased graduation requirements in mathematics, science, foreign languages, and technology; harsher grading; less leniency.

The restructuring of mainstream education has come at a time of intense pressure to restructure special education, as well. Many researchers, practitioners, and policymakers in the special education community have been calling for a restructuring of services for "hard-to-teach" students and have proposed that regular education classrooms can be made to work effectively for *all* students. That pressure to return students with disabilities to mainstream instruction is known as the *regular education initiative* (Will, 1986). Advocates of the regular education initiative (REI) assume that schools are prepared to accept a wider range of abilities and to deliver a diversity of educational options within the regular classroom.

The reality is quite different, especially at the high school level, because the restructuring effort in special education is simply not compatible with the restructuring effort in regular education. The mainstream reform effort sets rigid standards for acceptable school behavior; special education reform asks mainstream teachers to expand their tolerance of individual behavioral differences. The mainstream reform effort increases the rigor of the curriculum; the special education reform asks teachers to be more flexible, more thoughtful, more selective in curriculum coverage. The mainstream reform effort introduces uniform testing programs and grading guidelines; the special education reform asks teachers to adapt testing procedures and grading standards to accommodate students with special needs.

Recognizing the impact of mainstream reform efforts on high school teachers and high school programs, Model Two calls for *increasing* the level of responsibility of special education personnel for educating students with learning disabilities in secondary schools. Five features define the Model Two high school program:

1. *All basic skills are taught by a special educator and instruction in basic skills is linked to transition planning.* Special education personnel would be responsible for teaching all English/reading and math courses required for graduation. These courses would not be simple modifications of the mainstream high school curriculum. Instead, the curriculum of these courses would address the functional skill needs of the students in the classes and be coordinated with the vocational education courses being taken by the students concurrently. Explicit discussions on the relevance of reading and math skills to vocational pursuits would be a regular part of the courses, as would discussions of job possibilities after completion of high school.

2. *Required "content" subjects are co-taught by special educators.* Students with learning disabilities would be scheduled to take science, social studies, or health in mainstream classes co-taught by a mainstream content subject specialist and a special education teacher. The curriculum would parallel the curriculum taught in other basic content courses in the mainstream but might utilize text material written at a more readable level. Also, the course might cover some material less deeply and some material more deeply than the more traditional mainstream counterpart.

3. *Vocational education is provided in the mainstream and coordinated with transition planning provided within special education.* Beginning in the freshman year of high school, students would be scheduled into regular vocational education courses. The first 2 years of vocational courses would involve extensive exploration of job possibilities, including some on-the-job internships to "try on" various jobs, and would be scheduled for two periods per day. By the junior year, exposure to vocational/technical training would continue to occupy two periods per day, but vocational training would become more intense and involve sustained training in one occupation for 2 years. At the same time, vocational education teachers would work closely with special education personnel on skills students need to master the vocational content. These skills would be reinforced in the basic skills courses being taken by students concurrently. Also, special education and vocational education personnel would work with the students' counselors to be certain that coordinated transition planning is taking place.

4. *All ninth-grade students with learning disabilities will take a required course on survival skills taught by a special educator.* A survival skills course would provide incoming ninth graders with an orientation to the rules and demands of high school and teach the students behavior control, teacher-pleasing behaviors, and study skills expected of a high school student.

5. *Students' schedules would reflect a light academic load in ninth grade to ensure successful completion of the first year of high school.* During ninth grade, students would be scheduled to complete two vocational education courses and the elective requirements in art or humanities would be delayed until eleventh and twelfth grades. This would reduce the academic press of that first year in high school and increase the likelihood that students will have a successful year.

Figure 17 provides a summary of a 4-year high school program for students with LD that meets basic requirements for graduation in the Commonwealth of Pennsylvania. Again, the schedule in Model Two assumes that students carry seven classes at a time.

Model Two would be especially suitable for students who enter high school with minimal competence in basic skills and who have no aspirations to attend college. It has several advantages:

1. Students with learning disabilities are sheltered from the demands of mainstream classes and are less likely to earn failing grades; if they earn passing grades in required courses, students are more likely to persist in school until graduation.
2. Required academic courses are distributed fairly evenly throughout the 4 years, and two additional courses in arts or humanities required for graduation are not scheduled until the junior and senior years so that the ninth-grade curriculum is not quite so formidable.
3. Students have at least two periods per day of more practical coursework with explicit future-oriented planning; if vocational education really does have holding power, vocational courses beginning as early as ninth grade should "hook" students who are at greatest risk for dropping out.
4. Students are likely to be interacting throughout the day with a smaller network of teachers and fellow students, creating a more personalized "school within a school" climate that also could function to hold students in school.
5. Students in Model Two will have been carefully prepared for the transition into the world of work or postsecondary job training and would have some immediately usable skills for entering the job market.

Although Model Two offers some distinct advantages for students with LD, it will be difficult to implement well because of staffing problems, as well as state and local school policy constraints. There are two staffing issues to consider. First, given the enhanced role of special education personnel in the model, a high school adopting Model Two may have to increase the numbers of its special education staff.

Year 1	Year 2	Year 3	Year 4
English/ Reading*	English/ Reading*	English/ Reading*	English/ Reading*
Math*	Math*	Math*	
Social Studies**	Social Studies**		Social Studies**
	Science**	Science**	Science**
Survival Skills*			
PE/Health*	PE	PE/Health*	PE
Voc Ed	Voc Ed	Voc Ed	Voc Ed
Voc Ed	Voc Ed	Voc Ed	Voc Ed
		Elective***	Elective***

*Courses taught by special education teacher.

**Courses co-taught by mainstream and special educators.

***These courses would have to meet graduation requirements of two credits in art and/or humanities.

Note: This schedule meets Pennsylvania requirements for graduation.

FIGURE 17   *Four-Year Course Schedule for Students with Learning Disabilities in Model Two*

Second, special education teacher preparation programs simply do not prepare special education teachers as high school content subject specialists, so teachers will not be prepared for instructional duties in science, social studies, and health. We have observed secondary school content subject classes being taught by special educators; the teachers are so ill-at-ease with the subject matter that they cannot provide interesting elaborations or explanations of the content, and they cannot answer students' questions accurately. Furthermore, special education teachers have probably not had training in models of co-teaching and collaboration. Students with learning disabilities who are in this model will be seriously shortchanged unless teacher preparation programs address these deficiencies or school districts provide content updates for special education personnel given these new assignments.

Issues at the policy level also plague Model Two. First, graduation requirements set at the state level often consist of more than course titles. Curricula are defined for courses that will count toward meeting graduation requirements. Courses taught by special education personnel to students with LD may, by design, deviate from the prescribed curriculum, to make them more relevant and more suitable to the students' skill and cognitive levels. A waiver may be required for these adapted courses to be counted toward high school graduation.

Second, a single high school may not have sufficient numbers of students with LD to warrant offering co-teaching the entire special education high school curriculum (four English courses, three math courses, three social studies courses, three science courses, and one health course) in a single year. Instead, co-teaching in social studies, science, and health courses may have to be offered on a rotating basis so that, over the course of four years, all courses will have been available to students with LD. This rotational system may make staffing easier, but students with LD who transfer in or out of a given high school during the 4 years may have difficulty getting all the courses they need.

CONCLUSIONS

The secondary school is a complex environment that many students find difficult to negotiate. For students with LD it presents formidable challenges. A poorly designed high school program can undermine students' self-concept and drive students from school before they are fully prepared. A well designed high school program provides opportunities to learn what has not yet been mastered, to develop social and interpersonal skills, to prepare for the world beyond public schooling.

An appropriate and effective secondary school program can fortify young people who have learning disabilities with the self-confidence and skills needed to function effectively in postsecondary education or employment, or in personal and social relationships. Our task is to organize schooling to provide opportunities for these things to happen regardless of the cost or how much change it requires of us. It is a challenging task, but it is a challenge we simply must meet.

I wish to acknowledge the support and cooperation of Dr. William Penn, Director of the Division for Exceptional Children, Pittsburgh Public Schools, without whom the work described in this article could not have been done. I also acknowledge grant support from OSEP through the divisions of Personnel Preparation and Innovation and Development (directed and field-initiated research), whose funds made much of this work possible.

REFERENCES

Alexander, D. F. (1985). The effect of study skill training on learning disabled students retelling of expository material. *Journal of Applied Behavior Analysis, 18*, 263–267.

Alley, G., & Deshler, D. (1979). *Teaching the learning disabled adolescent: Strategies and methods.* Denver: Love Publishing.

Association for Children and Adults with Learning Disabilities. (1982, September/October). *ACLD vocational committee survey of learning disabled adults: Preliminary report. ACLD News Briefs,* pp. 10–13.

Bachman, J. G. (1972). Anti-dropout campaign and other misanthropies. *Society, 9.*

Barrett, D. (1986). *An analysis of policy variables relating to secondary learning disabled students who are mainstreamed into academic content areas.* Unpublished doctoral dissertation, University of Pittsburgh.

Bradley, L., & Bryant, P. (1985). *Rhyme and reason in reading and spelling.* Ann Arbor: University of Michigan Press.

Brown, G. M., Kerr, M. M., Zigmond, N., & Harris, A. L. (1984). What's important for student success in high school? "Successful" and "unsuccessful" students discuss school survival skills. *High School Journal, 68*(1), 10–17.

Calfee, R. (1976). Sources of dependency in cognitive processes. In D. Klahr (Ed.), *Cognition and Instruction.* New York: Erlbaum.

Cawley, J. F., Fitzmaurice-Hayes, A. M., & Shaw, R. A. (1988). *Mathematics for the mildly handicapped: A guide to curriculum and instruction.* Boston: Allyn and Bacon.

Cawley, J. F., Fitzmaurice, A. M., Shaw, R. A., Kahn, H., & Bates, H. III, (1978). Mathematics and learning disabled youth: The upper grade levels. *Learning Disability Quarterly, 1,* 37–52.

Cawley, J. F., Fitzmaurice, A. M., Shaw, R. A., Kahn, H., & Bates, H. III, (1979a). LD youth and mathematics: A review of characteristics. *Learning Disability Journal, 2,* 29–44.

Cawley, J. F., Fitzmaurice, A. M., Shaw, R. A., Kahn, H., & Bates, H. III, (1979b). Math word problems: Suggestions for LD students. *Learning Disability Quarterly, 2,* 25–41.

Cervantes, L. F. (1965). *The dropout.* Ann Arbor: University of Michigan Press.

Cobb, R., & Crump, W. (1984). *Post-school status of young adults identified as learning disabled while enrolled in learning disabilities programs (Final report U.S.D.E. Grant No. G008302185).* Tuscaloosa: University of Alabama.

Combs, J., & Cooley, W. (1968). Dropouts in high school and after school. *American Educational Research Journal, 5,* 343–363.

Critchley, M. (1964). *Developmental dyslexia.* Springfield, IL: Charles C. Thomas.

Curley, T. J. (1971, March). *The social system: Contributor or inhibitor to the school dropout* (ED 049-344). Washington, DC: U.S. Dept. of Health, Education, and Welfare.

Cuthbertson, E. (1978). *An analysis of secondary testing and grading procedures.* Unpublished master's thesis, University of Kansas, Lawrence.

Dean, J. S. (1973, October). A plan to save dropouts: School-within-a-school. *Clearing House, 48,* 98–99.

deBettencourt, L., Zigmond, N., & Thornton, H. S. (1989). Follow-up of post-secondary age rural learning disabled graduates and dropouts. *Exceptional Children, 56*(1), 40–49.

Deno, S. L., & Mirkin, P. K. (1977). *Data-based program modification: A manual.* Reston, VA: Council for Exceptional Children.

Deshler, D. D., Lowrey, N., & Alley, G. R. (1979). Preparing alternatives for LD adolescents: A nationwide survey. *Academic Therapy, 14,* 389–397.

Donahoe, K., & Zigmond, N. (1990). High school grades of urban LD students and low achieving peers. *Exceptionality, 1,* 17–27.

Fardig, D., Algozzine, R., Schwartz, S., Hensel, J., & Westling, D. (1985). Post-secondary vocational adjustment of rural, mildly handicapped students. *Exceptional Children, 52*(2), 115–121.

Fayne, H. R., & Bryant, N. D. (1981). Relative effects of various word synthesis strategies on the phonics achievement of learning disabled youngsters. *Journal of Learning Disabilities, 73,* 616–623.

Fuchs, L. S., Hamlett, C. L., Fuchs, D., Stecker, P. M., & Ferguson, C. (1988). Conducting curriculum-based measurement with computerized data collection: Effects of efficiency and teacher satisfaction. *Journal of Special Education Technology, 9*(2), 73–86.

Glass, G. G. (1978). *Glass-analysis for decoding only.* Garden City, NY: Easier to Learn, Inc.

Graden, J. L., Casey, A., & Bonstrom, O. (1985). Implementing a prereferral intervention system: Part 2. The data. *Exceptional Children, 51,* 487–496.

Graham, S., & Harris, K. R. (1989a). Cognitive training: Implications for written language. In J. Hughes & R. Hall (Eds.), *Cognitive behavioral psychology in the schools: A comprehensive handbook* (pp. 247–279). New York: Guilford.

Graham, S., & Harris, K. R. (1989b). Improving learning disabled students' skills at composing essays: Self-instructional strategy training. *Exceptional Children, 56*(3), 201–214.

Graham, S., & Johnson, L. A. (1989). Teaching reading to learning disabled students: A review of research-supported procedures. *Focus on Exceptional Children, 21*(6), 1–12.

Gregory, J. F., Shanahan, T., & Walberg, H. (1986). A profile of learning disabled twelfth-graders in regular classes. *Learning Disability Quarterly, 9*(1), 33–42.

Hammontree, T. (1978). Profile of a dropout. *Florida Vocational Journal, 3,* 26–28.

Hartwell, L. K., Wiseman, D. E., & Van Reusen, A. (1979). Modifying course content for mildly handicapped students at the secondary level. *Teaching Exceptional Children, 12,* 28–32.

Hasazi, S., Gordon, L., & Roe, C. (1985). Factors associated with the employment status of handicapped youth exiting high school from 1979 to 1983. *Exceptional Children, 51*(6), 455–469.

Hewitt, J. D., & Johnson, W. S. (1979). Dropping out in Middletown. *High School Journal, 62,* 252–256.

Hill, C. R. (1979). Capacities, opportunities, and educational investments: The case of the high school dropout. *Review of Economics & Statistics, 61,* 9–20.

Hoffman, F. J., Sheldon, K. L., Minskoff, E. H., Sautter, S. W., Steidle, E. F., Baker, D. P., Bailey, M. B., & Echols, L. D. (1987). Needs of learning disabled adults. *Journal of Learning Disabilities, 20*(1), 43–52.

Howell, F., & Frese, W. (1982). Early transition into adult roles: Some antecedents and outcomes. *American Educational Research Journal, 19*(1), 51–73.

Howell, K., & Morehead, M. K. (1987). *Curriculum based evaluation in special and remedial education.* Columbus, OH: Merrill Publishing Co.

Johnson, D. J., & Myklebust, H. R. (1967). *Learning disabilities.* New York: Grune & Stratton.

Johnson, D. W., & Johnson, R. T. (1978). Cooperative, competitive, and individualistic learning. *Journal of Research & Development in Education, 12*(1), 3–15.

Kaplan, J., & Luck, E. (1977). The dropout phenomenon as a social problem. *Education Forum, 42,* 41–56.

Kerr, M. M., Zigmond, N., Schaeffer, A., & Brown, G. (1986). An observational follow-up of successful and unsuccessful high school students. *High School Journal, 70*(1), 20–24.

Kowalski, C., & Cangemi, J. (1974). High school dropouts—A lost resource. *College Student Journal, 8,* 71–74.

Kozol, J. (1985). *Illiterate America.* New York: Plume Publishers.

Laurie, T., Buchwach, L., Silverman, R., & Zigmond, N. (1978). Teaching secondary learning disabled students in the mainstream, *Learning Disability Quarterly, 1*(4), 67-72.

Levin, E. K., Zigmond, N., & Birch, J. W. (1985). A follow-up study of 52 learning disabled adolescents. *Journal of Learning Disabilities, 18,* 2–7.

Lloyd, D. N. (1976). Concurrent prediction of dropout and grade of withdrawal. *Educational & Psychological Measurement, 36,* 983–990.

Lloyd, J. W., & Keller, C. E. (1989). Effective mathematics instruction: Development, instruction, and programs. *Focus on Exceptional Children, 21*(7), 1–10.

Mahood, W. (1981, January). Born losers: School dropouts and pushouts. *National Association of Secondary School Principals Bulletin, 65,* 54–57.

Mare, R. D. (1980). Social background and school continuation decisions. *Journal of American Statistical Association, 75,* 195–305.

McKeown, M., & Beck, I. (1988). Learning vocabulary: Different ways for different goals. *Remedial & Special Education, 9,* 42–52.

Miller, S. E., Leinhardt, G., & Zigmond, N. (1988). Influencing engagement through accommodation: An ethnographic study of at-risk students. *American Educational Research Journal, 25*(4), 465–488.

Moran, M. R. (1980). *An investigation of the demands of oral language skills of learning disabled students in secondary classrooms* (Research Report #1). Lawrence: University of Kansas, Institute for Research in Learning Disabilities.

Morrow, D., Thornton, H., & Zigmond, N. (1988). *Graduation and post-secondary adjustment: Follow-up of urban-bound learning disabled students.* Final Report. Pittsburgh: University of Pittsburgh.

National Commission on Excellence in Education. (1983). *A nation at risk: The imperative for educational reform.* Washington, DC: U.S. Dept. of Education.

Nickerson, R. S. (1985). *Adult literacy and technology* (Report No. 351). Champaign, IL: University of Illinois, Center for the Study of Reading. (ERIC Document Reproduction Service No. ED 266 420).

Norman, C. A., & Zigmond, N. (1980). Characteristics of children labeled and served as learning disabled in school systems affiliated with child service demonstration centers. *Journal of Learning Disabilities, 13,* 542–547.

O'Shea, L. J., Sindelar, P. T., & O'Shea, D. J. (1987). The effects of repeated readings and attentional cues on the reading fluency and comprehension of learning disabled readers. *Learning Disabilities Research, 2,* 103–109.

Palinscar, A. S., & Brown, A. L. (1984). Reciprocal teaching of comprehension-fostering and comprehension-monitoring activities. *Cognition & Instruction, 1,* 117–175.

Polsgrove, L., & McNeil, M. (1989). The consultation process: Research and practice. *Remedial & Special Education, 10*(1), 6–13.

Riegel, R. H., & Mathey, J. P. (1980). *Mainstreaming at the secondary level: Seven models that work* (Bulletin #1427). Wayne County, MI: Intermediate School District.

Rumberger, R. W. (1983). Dropping out of high school: The influence of race, sex, and family background. *American Educational Research Journal, 20*(2), 199–220.

Rumberger, R. W. (1987). High school dropouts: A review of issues and evidence. *Review of Educational Research, 57,* 101–121.

Schalock, R. L., Wolzen, B., Ross, J., Elliott, B., Werbel, C., & Peterson, J. (1986). Post-secondary community placement of handicapped students: A five year follow-up. *Learning Disability Quarterly, 9*(4), 295–303.

Schreiber, D. (1962). School dropouts. *National Educational Association Journal, 51,* 50–59.

Schumaker, J. B., Deshler, D. D., Alley, G. R., Warner, M. M., & Denton, P. H. (1982). Multipass: A learning strategy for improving reading comprehension. *Learning Disability Quarterly, 5,* 295–304.

Silverman, R., Zigmond, N., & Sansone, J. (1981). Teaching coping skills: A school survival skills curriculum for adolescents with learning disabilities. *Focus on Exceptional Children, 13*(6), 1–20.

Stoughton, C. R., & Grady, B. R. (1978, Fall). How many students will drop out and why? *North Central Association Quarterly, 53,* 312–315.

Thornton, H. (1987). *A follow-up study of learning disabled young adults who participated in mainstream vocational education programs.* Unpublished doctoral dissertation, University of Pittsburgh.

Thornton, H., & Zigmond, N. (1986). Follow-up of post-secondary age LD graduates and dropouts. *LD Research, 1*(1), 50–55.

Thornton, H. S., & Zigmond, N. (1987a, April). *Predictors of dropout and unemployment among LD high school youth: The holding power of secondary vocational education for LD students.* Paper presented at annual meeting of American Educational Research Association, Washington, DC.

Thornton, H. S., & Zigmond, N. (1987b, April). *Post-secondary follow-up of learning disabled and non-handicapped completers of mainstream vocational education programs.* Paper presented at annual meeting of American Educational Research Association, Washington, DC.

Thornton, H. S., & Zigmond, N. (1988). Secondary vocational training for LD students and its relationship to school completion status and post school outcomes. *Illinois School Journal, 67*(2), 37–54.

Tseng, M. S. (1972). Comparisons of selected personality and vocational variables of high school students and dropouts. *Journal of Educational Research, 65* (10), 462–466.

U. S. Department of Education. (1988). *To assure the free appropriate public education of all handicapped children: Tenth annual report to Congress on the implementation of the Education of the Handicapped Act.* Washington, DC: Government Printing Office.

U. S. Department of Education. (1989). *To assure the free appropriate public education of all handicapped children: Eleventh annual report to Congress on the implementation of the Education of the Handicapped Act.* Washington, DC: Government Printing Office.

Warner, M. M., Alley, G. R., Schumaker, J. B., Deshler, D. D., & Clark, F. L. (1980). *An epidemiological study of learning disabled adolescents in secondary schools: Achievement and ability, socioeconomic status, and school experiences* (Research Report #13). Lawrence: University of Kansas, Institute for Research in Learning Disabilities.

Weber, J., & Silvani-Lacey (1983). *Building basic skills: The dropout.* Columbus: Ohio State University, National Center for Research in Vocational Education.

Wehlage, G. G., & Rutter, R. A. (1986). Dropping out: How much does school contribute to the problem? *Teachers College Record, 87,* 374–392.

Wehlage, G. G., Rutter, R. A., Smith, G. A., Lesko, N., & Fernandez, R. R. (1989). *Reducing the risk: Schools as communities of support.* New York: Falmer Press.

West, J. F., & Idol, L. (1987). School consultation (Part 1): An inter-disciplinary perspective on theory, models, and research. *Journal of Learning Disabilities, 20,* 388–408.

White, W., Schumaker, J., Warner, M., Alley, G., & Deshler, D. (1980). *The current status of young adults identified as learning disabled during their school career* (Research Report #21). Lawrence: University of Kansas, Institute for Research in Learning Disabilities.

Will, M. (1986). *Educating students with learning problems: A shared responsibility.* Washington, DC: Office of Special Education and Rehabilitative Services, U. S. Department of Education.

Williams, J. P. (1980). Teaching decoding with an emphasis on phoneme analysis and phoneme blending. *Journal of Educational Psychology, 73,* 697–704.

Wong, B. Y. L. (1986). Metacognition and special education: A review of a view. *Journal of Special Education, 20*(1), 9–29.

Zigmond, N. (1978). A prototype of comprehensive services for secondary students with learning disabilities. *Learning Disability Quarterly, 1*(1), 39–49.

Zigmond, N. (1988, April). *Evaluating staff development initiatives using direct observations of teacher and student behavior.* Paper presented at annual meeting of American Educational Research Association, New Orleans.

Zigmond, N., Kerr, M. M., Brown, G. M., & Harris, A. L. (1984). *School survival skills in secondary school age special education students.* Presented at annual meeting of the American Educational Research Association, New Orleans.

Zigmond, N., Kerr, M. M., & Schaeffer, A. L. (1988). Behavior patterns of learning disabled adolescents in high school academic classes. *Remedial & Special Education, 9*(2), 6–11.

Zigmond, N., Kerr, M. M., Schaeffer, A. L., Farra, H. E., & Brown, G. M. (1986). *The school survival skills curriculum.* Pittsburgh: University of Pittsburgh.

Zigmond, N., Levin, E., & Laurie, T. E. (1985). Managing the mainstream: An analysis for teacher attitudes and student performance in mainstream high school programs. *Journal of Learning Disabilities, 18*(9), 535–541.

Zigmond, N., & Thornton, H. S. (1985). Follow-up of post-secondary age LD graduates and dropouts. *Learning Disabilities Research, 1*(1), 50–55.

Zigmond, N., & Thornton, H. (1988)). Learning disabilities in adolescents and adults. In K. Kavale (Ed.), *Learning disabilities: State of the art and practice.* San Diego: College Hill Press.

Naomi Zigmond is affiliated with the Department of Instruction and Learning at the University of Pittsburgh.

○ 8 ○

The innovative technology of the 1990s will involve videodisc instruction, the authors maintain. They describe a naturalistic study of this technology with seven high school teachers, dealing with the level of implementation, teacher reactions, and student achievement. The research presented here offers a real challenge to special education because of the generally positive results and the surprising level of acceptance by teachers.

Innovative Technology for Secondary Students with Learning Disabilities

John Woodward and Russell Gersten

Over the past decade, public schools have spent approximately $2 billion for microcomputers. Acquisitions in special education alone grew more than 330% from 1983 to 1985 (Blaschke, 1985). Although 96% of American schools have microcomputers, the typical school has a ratio of only 1 computer per 30 students. Furthermore, most schools house their 10–20 computers in a single computer lab, thus limiting computer use to an average of about 15 minutes (min) per day per student. This growth has spawned an array of frustrations—some logistical, some instructional (Buckeley, 1988; Rothman, 1988; West, 1988).

Recent evaluations of technology use in education concluded that computers are failing as educational aids (Buckeley, 1988; Snider, 1986). Early in the 1980s, visionaries (Bork, 1981; Papert, 1980) claimed that computers would revolutionize learning. More recently, critics of educational technology (Cuban, 1986) have pointed out that the early sanguine predictions are similar to those that accompanied previous technological innovations, such as instructional television. Once initial enthusiasm palled, the educational community used these technologies at an extremely modest level, and their impact on improving instruction has been minimal.

Some microcomputer proponents are trying to sort out what is currently happening to their "revolution" in the schools. Reasons expressed for the modest acceptance of microcomputers in the schools vary. Hofmeister (1984), in particular, has stressed the poor quality of most instructional software; a view which is now more widely shared in schools (Buckeley, 1988). Semmel and Lieber (1986) stated that the early claims about the superiority of computer-assisted instruction (CAI) as an alternative to traditional instruction were exaggerated.

Perhaps the most perceptive—and indicting—analyses have come from Cuban (1986), Cohen (1987), and Wolcott (1981). These researchers argued that computers are but another in a set of educational innovations that have largely ignored the culture of schools. Cuban stressed that computers have been forced on schools in a top-down fashion. Computers have commonly been deployed in classrooms and labs in a way that doesn't mesh well with the various demands and routines of a teacher's day. This lack of sensitivity to the realities and routines of classroom learning has resulted in a revolution that has been, at least for the moment, temporarily derailed. These views seem to apply to special education as well as regular education.

PROBLEMS AND ISSUES IN TECHNOLOGY USE IN SECONDARY SPECIAL EDUCATION

One of the most recent surveys of microcomputer use at the secondary level indicates that students in special education spend as much time on computers as students with average ability (Becker & Sterling, 1987). However, they engage in very different activities on the computer than do their peers. On the average, secondary students use drill-and-practice computer programs only 13% of the time. In contrast, secondary students in special education classes spend most of their computer time on drill and practice, mainly in the areas of math and language arts programs (Becker & Sterling; Okolo, Rieth, Polsgrove, Bahr, & Yerkes, 1985). Where computers were not used for drill and practice, the main intent of computer use with students in special education was to improve motivation, self-confidence, and self-discipline. On the other hand, when working with other secondary students, teachers' main goals were programming, computer literacy, and word processing (Becker, 1987).

We would like to emphasize several key points about the use of technology in high schools, and with high-school students in special education. The first point is seemingly obvious: Technology use in all schools fundamentally involves microcomputers. Rarely do educators use alternate technologies, such as videodisc instruction, or more elaborate uses, such as telecommunications or information retrieval from commercial databases. Second, access to these computers is typically very limited, possibly undercutting their value as tools for instructional delivery. This is true for both special education students and other students. Third, students with mild disabilities are unique among secondary students because they predominantly use microcomputers for drill and practice. However, anything beyond the drill-and-practice level of instruction, be it through microcomputers or other forms of computer technology, is rare for these students.

One of the few studies of microcomputer use in secondary special education (Rieth, Bahr, Okolo, Polsgrove, & Eckert, 1988) reveals that even though secondary special education teachers extensively supervise their students during computer use, very limited, substantive academic interaction occurs. Although students tend to be engaged at high rates, it is far from clear that students are successful at their work on the computer or that they understand the content of the CAI. Furthermore, there is little evidence that teachers are able to successfully integrate CAI with their traditional curriculum. These factors, along with the typically high ratio of students to computers (about 30 : 1) and the overreliance on drill-and-practice programs, combine to make computer-based instruction a poor fit with traditional secondary-level instruction.

VIDEODISC INSTRUCTION

An emerging alternative to conventional CAI is videodisc technology. If offers a vastly superior presentational format than do microcomputers. One distinct feature that differentiates videodiscs from microcomputers is the enhanced graphics capabilities. Videodiscs can store up to 30 min of continuous motion pictures per side or 54,000 photographic quality frames. The stored images may appear as slides, archival film, videotape segments, and state-of-the-art computer graphics—in any combination. A second appeal is narration, allowing students the opportunity to watch presentations rather than, for example, read from text and examine static diagrams or charts. All these features go well beyond the capabilities of today's microcomputers.

A further attraction is that teachers can operate a videodisc in the same fashion as a video cassette recorder; thus the technology is relatively easy to use. This last point is not trivial. Teachers with limited technical expertise are understandably bewildered when they encounter "DOS error" or scrambled letters on the computer monitor screen.

Finally, videodisc technology can facilitate group instruction. A videodisc can be operated from a distance as the teacher walks around the classroom. The ratio of one videodisc player and its program to a classroom is satisfactory, as opposed to one of the main logistical problems associated with microcomputers, which typically demand a one-to-one interaction. The teacher positions the videodisc player and television monitor in the front of the room and, with a remote control, operates the program from a distance. The teacher can then circulate among the students, monitoring individual work and giving substantive feedback.

Some educational developers have been drawn to the videodisc medium because of its potential for embedding research-based effective teaching techniques into the medium. Software such as *Mastering Fractions* (Systems Impact, 1986), the subject of the current evaluation study, was designed following empirically derived principles of effective instruction (Brophy & Good, 1986; Leinhardt & Smith, 1985). These include breaking each problem-solving process into small steps, using extensive models of problem-solving strategies, and showing a wide range of examples. Other steps involve review of relevant preskills, cumulative review, discrimination practice, and frequent assessment of student understanding of new material presented. The videodisc program differs from more traditional approaches by teaching fractions concepts and operations in more depth and by providing more practice.

The videodisc curriculum used in this study was based on many components of the Good, Grouws, and Ebmeier (1983) model of effective mathematics instruction. To this extent, this program was somewhat unusual and certainly not representative of instructional videodiscs as a whole. One of the cornerstones of this model is the use of guided practice to frequently assess student understanding of each small instructional unit presented. Checks for Student Progress (CSPs) are incorporated into each lesson of the videodisc curriculum. These CSPs enable teachers to determine when brief review or remediation activities are necessary. In this respect, the program was conceptually quite different from other, more typical videodisc programs, which tend to contain many archival images and film clips and function as highly flexible instructional supplements (e.g., *Windows on Science*, Optical Data, 1988).

The use of videodisc technology for group instruction requires significant role shifts for teachers. The videodisc becomes the source of initial explanations, graphic demonstrations, and guided practice problems. This feature frees the teacher from the task of curriculum presentations and allows him or her to concentrate on monitoring the group and on individual assistance. The videodisc program includes a substantial portion of traditional instruction—the portion typically devoted to curriculum presentation through problems on the chalkboard or through a lecture.

For example, following a 3-min presentation of the concept of reducing fractions that involves computer graphics and narration, the videodisc program presents a set of two to four guided practice problems. Each set is a still frame, and the teacher advances to the next frame when all the students are ready. Students copy the problems from the screen onto paper at their desks and work the problems; the teacher then presents the next frame showing the same problems and their answers. The videodisc then shows another set of problems or presents a "decision menu" for the teacher, directing her to different sections of the videodisc depending on student performance over the set of guided practice problems. This interactive format is very different from previous educational technologies cited by Cuban (1986), especially educational television.

A recent controlled experimental study by Kelly, Carnine, Gersten, and Grossen (1986) of the *Mastering Fractions* (1986) videodisc program demonstrated significant positive effects on student achievement when the system was used to teach basic fractions concepts to secondary students in remedial and special education programs. Results of the study showed superior performance of students taught with the videodisc on a criterion-reference posttest. Effects were maintained on a measure given several weeks later. Rates of academic engagement were significantly higher for the videodisc students. However, this study used highly trained experimental teachers, who were carefully monitored by the researchers. When *Mastering Fractions* has been used under less controlled conditions, noticeable variation in the way the program has been implemented has been observed (Hasselbring, Sherwood, & Bransford, 1986). It was a growing concern for the use of this particular videodisc program—which is highly prescriptive in its implementation—in more typical, day-to-day settings that led us to the following study.

Research on educational innovation and school improvement (Fullan, 1982) suggests that to analyze a change effort, such as the use of new educational technologies, one must first describe and analyze the context. This involves examining the instructional materials used and the staff development provided (Loucks & Zacchei, 1983). This type of research entails not only observations of how teachers implement the innovation, but also a probing of teachers' attitudes and beliefs toward it. A comprehensive, multifaceted evaluation should also examine the impact of the innovation on student learning. Fullan (1982) correctly noted that students, the ultimate recipients of new instructional programs, are typically neglected as sources for reactions to innovation.

Therefore, a range of instruments were developed to capture the implementation. We assessed the level of implementation of the program by the teacher, along with transfer of training following the videodisc experience. We probed teachers' reactions and perceptions through semi-structured interviews. Student achievement was documented through a curriculum-referenced test covering the major topics in fractions.

We made a special effort to interview the 57 students who participated in the study. Because the program required far greater active student involvement than traditional instruction, it was important to document the students' reactions in a variety of ways. Finally, we assessed whether use of the innovation had any transfer effects (i.e., any impact on teachers' conventional instruction).

This article reports on a study of technology use in special education classes at the secondary level—an empirically validated videodisc program—using a multifaceted approach. Our concern was less an evaluation of how well students learned with the new technology (student learning has been documented by Kelly et al., 1986) than an evaluation of how teachers used it; what factors led to successful implementation; and to what extent the technology fit into teachers' current classroom situation.

METHOD

Subjects and Setting

Before the 1987-88 school year began, secondary special education teachers in a large district were contacted regarding a new fractions program. Only a small subsample of the district's secondary special education teachers were eligible to participate in this study, either because they were not scheduled to teach fractions in the fall or because they were unavailable for the initial in-service session. Of the eight teachers contacted, only one declined to use the curriculum. All seven participating teachers taught mathematics in secondary resource room programs for students with mild disabilities. The average teaching experience was 11.7 years, with an average of 7.2 years in special education and 9 years of teaching mathematics.

The study took place in one of the 8 largest districts in the United States. As in most large urban districts, the student population is diverse; approximately 45% of the students were minority. The seven school sites involved in this study ranged from upper middle-income neighborhoods to inner-city, low-income settings.

Only one section of Basic Math, per teacher, was used for this study. Teachers were free, however, to use the curriculum with other sections of this course; and four teachers did so. These classes typically consisted of 6 to 15 students. All students were eligible for the study except those who performed poorly on a test of basic computation skills (e.g., simple addition and subtraction). Three students were excluded for this reason. A total of 57 students participated over the 6-week intervention period. All were classified as learning disabled; all were receiving special mathematics instruction as specified by their individualized education programs (IEPs).

Intervention Procedures

Teacher Training

Participating teachers attended two 1-hour (hr) training sessions before implementation. These sessions included an overview of videodisc technology, an introduction to the fractions curriculum, a demonstration of how to operate the videodisc equipment, and guidelines for implementation of the program in the classroom.

The first session allowed participants to learn some of the theory behind the program (Showers, Joyce, & Bennett, 1987), provided a demonstration of what a typical lesson should look like, and provided limited practice with the new technology. The quantity and nature of the training was designed to parallel the amount generally provided by publishers of standard curricula.

The second session allocated approximately 30 min for hands-on practice with the videodisc equipment. The trainers encouraged teachers to spend time familiarizing themselves with the equipment and with the content of the lessons before presenting the first lesson to their students.

Four specific aspects of implementation were stressed during the training: (a) spending at least 45 min of the class period for the lesson presentation and corresponding workbook exercises; (b) use of *guided practice* to assess student comprehension at the three to four designated points during each lesson (CSPs); (c) monitoring students' work throughout all segments of the lesson; and (d) teaching to mastery. Trainers stressed the importance of student mastery of the material, rather than "automatic" progress of one lesson per day; and they showed teachers how to use the "remediation options" in the program.

Program Implementation

Beginning in early October, the seven participating teachers used the *Mastering Fractions* program with their students for a period of 6 weeks. The number of lessons teachers covered in this time was contingent on the day-to-day progress of their students. At the end of the implementation, most teachers had completed approximately 24 of the 35 lessons of the University of Oregon program.

Throughout the study, an individual knowledgeable in curriculum implementation and the technology was available to assist teachers with questions about the program, particularly the logistical ones (e.g., how to operate the remote control device and where to position the monitor for optimal viewing). Teachers voluntarily asked for assistance or feedback. The facilitator was often able to use "How am I doing?" situations for constructive feedback. Some teachers asked the facilitator for assistance four or five times in the 6 weeks of implementation; others needed help only once to deal with specific technical problems or mechanical problems with the videodisc technology.

Measures

Measures of Teachers' Implementation of the Innovation

Each teacher was observed for two consecutive lessons during the 4th or 5th week of implementation. The observers were two researchers, one of whom was an expert in the program and the other an experienced educational consultant who was highly familiar with the content and teaching style of the videodisc curriculum. Implementation was assessed with the Videodisc Implementation Observational Scale. Table 1 presents the specific items on the scale. Observers completed this form after a full 45-min observation. The first 4 items were yes/no items; the latter 5 items were completed on a 1 to 3 scale, (1 was never, 2 sometimes, 3 always). Interobserver reliability for the observational system was .87.

TABLE 1 Videodisc Observation Items

Issue	Mean Percent of Observed Behaviors	
1. Teacher demonstrates familiarity with the disc player and its operations.	92.2	
2. Students are seated so that the screen is clearly visible.	100.0	
3. The teacher uses the program the entire period (at least 45 min.).	66.6[a]	
4. Teacher uses the Check for Student Progress (guided practice) aspect of the lesson at designated times.	100.0	

Issue	Mean Rating on 1-3-Point Scale	(SD)
5. The teacher provides specific remediation activities at designated points in the videodisc lesson.	2.66	(.52)
6. The teacher gives students sufficient time to work and check their answers.	2.83	(.19)
7. The teacher proceeds through the lesson at a brisk pace.	2.58	(.49)
8. The students respond as a group to the narrator's questions.	2.00	(.35)
9. The teacher circulates around the room monitoring students.	2.86	(.24)

Note: N = 7 teachers, 2 observations per teacher.
[a]*Not applicable for 2 observations.*

The observational system also included direct counts of several variables. The observers recorded (a) the number of explanations teachers provided that were consistent with the language and terminology of the videodisc curriculum; (b) the number of explanations that used contradictory language or confusing language; and (c) all instances of teacher praise and criticism. Every 5 min they recorded the percentage of students academically engaged and those off task. Finally, they collected the daily seatwork, which the observer scored to obtain a measure of student success rate.

Teachers' Reactions and Perceptions: Semi-structured Interviews

At the end of the study, a semi-structured 40–50-min interview was administered to all teachers by the researchers. The 17-item interview contained questions with yes/no answers, such as "Do you find the videodisc itself hard to use?" and "Does it end up slowing down progress?" as well as more open-ended questions, such as "What are the best features of the program?" and "What are the major ways that it is different from how you taught fractions before?" Finally, researchers asked teachers to give an overall assessment on a scale from 1 to 5 of the experience of using the videodisc program to teach fractions to these students (see Tables 2 and 3).

TABLE 2 Teachers' Perceptions of Use of Interactive Videodisc to Teach Fractions

Perception	Percent of Teachers Who Answered Yes
A. Technical Issues	
1. Do you find the videodisc itself hard to use?	0
2. Do you have problems using the remote control?	14
3. Do you get confused trying to make the corrrect choices at the decision menu when it asks if 1/5 of the students missed the problems?	14
4. How about remediation after quizzes?	43
B. Utility of Remediation and Guided Practice in the Videodisc	
5. Do you think it helps students master the material?	86
6. Does it end up slowing down progress?	14
7. Do you use these frequently to play back chapters that the students need additional practice on?	43
C. Overall Perceptions	
8. Do students participate more than they did in your regular curriculum?	86
9. Do the students seem to be mastering the skills?	100
10. How would you rate your experience with the program overall on a scale of 1 to 5, with 5 being the highest and 1 being the lowest?	4.5

Transfer of Training Following the Videodisc Experience

A final concern of this study was what effect, if any, the experience of using the videodisc would have on the instructional practices of the seven participating teachers when they returned to conventional curriculum materials. To gauge the effect of the program, teachers were observed teaching the target class three times before the intervention and three times 2 weeks following their use of the *Mastering Fractions* program.

During the observed lessons, teachers used conventional print curricula, as well as teacher-developed dittos. The observational scale used selected variables from the research on effective mathematics instruction for low-achieving students (Good et al., 1983). The list of observed variables is found in Table 4. This observational system was developed 9 months before the study began.

Impact of the Program on Students: Achievement and Reactions

Students were tested before and 30 days after implementation on a curriculum-referenced test that covered all major topics in the curriculum—the meaning of fractions, equiva-

TABLE 3   Open-Ended Questions

Question and Response[a]	Percent of Teachers Responding
1. What are the best features of the program?	
A. Graphics as a means of demonstrating concepts	100
B. Special effects	86
C. Design of the curriculum/orchestration of skills and activities	57
D. Remediation	29
2. What are its weakest features?	
A. Too juvenile or oriented to young students	14
B. Too much paperwork	43
3. What are the biggest ways that it is different from how you taught fractions before?	
A. Things are broken into smaller steps	71
B. More monitoring of student work than before	43
4. What changes have you seen in the students? Improved work habits	86
5. What kind of future do you think something like the videodisc has in the schools? Great	100
6. Do you like the way everything is laid out for you, the way everything is structured?	100
7. Some people have reacted to this kind of use of the videodisc by saying that it will "replace" the teacher. What do you think about this kind of reaction?	
A. It won't replace the teacher.	86
B. You always need a human factor, someone to make decisions.	43

[a]*A "key word" approach was used to classify responses.*

**TABLE 4   *Transfer of Teaching Skills:
Results of Classroom Observations***

Issue	Before Videodisc		After Videodisc	
	Mean	SD	Mean	SD
1. Number of problems modeled**	.43	.93	2.43	2.17
2. Number of guided practice problems*	3.14	2.87	9.79	4.40
3. Number of product questions	13.67	7.38	12.32	4.13
4. Number of process questions***	2.83	2.08	1.65	.36
5. Number of logistical or nonacademic questions*	4.73	1.18	2.02	1.80
6. Number of probing questions during corrections	9.14	5.50	10.21	4.59
7. Amount of praising	14.96	6.31	14.84	5.52
8. Amount of criticisms	1.64	1.92	2.01	1.08
9. Success rate on independent work*	68.75	11.45	83.04	5.56

*$p < .01$. **$p < .05$. ***$p < .15$.

lence of fractions, and computations involving fractions with like and unlike denominators. The coefficient alpha reliability of this test is .98 (Kelly, Gersten, & Carnine, 1990).

In addition, a research assistant interviewed the students during the final week of implementation. This 5–10 min interview consisted of seven questions. The interviewer asked students to describe their impressions of the program and the experience of learning with the interactive videodisc medium.

RESULTS

Teachers' Implementation of the Innovation: Observational Rating Scale Findings

Table 1 shows observed level of videodisc implementation by the end of the 4th week of the study. Results on the first four items were yes/no. Items 5 through 9 were completed on a 3-point scale, where 1 was never, 2 sometimes, and 3 always.

After 4 weeks of use, teachers were implementing most major components of the program at an acceptable level. They appeared familiar and comfortable with the remote control device and the basic operation of the videodisc player. All teachers used the CSPs (i.e., guided practice) component daily. Students were seated so that they could see the screen. There was only one area in which teachers demonstrated problems: Two teachers did spend part of each period with other math activities (such as math fact games) or spent time in nonacademic activities.

The lower half of Table 1 shows the results of rating scale items. These address the more subtle and sophisticated instructional techniques. Most of the time (mean of 2.68 on a 3-point scale), the teachers provided the remediation activities specified in the program at the designated points. Teachers virtually always gave students time to check their work when the answers to problem sets were presented on the screen; and, as instructed, the teachers spent a considerable amount of time circulating around the room to monitor independent student work.

The videodisc procedures for guided practice, careful monitoring of students' independent work, and provision of brief remedial mini-lessons whenever students experienced difficulty all appear to be implemented at an extremely high level. Overall, the observation data indicate that teachers tended to exhibit the research-based effective teaching techniques that were intended by the program developers.

Direct Observational Measures

One concern, before the study began, was the extent to which teachers would provide explanations of fractions concepts in their own words, a practice that might contradict the consistent wording used in the videodisc curriculum and, thus, confuse the students. Expert judgment was used to determine the consistency of the teacher explanations to that of the program, and the mean number of consistent explanations for any given period was 8.7, whereas the mean number of inconsistent explanations was 3.4. This ratio of consistency to inconsistency is approximately 2.5 : 1. Though the mean number of inconsistent explanations is potentially troublesome, it is still surprising how much more often the teachers explained fractions concepts in the same way as the program, especially considering the fact that all of the teachers had been teaching fractions in a more traditional manner for many years.

Finally, evidence from the classroom observations showed that the videodisc program was used in a noncritical atmosphere. Average number of teacher criticisms to students (e.g., insults, expressions of disgust or anger, harsh feedback) was approximately one per period.

Teachers' Perceptions of the Videodisc Experience: Findings from Semi-Structured Interviews

Table 2 presents the results for the questions with fairly clear-cut yes/no responses. Table 3 uses a key word method to summarize results on the more open-ended questions.

Technical and Logistical Issues

All seven teachers found the interactive videodisc easy to use. Considering the complexity of most educational technologies, and the fact that only one of the teachers had previous experience using any type of educational technology up to this point, this is an unusual finding. In one teacher's words, it was only a bit more difficult to use than a home VCR.

Teachers experienced some implementation problems, however. One of the seven had problems with the remote control (item 2). A few teachers were initially confused with the logistics of using the decision menus for remediation and review. They indicated that these problems diminished with practice. By the end of the study, all felt comfortable with the procedure.

Utility of Remediation Activities and Guided Practice (CSPs)

All teachers but one thought the extensive use of remediation and guided practice incorporated into the program helped students really master the material. One of the seven felt the extensive use of remediation and guided practice slowed down overall class progress slightly, however. This is a constant dilemma for those employing any type of instructional model combining mastery learning and group instruction.

Three of the seven teachers needed to frequently play back lesson segments for review and remediation purposes. For the other four, the pace of the curriculum was such that remediation activities were rarely needed. Thus, even though the majority of the teachers liked the concept of guided practice checks every 5 min or so, not all the teachers had an opportunity to really try them out. The observers also reported (Table 1) that teachers were implementing the guided practice and remediation segments properly.

Perceptions of the Overall Utility of the Videodisc Curriculum

All seven special education teachers felt that the students were mastering the skills. As mentioned earlier, these teachers had previously found fractions one of the most difficult topics in mathematics to teach and were dissatisfied with most existing curricula. All but one of the teachers felt that students participated more in the lesson with the videodisc than with conventional instruction. In years past, many students had failed to learn several of the major topics covered. During the open-ended segment of the interviews, teachers indicated the specific strategies that they found to be successful—the use of a number line, the instructional strategy for finding least common denominator, and the teaching of improper fractions. Finally, teachers were asked to provide a global rating of the videodisc curriculum on a 1 to 5 scale. The mean score was 4.5, an above-average assessment for an innovative practice.

Results on Open-Ended Items

Table 3 presents a brief summary of how teachers responded to the open-ended questions. They unanimously found the graphics and special effects to be the best features of the curriculum. They all mentioned how the computer graphics could visually demonstrate relationships and concepts much more elegantly, with many more examples, and much more quickly than they could with a chalkboard or colored paper and scissors. They also expressed that the students seemed much more interested and attentive to the bright colors and visual excitement of the graphic displays.

More than half the teachers also were sensitive to the design of the curriculum. They talked about the orchestration of skills across many lessons, the range of activities incorporated into each lesson, and how this curriculum was designed so differently from conventional texts, which tend to focus on only one topic per lesson with minimal review. They pointed out that the constant review was essential for low-achieving students, and that the variety of activities with a lesson helped keep the student interested.

The teachers generally felt this type of subtle orchestration of skills would be extremely difficult, if not impossible, without the aid of technology. Finally, two of the seven teachers mentioned the provision for remediation as one of the best features of the curriculum.

One factor emerged as a weak feature of the program. Three of the seven teachers felt there was too much paperwork involved in the rather complex mastery learning system that involved daily checks of independent seatwork, as well as group checks of daily quiz performance.

We next asked teachers to indicate how teaching with the interactive videodisc curriculum was different from their conventional curriculum. The majority of the teachers pinpointed that things were broken into much smaller steps than is typical. The teachers cited the advantage of such an approach for teaching low-performing students.

Several of the teachers also felt that with this curriculum, they were able to monitor students' work more frequently and more precisely than before. They talked about how their role had shifted from an individual who primarily explains and demonstrates new concepts to one who primarily makes sure students understand the new material and helps those students with problems. All seven teachers thought the interactive videodisc had great potential for future use in both special education and regular classroom instruction, particularly in the areas of mathematics and science.

The videodisc curriculum is much more directive about teacher behavior than is conventional instruction; and the role of the teacher is much more precisely defined. We inquired how teachers felt about this. All seven teachers liked the way everything was structured and laid out for them. They all felt that as a result of the videodisc, they did "less talking" and explaining. As one teacher put it, "To be honest, I used to get only 15 minutes of instruction out of a regular period [45 minutes]. With this program, I get 45 minutes of teaching."

When some individuals first see the videodisc program, they think that teachers won't like it, that, essentially, it replaces the teacher. We asked the teachers whether they felt "replaced" by the videodisc. All but one said no. They saw their role as providers of feedback and support as essential. They also saw the importance of what several called "the human factor," the need for an adult to make instructional decisions.

Transfer of Training Following the Videodisc Program

Observers documented teacher performance across a variety of effective teaching behaviors. Table 4 shows performance on these behaviors before and after the intervention.

Perhaps the most evident and important effect of the program was the change in the number of problems modeled by the teacher before assigning independent work and the number of guided practice problems. The videodisc curriculum stressed the use of (a) presentation of numerous models of each problem type, and (b) the use of guided practice before asking students to work on their own. Teachers incorporated this approach into their day-to-day teaching.

A correlated t-test showed significant increases in the modeling of strategies ($t = 2.13$, $df = 6$) and use of guided practice ($t = 4.27$, $df = 6$). This growth corresponded with a dramatic improvement in student accuracy on independent work, from a mean of 68.75% before implementation to a mean of 83.04% after implementation ($t = 3.03$). One of the primary features of the videodisc program is ensuring a high student success rate through step-by-step instruction. The fact that this carried over to conventional instruction is a very positive sign.

There appeared to be little change in the number or type of questions asked, with one exception. Teachers asked significantly fewer logistical/noninstructional questions ($t = 3.46$, $df = 6$). Teachers continued to conduct their classrooms in a cordial manner, with a relatively high ratio of praise to criticisms (approximately 4 : 1).

Effects of the Videodisc Program on Student Achievement

A criterion-reference test developed by the program writers was used as a pretest and posttest measure of achievement. Table 5 shows the mean pretest, posttest, and gain scores for the students, with fewer than five absences during the course of the study. The mean pretest performance was quite low, 29.4 ($SD = 9.38$). The mean posttest was considerably higher (mean = 79.0, $SD = 10.08$). This resulted in an overall mean gain score of 49.7 ($SD = 8.81$).

Using a score of 80% on the posttest as an acceptable level of performance, almost two thirds of the students (64%) reached or exceeded criterion performance on the posttest. These data reveal consistent, marked improvement across the seven secondary special education classrooms. The mean level of performance is somewhat less than what was found in the previous, more controlled experimental study of the fractions curriculum (i.e., Kelly et al., 1986), where the mean was 95%. However, the current findings are at a reasonable performance level, especially considering that these were all special education students.

Observational data indicate that students were engaged in academic activities at a reasonable rate—with an on-task rate of 78% ($SD = 4.4$). This was only a modest increase from the engagement rate observed prior to instruction of 75.5%. However, observational notes indicated that there were times when several students in the group would be waiting for others to finish up their guided practice exercises.

Student seatwork was collected after each observation. Students tended to be quite successful in their independent work. On the average, the student success rate for independent seatwork was 82% ($SD = 7.37$).

TABLE 5 *Mean Videodisc Achievement Results for Students with Mild Disabilities*

Teacher	N	Mean Pretest	(SD)	Mean Posttest	(SD)	Gain
1	7	35	(21.2)	68	(18.2)	33
2	6	43	(21.9)	87	(8.8)	44
3	7	15	(20.7)	64	(19.9)	49
4	6	33	(18.6)	85	(11.8)	52
5	7	29	(10.3)	84	(7.3)	55
6	7	20	(14.8)	75	(14.1)	55
7	6	31	(18.3)	90	(7.1)	59
Total	57	29.4	—	79	—	49.6

Student Interviews

Table 6 presents the main questions and open-ended responses from an individually conducted, 10-min interview. Students were consistently positive about the program, not only in their general reactions to the curriculum, but as a way to learn math. Almost 90% of the students felt more self-assured in their ability to work fraction problems, and almost the same percentage would like to continue to learn fractions in this way. Researchers were particularly concerned with how students would feel about answering aloud. Less than one third of the students had a negative reaction to answering aloud, whereas over half had a neutral reaction. This kind of reaction corresponds to the observational data, which revealed that teachers typically had students answer aloud only some of the time. It is difficult to say at this point how important this practice is at the secondary level.

One final concern was the amount of step-by-step instruction that was built into the program. There is a considerable amount of cumulative review and additional practice

TABLE 6   Student Interview Data (N = 57)

Question and Response	Percent of Students Responding
1. In general, what was your reaction to the videodisc math program?	
Negative to neutral	14.1
OK to good	78.9
Loved it	3.5
2. Do you think that it is a good way to teach math?	
Yes	96.5
No	3.5
3. What did you like best about the videodisc program?	
The graphics and use of a TV	38.5
The way the teacher taught	19.3
It wasn't boring	12.3
4. What didn't you like about the program?	
It was OK the way it was	47.7
Too much writing	14.0
Too much repetition	14.0
5. How did you feel about answering aloud so often?	
Negative	29.8
Neutral to OK	52.7
Good	17.5
6. Do you think that you know how to do fractions now?	
Yes	89.4
No	5.3
Not sure	5.3
7. Would you like to continue to learn fractions this way?	
Yes	87.7
No	12.3

problems for students who fall below criterion on unit tests or guided practice problems. Approximately one sixth of the students thought that there was too much repetition, while almost half thought it was acceptable the way it was. The only other common concern was the amount of writing, not only the copying of problems from the screen, but the worksheets and tests that accompanied the program.

DISCUSSION

The unexpectedly positive reaction to the videodisc program can be traced to several sources. First, as an innovation, it met explicit teacher needs. It provided a better, more effective way to teach fractions to secondary students with learning disabilities. All teachers felt that the new curriculum was more effective than anything they had used previously and that most of their students were actually understanding the concepts.

The National Assessment of Educational Progress (see National Council of Teachers of Mathematics, 1988) has consistently shown that many secondary students never learn fractions. For most of the students in the study, this was the third time they had been taught a unit on fractions. The fact that the majority were finally succeeding in learning these difficult concepts was a major refrain of teachers' interviews. Fractions instruction had been a difficult instructional area for these teachers for many years. As the research of Guskey (1984) and Berman and McLaughlin (1976) has found, teachers' attitudes toward new instructional practices are largely shaped by how well the new program succeeds with their students, especially students who are difficult to teach, such as those in the current study.

Overall, one positive effect of the videodisc implementation was a transfer of teaching skills to conventional practices. After using the program, teachers tended to model more problems and provide more guided practice. Their teaching styles tended to become more interactive. Some researchers in the area of school change have argued that this transfer should be a main goal of training in a new strategy or instructional technique (Showers et al., 1987).

In this study, teachers' enthusiasm was appreciably higher, and more consistent, than that found by the earlier work on research-based practices, such as mastery learning (Duckworth & Fielding, 1985; Guskey, 1984) and direct instruction (Gersten, Carnine, Zoref, and Cronin, 1986). Several factors might help explain this finding.

First, teachers were being asked to use the videodisc for just one subject area and for only one or two periods a day. The relatively small scope of the intervention reduced stress and enhanced the likelihood of initial success (Fullan, 1982; Huberman & Miles, 1984). Furthermore, a modest amount of knowledgeable, follow-up technical assistance was available. This seemed to make a considerable difference in the level of implementation (Cox 1983; Huberman & Miles; Loucks & Zacchei, 1983; Showers et al., 1987). The participating teachers repeatedly commented on how they enjoyed the fact that a facilitator was available to answer questions, to give them a sense of how they were using the program, and to clarify why the program was designed the way it was.

In addition, it is evident that all teachers found the videodisc technology easy to use. After 1 or 2 days of some minor confusion (e.g., how to use particular remote control buttons or how to read decision menus), teachers felt comfortable with the remote control device and the basic operation of the program.

Finally, several of the teachers indicated how the videodisc freed them to perform other teaching functions with more precision. They were able to monitor carefully how all students were doing; provide praise and encouragement to students for effort; or provide brief, focused tutorial sessions. The structure of the videodisc allowed them to teach in a more interactive fashion and to more closely follow the model of teaching that research has found to be effective, particularly for low achieving students (Brophy & Good, 1986).

Relationship to Executive Functions of Teaching

The main reason for the lack of serious implementation problems may be that the interactive videodisc curriculum was designed to be consonant with conventional classroom organization and structure. In their review of the research on educational innovation, Loucks and Zacchei (1983) concluded that educational innovations are much more likely to succeed if they do not conflict radically with traditional organization of classrooms and the instructional strategies teachers employ. The videodisc lessons fit traditional ideas of what a class routine is like and what teaching is like.

Teachers still taught the entire group, and still were able to perform typical teaching functions—monitoring seatwork, checking for understanding, motivating students, and providing individual tutorials to students who were experiencing difficulties. Whereas many other technological innovations call for radical restructuring of the teachers' role and the mode of instructional delivery, the videodisc curriculum accentuates or improves on the existing method of teaching. In a sense, videodisc technology is more consistent with the culture of the classroom that Cuban (1986) describes than, for example, the banks of microcomputers in a typical computer lab. The role of a teacher and the nature of his or her relationships to students are radically different in a computer lab from those relationships in a conventional classroom.

Though the role the teacher played in this study was within the bounds of typical classroom instruction, there were appreciable shifts. Teachers focused almost exclusively on monitoring student progress, providing support, and providing remediation. The videodisc software did all the initial demonstrations of new concepts; presented the practice examples; and showed students how to solve problems, how to estimate, and how to check their work. Teachers did not seem to resent these shifts.

During the interviews, teachers were asked to reflect on how this approach compared with conventional practices. On several occasions, they referred to the efficient and effective management of time and the way the curriculum broke instruction into discrete, well-sequenced steps. Many teachers described how they would incorporate segments of the program—especially the use of a number line—into the way they would teach fractions again. In fact, the observational data revealed that, at the conclusion of the study, teachers did incorporate some of the videodisc's practices into their conventional teaching.

Much of the data points to issues raised by Berliner (1985) in his essay on executive functions of teaching. Day-to-day instruction is a complicated, all-consuming activity. Rarely do teachers have the time or resources to do one aspect of teaching well—be it classroom management, individual tutoring, modeling new concepts to the class as a whole, or giving corrective feedback. To the extent that technology-based programs such as the one used in this study can relieve teachers of some of their many obligations and, at the same time, provide expertise in one area, the quality of classroom instruction can be dramatically affected.

In no way does this imply that videodisc instruction should be used in all subject areas, as a constant companion throughout the day. Also, this particular program was unusual insofar as it had been empirically validated in controlled settings prior to this study. A recent comparison of videodisc programs (Woodward, 1990) has strongly suggested major differences in the effectiveness of this kind of technology in teaching content area material. Principles of curriculum design are clearly a major factor that influence educational outcomes.

Videodiscs, then, are *not* the hidden remedy to a flagging computer revolution in the schools. Rather, as a modest innovation that blends the power of a particular technology, especially its graphics capabilities, with carefully designed instruction, videodisc technology is a partial solution to the problem of effectively teaching a difficult subject area like fractions. It can not only free the teacher to perform other executive functions, but it can provide high-quality instruction in the mode of curriculum presentation. Rather than pitting instructional technology against traditional practices, the technology contributes within the framework of Berliner's executive functions.

REFERENCES

Becker, H. (1987). Using computers for instruction. *Byte, 12*(2), 149–162.

Becker, H., & Sterling, C. (1987). Equity in school computer use: National data and neglected considerations. *Journal of Educational Computing Research, 3*(3), 289–311.

Berliner, D. (1985). The executive functions of teaching. In J. Osborn, P. Wilson, & R. Anderson (Eds.), *Reading education: Foundations for a literate America* (pp. 87–108). Lexington, MA: Lexington Books.

Berman, P., & McLaughlin, M. (1976). Implementation of educational innovations. *Educational Forum, 40*(3), 345–370.

Blaschke, C. (1985) Technology trends in special education. *T.H.E. Journal, 14*(2), 73–77.

Bork, A. (1981). Educational technology and the future. *Journal of Educational Technology Systems, 10*(1), 3–19.

Brophy, J., & Good, T. L. (1986). Teacher and student achievement. In M. Wittrock (Ed.), *The third handbook of research on teaching* (pp. 328–375). New York: Macmillan.

Buckeley, W. (1988, June 16). Computers failing as teaching aids. *The Wall Street Journal*, p. 15.

Cohen, D. (1987). Educational technology, policy, and practice. *Educational Evaluation and Policy Analysis, 9*(2), 153–170.

Cox, P. (1983). Complementary roles in successful change. *Educational Leadership, 41*(3), 10–13.

Cuban, L. (1986). *Teachers and machines: The classroom use of technology since 1920.* New York: Teachers College Press.

Duckworth, K., & Fielding, G. (1985). *Management implications of teachers' design and use of tests in high school classes.* (Final Report to the National Institute of Education.) Eugene: University of Oregon, Center for Education Policy and Management.

Fullan, M. (1982). *The meaning of educational change*. New York: Teachers College Press.

Gersten, R., Carnine, D., Zoref, L., & Cronin, D. (1986). A multifaceted study of change in seven inner-city schools. *Elementary School Journal, 86*(3), 257–276.

Good, T. L., Grouws, D. A., & Ebmeier, H. (1983). *Active mathematics teaching*. New York: Longman.

Guskey, T. R. (1984). The influence of change in the instructional effectiveness upon the affective characteristics of teachers. *American Educational Research Journal, 21*(2), 245–259.

Hasselbring, T., Sherwood, B., & Bransford, J. (1986). *An evaluation of the* Mastering Fractions *level-one instructional videodisc program*. Nashville: George Peabody College of Vanderbilt University, The Learning Technology Center.

Hofmeister, A. (1984). Special education in the information age. *Peabody Journal of Education, 62*(1), 5–22.

Huberman, A., & Miles, M. (1984). *Innovation up close: How school improvement works*. New York: Plenum.

Kelly, B., Carnine, D. W., Gersten, R., & Grossen, B. (1986). The effectiveness of videodisc instruction in teaching fractions to learning handicapped and remedial high school students. *Journal of Special Education Technology, 8*(2) 5–17.

Kelly, B., Gersten, R., & Carnine, D. (1990). Student error patterns as a function of curriculum design: Teaching fractions to remedial high school students and high school students with learning disabilities. *Journal of Learning Disabilities, 23* (1), 23–29.

Leinhardt, G., & Smith, D. (1985). Expertise in mathematics instruction: Subject matter knowledge. *Journal of Educational Psychology, 77*(3), 247–271.

Loucks, S. F., & Zacchei, D. A. (1983). Applying our findings to today's innovations. *Educational Leadership, 41*(3), 28–31.

National Council of Teachers of Mathematics. (1988). NAEP: Results of the fourth mathematics assessment. *Educational Week*, 28–29.

Okolo, C., Rieth, H., Polsgrove, L., Bahr, C., & Yerkes, K. (1985). *An analysis of secondary special education teachers' attitudes toward computer-based instruction* (Research Rep. No. 103). Nashville, TN: Vanderbilt University.

Optical Data. (1988). *Windows on science* [videodisc program]. Orangewood, NJ: Author.

Papert, S. (1980). *Mindstorms*. New York: Basic Books.

Rieth, H., Bahr, C., Okolo, C., Polsgrove, L., & Eckert, R. (1988). An analysis of the secondary special education classroom ecology. *Journal of Educational Computing Research, 4*(4), 425–441.

Rothman, R. (1988, April 13). 'Computer competence' still rare among students, assessment finds. *Education Week*, pp. 1, 20.

Semmel, M., & Lieber, J. (1986). Computer applications in instruction. *Focus on Exceptional Children, 18*(9), 1–12.

Showers, B., Joyce, B., & Bennett, B. (1987). Synthesis of research on staff development: A framework for future study and state-of-the-art analysis. *Educational Leadership, 45*(2), 11–23.

Snider, W. (1986, January 11). Computers: A change in course? *Education Week*, pp. 1, 14.

Systems Impact, Inc. (1986). *Mastering fractions* [videodisc program]. Washington, DC: Author.

West, P. (1988, October 24). Chiefs eye barriers to technology. *Education Week*, p. 5.

Wolcott, H. (1981). Is there life after technology? Some lessons on change. *Educational Technology, 5*, 24–28.

Woodward, J. (1990). *Causal discourse and its effect on recall and understanding in science* (Tech. Rep. #12). Eugene: University of Oregon, Instructional Research.

John Woodward is a senior research associate and Russell Gersten (CEC OR Federation) is a professor in the College of Education at the University of Oregon, Eugene.

Part Two:
Emerging Challenges

*T*HERE ARE A NUMBER of emerging challenges that special education professionals and their colleagues in general education must face today. Perhaps the greatest challenge for both professional fields is the changing conceptualization of knoweldge in the social sciences. As the lead article in this section explains, the redefinition of social scientific knowledge is creating a crisis in professions like special education and general education, which base their knowledge, skills, and practices on theoretical knowledge produced by the social sciences. Although on the surface this has negative implications for both fields, it also opens up the possibility of reformulating special education and general education theory and practice in ways that may permit public education to serve the needs of all students more adequately.

Another emerging challenge for special and general educators is the existence of students who present instructional problems that special education has not had to respond to in the past. Some students apparently cannot sustain attention long enough to acquire the information necessary to achieve specified outcomes at age or grade levels. Others have problems associated with traumatic brain injury. Brain injuries may have clear origins if they result from automobile, bicycle, and skateboarding accidents, but other, subtle types of brain injury may accumulate over the years from physical abuse within the home or school setting. Whether the head injury is caused by a single traumatic event or a series of events over time, the students present instructional challenges that general and special educators have not encountered before. Nevertheless, these students have unique needs that require specially designed instruction and are accommodated under the legislation serving students with disabilities.

Many will not see the least restrictive environment for students with severe and complex disabilities as relevant to emerging challenges because it has been the subject of ongoing debate. On the other hand, the preference for including students with severe disabilities in general education classrooms is becoming stronger as time goes by. Therefore, special educators will have to determine effective ways of including students with severe disabilities into general education classrooms that may not provide the curriculum they need. In this sense, special educators are on the spot to determine what parts of the ongoing curriculum can be inclusive and what aspects of the curriculum have to be parallel.

In this emerging challenge, professionals clearly must differentiate the intensity of instruction needed and the site in which that instruction is delivered. Too often we have assumed that intensity requires a similar level of restrictiveness or removal from more regular settings for instruction. That is probably an error of judgment that should not be replicated as we move into the next century. In terms of instructional services for students with severe disabilities, instructional intensity can be at a high level in a general education classroom. One need not move a student who needs intensive services into the most restrictive setting to provide it. Because special educators are becoming more and more aware of the importance of consultation and collaboration among colleagues and traveling support services to students' home schools, the massing of large numbers of people under a single roof to accommodate students with severe disabilities is no longer necessary.

Clearly, this is an emerging challenge and one that will be the subject of heated debate in the coming years. One can only hope that this debate will generate new knowledge and professional skills to serve students with severe disabilities. Obviously these students are few in number, but they reflect many, many needs as compared to the population of students most special educators serve today.

Another emerging challenge, one of perhaps more significant numbers than students with attention deficit disorders, traumatic brain injury, and severe disabilities, is presented by those who have chronic and clinically severe depression. Too often special educators have thought that depression is a condition of adults. In that thinking, we have seriously ignored the implications of depression upon children's ability to adjust to home, community, and school expectations. Depression is extremely debilitating because it consumes energy that otherwise could be devoted to learning new skills and new ways to be independent. Professional special educators clearly must be alert to the presence of depression, be able to identify it, assess its acuteness and chronicity, and find ways to deal with it in a constructive manner before it controls the student's entire life.

All of these emerging challenges require special educators to reach out to colleagues in other professions and work together in teams that represent a truly interdisciplinary concept. This concept requires more than just sharing information among disciplines— as important as that might be as a first step toward a full and comprehensive intervention program for students who may require it. Because of economic issues and the availability of professionals these teams will have to commit to sharing not only knowledge but also skills with each other. The nurse will have to share some skills with the special educator. The special educator may become an expert in feeding procedures so the nutritionist will not have to be present every time a student needs to be fed. The physical therapist may have to teach some skills to the teacher and paraprofessional so physical therapy activities can be carried on more than once or twice a week. These examples illustrate the multidisciplinary approach necessary for students included in the current emerging challenges to be successful in the schools.

Special educators must consider many emerging challenges. The articles in this section represent a few of the more important ones. There are others. For example, how much more can special education expand to meet instructional and related needs of additional children who will be classified as disabled? The answer will require in-depth analyses from many perspectives. One is obviously economic: program costs. Another is public policy: a commitment to provide appropriate education to all children. Another is systemic: an organized way of providing learning experiences that do not require unnecessary duplication of intensive professional time and effort.

The articles in this section represent emerging challenges. We believe they will enable our colleagues to go beyond them and identify and respond to other challenges in the future. These confrontations produce program changes, most of which keep special educators at the front of functional reform efforts.

○9○

Because professional knowledge is grounded in the theoretical knowledge of the social sciences, a reconceptualization of the nature and limits of social scientific knowledge over the past thirty years has thrown professional fields like special education into a state of crisis. Although a crisis in professional knowledge carries a negative connotation, the author explains that it is a necessary prelude to the growth of knowledge and progress in scientific and professional communities. After tracing the theoretical grounding of traditional special education knowledge, he describes the revolutionary developments that are redefining social scientific knowledge, characterizes an alternative form of knowledge for grounding special education theory and practice, and recommends a mode of inquiry for achieving the necessary reorientation of the field.

The Crisis in Special Education Knowledge: A Perspective on Perspective

Thomas M. Skrtic

The profession of special education is composed of a number of subfields that are organized around categories of exceptionality or disability. As such, each subfield is premised on a somewhat unique body of professional knowledge that reflects presumed differences among types of exceptionality. Nevertheless, behind the surface differences each sub-field subscribes to a common foundation of basic special education knowledge. What is of interest here is this foundation of basic professional knowledge, which I will refer to simply as special education knowledge.

A major challenge in discussing special education knowledge is deciding on whose version of it to accept as the genuine article. To draw a crude analogy, asking the special education community about the nature of its professional knowledge is like asking a school of fish about the nature of water. Special educators rarely can be depended upon

The original version of this article, which appeared in March of 1986 as Volume 18, Number 7, of *Focus on Exceptional Children* (pp. 1-16), has been edited somewhat in the interest of clarity, and a new concluding section has been added that relates the original argument to the contemporary situation in the field.

for an adequate answer because special education knowledge is so basic to them that it is largely taken for granted. Thus, it will be helpful to bring a number of perspectives to bear upon the subject, which I will do by considering some of the criticisms of traditional special education knowledge. As we will see, there is no shortage of such criticism.

Like all professional knowledge, special education knowledge is premised on the positivist theory of knowledge, which yields the following hierarchical model of professional knowledge.

1. An *underlying discipline* or *basic science* component upon which the practice rests or from which it is developed.
2. An *applied science* or "engineering" component from which many of the day-to-day diagnostic procedures and problem-solutions are derived.
3. A *skills and attitudinal* component that concerns the actual performance of services to the client, using the underlying basic and applied knowledge. (Schein, 1972, p. 43)

According to the model, special education knowledge is grounded in the *theoretical knowledge* of an underlying discipline or basic science. At the applied science level of the model, theoretical knowledge is translated into *applied knowledge*, or the models and procedures that guide and shape special education practice. Finally, special education's theoretically grounded applied knowledge yields *practical knowledge*, which is transmitted to special education practitioners—in the form of skills and attitudes—through an extended program of professional education. The performance of special education professional services to clients is based on practical knowledge, which is conceptualized as the result of applying theoretical knowledge to the problems of special education practice.

Historically, there have been two general types of criticism of special education knowledge—practical and theoretical. Practical criticism refers to criticism of special education practical knowledge and applied knowledge—that is, both the skills and attitudes of special education practitioners and the models and procedures upon which they are premised. Theoretical criticism refers to criticism of special education theoretical knowledge and applied knowledge—that is, both to the field's models and procedures and the theories in which they are grounded.

PRACTICAL CRITICISM OF SPECIAL EDUCATION KNOWLEDGE

Of the two general types of criticism, practical criticism has been more visible and has had a greater impact on the way special education services are delivered to students. Practical criticism, centered on the actual practice of special education, has been mounted by parents, consumers and advocates, and, to some extent, by special educators themselves (e.g., Dunn, 1968; Blatt & Kaplan, 1966). Historically, critical debate has revolved around the relationship between regular and special education in terms of the identification, placement, and education of students with disabilities. In fact, much of today's special education practice has evolved as a response to yesterday's practical criticism. Although this mutually-shaping relationship between practical criticism and changes in practice can be traced over the entire history of special education, its most notable phase was the period from the early 1960s to the mid-1970s.

At the height of the social-political ferment of the 1960s, parents and special education consumers and advocates used the period's increased sensitivity to human and civil rights to mount a case against special education as it was practiced at that time. This particular round of practical criticism led to victories in courtrooms and statehouses across the country and eventually in the U.S. Congress, which ultimately redefined special education practice under the rubric of the statutory mandate of Public Law 94-142, The Education for All Handicapped Children Act of 1975 (EHA).

The EHA mandates a free, appropriate public education for all students with disabilities in the least restrictive—most integrated—environment possible. It changed special education practice by changing its structural relationship to regular education and by extending to students and their parents certain constitutional rights and procedural safeguards, including due process of law. Of course, the EHA did not end critical commentary on special education practice. Public debate and legal action over the precise meaning of "appropriate education" and "least restrictive environment," among other concepts, have continued over the 10 years of the law's implementation (Turnbull, 1986). But the point is that practical criticism led to changes in special education practice. It is important to note, however, that the changes brought about by the EHA did not result from theoretical criticism. The law and the changes in practice that have resulted from it were the product of practical criticism, that is, moral, ethical, legal, and political arguments against special education models, procedures, and practices (Ballard-Campbell & Semmel, 1981; Biklen, 1985), and not of arguments against the theoretical knowledge in which they were grounded.

THEORETICAL CRITICISM OF SPECIAL EDUCATION KNOWLEDGE

Ultimately, theoretical criticism of special education knowledge is also criticism of special education practice. But, as I am using the term, it is essentially criticism of the field's grounding theoretical knowledge and the manner in which it is used at the applied science level of the profession. Thus, the targets of theoretical criticism are special education applied researchers and policymakers at universities and at all levels of government. Whereas practical criticism of special education has been mounted primarily by parents, consumers, and advocates, theoretical criticism largely has come from social scientists who have made one of three claims: that special education is atheoretical, that it confounds theory, or that it is premised on the wrong theory.

The Atheoretical Claim

The first type of theoretical criticism is based on the claim that special education applied research and practice operate in the absence of any guiding theory (e.g., Bogdan & Kugelmass, 1984; Rist & Harrell, 1982; Tomlinson, 1982). It is argued that, instead of being grounded in the theories of an underlying discipline or basic science, special education applied research and practice are guided by a narrow set of unconscious assumptions. Bogdan and Kugelmass (1984) summarized these assumptions as follows:

(1) Disability is a condition that individuals have; (2) disabled/typical is a useful and objective distinction; (3) special education is a rationally conceived and coordinated system of services that help children labeled disabled; (4) progress in the field is made by improving diagnosis, intervention and technology. (p. 173)

While not denying that these unconscious assumptions guide special education research and practice, the "atheoretical" part of Bogdan and Kugelmass' claim cannot be justified. As we will see below, the first two assumptions derive directly from theories of deviance in the disciplines of psychology and biology. The third assumption actually has two theoretical sources. The first source is the positivist theory of knowledge that underwrites the dominant model of professional knowledge (Schön, 1984; Schein, 1972; Glazer, 1974). Special educators, like all professionals, implicitly believe that their knowledge is the end product of a rational system of knowledge production. The second source of this assumption is the theory of organizational rationality, which until recently has dominated thinking and writing about all organizations, including schools (see Clark, 1985; Weick, 1985). It has been so central to the organization of industrialized societies that it permeates the consciousness of all industrialized people as a norm for organized activity per se. Finally, the fourth assumption about the nature of progress derives from the notion of cumulative knowledge that underwrites the positivist theory of knowledge, as well as the dominant conceptualization of scientific progress (discussed below). The point is that, although special education research and practice are guided by unconscious assumptions, one can hardly claim that these beliefs have no theoretical basis at all. The real problem for special education is the unconscious—and thus uncritical—nature of these assumptions, and not whether they are grounded in theory.

The Confounded Theory Claim

The second type of theoretical criticism is based on the claim that special education applied research and practice confound theories. Perhaps the best example of this type of criticism is Mercer's (1973) explanation of the way biological and psychological theories of deviance are confounded within the clinical perspective of mental retardation. Derived from medicine and psychology, the clinical perspective is the familiar frame of reference that guides research and practice in all of the helping professions. It contains two contrasting theories of "normal/abnormal": the pathological model from medicine (biology), and the statistical model from psychology.

The pathological model defines normal/abnormal according to the presence or absence of observable biological symptoms. Biological processes that interfere with system preservation are "bad," or pathological; those that enhance the life of the organism are "good," or healthy. Thus, the pathological model is bipolar: At one pole is normal (i.e., the absence of pathological symptoms and health); at the other pole is abnormal (i.e., the presence of pathological symptoms and illness or "unhealth"). The pathological model is essentially evaluative: To be abnormal is to be unhealthy; this is "bad" and should be prevented or alleviated.

The statistical model is based on the concept of the normal curve, that is, the idea that an individual's attributes can be described by his or her relative position in a frequency distribution of other persons measured on those attributes. Whereas the pathological model defines abnormality as the presence of observable pathological symptoms, the statistical model defines abnormality according to the extent to which an individual varies from the average of a population on a particular attribute. Unlike the bipolar pathological model, which defines only one type of abnormality, the statistical model defines two types of abnormality: abnormally large and abnormally small amounts of the measured characteristic. Whereas the pathological model is evaluative (pathological signs are always "bad"), the statistical model is evaluatively neutral; whether large or small amounts are good or bad depends on the attribute being measured. And whether it is good or bad to have large or small amounts of a particular attribute is defined by society.

Both models are used to define mental retardation—the pathological model for assessing biological manifestations and the statistical model for assessing behavioral manifestations, which are not comprehensible within the pathological model. Although instances of moderate to severe/profound mental retardation are associated with observable patterns of biological symptoms, and are thus comprehensible under the pathological model, most individuals labeled "mildly mentally retarded" do not show any biological signs. In these instances the statistical model is used and a low score on an intelligence (IQ) test is accepted as a symptom of pathology. The problem is that when the models are used in conjunction with one another, the tendency is to transpose them, turning behavioral patterns into pathological signs. Mercer (1973) explained the confusion by saying that:

> The implicit logic that underlies this transformation is as follows: Low IQ = "bad" in American society: a social evaluation. "Bad" = pathology in the pathological model. Therefore, low IQ = pathology. Thus, IQ, which is not a biological manifestation but is a behavioral score based on responses to a series of questions, becomes conceptually transposed into a pathological sign carrying all of the implications of the pathological model. (pp. 5–6)

Although Mercer identified a number of negative implications of the conceptual transposition, the primary implication—and the point of interest here—is the fact that the clinical perspective regards mental retardation as a pathological condition, as an objective attribute of the individual. Although Mercer limited her criticism to the area of mental retardation, the same type of criticism has been leveled against special education research and practice in the areas of learning disabilities (Rist & Harrell, 1982; Schrag & Divorky, 1975) and emotional disturbance (Algozzine, 1976, 1977; Apter, 1982; Hobbs, 1975; Rhodes, 1970; Ross, 1980; Swap, 1978) which, together with mild mental retardation, make up the majority of all students identified as disabled.

The Wrong Theory Claim

The third type of theoretical criticism rests on the claim that special education knowledge is based on the wrong theory, or that it relies too narrowly on one or more theories to the exclusion of others. Most instances of this type of criticism have been mounted by sociologists and political scientists who argue that special education relies too heavily or exclusively on theories derived from the discipline of psychology and the associated disciplines behind the field of medicine (ultimately, biology). The argument is that, by their very nature, these disciplines place the root cause of deviance within the person, and exclude from consideration causal factors that lie in the larger social and political processes external to the individual. In addition, social scientists view diagnostic and instructional models and practices based solely in the behavioral and biological sciences as superficial because they do little to assess, alter, or circumvent the social-political-cultural context of "disability."

Whereas the behavioral and biological sciences study organisms and consider disability to be an objective condition that people have, the social sciences study social and political systems and processes and consider deviance to be a subjective condition that is socially constructed and maintained (see Gould, 1982; Szasz, 1961; Goffman, 1961, 1963; Scheff, 1966; Scott, 1969; Braginsky & Braginsky, 1971; Lemert, 1967; Davis, 1963; Wiseman, 1970; Bogdan, 1984; Gubrium, 1975; Biklen, 1977; Taylor & Bogdan, 1977). And this is more than an academic argument. Many of the social scientists who raise the issue are ultimately concerned with the impact of social and political processes on people and society. From their perspective, special education in industrialized societies is largely an arm of education that creates, and works against the social-political interests of, powerless groups (Sarason & Doris, 1979; Barton & Tomlinson, 1984; Tomlinson, 1982; Farber, 1968).

THE IMPACT OF CRITICISM OF SPECIAL EDUCATION KNOWLEDGE

Practical criticism was successful in bringing about changes in the way special education is practiced in public education, as those changes have been embodied in the EHA. But criticism of special education's practical knowledge does not resort to a critique of special education's theoretical knowledge and thus has had no effect on the field's unconscious assumptions. That is, although the EHA brought about substantial changes in the organization and practice of special education, it rests on the same set of basic beliefs about the nature of disability, diagnosis, special education, and progress in the field. The first three assumptions—that disabilities are conditions people have, that disabled/typical is a useful and objective distinction, and that special education is a rational system that helps students labeled disabled—stand unaltered. Moreover, the EHA is perceived as a rational improvement in diagnostic and instructional technologies, and thus as an example of progress according to the fourth assumption.

Unlike practical criticism, which at least has resulted in apparent changes in the organization and practice of special education, theoretical criticism has had few, if any, meaningful consequences for research or practice in special education. People from a number of disciplines and fields, including special education, have criticized special education's unconscious assumptions, or have attempted to convince the professional community of special education to expand its disciplinary base to include social and political theories of deviance. But no general movement has been launched to alter special education policy and practice or to reorient its research based on these insights.

Discussing the impact of theoretical criticism on special education applied research and practice, Bogdan and Kugelmass (1984, p. 173) summarized the state of affairs succinctly by saying that: "In short, most research has been *for* special education (serving the field as it conceived of itself), not *of* special education, that is looking at the field from an alternative vantage point." Special education applied research leaves unanswered, and treats as unproblematic, fundamental questions about its unconscious assumptions.

Thus, on one hand practical criticism has resulted in apparent changes in the way special education is practiced but has had no effect on theory or the taken-for-granted assumptions that derive from it. On the other hand, theoretical criticism has had virtually no impact on theory, research, or practice in special education. Special education practice has been altered by the EHA, but only within the frame of reference of special education's traditional assumptions about the nature of disability, diagnosis, special education, and progress. Does the EHA represent progress? Undoubtedly it does. But this is only a limited sort of progress—progress *within* a particular frame of reference or set of basic assumptions.

Real progress in special education will require a different frame of reference. At a minimum, it will require that special education take seriously the critics of its theoretical and applied knowledge, and thus of its taken-for-granted assumptions. It will require criticism in the classical sense—self-reflective examination of the limits and validity of special education knowledge. But the problem is that the professional community of special education will not readily accept theoretical criticism, precisely because it contradicts the field's taken-for-granted assumptions about the nature of disability, diagnosis, special education, and progress.

Of course, one could argue that, as a professional community, special education demonstrated its ability to accept criticism—and even to engage in self-criticism—during the period leading to passage of the EHA. But most of that was practical criticism or criticism that could be deflected onto the regular education system. Special education could accept it because at bottom it did not contradict its basic assumptions. Theoretical criticism is more difficult to accept because it contradicts those assumptions. Moreover, the problem is more than an inability to accept theoretical criticism. It is largely an inability to comprehend it.

Professionals in all fields are prepared for practice—whether practice is service delivery or applied research—through a process that shapes their thought and behavior to conform to the established knowledge tradition of the profession. The process requires total submission to the authority of the profession and thus an acceptance of the legitimacy of the profession's knowledge on faith. Professional induction is the efficient inculcation of the inductee with a commitment to a particular way of seeing the world and operating on it (Schein, 1972; Schön, 1984).

Special education professionals—teachers, administrators, teacher trainers, applied researchers—ordinarily have difficulty understanding theoretical criticism because it is based on a view of the world and special education that falls outside of the field's established knowledge tradition. Persons inside the professional community and their theoretical critics on the outside literally are inhabitants of different conceptual worlds. They slice up the social world differently; they speak different languages and employ different concepts. Moreover, professional autonomy means that there is little to compel the special education professional community to listen to its critics. All judgments as to the adequacy of special education knowledge are left to the profession itself. And, of course, special education's inability to see itself as others do is not particularly unusual. This is an inherent characteristic of all professional communities. They all create and maintain their own conventionally-based reality. Each is an insulated subculture of conventional knowledge. Each is a way of seeing.

THE CASE FOR MULTIDISCIPLINARY
SPECIAL EDUCATION KNOWLEDGE

One can demonstrate that special education *can* view itself from alternative vantage-points by using either a longitudinal or a cross-sectional approach. The longitudinal approach looks at the same entity over time. To understand that special education can be viewed in different ways, one need only compare special education today with what it was at any given point in its past history. In this sense, the history of special education is the history of the redefinition of special education practice. We can see, for example, that special education practice in the 1940s was substantially different than it was in the 1960s, or than it is today. Here again, however, these changes have been largely changes in practice. The field's theoretical knowledge—and thus its unconscious assumptions—have not changed.

In contrast, the cross-sectional approach looks at one entity from different perspectives. Conventional special education knowledge about the nature of disability and diagnosis is the result of the particular disciplinary base of theoretical knowledge that grounds the field and the manner in which it has been applied. Given the positivist model of professional knowledge and the nature of professional education, the special education professional community not surprisingly is deeply committed to a biological-psychological conceptualization of deviance. Nevertheless, we know that there are alternative theoretical conceptualizations of deviance, and thus that alternative forms of special education knowledge are possible. There is a substantial body of literature on sociological, political, and cultural theories of deviance, and thus many different ways to conceptualize special education and the traditional notion of "disability."

Once one accepts the position that special education and disability can be viewed in alternative ways and, more important, that each perspective has different implications for students labeled disabled and their parents and families, the argument that special education *should* consider itself and its professional knowledge from alternative vantage points is self-evident on ethical and moral grounds. For special education to continue to rely on an exclusively biological/psychological explanation of disability has no defensible argument.

Contemporary special education knowledge is not inherently correct. It is a matter of history—a history that could have taken a different course. For example, if special education knowledge were grounded in the theoretical knowledge of sociology, political science, anthropology, psychology, and biology, instead of in psychology and biology, members of the professional community would think and act in very different ways. They would inhabit a different conceptual world, speak a different language, and employ different concepts. If this were so, the very notion of disability and the approach taken would be substantially different. Intervention would not be directed exclusively at students, but would just as likely be directed at conceptual and material structures, systems, and processes external to the individual. Things such as organizations, institutions, and belief systems would be targets for intervention, and not just children and youth.

Given these arguments, special education should expand its disciplinary base beyond psychology and biology to include the various social, political, and cultural sciences. Like most of the theoretical critics cited above, I believe that special education should be multidisciplinary. It is important to note, however, that "multidisciplinary" is not the same as "interdisciplinary." Interdisciplinary refers to collaboration among professionals in the performance of services to clients. The case for interdisciplinary professional practice is a familiar argument by now and is based on the fact that many of the challenges society faces today are so complex that no single profession can deal with them effectively (see Schein, 1972). I do not want to minimize the need for interdisciplinary professional *practice*. Given the complexity of problems in special education practice, interdisciplinary collaboration—among regular and special education practitioners, among various types of special educators, and among special education and related services professionals—is a necessity. But the point of this discussion is that special education *knowledge* should be multidisciplinary as well. And to achieve this status the field of special education would need to engage in a substantive reorientation of its theoretical, applied, and practical knowledge, as well as a corresponding revision in its professional education curriculum.

Such a reorientation would begin with a multidisciplinary theoretical critique of special education knowledge—that is, a self-reflective examination of the limits and validity of traditional special education knowledge from the alternative perspectives of the various social sciences, an examination that would be facilitated greatly by the fact that a number of alternative disciplinary analyses currently exist. Moreover, to be adequate this substantially top-down theoretical analysis must be informed by the essentially bottom-up practical criticism of current special education practice, thus uniting in one democratized discourse the interests and insights of theorists, applied scientists, practitioners, parents, and special education consumers and advocates.

Although such a multidisciplinary theoretical critique and multidisciplinary reorientation is necessary, it would not be sufficient to reconceptualize special education knowledge. Today, theoretical criticism and a multidisciplinary orientation are simply not enough.

METATHEORETICAL CRITICISM OF
SPECIAL EDUCATION KNOWLEDGE

A multidisciplinary theoretical critique and multidisciplinary reorientation of special education knowledge is not sufficient because the very notions of "theory" and "discipline" themselves are under attack today. A reconceptualization of special education knowledge must go beyond theoretical criticism: It must be based on a "metatheoretical" critique. Understanding what I mean by metatheoretical criticism requires the introduction of several additional concepts. Central among these are the concepts of paradigm and paradigm shift.

Paradigms and Paradigm Shifts

For the past two decades the terms paradigm and paradigm shift have been associated most often with the influential work of Thomas Kuhn (1962, 1970a). Kuhn used these concepts to reconceptualize the nature of progress in the physical or "hard" sciences, such as physics and chemistry. Kuhn reserved his analysis exclusively for the physical sciences, making no claim for its application to the social sciences. Nevertheless, his work has had a profound effect on the social sciences, despite his reluctance to apply it there.

Although the concept of a paradigm was the central element in Kuhn's analysis of scientific progress, he was neither clear nor consistent about what he meant by it. Masterman (1970) counted more than 20 different uses of the term in Kuhn's original work, which she reduced to three broad types of paradigms: the metaphysical, the sociological, and the construct paradigm. Of the three types of paradigms, the metaphysical paradigm represents the broadest use of the term and subsumes the other two. A metaphysical paradigm is a total world view or gestalt within a given scientific community or subcommunity.

> The metaphysical paradigm is the broadest unit of consensus within a given science. It serves to define the broad parameters of the field, or subareas within a field, giving the scientist a broad orientation from which to operate. (Ritzer, 1980, p.5)

In this sense, Kuhn used paradigm to mean a way of seeing, a general organizing principle governing perception, a "map" that describes for scientists which entities exist (and which do not) and how they behave.

Broadly construed, then, a paradigm is a set of explicit or implicit metatheoretical presuppositions that scientists use to provide coherence to their picture of the world and how it works. These presuppositions are *meta*theoretical because they are more fundamental than theories themselves. They are more fundamental than theories because observation—which, according to the conventional view, is the rock bottom upon which theory is founded (see Feigl, 1970)—is itself strongly influenced by a prior conceptual system of metatheoretical assumptions (see Mulkay, 1979; Shimony, 1977).

A metaphysical or metatheoretical paradigm (hereafter simply paradigm) can be thought of as a special lens through which the world can be viewed. This lens has the peculiar property that, while it may enhance the clarity with which some things can be viewed, it does not allow one to view other things. A paradigm is a particular lens, a particular way of seeing. A paradigm shift occurs when we abandon one way of seeing for a different one. The new lens or paradigm provides a different way of seeing the world and making sense of it.

Kuhn revolutionized our understanding of science and scientific knowledge by using the concepts of paradigm and paradigm shift to distinguish between continuous and discontinuous scientific progress. Continuous scientific progress—what Kuhn called "normal science"—progresses by gradual additions to a knowledge base. Normal science is a highly cumulative enterprise that refines, extends, and articulates a paradigm that already exists. An accepted paradigm is essential for scientific work because it unrandomizes nature and thus permits scientists to know what data are, what methods and instruments are necessary to retrieve them, and what concepts are relevant to their interpretation (Kuhn, 1970a).

Although normal science or continuous scientific progress is the typical image of scientific work, Kuhn's thesis is that it is only a necessary prelude to discontinuous scientific progress—real scientific discovery that uncovers new and unsuspected phenomena and invents radical new theories. Discontinuous scientific progress—what Kuhn called "revolutionary science"—is characterized by discontinuous breakthroughs that demand an entirely new paradigm or set of metatheoretical assumptions for understanding data. Discoveries of this sort begin with the recognition and extended exploration of an anomaly, which is a violation of the paradigm-induced expectations of normal science. When the anomaly comes to be seen as more than just another normal science problem, the transition to paradigm crisis has begun. As the anomaly continues to resist, many of the field's most eminent scientists come to view its resolution as *the* subject matter of their field, which intensifies the crisis to the point where the rules of normal science are blurred. The paradigm exists, but few practitioners can now agree entirely about what it is.

Loosening of the paradigm's rules give rise to extraordinary research and philosophical analysis. Extraordinary research includes attempts to isolate and magnify the anomaly, random experimentation, and generation of speculative theories. Philosophical analysis is directed toward exposing—often for the first time—the metatheoretical assumptions that underwrite the current paradigm and the contemporary research tradition. Together, extraordinary research and philosophical analysis loosen the paradigm's stereotypes and begin to provide the incremental data necessary for a fundamental paradigm shift. Sometimes the structure these procedures give the anomaly foreshadows the shape of the new paradigm. More often, however, the new paradigm emerges all at once—"sometimes in the middle of the night, in the mind of a [scientist] deeply immersed in crisis" (Kuhn, 1970a, p. 90). In any event, the shift to a new paradigm is revolutionary science. Normal science rests on the mutual acceptance of a given paradigm among a community of scientists; revolutionary science requires a paradigm shift. After the shift, the stage is set for the process to repeat itself.

Kuhn's view of scientific progress as discontinuous placed him at odds with the prevailing positivist view of scientific progress and the continuous, cumulative growth of knowledge. He replaced the conventional assumption that science produces knowledge that is cumulative, convergent, and objective with the idea that science and scientific knowledge are discontinuous, divergent, and inherently subjective.

The Subjectivity of Science and Scientific Knowledge

A key element in Kuhn's original work was that the process by which one paradigm replaces another one is essentially a political phenomenon, a process of persuasion and conversion in which the victorious paradigm is the one that wins the most converts (Ritzer, 1980). Thus, nonrational and subjective factors may affect and even determine the emergence of a new paradigm. In the face of criticisms that he overemphasized nonrationality in scientific work (Lakatos & Musgrave, 1970), Kuhn subsequently retreated somewhat from this position (Kuhn, 1970b). Nevertheless, it was this aspect of his analysis that was most attractive to those who have extended his work.

Using Kuhn's thesis to frame their work, proponents have argued that indeed paradigms in the physical sciences rise and fall as a result of subjective, not objective, factors (e.g., Bloor, 1976; Law, 1975; Phillips, 1973; Knorr, Krohn, & Whitley, 1981). Krohn (1981) summarized the first body of empirical work on scientific practice—the ethnographic and detailed historical study of actual scientific activity—by saying that "[physical] scientists are literally constructing their world rather than merely describing it" (p. xi). Kuhn's work was important for what it had to say about the role of culture and tradition in the production of knowledge. His analysis of the conventional nature of knowledge and the nature of convention itself contradicted the common perception that science and knowledge are objective, and advanced the idea that both depend on their cultural context for meaning and interpretation.

Barnes (1982) noted the significance of the subculture in science, and the communal activity of the organized practitioners who sustain it, when he said that "the culture is far more than the setting for scientific research; it is the research itself" (p. 10). The image of the scientist as an objective and impersonal observer engaged in the process of knowledge discovery is being replaced by the image of the scientist as craftperson who, bound by the culture of a particular place and time, creates knowledge that is of temporary utility and validity (Ravetz, 1971). This revised image of science and scientific work has necessarily caused a revision in the very legacy of scientific knowledge. Once conceived as "a separate verbal and symbolic high culture [with] the power to reveal, order and enlighten . . . [it] is being brought down to earth, demystified as a human construction, in the natural as well as the social [sciences] (Krohn, 1981, p. xii).

At this point we can begin to see the parallels between the work of basic scientists and that of applied scientists and professional practitioners. The latter groups are assumed to operate on the basis of received knowledge—that is, knowledge that each accepts on faith from higher levels in the hierarchy of professional knowledge. Although this is the case for applied researchers and professional practitioners, the assumption had been that the theoretical knowledge of the basic scientist is itself objective knowledge about reality. The key point to grasp is that, like the applied scientist and professional practitioner, basic scientists operate on the basis of received knowledge. Theirs is not objective knowledge of reality, but rather knowledge received by looking at the world through the lens of a particular paradigm or set of metatheoretical assumptions.

From this and Kuhn's corresponding description of scientific education, we can see now that the education of all three groups—basic scientists, applied researchers, and professional practitioners—is a matter of being inducted into a subculture of conventional knowledge, which is received on faith as the only way of unrandomizing the complexity of a particular world of practice. Like the craftperson, the members of each group are bound by the culture of a particular place and time. Like the image of science and the legacy of scientific knowledge, the role of basic scientist has been demystified and brought down to earth.

Social Scientific Thought

Although Kuhn reserved his conception of paradigms and paradigm shifts exclusively for the physical sciences, extensions of his work permit us to understand the social sciences in terms of their paradigmatic status. Masterman (1970) made an important contribution in this regard by using the paradigm concept to differentiate among four types of sciences: paradigmatic, nonparadigmatic, dual paradigmatic, and multiple paradigmatic. For Masterman, a paradigmatic science is one having broad consensus within the scientific community on a particular paradigm. Physics is the primary example of a science achieving the paradigmatic state. Until the birth of the Einsteinian paradigm in this century, physics was dominated by the Newtonian paradigm. Although some scientists doubted the Newtonian paradigm, physics during the period between Newton and Einstein is perhaps as close as a science can come to the paradigmatic state (see Clark, 1971).

Nonparadigmatic science is the situation in which no consensus exists on a paradigm. Before Newton, physics presumably lacked consensus and therefore was, at that point in its development, a nonparadigmatic science. The dual paradigmatic state exits immediately before a Kuhnian scientific revolution, when two paradigms—the older, crisis-ridden paradigm and the new, emerging paradigm—are vying for the dominance that only one of them ultimately will achieve. The Newtonian paradigm dominated physics until increasing anomalies set it up for defeat by the Einsteinian paradigm, but at the point when both paradigms were competing for dominance, physics was a dual paradigm science.

The final type of science discussed by Masterman is a multiple paradigmatic science, a situation in which several viable paradigms compete unsuccessfully for dominance within the scientific community. The multiple paradigm state is particularly important for our purposes because it permits differentiation between the physical and social sciences on the basis of their paradigmatic status. The various physical sciences (more or less) are paradigmatic sciences. The birth of a particular physical science can be thought of as the point at which it emerged from a nonparadigmatic state and achieved its paradigmatic status. From there, its history is a series of discontinuous progressions in which normal science—now possible because of paradigmatic consensus—produces the anomalies necessary to create a crisis big enough to yield a scientific revolution and thus a new paradigm.

The social sciences are multiple paradigm sciences. Unlike the physical sciences, in which one paradigm dominates until crisis and revolution replace it with another one, multiple paradigms co-exist in the social sciences. This means that scientific revolutions in the Kuhnian sense are virtually impossible in the social sciences because there is no dominant paradigm to be overthrown. Although the social sciences always have had revolutionary ways to think, all of the paradigms for thinking about the social world emerged—relative to the way physical science paradigms emerge—more or less together. Each one is a viable way to understand the social world, and each has had its own followers. Allegiances have shifted throughout history, and one or another paradigm has dominated particular regions of the globe. But no general consensus—and thus no single dominant paradigm of social scientific thought—has been reached. Not only has this precluded revolutionary science, but it also has made normal science more difficult because, as Ritzer (1980) noted, social scientists are forced to spend an inordinate amount of energy engaging in the politics of winning converts and defending their flanks against attacks from rival paradigms.

Burrell and Morgan (1979) conceptualized the multiple paradigms in the social sciences by considering the relations between two dimensions of intellectual tradition: philosophy of science and theories of society. Philosophy of science is a branch of philosophy that studies the reasoning processes behind the concepts, presuppositions, and methodology of science. Among other things, philosophers of science are concerned with the consequences of scientific knowledge for matters such as the perception of reality and the validity and limits of knowledge (Angeles, 1981). Burrell and Morgan used four traditional strands of debate within philosophy of science to formulate the philosophy of science or "objective-subjective" dimension of their analysis: ontology (the nature of reality), epistemology (the nature of knowledge), human nature (the nature of human action), and methodology (the nature of inquiry). Table 1 presents the extreme positions on each of the four strands of debate.

TABLE 1   *The Objective-Subjective Dimension*

Subjectivist Social Science		Objectivist Social Science
Nominalism	ontology	Realism
Anti-positivism	epistemology	Positivism
Voluntarism	human nature	Determinism
Idiographic	methodology	Nomothetic

Source: Burrell and Morgan (1979, p. 3).

According to Burrell and Morgan (also see Morgan & Smircich, 1980) the realist assumes that the social world exists "out there," independent of an individual's appreciation of it, and that it is virtually as hard and concrete as the physical world. The nominalist, in contrast, assumes that the social world external to individual cognition is made up of names, concepts, and labels that serve as tools for describing, interpreting, and negotiating the external world. The positivist seeks to explain and predict social events by searching for regularities and determinate causal relationships. Growth of knowledge is seen as an essentially cumulative process in which new information is added to the existing stock of knowledge and false hypotheses are eliminated. The anti-positivist, conversely, assumes the social world to be essentially relativistic—understandable, but only from the point of view of the individuals directly involved in the activities to be investigated. Anti-positivists reject the notion of "observer" as a valid vantage point for understanding human activities.

Determinists assume that humans respond mechanistically or even deterministically to the situations encountered in their external world. Voluntarists ascribe a much more creative human role. Free will and autonomy are assumed and humans are seen as creating their environments, controlling them rather than being controlled by them. Nomothetic methodologies are adopted by social scientists who treat the social world as if it were a hard, objective, external reality. The search is for universal laws that explain and govern the concrete, objective social reality that is presumed to exist. Idiographic methodologies are adopted by those who assume the importance of the subjective experience of individuals in constructing their social world. The principal concern for social scientists using idiographic methodologies is to understand the ways individuals socialy construct, modify, and interpret the social world in which they find themselves.

The extreme positions of the objective-subjective dimension are reflected in two major intellectual traditions that have dominated social science during the modern era, or roughly the past two centuries. Objectivist social science is logical positivism, the dominant position in the West, which:

> reflects the attempt to apply the models and methods of the natural sciences to the study of human affairs. It treats the social world as if it were the natural world, adopting a "realist" approach to ontology . . . backed up by a "positivist" epistemology, relatively "deterministic" views of human nature and the use of "nonmothetic" methodologies. (Burrell & Morgan, 1979, p. 7)

The subjectivist position, German idealism, stands in complete opposition to positivism in that:

> it is based upon the premise that the ultimate reality of the universe lies in "spirit" or "idea" rather than in the data of sense perception. It is essentially "nominalist" in its approach to social reality . . . "antipositivist" in epistemology, "voluntarist" with regard to human nature and it favors idiographic methods as a foundation for social analysis. (Burrell & Morgan, 1979, p. 7)

Burrell and Morgan used the terms "sociology of regulation" and "sociology of radical change" to describe the extreme positions on their "nature of society," or "order-conflict," dimension. Table 2 differentiates between the two positions by comparing the issues with which each is concerned.

TABLE 2   The Order–Conflict Dimension

The sociology of **regulation** is concerned with:	The sociology of **radical change** is concerned with:
The status quo	Radical change
Social order	Structural conflict
Consensus	Domination
Social integration	Contradiction
Solidarity	Emancipation
Need satisfaction	Deprivation
Actuality	Potentiality

Source: Adapted from Burrell and Morgan (1979, p. 18).

Sociology of regulation—the dominant position in the West—reflects the value position of theorists who are concerned about explaining society's underlying unity and cohesion. Conversely, theorists of the sociology of radical change view modern society as being characterized by conflict, modes of domination, and contradiction. They are concerned with people's emancipation from existing social and ideological structures.

Ritzer (1980) proposed another way to think about the same intellectual territory covered in the Burrell and Morgan analysis. He used the same objective-subjective dimension but, in place of Burrell and Morgan's order-conflict dimension, substituted a "levels of social reality" or "macroscopic-microscopic" dimension in which the magnitude of social phenomena—ranging from total world systems (macro) to individual thought and action (micro)—differentiates among theoretical positions. Ritzer's microscopic level corresponds to the order end of Burrell and Morgan's order-conflict dimension, and his macroscopic level corresponds to the conflict position. In either case, when the two dimensions are related orthogonally, they produce a conceptual map of four paradigms of social scientific thought (see Figure 1), each of which is based on a mutually exclusive view of the social world and how it might be investigated. Each of the four paradigms— what I will refer to, following Burrell and Morgan, as the functionalist, interpretivist, humanist, and structuralist paradigms—rests on a fundamentally different set of metatheoretical assumptions about the nature of science and of society, that is, fundamentally different metatheoretical assumptions about the nature of social science itself.

The functionalist paradigm is the dominant framework for social science in the Western world. It is firmly grounded in the sociology of regulation, takes a more or less microscopic view of social reality, and studies its subject matter from an objectivist point of view. It seeks to provide rational explanations of social affairs using an approach to science premised in the tradition of logical positivism. As such, it:

> reflects the attempt, *par excellence*, to apply the models and methods of the natural sciences to the study of human affairs. . . . The functionalist approach to social science tends to assume that the social world is composed of relatively concrete empirical artifacts and relationships which can be identified, studied and measured through approaches derived from the natural sciences. (Burrell & Morgan, 1979, p. 26)

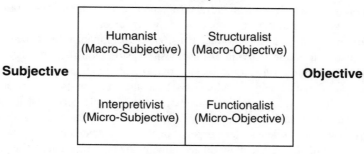

FIGURE 1   *Four Paradigms of Social Scientific Thought*

Source: Adapted from Burrell and Morgan (1979, p. 29) and Ritzer (1980, p. 239).

The functionalist paradigm is equivalent to what Ritzer (1980) referred to as the "micro-objective" approach to social science. Theorists operating from this vantage point are concerned with explaining social life by concentrating on microscopic social phenomena such as patterns of behavior, action, and interaction.

Interpretivist theorists are only implicitly committed to regulation and order. They assume that the social world is cohesive, ordered, and integrated but, unlike the functionalists, they are oriented toward understanding the ongoing processes through which humans subjectively construct their social world. The interpretivist paradigm addresses the same social issues as the functionalist paradigm, but it is concerned with understanding the essence of the everyday world as an emergent social process. When a social world outside the consciousness of the individual is recognized, it is regarded as a network of assumptions and intersubjectively shared meanings. The interpretivist paradigm corresponds to Ritzer's (1980) micro-subjective perspective. Theorists of this persuasion are concerned with understanding the various facets of the social construction of reality—the way people create and share meaning (see Berger & Luckmann, 1967).

Although humanists share a view of social science with the interpretive paradigm, their frame of reference is the sociology of radical change. The humanist paradigm views society with a concern for transcending the limitations of existing social structures. Humanism views the ideological structures with which people interact as a screen between them and their true consciousness. Thus society is viewed as being antihuman—as inhibiting human development and fulfillment. Humanist theorizing centers on a critique of the status quo, using what Ritzer (1980) called the "macro-subjective" approach to social science. As such, humanists concentrate on the influence of ideological structures—culture, norms, and values—on human thought and action.

Like humanism, the structuralist paradigm mounts a critique of the status quo and advocates change. But it takes this stance from the perspective of the objectivist, thus sharing an approach to social science with the functionalist paradigm. Structuralists view contemporary society as being characterized by fundamental conflicts that generate change through political and economic crises. Whereas humanists are concerned with ideological structures and individual consciousness, structuralists focus their critique upon material structures—including social arrangements—and are concerned with the consciousness of entire classes of individuals. Structuralist theorists work from Ritzer's (1980) "macro-objective" perspective and thus approach social science with a concern to explain social entities such as the economy, law, architecture, technology, and language.

The approach social scientists take depends on their metatheoretical assumptions with respect to the nature of the social world and how it may be investigated. The particular combination of metatheoretical assumptions explicitly or, as is most often the case, implicitly defines the paradigm and provides the frame of reference of social scientists who work within it (Burrell & Morgan, 1979; Ritzer, 1980). Each paradigm produces knowledge that is based on a unique brand of insight. Each paradigm is a way of seeing.

The Paradigm Shift in Science and Civilization

Using the scheme presented in Figure 1 as a backdrop, we can begin to see the radical implications of the ideas of paradigms and paradigm shifts. From Kuhn, and the extensions of his original work, we can see that the very notions of paradigm and paradigm shift support a subjectivist philosophy of science. Whether we think of the process of total paradigm replacement in the physical sciences, or the process of competitive co-existence among multiple paradigms in the social sciences, the idea that paradigms exist in the minds of humans, who then operate under their received meaning, is the type of thinking about knowing that is possible only from a subjectivist view of science and knowledge. The concepts of paradigm and paradigm shift are comprehensible only from the interpretivist and humanist paradigms. They are conceptually impossible in the two objectivist paradigms because they presuppose a single objective social reality.

Further evidence for a paradigm shift in the physical and social sciences was provided by Schwartz and Ogilvy (1979) in their analysis of the 20th century Kuhnian paradigm shifts in physics, chemistry, brain theory, ecology, evolution, mathematics, philosophy, politics, psychology, linguistics, religion, consciousness, and the arts. They argued that, taken together, the manifestations of these disciplinary shifts characterize an emergent world view in the formal disciplines that is moving away from objectivism and positivism and toward a subjectivist view of science and knowledge.

At yet a broader level of human consciousness, Schwartz and Ogilvy (1979) argued that the values inherent in the disciplinary paradigm shifts foreshadow an emergent shift in the entire consciousness of Western civilization. Evidence supporting this assertion, of course, is all around us. Our current world view is the result of the 17th century scientific revolutions that collectively became the Enlightenment. The Newtonian world view emanating from that paradigm shift is reflected today in every aspect of our social order. Its models and metaphors are embedded in our language, our history, and our image of science. These mental maps of the world are the foundations of Western values and beliefs—the very values and beliefs that made the functionalist paradigm the dominant social science paradigm in the West. In the future, according to Schwartz and Ogilvy, Western values and beliefs will conform more to the subjectivist metatheoretical assumptions than the traditional objectivist ones.

The Meta-Leap to Antifoundational Knowledge

Although science and civilization have shifted paradigms before, the current paradigm shift is even more revolutionary because this time, as Schwartz and Ogilvy (1979) noted, the patterns of change have themselves changed. Not only do we appear to be at the threshold of a new paradigm or world view, but we know that there *are* paradigms. This awareness itself is part of the new paradigm because a shift to the subjectivist outlook was required before a paradigm or a paradigm shift could be comprehended. Our current paradigm amounts to the view that there are no such things as paradigms; only the "facts" are important—seeing is believing. Today, however, Western science has begun to take seriously the proposition that what we believe shapes what we see, and that the notion of an objective science is illusionary. Until this century, the assumption was that we could study the social world objectively by using the methods and models of the physical sciences. Now we have discovered that, even in the physical world, inquiry affects results. Our disciplines themselves are not neutral to the world. Believing is seeing.

The common view that social science is a neutral, technical process that reveals or discovers knowledge is being replaced by an appreciation of social science as a distinctively human process through which knowledge is created. Historically, debate in the social sciences has been premised on a foundational view of knowledge, which has led to arguments over the "best" way of doing research or the "best" theory to explain social phenomena. But today, debate is moving beyond consideration of a single research method, theory, or paradigm, and social scientists are beginning to call for an antifoundational, reflective discourse about and appreciation of the variety of available research logics, theoretical positions, and paradigmatic perspectives (see Morgan, 1983; Soltis, 1984). Moreover, recognition of the selection of a particular research strategy, theory, or paradigm as problematic and value-laden is forcing us to recognize social science as a political, moral, and ethical undertaking as much as a technical one.

The Paradigmatic Status of Special Education Knowledge

Special education's disciplinary base in biology and psychology yields an approach to diagnosis and intervention that is premised on diagnostic-prescriptive teaching and behavioristic theory. Diagnostic-prescriptive teaching is the attempt to design instructional programs on the basis of test performance. Of the two models within the diagnostic-prescriptive approach—ability-training and task-analysis—Salvia and Ysseldyke (1981) noted the preference in special education for the latter because of the lack of reliable and valid norm-referenced assessment devices necessary to actualize the ability training model.

The task-analysis model is based on the application of behavioristic theory to instruction in specific skills. Complex instructional goals are task-analyzed into subskills and taught using a hierarchy of behavioral procedures for skill acquisition (see White & Haring, 1976). The teacher is conceptualized as a technician applying a technology of teaching commonly referred to as "systematic instruction," which is based on:

> the experimental analysis of behavior, which, as a scientific discipline, sought to find a systematic interpretation of human behavior based on generalized principles, or laws, of behavior. The goal of this search for laws of behavior was much the same as in any other branch of science—to make reliable predictions (Skinner, 1953). The development of behavior analysis has been rigorously scientific, beginning with basic laboratory research and slowly generalizing the results to social situations. (Haring, 1978, p. 21)

Burrell and Morgan (1979) locate behaviorism in the extreme objectivist region of the functionalist paradigm.

> Skinner's perspective is a highly coherent and consistent one in terms of the four strands of the subjective-objective dimension of our analytical scheme. Ontologically, his view is firmly realist; epistemologically, his work is the archetype of positivism; his view of human nature reflects a determinism of an extreme form; the highly nomothetic methodology reflected in his experimental approach is congruent with these other assumptions. (Burrell & Morgan, 1979, p. 103)

This places special education knowledge in the most extreme objectivist region of the functionalist paradigm, as shown in Figure 2 (see also Heshusius, 1982).

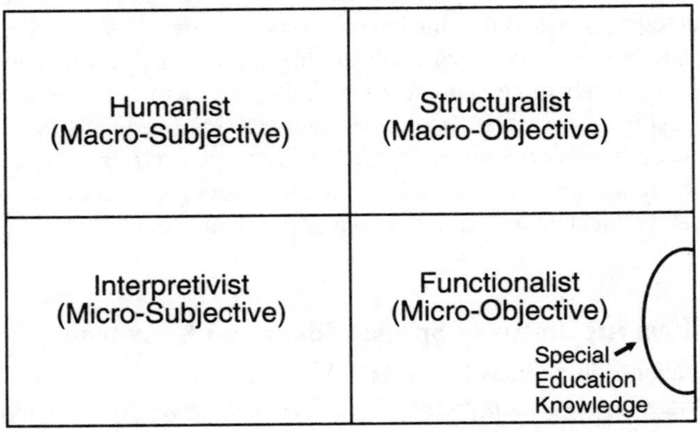

Humanist (Macro-Subjective)	Structuralist (Macro-Objective)
Interpretivist (Micro-Subjective)	Functionalist (Micro-Objective) Special Education Knowledge

FIGURE 2   PARADIGMATIC STATUS OF SPECIAL EDUCATION KNOWLEDGE

THE CASE FOR MULTIPARADIGMATIC, MULTIDISCIPLINARY SPECIAL EDUCATION KNOWLEDGE

Special education can and should view itself from alternative perspectives. The fact that special education can view itself from alternative perspectives was demonstrated above using both a longitudinal and a cross-sectional explanation. The cross-sectional explanation can be extended at this point by noting that, in addition to the possibility of considering special education knowledge from a number of alternative *disciplines*, the very nature of those disciplines requires that special education knowledge be considered from the multiple *paradigms* of social scientific thought. As we have seen, to view any of the social science disciplines as a unitary body of thought is simply inadequate.

Once one accepts the position that special education can be viewed from alternative disciplinary perspectives, and that each of these perspectives has different implications for students labeled disabled and their parents and families, there is no morally or ethically defensible argument for special education to continue to rely on an exclusively biological/psychological interpretation of disability. At this point we can extend this argument by referring to the multiple paradigmatic status of the social sciences and the notion of antifoundational knowledge. As we know, the social disciplines are multiple paradigm sciences, which means that no particular paradigm can be inherently correct. Given this, and the fact that each paradigm has different implications for students labeled disabled and their parents and families, there is no morally or ethically defensible argument for special education to continue to rely exclusively on a functionalist conceptualization of the social sciences.

Given this line of argument, special education should expand its disciplinary base beyond psychology and biology to include the various social, political, and cultural sciences. That is, at a minimum, special education knowledge should be multidisciplinary. However, given the multiparadigmatic status of the social sciences and the implications of antifoundationalism, an adequate response would require that special education models and practices be grounded in knowledge that is multiparadigmatic as well as multidisciplinary. The process of achieving such a grounding would begin with a multiparadigmatic, metatheoretical critique of current special education knowledge and practices—that is, an antifoundational, self-reflective examination from the alternative perspectives of the multiple paradigms of the social, political, and cultural sciences—and would be sustained by an ongoing democratized discourse among metatheorists, theorists, applied scientists, practitioners, parents, and special education consumers and advocates. In principle, the process would result in a multiparadigmatic, multidisciplinary reorientation of special education knowledge and a corresponding modification of special education's professional education curriculum, which would produce special education professionals who think and act in ways that are substantially different from their contemporary counterparts.

However, there are a number of factors working against the possibility of such a reorientation of special education knowledge. Paradigm shifts take time and are bitterly resisted. Moreover, the meta-leap to antifoundational knowledge itself requires a prior paradigm shift from objectivism to subjectivism. Nevertheless, there are some encouraging developments on both of these fronts in the social sciences, as we have seen. Moreover, there even has been some movement toward subjectivism in the field of special education, both at the level of practice (Heshusius, 1982) and at the level of applied research (Stainback & Stainback, 1984). In both cases, the argument has been for a shift from the functionalist to the interpretivist paradigm (refer to Figure 2), which of course reflects the broader trend toward subjectivism in science and civilization.

As might be expected from the foregoing discussion, the reaction of the special education community to these proposals has been decidedly negative (see Ulman & Rosenberg, 1986; Simpson & Eaves, 1985). In both reaction papers, the authors implicitly defend the prevailing functionalist paradigm by evaluating and dismissing the interpretivist proposals exclusively on the basis of functionalist criteria, which they take to be foundational and thus the only criteria that exist. The reactions show no recognition of the possibility of alternative frames of reference, to say nothing of the possibility of antifoundational knowledge. Although the original proposals and the advocates' responses to the defenders' reactions to them (Heshusius, 1986; Stainback & Sainback, 1985) were informative and thought provoking, the exchange could hardly be called a discourse. Exchanges like this serve the purpose of educating the field and introducing anomalies, but what is needed is a sustained discourse in which all participants recognize the multiple paradigm status of the social sciences and the moral and political implications of the meta-leap to antifoundational knowledge.

If an informed discourse such as this could be initiated and sustained in a manner that would enhance special education's capacity for reflective self-criticism, two additional problems potentially would arise. First, there is the danger of the discourse becoming a substitute for action. Given the moral and political implications of the nature of special education knowledge, we do not have the luxury of time; every day counts. Second, there is the danger that the discourse will remain at the level of paradigms. As Morgan and Smircich (1980) noted, such a discourse can result in merely replacing one dominant paradigm with another one. We must not lose sight of the implications of antifoundational knowledge. The discourse must be raised to the meta-level and not be permitted to degenerate into a narrow debate over "the best paradigm."

Finally, even if an informed, antifoundational discourse could be mounted and sustained in the field of special education, it would not be sufficient to substantially alter actual practices. Special education is not an island. It is merely a subsystem within the larger system of public education. Criticism of special education knowledge and practices necessarily will spill over into criticism of the knowledge base and practices of general education. In a sense, this article is a start in that direction, for virtually everything that has been said about special education knowledge applies equally well to general education knowledge.

In summary, I am arguing that special education knowledge should be multiparadigmatic and multidisciplinary. Achieving such a reorientation will require a multiparadigmatic, metatheoretical critique of current special education knowledge in the context of a democratized discourse on the implications of choosing a frame of reference for students and their parents and families. And it will be essential to expand the critique and the discourse to the entire system of public education in this country.

THE SITUATION TODAY

A crisis in knowledge is a necessary prelude to the growth of knowledge and thus the driving force behind progress in the physical sciences (Kuhn, 1970a), the social sciences (Barnes, 1982), and the professions (Schön, 1983). By calling the traditional practices of a scientific or professional community into question, a crisis in knowledge frees its members from conventional thinking, which permits them to consider alternative perspectives upon which to base new practices. Indeed, progress in the field of special education is a case in point: Special educators could not have developed the practices associated with the EHA and mainstreaming if they had not lost confidence in those associated with the traditional special classroom model. As we have seen, however, professional practices are grounded in theories that are themselves shaped by a larger network of implicit metatheories. And because the professions largely take their grounding knowledge for granted, a common problem is that new professional practices tend to be based on old assumptions, which means that they do not necessarily result in better services to clients. Unfortunately, special education is a case in point for this phenomenon as well (see Skrtic, 1987, 1988a).

Special education's first crisis in knowledge began in the 1960s when the practices associated with the special classroom model were criticized for being racially biased, instructionally ineffective, and psychologically and socially damaging (Dunn, 1968; Johnson, 1962). That crisis ended in 1975 with the enactment of the EHA and the broad adoption of the mainstreaming model, both of which were intended to solve the problems associated with the special classroom model (Abeson & Zettle, 1977; Dunn, 1968). Over the past several years, however, a second crisis has emerged. This one stems from a growing recognition in the field that the practices associated with the EHA and mainstreaming have created virtually the same problems as the special classroom model (see Heller, Holtzman & Messick, 1982; Wang, Reynolds & Walberg, 1987). Although no one in the special education community is questioning the fact that some positive changes have occurred since 1975, the implication is that, rather than solving the problems of the 1960s, the EHA and mainstreaming merely reproduced them in the 1980s and 1990s.

Special education reproduced the problems it intended to solve because its case against the special classroom model was based on practical criticism rather than theoretical criticism. That is, it was based on a critique of traditional practices rather than a critique of those practices *and* the assumptions in which they are grounded. Although the practices associated with mainstreaming are different from those of the special classroom model, they reproduced the problems they were intended to solve because they are premised on the same assumptions about the nature of disability, diagnosis, special education, and progress (Skrtic, 1988a). Moreover, the danger today is that special education's current confrontation with uncertainty is following the same pattern. That is, the controversy over the adequacy of mainstreaming and the feasibility of the new "regular education initiative" or "inclusion" model (see, e.g., Gartner & Lipsky, 1987; Kauffman, 1989; Kauffman, Gerber & Semmel, 1988; Reynolds, Wang & Walberg, 1987) is taking place at the level of practices rather than at the level of grounding assumptions (Skrtic, 1987, 1991a, 1991b).

If the special education community is to avoid reproducing its current problems in the next century, it must initiate and sustain a critical discourse, that is, it must engage in a form of problem analysis and resolution that questions special education practices *and* the taken-for-granted assumptions in which they are grounded. The value of such a discourse is the realization that changing special education practices in ways that do not reproduce current problems requires changing the assumptions upon which those practices are based. The mere existence of a critical discourse is not sufficient, however. As we have seen, the critical discourse on special education in the social sciences has had virtually no effect on special education practices or assumptions (Bogdan & Kuglemass, 1984; Skrtic, 1988a). One problem, of course, is that professionals tend to reject critical discourses because, by their very nature, they question their taken-for-granted assumptions. Furthermore, the insights contained in such discourses are difficult for professionals to use because they are presented in unfamiliar theoretical languages and are thus largely incomprehensible to the members of the professional community.

The advantage today is that a critical discourse has emerged within the field of special education (e.g., Bogdan & Knoll, 1988; Ferguson, 1987; Heshusius, 1986; Iano, 1986, 1987; Janesick, 1988; Poplin, 1987; Skrtic, 1988a, 1988b; Sleeter, 1986; Sigmon, 1987). Of course, a critical discourse within the field is no panacea. Like the one in the social sciences, it too questions taken-for-granted assumptions and is carried out in largely unfamiliar theoretical languages (see Skrtic, 1991a, in press). Nevertheless, a critical discourse carried out by fellow special educators has been more difficult for the field to reject out of hand. This has increased the degree to which theoretical insights are being used to inform practical criticism of the ethics and efficacy of special education practices—that is, used to interpret empirical evidence produced by the field itself, according to its traditional assumptions and in its traditional language (see Skrtic, 1991a, in press). Under these conditions, a critical orientation within the field may in the long run produce an expanded discourse that is both critical *and* comprehensible to the special education professional community.

An expanded discourse of this sort is necessary if special education is to break the cycle of reproducing itself and its problems, but it is not sufficient. This is so because, although special education's emerging theoretical discourse is *critical,* it is not *pragmatic*. It is critical because it questions the field's assumptions and provides alternative theories for interpreting data and conceptualizing solutions. It is not pragmatic because it does not solve the problem of choosing among the various theories that are put forth in the discourse. To be critical *and* pragmatic the expanded discourse must not only look behind practices to expose the unquestioned assumptions or theories in which they are grounded, it must also look behind the theories themselves (see Skrtic, 1991a, 1991b). That is, it must expose and question the metatheoretical assumptions in which the various theories are grounded, which is the sort of antifoundational discourse that is implied by the notion of a multiparadigmatic, multidisciplinary reorientation of special education knowledge.

The goal of an antifoundational discourse is not truth or certainty; it is edification. It is a pedagogical process of remaking ourselves as we think about our knowledge and our practices in unconventional ways (Gadamer, 1975). Such a discourse is edifying because it forces professionals to face the fact that everything they think, do, say, write, and read as professionals is shaped by convention; that is, it forces professionals to see that they can only know their knowledge and their practices and, ultimately, their clients and themselves "under optional descriptions" (Rorty, 1979, p. 379). Put simply, an antifoundational discourse is the attempt to:

> redescribe lots and lots of things in new ways, until you...tempt the rising generation to . . . look for . . . new [theories, models, and practices]. . . . It says things like "try thinking of it this way"—or more specifically, "try to ignore the apparently futile traditional questions by substituting the following new and possibly interesting questions" (Rorty, 1989, p. 9).

An antifoundational discourse is a method for deconstructing and reconstructing professional knowledge and practices under conditions of uncertainty. Given the uncertainty in special education and general education today, I believe that such a discourse is precisely what we need to deconstruct 20th century public education and to reconstruct it for the emerging historical contingencies of the 21st century.

REFERENCES

Abeson, A., & Zettel, J. (1977). The end of the quiet revolution: The Education for All Handicapped Children Act of 1975. *Exceptional Children, 44* (2), 115–128.

Algozzine, B. (1976). The disturbing child: What you see is what you get? *Alberta Journal of Education Research, 22,* 330–333.

Algozzine, B. (1977). The emotionally disturbed child: Disturbed or disturbing? *Journal of Abnormal Child Psychology, 5* (2), 205–211.

Angeles, P.A. 1981. *Dictionary of philosophy.* New York: Barnes and Noble Books.

Apter, S.J. (1982). *Troubled children, troubled systems.* New York: Pergamon Press.

Ballard-Campbell, M., & Semmel, M. (1981). Policy research and special education: Research issues affecting policy formation and implementation. *Exceptional Education Quarterly, 2*(2), 59-68.

Barnes, B. (1982). *T.S. Kuhn and social science.* New York: Columbia University Press.

Barton, L., & Tomlinson, S. (Eds.). 1984. *Special education and social interests.* London: Croom-Helm.

Berger, P.L., & Luckmann, L. (1967). *The social construction of reality.* New York: Doubleday.

Biklen, D. (1977). Exclusion. In B. Blatt, D. Biklen, and R. Bodgan (Eds.), *An alternative textbook in special education.* Denver: Love Publishing.

Biklen, D. (Ed.). (1985). *Achieving the complete school: Strategies for effective mainstreaming.* New York: Columbia University.

Blatt, B., & Kaplan, F. (1966). *Christmas in purgatory.* Boston: Allyn & Bacon.

Bloor, D.C. (1976). *Knowledge and social imagery.* London: Routledge & Kegan Paul.

Bogdan, R. (1984). *Being different; The autobiography of Jane Fry.* New York: John Wiley.

Bogdan, R., & Knoll, J. (1988). The sociology of disability. In E.L. Meyen and T.M. Skrtic (Eds.), *Exceptional children and youth: An introduction,* pp. 449–477. Denver: Love Publishing.

Bogdan, R., & Kugelmass, J. (1984). Case studies of mainstreaming: A symbolic interactionist approach to special schooling. In L. Barton and S. Tomlinson (Eds.), *Special education and social interests* (pp. 173–191). London: Croom-Helm.

Braginsky, D., & Braginsky, B. (1971). *Hansels and Gretels.* New York: Holt, Rinehart & Winston.

Burrell, G., & Morgan, G. (1979). *Sociological paradigms and organizational analysis.* London: Heinemann Educational Books Ltd.

Clark, D.L. (1985). Emerging paradigms in organizational theory and research. In Y.S. Lincoln (Ed.), *Organizational theory and inquiry: The paradigm revolution* (pp. 43-78). Beverly Hills, CA: Sage Publications.

Clark, R. (1971). *Einstein: The life and times.* New York: Avon Books.

Davis, F. (1963). *Passage through crisis.* Indianapolis: Bobbs-Merrill.

Dunn, L.M. (1968). Special education for the mildly retarded: Is much of it justifiable? *Exceptional Children, 35*(1), 5–22.

Farber, B. (1968). *Mental retardation: Its social context and social consequences.* Boston: Houghton Mifflin.

Feigl, H. (1970). The "orthodox" view of theories: Remarks in defense as well as critique. In Radnew & Winokur (Eds.), *Minnesota studies in the philosophy of science* (Vol. 4). Minneapolis: University of Minnesota Press.

Ferguson, P.M. (1987). The social construction of mental retardation. *Social Policy, 18*(1), 51–56.

Gadamer, H. G. (1975). *Truth and method.* G. Barden and J. Cumming (Eds. and Trans.). New York: Seabury Press.

Gartner, A., & Lipsky, D.K. (1987). Beyond special education: Toward a quality system for all students. *Harvard Educational Review, 57*(4), 367–390.

Glazer, N. (1974). The schools of the minor professions. *Minerva, 12,* (3), 346–364.

Goffman, E. (1961). *Asylums: Essays on the social situation of mental patients and other inmates.* Garden City, New York: Doubleday/Anchor Books.

Goffman, E. (1963). *Stigma.* Englewood Cliffs, NJ: Prentice-Hall.

Gould, S.J. (1982). *The mismeasure of man.* New York: W.W. Norton.

Gubrium, J. (1975). *Living and dying at Murray Manor.* New York: St. Martin's Press.

Haring, N.G. (1978). *Behavior of exceptional children: An introduction to special education.* Columbus, OH: Charles E. Merrill.

Heller, K., Holtzman, W., & Messick, S. (1982). *Placing children in special education: A strategy for equity.* Washington, D.C.: National Academy of Sciences Press.

Heshusius, L. (1982). At the heart of the advocacy dilemma: A mechanistic world view. *Exceptional Children, 49*(1), 6–13.

Heshusius, L. (1986). Paradigm shifts and special education: A response to Ulman and Rosenberg. *Exceptional Children, 52*(5), 461–465.

Hobbs, N. (1975). *The futures of children: Categories, labels, and their consequences.* San Francisco: Jossey-Bass.

Iano, R.P. (1986). The study and development of teaching: With implications for the advancement of special education. *Remedial and Special Education, 7*(5), 50–61.

Iano, R.P. (1987). Rebuttal: Neither the absolute certainty of prescriptive law nor a surrender to mysticism. *Remedial and Special Education, 18*(1), 51–56.

Janesick, V.J., (1988). Our multicultural society. In E.L. Meyen and T.M. Skrtic (Eds.), *Exceptional children and youth: An introduction,* pp. 519–535. Denver: Love Publishing.

Johnson, G.O. (1962). Special education for the mentally handicapped—A paradox. *Exceptional Children, 29*(2), 62–69.

Kauffman, J.M. (1989). The regular education initiative as Reagan-Bush education policy: A trickle-down theory of education of the hard-to-teach. *Journal of Special Education, 23*(3), 256–278.

Kauffman, J. M., Gerber, M. M., & Semmel, M. I. (1988). Arguable assumptions underlying the regular education initiative. *Journal of Learning Disabilities, 21*(1), 6–11.

Knorr, K.D., Krohn, R., & Whitley, R. (Eds.). (1981). *The social process of scientific investigation.* Boston: D. Reidel Publishing.

Krohn, R. (1981). Introduction: Toward the empirical study of scientific practice. In K.D. Knorr, R. Krohn, & R. Whitley (Eds.), *The social process of scientific investigation* (pp. vii–xxv). Boston: D. Reidel Publishing.

Kuhn, T.S. (1962). *The structure of scientific revolutions* (1st ed.). Chicago: University of Chicago Press.

Kuhn, T.S. (1970a). *The structure of scientific revolutions* (2nd ed.). Chicago: University of Chicago Press.

Kuhn, T.S. (1970b). Reflections on my critics. In I. Lakatos and A. Musgrave (Eds.), *Criticism and the growth of knowledge.* Cambridge: Cambridge University Press.

Lakatos, I., & Musgrave, A. (1970). *Criticism and the growth of knowledge.* Cambridge: Cambridge University Press.

Law, J. (1975). Is epistemology redundant? *Philosophy of the Social Sciences, 5,* 317–337.

Lemert, E. (1967). *Human deviance, social problems, and social control.* Englewood Cliffs, NJ: Prentice-Hall.

Masterman, M. (1970). The nature of a paradigm. In I. Lakotos and A. Musgrave (Eds.), *Criticism and the growth of knowledge.* Cambridge: Cambridge University Press.

Mercer, J.R. (1973). *Labeling the mentally retarded.* Berkeley: University of California Press.

Morgan, G. (Ed.). (1983) *Beyond method: Strategies for social research.* Beverly Hills, CA: Sage Publications.

Morgan, G., & Smircich, L. (1980). The case for qualitative research. *Academy of Management Review, 5,* 491–500.

Mulkay, M.J. (1979). *Science and the sociology of knowledge.* London: Allen & Unwin.

Phillips, D. (1973). Paradigms, falsifications and sociology. *Acta Sociologica, 16,* 13–31.

Poplin, M.S. (1987). Self-imposed blindness: The scientific method in education. *Remedial and Special Education, 8*(6), 31–37.

Ravetz, J.R. (1971). *Scientific knowledge and its social problems.* Oxford: Clarendon Press.

Reynolds, M. C., Wang, M. C., & Walberg, H. J. (1987). The necessary restructuring of special and general education. *Exceptional Children, 53,* 391–398.

Rhodes, W.C. (1970). A community participation analysis of emotional disturbance. *Exceptional Children, 36,* 306–314.

Rist, R., & Harrell, J. (1982). Labeling and the learning disabled child: The social ecology of educational practice. *American Journal of Orthopsychiatry, 52* (1), 146–160.

Ritzer, G. (1980) *Sociology: A multiple paradigm science.* Boston: Allyn & Bacon.

Rorty, R. (1979). *Philosophy and the mirror of nature.* Princeton, NJ: Princeton University Press.

Rorty, R. (1989). *Contingency, irony, and solidarity.* New York: Cambridge University Press.

Ross, A.O. (1980). *Psychological disorders of children.* New York: McGraw-Hill.

Salvia, J., & Ysseldyke, J.E. (1981). *Assessment in special and remedial education.* Boston: Houghton Mifflin.

Sarason, S.B., & Doris, J. (1979). *Educational handicap, public policy, and social history.* New York: Free Press.

Scheff, T.J. (1966). *Being mentally ill: A sociological theory.* Chicago: Aldine Publishing.

Schein, E.H. (1972). *Professional education.* New York: McGraw-Hill.

Schön, D.A. (1984). *The crisis of professional knowledge and the pursuit of an epistemology of practice* (Report for the Harvard Business School). Cambridge: Harvard.

Schön, D.A. (1983). *The reflective practitioner: How professionals think in action.* New York: Basic Books.

Schrag, P., & Divorky, D. (1975). *The myth of the hyperactive child.* New York: Pantheon.

Schwartz, P., & Ogilvy, J. (1979). *The emergent paradigm: changing patterns of thought and belief.* Menlo Park, CA: SRI International.

Scott, R. (1969). *The making of blind men.* New York: Russell Sage Foundation.

Shimony, A. (1977). Is observation theory-laden? A problem in naturalistc epistemology. In R.G. Colodny (Ed.), *Logic, laws and life.* Pittsburgh: University of Pittsburgh Press.

Sigmon, S.B. (1987). *Radical analysis of special education: Focus on historical development and learning disabilities.* London: Falmer Press.

Simpson, R.G., & Eaves, R.C. (1985). Do we need more qualitative research or more good research? A reaction to Stainback and Stainback, *Exceptional Children, 51* (4), 324–329.

Skinner, B.F. (1953). *Science and human behavior.* New York: Free Press.

Skrtic, T.M. (1987). An organizational analysis of special education reform. *Counterpoint, 8*(2), 15–19.

Skrtic, T.M. (1988a). The crisis in special education knowledge. In E.L. Meyen and T.M. Skrtic (Eds.), *Exceptional children and youth: An introduction.* Denver: Love Publishing.

Skrtic, T. M. (1988b). The organizational context of special education. In E. L. Meyen and T. M. Skrtic (Eds.). *Exceptional children and youth: An introduction.* Denver: Love Publishing.

Skrtic, T. M. (1991a). *Behind special education: A critical analysis of professional culture and school organization.* Denver: Love Publishing.

Skrtic, T. M. (1991b). The special education paradox: Equity as the way to excellence. *Harvard Educational Review, 61*(2), 148–206.

Skrtic, T. M. (in press). *Exploring the theory/practice link in special education: A metatheoretical genealogy.* New York: Teachers College Press.

Sleeter, C. E. (1986). Learning disabilities: The social construction of a special education category. *Exceptional Children, 53,* 46–54.

Soltis, J.F. (1984). On the nature of educational research. *Educational Researcher, 13*(10), 5–10.

Stainback, S., & Stainback, W. (1984). Broadening the research perspective in special education. *Exceptional Children, 50,* 400–408.

Stainback, S., & Stainback, W. (1985). Quantitative and qualitative methodologies: Competitive or complementary? A response to Simpson and Eaves. *Exceptional Children, 51*(4), 330–334.

Swap, S. (1978). The ecological model of emotional disturbance in children: A status report and proposed synthesis. *Behavioral Disorders, 3*(3), 156–186.

Szasz, T.S. (1961). *The myth of mental illness.* New York: Hoeber-Harper.

Taylor, S., & Bogdan, R. (1977). A phenomenological approach to "mental retardation." In B. Blatt, D. Biklen, and R. Bogdan (Eds.), *An alternative textbook in special education.* Denver: Love Publishing.

Tomlinson, S. (1982). *A sociology of special education.* Boston: Routledge & Kegan Paul.

Turnbull, H.R. (1986). *Free appropriate education: The law and children with disabilities.* Denver: Love Publishing.

Ulman, J.D., & Rosenberg, M.S. (1986). Science and superstition in special education. *Exceptional Children, 52*(5), 459–460.

Wang, M.C., Reynolds, M.C., & Walberg, H.J. (1987). *Handbook of special Education: Research and Practice (Vol. I: Learner characteristics and adaptive education).* Oxford, England: Pergamon Press.

Weick, K.L. (1985). Sources of order in underorganized systems. In Y.S. Lincoln (Ed.), *Organizational theory and inquiry: The paradigm revolution* (pp. 106–136). Beverly Hill, CA: Sage Publications.

White, O.R., & Haring, N.G. (1976). *Exceptional teaching: A multimedia training package.* Columbus, OH: Charles E. Merrill.

Wiseman, J. (1970). *Stations of the lost.* Englewood Cliffs, NJ: Prentice-Hall.

Tom Skrtic is a professor of special education at the University of Kansas, Lawrence.

$\circ$ **10** $\circ$

Curriculum-based measurement (CBM) is a set of procedures with the potential to greatly improve instruction and evaluation of instruction in general and special education. Shinn and Hubbard explain the differences in curriculum-based measurement and curriculum-based assessment, two concepts that often have been used interchangeably in the field of special education. They explain how these practices can improve the linkage of information that is collected in the assessment process and the instruction of children with special needs.

Curriculum-Based Measurement and Problem-Solving Assessment: Basic Procedures and Outcomes

Mark R. Shinn and Dawn D. Hubbard

More than 15 years after the passage of the Education for All Handicapped Children Act (EAHCA), assessment and testing practices with students who have mild handicaps remain essentially unchanged. Testing is characterized by a high reliance on commercially available, published norm-referenced tests (PNTs) of aptitude, achievement, and specific "abilities" (Reschly, Genshaft, & Binder, 1987). The lack of change is disturbing to many educators, as historically these practices have generated considerable controversy and little evidence of efficacy (Bersoff, 1973).

Most of the controversy has centered on appropriateness of PNTs to identify students as learning disabled (LD), educably mentally retarded (EMR) or low achieving (Gerber & Semmel, 1984; Heller, Holtzman, & Messick, 1982; Ysseldyke, Algozzine, Shinn, & McGue, 1982; Ysseldyke & Thurlow, 1984). Their accuracy and efficacy to diagnose students differentially among disability categories has been the subject of many research articles and much special education placement litigation (e.g., Reschly, Kicklighter, & McKee, 1988c). The focus on PNTs in identification has obscured a more important question, however. Can the data derived from current testing practices be used to: (a) *develop* more effective interventions, and (b) *evaluate the effectiveness* of any specific intervention implemented (Deno, 1986; 1989)? Measurement experts summarizing litigation (e.g., Reschly, Kicklighter, & McKee, 1988a; 1988b; 1988c) concluded that the link to intervention planning and evaluation is what will form the basis for promoting assessment practices as useful.

A number of resources detail why information derived from PNTs is difficult to link to intervention planning and intervention evaluation (e.g., Marston, 1989; Shinn, Nolet, & Knutson, 1990). Stated briefly, to be useful for planning instructional interventions, a test must provide information about what skills, task preskills, or problem-solving algorithms a student does and does not demonstrate that are essential for success in the curriculum the student is expected to learn (Howell & Morehead, 1987). Key features of tests to be used for these purposes include high content validity, enough items to reliably detect error and success patterns, and response formats that rely on production-type responses (e.g., writing answers to math problems). To be useful for evaluating effectiveness of the intervention, a test must be capable of being used to write long-term (i.e., annual) goals and be used on a repeated and frequent basis so that effective interventions are maintained and ineffective interventions are modified.

Key features again include content validity, a sufficient number of items drawn from the curriculum, and production-type responses. Content validity ensures that decisions are made on the basis of what students are expected to learn. A sufficient number of items is necessary so that the test is "sensitive" to change. Production-type responses allow for a careful analysis of a student's pattern of successes and errors that facilitates modifications of the current intervention, if necessary (Howell & Morehead, 1987).

As detailed in Figure 1, PNTs, at best, can be used to describe the severity of an academic problem relative to the academic performance of what is typically a nationally normed sample. The utility of this use of PNTs is most defensible when the test has high content validity. Even with PNTs that have high content validity, however, information for intervention planning and evaluation is lacking or must be extrapolated or collected via devices and methods in addition to or *after* a special education certification/eligibility decision has been made.

CURRICULUM-BASED ASSESSMENT AS A VIABLE ALTERNATIVE

One of the most frequently proposed solutions to using PNTs is curriculum-based assessment (CBA). CBA has been promoted because of its purported linkage of assessment and intervention (Reschly et al., 1988c) and because of its emphasis on data for intervention planning (Tucker, 1985). Unfortunately, CBA is *not* one set of unified testing strategies or procedures. Instead, CBA approaches range from testing procedures that resemble teacher-made criterion-referenced tests (Criterion-referenced curriculum-based assessment, C-R CBA, Blankenship, 1985) to procedures designed to determine a student's frustrational, instructional, and independent academic levels (Curriculum-Based Assessment for Instructional Design, C-BAID, Gickling & Thompson, 1985), and to a set of short-duration fluency measures of reading, written expression, spelling, and mathematics computation (Curriculum-Based Measurement, CBM, Deno, 1985, 1986; Shinn, 1989a).

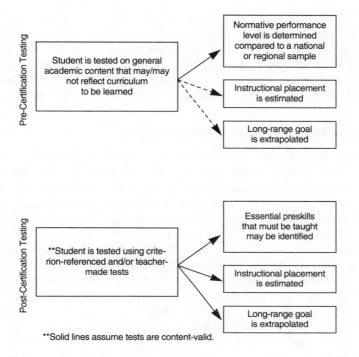

FIGURE 1   Current Eligibility Determination and Intervention Planning Assessment Strategies and Potential Contributions to Problem-Solving Decision Making

These CBA testing approaches are similar in that they rely on students' curriculum as the basis for constructing testing materials and decision making. The approaches differ on a number of critical dimensions, however, including philosophical assumptions underlying the assessment process, kinds of data collected, availability of technical adequacy data, and decision-making focus (for more detail, see Shinn, Rosenfield, & Knutson, 1989). Each CBA approach is designed to affect and improve academic interventions. Exactly how this is accomplished differs, though. Pragmatically, the approaches are not competitive; they can be used collaboratively and comprehensively to plan and evaluate academic interventions.

With the exception of CBM, CBA approaches emphasize the collection of student performance data for intervention planning that are not *directly* useful or validated for determining special education eligibility (Shinn, Rosenfield, & Knutson, 1989; Shinn & Good, in press). The procedures emphasize information useful for planning the instructional content (the "what to teach" component) of an intervention plan. The assessment strategies correspond to the kinds of information collected by special education teachers after the certification decision is made, as represented in Figure 1. Sequentially, the timing of CBA data collection need not occur after the eligibility determination, though.

At best, these CBA approaches contribute only indirectly to special education certification decisions. Therefore, the direct linkage between special education eligibility and intervention—one of the quality assessment indicators proposed by Reschly et al. (1988c)—is not evident. Furthermore, most CBA strategies have not been demonstrated to be useful for evaluating the effectiveness of interventions for specific students. As a result, they fail to meet Reschly et al.'s (1988c) second criterion for good assessment practice.

CURRICULUM-BASED MEASUREMENT

Curriculum-Based Measurement is the only CBA strategy to meet Reschly et al.'s criteria of linking information collected for eligibility determination to intervention planning and usefulness for evaluating intervention effectiveness. As developed by Deno (1985, 1986, 1989) and others (e.g., Fuchs, 1989, Fuchs, Hamlett, Fuchs, Stecker, & Ferguson, 1988; Germann & Tindal, 1985; Marston & Magnusson, 1985; Shinn, 1989a; Wesson, 1987), CBM is a set of short- duration (1–3 minutes) fluency tests in the basic skill areas of reading, spelling, mathematics computation, and written expression, used in a standardized manner to facilitate problem-solving assessment.

The basic CBM measures, testing durations, scoring metrics, and sample investigations of their technical adequacy (reliability and validity) are presented in Table 1. An extensive program of research has been conducted for more than 12 years supporting these measures as reliable and valid indicators of student progress in the basic skill areas. For example, in reading, the number of words read correctly has been validated as an accurate measure of a student's general reading skill, including reading comprehension. For more detail on technical adequacy, see the extensive review by Marston (1989).

In contrast to Figure 1, CBM links the assessment data collected for special education (or other special programs) eligibility to intervention by testing a referred student repeatedly in successive levels of the general education curriculum in which the student is having difficulty. This testing process is called Survey-Level Assessment (SLA). As with PNTs, data derived from CBM SLA may assist in determining a student's eligibility for special education services by providing an index of normative performance. Rather than testing referred students on tests assumed to be content-valid and making comparisons to a norm group that may or may not represent the referred students' learning experiences and opportunities within the specific curriculum, CBM tests students in the curriculum they are expected to learn. Performance is then compared directly to how other students perform in that curriculum. And while CBM provides equivalent, but more *direct* information for eligibility, the data also allow for initial decisions about intervention to be made, as presented in Figure 2.

By testing students in successive levels of the curriculum, the level in which a student performs *successfully* can be identified for instructional placement purposes. This strategy of directly testing students until they are successful is in stark contrast to PNTs, which usually confirm that the referred student is unsuccessful on the test tasks. SLA also facilitates discussion of the level of the curriculum in which the student would be expected to perform in 1 year. Once this curriculum level has been identified, the annual

**TABLE 1   A Description of the Basic Curriculum-Based Measures
In Reading, Spelling, Mathematics Computation,
and Written Expression**

Area	Testing Duration	Description and Types of Scores Derived	Sample Technical Adequacy Information
Reading	1 minute	Students read passages orally, and the number of words read correctly and errors are counted.	Deno, Mirkin, & Chiang (1982); Fuchs, Fuchs, & Maxwell (1988)
Spelling	2 minutes	Students write words that are dictated orally, and the number of words spelled correctly and correct letter sequences are counted.	Deno, Marston, Mirkin, Lowry, Sindelar, & Jenkins (1982); Marston, Lowry, Deno, & Mirkin (1981)
Mathematics Computation	2-5 minutes	Students write answers to computation problems, and number of correct digits are counted.	Fuchs & Fuchs (1987a); Marston, Fuchs, & Deno (1986)
Written Expression	3 minutes	After being given a story starter or topic sentence, students write a story. Number of words written, spelled correctly, and correct word sequences may be counted.	Deno, Marston, & Mirkin (1982)

goal of the individualized education program (IEP) can be written. Once goals have been established, the initial intervention plan can be evaluated on a continuous and frequent basis, allowing ineffective interventions to be identified and modified and effective treatments to be continued with confidence. Finally, the extensive amount of information about how the student performs (i.e., what the student does/does not do successfully) in the curriculum can be analyzed to form hypotheses about what essential curricular skills the student already has mastered and those that must be taught.

Basic Assumptions of CBM and Problem-Solving Assessment

The use of CBM is more than just employing a new set of "tests." Instead, it is a commitment to a new way of viewing school problems and their solutions through a Problem-Solving model (Deno, 1989; Shinn & Good, in press). The Problem-Solving model is predicated on seven assumptions.

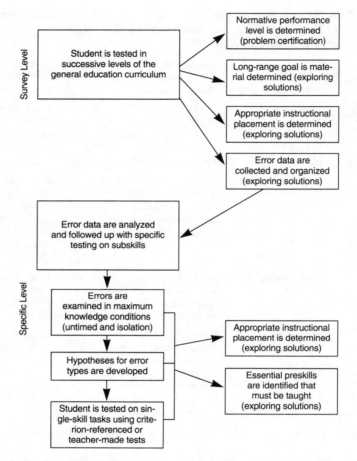

FIGURE 2   *Linking Eligibility Determination and Intervention*

First is an inherent assumption that special education, like other remedial programs, is a *problem-solving system* for general education. It is designed to remediate some of the problems that general education, as currently structured, is ill equipped to resolve. For example, general education in most schools is not designed to meet the needs of a population with diverse academic skills (Gerber & Semmel, 1984). Special education for students with mild handicaps attempts to remediate many of these problems.

Second, problems are *defined situationally*. A problem is defined as a significant discrepancy between what is expected in the environment and what occurs. Academic problems are defined by the lack of success for a specific student within a specific general education curriculum compared to students in that same environment who are performing successfully in the curriculum. Therefore, problems have to be defined by the discrepancy in the general education curriculum compared to peers rather than an internal discrepancy residing within the student. When situations change, what was a problem may no longer be one and vice versa.

Third, the Problem-Solving model takes a *value position* that some students need additional resources (e.g., special education) to profit from education. Although decisions about who needs additional resources can be data-based, changes in financial resources, service delivery models, or the knowledge base may result in a change in our conceptions as to who receives special education services.

Fourth, identifying problems is not enough; special education, in and of itself, is not an intervention. As a result, interventions have to be planned in detail.

Fifth, with our current assessment technology and scientific data base, unfortunately, we cannot predict with certainty an intervention that will be effective with any given student. Based on test results, we cannot identify a student as an auditory learner or a sequential learner and prescribe the intervention that is certain to work (for more information, see Deno, 1990).

Sixth, because of the uncertain effects of any intervention, the treatment outcomes for specific students must be evaluated frequently and in a timely manner. Effective interventions should be maintained. Ineffective interventions should be modified as soon as possible.

Seventh, problems are resolved when the discrepancy between what is expected and what occurs is no longer significant. For academic problems, typically, that means that a student performs in the general education curriculum at a level commensurate with peers in the same environment.

Steps and Issues

The Problem-Solving model is divided into five sequential steps, presented in Table 2. Each step is characterized by a different set of conceptual issues that dictate collection of different types of CBM data.

Specific CBM Problem-Solving Procedures

Problem Identification and Certification

A potential need for additional instructional resources to resolve an academic problem typically is stimulated by a general education teacher making a referral for assistance to a specialized remedial program such as Chapter 1 or special education. Referral to assistance programs such as Chapter 1 is relatively uncontroversial. Referral to special education has been and remains controversial, in large part because of the stigmatizing labels used and the testing procedures by which those labels are decided. Nevertheless, dramatic changes are needed in determining who receives special education services, and such services unfortunately must be accompanied by labels that place the problem solely within the student (e.g., learning disabilities).

As with any program with limited resources, educators must determine who needs specialized assistance so students may benefit from their education. It has been argued per-

**TABLE 2 CBM Problem-Solving Model Decisions,
Measurement Activities, and Evaluation Activities**

Problem-Solving Decision	Measurement Activities	Evaluation Activities
1. Problem identification (Screening)	Observe and record student differences, if any, between actual and expected performance.	Decide that a performance discrepancy exists.
2. Problem certification (Eligibility determination)	Describe the differences between actual and expected performance in context of the likelihood of general education resources solving the problem.	Decide if discrepancies are important enough that special services may be required to resolve problems.
3. Exploring alternative solutions (IEP goal setting and intervention planning)	Determine probable performance improvements (goals) and costs associated with various interventions.	Select the program reform (i.e., intervention) to be tested.
4. Evaluating solutions and making modifications (Progress monitoring)	Monitor implementation and student performance changes.	Determine whether intervention is effective or should be modified.
5. Problem solution (Program termination)	Observe and record student differences, if any, between actual and expected performance.	Decide that exisiting discrepancies, if any, are not important and program may be terminated.

Source: From "Curriculum-Based Measurement and Alternative Special Education Services: A Fundamental and Direct Relationship" (p. 13) by S. L. Deno, 1989, *Curriculum-Based Measurement: Assessing Special Children*, edited by M. R. Shinn, New York: Guilford Press. Copyright ©1989 by The Guilford Press. Adapted by permission.

suasively (e.g., Gerber & Semmel, 1984) and from a data-based perspective that schools serve students with severe achievement needs in special education programs. For example, Shinn, Tindal, and Spira (1987) demonstrated that students referred by their general education teachers for learning disabilities services in reading typically perform below the 5th percentile, compared to local norms in the reading curriculum. Other studies have demonstrated that students actually placed in learning disabilities programs typically perform below the 3rd percentile, compared to local norms in the curriculum (Shinn, Tindal, Spira, & Marston, 1987).

The Problem-Solving model begins with a decision that a potential problem is *important enough* to investigate further. At the point that someone (often a general education teacher) has concerns over performance in the curriculum, CBM can be used to de-

TABLE 3　Results of CBM Problem Identification for Desireé

Academic Area		Day 1	Day 2	Day 3	Median	Peer Median
Reading	Passage 1	22	16	11		
	Passage 2	14	15	11		
	Passage 3	18	12	14		
	Daily Median	18	15	11	15 WRC*	75 WRC*
Math Grade	3 Problems	19	20	14	19 CD**	26 CD**

*WRC= words read correctly
**CD= correct digits

termine if the student's skills are sufficiently different from other students to warrant further investigation. As shown in Table 2, a problem is defined as a significant difference between expected performance in the general education curriculum and how the referred student performs. CBM is used to operationalize this conceptual model by having referred students take probes derived from the general education curriculum that typical students are expected to learn. The referred student's scores then are compared to local norms developed from same-grade peers using those same probes.

Consider the case of Desireé, a third-grade student referred because her classroom teacher had serious concerns about progress in reading and mathematics. Because no obvious reasons could explain the teacher's concerns (e.g., poor school attendance, vision or hearing difficulties), Desireé was tested using a series of probes derived from her general education reading (Ginn) and math (Heath) curricula. Typical third-grade students were expected to be reading Ginn Level 8, and school district norms had been developed on this level of the reading series (see Shinn, 1989b, for more detail on the local norming process). Desiree read three different passages each day for 3 days in a 5-day period. Her nine scores are presented in Table 3 and summarized by determining her median performance across the passages.

Desireé also completed three different forms of probes derived from the computational objectives for the Grade 3 Heath curriculum. Her scores on these probes also are presented in Table 3. To determine if a problem requiring further assessment existed, Desireé's scores were compared to third-grade peers in her school district. The median score of the third-grade local norms also is displayed in Table 3. In this example, if Desireé's scores consistently fell below half the level of typical grade-level peers, a problem worth warranting investigation would be identified.

To facilitate communication with general education teachers, parents, administrators, and the students themselves, the Problem Identification data are displayed graphically. Desireé's results are presented in Figure 3.

Desireé performed consistently below the cutting score only in the area of reading. Although her score in mathematics was below the median of her peers, it was not considered to be sufficiently different from other students to warrant additional investigation.

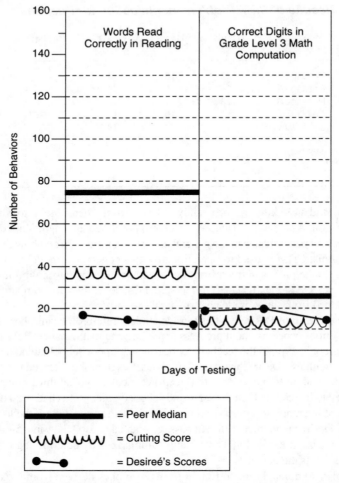

**FIGURE 3 *Use of CBM Comparing Desireé to Same-Grade General
Education Peers***

Because all the math probes required Desiree to write answers to the computational
problems, however, the specific responses could be analyzed to determine if she had
areas of weakness that could be shared with her general education teacher for improved
performance.

As a result of the Problem Identification decision-making process, a problem of potentially serious magnitude was observed only in reading. Consequently, Desireé was
administered a Survey-Level Assessment from successive levels of her general education
curriculum using CBM as part of the Problem Certification decision-making process. As
shown in Table 2, Problem Certification is conceptualized as determining if the difference

between expected performance and observed performance in the curriculum is serious enough that a multidisciplinary team considers it unlikely that the problem will be resolved in general education. Then the student may be considered eligible for special education, assuming that procedural state and federal requirements are met.

Consider a fifth-grade student who is placed appropriately in a fifth-grade reader. No additional resources should be required in general education for the student to acquire the expected reading skills, assuming instruction is adequate and the student is motivated. The need for additional resources is less clear for a fifth-grade student who is placed appropriately in a third-grade reader. The general education classroom should have resources (e.g., instructional alternatives, peer tutoring or cooperative learning programs, more individualized assistance) to accommodate that student in the general education classroom. In reality, however, the resources to accommodate the student may vary considerably from district to district and even from school to school. As currently structured, general education may not facilitate the student learning the reading curriculum, so additional resources outside of general education may be necessary.

Finally, consider the fifth-grade student who is placed appropriately in a beginning first-grade reader. It seems unlikely that in most settings, at least as currently structured, general education would have sufficient resources to facilitate the student mastering the reading curriculum. In this circumstance, the intensive and extensive resources provided by special education may be required.

The process of Problem Certification decision making using CBM relies on the SLA to identify the magnitude of the problem. In Desireé's case, she was given at least three randomly selected passages in each of a number of successively lower levels of the Ginn reading curriculum. Her scores in Ginn 8 were already available from the Problem Identification process, so the SLA began by testing her at the next lower level (Ginn 7). One of the major goals of the SLA is to determine a level of the curriculum in which Desiree is "successful."

This decision is operationalized in reading by identifying the highest level of the curriculum (i.e., instructional placement) where she could be placed and expected to profit from instruction. If the student were to be placed in third- through sixth-grade material, it would be desirable to be reading 70-100 words correctly per minute with no more than 4–6 errors (95% accuracy). If the student were to be placed in first- or second-grade material, it would be desirable to be reading 40–60 words correctly per minute with no more than 4–6 errors (90% accuracy).

On a single testing occasion, Desireé read passages beginning at Level 8 through Level 4. Her scores are shown in Table 4. For ease of interpretation, only the number of words she read correctly are included. According to the reading instructional placement guidelines, Desireé most likely should be placed in a Ginn 4 reader, material expected for typical first-grade students. One conclusion that can be reached is that Desireé performs about 2 years behind curricular expectations in reading.

The potential magnitude of the problem also is defined relative to local normative performance in the reading curriculum. Local norms were developed for the school district from the expected level of the Ginn series representative of each grade. For exam-

TABLE 4   Results of Survey-Level Assessment and Problem Certification for Desireé

Grade Material to be Learned	Level of Ginn Curriculum	Desireés Median Performance	Grade-Level Peer Performance	Desireés Percentile Rank
3	8	15	87	5
2	7	20	*	
	6	22	58	14
1	5	36	*	
	4	40	23	73

*Local norms, developed from only one level of curriculum per grade level. Therefore, no norms are available for these curriculum levels.

ple, second-grade students were normed using Level 7 of the Ginn curriculum, the expected level representative of most second-grade students during the school year. The appropriate interpretive score is the percentile rank, also shown in Table 4. Desireé performed well below typical third- and second-grade students, but read above the median of typical first-grade students at this time of the school year.

Decisions about Problem Certification using CBM usually are made on the basis of percentile rank criteria (Marston & Magnusson, 1988; Shinn, 1989b). In Desireé's school district, she could be considered eligible for special education if her scores were below the 16th percentile of students one grade-level below her current grade placement. In this instance, Desireé could be considered eligible because she performed at the 5th percentile of second graders, well below the 16th percentile. Desireé's results in reading compared to the range of reading scores from local norms are presented in Figure 4. The figure communicates clearly that she performs outside the range of typical third and second graders, but performs above typical first graders in the Ginn series.

Eligibility is but one part of the Problem Certification decision. The second part is *need*. A student may be eligible for special education, but not need the services. This decision is made only by examining Desireé's instructional needs in the context of resources available in general education that may be used to affect her learning positively. Only after it has been demonstrated to be unlikely that she could benefit from those resources should she be considered for special education. In this case, the multidisciplinary team decided it was unlikely that Desireé would benefit from reading instruction in general education regardless of what resources were brought to bear. Therefore, Desireé was provided special education with an IEP in reading.

Exploring and Evaluating Solutions

The data collected for Problem Identification and Certification decisions are linked directly to Exploring and Evaluating Solutions decisions. In Exploring Solutions, an initial intervention is planned with respect to the "what" to teach (e.g., content of instruction, type and level of curriculum to be used) and the "how" to teach (e.g., what teaching strategies will be used). CBM Problem Identification and Problem Certification data can as-

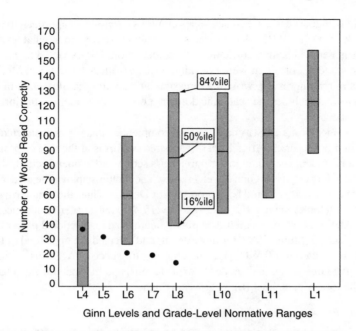

FIGURE 4   *Comparing Desireé to Same- and Other-Grade General Education Peers in Reading*

sist in the intervention planning process by providing information regarding specific skills the student does or does not demonstrate (Howell & Morehead, 1987; see Figure 2). The major strength of CBM, however, is in evaluating outcomes. CBM was developed to provide teachers with a set of procedures so they may make frequent and routine decisions about whether and when to modify a student's instructional program (Deno, 1985).

In Exploring Solution decisions, the first task is to develop annual goals for the student. Fuchs and Shinn (1989) state that "specification of a goal precedes and defines the CBM monitoring of student progress and instructional effectiveness" (p. 130). A compelling reason to use CBM data to write goals comes from the Education for All Handicapped Children Act (1975). This act requires that an IEP identify each special education student's needs in terms of goals and objectives (Bateman & Herr, 1981) and identify "appropriate criteria and evaluation procedures" for determining progress toward these goals (Sect. 121a.316e). Yet, almost 16 years after implementation of the Act, current IEPs fail to demonstrate significant improvement in quality over initial implementation (Smith, 1990). Too often, IEP goals are written without current student performance data. IEP goals are frequently vague, lacking observable, measurable outcomes (e.g., "Will improve 1 year in reading"), or are overly specific and detail a series of short-term instructional objectives (e.g., "Will master C-V-C words with 80% accuracy"). As a result, *systematic* evaluation of an individual's special education intervention is precluded.

Writing IEP goals using CBM strategies employs a *long-term* approach to measurement (Fuchs & Deno, 1991). A decision is made about where and at what level of success in the general education curriculum the student would be expected to perform in 1 year if the student's program were considered successful. A basic format for IEP annual goals in reading, math, written expression, and spelling is illustrated in Table 5. The basic format includes the academic domain, conditions, student behavior, and criterion for success.

If we consider Desireé's SLA data, it was recommended that she be instructed in Level 4 of the Ginn basal series. After 1 year, if Desireé performs at the rate of progress expected of any student according to the publisher's scope-and-sequence chart, she would be expected to be placed in a Ginn Level 7 reader. The multidisciplinary team decided this expected rate of progress would be appropriate for Desireé. Thus, the long-term goal material identified for her annual IEP goal was Level 7. Next, the criterion for success must be identified. For Desiree, the multidisciplinary team used instructional placement standards (see Fuchs & Shinn, 1989, for more detail) and selected the upper end of the range for grades 1-2 material (60 WCM) as the criterion for success. After discussion of the SLA data, the Ginn scope-and-sequence expectations, and the specific expectations for Desireé, the following annual IEP goal was written:

TABLE 5　Basic Format for Annual IEP Goals in Reading, Math, Written Expression, and Spelling

Academic Area	Conditions	Behavior	Criterion
Reading	In *(number of weeks until annual review)*, when given a randomly selected passage from *(level and name of reading series)*,	student will read aloud	at *(number of words per minute correct/ # of errors)*.
Math	In *(number of weeks until annual review)*, when given randomly selected problems from *(level and name of math series)* for 2 minutes,	student will write	*(number of correct digits)*.
Written Expression	In *(number of weeks until annual review)*, when given a story starter or topic sentence and 3 minutes in which to write,	student will write	a total of *(number of words or letter sequences)*.
Spelling	In *(number of weeks until annual review)*, when dictated randomly selected words from *(level and name of spelling series)* for 2 minutes,	student will write	*(number of correct letter sequences)*.

Source: From "Writing CBM IEP Objectives" (p. 136) by L. S. Fuchs and M. R. Shinn, 1989, *Curriculum-Based Measurement: Assessing Special Children*, edited by M.R. Shinn. New York: Guilford Press. Copyright ©1989 by The Guilford Press. Reprinted by permission.

In 32 weeks, when given a randomly selected passage from Level 7 of the Ginn reading series, Desireé will read aloud at a rate of 60 words per minute correct with 4 or fewer errors.

One advantage of measuring Desireé's reading proficiency in long-term goal material is the emphasis on broad, rather than specific, curricular achievement (Fuchs & Fuchs, 1986a; Fuchs & Deno, 1991). In addition, measuring Desireé's performance in annual goal material, in contrast to short-term objectives, is more logistically feasible, assesses for retention and generalization, represents meaningful growth in the curriculum, and is supported by technical adequacy data (for more detail see Fuchs, in press; Fuchs & Deno, 1991).

Writing IEP goals using CBM data can be accomplished through a variety of strategies. The first set of strategies involves establishing the IEP annual goal(s) in the absence of local norms. These strategies include expert judgment, dynamic aim, and instructional placement standards.

The second strategy utilizes local norms to establish the criterion for success. All the strategies use the information collected from the SLA data, as this provides the legally required current performance data across levels of the curriculum.

Goal-writing strategies without local norms. The use of "expert judgment" is premised on the expectation that the student will "do more in more difficult material" in 1 year. The multidisciplinary team makes a "best guess" about the annual goal material, the level of the curriculum at which the student would be expected to be performing in 1 year. This level becomes the measurement material for evaluating student progress. A criterion for success also must be specified. As broad guidelines for using the expert judgment approach: (a) the annual goal material must be at least one curriculum level beyond the student's current instructional placement, and (b) the criterion for success must be higher than the student's current performance in the annual goal material (Fuchs & Fuchs, 1986a). In the case of Desireé, this strategy would require selecting, at the very minimum, Level 5 as the annual goal material and a criterion for success greater than 36 WPM. Goals written using this method usually are significantly more ambitious than these minimal standards. In the absence of more objective data (e.g., instructional placement criteria, local norms), this strategy is straightforward and encourages writing ambitious and realistic goals.

The *dynamic aim* approach is a variation of the expert judgment approach. This strategy originates with the original "best guess," but the criterion for success is adjusted based on the student's rate of progress. For example, suppose Desireé's IEP goal stated that in 1 year, given passages from Ginn Level 6, Desireé will read aloud at a rate of 50 WPM with 4 or fewer errors. The dynamic aim approach would require frequently evaluating Desireé's performance compared to the goal of 50 WPM and adjusting the criterion for success (i.e., 50 WPM) based on her projected rate of progress. If her rate of progress suggests that she will exceed 50 WPM, the goal would be raised. On the other hand, if her rate of progress suggests that she will not meet the goal, the 50 WPM goal would be retained and an instructional change would be made. Teachers who utilize a dynamic aim approach have been shown to raise goals more frequently, employ more ambitious goals, and obtain greater student achievement outcomes, as compared to teachers using an approach in which goals are not raised if rate of progress exceeds the goal (Fuchs, Fuchs, & Hamlett, 1989b).

A third strategy involves using *instructional placement standards* as guidelines for determining the level of the general education curriculum in which a student would be placed for instructional purposes, the annual goal level of the curriculum, and the criterion for success. To date, CBM instructional placement standards have been proposed only in the area of reading. This approach follows the same general guidelines that were set forth in the expert judgment strategy, but are more data-based. First, the level of the general education curriculum in which the student would be expected to be successful is identified. Although the special education student may not receive instruction in this curriculum, identifying instructional level serves as the index to current performance in the mainstream curriculum. Once that level has been established, the multidisciplinary team can discuss how much progress in the general education curriculum would be expected in 1 year, if the program were successful. The level of the general education curriculum where the student would be expected to perform corresponds to the annual goal material. The criterion for success equals the instructional placement standard for that level of the curriculum (for more detail, see Fuchs & Shinn, 1989).

As discussed in the section on Problem Identification and Problem Certification, for Desireé, the suggested instructional placement would be Ginn Level 4, because this was the highest level of first- or second-grade curriculum in which she read at least 40 WPM correct. The instructional placement standards also are used as a guideline for determining criteria for success in the IEP goal material. If Level 7 were selected as the annual goal-level material, it would be recommended that Desireé read at least 40 WPM correct as the criterion for success. In Desireé's case, the multidisciplinary team identified the upper end (60 WRC) of the instructional placement standards as the criterion for success.

Goal writing strategies using local norms. The availability of local norms assists with establishing more data-based criteria for success in the annual goal material. Expectations about student progress are tied to the performance of typical general education peers. Guidelines for this approach again require specification of the level of the general education curriculum at which the student would be expected to be performing in 1 year. The criterion for success in that material is the median score of typical general education students in that material. For example, if the multidisciplinary team decided that in 1 year Desireé would be expected to perform in the third-grade level of the curriculum (Level 8), the criterion for success would be 87, the normative score of students at that grade (see Table 5).

Evaluating Solutions

Procedures for Data Collection

Once data-based annual IEP goal(s) are written, a standard is provided for evaluating the initial intervention's effectiveness. Effectiveness is evaluated by routinely and frequently collecting and analyzing student data. Annual goals in the IEP are translated into a graph to provide a visual representation of the goal and actual student perfor-

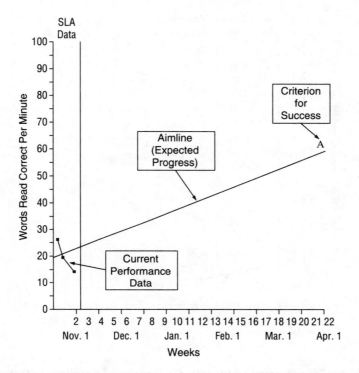

FIGURE 5 *Desireé's Annual IEP Goal Translated into a Graph for Monitoring Intervention Effectiveness*

mance, as shown in Figure 5. The graph includes: (a) time frame (horizontal axis), (b) unit of measurement (vertical axis), (c) criterion for success, and (d) current performance data from the material specified in the annual goal (from SLA). The line drawn from the student's current performance data to the criterion for success represents the expected rate of progress, or *aimline*.

Frequency of measurement. Use of CBM is predicated on the notion that student outcomes are examined on an ongoing and frequent basis. Every time a student is tested, the results are graphed as shown in Figure 6. In Desireé's case, two times each week she was tested by reading a passage randomly sampled from the level of the curriculum specified in her annual IEP goal. In this instance it was Ginn Level 7. As shown in Figure 6, the initial instructional program implemented for 5 weeks was not effective. In fact, the intervention was having a detrimental effect on her reading achievement. Her estimated rate of progress, shown by the *trendline*, was decreasing. The trendline is drawn through each of Desireé's scores to represent her estimated rate of progress. Because her actual rate of progress was much less than her expected rate of progress, a change in her instructional program was required.

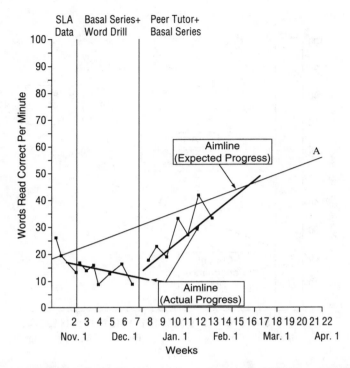

FIGURE 6   *Effectiveness of Desireé's Reading Intervention Relative to Rate of Progress Toward Annual Goal*

The change in intervention was effective. Not only was Desireé now improving in her general reading skills, but her actual rate of progress was exceeding her expected rate. Collecting student performance data frequently allowed Desireé's teacher to change the instructional program when it was shown to be ineffective.

Determining how frequently CBM data should be collected involves appraising both technical and practical considerations. *Technical considerations* refer to evidence supporting the use of data to make reliable decisions regarding student progress. The major tool in making this decision is the trendline (Fuchs, 1989). Among the technical issues regarding use of a trendline are the number of data points required to estimate actual progress reliably and how to organize the data for interpretation. An ideal trendline would allow reliable decisions to be made with a few number of data points. This would enable teachers to avoid maintaining an ineffective instructional program for long periods. A minimum of 10 data points (Good & Shinn, 1990) is necessary to estimate a reliable performance trend.

Practical considerations also are important. Although collecting data on student performance daily may be technically advantageous so that the minimum number of data points for trend estimation can accrue rapidly, this may not be feasible. Research has suggested that measuring student performance twice weekly may be sufficient to make appropriate decisions (Fuchs & Fuchs, 1986b). No additional student achievement benefits as a function of frequency of measurement were found for monitoring twice weekly or three times weekly or daily (Fuchs & Fuchs, 1986b). Therefore, it is recommended that special education practitioners collect student performance data twice weekly so the requisite 10 data points can be collected in a little over a month (5 weeks). This time frame allows adequate time for demonstrating instructional effects and the modification of ineffective programs.

Data collection strategies. Various methods have been utilized to collect CBM student performance data. Most frequently, teachers collect and score the data. The usefulness of having teachers meaningfully involved in collecting and evaluating student data has been documented in terms of greater positive effects on student achievement (Fuchs, Deno, & Mirkin, 1984; Fuchs & Fuchs, 1986b). Some special education teachers, however, express reluctance, at least initially, to use CBM progress monitoring strategies because they perceive the amount of time involved to be excessive (Wesson, King, & Deno, 1984). The *perception* of progress monitoring being time consuming does not match the data, however. Fuchs (1987) found that teachers spent an average of only 2 minutes and 15 seconds collecting a 1-minute sample of reading, including preparation, administration, scoring, and graphing of student data. Other research corroborates these findings for teachers who monitor student progress using CBM (Marston & Magnusson, 1985; Wesson, Fuchs, Tindal, Mirkin, & Deno, 1986).

Although it is logistically feasible for teachers to collect, score, and analyze CBM data, other strategies may increase efficiency. One approach has emphasized computer-managed instruction (CMI; Fuchs, 1988), which uses computer software programs to collect, graph, and analyze student performance data (Fuchs, Hamlett, & Fuchs, 1990). CMI creates an information management system to assist teachers in evaluating students' progress towards the CBM annual IEP goal. In a study that compared utilizing the computer software program to teacher-managed CBM practices (Fuchs, Fuchs, Hamlett, & Hasselbring, 1987), teachers reported that computers were more efficient than scoring, graphing, and evaluating student data by hand. Although the teachers perceived increased efficiency by using the computer software program, the research results suggested that the use of computers actually decreased teachers' efficiency in charting student performance. Using the computer program, however, may minimize teacher time devoted to analyzing student performance (Fuchs, Fuchs, Hamlett & Hasselbring, 1987).

The use of student peers also has been investigated as an option to reduce teacher data collection time and allow teachers to devote more time to interpreting the obtained information. Moreover, it has been hypothesized that potential benefits to peer tutors from collecting student data may accrue in terms of their own achievement and self-concept gains. Research related to training general education students to monitor reading using CBM procedures suggests that they can be trained to be reliable data collectors. Trained student monitors have been shown to be as accurate as adults, with interrater agreement percentages between students and trained adults ranging from 96.6% to 97.7% (Bentz,

Shinn, & Gleason, 1990) and 86.2% to 100% (Knutson, 1990). Concerns have been raised, however, about the amount of time needed to train and frequently monitor student data collectors to assure high levels of reliability over time (Knutson, 1990). Again, in making CBM procedures more time-efficient, the qualitative information that teachers gain through direct scoring of student protocols is forfeited and should be taken into account when considering alternatives.

Determining intervention effectiveness. Data are collected in an ongoing manner to provide information regarding a student's progress toward the annual IEP goal(s). Teachers ultimately must make *decisions* about whether a program is effective, based on the data. Program effectiveness decisions are made by summarizing actual student performance and choosing an evaluation framework, either goal- or experimental-based.

Summarizing actual student progress is accomplished in two ways: (a) using a split-middle trendline (SM) or (b) using an ordinary-least-squares trendline (OLS). The SM and OLS differ in the way they are calculated. The SM requires few calculations and is trained easily (White, 1974). The OLS requires a programmable calculator or a microcomputer. In a study comparing the accuracy of SM and OLS procedures, results indicated that the OLS method was superior to the SM method for reading CBM data (Good & Shinn, 1990). More specifically, the OLS estimates were superior in their ability to estimate with smaller numbers of data points (10) and for longer periods into the future (6 weeks). These data suggest that an OLS method for evaluating student performance and making instructional decisions is best.

Goal-based data evaluation is the most common evaluation approach (see Fuchs, Fuchs, & Hamlett, 1989b). In the goal-based evaluation framework, the annual IEP goal is translated into the aimline of expected rate of progress. This aimline is used as the reference for success and decisions are made according to the student's progress toward this line. This evaluation approach is illustrated in Figure 6. To determine whether Desireé is making progress toward her goal, decision rules are applied when a predetermined number of data points have been collected. The rules applied would be in accordance with the slope of the trendline (either exceeding or failing to meet projected aimline), as explained previously. A variation to using a trendline with this approach is the 3-day rule (see White & Haring, 1980). The 3-day rule states that if the student's data points fall below the aimline for 3 consecutive monitoring days, an instructional change is warranted. Conversely, if the data points fall above the line for 3 consecutive monitoring days, the goal should be raised.

An experimental-based approach to evaluating student performance (see Hamlett, Fuchs, Stecher, & Ferguson, Fuchs, 1988) also can be used to determine intervention effectiveness. This approach requires that an instructional change be made after collecting a predetermined number of data points (e.g., 10), regardless of student progress. Changes in student programs are made routinely to: (a) test the effectiveness of different instructional strategies, and (b) potentially effect a greater rate of progress than would be obtained even if an effective program were maintained (Fuchs, 1988). A student's slope of improvement for each intervention is compared to determine which intervention had the greatest effect on student progress. The teaching approach that had the greatest effect on student performance then is implemented. Research comparing the goal-based and experimental-based methods indicates that the goal-based approach has a greater impact on student achievement, and teachers using this approach implement the monitoring and data-management procedures more accurately (Fuchs, 1988).

Problem Solution

If interventions are effective, educators can expect that ultimately a problem will be resolved. In the Problem-Solving model, this decision is reached when the initial severe discrepancy between what was expected and what was occurring is no longer severe. In special education, this decision is akin to making a decision that a student no longer needs special education services and can benefit from education in the general education classroom. The limited research data on special education exit rates suggest that few students are returned to general education annually (Shinn, 1988; Rodden-Nord, Shinn, & Good, 1992). Whether this outcome is due to the limited effectiveness of special education intervention programs, poor assessment practices, or an interaction of the two has not been determined. Some school-based personnel (e.g., Allen, 1989) have argued that Problem Solution decisions are not made because relevant data are not collected to suggest that a special education student can perform successfully in the general education curriculum.

CBM can be used to assist in making Problem Solution decisions in two ways. *First,* student progress toward the annual IEP goal is examined formally. This process entails evaluation of the graphed data, typically in relationship to the expected rate of progress shown by the aimline. In Figure 6, failure of the intervention implemented initially to resolve Desireé's reading problem was identified as part of the Problem Solution decision in mid-December.

Second, CBM can be used to repeat quarterly the Problem Identification peer-referenced testing activities. Special education students are tested on one day in the typical level of the curriculum from their grade placement and compared to same-grade students. At the time the first peer-referenced testing took place, Desireé had not reduced the discrepancy from her third-grade students as she continued to score at the 5th percentile.

At the time of the annual review, special education students are given another SLA, in which they are tested in successive levels of the curriculum. These data allow decisions to be made regarding reduced discrepancies from same-grade and lower-grade students in the curriculum. The data also serve as current performance data for writing new annual IEP goals.

In Desireé's case, by the end of the school year, not only had she exceeded greatly her expected rate of progress on the IEP but she also had reduced significantly the discrepancy from her peers in the curriculum. At the beginning of the year, she had performed at the 5th percentile of same-grade peers. By the expiration of her IEP, she performed at the 38th percentile relative to same-grade peers. Because of her rapid rate of progress in special education, as evidenced by the IEP graph and her reduced discrepancy, Desireé was exited from special education.

RESEARCH OUTCOMES OF CBM AND
PROBLEM-SOLVING MODEL IMPLEMENTATION

A number of studies have examined components of CBM implementation (e.g., the effects of specific goal-setting strategies on student achievement in reading) and on implementation of CBM in a Problem-Solving model for special education decision making. The current research results reported here are interpreted in a unit of analysis called *effect size* (ES). Effect size is determined by taking the difference in scores between group means (e.g., experimental and control groups) divided by the standard deviation of the control group (Kavale & Forness, 1987). ES will be used to discuss differences in CBM performance for descriptive and experimental studies. For descriptive studies, an ES represents the mean performance differences between groups of students.

For example, Shinn, Ysseldyke, Deno, and Tindal (1986) compared the CBM reading scores of fifth-grade students in learning disabilities programs and other low-achievers. They found an ES of −1.3. This score is interpreted as meaning that the typical LD student performed 1.3 standard deviations below the typical low achiever on CBM reading probes. In terms of percentile ranks, an ES of this magnitude means that the typical LD student performed at approximately the 10th percentile rank of low-achieving students.

For the experimental studies, Fuchs and Fuchs (1986b) explain an effect size of approximately one-half standard deviation (.52) as meaning that "in terms of the standard normal curve and an achievement test scale with a population mean of 100 and standard deviation of 15, one might expect the [intervention X] to increase the typical achievement outcome score from 100 to approximately 107.5" (p. 436). Achievement gains of this magnitude suggest that a student who would be expected to perform at the 50th percentile without the treatment would be expected to perform at the 69th percentile with the treatment.

Problem Identification/Problem Certification Research Outcomes

Outcome investigations regarding the use of CBM to make Problem Identification and Problem Certification decisions have been undertaken in three broad areas: (a) the utility of using CBM measures to differentiate students with mild handicaps (e.g., learning disabilities) from low-achieving and typical general education students, (b) the effects on special education assessment and placement practices, and (c) effects on the practices of school psychologists.

Using CBM to Differentiate Groups of Students

Four studies have investigated the usefulness of CBM to differentiate students referred for or placed in special education from other groups such as low achievers (e.g., Chapter 1 students) and typical students. One study investigated the achievement characteristics of students referred for special education services in reading. Three studies examined whether CBM provides clear and reliable differentiation among students placed in special education, Chapter 1, and general-education-only students. If the measures are to be validated for Problem Identification and Certification decisions, differences should be observed among groups of students that educators classify differentially.

The achievement characteristics of students referred for special education because of reading problems were studied by Shinn, Tindal, and Spira (1987). They examined the performance of referred students grades 2–6 on grade-level CBM reading tasks compared to local norms of general education students in the same school district. ESs across grades ranged from –1.6 to –1.0. When translated into percentiles, these ESs ranged from the 5.5th to the 15.9th percentile. The typical referred student performed at about the 8th percentile of general education peers. The authors concluded that referred students are characterized by extremely low achievement in the general education curriculum compared to other students and that CBM reliably indexes these achievement differences.

CBM also reliably differentiates groups of students classified by more traditional procedures. As presented earlier, Shinn, Ysseldyke, Deno, and Tindal (1986) found significant differences between LD students and low achievers on CBM reading, spelling, and written expression problems. In reading, the typical fifth-grade LD student across five districts performed at the 9.7th percentile rank of low-achieving students. More than 90% of low achievers would be expected to earn CBM reading scores above the typical student placed in LD programs.

Shinn and Marston (1985) researched differences on CBM measures of reading, spelling, math computation, and written expression among students placed in programs for mild handicaps (MH), Chapter 1 students, and typical general education students in grades 4–6. ESs across grades showed that students in MH programs performed at extremely low levels compared to general education peers and Chapter 1 students. In reading, for example, ESs ranged from –2.3 to –2.4 relative to general education peers; the typical MH student performed at the 1st percentile of general education students. When MH students were compared to Chapter 1 students, ESs ranged from –.2 to –1.5, with the differences increasing by grade level; the typical MH student performed at the 17th percentile of Chapter 1 students. More than 83% of Chapter 1 students outperformed the MH students in reading. Chapter 1 students also were differentiated reliably from general education students. By grade, the ESs ranged from –.9 to –1.5, with the typical percentile rank corresponding to the 16th percentile compared to general education peers.

Finally, CBM was used to study potential CBM reading differences between all students in a school system, grades 1 to 6, who had been placed in programs for learning disabilities via traditional ability-achievement discrepancy procedures (Shinn, Tindal, Spira, & Marston, 1987) and Chapter 1 and typical general education students. When comparing LD students to general education peers, ESs ranged from –1.1 at grade 1 to –2.2; the typical LD student performed at the 3rd percentile of general education students. In comparison to Chapter 1 students, ESs ranged from –.2 at grade 1 to –1.5 with the differences increasing by grade level; again, the typical LD student performed at the 17th percentile of Chapter 1 students. As in the previous studies, Chapter 1 students were differentiated reliably from general education students. By grade, the ESs ranged from –.7 to –1.4 with the typical percentile rank corresponding to the 14th percentile compared to general education peers.

In each of these studies, the authors concluded that CBM could be used to differentiate groups into different types of educational services in much the same way as the school had classified students in the past, but more in line with the benefits of the Problem-Solving model approach.

Effects on Assessment and Placement Practices

Marston and Magnusson (1988) summarized the effects of using CBM within a Problem-Solving model on eligibility assessment and special education placement practices. The number of students referred for special education who actually were assessed for eligibility determination decreased by almost half when systematic Problem Identification decisions were made. In contrast to practices in which almost all referrals are tested for special education eligibility, Marston and Magnusson (1988) reported rates of 45 to 65% of referred students being tested. Actual eligibility rates also dropped to approximately 25 to 45% of all referrals—again a figure quite in contrast to national referral placement rates of 75 to 92% (Algozzine, Christenson, & Ysseldyke, 1982). Germann and Tindal (1985) reported special education placement figures that closely paralleled their state and national levels.

Effects on School Psychology Practices

Changes in the assessment and service delivery practices of school psychologists after implementation of CBM within a problem-solving model have been noted by Canter (1991) and Marston and Magnusson (1988). Canter (1991) reported changes in school psychologists' assessment practices. Rather than routinely testing every referral to determine special education eligibility, in the Problem-Solving model school psychologists tested students only when there were specific assessment questions. Only half of the cases on the typical school psychologist's load involved testing, and only half of those involved assessment of learning aptitude (i.e., intelligence). In addition, Canter (1991) detailed qualitative changes in the types of data collected when testing was conducted.

With the decreased time in routine eligibility testing, Marston and Magnusson (1988) observed corresponding increases in school psychologists' consultation activities from 12 to 36% of their time within 3 years, and a similar increase from 1.5 to 10% for direct services (e.g., counseling). Canter (1991) reported that in subsequent years school psychologists' consultation time increased further to 52% of their time.

Exploring and Evaluating Solutions

The outcomes of using CBM to write data-based annual IEP goals and monitor intervention effectiveness have been examined in three broad areas: (a) student achievement outcomes, (b) changes in teaching practices, and (c) students' goal awareness. Most of the experimental work has been conducted by Lynn Fuchs and associates at Vanderbilt University and typically are interpreted as ES units.

Effects on Student Achievement

A number of studies have demonstrated effect sizes related to student achievement and CBM. These studies, summarized in Table 6, include the use of CBM procedures to monitor student achievement by having teachers collect CBM data: (a) without instruction on how to use the information (informal decision making), (b) with systematic rules for making intervention effectiveness decisions and instructional changes, and (c) by providing feedback about how the students performed on specific required curricular skills (instructional enhancements).

These studies indicate, at a broad level, that the ESs associated with using CBM and data evaluation and decision rules produce significant and socially meaningful achievement gains. Most of the studies comparing the role of feedback systems (i.e., feedback regarding programmatic changes, qualitative feedback on student progress, and so on) indicate that teacher involvement in the evaluation process has a greater influence on student achievement than measurement that does not require teacher involvement.

Informal decision making regarding student progress. The process of collecting CBM student performance data without specific decision-making strategies for determining when a program is ineffective and requires modification seems to have mild effects on student achievement. Overall, individuals whose progress is monitored using CBM over time can be expected to make modest gains (average ES = .36, increases from 50th to 63rd percentile) over those students whose progress is monitored using traditional methods (e.g., teacher judgment, student workbooks, and so on). In some circumstances, using CBM without specific strategies to make program improvements does not impact student achievement. For example, in a study by Fuchs, Fuchs, and Hamlett (1989c), an ES of .36 was found not to be reliably different from students whose progress was monitored using traditional methods. In a meta-analysis of systematic formative evaluation studies, ESs up to .70 (i.e., increases from 50th to 76th percentile) have been noted, but how many studies included a data collection-only group is unclear (Fuchs & Fuchs, 1986b).

Systematic decision-making strategies. Student achievement can be maximized by *using* CBM data and systematic decision rules to indicate *when* a change in an instructional program is required. Several studies have investigated systematic strategies designed to get teachers to make instructional changes in response to students' progress. The research has focused on feedback methods indicating to teachers that an instructional program is ineffective and a change is due, including: (a) the amount and type of feedback given regarding programmatic changes and student performance, and (b) the type of goal structure used.

Most frequently, computers have been used to indicate when an instructional change is required (e.g., Fuchs, Fuchs, & Hamlett, 1989d). The computer compares a student's actual rate of progress with the expected rate of progress toward the IEP annual goal. When actual progress is less than expected progress, the computer signals to teachers that a program change is required. Outcomes of using CBM and this computer feedback system are ESs in the magnitude of .72. This growth represents an increase from the 50th to the 77th percentile, compared to using traditional methods. Other research has ex-

TABLE 6 Summary of Effect Sizes Related to Student Achievement and Curriculum-Based Measurement

Study	Domain	Group or Experimental Conditions	Effect Size
Fuchs & Fuchs (1986b)	Meta-analysis of systematic formative evaluation	Effects on achievement using progress monitoring	Average = .70
		Effects on achievement using data evaluation and decision rules	Average = .91
		Effects on achievement using teacher judgment	Average = .42
		Effects on achievement using graphic display	Average = .70
		Effects on achievement using recorded data	Average = .26
Fuchs & Fuchs (1987b)	Meta-analysis of graphing student data	Effects on achievement using equal-interval paper	Average = .46
		Effects on achievement using ratio-scaled paper	Average = .53
Fuchs, Deno, & Mirkin (1984)	Reading	G1. CBM monitoring G2. Traditional monitoring	Words read correctly = .92
Fuchs (1988)	Spelling	G1. Goal-based structure G2. Experimental structure	*WSC = .67 **CLS = 1.05
Fuchs, Fuchs, & Hamlett (1989d)	Reading	G1. Performance + quality feedback G2. Performance only	Retell matched words = .67
Fuchs, Fuchs, & Hamlett (1989a)	Spelling	G1. Enhanced feedback CBM G2. Unenhanced feedback CBM G3. Control	1 vs. 3 = .45 1 vs. 2 = .22 2 vs. 3 = .23
Fuchs, Fuchs, & Hamlett (1989c)	Reading	G1. Measurement + evaluation G2. Measurement only G3. Control	1 vs. 3 = .72 1 vs. 2 = .21 2 vs. 3 = .36
Fuchs, Fuchs, & Hamlett (1989b)	Math	G1. Dynamic goal structure G2. Static goal structure G3. Control	1 vs. 3 = .52 1 vs. 2 = .28 2 vs. 3 = .25
Fuchs, Fuchs, Hamlett, & Stecker (1990)	Math	G1. Performance + skills analysis G2. Performance only G3. Control	1 vs. 3 = .67 1 vs. 2 = .55 2 vs. 3 = .26

*WSC = words spelled correctly
**CLS = correct letter sequences

plored using computer feedback after teachers make initial program effectiveness decisions. In the area of spelling, Fuchs, Fuchs, and Hamlett (1989a) provided feedback to teachers by the computer automatically or required teachers to make an initial decision about when and what to change. The computer then gave feedback regarding the correctness of the teacher's initial decision. Results indicated that spelling achievement was greater with students of teachers who were required to make initial decisions with subsequent computer feedback.

Varying computer feedback using different CBM goal structures also has been explored. Fuchs, Fuchs, and Hamlett (1989b) compared a dynamic goal structure approach to a static goal structure approach. The computerized feedback was the same for both groups, but the dynamic goal structure group received computerized feedback that required teachers to raise the goal when estimated student progress exceeded the aimline. The static goal structure did not require the teachers to increase goals in response to progress that exceeded the anticipated aimline. The results indicated that the dynamic goal approach had greater effects on student achievement than the static goal structure or the control group as measured by CBM math measures (Fuchs, Fuchs, & Hamlett, 1989b). The effect size magnitude associated with the dynamic goal CBM procedures was .52 (approximately one half standard deviation), or the difference from the 50th to the 69th percentile.

Instructional enhancements. Research on CBM and in Exploring and Evaluating Solutions, to this point, has examined the outcomes of collecting CBM data with informal and systematic decision-making strategies. The latter were designed to tell teachers explicitly that instructional changes are necessary because the current instructional program was not effective. The focus of decision making has been on *when* to change rather than *what* to change. Use of CBM has been explored further in terms of providing specific information designed to tell teachers what parts of their instructional program to change. This type of information is referred to as a skills analysis, or an *instructional enhancement.* Most often, teachers have been provided with skills analysis information obtained from the student's performance on weekly probes. The skills analysis gives teachers specific information regarding skills required in the curriculum that have/have not been demonstrated. As shown in Table 6, research in this area corroborates earlier findings that teachers who use direct and frequent measurement affect student outcomes to a greater degree than teachers who use traditional means of monitoring progress.

In the areas of math and reading, teachers who use CBM *and* receive skills analysis information effected greater growth, compared to teachers who monitored and evaluated student progress and the control group (Fuchs, Fuchs, & Hamlett 1989d; Fuchs, Fuchs, & Hamlett, & Stecker, 1990). The skills analysis information for math included specific math problem types (e.g., addition basic facts, sums to 18) that were attempted at least 75% of the time on the probes with at least 85% accuracy. The ES magnitude associated with CBM skills analysis was .67 compared to the control group, and .55 compared to CBM teachers who did not receive the skills analysis. In reading, the skills analysis information consisted of a structured analysis of story components included in students' recalls. The ES magnitude associated with CBM skills analysis was .67 compared to

CBM teachers who did not receive the skills analysis. In terms of the standard normal curve, this result would be associated with increases from the 50th to the 75th percentile.

Research in spelling indicates that CBM skills analysis can effect student achievment, but the skills analysis information does not have to include recommendations as to *what* to change (Fuchs, Fuchs, Hamlett, & Allinder, 1991a; 1991b). Fuchs, Fuchs, Hamlett, and Allinder (1991a) demonstrated support for earlier findings that CBM skills analysis effects greater student achievement. The skills analysis information provided teachers the lists of words administered to the student, the student's response, and the three most frequent types of errors the student had made. A variation of the skills analysis information in spelling was explored by providing the teacher a recommended teaching adjustment along with detailed instructions for how to implement it (Fuchs, Fuchs, Hamlett, & Allinder, 1991b). When compared to teachers employing traditional monitoring strategies, teachers who received skills analysis information versus teachers who received the revised skills analysis information both showed greater achievement gains, but did not significantly differ from each other. The comparability of the two CBM groups may suggest that in the area of spelling, specific recommendations for instructional planning may not be necessary or sufficient.

Effects on Students' Goal Awareness

Students' knowledge of their progress generally has been suggested as a means of making the student aware of teachers' expectations, offering motivation as a means of accomplishing their goal, and in some way serving as an exercise in self-monitoring. Erez (1977), for example, suggests that goals and knowledge of performance toward goals are necessary to improve student performance.

In a study examining the effects of CBM on teacher behavior and student achievement (Fuchs, Deno, & Mirkin, 1984), student awareness of learning also was examined. Awareness was measured by asking students if they knew their goals and if they could judge whether they would meet their goals. Results indicated that students who were monitored using CBM procedures in reading were more knowledgeable about their learning. Similarly, students using CBM in spelling described their goals more specifically than students who were monitored using traditional methods (Fuchs, Butterworth, & Fuchs, 1989). In addition, achievement gains were greater for students in the CBM groups than students being monitored using traditional methods. It was suggested that the differences in achievement gains were not attributable to differences in student perceptions of goal attainment but, rather, that they may be related to the student's knowledge of goals and perceptions of teacher feedback concerning progress (Fuchs, Butterworth, & Fuchs, 1989).

Effects on Teaching Practices

Although much attention has been directed at student achievement outcomes, teacher behavior also has been shown to be affected by CBM monitoring procedures. Changes have been demonstrated in terms of compliance with CBM procedures, responding to student data, and varying individual instructional planning and delivery.

The extent to which teachers implement CBM procedures has been determined most commonly using the Modified Accuracy of Implementation Rating Scale (MAIRS; Fuchs, 1986). This scale consists of 11 items assessing compliance with each component of the CBM procedure, ranging from placing students in goal-level material to changing instructional programs when told to do so. The degree to which teachers comply with the CBM procedures has been comparable across a variety of experimental conditions (Fuchs, Fuchs, Hamlett, & Allinder, 1991b; Fuchs, Fuchs, Hamlett, & Stecker, 1990; Fuchs, Fuchs, & Hamlett, 1989b; Fuchs, 1988). But differences in compliance have been found, relating to evaluation approach (e.g., goal- versus experimental-based) (Fuchs, Fuchs, & Hamlett, 1989a) and evaluation method (e.g., 3-day decision rule) (Fuchs, 1989).

Using CBM data to make progress monitoring and instructional effectiveness decisions has been shown to affect teachers' instructional planning and teaching. Teachers who received CBM data and qualitative feedback regarding student performance wrote more specific instructional plans (Fuchs, Fuchs, & Hamlett; 1989a; Fuchs, Fuchs, Hamlett & Stecker, 1990). In addition, teachers also increased their accuracy with identification of phonetic spelling errors (Fuchs, Allinder, Hamlett, & Fuchs, 1990).

The implications of this research are encouraging not only in terms of instructional planning, but also with regard to changes in teaching. Teachers using CBM have been found to make more instructional changes in students' programs (e.g., Fuchs, Deno, & Mirkin, 1984; Fuchs, Fuchs, Hamlett, & Allinder, 1991b), which may be one of the variables associated with greater student achievement gains. The effect of progress monitoring on the structure of instruction also has been explored. Variables examined included instructional grouping, teacher-directed learning, active academic responding, and prompting (Deno, King, Skiba, Sevcik, & Wesson, 1983). Teachers who used CBM monitoring procedures demonstrated increased structure in instructional delivery (Fuchs, Deno, & Mirkin, 1984).

Teacher attitudes regarding student progress and instructional programs also have changed when utilizing CBM progress monitoring procedures. Teachers were more realistic about student progress (Fuchs, Deno, & Mirkin, 1984) and more open to trying new interventions when a student was not making adequate progress (Fuchs, Deno, & Mirkin, 1984; Marston & Magnusson, 1988).

Problem Solution Research Outcomes

Research on Problem Solution decisions for all assessment practices remains limited. Research on the use of CBM to make this decision is increasing and can be divided into two broad areas: (a) effects on percentages of students exited from special education, and (b) preliminary research on identifying potential candidates for reintegration into general education. Significant increases in special education exit rates have been observed when data relevant to performance in general education curriculum are used in decision making. Marston and Magnusson (1988) reported an increase in the percentage of students exited yearly from special education resource rooms to 20% from 4%.

Preliminary research on using CBM to identify potential candidates for reintegration shows promise. Shinn, Habedank, Rodden-Nord, and Knutson (in press) examined the percentage of special education students served in resource rooms with an IEP objective in reading who read grade-level curricular materials in the range of low reading group general education students from their grade placement. The outcomes estimated that approximately 40% of the special education students read as well as or better than at least one of the low reading group students. These data suggest that these special education students should be considered for return to general education for reading instruction. Rodden-Nord, Shinn, and Good (1992) researched the effects of these kinds of CBM data on general education teachers' attitudes about reintegrating special education students back into their classrooms for reading instruction. When provided with CBM data indicative of reading skills commensurate with low reading group students, general education teachers' attitudes about reintegration changed positively and significantly. Teachers reported that they were very willing to reintegrate the special education student.

CONCLUSION

CBM meets the criteria proposed by Reschly, Kicklighter, and McKee (1988c) for a useful assessment system, that the data collected for special education eligibility be linked to intervention planning *and* evaluation. CBM typically is used not as a series of tests added to an educator's testing "armament." Instead, it is to be used within a problem-solving model. Using CBM in this manner has a number of positive demonstrated outcomes for each of the five steps of the model proposed here. Most important, students' achievement is affected. When educators write data-based long-term goals and adjust their interventions as a result of students' rates of progress, significant and meaningful changes in student outcomes are observed. Given the legal requirement for evaluation of progress toward annual goals, the field of special education's documented lack of improvement in this area, and the strong potential for changes in student outcomes upon implementation, special education systems should place a high priority on training and implementating of CBM and problem-solving decision-making strategies.

Development of this paper was supported by grant no. 8029D80051–91 from the U.S. Department of Education, Special Education Programs, to provide leadership training in curriculum-based assessment. The views expressed within this paper are not necessarily those of the U.S. DOE.

REFERENCES

Algozzine, B., Christenson, S., & Ysseldyke, J. (1982). Probabilities associated with the referral to placement process. *Teacher Education & Special Education, 5,* 19–23.

Allen, D. (1989). Periodic and annual reviews and decisions to terminate special education services. In M. R. Shinn (Ed.), *Curriculum-based measurement: Assessing special children* (pp. 184–203). New York: Guilford.

Bateman, B., & Herr, C. (1981). Law and special education. In J. Kauffman & D. Hallahan (Eds.), *Handbook of special education* (pp. 330–360). Englewood Cliffs, NJ: Prentice Hall.

Bentz, J., Shinn, M., & Gleason, M. M. (1990). Training general education pupils to monitor reading using curriculum-based measurement procedures. *School Psychology Review, 19*(1), 23–32.

Bersoff, D. (1973). Silk purses into sow's ears. *American Psychologist, 10,* 892–899.

Blankenship, C. (1985). Using curriculum-based assessment data to make instructional decisions. *Exceptional Children, 52,* 233–238.

Canter, A. (1991). Effective psychological services for all students: A data-based model of service delivery. In G. Stoner, M. R. Shinn, & H. M. Walker (Eds.), *Interventions for achievement and behavior problems* (pp. 49–78). Silver Spring, MD: National Association of School Psychologists.

Deno, S. L. (1985). Curriculum-based measurement: The emerging alternative. *Exceptional Children, 52,* 219–232.

Deno, S. L. (1986). Formative evaluation of individual student programs: A new role for school psychologists. *School Psychology Review, 15,* 358–374.

Deno, S. L. (1989). Curriculum-based measurement and alternative special education services: A fundamental and direct relationship. In M. R. Shinn (Ed.), *Curriculum-based measurement: Assessing special children* (pp. 1–17). New York: Guilford.

Deno, S. L. (1990). Individual differences and individual difference: The essential difference of special education. *Journal of Special Education, 24*(2), 160–173.

Deno, S. L., King, R., Skiba, R., Sevcik, B., & Wesson, C. (1983). *The structure of instruction rating scale (SIRS): Development and technical characteristics* (Research Rep. No. 107). Minneapolis: University of Minnesota Institute for Research on Learning Disabilities.

Deno, S. L., Marston, D., & Mirkin, P. (1982). Valid measurement procedures for continuous evaluation of written expression. *Exceptional Children, 483,* 68–371.

Deno, S. L., Marston, D., Mirkin, P. K., Lowry, L., Sindelar, P., & Jenkins, J. (1982). *The use of standard tasks to measure achievement in reading, spelling, and written expression: A normative and developmental study.* Minneapolis: University of Minnesota Institute for Research on Learning Disabilities.

Deno, S. L., Mirkin, P., & Chiang, B. (1982). Identifying valid measures of reading. *Exceptional Children, 49,* 36–45.

Education for All Handicapped Children Act of 1975 (PL 94–142, 29 Nov. 1975) *United States Statutes at Large,* 79, pp. 27–52.

Erez, M. (1977). Feedback: A necessary condition for the goal setting-performance relationship. *Journal of Applied Psychology, 62,* 624–627.

Fuchs, L. S. (1986). *Effects of teacher training procedures on data-based instructional management implementation.* (Unpublished manuscript available from L. S. Fuchs, Box 328, Peabody College, Vanderbilt University, Nashville, TN 37203).

Fuchs, L. S. (1988). Effects of computer-managed instruction on teacher's implementation of systematic monitoring programs and student achievement. *Journal of Educational Research, 81,* 294–304.

Fuchs, L. S. (1989). Evaluating solutions: Monitoring progress and revising intervention plans. In M. R. Shinn (Ed.), *Curriculum-based measurement: Assessing special children* (pp. 155–183). New York: Guilford.

Fuchs, L. S. (in press). Enhancing instructional programming and student achievement with curriculum-based measurement. In J. Kramer (Ed.), *Curriculum-based assessment: Examining old problems, evaluating new solutions.* Hillsdale, NJ: Erlbaum.

Fuchs, L. S., Allinder, R. M., Hamlett, C. L., & Fuchs, D. (1990). An analysis of spelling curricula and teachers' skills in identifying error types. *Remedial & Special Education, 11*(1), 42–51.

Fuchs, L. S., Butterworth, J. R., & Fuchs, D. (1989). Effects of ongoing curriculum-based measurement on student awareness of goals and progress. *Education & Treatment of Children, 12*(1), 63–72.

Fuchs, L. S., & Deno, S. L. (1991). Paradigmatic distinctions between instructionally relevant measurement models. *Exceptional Children, 57*(6), 488–500.

Fuchs, L. S., Deno, S. L., & Mirkin, P. (1984). The effects of frequent curriculum-based measurement and evaluation on pedagogy, student achievement and student awareness of learning. *American Educational Research Journal, 21,* 449–460.

Fuchs, L. S., & Fuchs, D. (1986a). Curriculum-based assessment of progress towards long-and short-term goals. *Journal of Special Education, 20,* 69–82.

Fuchs, L. S., & Fuchs, D. (1986b). Effects of systematic formative evaluation on student achievement: A meta-analysis. *Exceptional Children, 53,* 199–208.

Fuchs, L. S., & Fuchs, D. (1987a). *Effects of curriculum-based measurement procedures in spelling and math*. (Unpublished manuscript available from L. S. Fuchs, Box 328, Peabody College, Vanderbilt University, Nashville, TN 37203).

Fuchs, L. S., & Fuchs, D. (1987b). The relation between methods of graphing student performance data and achievement: A meta-analysis. *Journal of Special Education Technology, 8*, 5–13.

Fuchs, L. S., Fuchs, D., & Hamlett, C. L. (1989a). Computers and curriculum-based measurement: Effects of teacher feedback systems. *School Psychology Review, 18*, 112–125.

Fuchs, L. S., Fuchs, D., & Hamlett, C. (1989b). Effects of alternative goal structures within curriculum-based measurement. *Exceptional Children, 55*, 429–438.

Fuchs, L. S., Fuchs, D., & Hamlett, C. L. (1989c). Effects of instrumental use of curriculum-based measurement to enhance instructional programs. *Remedial & Special Education, 10*(2), 43–52.

Fuchs, L. S., Fuchs, D., & Hamlett, C. L. (1989d). Monitoring reading growth using student recalls: Effects of two teacher feedback systems. *Journal of Educational Research, 83*(2), 103–110.

Fuchs, L. S., Fuchs, D., Hamlett, C. L., & Allinder, R. M. (1991a). The contribution of skills analysis to curriculum-based measurement in spelling. *Exceptional Children, 57*(5), 443–452.

Fuchs, L. S., Fuchs, D., Hamlett, C. L., & Allinder, R. M. (1991b). Effects of expert system advice within curriculum-based measurement on teacher planning and student achievement in spelling. *School Psychology Review, 20*(1), 49–66.

Fuchs, L. S., Fuchs, D., Hamlett, C. L., & Hasselbring, T. S. (1987). Using computers with curriculum-based progress monitoring: Effects on teacher efficiency and satisfaction. *Journal of Educational Technology, 8*, 14–27.

Fuchs, L. S., Fuchs, D., Hamlett, C. L., & Stecker, P. M. (1990). The role of skills analysis in curriculum-based measurement in math. *School Psychology Review, 19*(1), 6–22.

Fuchs, L. S., Fuchs, D., & Maxwell, L. (1988). The validity of informal reading comprehension measures. *Remedial & Special Education, 9*, 20–28.

Fuchs, L. S., Hamlett, C. L., & Fuchs, D. (1990). *Monitoring basic skills progress* [Computer program]. Austin, TX: PRO-ED.

Fuchs, L. S., Hamlett, C. L., Fuchs, D., Stecker, P. M., & Ferguson, C. (1988). Conducting curriculum-based measurement with computerized data collection: Effects on efficiency and teacher satisfaction. *Journal of Special Education Technology, 9*(2), 73–86.

Fuchs, L. S., & Shinn, M. R. (1989). Writing CBM IEP objectives. In M. R. Shinn (Ed.), *Curriculum-based measurement: Assessing special children* (pp. 132–154). New York: Guilford.

Gerber, M., & Semmel, M. (1984). Teachers as imperfect test: Reconceptualizing the referral process. *Educational Psychologist, 19*, 137–148.

Germann, G., & Tindal, G. (1985). An application of curriculum based assessment: The use of direct and repeated measurement. *Exceptional Children, 52*, 244–265.

Gickling, E., & Thompson, V. (1985). A personal view of curriculum-based assessment. *Exceptional Children, 52*, 153–165.

Good, R. H., & Shinn, M. R. (1990). Forecasting accuracy of slope estimates for reading curriculum-based measurement: Empirical evidence. *Behavioral Assessment, 12*, 179–193.

Heller, K. A., Holtzman, W., & Messick, S. (1982). *Placing children in special education: A strategy for equity*. Washington, DC: National Academy Press.

Howell, K. W., & Morehead, M. K. (1987). *Curriculum-based evaluation for special and remedial education*. Columbus, OH: Merrill.

Kavale, K. A., & Forness, S. R. (1987). Substance over style: Assessing the efficacy of modality testing and teaching. *Exceptional Children, 54*(3), 228–239.

Knutson, N. (1990). *Teaching low-performing students to monitor the reading progress of their cross-age peers*. Unpublished doctoral dissertation, University of Oregon, Eugene.

Marston, D. (1989). Curriculum-based measurement: What is it and why do it? In M. R. Shinn (Ed.), *Curriculum-based measurement: Assessing special children* (pp. 18–78). New York: Guilford Press.

Marston, D., Fuchs, L. S., & Deno, S. L. (1986). A comparison of standardized achievement tests and direct measurement techniques in measuring student progress. *Diagnostique, 11*, 77–90.

Marston, D., Lowry, L., Deno, S. L., & Mirkin, P. K. (1981). *An analysis of learning trends in simple measures of reading, spelling, and written expression: A longitudinal study* (Research Rep. No. 49). Minneapolis: University of Minnesota Institute for Research on Learning Disabilities.

Marston, D., & Magnusson, D. (1985). Implementing curriculum-based measurement in special and regular education settings. *Exceptional Children, 52*, 266–276.

Marston, D., & Magnusson, D. (1988). Curriculum-based assessment: District-level implementation. In J. Graden, J. Zins, & M. Curtis (Eds.), *Alternative educational delivery systems: Enhancing instructional options for all students* (pp. 137–172). Washington, DC: National Association of School Psychologists.

Reschly, D. J., Genshaft, J., & Binder, M. S. (1987). *The 1986 NASP survey: Comparison of practitioners, NASP leadership, and university faculty on key issues.* Washington, DC: National Association of School Psychologists.

Reschly, D. J., Kicklighter, R., & McKee, P. (1988a). Recent placement litigation, Part I, Regular education grouping: Comparison of Marshall (1984, 1985) and Hobson (1967, 1969). *School Psychology Review, 17,* 9–21.

Reschly, D. J., Kicklighter, R., & McKee, P. (1988b). Recent placement litigation, Part II, Minority EMR over-representation: Comparison of Larry P. (1979, 1984, 1986) with Marshall (1984, 1985) and S-1 (1986). *School Psychology Review, 17,* 22–49.

Reschly, D. J., Kicklighter, R., & McKee, P. (1988c). Recent placement litigation, Part III, Analysis of differences in Larry P., Marshall, and S-1 and implications for future practices. *School Psychology Review, 17,* 39–50.

Rodden-Nord, K., Shinn, M. R., & Good, R. H. (1992). Effects of classroom performance data on general education teachers' attitudes towards reintegrating students with learning disabilities. *School Psychology Review, 21*(1), 138–154.

Shinn, M. R. (1988). Development of curriculum-based local norms for use in special education decision making. *School Psychology Review, 17,* 61–80.

Shinn, M. R. (Ed.). (1989a). *Curriculum-based measurement: Assessing special children.* New York: Guilford.

Shinn, M. R. (1989b). Identifying and defining academic problems: CBM screening and eligibility procedures. In M. R. Shinn (Ed.), *Curriculum-based measurement: Assessing special children* (pp. 90–129). New York: Guilford.

Shinn, M. R., & Good, R. H. (in press). CBA: An assessment of its current status and a prognosis for its future. In J. Kramer (Ed.), *Curriculum-based assessment: Examining old problems, evaluating new solutions.* Hillsdale, NJ: Erlbaum.

Shinn, M.R., Habedank, L., Rodden-Nord, K., & Knutson, N. (in press). Using curriculum-based measurement to identify potential candidates for reintegration into general education. *The Journal of Special Education.*

Shinn, M. R., & Marston, D. (1985). Differentiating mildly handicapped, low-achieving and regular education students: A curriculum-based approach. *Remedial & Special Education, 6,* 31–45.

Shinn, M. R., Nolet, V., & Knutson, N. (1990). Best practices in curriculum-based measurement. In A. Thomas & J. Grimes (Eds.), *Best practices in school psychology* (pp. 287–308). Washington DC: National Association of School Psychologists.

Shinn, M. R., Rosenfield, S., & Knutson, N. (1989). Curriculum-based assessment: A comparison and integration of models. *School Psychology Review.*

Shinn, M. R., Tindal, G., & Spira, D. (1987). Special education referrals as an index of teacher tolerance: Are teachers imperfect tests? *Exceptional Children, 54,* 32–40.

Shinn, M., Tindal, G., Spira, D., & Marston, D. (1987). Practice of learning disabilities as social policy. *Learning Disabilities Quarterly, 10*(1), 17–28.

Shinn, M. R., Ysseldyke, J., Deno, S. L., & Tindal, G. (1986). A comparison of differences between students labeled learning disabled and low achieving on measures of classroom performance. *Journal of Learning Disabilities, 19,* 545–552.

Smith, S. W. (1990). Individualized educational programs (IEPs) in special education: From intent to acquiescence. *Exceptional Children, 57*(1), 6–14.

Tindal, G., Fuchs, L. S., Christenson, S., Mirkin, P. K., & Deno, S. L. (1981). *The relationship between student achievement and teacher assessment of short- or long-term goals* (Research Rep. No. 61). Minneapolis: University of Minnesota, Institute for Research on Learning Disabilities. (ERIC Document Reproduction Service No. Ed 218 846).

Tucker, J. (1985). Curriculum-based assessment: An introduction. *Exceptional Children, 52,* 199–204.

Wesson, C. (1987). Increasing efficiency. *Teaching Exceptional Children, 20,* 46–47.

Wesson, C., Fuchs, L., Tindal, G., Mirkin, P., & Deno, S. L. (1986). Facilitating the efficiency of ongoing curriculum-based measurement. *Teacher Education & Special Education, 9,* 166–172.

Wesson, C. L., King, R. P., & Deno, S. L. (1984). Direct and repeated measurement of student performance: If it's good for us, why don't we do it? *Learning Disability Quarterly, 7,* 45–48.

White, O. R. (1974). *Evaluating educational process.* Unpublished manuscript, University of Washington, Child Developmental and Mental Retardation Center, Experimental Education Unit, Seattle.

White, O. R., & Haring, N. G. (1980). *Exceptional teaching* (2nd ed.). Columbus, OH: Merrill.

Ysseldyke, J. E., Algozzine, B., Shinn, M. R., & McGue, M. (1982). Similarities and differences between low achievers and students labeled learning disabled. *Journal of Special Education, 16,* 73–85.

Ysseldyke, J. E., & Thurlow, M. L. (1984). Assessment practices in special education: Adequacy and appropriateness. *Educational Psychologist, 9,* 123–136.

Mark Shinn is with the School Psychology Program, Division of Special Education and Rehabilitation, at the University of Oregon, Eugene. Dawn Hubbard is a doctoral student in the School Psychology Program at the University of Oregon, Eugene.

○ 11 ○

The discussion in this article first points out the inability of norm-referenced tests to effectively predict or identify effective instructional outcomes for students with mild disabilities. It then points to functional dimensions related to the school curriculum and social competencies necessary for effective programs for those with mild disabilities. Reschly suggests an approach employing curriculum-based instruction, along with seven principles from the instructional effectiveness literature, which will greatly aid special education and regular education teachers in improving instruction.

Special Education Decision Making and Functional/Behavioral Assessment

Daniel J. Reschly

INTRODUCTION

A strong position is advanced in this chapter regarding the kind of assessment that should be used with students classified now as having mild disabilities. Functional, behavioral assessment is seen as preferable to norm-referenced, standardized tests on the dimensions of diagnostic utility, intervention implications, and treatment validity. The critical deficiencies in standardized, norm-referenced tests are the absence of treatment validity and clear intervention implications. The alternative, functional/behavioral assessment, has the major advantages of intervention implications and treatment validity, as well as diagnostic utility that is equal to that of conventional standardized tests.

Functional assessment is defined here as information-gathering procedures that have direct applicability to the definition of problem behaviors, determination of current levels of problem behavior, the development and design of interventions, the monitoring of intervention implementation, and the evaluation of intervention outcomes. Functional assessment procedures typically have the characteristics of being direct measures applied in the natural setting, of the utilization of small units of behavior, of focus on observable behaviors, of repeatable measurement procedures, and of social validity (Shapiro & Kratochwill, 1988).

THE CONTEXT OF ASSESSMENT

Standardized tests of achievement and ability have dominated special education assessment since the development of standardized tests early in the twentieth century. A recent national survey indicated that school psychologists devoted approximately 65 percent of their time to various activities related to determining and maintaining special education eligibility (Reschly, Genshaft, & Binder, 1987). The most frequently used measure for school psychologists was the Wechsler Intelligence Scale for Children—Revised (WISC-R). The WISC-R, along with the Woodcock Johnson Achievement Battery, are the two most widely used measures in special education assessment.

These measures typically yield information indicating the relative standing of students in comparison to a national representative sample of like-age persons. The relative-standing information is then used to determine whether the student meets certain eligibility requirements for classifications such as mild mental retardation (MMR), specific learning disability (LD), or behavior disorder (BD). Although not directly related to the classification criteria for behavior disorder, achievement, ability, and cognitive processing measures typically are given to students who ultimately are classified as BD or severe emotionally disturbed (ED).

In recent years the cost and benefits of traditional educational assessment have been examined critically. The results of this examination are not encouraging regarding norm-referenced tests. First, the administration of standardized tests for the purposes of determining eligibility is expensive, time consuming, and incompatible with other services (e.g., prereferral interventions) that might lead to the resolution of problems in regular education. In the early 1980s, Shepard and Smith (1983) estimated the cost of establishing and maintaining special education eligibility, of which intellectual and achievement testing was a major part, at approximately $1,200 per student. It is doubtful whether the benefits of standardized norm-referenced tests justify these large costs.

DIAGNOSTIC UTILITY: NORM-REFERENCED TESTS

The costs/benefits question can best be answered through an examination of the decisions that currently are made with standardized, norm-referenced tests. These tests are used most often in the determination of eligibility for special education. Determination of eligibility serves to trigger the delivery of expensive services that are designed to ameliorate, compensate for, or substantially improve dysfunctional patterns of behavior. Eligibility determination involves the assignment of a particular classification (label), a critical component of current service delivery. Evidence cited later, however, indicates that functional assessment procedures are more efficient in determining eligibility.

Information from standardized norm-referenced tests is also applied, but to a lesser extent, to the planning of programs and the design of interventions for students with handicaps. The information from standardized tests may be used to establish the general levels of functioning as well as to delineate general goals for intervention outcomes. Some limited information also may be provided regarding specific objectives and approaches that might be used to design interventions (see later discussion).

Finally, traditional standardized tests of achievement are often used as part of the annual evaluation and in triannual reevaluations of students classified as handicapped. These tests are particularly ill suited for the annual evaluation of programs because the score scales typically are not sensitive to growth in skills. The score scales (e.g., percentile ranks, standard scores, or age/grade equivalents) indicate relative standing within some national normative group, not the specific skills that the student has or has not attained. The use of these measures in triannual evaluations is typically devoted to reaffirming eligibility and to establishing general program goals.

Although wide variations exist across states, the determination of eligibility typically involves approximately eleven handicapping conditions. The vast majority of students in school settings classified as handicapped have mild disabilities such as LD, MMR, or ED/BD. Recent estimates suggest that from 80 to 90 percent of all students served in special education have mild disabilities (Algozzine & Korinek, 1985; Reschly, 1988). The common characteristics of students with mild disabilities are: (1) achievement problems; (2) no identifiable biological anomalies; (3) identification in school (not in preschool or adult years); (4) social skills problems; and (5) normal behaviors in most social roles. These disabilities are understood far better from a social system than by a medical model paradigm (J. Mercer, 1979; Reschly, 1987).

The *reliability* of current classifications of students as mildly handicapped is less than impressive. Although it is unlikely that a student performing at the average or above-average levels will be classified as handicapped, differentiations between categories of handicapped students, between slow learners and handicapped students, or between culturally different and handicapped students are notoriously unreliable. Some of the reasons for this unreliability have to do with the quality of the assessment procedures and the measurement approaches used in determining the eligibility of referred students for various categories of the handicapped (Coles, 1978; Shepard, 1983; Ysseldyke, Thurlow, Graden, Wesson, Algozzine, & Deno, 1983). If unreliable assessment procedures are used to operationalize classification criteria, the resulting classifications cannot help but be unreliable.

A second source of unreliability in current classification with the mildly handicapped is the enormous variations in definitions and in the implementation of classification criteria across states and, in several instances, across districts within states. It is entirely possible for a student to be classified as LD in one state (or in one district), move across the state line or transfer school districts, and have that classification changed either to another mild handicap or to slow learner/low achiever (Mercer, King-Sears, & Mercer, 1990; Patrick & Reschly, 1982; Smith, Wood, & Grimes, 1988).

In addition to variations in classification criteria are a host of systems factors such as differences in teacher tolerance for individual differences in learning and behavior, variations in screening of referrals in local school buildings, and variations in the degree to which students deemed eligible for special education are actually placed in programs (Hersh & Walker, 1983; MacMillan, Meyers, & Morrison, 1980). Perhaps the system factors are not surprising in view of the wide variations of classification criteria used across the United States as well as the disagreement among experts in defining learning problems (see Tucker, Stevens, & Ysseldyke, 1983). The widely divergent views of LD experts also included markedly varying estimates of LD prevalence, varying from 1 to 3 percent to as high as 50 percent.

The final issue with reliability has to do with the consistency and accuracy with which students with learning problems can be classified into different categories of handicap. There is considerable literature suggesting that the mild handicapping categories of LD, MMR, and BD/ED have similarities both in characteristics of students and in the programs needed by students (Gajar, 1979; Neissworth & Grier, 1975; Epps, Ysseldyke, & McGue, 1984; Jenkins, Pious, & Peterson, 1988). Recent Iowa studies of mildly handicapped students classified as MMR, BD, or LD indicate that the educational programs provided for such students were far more similar than different (Reiher & Reschly, 1990; Reschly et al., 1988). For example, the top IEP goals for students across the three categories were reading and mathematics. There was little basis to differentiate programs for MMR, LD, or BD, including a careful examination of adaptive behavior and the interventions for behavioral problems. The unanswered question then is, Does the differential diagnosis, an expensive activity, lead to a reliable classification that has most important implications for treatment?

The *validity* of a classification such as LD is determined by the degree to which a category is related to the determination of treatment, the treatment outcome, and/or to prevention (Cromwell, Blashfield, & Strauss, 1975). The traditional categories for students with mild handicaps are not valid using these criteria. There is virtual unanimity regarding low usefulness of the information gathered during eligibility determination for decisions about instruction or treatment. The information needed to determine whether the student is eligible to be classified as LD, MMR, or ED, typically does not translate readily into general goals, specific objectives, monitoring of interventions, or evaluating outcomes. Furthermore, considerable evidence now exists to suggest that the educational interventions provided to students in the different categories of handicap are far more alike than different (see prior paragraph). Clearly, there is no evidence to substantiate that eligibility determination has a large impact on instructional design and treatment planning.

Recent evidence further suggests that effective instructional programming or psychological treatment utilizes the same principles and very often the same procedures regardless of whether the student is classified as LD, MMR, ED, slow learner, or educationally disadvantaged (Carter, 1984; Epps & Tindall, 1987). The absence of treatment implications and differential programming by category has led some scholars to rather cynical, but perhaps accurate, characterizations of current classification practices (Gelb & Mizokowa, 1986; Shinn, Tindall, Spira, & Marston, 1987; Sleeter, 1986).

SUMMARY

The principal special education outcome of current standardized tests of achievement, ability, and cognitive processing is determination of eligibility for special education through assignment of the student to a particular diagnosis. The most frequent traditional diagnosis is a mild handicap; that is, 80 to 90 percent of the students in special education are diagnosed as LD, MMR, or BD/ED. Increasing evidence leads to skepticism about the reliability or the validity of these classifications. If the classifications are unreliable and invalid, then the use of the traditional standardized test is equally unreliable and invalid. Alternatives need to be pursued.

DIAGNOSTIC UTILITY: FUNCTIONAL MEASURES

Although the major purpose of functional/behavioral assessment procedures is *not* diagnosis, recent evidence suggests that traditional classification of children can be carried out as effectively with functional measures. Different classification criteria might be used with functional/behavioral measures. The criteria, resistance to interventions and discrepancies on functional dimensions, would identify virtually the same students as eligible for special education.

Resistance to Interventions

One criterion for determining whether a student has a mild educational disability should be the degree to which the problem(s) exhibited cannot be satisfactorily resolved within regular education settings. Gresham (in press) suggests that the concept of "resistance to intervention" is a critical component of determining whether students' behavioral problems can be regarded as handicapped. The critical factors in resistance to extinction involve a careful behavioral assessment followed by interventions that are examined carefully regarding relative strength, acceptability, integrity, and effectiveness.

Although most states now require that "prereferral interventions" be implemented prior to the consideration of classification, the fact of the matter is that the vast majority of these prereferral interventions lack essential features of effective treatment (Reschly, Robinson, & Ward, 1990). The essential features of sound interventions have been defined in context of collaborative problem solving through consultation (Reschly, 1989).

Effective treatment or intervention requires a definition of the behavioral problem. Then a measure must be selected or developed that directly assesses the target behavior, that can be used repeatedly, and that will reflect the effects of interventions. The intervention must be developed around sound principles of effective instructional or behavioral change. The treatment must be implemented over a reasonable period of time, usually defined as at least several weeks. Progress monitoring using the behavioral measure with, as necessary, revision of the intervention must be performed, followed by evaluation of outcomes. Interventions applied in regular education settings typically lack several of these essential features.

Functional assessment is critical to effective interventions and to assessing the degree to which the behavioral problem exhibited by the student is resistant to systematic interventions in regular education. The functional assessment data gathered during this intervention phase provide the basis for the definition of the problem behavior and for subsequent diagnostic activities.

Functional Dimensions

The dimensions of behavior that should serve as the basis for determining whether students exhibit disabilities should be directly related to the school curriculum and to critical social competencies required for adequate performance in current and future daily life activities. The academic curriculum interventions should include the critical areas of reading, mathematics, written expression, and spelling. Although there are different approaches to curriculum-based assessment and measurement (Shinn, Rosenfield, & Knutson, 1989) a number of common features have emerged. These common features included the use of relatively small units of analysis, evaluation devices developed from the curriculum that is used in regular education, and frequent measurement of progress. Furthermore, determination of whether the student is classified as exhibiting a disability is frequently based on discrepancies from classroom, school building, or district averages using the curriculum-based measures. The focus on measures from academic curricula facilitates a close relationship between special and regular education services as well as a clear match between the assessment and curriculum.

Social competencies are the second set of functional dimensions in which students considered for possible classification as mildly handicapped should be assessed. The social competency dimensions are critical to the child's acceptability in the classroom, peer relationships, the efficiency and success of academic efforts, current life adjustment, and future social and vocational success. Critical dimensions for social competency include skills associated with independent functioning, social functioning, functional academic or practical cognitive skills, and vocational occupational competencies (Reschly, 1990). The social functioning domain can be further organized around critical social skills components associated with school performance and current adjustment. Although several different terms have been attached to the social skills components, there appears to be consensus regarding the importance of three components (Walker & McConnell, 1988; Gresham & Elliot, 1990):

1. *"School survival skills"*: Defined as behaviors essential to or strongly supportive of academic achievement. Examples include following directions, being able to work independently, task behavior, and asking/answering questions appropriately.
2. *"School social behaviors"*: Defined as behaviors essential to effective functioning in classrooms and other settings and to the maintenance of positive relationships with adults. Some examples include control of impulsive behaviors, minimizing aggressing behaviors, expressing feelings properly, and gaining attention appropriately.
3. *"Peer relationships"*: Defined as behaviors that lead to positive relationships and peer acceptance. Examples include joining others, social graces, a positive behavior toward others, and conversational skills.

Evidence gathered since 1985 suggests that the overwhelming majority of students classified as mildly handicapped could be identified through use of functional measures such as curriculum-based measurement or behavioral observation, applied over the dimensions just described (Shinn, Tindal, & Stein, 1988; Germann & Tindel, 1985; Marston & Magnusson, 1988; Wilson, Schendel, & Ulman, in press).

Two major advantages would be realized through using functional assessment procedures over dimensions of behavior directly related to classroom performance. First, the information gathered would reflect the effort to develop interventions in regular education and provide the basis for further efforts to intervene with the student through the specialized programming associated with special education. Second, the separation in regular and special education would be reduced because the functional assessment measures cited here are typically drawn from the regular education curriculum and the basis for defining the student's problem is usually a discrepancy from typical patterns of behavior for peers in the same setting.

The prior literature in this area suggests that the functional assessment procedures will find the same students. That is, the same students, now identified through expensive, time-consuming measures that have relatively little, if any, relevance to intervention, will be identified through the use of the functional assessment procedures (Germann & Tindal, 1985; Marston & Magnusson, 1988; Shinn et al., 1988; Wilson et al., in press).

Note that there is no claim for perfection or near perfection in identifying students as LD, MMR, or ED/BD. Those classifications ought to be eliminated in favor of a more generic conception of mild handicap. Rather, what is claimed is that the same students now identified as mildly handicapped will also be identified using the functional assessment procedures. Furthermore, the functional assessment procedures will be as accurate as the traditional measures, including the newer measures of cognitive processing, in identifying students as mildly handicapped or in identifying them as LD, BD/ED, or MMR. Finding the same students and generating information useful for interventions is the major advantage of functional assessment.

TREATMENT IMPLICATIONS

Sharp contrasts exist between the treatment implications of traditional achievement, cognitive processing, and ability measures and the functional/behavioral assessment procedures. Treatment implications involve basic questions regarding: (1) the goals and objectives of interventions; (2) the methodology or approaches to designing the intervention; (3) the monitoring of progress during the course of intervention along with the course of intervention; and (4) the evaluation of outcomes. On each of these dimensions norm-referenced measures are considerably inferior to functional assessment procedures.

Treatment Implications:
Traditional Assessment

The more recently conceptualized cognitive measures (Das & Naglieri, in press; Naglieri, Das, & Jarman, 1990) as well as traditional measures of achievement and ability (Sattler, 1988), appear to have three kinds of treatment implications. Unfortunately, little evidence substantiates the efficacy of any of these treatment implications.

The first treatment implication comes from the appropriate diagnosis or classification of children's learning and/or behavioral problems into traditional categories such as those suggested in the Education of the Handicapped Act or the American Psychiatric Association Diagnostic and Statistical Manual III-R (American Psychiatric Association, 1988). Naglieri et al. (1990) reviewed evidence suggesting that reliable differences on cognitive processing profiles were obtained for students classified in certain traditional categories. The differences were, however, relatively small (Reschly & Wilson, 1990), and no data had been reported concerning improved treatment implications associated with the categories. No evidence has been reported to refute the prior generalization that students classified as LD, MMR, and ED/BD have highly similar needs and effective programs for each of these diagnoses are built around the same intervention principles. The newer cognitive measures may provide slightly more reliable classification of students, but the treatment implications have yet to be delineated.

A second use of traditional and recently developed norm-referenced procedures has been to identify cognitive processes that need to be remediated. This approach is sometimes called deficit training. The deficit training approaches were criticized severely in the mid-1970s by Hammill and associates (Hammill & Larsen, 1974, 1978). Remediation of processing deficits continues to be debated (see Dunn, 1990; Kavale & Forness, 1987, 1990). Although much heat has been generated in this debate, advocates of process deficit remediation have not been able to show that changing or improving cognitive processing leads to improved educational performance. Indeed, the typical outcome of such deficit remediation has been to show that the skill improvement is restricted to criterion measures that match closely the training materials. Unless these changes in processing competencies generalize to relevant areas of learning such as academic achievement, the processing remediation must be regarded as having undemonstrated benefits for students. The recent cognitive processing instruments such as the Cognitive Assessment System (Naglieri et al., 1990) appear to be predicated on the assumption of broad positive effects associated with training cognitive processes. Those effects have not been demonstrated.

The selection of intervention or teaching methodology is a third area in which traditional measures of achievement, ability, or cognitive processing might be used. The selection of methodology rests on the assumption of Aptitude by Treatment Interaction (ATI). Aptitude by treatment interaction means that matching methodology to the students processing strength will lead to maximum education benefits, whereas mismatching will lead to less desirable outcomes. The ATI notion is implicitly attractive and seems inherently sensible.

The only problem with this very attractive idea is that there is little or no evidence to suggest that it works (Arter & Jenkins, 1979; Ayres & Cooley, 1986; Ayres, Cooley, & Severson, 1988; Colarusso, 1987; Reschly & Gresham, 1989; Teeter, 1987, 1989). Indeed, some studies seem to show that "mismatching" may have more benefits than matching (Ayres & Cooley, 1986). I am not arguing for "mismatching"; my purpose is to point to the absence of evidence to substantiate the value of either traditional measures or more recently developed measures of cognitive processing for designing interventions. Intervention implications must be demonstrated, not assumed.

FUNCTIONAL ASSESSMENT INTERVENTION IMPLICATIONS

Emphasis on functional assessment procedures facilitates the application of the available knowledge on effective instruction or psychological interventions. That knowledge base is similar in many ways to the major findings in the effective schools literature. Application of that knowledge base in special education programs has been emphasized in the recent work of a number of investigators and reviewers (Bickel & Bickel, 1986; Christenson, Ysseldyke, & Thurlow, 1989; Epps & Tindal, 1987; Fuchs, Deno, & Mirkin, 1984; Fuchs & Fuchs, 1986; Fuchs, Fuchs, & Deno, 1985; Gerstein, Woodward, & Darch, 1986; Leinhardt, Bickel, & Pallay, 1982; Marston, 1988; Morsink, Soar, Soar, & Thomas, 1986). There is a body of knowledge that is clearly related to the effectiveness of instructional interventions or psychological treatments. Effective instruction or psychological treatment nearly always involves carefully designed changes in environmental events. Functional assessment procedures, in contrast to traditional measures, focus on environmental conditions rather than on presumed internal attributes of individuals.

Based on the effective schools research and the special education literature (see references cited in previous paragraph) at least seven variables are involved in effective instruction/interventions. The application of each variable is facilitated by functional assessment procedures. These variables are as follows:

1. *Instruction must be provided at the student's level of skill development in the regular education curriculum.* The functional assessment procedures, particularly curriculum-based measurement, enable precise identification of the student's level of skills within the existing curriculum. This information at first glance may appear to be redundant. Don't teachers already know students' skills levels? In fact, curriculum-based measurement studies indicate that teachers know which students are considerably behind their peers, but they cannot pinpoint the students' level of skills within the regular education curriculum. This is more understandable when we consider that the students of greatest concern to special educators may be two or more years behind their regular classroom peers with whom regular classroom teachers are familiar. In contrast, traditional measures provide little information on level of skill development in the regular education curriculum.

2. *The establishment of clear objectives and high expectations is a second crucial element of effective interventions.* Establishment of objectives is facilitated by precise knowledge of current levels of performance as well as knowledge of the scope and sequence of a curriculum. Functional assessment using curriculum-based measures can yield good information on both.

3. *Clear focus on the development of skills is essential to effective intervention.* Many traditional measures focus on students' deficits or on internal attributes that cannot be

changed directly through interventions. Functional measures focus on skills that can be taught or behavioral competencies that can be developed through interventions.

4. *Systematic, intentional instruction to promote skill development leads to greater intervention success.* Direct, intentional instruction is facilitated by knowing what is to be learned and the student's current level of skills. Systematic, intentional instruction is one of the most powerful influences on intervention outcomes.

5. *Continuous or frequent monitoring of progress significantly enhances interventions.* The effective schools and instructional intervention outcome literature both identify frequent progress monitoring along with feedback to students and teachers as critical to successful programming. Functional assessment measures such as curriculum-based measures, permanent product data, or behavior observations are, by their nature, capable of being used repeatedly. In contrast, traditional measures typically cannot be used repeatedly, and they do not yield information useful in making decisions about the effectiveness of interventions.

6. *Revisions of programs based on progress-monitoring data insignificantly improves intervention outcomes.* Students who are not meeting goals should generally receive greater instructional or intervention intensity. Students who are exceeding goals should have their goals increased in order to maximize outcomes. The development of decision rules for making revisions in programs markedly enhances outcomes (Fuchs & Fuchs, 1986).

7. *Reinforcement for learning has a powerful effect on intervention effectiveness* (Walberg, 1984). Indeed, reinforcement for learning appeared in Walberg's meta-analysis as the single most important environmental variable available to change agents.

Functional assessment procedures provide the kind of information required for effective interventions. Indeed, functional assessment procedures have a nearly symbiotic relationship with the elements of effective intervention just described. For several of the elements, it is impossible to think of other than functional assessment procedures. In contrast, traditional measures of ability, achievement, and cognitive processes simply do not yield information that is relevant to implementation of these critical variables.

TREATMENT VALIDITY

The ultimate criterion for any assessment procedure has to be treatment validity or an outcomes criterion (Reschly, 1979).

The treatment validity of functional assessment procedures is well established in the behavior therapy literature (Witt, Elliot, Gresham, 1988; Fuchs & Fuchs, 1986; Shapiro, 1989; Shinn, 1989). Fuchs and Fuchs' meta-analysis (1986) provided some of the most impressive evidence to date concerning the beneficial effects of curriculum-based measurement, frequent progress monitoring with decision rules, and the use of reinforcement. Formative evaluation using functional assessment procedures has excellent treatment validity.

In sharp contrast, traditional measures of ability, achievement, and cognitive processes have little or no treatment validity. A Buros Mental Measurement Yearbook had this conclusion, "In short, the WISC-R lacks treatment validity in that its use does not enhance remedial interventions for children who show specific academic skill deficiencies. . . . For a test to have treatment validity, it must lead to better treatments (i.e., better educational programs, teaching strategies, etc." (Witt & Gresham, 1985, p. 1717). Traditional measures are most vulnerable to criticism on the issue of treatment validity. Despite numerous efforts, originating in a variety of theoretical orientations, there is little established treatment validity for the traditional measures.

CONCLUSIONS

If we establish our ultimate criterion as demonstrated benefits to students with learning and behavioral problems, then functional assessment procedures must be acknowledged as considerably preferable to standardized, norm-referenced measures of ability, achievement, and cognitive processes. Although there are recent improvements in cognitive processing instruments and in traditional measures of ability (Das & Naglieri, in press; Woodcock & Johnson, 1989) these measures are clearly inferior to functional assessment procedures using the criteria of treatment validity and intervention implications. The relative advantages of the two classes of instruments for diagnostic or classification decision making are arguable. That argument, however, does not need to be resolved until the classifications, that is, LD, ED/BD, or MMR, have greater validity as diagnostic constructs. When an instrument does a good job of diagnosing a particular condition but the diagnostic construct itself is invalid, that instrument has little utility for the individual (Cromwell et al., 1975). If our goal is effective treatment for individual students with learning and behavior problems, and I cannot imagine another goal with higher priority, then functional assessment procedures must be regarded as superior to norm-referenced standardized measures of achievement, and cognitive processes.

REFERENCES

Algozzine, B., & Korinek, L. (1985). Where is special education for students with high prevalence handicaps going? *Exceptional Children, 51*, 388–394.

American Psychiatric Association. (1988). *Diagnostic and Statistical Manual III-R*. Washington, DC: American Psychiatric Association.

Arter, J. A., & Jenkins, J. R. (1979). Differential diagnosis—prescriptive teaching: A critical appraisal. *Review of Education Research, 49*, 517–555.

Ayres, R. R., & Cooley, E. J. (1986). Sequential versus simultaneous processing on the K-ABC: Validity in predicting learning success. *Journal of Psychoeducational Assessment, 4*, 211–220.

Ayres, R. R., Cooley, E. J., & Severson, H. H. (1988). Educational translation of the Kaufman Assessment Battery for Children: A construct validity study. *School Psychology Review, 17*, 113–124.

Bickel, W. E., & Bickel, D. D. (1986). Effective schools, classrooms, and instruction: Implications for special education. *Exceptional Children, 52*, 489–500.

Carter, L. F. (1984). The sustaining effects study of compensatory and elementary education. *Educational Researcher, 13*, 4–13.

Christenson, S. L., Ysseldyke, J. E., & Thurlow, M. L. (1989). Critical instructional factors for students with mild handicaps. *Remedial and Special Education, 10*, 21–31.

Colarusso, R. P. (1987). Diagnostic-prescriptive teaching. In M. C. Wang, M. C. Reynolds, & H. J. Walberg (eds.), *The handbook of special education: Research and practice* (Vol. I) (pp. 155–166). Oxford, England: Pergamon Press.

Coles, G. S. (1978). The learning disabilities test battery: Empirical and social issues. *Harvard Educational Review, 48*, 313–340.

Cromwell, R., Blashfield, R., & Strauss, J. (1975). Criteria for classification systems. In N. Hobbs (ed.), *Issues in the classification of children* (pp. 4–25). San Francisco, CA: Jossey-Bass.

Das, J. P., & Naglieri, J. A. (in press). Das-Naglieri: Cognitive Assessment System.

Dunn, R. (1990). Bias over substance: A critical analysis of Kavale and Forness's report on modality-based instruction. *Exceptional Children, 56*, 352–356.

Epps, S. & Tindal, G. (1987). The effectiveness of differential programming in serving students with mild handicaps. In M. C. Wang, M. C. Reynolds, & H. J. Walberg (eds.), *Handbook of special education: Research and practice* (Vol. I) (pp. 213–248). Oxford, England: Pergamon Press.

Epps, S., Ysseldyke, J., & McGue, M. (1984). Differentiating LD and non-LD students: "I know one when I see one." *Learning Disability Quarterly, 7*, 89–101.

Fuchs, L. S., Deno, S. L., & Mirkin, P. K. (1984). The effects of frequent curriculum-based measurement and evaluation on pedagogy, student achievement, and student awareness of learning. *American Educational Research Journal, 21*, 449–460.

Fuchs, L. S., & Fuchs, D. (1986). Effects of systematic formative evaluation: A meta-analysis. *Exceptional Children, 53*, 199–208.

Fuchs, L. S., Fuchs, D., & Deno, S. L. (1985). Importance of goal ambitiousness and goal mastery to student achievement. *Exceptional Children, 52*, 63–71.

Gajar, A. (1979). Educable mentally retarded, learning disabled, and emotionally disturbed: Similarities and differences. *Exceptional Children, 45*, 470–472.

Gelb, S. A., & Mizokawa, D. T. (1986). Special education and social structure: The commonality of "exceptionality." *American Educational Research Journal, 23*, 543–557.

Germann, G., & Tindal, G. (1985). An application of curriculum-based measurement: The use of direct and repeated measurement. *Exceptional Children, 52*, 244–265.

Gerstein, R., Woodward, J., & Darch, C. (1986). Direct instruction: A research-based approach to curriculum design and teaching. *Exceptional Children, 53*, 17–31.

Gresham, F. M. (in press). Conceptualization behavior disorders in terms of resistance to interventions. *Journal of School Psychology.*

Gresham, F. M., & Elliot, S. N. (1990). *Social skills rating systems*. Circle Pines, MN: American Guidance Service.

Hammill, D., & Larsen, S. (1974). The effectiveness of psycholinguistic training. *Exceptional Children, 41*, 5–14.

Hammill, D., & Larsen, S. (1978). The effectiveness of psycholinguistic training: A reaffirmation of position. *Exceptional Children, 44*, 402–414.

Hersh, R. H., & Walker, H. M. (1983). Great expectations: Making schools effective for all children. *Policy Studies Review, 2*, 147–188.

Jenkins, J. R., Pious, C. G., & Peterson, D. L. (1988). Categorical programs for remedial and handicapped students. *Exceptional Children, 55*, 147–158.

Kavale, K. A., & Forness, S. R. (1987). Substance over style: Assessing the efficacy of modality testing and teaching. *Exceptional Children, 54*, 228–239.

Kavale, K. A., & Forness, S. R. (1990). Substance over style: A rejoinder to Dunn's animadversions. *Exceptional Children, 56*, 357–361.

Leinhardt, G., Bickel, W., & Pallay, A. (1982). Unlabeled but still entitled: Toward more effective remediation. *Teachers College Record, 84*, 391–422.

MacMillan, D., Meyers, C. E., & Morrison, G. (1980). System-identification of mildly mentally retarded children: Implications for interpreting and conducting research. *American Journal of Mental Deficiency, 85*, 108–115.

Marston, D. (1988). Measuring progress on IEPs: A comparison of graphing approaches. *Exceptional Children, 55*, 38–44.

Marston, D., & Magnusson, D. (1988). Curriculum based measurement: District level implementation. In J. L. Graden, J. E. Zins, and M. J. Curtis (eds.), *Alternative educational delivery systems: Enhancing instructional options for all students* (pp. 137–172). Washington, DC: National Association of School Psychologists.

Mercer, C. D., King-Sears, P., & Mercer, A. R. (1990). Learning disabilities definitions and criteria used by state education departments. *Learning Disability Quarterly, 13,* 141–152.

Mercer, J. (1979). *System of multicultural pluralistic assessment technical manual.* San Antonio, TX: Psychological Corporation.

Morsink, C. V., Soar, R. S., Soar, R. M., & Thomas, R. (1986). Research on teaching: Opening the door to special education classrooms. *Exceptional Children, 53,* 32–40.

Naglieri, J. A., Das, J. P., & Jarman, R. F. (1990). Planning, attention, simultaneous, and successive cognitive processes as a model for assessment. *School Psychology Review, 19,* 413–426.

Neissworth, J., & Greer, J. (1975). Functional similarities of learning disability and mild retardation. *Exceptional Children, 42,* 17–21.

Patrick, J., & Reschly, D. (1982). Relationship of state educational criteria and demographic variables to school-system prevalence of mental retardation. *American Journal of Mental Deficiency, 86,* 351–360.

Reiher, T., & Reschly, D. (1990). *The Iowa behavioral disorders research project: Final report.* Des Moines, IA: Bureau of Special Education, Iowa Department of Education.

Reschly, D. (1979). Nonbiased assessment. In G. Phye & D. Reschly (eds.), *School psychology: Perspectives and issues* (pp. 215–253). New York: Academic Press.

Reschly, D. J. (1987). Learning characteristics of mildly handicapped students: Implications for classification, placement, and programming. In M. C. Wang, M. C. Reynolds, & H. J. Walberg (eds.), *The handbook of special education: Research and practice* (Vol. I) (pp. 35–38). Oxford, England: Pergamon Press.

Reschly, D. J. (1988). Special education reform: School psychology revolution. *School Psychology Review, 17,* 459–475.

Reschly, D. J. (1989). *Consultation techniques for collaborative problem solving workshop manual* (p. 97). Department of Psychology, Iowa State University, Ames, IA 50011-3180.

Reschly, D. J. (1990). Adaptive behavior. In A. Thomas & J. Grimes (eds.), *Best practices in school psychology* (2nd ed.). Washington, DC: National Association of School Psychologists.

Reschly, D. J., Genshaft, J., & Binder, M. S. (1987). *The 1906 NASP survey: Comparison of practitioners, NASP leadership, and university faculty on key issues.* Washington, DC: National Association of School Psychologists. ED300733.

Reschly, D. J., & Gresham, F. M. (1989). Current neuropsychological diagnosis of learning problems: A leap of faith. In C. R. Reynolds & E. Fletcher-Janzen (eds.), *Handbook of clinical child neuropsychology* (pp. 503–519). New York: Plenum Press.

Reschly, D. J., Robinson, G. A., Volmer, L. M., & Wilson, L. R. (1988). *Iowa Mental disabilities research project final report and executive summary.* Des Moines, IA: Iowa Department of Education, Bureau of Special Education.

Reschly, D. J., Robinson, G. A., & Ward, S. (1990). *Evaluation of the Iowa renewed service delivery system: Research report #1.* Des Moines, IA: Bureau of Special Education, Iowa Department of Education.

Reschly, D. J., & Wilson, M. S. (1990). Cognitive processing vs. traditional intelligence: Diagnostic utility, intervention implications, and treatment validity. *School Psychology Review, 19*(4), 339–352.

Sattler, J. M. (1988). *Assessment of children* (3rd ed.). San Diego, CA: Jerome Sattler Publisher.

Shapiro, E.S. (ed.) (1989). *Academic skills problems: Direct assessment and intervention.* New York: Guilford Press.

Shapiro, E. S., & Kratochwill, T. R. (eds.) (1988). *Behavioral assessment in schools: Conceptual foundations and practical applications.* New York: Guilford Press.

Shepard, L. A. (1983). The role of measurement in educational policy: Lessons from the identification of learning disabilities. *Educational Measurement: Issues and Practices, 2,* 4–8.

Shepard, L. A., & Smith, M. L. (1983). An evaluation of the identification of learning disabled students in Colorado. *Learning Disability Quarterly, 6,* 115–127.

Shinn, M. R. (ed.) (1989). *Curriculum-based measurement: Assessing special children.* New York: Guilford Press.

Shinn, M. R., Rosenfield, S., & Knutson, N. (1989). Curriculum-based assessment: A comparison of models. *School Psychology Review, 18,* 299–316.

Shinn, M. R., Tindal, G. A., Spira, D., & Marston, D. (1987). Practice of learning disabilities as social policy. *Learning Disabilities Quarterly, 10,* 17–28.

Shinn, M. R., Tindal, G. A., & Stein, S. (1988). Curriculum based measurement and the identification of mildly handicapped students. *Professional School Psychology, 3,* 69–85.

Sleeter, C. (1986). Learning disabilities: The social construction of a special education category. *Exceptional Children, 53,* 46–54.

Smith, C. R., Wood, F. H., & Grimes, J. (1988). Issues in the identification and placement of behaviorally disordered students. In M. C. Wang, M. C. Reynolds, & H. J. Walberg (eds.), *The handbook of special education: Research and practice* (Vol. II) (pp. 95–123). Oxford, England: Pergamon Press.

Teeter, P. A. (1987). Review of neuropsychological assessment and intervention with children and adolescents. *School Psychology Review, 16,* 582–583.

Teeter, P. A. (1989). Neuropsychological approaches to the remediation of educational deficits. In C. R. Reynolds, & E. Fletcher-Janzen (eds.), *Handbook of clinical child neuropsychology* (pp. 357–376). New York: Plenum Press.

Tucker, J., Stevens, L., & Ysseldyke, J. E. (1983). Learning disabilities: The experts speak out. *Journal of Learning Disabilities, 16,* 6–14.

Walberg, H. J. (1984). Improving the productivity of America's schools. *Educational Leadership, 41,* 19–30.

Walker, H. M., & McConnell, S. (1988). *Walker-McConnell scale of social competence and school adjustment.* Austin, TX: PRO-ED.

Wilson, M. S., Schendel, J., & Ulman, J. (in press). Curriculum-based measures, teacher ratings, and group achievement scores: Alternative screening measures. *Journal of School Psychology.*

Witt, S., Elliot, S., & Gresham, F. (1988). *The handbook of behavior therapy in education.* New York: Guilford Press.

Witt, J. S., & Gresham, F. M. (1985). Review of the Wechsler Intelligence Scale for Children—Revised. In J. Mitchell (ed.), *Ninth mental measurements yearbook* (pp. 1716–1719). Lincoln, NE: Buros Institute.

Woodcock, R. B., & Johnson, M. B. (1989). *Woodcock-Johnson Psycho-educational Battery—Revised.* Allen, TX: DLM Teaching Resources.

Ysseldyke, J. E., Thurlow, M., Graden, J., Wesson, C., Algozzine, B., & Deno, S. (1983). Generalizations from five years of research on assessment and decision making: The University of Minnesota Institute. *Exceptional Education Quarterly, 4,* 75–93.

Daniel Reschly is a distinguished professor in the department of psychology at Iowa State University, Ames.

∘ 12 ∘

Attention deficit disorder (ADD) and similar terminology describe an increasing childhood problem in learning and one of the newest areas of emphasis in special needs children. The Lerners review the history of ADD over 50 years and its present emphasis in the Individuals with Disabilities Act (IDEA). They offer identification and treatment approaches. The authors point out that the varied terminology will result in some children being served through special education and another large group being served through modifications and programs in regular education.

Attention Deficit Disorder: Issues and Questions

Janet W. Lerner and Sue R. Lerner

Attention deficit disorder (ADD) is one of the most common disorders of childhood, accounting for half of all child referrals to outpatient mental health clinics. With increasing frequency, physicians and psychologists are identifying the syndrome of ADD in children (DuPaul, Barkley, & McMurray, 1991; Frick & Lahey, 1991). Terminology in this field can be disconcerting because of the variety of terms, in addition to ADD, used to refer to this condition: attention-deficit hyperactivity disorder (ADHD), attention deficit disorder with hyperactivity (ADDH), and others. Following the suggestion of Henker and Whalen (1989) that these different terms represent a family of disorders and should be used interchangeably, ADD is used in this article to refer to the entire family of disorders.

We do not intend to cover every part of the complex phenomenon of ADD but, rather, to examine it from the educator's perspective. This article covers dimensions of ADD of value to educators, namely ADD and special education legislation, the history of ADD, associated conditions, assessment, treatment, and current issues.

Although the terminology, definition, and diagnostic criteria have varied over the past 50 years that the condition has been reported in the literature, individuals with ADD are usually characterized as having difficulty staying on task, focusing attention, and completing work. In addition, they often display symptoms of age-inappropriate hyperactive behavior, are easily distracted, racing from one idea or interest to another, or produce sloppy and carelessly done work. They impart the impression that they are not listening or have not heard what they have been told.

For parents, physicians, psychologists, educators, legislators, and for the children themselves, the issues and questions surrounding ADD are complex and controversial. Physicians and psychologists increasingly diagnose ADD in children, yet the precise nature of the disorder and its treatment remain enigmatic. Parents tend to accept with relief a physician's diagnosis of ADD for their child because it is a known diagnostic medical entity, but their relief is soon replaced by anxiety and frustration as physicians, psychologists, parents, and educators attempt to clarify the implications of the diagnosis and come up with the most reasonable and effective treatments (Frick & Lahey, 1991; Shaywitz & Shaywitz, 1991).

ADD AND SPECIAL EDUCATION LEGISLATION

The two federal laws that are especially pertinent for children with ADD in the schools are (a) the Individuals with Disabilities Education Act (IDEA) and (b) Section 504 of the Rehabilitation Act.

Individuals with Disabilities Education Act (IDEA)

In October of 1990, Congress passed the Individuals with Disabilities Act (IDEA) (Public Law 101–476). This law is a reauthorization of Public Law 94–142, Education of the Handicapped Act (EHA), which has served the special education community for more than 12 years. In the reauthorization, the title of the law was changed to the Individuals with Disabilities Act (highlighting "individuals" instead of "children" and "disabilities" instead of "handicaps"). The most controversial debate surrounding IDEA was whether the law should or should not identify ADD as a separate disability. Advocates of identifying ADD as a separate category argue that ADD is an identifiable condition recognized by the medical field and that children with ADD are not adequately served (Barkley, 1990; Thomas, 1990). Opponents of identifying ADD as a separate category within the law argue that children with ADD can already be served under other disability categories, such as learning disabilities (LD), emotional disturbances (ED), or other health impaired (OHI), and therefore a separate category for ADD is unneeded (ED Issues/Questions on Attention Deficit Disorder, 1990; Council for Exceptional Children, 1991; Council for Learning Disabilities, 1991; Learning Disabilities Association, 1991).

Recognition of ADD as a Disability under IDEA

ADD was finally recognized as a disability under the Individuals with Disabilities Act (IDEA) on September 16, 1991 in a Policy Memorandum issued by the U.S. Department of Education. The Department of Education expressly recognized children with attention deficit disorder (ADD/ADHD) as eligible for special education and related services under federal law when ADD impairs educational performance or learning. The policy memorandum stated that ADD does not need to be added as a separate disability category because children with ADD who require special education and related services can meet the eligibility criteria for services under existing categories of IDEA. If the primary disability is ADD, students are eligible under statutes and regulations of the category "Other Health Impaired" (Education of the Handicapped, 1991). For some children with ADD, the primary disability area for eligibility will be learning disabilities or emotional disturbances.

Leading up to the recognition of ADD by the U.S. Department of Education were several critical events. Congress did not include ADD when IDEA was passed in October 1990, but opted to obtain more information on the current issues surrounding children with ADD. The Department of Education was directed to hold public hearings and seek public response to several questions dealing with Attention Deficit Disorder, including the degree to which children with ADD are currently excluded from special education services, unique characteristics of children with ADD, recommended criteria for the identification of children with ADD, and protection issues regarding misclassification of minority students (OSEP sends notice of inquiry summary, 1991). The specific questions for public hearings are listed in the accompanying box.

Questions About ADD for Public Inquiry Under IDEA

As directed in IDEA (PL 101–476), the Department of Education held public hearings on 12 questions about ADD:

1. Are children with ADD now being excluded from special education programs?

2. To what extent are children with ADD identified within the existing disability categories?

3. Do children with ADD have unique characteristics not reflected in the existing categories? If so, to what extent do these characteristics require separate evaluation criteria, special preparation for teachers and staff, and distinct education programs and services.

4. What education programs and/or services are school districts now providing to children diagnosed with ADD, either in special education or in general education programs?

5. How should attention deficit disorder be described for purposes of qualifying a child for special education services?

6. What criteria should be included in the definition to qualify children with ADD whose disability is as severe as those of other children eligible for special education?

7. What specific manifestations of ADD should be included in the definition?

8. Should the definition include factors producing inattentive behaviors that alone should not make a child eligible for special education under the definition of ADD?

9. Should the definition address the concurrence of ADD with other disabilities?

10. Should guidelines be provided to state and local education agencies on their obligation to evaluate a child thought to have ADD?

11. Who should be authorized to conduct such evaluations, and should they be conducted by more than one person?

12. What should be in the definition, and should any additional steps be taken to ensure that children from racial, ethnic, and linguistic minorities are not misclassified?

ADD as a Separate Category: Pros and Cons

The intense debate about establishing ADD as a separate category of disability in the federal legislation of IDEA underscores basic differences of opinion. Support for a separate category for ADD comes from certain parent groups (e.g., *CH.A.D.D.: Children with Hyperactivity Attention Deficit Disorders*) and some medical professionals (Barkley, 1990; Thomas, 1990). Opponents of this action include other parent groups (e.g., *LDA: Learning Disabilities Association*) and some special education entities (e.g., Council for Exceptional Children). In part, this difference is due to the sources of authority for these two groups. For medical professionals and psychologists, the *Diagnostic and Statistical Manual of Mental Disorders (DSM),* published by the American Psychiatric Association, is the basic source of nomenclature, definitions, and criteria. In contrast, special educators and school personnel are inclined to look at rulings from the IDEA legislation. In effect, two classification systems are competing (Schaughency & Rothlind, 1991).

Responses to the Public Inquiry

The public inquiry on ADD generated more than 2,000 responses, which were summarized by the Department of Education's Office of Special Education Programs (OSEP) and sent to Congress on May 17, 1991. The responses revealed a diversity of opinion surrounding each question. For example, the question on whether children with ADD are being excluded from special education services prompted the following diverse responses (OSEP sends notice, 1991):

❏ Parents described personal experiences in which their child was denied services on the basis of an ADD diagnosis.

❏ Children with ADD were being served under an existing category (such as learning disabilities or emotional disturbances), and the ADD problem was not being addressed.

❏ Concern was expressed about the effect of a delay in identification and service delivery to children with ADD, resulting in the development of secondary handicapping conditions over time.

❏ Students with ADD are being served currently and are not excluded from services.

❏ The regular education program should be able to effectively address the needs of students with ADD if the problems are not significant enough to qualify them for special education.

In responses to the question of who should be authorized to conduct an assessment of a child having or suspected of having ADD, the diverse opinions included: only a physician, only educators, a multidisciplinary approach including both medical and educational assessment.

In its summary report, OSEP made no recommendations to Congress on whether to include ADD as a separate category of disability under IDEA. In the OSEP report, the Director of Policy and Planning for OSEP, Patty Guard, said:

OSEP recognizes the consistent confusion regarding obligations to evaluate children with ADD and the circumstances under which children with ADD are eligible for services under Part B. OSEP will issue a joint memo with the Office of Civil Rights regarding these obligations to provide assessment of children suspected of having ADD. (p. 160)

With the September 16, 1991 Policy Memorandum issued by the U.S. Department of Education, ADD is recognized in IDEA under the categories of learning disabilities (LD), emotional disturbance (ED), or "other health impaired" (OHI). This means that children with ADD can be served under the law even if they do not meet the eligibility criteria for learning disabilities or emotional disturbances (Parker, 1990; Teeter, 1991).

Section 504 of the Rehabilitation Act

Accommodations for children with ADD in the schools can also be provided through another federal law, Section 504 of the Rehabilitation Act of 1973. Enforced by the Office of Civil Rights (OCR) of the U.S. Department of Education, this law is a civil rights act that protects the civil and constitutional rights of handicapped individuals. This law is sometimes called the "curb cut" law because it is the legal basis of the mandated curb cuts in streets that allow wheelchairs (as well as strollers, bicycles, and so on) to more easily go from street to sidewalk. Section 504 of the Rehabilitation Act (PL 93–112), first passed by Congress in 1973, was expanded in 1978 to cover schools. The law states:

No otherwise qualified handicapped individual . . . shall, solely by reason of his/her handicap, be excluded from participation in, be denied the benefits of, or be subject to discrimination under any program or activity receiving federal financial assistance.

Section 504 covers a broader population of individuals with handicaps than the Individuals with Disabilities Education Act (Madsen, 1990). As related to the educational setting, students with handicaps may not be receiving services from special education teachers but still require assistance in school because of their handicapping condition. A child with ADD is a "qualified handicapped person" under Section 504 if (a) the child is between the ages of 3 and 21, and (b) the handicapping condition substantially limits the child's ability to learn or to otherwise benefit from his or her education program.

If a school district regards a student as handicapped or if the student has previously been in a special education program, he or she qualifies for *accommodations* under Section 504. Many students currently served under Section 504 have physical disabilities and are provided barrier-free environments. Students who have documented health problems such as attention deficit disorders, as well as students who have identified learning disabilities but do not qualify for services under a district's severe eligibility specifications, can meet criteria to be served under Section 504. These students require specific accommodations to benefit from the educational process.

School districts should be aware of their obligations under Section 504, develop procedures for administering to their special needs students, and provide school staff with the techniques necessary to accommodate them. Classroom teachers can provide accommodations through classroom modifications, curriculum adaptations, time management, and delivery of instruction. School administrators can provide for the needs of children with ADD without major changes in school procedure (Reeves, 1990; Teeter, 1991).

By implementing Section 504, students with learning disabilities are able to enroll in college and postsecondary schools in steadily increasing numbers (Vogel, 1987). A recent survey shows that many colleges and postsecondary schools provide Section 504 access services for students with learning disabilities (Bursuck, Rose, Cowen, & Yahaya, 1989). Section 504 college services include taped textbooks, note takers, counseling, individualized education plans, and basic skills instruction in reading, math, and language.

HISTORY OF ADD

Tracing the history of ADD offers an explanation of the origins of the various terms used to describe this syndrome and an historical perspective of the evolving theories. In the past 50 years, as researchers and clinicians wrote about the condition, many theories and terms evolved, including (a) brain damage syndrome, (b) minimal brain dysfunction (MBD), (c) hyperkinetic reaction of childhood, (d) attention deficit disorder with hyperactivity (ADDH) and attention deficit disorder without hyperactivity (ADD/noH), and (e) attention-deficit hyperactivity disorder (ADHD) and undifferentiated attention-deficit disorder (U-ADD) (Cantwell & Baker, 1991; Frick & Lahey, 1991; Lahey & Carlson, 1991; Shaywitz, 1987; Shaywitz & Shaywitz, 1988; Silver, 1990; Silver & Hagin, 1990). A brief historical overview of the diagnostic terminology used over the years is summarized in Table 1.

Brain Damage Syndrome

The first report in the medical literature was an article by Still (1902), who described children with what he termed "morbid defects in moral control." His descriptions were remarkably similar to diagnostic criteria used today. Other investigators of that era were also beginning to link this behavior to traumatic brain injury and other childhood central nervous system infections (Goldstein, 1936; Meyer, 1904).

In the 1930s and 1940s, work on a specific behavioral syndrome in children arising from brain damage led to influential publications by Werner and Strauss (1941) and Strauss and Lehtinen (1947). Surveying a population of mentally defective, institutionalized children and using case history information and a neurological examination, those researchers linked the learning problems and symptomatic behaviors of some of these children to brain damage. They hypothesized that the insult to the brain could occur before, during, or after birth. The behaviors of the brain-damaged children were described as hyperactive, distractible, impulsive, emotionally labile, and perserverative. The work of Strauss & Lehtinen (1947) alerted many physicians and educators to an alternative diagnosis for children who previously had been given other labels and to parents who had been blamed for the child's behavior.

TABLE 1 Historical Overview of Attention Deficit Disorder

Date	Diagnostic Terminology	Source	Characteristics
1941, 1947	Brain damage syndrome	Werner & Strauss	Hyperactivity, distractibility, impulsivity, emotionality unstable perserveration.
1962	Minimal brain dysfunction (MBD)	Clements & Peters	Soft neurological indicators, specific learning deficits, hyperkinesis, impulsivity, short attention span.
1968	Hyperkinetic reaction of childhood	DSM II	Hyperactivity
1980	Attention deficit disorder with hyperactivity (ADDH)	DSM III	(a) Inattention, impulsivity, motor hyperactivity (b) Onset before age 7 (c) Duration of at least 6 months
	Attention deficit disorder without hyperactivity (ADD/noH)		Inattention, disorganization, difficulty completing tasks
1987	Attention-deficit hyperactivity disorder (ADHD)	DSM III-R	Any 8 of a set of 14 symptoms
	Undifferentiated attention deficit disorder (U-ADD)		Developmentally inappropriate and marked inattention
1991	Attention deficit disorder (ADD)	Policy Memorandum, U.S. Department of Education	IDEA, Part B— Other Health Impaired
In process		DSM IV	

Sources: Diagnostic and Statistical Manual of Mental Disorders (2nd ed.; 3rd ed.; 3rd ed., rev.; 4th ed.), 1968; 1980; 1987; and in process, Washington, DC: American Psychiatric Association. "Minimal Brain Dysfunction in the School-Aged Child" by S. D. Clements and J. E. Peters, 1962, *Archives of General Psychiatry, 6*, pp. 185–187. *Psychopathology and Education in Brain-Injured Children* by A. S. Strauss and L. E. Lehtinen, 1947, New York: Grune & Stratton. "Pathology of the Figure-Background Relation in the Child" by H. Werner and A. S. Strauss, 1941, *Journal of Abnormal & Social Psychology, 36*, p. 234–248. U.S. Department of Education, Policy Memorandum, September 16, 1991.

Minimal Brain Dysfunction (MBD)

By the 1950s the medical literature reported that verifying brain damage in children with learning and behavioral problems was difficult and that these children looked normal. To differentiate this condition from true or gross brain damage, scholars suggested the term "minimal brain damage," a designation indicating that the brain damage was slight (Cantwell & Baker, 1991; Laufer & Denhoff, 1957; Shaywitz & Shaywitz, 1991; Silver, 1990).

An elaboration of this concept, suggested by Clements and Peters (1962), was "minimal brain dysfunction," a term implying that these individuals did not have brain damage but, rather, difficulty with the way the brain functioned (Silver, 1990). In 1966, a report sponsored by the National Institute of Health (NIH) recommended that the term "minimal brain damage" be discarded and replaced by "minimal brain dysfunction" (MBD) (Clements, 1966). The definition of MBD was:

> Children of near-average, average, or above-average general intelligence with certain learning or behavioral disabilities ranging from mild to severe, which are associated with deviations of function of the central nervous system. These deviations may manifest themselves by various combinations of impairment in perception, conceptualization, language, memory, and control of attention, impulse, or motor function. (p. 9)

The concept of MBD was appealing to psychiatrists, neurologists, and psychologists because it allowed them to note neurological deviations of a subtle nature. The symptoms of MBD included specific learning deficits, hyperkinesis, impulsivity, and short attention span, and the diagnosis included evidence of "equivocal" neurological signs and an electroencephalogram (EEG) that is borderline or abnormal.

Hyperkinetic Reaction of Childhood

The concept of MBD proved to be controversial because it was not operational and lacked sufficient guidelines for diagnosis. What was needed was a rigorous set of diagnostic criteria to identify the disorder. In 1968 the beginnings of a set of diagnostic criteria appeared in the second edition of the *Diagnostic and Statistical Manual of Mental Disorders* (DSM II) (American Psychiatric Association, 1968). The term "hyperkinetic reaction of childhood" was used to describe the hyperactive child. The disorder was characterized by overactivity, restlessness, distractibility, and short attention span (Silver, 1990).

Attention Deficit Disorder: ADDH and ADD/noH

The third edition of the *Diagnostic and Statistical Manual of Mental Disorders* (DSM III) (American Psychiatric Association, 1980) is considered a significant advance in the validity of diagnosis of attention deficit disorder (Cantwell & Baker, 1991; Shaywitz & Shaywitz, 1988). DSM III shifted the focus to attentional problems rather than activity problems, and it established the term "attentional deficit disorder." The role of attention in learning and within the larger cognitive system is complex. Attention impacts the rest of the system by what information it allows in at the sensory level, by how information is managed in short-term working memory, how information is encoded into long-term memory, and how information is retrieved from long-term memory (Cherkes-Julkowski, Stolzengerg, & Segal, 1991; Torgesen, Kistner, & Morgan, 1987).

In DSM III, two types of ADD were noted: (a) ADD with hyperactivity (ADDH) and (b) ADD without hyperactivity (ADD/noH). To establish the diagnosis of ADDH, the child had to show evidence of three criteria: (a) inattention, (b) impulsivity, and (c) motor hyperactivity. DSM III specified behaviors for each of the three criteria. The diagnosis of ADD/noH was for children who exhibited attentional deficits and impulsivity but no hyperactivity. Other diagnostic criteria for both ADDH and ADD/noH specified the age of onset as prior to 7 years and a duration of at least 6 months.

Attention Deficit Hyperactivity Disorder (ADHD)

In 1987, publication of the *Diagnostic and Statistical Manual of Mental Disorders-Revised* (DSM III-R) (American Psychiatric Association, 1987) revealed further modifications. The term "attention-deficit hyperactivity disorder" (ADHD) was used to reflect recent research showing that distractibility was a primary issue but hyperactivity was also an important factor in this disorder (Silver, 1990). For a diagnosis of ADHD, DSM III-R allowed any 8 symptoms to be identified from a set of a possible 14. Also, it kept the criteria for age of onset as prior to 7 years and duration of the behavior for at least 6 months. The diagnostic criteria for ADHD specified in DSM III-R are shown in the chart on the following page.

The type of ADD without hyperactivity (noted in DSM III) was relegated to minor status in DSM III-R (Barkley, DuPaul, & McMurray, 1991). Instead, DSM III-R describes a category called "undifferentiated attention-deficit disorders (U-ADD)," which roughly corresponds to children identified as ADD/noH in DSM III. Epstein, Shaywitz, Shaywitz, and Woolston (1991) believe these children are an underidentified, underserved group at significant risk for long-term academic, social, and emotional difficulties. Children with ADD/noH are far less visible and less likely to come to the attention of parents, educators, or other professionals; but, at the same time, they may be at much greater risk for school failure and social failure than children who have ADD with hyperactivity (Shaywitz, 1987).

Recent studies show that children with attention deficit disorders without hyperactivity represent a distinct category of ADD (Barkley et al., 1991; Lahey & Carlson, 1991; Schaughency & Rothlind, 1991). Compared to children having hyperactivity with attention deficit disorders, these children exhibit less serious conduct problems, are less impulsive, are more likely to be characterized as sluggish and drowsy, are less rejected by peers but more socially withdrawn, and are more likely to show depressed moods and symptoms of anxiety disorder. Many researchers recommend that ADD without hyperactivity represents a clinically meaningful entity and should be included as a distinct diagnostic category in DSM IV, which is currently in development (Epstein et al., 1991).

ASSOCIATED CONDITIONS

The classification of children with ADD is intrinsically related to classification efforts for other learning and behavior disorders (Fletcher, Morris & Francis, 1991). To be eligible for services under IDEA, a child must be classified under one of three existing disabilities: (a) specific learning disabilities (LD), (b) seriously emotionally disturbed (ED), or (c) other health impaired (OHI). August and Garfinkel (1989) designated two sub-

Diagnostic Criteria for Attention-Deficit Hyperactivity Disorder (DSM III-R)

Note: Consider a criterion met only if the behavior is considerably more frequent than that of most people of the same mental age.

A. A disturbance of at least six months during which at least eight of the following are present:

  1. often fidgets with hands or feet or squirms in seat (in adolescents may be limited to subjective feelings of restlessness)
  2. has difficulty remaining seated when required to do so
  3. is easily distracted by extraneous stimuli
  4. has difficulty awaiting turn in games or group situations
  5. often blurts out answers to questions before they have been completed
  6. has difficulty following through on instructions from others (not due to oppositional behavior or failure of comprehension); e.g., fails to finish chores
  7. has difficulty sustaining attention in tasks or play activities
  8. often shifts from one uncompleted activity to another

  9. has difficulty playing quietly
  10. often talks excessively
  11. often interrupts or intrudes on others; e.g., butts into other children's games
  12. often does not seem to listen to what is being said to him or her
  13. often loses things necessary for tasks or activities at school or at home (e.g., toys, pencils, books, assignments)
  14. often engages in physically dangerous activities without considering possible consequences (not for the purpose of thrill-seeking); e.g., runs into street without looking

  Note: The above items are listed in descending order of discriminating power based on data from a national field trial of the DSM III-R criteria for disruptive behavior disorders.

B. Onset before the age of 7
C. Does not meet the criteria for a pervasive developmental disorder

---

Criteria for Severity of Attention-Deficit Hyperactivity Disorder (pp. 52-53):

Mild: Few, if any, symptoms in excess of those required to make the diagnosis and only minimal or no impairment in school and social functioning

Moderate: Symptoms or functional impairment intermediate between "mild" and "severe"

Severe: Many symptoms in excess of those required to make the diagnosis and significant and pervasive impairment in functioning at home and school with age peers

---

The *Diagnostic and Statistical Manual* III-R (1987) also defines *undifferentiated attention-deficit disorder* as (p. 95):

A residual category for disturbances in which the predominant feature is the persistence of developmentally inappropriate and marked inattention that is not a symptom of another disorder, such as mental retardation or attention-deficit hyperactivity disorder, or a disorganized and chaotic environment. Some of the disturbances that in DSM-III would have been categorized as attention deficit disorder without hyperactivity would be included in this category. Research is necessary to determine if this is a valid diagnostic category and, if so, how it should be defined.

Source: From *Diagnostic and Statistical Manual of Mental Disorders* (3rd ed., rev.), 1987, Washington, DC: American Psychiatric Association.

types of ADHD: "behavioral" and "cognitive." The cognitive subtype is associated with LD and is characterized by severe academic underachievement and neuropsychological skill deficits having to do with encoding the retrieval of linguistic information. The behavioral subtype is characterized by conduct disorders and aggressive behavior, in addition to inattention, impulsivity, and overactivity.

Learning Disabilities and ADD

Accumulating evidence indicates a significant overlap between ADD and learning disabilities (LD). ADD is not a learning disability, but it is a disorder associated with learning disabilities (Silver, 1990). The relationship between LD and ADD is still unclear, with varying co-occurrence estimates (Shaywitz, 1987). A major problem is the inconsistent criteria used to diagnose both ADD and LD. Each is presumed to stem from a neurological disorder. With LD, it impacts the basic psychological processes involved in academic functioning. With ADD, it is manifested in hyperactivity (controlling motor activity level), distractibility (determining which external stimuli are relevant or not relevant), and impulsivity (reflecting before acting) (Shaywitz & Shaywitz, 1988; Silver, 1990). One study shows that children with untreated ADD (children who were not prescribed medication) were difficult to differentiate from those who had forms of learning disabilities (Cherkes-Julkowski & Stolzengerg, 1991).

Current estimates of co-occurrence of ADD and LD vary widely. A substantial proportion of ADD children (23–30%) have difficulties achieving up to a level predicted by their age and general intelligence (Epstein et al., 1991; Frick & Lahey, 1991; Shaywitz & Shaywitz, 1991). Moreover, between 15 and 20% of children and adolescents with learning disabilities will have ADD (Silver, 1990). Studies also show that 33% of LD students exhibit hyperactivity and that 11% of ADD children have significant problems in reading or arithmetic (Shaywitz & Shaywitz, 1988). The question of co-occurrence of ADD and LD and their mechanisms of interaction is important and merits further study.

Behavior/Emotional Disorders and ADD

The most significant problems associated with ADHD are aggressive and antisocial behaviors. Between 30 and 90% of children diagnosed with ADHD have significant conduct problems (Frick & Lahey, 1991). Many children with ADHD are referred by schools or parents for evaluation and treatment because of behavioral problems. These difficulties are often related to inattentiveness, overactivity, and impulsivity. The children require adult attention at home and school for behaviors such as noncompliance, excessive and inappropriate verbalizations, not completing or attending to tasks, and disturbing other children. In addition, their intrusiveness and bossiness, coupled at times with aggressive behavior and poor social skills, lead to unsatisfactory peer relations and often to outright peer rejection (Abikoff, 1991).

Under current federal law (IDEA), children with ADD may be classified and receive services under the disability category of *seriously emotionally disturbed*. The term used in DSM III-R and preferred by many medical specialists and psychologists is *conduct disorders*.

In the public inquiry on ADD, more than 800 people responded to the question concerning the extent to which children with ADD are being identified within existing disability categories (OSEP, 1991). Many commenters expressed the view that the existing disability categories are not sufficient to appropriately identify children with ADD. Parents often noted their reservations about identifying their children as emotionally handicapped. The responses reveal that parents do not like the term "behavior disorders." They are embarrassed by it and feel their child does not need the stigma that they perceive is attached. Many parents refuse placement when the classification of "seriously emotionally disturbed" is the only alternative. Teachers often report that the classroom behaviors of ADD children are considerably different from those of other ED children.

Other Health Impaired (OHI)

The disability category of *other health impaired* (OHI) offers the third option under IDEA for identifying and providing services to children with ADD (Teeter, 1991; Thomas, 1990). Although this is now an option, few children with ADD are presently identified under this category, and only a small percentage of the total school population (about .12%) is served under OHI (U.S. Department of Education, 1991, p. A-49). Of course, as more ADD children are identified under OHI, this percentage will increase substantially.

Children with health impairments require ongoing medical attention, stemming from a wide variety of conditions. Traditionally, the conditions under OHI include asthma, cystic fibrosis, heart defects, cancer, diabetes, and hemophilia. These conditions may not interfere with the child's ability to participate in regular classroom activities and may not require curricular adaptations, but they can require medication or special medical treatment. Teachers working with OHI children should know about medical procedures needed at school, limitations on activities, and emergency procedures that may be necessary if problems arise (Kirk & Gallagher, 1989). How children with ADD will be identified and served under the disability category of OHI will require further study and investigation.

ASSESSMENT

ADD is a behavioral diagnosis, requiring multimethod behavioral assessment. The goal of assessment is to make appropriate administrative decisions about eligibility for services and to facilitate linkages with other professionals and agencies, as appropriate (Schaughency & Rothlind, 1991). Schools are in a unique position to contribute to the identification and assessment of children with ADD. Because children spend 6 hours a day, 5 days a week, and 40 weeks per year in school, the school setting is important. Children can be observed doing a variety of academic and social tasks across a number of settings, and observed by multiple peers and adults. The child's problem is often first noted by the teacher after the child enters school. Moreover, studies show that teachers are able to distinguish between children with and without symptoms of ADD. Thus, a wealth of clinical information is available through the schools (Atkins & Pelham, 1991).

In school-based assessment of ADD, multiple measures should be used, including teacher rating scales, direct observations in classrooms and playgrounds, peer rating and sociometric measures, and academic performance (Atkins & Pelham, 1991; Schaughency & Rothlind, 1991).

Teacher Rating Scales

Because teacher ratings are the most easily obtained measure of the child's classroom behavior, they are the predominant method of collecting information. Some teacher rating scales are:

❑ *Conners Teacher Rating Scale (CTRS)* (Conners, 1969). The CTRS is one of the most frequently used scales designed to assess teacher perceptions of hyperactivity and related problems. The CTRS contains 39 items, which rate five factors: daydreaming-inattentive, hyperactive, conduct problems, anxious-fearful, and social-cooperative.

❑ *Hyperkinesis Index, Abbreviated or Short-Form* (Conners, 1973). The Hyperkinesis Index consists of 10 items from the original CTRS. A score of 15 of a possible 30 is considered the cutoff for classifying a child as hyperactive (Werry et al., 1975).

❑ *IOWA-Conners Rating Scale* (Loney & Milich, 1982). The IOWA-Conners Rating Scale consists of 10 items from the original 39 items of the CTRS. Five of the items are designed to measure inattention/overactivity, and the five remaining items measure aggression. Empirical evaluations have demonstrated considerable evidence for the IOWA-Conner's validity as a measure of ADHD (Atkins & Milich, 1988).

Direct Observations

Direct observation of classroom and playground behavior has been an important aspect of school-based assessment of ADHD. In direct observation, trained observers watch in a classroom situation and note specific targeted behaviors, through time-sampling methods. Direct observations are less subjective than ratings because they provide clearly defined measures that minimize inference on the observers' part. Research shows that direct observation methods do document differences between children with and without hyperactivity on objective measures of classroom behaviors (Abikoff, Gittelman, & Klein, 1980). Although direct observation methods are especially useful for research purposes, the method is costly for general assessment purposes.

Peer Ratings and Sociometrics

Children with ADD often have problems in social relations. Two common measures of peer acceptance are *peer nominations* and *peer ratings*. In peer nominations, children are asked to nominate a predetermined number of classmates (usually three) as those whom they most like and those whom they least like. In peer ratings, classmates rate specific behaviors. On both of these measures, children with ADD are rated as less popular and more disliked. Children with ADD who are also aggressive generate the most negative peer evaluations (Pelham & Milich, 1984).

Measures of Academic Performance

Measures of academic achievement and performance also add to the assessment picture. For example, if the item related to attention is the behavior "fails to finish things he starts," an assessment of the various classroom tasks the child is required to do adds significant diagnostic information (Atkins & Pelham, 1991).

TREATMENT

Most experts recommend a multimodal treatment for ADD. It should include combined therapies of medication, education, family counseling, and parent training.

Medical Treatment

Psychopharmalogical therapy, or the use of medication, has proven effective in treating ADD. Psychostimulant medications (central nervous system stimulant drugs) are given most frequently. The stimulant medications have a higher probability of success and have been studied most extensively (Anastopoulos, DuPaul, & Barkley, 1991; DuPaul, Barkley, & McMurray, 1991; Swanson, Cantwell, Lerner, McBurnett, & Hanna, 1991). The psychostimulant medications include Ritalin, Dexedrine, and Cylert (See Table 2). About 60–90% of the children with ADD are prescribed a regimen of stimulant therapy at some point during their school-age years, most often Ritalin (Landau & Moore, 1991). By some estimates, stimulant medications improve attention and reduce overactivity and even aggression in 70–80% of ADD children (Silver, 1990; Parker, 1988). With less frequency, antidepressant medications are used with a favorable response. These include Trofanil (imipramine) and Desipramine (norpramine) (Pliszke, 1987; Shaywitz & Shaywitz, 1988).

Psychostimulant medications increase the arousal or alertness of the central nervous system. The way in which stimulant medication alters deficits of ADD children in the domains of inattention, impulsivity, and overactivity is complex and still under study.

Research reviews on the effectiveness of stimulant medication consistently demonstrate that it improves children's classroom manageability and attention (Barkley, 1977; DuPaul et al., 1991; Gittelman-Klein & Klein, 1987). Recent studies suggest that medication also increases academic productivity (Swanson, Cantwell, Lerner, McBurnett, & Hanna, 1991). More than 70% of children with ADD taking these medications show behavioral, academic, and attention improvements, according to parent/teacher ratings, laboratory task performance, and direct observations (Anastopoulos et al., 1991).

Cherkes-Julkowski and Stolzengerg (1991) compared 21 ADD children who received medication with 20 ADD children who did not receive medication and found that the

TABLE 2 Psychostimulant Medications

Brand Name*	Dosage Regimen	Dose Range
Ritalin (methylphenidate)	Twice daily**	2.5 mg to 25 mg
Dexedrine (d-amphetamine)	Once daily	2.5 mg to 20 mg
Cylert (pemoline)	Once daily	18.75 mg to 112.5 mg

*Generic name in parenthesis.
**Slow-release dosage can be given once daily.

Source: From "Therapeutic Effects of Medication on ADHD: Implications for School Psychologists" by G. DuPaul, R. Barkley, and M. McMurray, 1991, *School Psychology Review, 20,* pp. 203–219.

medicated ADD group performed better in certain areas, particularly as related to working memory. But their data suggest the need for intervention beyond medication alone for children with ADD.

Current research focuses on differences between the responses of ADD children with hyperactivity (ADHD) and ADD children without hyperactivity (ADD/noH). One study of treatment responses to Ritalin (methylphenidate), conducted by Barkley et al. (1991), indicates that ADHD children respond differently to the medication than ADD/noH children. This study compared the responses of 23 ADHD children and 17 ADD/noH children to various dosages of Ritalin (methylphenidate). The majority of the ADHD children responded positively, primarily to the moderate to high doses of methylphenidate, whereas the ADD/noH children had minimal or no response or did best on the low dose of medication. The researchers concluded that the ADD/noH children may have a qualitatively different impairment in attention than ADHD children.

Diminished self-esteem is commonly associated with attention deficit disorder. Kelly et al. (1991) conducted a study of the changes in self-esteem of 21 ADD children, ages 8 to 12. Their research showed that initial self-esteem was low in 30% of the subjects, intermediate in 55%, and high in 15%. The children were assessed after a short-term course of treatment of Ritalin (methylphenidate) or a placebo, in a double-blind crossover fashion. No significant changes in self-esteem were noted after the one-month course of treatment, but at long-term follow-up (averaging 16 months), self-esteem improved significantly. Long-term treatment consisted of multimodal management, including medical management, supportive counseling, and referral for psychosocial and educational assistance.

The most frequently reported *side effects* of stimulant medications given to children with ADD are insomnia or sleep disturbances, and decreased appetite, but these are temporary. In addition, a slowing in height growth was noted in some studies when the child

received high doses over a long duration. Other studies show that when medication is reduced or is omitted for holiday periods, growth catches up. Of more concern is the onset
of Tourette's syndrome or tics in some patients. Physicians, teachers, and parents should
be alert to symptoms of tics so that medication can be eliminated or changed if this symptom appears (Silver & Hagin, 1990).

Educational Treatment

Educational treatment for ADD is part of a total multimodal treatment approach. ADD
is treatable through specialized, behaviorally based interventions in the educational setting, in conjunction with medication. Educational procedures include those used in special education for children with learning disabilities and behavioral disorders, modifications in the child's environment and assigned tasks, behavioral management methods,
and cognitive training (Abramowitz & O'Leary, 1991; McBurnett & Pfiffner, 1991;
Newby & Fischer, 1991; Pfiffner & Barkley, 1990).

Importance of the Teacher's Understanding of ADD

In addition to acquiring knowledge about ADD and its associated behaviors, teachers
should recognize their own reactions to a child with ADD. Because of their impulsiveness, loud presence in the classroom, and persistence of their questions, comments, and
demands, ADD children try teachers' patience and tend to become unpopular members
of the classroom group. Teachers have to understand that much of this behavior is not
intentional, not part of a ploy to defy educational authority. ADD children's activity level,
annoying as it is to people around the youngster, is not always under voluntary control
(Silver & Hagin, 1990).

Special Education Instruction

If the child is eligible for special education, educational intervention is likely to follow the
methods used in that category of disability. If the child is identified as having a learning
disability, many of the procedures and methods are similar to those for treating a learning disability. If the child is identified as having a conduct disorder, the methods likely
are those applied to children with an emotional disturbance. If children are identified in
the category of other health impaired (OHI), educational management has not yet been
clearly established (Goldstein & Goldstein, 1990; Parker, 1988; Silver, 1990). If a child
is not identified for special education, accommodations can be made within the regular
classroom, in the form of classroom modifications, curriculum adaptations, time management, and delivery of instruction.

   Behavioral Intervention Strategies. One behavioral approach for children with ADD
entails *modifying the environment and the task.* Several research studies have explored
the effect of variables in the classroom setting and environment on the attention and hyperactivity of children with ADD. A summary of the findings of this research
(Abramowitz & O'Leary, 1991), shows that children with ADD are distracted by classroom noise, by tasks that are too difficult, and by tasks that are paced by others (as op-

posed to self-paced tasks). Attention is facilitated through greater task structure and increasing stimulation by adding color, shape, and texture. The research also shows that children attend better when class size is small; and their attention is higher in the resource room than in the regular classroom and during direct instruction (rather than seatwork).

Another approach, *behavioral management*, uses contingency management strategies, which apply consequences contingent on specific child behaviors. This approach has generated much research on children with ADD. Abramowitz and O'Leary (1991) review several different contingency management strategies with children who have ADD: contingent teacher attention, classroom token economies, home-school contingencies, peer-mediated interventions, time-out contingencies, and reductive procedures based on reinforcement.

❑ *Contingent teacher attention* calls for frequent verbal feedback (positive and negative) and nonverbal feedback (nods, frowns, smiles, and pats of approval). A combination of praising appropriate behavior while ignoring inappropriate behavior can successfully reduce classroom disruptiveness.

❑ *Classroom token economies* involve awarding or removing tokens or points to children contingent upon specific desirable or undesirable behaviors, which motivates youngsters and improves on-task behavior and academic achievement.

❑ *Home-school contingencies* combine the efforts of school and parents to improve children's classroom behavior. Teachers complete a brief daily checklist of three to five items, indicating whether the child met the goals for that day. The checklist is sent home, signed by parents, and returned. Parents provide appropriate consequences at home by applying contingencies that have been developed in advance. The advantage of this strategy is that it encompasses two environments, the school and the home.

❑ *Peer-mediated intervention* draws upon classmates of the ADD child as contingency managers. Peers are trained to praise appropriate behavior and ignore inappropriate behavior. Enlisting peer cooperation has proven to be efficient and successful in modifying the behavior of a target child (Abramowitz & O'Leary, 1991).

❑ *Time-out from positive reinforcement* is a method of mild punishment in which the child is removed from the instructional setting for a brief period. Although it is well documented as a powerful and effective method of contingency management, time-out is controversial and can be misused. Abramowitz and O'Leary (1991) recommend that it be reserved for only the most disruptive classroom behaviors and administered only by highly trained staff.

❑ *Reductive procedures based on reinforcement* involve the use of reinforcers to reduce rates of inappropriate behavior. These techniques employ various schedules, timings, and rates of providing reinforcement. Abramowitz and O'Leary (1991) believe that the methods can be effective with children with ADD, particularly when they have associated conduct disorders.

Cognitive Training. Over the past 10 years, cognitive training has emerged as a major instructional procedure to teach children to act as their own behavior change agents. Two categories of behavior are targeted through cognitive-behavioral instruction: (a) teaching students self-monitoring and self-reinforcement strategies (Kendall & Braswell, 1985; Meichenbaum, 1977; Meichenbaum & Goodman, 1971); and (b) teaching students self-instructional and problem-solving cognitive skills (Abikoff, 1991; Deshler & Schumaker, 1986). The strategy intervention model (SIM) has been researched extensively to help students with learning disabilities (Deshler & Schumaker, 1986). Its goal is to help students learn the strategies that effective learners use to control their own behavior and learning. These strategies include self-instructional training, cognitive modeling, self-monitoring, self-reinforcement, and cognitive and interpersonal problem solving (Harris & Pressley, 1991).

The central goal of cognitive training for children with ADD is the development of self-control skills and reflective problem-solving strategies, both of which are presumed to be deficient in children with ADD. These deficiencies are thought to account for difficulties in regulating attentive, impulsive, and interpersonal behaviors (Abikoff, 1991). The method is also referred to as *cognitive behavior modification* because students learn to control and modify their own behavior through self-behavior modification techniques (Meichenbaum, 1977), and *learning strategies* because students acquire methods that help them learn how to control their learning behavior (Deshler & Schumaker, 1986).

Among the models of cognitive training, the learning strategies model developed at the University of Kansas Institute on Learning Disabilities offers a structure that has gained wide popularity (Ellis, Deshler, Lenz, Clark, & Schumaker, 1991). This model has eight steps, as presented in Table 3.

Cognitive training methods used on children with learning disabilities and low-achieving children are effective in teaching academic skills (Ellis et al., 1991). Only a few studies, however, have targeted improving the cognitive behavior of ADD children. Some studies suggest that cognitive training for ADD children may be a useful adjunct to medical treatment or may be helpful when children are tapered off medication (Shaywitz & Shaywitz, 1988).

Family Counseling and Parent Training

The ADD child and the family may benefit from family counseling to help repair injured self-esteem, overcome feelings of demoralization or depression, or learn more effective behavior approaches. Family problems can relate to the parents' handling of the child or adolescent, to the stress created within the family, or to problems with siblings (Parker, 1988). Parent training is often recommended as a treatment for children with ADD (Newby & Fischer, 1991).

Being a parent is not easy, and having a child with a disability is even more difficult. When the disability is invisible, as in ADD, it creates even more stress for the parent. Parents may have difficulty accepting the reality that their child has a disability. A parent may show evidence of *denial,* refusing to accept the existence of the problem. As parents con-

TABLE 3   Cognitive Training: Steps of the Learning Strategies Model

Step 1: Give pretest and obtain commitments
Assess student's present level of work.

Step 2: Describe the procedure
Give student the rationale for the procedure.

Step 3: Model the procedure
Demonstrate the procedure by talking aloud the thought process.

Step 4: Engage student in verbal rehearsal
Have student go through the procedure by talking aloud

Step 5: Introduce controlled practice and feedback
Have student practice the procedure in controlled, easy situation.

Step 6: Give grade-appropriate practice and feedback
Have student practice the procedure in more difficult situation.

Step 7: Administer posttest and obtain commitment to generalize
Test student on learning.

Step 8: Promote generalization
Help student become aware of other situations and strategies for using the learning strategy.

Source: From "An Instructional Model for Teaching Learning Strategies" by E.S. Ellis, D.D. Deshler, B.K. Lenz, J.B. Schumaker, and F.L. Clark, 1991, *Focus on Exceptional Children, 23*(6), p. 11.

tinue to struggle with the problem, they may become *angry* or feel *guilty.* The anger can be directed toward teachers and others; the guilt may lead to self-critical behavior or the need to do more for the child to make up for the child's problem (Silver, 1989).

In family therapy, parents first need information about their child, including medical, educational, psychological, and psychiatric data. The nature of ADD should be explained. Existing emotional, social, or family problems should be clarified and related to ADD. A treatment plan should be formulated and parents counseled on the necessity of becoming advocates for their son or daughter. Full evaluative information should be shared with the child or adolescent, who must understand the reasons for the difficulties and understand the reasons for the treatment plan (Silver, 1989).

Parents have a critical role to play in helping their child. They need to understand how the problem impacts on family activities. They might think about what the child is good at and the areas in which the child has difficulty. They can then apply this knowledge to planning for many activities that will lead to success in school and academics and making friends and establishing social relationships. Specifically, this could include choosing a camp or selecting sports activities and facilitating outside group activities.

If the child's emotional problems are believed to be secondary to ADD, the focus should be on establishing the necessary educational programs and clarifying the nature of the problem with the individual and the family. If the secondary psychological problems have become so established that they now have a life of their own, however, they must be treated, and psychotherapy may be necessary. Clinicians must understand how ADD interferes with peer and family interactions so it can be explained to the child and become useful in problem solving (Silver, 1989).

CURRENT ISSUES

Extensive research and new methods of assessment and treatment regarding ADD make it a dynamic and rapidly changing discipline. Some areas of recent study are gender issues, ADD characteristics at different age levels, social deficits, and cross-generational findings.

Gender Issues

Many more boys than girls are identified as having ADD. In studies comparing sex ratios, boys outnumber girls, with a range between twice as many to eight times as many boys (Shaywitz & Shaywitz, 1988). Many of the clinical characteristics found in girls are similar to those described for boys, but some differences are apparent. Girls with ADD have more cognitive and language deficits and greater social liability. Boys with ADD show more physical aggression and loss of control (Berry, Shaywitz, & Shaywitz, 1985; Shaywitz, 1987).

The reasons for these gender differences remain speculative. ADD may have biological roots, with males being more vulnerable to ADD. Or ADD may entail cultural bias, with more referral of boys than girls because boys tend to show more disruptive behaviors that are troublesome to adults. Also, boys may be under more pressure than girls to succeed at school, making them more vulnerable to effects of stress. Some researchers suspect that girls with ADD are an underidentified and underserved group at significant risk for long-term academic, social, and emotional difficulties (Shaywitz & Shaywitz, 1988).

Developmental Characteristics of ADD

ADD has different manifestations as the child matures, and the symptoms show a developmental trend. The disorder appears at an early age and often persists into later life. Many children with ADD do not outgrow the problem, but the characteristics change at different stages of life. Until age 3, activity level increases, but then it slows down. By adolescence, gross motor hyperactivity is no longer present, although attentional deficits persist. Certain symptoms, such as hyperactivity, may diminish, but others, such as academic difficulties, behavioral problems, poor peer acceptance, low self-esteem, and at times, depression, are evident. Secondary problems often become more prominent. Although many of the symptoms persist, previously hyperactive young adults fare better in the workplace than they did in the classroom (Shaywitz, 1987; Teeter, 1991; Weiss & Hechtman, 1986).

Some of the developmental characteristics of ADD at different stages are (Campbell, 1990; Teeter, 1991):

❑ *Infancy:* excessive crying, undue sensitivity, difficult to soothe.

❑ *Toddler:* stressful mother-child interaction; less compliant.

❑ *Preschool:* excessive activity; noncompliant, difficult to toilet train; shifts activities in free play; high activity levels during structured activities, impulsive responding, negative encounters with others.

❑ *Elementary ages:* poor school performance, failure to finish assignments; disruptive in class, poor social relations, aggressive, possible opposition behavior, low attention, easily frustrated.

❑ *Adolescence:* problems with following rules and assuming responsibilities, more conduct problems, social problems, antisocial behavior, self-control problems, academic failure.

❑ *Adult:* social problems, depression, low self-esteem.

These changes in symptoms during different age levels suggest different treatment needs. During infancy and toddler stages, treatment should focus on building positive parent-child relationships. During the preschool stage, parent training should emphasize consistent and firm limit setting, with reasonable and fair expectations. Social skills training for preschool children may also be necessary so the child can learn to share and take turns and not to grab toys or hit others. During the elementary years, ADD children may need extra instructional opportunities and behavior management to counter their disruptive behavior in the classroom. In the adolescent stage, interventions should be directed toward improved academic competencies, how to handle social situations and pressures, conflict resolution, and self-control cognitive and behavioral strategies (Teeter, 1991).

Social Deficits

Many children with ADD have serious interpersonal difficulties and experience peer rejection. Although not all children with ADD have social skills deficits, it is a problem for many. Children with ADD with hyperactivity (ADDH) as well as those with ADD without hyperactivity (ADD/noH) score lower than their peers on popularity ratings, but the ADDH children rate lower in popularity and peers actively dislike them. Hyperactive children are likely to be intrusive, boisterous, annoying, and generally aversive to peers and others; children with ADD/noH tend to be more socially withdrawn (Lahey & Carlson, 1991; Landau & Moore, 1991; Shaywitz & Shaywitz, 1988).

Attention to social problems is important because peer relations are predictive of most accepted outcome measures of adolescent and adult mental health as employed in clinical research. Social rejection may lead to secondary symptoms including poor self-esteem, depression, and antisocial behaviors. Moreover, early disturbed peer relations predict premature dropping out of school, juvenile delinquency, job termination, bad conduct discharges from the military, police contacts, and psychiatric hospitalizations. Early peer problems not only indicate concurrent difficulties for the child but also represent a significant at-risk marker for later emotional and behavioral disturbance (Landau & Moore, 1991; Parker & Asher, 1987; Shaywitz & Shaywitz, 1988).

Treatment for social skills deficits includes psychopharmalogical treatment, behavioral interventions, cognitive-behavioral interventions, and combination therapies (Landau & Moore, 1991). Psychopharmalogical treatment with stimulant medication, usually Ritalin, has been found to be effective in reducing hyperactivity. And less hyperactivity enhances the child's social acceptance (Whalen & Henker, 1991).

Behavioral interventions to improve the social functioning of children with ADD employ an array of behavior modification and reinforcement methods. Cognitive-behavior interventions focus on teaching cognitive and self-instructional strategies for negotiating interpersonal exchanges. Because this is a relatively new approach to improving social competencies, research is needed to substantiate its efficacy.

Finally, combining several therapies concurrently may reinforce the efficacy of treatment. Although few studies have examined the combined effects of several therapies on social functioning, the combination approach looks promising (Landau & Moore, 1991).

Cross-Generational Findings

Evidence from a number of investigations points to a strong genetic influence in ADD. Family studies, twin studies, foster child rearing studies, and neurochemical studies suggest that the child is born that way. Others in the family—fathers, uncles, siblings—often report having had similar problems (Shaywitz, 1987; Shaywitz & Shaywitz, 1988). The genetic/biological factors may be related to abnormalities in neurological function, in particular to disturbances in brain neurochemistry involving a class of brain neurochemicals called neurotransmitters.

SUMMARY

Because so many children are being diagnosed with attention deficit disorders (ADD), educators should become familiar with the condition. Special education legislation, specifically the Individuals with Disabilities Education Act (IDEA) and Section 504 of the Rehabilitation Act recognize ADD. Children can be served under learning disabilities, serious emotional disturbances, or other health impaired.

The literature reveals several historical phases in the thinking about this disorder, reflected in the terms brain damage syndrome, minimal brain dysfunction (MBD), hyperkinetic reaction of childhood, attention deficit disorders: ADDH and ADD/noH, and attention-deficit hyperactivity disorder (ADHD).

Methods of school assessment include teacher rating scales, direct observation, peer ratings and sociometrics, and measures of academic performance. Treatment may consist of medical, educational, family counseling, and parent training methods. Most experts believe that a combination of methods is the most effective approach.

Current issues affecting ADD include gender differences, developmental characteristics of ADD, social deficits, and cross-generational research. ADD remains a complex and puzzling condition for many children in the schools, and much research remains to be accomplished on all fronts.

REFERENCES

Abikoff, H. (1991). Cognitive training in ADHD children: Less to it than meets the eye. *Journal of Learning Disabilities, 24,* 205–209.

Abikoff, H., Gittelman, R., & Klein, D. (1980). Classroom observation code for hyperactive children: A replication of validity. *Journal of Consulting & Clinical Psychology, 48,* 772–783.

Abramowitz, A. J., & O'Leary, S. G. (1991). Behavior interventions for the classroom: Implications for students with ADHD. *School Psychology Review, 20,* 221–235.

American Psychiatric Association (1968). *Diagnostic and statistical manual of mental disorders* (2nd ed.) (DSM II). Washington, DC: APA.

American Psychiatric Association (1980). *Diagnostic and statistical manual of mental disorders* (3rd ed.) (DSM III). Washington, DC: APA.

American Psychiatric Association (1987). *Diagnostic and statistical manual of mental disorders* (3rd ed., rev.) (DSM III-R). Washington, DC: APA.

American Psychiatric Association (in process). *Diagnostic and statistical manual of mental disorders* (4th ed.) (DSM IV). Washington, DC: APA.

Anastopoulos, A., DuPaul, G., & Barkley, R. (1991). Stimulant medication and parent training therapies for attention deficit-hyperactivity disorder. *Journal of Learning Disabilities, 24,* 210–218.

Atkins, M. S., & Milich, R. (1988). The IOWA-Conners Teacher Rating Scale. In M. Hersen & A. Bellack (Eds.), *Dictionary of behavioral assessment techniques* (pp. 273–274). New York: Pergamon Press.

Atkins, M. S., & Pelham, W. E. (1991). School-based assessment of attention deficit-hyperactivity disorder. *Journal of Learning Disabilities, 24,* 197–204.

August, G. L., & Garfinkel, B. D. (1989). Behavioral and cognitive subtypes of ADHD. *Journal of the American Academic of Child & Adolescent Psychiatry, 28,* 739–748.

Barkley, R. A. (1977). A review of stimulant drug research with hyperactive children. *Journal of Child Psychology and Psychiatry, 18,* 137–165.

Barkley, R. A. (1990). *Attention deficit hyperactivity disorders: A handbook for diagnosis and treatment.* New York: Guilford Press.

Barkley, R. A., DuPaul, G. J., & McMurray, M. B. (1991). Attention deficit disorder with and without hyperactivity: Clinical response to three dose levels of methylphenidate. *Pediatrics, 87*(4), 519–531.

Berry, C. A., Shaywitz, S. E., & Shaywitz, B. A. (1985). Girls with attention deficit disorder: A silent minority? A report on the behavioral and cognitive characteristics. *Pediatrics, 76,* 807–809.

Bursuck, W. D., Rose, E., Cowen, S., & Yahaya, M. (1989). Nationwide survey of postsecondary education services for students with learning disabilities. *Exceptional Children, 56,* 236–254.

Campbell, S. B. (1990). The socialization and social development of hyperactive children. In M. Lewis & S. Miller (Eds.), *Handbook of developmental psychopathology* (pp. 77–92), New York: Plenum Press.

Cantwell, D. P., & Baker, L. (1991). Association between attention deficit-hyperactivity disorder and learning disorders. *Journal of Learning Disabilities, 24,* 88–95.

Cherkes-Julkowski, M., & Stolzengerg, J. (1991). The learning disability of attention deficit disorder. *Learning Disabilities: A Multidisciplinary Journal, 2*(1), 8–15.

Cherkes-Julkowski, M., Stolzengerg, J., & Segal, L. (1991). Prompted cognitive testing as a diagnostic compensation for attentional deficits: The Raven Standard Progressive Matrices and attention deficit disorder. *Learning Disabilities: A Multidisciplinary Journal, 2*(1), 1–7.

Clements, P. (1966). *Minimal brain dysfunction in children* (NINDS Monograph No. 3, Public Health Bulletin No. 1415). Washgton, DC: U.S. Department of Health, Education, and Welfare.

Clements, S. D., & Peters, J. E. (1962). Minimal brain dysfunciton in the school-aged child. *Archives of General Psychiatry, 6,* 185–187.

Clements, S. D., & Peters, J. E. (1966). *Minimal brain dysfunction in children: Terminology and identification* (Public Health Service Publication No. 1415). Washington, DC: U.S. Department of Health, Education, and Welfare.

Conners, C. K. (1969). A teacher rating scale for use in drug studies with children. *American Journal of Psychiatry, 126,* 884–888.

Conners, C. K. (1973). Rating scales for use in drug studies with children (special issue). *Psychopharmacology Bulletin,* pp. 24–84.

Council for Exceptional Children (1991). CEC Response to Notice of Inquiry: Children with ADD. *CEC News.* April 17.

Council for Learning Disabilities: CLD (1991). Letter to Office of Special Education Programs in response to Notice of Inquiry: Attention Deficit Disorder, March 26.

Deshler, D. D., & Schumaker, J. B. (1986). Learning strategies: An instructional alternative for low-achieving adolescents. *Exceptional Children, 52,* 583–590.

DuPaul, G. J., Barkley, R. A., & McMurray, M. B. (1991). Therapeutic effects of medication on ADHD: Implications for school psychologists. *School Psychology Review, 20,* 203–219.

(1990, Dec.). ED issues/questions on attention deficit disorder. *Education of the Handicapped, 16*(25), 1–2.

(1991, Sept.). ED clarifies stance on ADD, Says students must be served. *Education of the Handicapped, 17,* 1, 3.

Ellis, E. S., Deshler, D. D., Lenz, B. K., Clark, F. L., & Schumaker, J. B. (1991). An instructional model for teaching learning strategies. *Focus on Exceptional Children, 23*(6), p. 11.

Epstein, M. A., Shaywitz, S. E., Shaywitz, B. A., & Woolston, J. L. (1991). The boundaries of attention deficit disorder. *Journal of Learning Disabilities, 24,* 78–86.

(1991). On the Public Policy Front. *Exceptional Children, 23*(3), 62.

Fletcher, J., Morris, R., & Francis, D. (1991). Methodological issues in the classification of attention-related disorders. *Journal of Learning Disabilities, 24,* 72–79.

Frick, P. J., & Lahey, B. B. (1991). Nature and characteristics of attention-deficit hyperactivity disorder. *School Psychology Review, 20,* 163–173.

Gittelman-Klein, R., & Klein, D. G. (1987). Pharmacotherapy of childhood hyperactivity: An update. In H. Y. Meltzer (Ed.), *Psychopharmacology—The third generation of progress* (pp. 1215–1224). New York: Raven Press.

Goldstein, K. (1936). Modification of behavior subsequent to cerebral lesion. *Psychiatric Quarterly, 10,* 539–610.

Goldstein, S., & Goldstein, M. (1990). *Managing attention disorders in children: A guide for practitioners.* New York: Wiley Interscience Press.

Harris, K. R., & Pressley, M. (1991). The nature of cognitive strategy instruction: Interactive strategy construction. *Exceptional Children, 57,* 391–404.

Henker, B., & Whalen, C. K. (1989). Hyperactivity and attention deficits. *American Psychologist, 44,* 215–223.

Kelly, P. C., Cohen, M. L., Walker, W. O., Caskey, O. L., & Atkinson, A. W. (1991). Self-esteem in children medically managed for attention deficit disorder. *Pediatrics, 83,* 211–217.

Kendall, P. C., & Braswell, L. (1985). *Cognitive behavioral therapy for impulsive children.* New York: Guilford.

Kirk, S., & Gallagher, J. (1989). *Educating exceptional children.* Boston: Houghton Mifflin.

Lahey, B. B., & Carlson, C. L. (1991). Validity of the diagnostic category of attention deficit disorder without hyperacitivity: A review of the literature. *Journal of Learning Disabilities, 24,* 110–120.

Landau, S., & Moore, L. A. (1991). Social skill deficits in children with attention-deficit hyperactivity disorder. *School Psychology Review, 20,* 235–251.

Laufer, M., & Denhoff, E. (1957). Hyperkinetic behavior syndrome in children. *Journal of Pediatrics, 50,* 463–474.

Learning Disabilities Association (1991). *LDA Legislative Update,* May 28.

Learning Disabilities Association (1991). Response to notice of inquiry regarding attention deficit disorder. *LDA Newsbriefs, 16*(3), 1, 5–7.

Loney, J., & Milich, R. (1982). Hyperactivity, inattention, and aggression in clinical practice. In M. Wolraich & D. K. Routh (Eds.), *Advances in behavioral pediatrics* (Vol. 2, pp. 113–137). Greenwich, CT: JAI Press.

Madsen, C. (1990). ADD/ADHD recognized as handicapping conditions under Section 504, Rehabilitation Act of 1973. *HAAD Enough,* Jan./Feb., 10–11.

McBurnett, K., & Pfiffner, L. J. (1991). ADHD and LD. *Journal of Learning Disabilities, 24,* 258–259.

Meichenbaum, D. (1977). *Cognitive-behavior modification: An integrative approach.* New York: Plenum Press.

Meichenbaum, D., & Goodman, J. (1971). Training impulsive children to talk to themselves: A means of developing self control. *Journal of Abnormal Psychology, 77,* 115–126.

Meyer, A. (1904). The anatomical facts and clinical varieties of traumatic insanity. *American Journal of Insanity, 60,* 373–441.

Newby, R. F., & Fischer, M. (1991). Parent training for families of children with ADHD. *School Psychology Review, 20,* 252–265.

OSEP sends notice of inquiry summary on ADD to Congress. (1991). *Special Educator, 6*(18), 255, 257.

Parker, H. C. (1988). *The ADD hyperactivity workbook for parents, teachers, and kids.* Plantation, FL: Impact Publications.

Parker, H. C. (1990). CH.A.D.D. Education position paper. *CH.A.D.D.: Children with Attention Deficit Disorders, 4*(1), 19–28.

Parker, J. G., & Asher, S. R. (1987). Peer relations and later personal adjustment: Are low-accepted children at risk? *Psychological Bulletin, 102,* 357–389.

Pelham, W. E., & Milich, R. (1984). Peer relations in children with hyperactivity/attention deficit disorder. *Journal of Learning Disabilities, 17,* 560–567.

Pfiffner, L. J., & Barkley, R. A. (1990). Classroom management methods. In R. A. Barkley (Ed.), *Attention deficit hyperactivity disorders: A handbook for diagnosis and treatment* (pp. 438–539). New York: Guilford Press.

Pliszke, S. R. (1987). Tricyclic antidepressants in the treatment of children with attention deficit disorder. *Journal of the American Academy of Child & Adolescent Psychiatry, 26,* 127–132.

Reeves, R. (1990, Sept./Oct.). Serving children with ADHD in the schools. *HAAD Enough,* pp. 3–4.

Schaughency, E. A., & Rothlind, J. (1991). Assessment and classification of attention-deficit hyperactivity disorders. *School Psychology Review, 20,* 187–202.

Shaywitz, B. (1987). Hyperactivity/attention deficit disorder. *Learning disabilities: A report to U.S. Congress.* Washington, DC: Interagency Committee on Learning Disabilities.

Shaywitz, S., & Shaywitz, B. (1988). Attention deficit disorder: Current perspectives. In J. Kavanagh & J. Truss (Eds.), *Learning disabilities: Proceedings of the national conference* (pp. 369–567). Parkton, MD: York Press.

Shaywitz, S., & Shaywitz, B. (1991). Introduction to the special series on attention deficit disorder. *Journal of Learning Disabilities, 24,* 68–71.

Silver, L. B. (1989). Psychological and family problems associated with learning disabilities: Assessment and intervention. *Journal of the American Academy of Child & Adolescent Psychiatry, 28,* 319–325.

Silver, L. B. (1990). Attention deficit-hyperactivity disorder: Is it a learning disability or a related disorder? *Journal of Learning Disabilities, 23,* 394–397.

Silver, A., & Hagin, R. (1990). *Disorders of learning in childhood.* New York: Wiley.

Still, G. E. (1902). The Coulstonian Lectures on some abnormal physical conditions in children. *Lancet,* 1:10018–12, 1007–82, 1163–68.

Strauss, A. A., & Lehtinen, L. E. (1947). *Psychopathology and education of the brain-injured child.* New York: Grune & Stratton.

Swanson, J. M., Cantwell, D., Lerner, M., McBurnett, K., & Hanna, G. (1991). Effects of stimulant medication on learning in children with ADHD. *Journal of Learning Disabilities, 24,* 219–230.

Teeter, P. A. (1991). Attention-deficit hyperactivity disorder: A psychoeducational paradigm. *School Psychology Review, 20,* 266–280.

Thomas, S. F. (1990). Washington highlights. *CH.A.D.D.ER, 4*(2), 7.

Torgesen, J. K., Kistner, J. A., & Morgan, S. (1987). Component processes in working memory. In J. G. Borkowski & J. D. Days (Eds.), *Cognition in special children: Comparative approaches to retardation, learning disability, and giftedness* (pp. 49–86). Norwood, NJ: Ablex.

U.S. Department of Education (1991). To assure the free appropriate public education of all children with disabilities (Thirteenth Annual Report to Congress on the Implementation of the Education of the Handicapped Act). Washington, DC: U.S. Government Printing Press.

Vogel, S. A. (1987). Issues and concerns in LD college programming. In D. J. Johnson & J. W. Blalock (Eds.), *Adults with learning disabilities*. Orlando, FL: Grune & Stratton.

Weiss, G., & Hechtman, L. T. (1986). *Hyperactive children grown up: Empirical findings and theoretical considerations*. New York: Guilford.

Werner, H., & Strauss, A. (1940). Causal factors in low performance. *American Journal of Mental Deficiency, 45*, 213–218.

Werner, H., & Strauss, A. S. (1941). Pathology of the figure-background relation in the child. *Journal of Abnormal & Social Psychology, 36*, 234–248.

Werry, J., Sprague, R., & Cohen, M. (1975). Conners Teaching Rating Scale for use in drug studies with children: An empirical study. *Journal of Abnormal Child Psychology, 3*, 217–229.

Whalen, C., & Henker, B. (1991). Social impact of stimulant treatment for hyperactive children. *Journal of Learning Disabilities, 24*, 231–241.

Janet Lerner is a professor of special education at Northeastern Illinois University in Chicago. Sue Lerner earned her Ph.D. at the University of Texas and is currently on the staff of the DayGlow Family Treatment Program in Austin, Texas.

○ 13 ○

Modern society has produced more cases of traumatic head injury, of which automobile accidents head the list. This article not only documents the increased numbers but also the tremendous progress through technology. Students are now far more likely to receive appropriate care that allows them to reenter school. The article presents the patterns of recovery following head injury and suggestions for transition programs.

Students with Traumatic Brain Injury: Making the Transition from Hospital to School

Mary P. Mira and Janet Siantz Tyler

THE NATURE OF TRAUMATIC BRAIN INJURY

Barbara's Accident: How It All Began

Sixteen-year-old Barbara lost control of her car on a rural road and slid into a moving delivery truck. Although she was restrained by a lap belt, she slammed sideways on impact, hitting her head against the side of the car. The driver surmised that Barbara was seriously injured and summoned an ambulance on the truck's radio.

Because they were not far from town, the paramedics arrived quickly. They noted her unconscious state and that she was moving her extremities and trunk in a writhing manner. Recognizing that this indicated a head injury, they phoned ahead to the regional medical helicopter service, which met them at the local hospital. After she was stabilized at the emergency room, Barbara was evacuated to the nearby university medical center. Less than an hour after the accident, she was in the neurosurgical operating room.

The Demographics of Head Injury

Barbara's case exemplifies several typical features of traumatic brain injury (TBI). First, she was an adolescent; head injuries occur most often in the 15–24-year age range (Kalsbeek, McLaurin, Harris, & Miller, 1980). Because TBI is almost as frequent in children under age 15 (Kalsbeek et al., 1980), the peak incidence occurs among children of school age. Second, Barbara was injured in a vehicular accident. Motor vehicle accidents, either pedestrian or passenger/vehicle accidents, are the most common cause of head injuries in adolescents (Kalsbeek et al., 1980). Other causes of TBI in children include falls (the most frequent cause in young children), bicycle accidents, and other recreational activities. Among the adolescent group, sports injuries and, in some regions, assaults also result in head injuries. As a female, Barbara is not representative, the male-to-female ratio in adolescent motor vehicle injuries is about 2:1 (Kraus, Fife, Cox, Ramstein, & Conroy, 1986).

TBI is regarded as a low-incidence problem, with many school administrators reporting no occurrence in their schools (Tyler & Mira, 1989). Nevertheless, one in 500 school-age children will be hospitalized each year because of a head injury, and by age 15, 3% of the student body will have sustained a head injury (Kalsbeek et al., 1980). An average metropolitan district can expect 90 to 100 children a year to suffer head injuries that will have educational impact. In a small rural community three or four children may be injured annually. Thus, TBI is a significant problem within the schools.

Another feature of TBI, illustrated by Barbara's case, is that even in rural areas trauma care is often excellent, allowing those who are seriously injured to receive emergency care immediately. Children who once would not have survived severe injuries are getting prompt care, recovering, and returning to school. Thus, we can anticipate that the number of TBI children returning to school will increase as medical services become more sophisticated.

The Nature of Barbara's Injuries

Shortly after admission to the neurosurgical service, a computerized tomography (CT) scan was performed on Barbara. This radiological procedure allowed the physicians to visualize various layers of the brain and determine the extent of the structural damage. The CT scan revealed several areas of damage. One area was deep within the brain in the region where many major blood vessels join. Another area of contusion (brain tissue damage) was on the left side, extending from the middle portion of the temporal lobe to the posterior portion of the frontal lobe (from above the ear toward the forehead). Still another region of contusion was on the right side near the back of the frontal lobe. The CT scan also indicated areas of swelling throughout the brain. Barbara's condition was critical, and she required ventilation assistance to breathe. She remained in a coma for 6 weeks.

Neuropathology for the Educator

Educators who understand what happens in a TBI are in a better position to appreciate cognitive outcomes in children returning to school following a TBI. Barbara's injuries illustrate what often happens in a closed head injury. When the head is slammed against a stationary object (in this case, the inside of the car), the brain slams against the inside of the skull at the point of impact. The brain keeps moving back and forth within the skull after the impact, slamming against the inside of the skull at the opposite side from the point of impact, tearing apart the brain substance. Because the inner surface of the skull contains a number of sharp, bony protrusions, bleeding and further contusion will occur as the brain rubs against these.

In addition to contusions from slamming, the forces within the skull following an impact pull, stretch, and rotate the brain along various planes and surfaces. This not only further disrupts tissue and blood vessels but also affects individual brain cells as fibers are stretched and often torn. The significant feature of such rotational and stretching forces is that these occur widely throughout the brain, affecting the brain diffusely and far removed from the original site of impact.

Thus, in a TBI widespread damage may be done beyond the point of impact. The stretching and tearing result in diffuse changes, which are not often visualized by procedures such as CT scans. The implication is that the effects of TBI are generalized; they affect more than one area of the brain and, therefore, affect more than one or two skills. Rotational shearing effects, which are permanent, occur even in mild head injuries. This *primary* damage represents permanent effects of the trauma on the brain; the damaged cells will not regenerate.

Secondary effects of the trauma to the brain further influence the individual's condition after injury. Bleeding and accumulation of blood may be present within the brain. Build-up of fluids in the tissue will result in swelling. This swelling causes increased pressure within the brain, which may further restrict blood flow through smaller vessels, leading to more cell damage. These secondary effects of trauma will subside when treated; as they do, the patient's condition will improve. This early, relatively rapid improvement is often erroneously interpreted as an indication that subsequent recovery will be as rapid and complete.

Barbara's injuries exemplify several of the neurological features discussed. A significant area of her brain, most likely at the point of impact, sustained tissue damage. A region of contusion also was found opposite this point, probably as a result of the brain's rebounding against the opposite wall. Other tissue, deeper within the brain, also was damaged. The extent of primary tissue damage suggested diffuse damage to brain fibers that were not visible on the CT scan. In addition, secondary damage occurred as a result of the brain swelling. Thus, we could anticipate that Barbara would show some marked and specific deficits, at least in the early phase of recovery. And, because of the diffuse and generalized damage, she would continue to show long-lasting, if subtle, residuals.

Barbara's head injury was classified as serious because she was not fully conscious and alert for 6 weeks. The length of coma is a major criteria for classifying severity of head injuries. Although no uniform system exists for classifying TBI severity, a frequently cited system follows:

Minor: Common bumps on the head with no evidence of concussion; generally, these cases are not seen by a physician.

Mild: Only brief loss of consciousness, if any, with accompanying symptoms of concussion such as vomiting, lethargy, or lack of recall of the injury.

Moderate: Evidence of concussion; loss of consciousness, less than 5 minutes.

Severe: Concussion or skull fracture; loss of consciousness 5–30 minutes.

Serious: Loss of consciousness more than 30 minutes; concussion or skull fracture and notable neurological sequelae (Klonoff, Low, & Clark, 1977).

RECOVERY FROM TRAUMATIC BRAIN INJURY

Barbara's Hospital Course

Barbara was hospitalized for 10 weeks. During that time her neurological status gradually improved. Her coma intensity gradually diminished over the first 6 weeks, and she became more and more responsive to lighter stimuli. By the end of the sixth week, she opened her eyes on command, made motor responses to commands, and indicated when she needed to be helped to the toilet.

Soon after admission, a tracheostomy tube was inserted through an opening in her neck to maintain an airway and help her breathe. Initially she was fed intravenously with nutrients delivered directly into her bloodstream. At the end of the fourth week, this was changed to a nasogastric tube, which delivered nutrients directly into her stomach, a physiologically more normal type of feeding. At the end of the sixth week, she pulled out the tracheostomy tube and began breathing on her own. She also began feeding by mouth at that time. At the beginning of the seventh week, she was alert, walking with assistance, answering simple questions, and responding socially with smiles and two- to three-word comments.

Patterns of Recovery Following Head Injury

Each child with a TBI progresses through the recovery process in a unique way. Recovery is influenced by the site and extent of the injuries to the brain, age, and other injuries or complications. Nevertheless, Barbara's recovery exemplifies the general recovery course.

Motor functions are among the first to improve, and gains in this area are often greater than initially expected (Brink, Garrett, Hale, Woo-Sam, & Nickel, 1970). In Barbara's case, walking to the bathroom with assistance was one of her first accomplishments. In most cases, communication skills improve rapidly (Marquardt, Stoll, & Sussman, 1988). The child may move rapidly from using short utterances to complex sentences. At discharge, children may appear to converse easily; however, more complex language skills, such as word finding, comprehending complex instructions, and formulating coherent and sequenced outputs, may continue to be problematic (Ylvisaker, 1986).

Measures of intelligence, particularly verbal IQ, may recover to near pretrauma level within several months (Rutter, 1981). IQ scores within the normal range following a TBI indicate only what the child retains of previously learned information; this does not necessarily indicate normal ability to process new information, to learn easily and organize inputs efficiently.

Recovery occurs more slowly and to a lesser degree in higher level cognitive activities (Rourke, Fisk, & Strang, 1986) and attention and memory (Levin & Eisenberg, 1979). After even a mild head injury, problems in these areas may persist for many months (Boll, 1983).

Recovery, particularly following moderate to severe head injury, is characterized by relatively rapid progress during the first few months, with continued observable changes over the first year (Chadwick, Rutter, Brown, Shaffer, & Traub, 1981). Improvement in cognitive, motor, and language functioning may continue through the second year at a slower rate, and in some cases, there will be evidence of improvement for several years after the injury (Klonoff et al., 1977).

Acute Rehabilitation Program

Children who have mild to moderate head injuries may be admitted to a general pediatric unit of the hospital. Those with more severe injuries, who require continuous monitoring of brain function, intubation, and other assistive devices, or those who have had brain surgery, will be under the care of neurosurgeons, often within an intensive care unit.

Once the child is medically stable, if residual motor or speech impairments are present, the child should be transferred to an acute rehabilitation program within the hospital. Here the child can receive a medically directed program of evaluation and treatment. He or she is evaluated for seizures, metabolic problems related to the brain damage, and orthopedic, feeding, and nutritional problems. The rehabilitation team, directed by a physician who specializes in rehabilitation medicine, develops a treatment program to maximize the extent and rate of the child's recovery. Physical, occupational, and speech therapists treat the child up to several times daily. Cognitive retraining, in the hospital classroom and in individual therapy, encourages recovery of residual cognitive skills. Other services that may be available in a comprehensive rehabilitation program include neuropsychologists who assess current brain functioning and plan cognitive retraining programs, psychologists who work with child and family, providing counseling and behavioral management services, and special educators who guide the relearning of academic material and prepare the child for reentry into school.

All of these specialists work with the child during the initial recovery period when the child is most responsive to interventions. Many children who could benefit from intense acute care rehabilitation do not receive these services because of the lack of availability in a community, or because a child without obvious deficits is erroneously assumed to be fully recovered.

Barbara's Rehabilitation and Education

Barbara began occupational and physical therapy within the first week of hospitalization. The therapists worked with her several times daily, using passive exercise to maintain and improve motor function. Daily speech and language therapy was begun during the fifth week, and in the seventh week Barbara began attending the hospital school daily. Included within the total rehabilitation program was a team consisting of a psychologist and two special educators devoted to the transition of children with TBI back into the school. By the sixth week this team began working with Barbara to assess her cognitive and behavioral status. The team also met with family members daily to provide information about TBI and the services Barbara might require upon school reentry. The reentry team also initiated collaboration between the rehabilitation team and her school.

Barbara was discharged from the hospital 10 weeks after the accident. Because it was near the end of the school year and because of her physical and endurance limitations, she did not return to school but instead continued her rehabilitation program as an outpatient for an additional 10 weeks during the summer. The program included homebound instruction provided by her school, which focused on her regaining previous academic skills, physical, occupational, and speech therapy, plus an academically based cognitive rehabilitation program.

This last program, developed and presented by the special educator from the hospital reentry team, used educational materials rather than isolated cognitive tasks to address her specific cognitive deficits in comprehension, memory, judgment, problem solving, organization, and sequencing. For example, to improve her reading and listening comprehension, activities were developed from the daily newspaper, in which she was to identify main ideas and locate sentences containing specific information. For memory practice the educator used exercises involving following directions, providing rapid retrieval, and reading for detail. Computer exercises provided practice in all areas. For example, one program asked Barbara to state whether a sentence was fact or opinion, a task that called upon her use of judgment.

Children may remain in a hospital-based acute rehabilitation program for several weeks or months. They then may continue rehabilitation therapies on an outpatient basis. Other children may require long-term treatment from a team of experts in pediatric head injury; these children may enter one of the residential programs at centers around the country that offer such specialized treatment.

SEQUELAE OF TRAUMATIC BRAIN INJURY

Effects of TBI on Barbara's Functioning

At the end of the summer, following the outpatient rehabilitation program, Barbara displayed a number of residual problems that had to be considered in developing her educational program. Physically her stamina was reduced; she required frequent rest breaks and was very tired by afternoon. She could endure only an hour and a half of sustained academic work. Her balance was poor, and her gait was clumsy, necessitating extra time to get from one place to another. She had reduced strength and dexterity of both arms, with marked incoordination of the right arm. Although she did not have seizures, she was placed on an anticonvulsant as a preventive measure for one year. She was restricted from all contact sports for one year, because her motor problems rendered her prone to further injury.

Barbara's language comprehension had returned to pretrauma levels, but her expressive skills were impaired. She spoke slowly, with diminished oral movement, and imprecise articulation reduced her intelligibility.

Throughout her rehabilitation Barbara was always cooperative, cheerful, polite, and willing to work in her therapies. She presented no problems of compliance or difficulty with impulse control. She occasionally was silly but could control this when cued.

Her measured IQ was approaching a documented pretrauma level within the average range. Her performance on neuropsychological evaluations was characterized by reduced efficiency on complex psychomotor tasks, normal sensory perceptual functioning, reduced mental processing speed, and impaired efficiency in problem solving in novel situations. She demonstrated good recovery of higher level cognitive skills such as generating hypotheses, concept formation, and effective use of feedback. Memory problems persisted, however. Although Barbara approached normal levels on short-term memory tasks, her recall of more complex units of information depended on her familiarity with the material. Delayed recall continued to be moderately impaired.

She made steady recovery of previously learned academic material. At the end of summer, on an individual achievement measure her scores in reading and math were within the average range, and written language and knowledge were slightly below average.

Those scores, however, did not reflect her difficulty with instructional material on a day-to-day basis. Barbara read and comprehended independently at the ninth grade level but comprehended only 60% of material at the tenth–eleventh grade level. In math, although computational skills were recovering, she continued to have difficulty with word problems and defining math concepts. Before the TBI she had some difficulty with written language, and she continued to have considerable difficulty in this area. She could not generate well-formulated written products or detect her errors in grammar, style, or spelling. Although she could perform several tasks at her grade level, her speed of information processing was well below what was expected for her grade.

Educationally Significant Effects of Head Injury

Long-term sequelae often are associated with moderate to severe TBI. Many times these problems occur following mild injuries as well. A number of medical problems also may be present at the time of school reentry. Approximately 5% of the children have seizures following a TBI, with the incidence increasing to 40% among children who have sustained severe injuries (Hauser, 1983). In some cases the seizures occur soon after the injury; in others the onset may be delayed for as long as a year (Brink, Imbus, & Woo-Sam, 1980; Hauser, 1983). For this reason many neurologists routinely place a child on prophylactic anticonvulsant medication for the first year.

Persistent headaches are reported in up to 20% of children following a TBI (Klonoff & Paris, 1974), as are reduced stamina and fatigue (Lezak, 1978). Another characteristic, which teachers may interpret as boredom, is frequent yawning, reflecting the effects of injury rather than lack of interest or insolence.

Whereas obvious motor problems may resolve relatively quickly, problems with the execution of refined and complex psychomotor movements, particularly when speed is involved, may persist (Bawden, Knights, & Winogron, 1985). These deficits have implications for the child in the classroom because they influence the degree to which the child can keep up with class procedures such as copying, organizing material, and producing significant amounts of work.

Continuing language problems may influence how the child functions in the classroom. Although deficits such as lack of speech, restricted expressive output, and problems of breath control, which may have been present right after the trauma, may subside rapidly, more subtle and long-standing difficulties with language comprehension and expression may be present. These include problems of word finding, organization of sequenced utterances, and comprehension breakdown as instructional complexity increases (Ylvisaker, 1986).

The cognitive and psychosocial sequelae of TBI are the most important for the child's success in school. Children who have been comatose for 24 hours or more generally demonstrate some residual cognitive effects (Levin & Eisenberg, 1979). The degree of cognitive deficit is related to the amount of damage to the brain (Chadwick et al., 1981; Levin & Eisenberg, 1979). Although measured IQ may return to premorbid levels, as it did in Barbara's case, certain cognitive functions may take several years to recover and may never do so completely. Other cognitive problems that may persist include difficulties with concept formation, organization of sensory inputs, dealing with complex instructions, organizing coherent verbal or written products, and flexibility in thinking (Rourke et al., 1986). These deficits are less obvious on cursory examination but have major effects on how the child functions in school and community (Haarbauer-Krupa, Moser, Smith, Sullivan & Szekeres, 1985).

Behavioral Sequelae of Head Injury

In the period immediately following a TBI, children may exhibit a number of behavioral reactions that interfere with treatment and distress family and friends. These include agitation and confusion, impulsiveness, noncompliance with treatment, impaired judgment, and lack of sustained interest and attention (Black, Blumer, Wellner, & Walker, 1971; Klonoff & Paris, 1974). The origins of these problems stem from several sources: abnormal brain activity, demands of therapy, and restrictions on activity. Further, the irritability withdrawal, and impaired judgment may lead to adverse reactions from others, creating a maladaptive cycle that goes beyond the actual injury effects (Rutter, 1981). As schools take on greater responsibility for children recovering from TBI, many of these children will become the school's responsibility while exhibiting these early recovery behavioral patterns.

TRANSITION TO SCHOOL

The School as a Vehicle for Rehabilitation

The child's return to school is not the end point of rehabilitation. Rather, school is an extension of the rehabilitation program begun in the hospital. Because recovery from TBI continues for many months and even years, the child will be back in school while recovery is still taking place. And because the skills that are recovering are sensitive to the kinds of training that is going on, what schools provide will influence how the child recovers. Also, by its nature the educational program offers many of the features that contribute positively to recovery: a regular schedule, commitment to training, and systematic building on previous skills. The availability within school of specialists trained to provide motor, language, and educational therapies is another positive feature.

The school plays another major role in the recovery of the child with TBI. Prigatano's (1987) formulations about the role of the workplace in the adults' recovery apply to children in school. Because school is the setting for new learning, it is the place where the child faces the limits on performance imposed by the TBI and begins to develop a more realistic view of his or her new self. As the child and school together are involved in this changing perception, the school's role is significant. For this reason alone, educators must have the knowledge and sensitivity to carry this out intelligently.

The school also is important to families of the child with TBI. Families find that the support network they established during the acute phase of recovery no longer exists when the child returns to school. (Slater & Rubenstein, 1987). Thus, educators must be sensitive to changes in the family's functioning and provide support whenever possible. Families of the returning TBI child also will have to be taught that they are expected to be involved in all stages of planning the child's educational program.

A Transition Model

All too often the child with TBI is discharged from the hospital directly to home and school, with minimal planning for the transition. The family has little information about the child's residual problems and how they will affect learning in school. Family members are thus poorly prepared to advocate for their child. The school may not receive any

Steps in Planning Barbara's Transition to School

Planning for reentry began while Barbara was still hospitalized. Throughout her rehabilitation there was collaboration between the hospital and her school. Even before her discharge from the hospital, the rehabilitation team and the reentry team, the staff from her school, and the family met together. The purpose of that meeting was to acquaint the school with her progress and needs and to discuss the kinds of services that would be available through the school.

At the end of Barbara's 10-week outpatient rehabilitation/educational program, she received a comprehensive evaluation, conducted collaboratively by hospital and school staff. The psychologists from her school and from the reentry team jointly conducted the assessment of cognitive and neuropsychological functioning. The homebound teacher from the school and the reentry team special educator jointly conducted assessment of her academic status and needs.

Just before the start of the school year, a reentry planning meeting took place at Barbara's school. Attending were the 15 school administrators and staff members who would have contact with her, a member of the reentry team, Barbara, and her parents. Taking into account the information provided by the hospital and her recent evaluation, the group developed an individualized education plan based on her physical, cognitive, and academic status. The plan provided the following educational modifications:

1. Reduced course load: Barbara enrolled in a limited number of academic courses with the understanding that others could be added.
2. Special scheduling: Barbara took her most taxing courses early in the day, when she was most alert.
3. Resource room: Barbara would begin and end the day in the resource room with an aide present to provide assistance.
4. Rest breaks: Barbara was allowed to rest in the nurse's office when she became fatigued.
5. Adaptive physical education: Barbara would receive adaptive PE with an aide present to assist her at all times, because of the danger of her falling.
6. Student aide: One of her friends would assist her in moving from one class to the next.
7. Extra set of books: Barbara was given an extra set of books to keep at home, to avoid having to carry them back and forth.
8. Lunch room provisions: Because Barbara was still physically unsteady, someone would carry her lunch tray and have her seated before the lunchroom crowds arrived.
9. Counseling: Meetings were scheduled with the school counselor, and she was given the option for other meetings as needed.
10. Other modifications: Barbara would be allowed to have someone take notes for her in her class and tape her lectures, and she would be able to take her exams in a setting other than the regular classroom, with extra time allowed. She also would have use of a computer to complete assignments.

At the initial IEP meeting the need to closely monitor Barbara's progress was noted. Thus, a schedule was established that provided for monthly IEP reviews for the first semester and every few months thereafter.

information about the student's recovery course until he or she is back in school. Without prior reentry planning there is a potential for educational disruptions as the student's special needs are gradually identified and accommodations made. The process of transition is a complex one requiring considerations at each of the many steps. A comprehensive review of this process is provided by Ylvisaker, Hartwick, and Stevens (1991).

In Barbara's case, her transition to school was guided by a comprehensive reentry program. Although hospital-based, it was financially supported by her state's Department of Education. The program included several components that are critical for a successful transition.

First, a designated person or team was to be responsible for the interchange of information between hospital and school. This allowed the rehabilitation staff to learn about Barbara's pretrauma functioning and about the services her school could offer. Also, the reentry team was responsible for communicating to Barbara's school staff information about her injury and recovery course; and it arranged the predischarge conferences attended by hospital and school personnel.

A second component of a comprehensive reentry model is the education of families about TBI. Families need information about ways in which their child's injury will affect learning, and about school resources to meet special needs. Education of families does not automatically occur throughout the course of rehabilitation. Members of the rehabilitation team may not know how schools function and what kinds of educational modifications the child's residual deficits may dictate.

A third important component of a comprehensive reentry program is the preparation of school personnel for the reentering child. School personnel have not been trained in the characteristics, needs, and programming requirements of children with TBI (Mira, Meck, & Tyler, 1988; Savage & Carter, 1984). Also, educators often do not receive the necessary information to plan an appropriate program for the returning child (Tyler & Mira, 1989). A comprehensive reentry program addresses this issue; it provides inservice training to educators and bridges the information gap between the medical and educational worlds.

The Reentry Process

Criteria for School Reentry
The timing of reentry to school should not be determined by the school calendar but instead by carefully determining the degree to which the student is able to participate in the school setting. Before returning to school, the child with a TBI should display the ability to carry out the following: (a) sustain attention to a task; (b) work for 30 minutes without a break; (c) tolerate the multiple stimuli in a normal classroom; (d) respond to instruction; (e) interact with the environment (Mira, Tyler, & Tucker, 1988).

Evaluation of the Student
An early step in the transition from the acute rehabilitation program to school is a comprehensive evaluation of the student's physical, educational, and social needs. Comprehensive assessment of a student with TBI is usually beyond the combined competence of the public school staff. A range of specialists, such as those from neurology, neuropsy-

chology, physical and occupational therapy, audiology, and ophthalmology should be included (Martin, 1988). Often these evaluations are conducted within the rehabilitation program, perhaps prior to discharge.

As much as possible, members of the school's diagnostic team should participate in the comprehensive assessment of the child. For example, the intelligence testing can be completed by the school psychologist and used in combination with the neuropsychological assessment to provide information on cognitive, linguistic, mnemonic, sensory, and perceptual motor skills (Fay & Janesheski, 1986). The information from this comprehensive evaluation constitutes important data for the school to consider when preparing the child's individualized education plan. Telzrow (1991) provides an overview of tests that school psychologists can use in their comprehensive assessment.

Staff Training

Before the student with TBI returns to school, all personnel who are likely to interact with the student will need information about TBI and how the injury has affected this specific student. Those who knew the student before the injury must be informed about how the child will be different. Those who worked with the child before often have difficulty understanding that the child may now have a different learning style, pattern of reacting, and physical status.

Although staff training may occur during the initial IEP meeting, inservice training programs should be in place to inform the staff about TBI and its ramifications (Savage & Carter, 1984). Increased understanding of the effects of TBI may lead to more appropriate evaluations and better planning for the child, which may prevent a negative cycle of failure from beginning (Boll, 1983). During the inservice training the staff should receive general information about TBI, characteristics of children so injured, outcomes, and educational programming strategies. In addition, the staff should receive comprehensive information about the student's educational history, the nature of the accident and resulting injuries, rehabilitation course, and residual deficits. The staff also must understand that children with TBI often change rapidly and that educational programs have to be constantly reviewed and changed to meet the student's current needs.

Training educators about TBI has become a part of many reentry programs (Jacobs, 1989). A number of written resources are available for educators (Begali, 1987; Mira, Tucker, & Tyler, 1992; National Head Injury Foundation, 1988; Rosen & Gerring, 1986), as well as training modules for those who educate teachers (Tyler, 1990).

The IEP Meeting

Because of physical and cognitive impairments, students who have sustained a TBI qualify for special education services and an individualized education program (IEP) under PL 94–142. To avoid educational disruptions, the student's IEP should be developed prior to school reentry. Unlike other children, for whom school observations and evaluations can provide most of the information for educational planning, much of the relevant data about needs of the student with TBI is provided by professionals outside of the school. Because team collaboration between rehabilitation and educational specialists is needed for the student with TBI to best continue recovery (Savage, 1987), input from hospital and school personnel should be considered jointly when planning for the student. Furthermore, because most school personnel at this point have limited knowledge about programming for students with TBI (Mira, Meck, & Tyler, 1988), they must consult with specialists from outside the team when developing the student's program.

Any student needing special services poses a challenge to a school district, but the child with TBI poses a unique challenge (Martin, 1988). TBI has only recently been assigned a separate special education category (Individuals with Disabilities Education Act, 1990), so many of these students may still be identified under other categories. Because students who have sustained a TBI have rapidly changing needs, however, these other categories often are inappropriate for children with TBI. Furthermore, the child with a TBI may respond differently to intervention programs designed for other groups (Ewing-Cobbs, Fletcher, & Levin, 1985).

Therefore, rather than trying to fit the child with a TBI into a specific category, the goal of the IEP meeting should be to identify the student's unique educational needs and to determine which available school resources can be integrated to provide the program to best meet those needs.

The initial IEP meeting is only the first step in providing for the child with a TBI. Because goals, strategies, priorities, and services have to be adjusted according to the specific, yet changing, needs of the individual student (Begali, 1987), the child's progress must be continually monitored. After an IEP is developed, the school staff must maintain a network to promote ongoing communication about the student's performance and changing needs (DePompei & Blosser, 1987). At the initial IEP meeting, review dates should be set up and the staff and family encouraged to meet more frequently if changes are necessary.

Placement and Program Modifications

Problems of stamina often preclude the child with a head injury from physically returning to school, even though the child is ready to begin some educational activities. Thus, following a TBI, children commonly reenter the school system via homebound instruction. Homebound instruction cannot consist of merely delivering class assignments to the student. The homebound teacher must be knowledgeable about the needs of students with TBI and be able to modify materials for the child's unique learning characteristics (Martin, 1988). The student also must have continuity in the necessary therapies as he or she makes the transition from rehabilitation program to school.

The student may return to school with a reduced schedule or modified course load, with classes and activities to be added as attention and stamina increase. It is important for the child to return to the world of school, even on a limited basis, as soon as possible, because school is the ideal place for the student's continued cognitive and social rehabilitation (Savage & Carter, 1984).

Returning to school following a head injury can be a difficult transition. The child will be leaving an environment where others have similar difficulties and entering a setting where the injuries will clearly set him or her apart from peers (Rosen & Gerring, 1986). Some suggested activities to help ease the transition include making visits to school prior to reentry, preparing the child to tell classmates about the accident and treatment regime, and playing a videotape of the child's rehabilitation.

Once back in school, the educational program of the child with a TBI may require modifications. The child may have to be placed differently from the pre-injury placement. As many as half of the students sustaining severe to serious TBI require special education placements (Mira, 1989; Walker, Luckhard, Owen, Easley-Bowman, & Scott, 1987). Children returning to a regular educational setting will more than likely require programming modifications. Barbara's case exemplifies some typical educational modifications. Compensations for lack of speed (e.g., extra time for exams) and physical restrictions (providing rest breaks and assistance in moving between classes) allowed Barbara to participate in regular education courses. Modifications such as these minimize the student's deficits and allow him or her to remain in a less restrictive school environment.

EDUCATIONAL OUTCOMES OF TBI

School Progress

After a severe or serious TBI, approximately half of the children will require special education (Mira, 1989), and those who return to the regular class require some form of modification (Walker et al.,1987). Without specialized planning and programming, many children with TBI experience disruptions in school progress. For example, Klonoff, Low, and Clark (1977) found that of the children who returned to the mainstream after a TBI (including those with mild injuries), 20% failed or withdrew from school after successive failures. Difficulties in academic areas and behavior problems may lead to these failures.

After a TBI, progress in specific academic areas is frequently disrupted. Scott (1984) found that following a TBI, students experienced a significant decline in all academic areas (reading comprehension, language/vocabulary, spelling, and arithmetic), with reading comprehension most greatly impaired. Similarly, Shaffer, Bijur, and Rutter (1980) reported that 1 to 2 year delays in reading comprehension are common in students with TBI.

Math is another academic area that often is affected by a TBI (Levin & Benton 1986). In TBI students he studied, Adams (1990) found that mathematic application was the academic achievement area most negatively affected. Problems with math may be attributable to computational deficiencies, focusing difficulties, and attention problems, as well as organizational difficulties. Long-term language difficulties may affect all areas of academic functioning. Expressive and written language disorders often interfere with the child's overall school performance (Ylvisaker, 1986).

Behavior problems also may interfere with school progress. Up to half of children with a severe TBI demonstrate behavioral problems (Brown, Chadwick, Shaffer, Rutter, & Traub, 1981). Although behavior problems can occur in children who were free of problems prior to their injury, those with behavior problems before their accident almost

Barbara's Educational Course

Following Barbara's reentry to school, the school and the reentry team monitored her progress via the scheduled review meetings. These meetings proved to be vital for recognizing and planning for problems that arose in several areas. First, Barbara's continued difficulties with short-term memory and ability to work independently required modification of classroom strategies. Another issue related to problems in administering and delivering her program. These included overlooking the inservice of new teachers who were not aware of Barbara's head injury and special needs, and disruptions of communication between family and school.

The value of the review meeting was recognized when difficulties arose after a major schedule change was made without a planning meeting. Adding two new courses to Barbara's schedule and dropping time in the resource room led to problems in her keeping up with her work, and lower grades.

When Barbara returned to school, she was relatively free of emotional or behavioral problems. During her first year back in school, however, she sometimes resisted the resource room services. This could have reflected a typical adolescent response to being different from her peers by needing special help. Her major psychosocial problem occurred at the end of her junior year, as she began realizing the extent of her disabilities. This, coupled with the fact that her friends were not as supportive as they were right after her injury, led to feelings of isolation and depression. A counseling program outside of the school aided her in dealing with these problems and moving out of the depression.

With careful monitoring and program revisions as needed, and continued use of resource services, Barbara completed her junior and senior years with passing grades in all subjects. With the help of summer school courses, she accumulated the needed credits to graduate with her class. Her plans included college the next fall at a small university near home that offered special assistance for students with handicapping conditions.

always show post-injury behavior difficulties (Rutter, 1981). Behavior problems may include emotional difficulties and socially inappropriate behaviors (Brown et al., 1981), as well as depression and withdrawal (Barin, Hanchett, Jacob, & Scott, 1985). Even though it is important for school personnel to help the child deal with behavioral problems, parents have reported that school personnel often fail to recognize or provide for the student's social-interactional needs after a TBI (Walker et al., 1987).

Long-term academic and behavioral problems following TBI require school personnel to plan programs that address the child's needs in these areas.

CONCLUSION

The transition from hospital to school may be a difficult process for children following a traumatic brain injury. In the case presented here, a student made a successful transition following a serious head injury. Barbara's case was typical in many respects (type of accident, age at type of accident, recovery patterns), but several factors contributed to her successful reentry into school.

One factor was that her hospital had a reentry program supported by the State Department of Education. The staff was trained in head injury and could devote time to planning an effective transition.

Second, Barbara's school district had a strong commitment to provide a program to meet her needs and regularly monitor her progress. Successful reentry requires school personnel to acknowledge that the child with the TBI is unique and will require specialized programming (Blosser & DePompei, 1989).

Third, Barbara's family was a positive feature in her recovery and reentry. The family's premorbid stability, response to the original trauma, and positive view of her rehabilitation program were assets in her adjustment to her post-injury impairments. Their ability to learn about Barbara's needs and the school resources enabled them to advocate effectively for her with the school.

Finally, Barbara did not have a prior history of any behavioral, learning, or attentional deficits that can complicate post-injury adjustment (Jaffe & Hays, 1986). She also remained free of significant behavior problems following the TBI, which encouraged all to maintain the intense transition program.

Although most of these factors are not within the school district's control, they all contribute to the successful school reentry of children following TBI, and therefore must be considered. If a formal reentry program is not in place, educators must take the initiative in establishing communication with rehabilitation programs and in obtaining the needed information from hospital personnel.

Educators can make the necessary commitment to provide the best possible program for the child by being knowledgeable about TBI and realizing that the child will require specialized programming. Furthermore, because the family plays such an important role in the child's recovery, school personnel can work with the student's family to further understanding of their child's post-injury impairments and implications for the child's learning. Finally, by recognizing that behavioral and academic problems are common following a TBI, educators can establish programs that will best meet the needs of the individual student.

REFERENCES

Adams, W. (1990, May). *Academic impact of mild head injury in children.* Paper presented at the North Coast Regional Conference of Society of Pediatric Psychology, Detroit.

Barin, J. J., Hanchett, J. M., Jacob, W. L., & Scott, M. B. (1985). Counseling the head injured patient. In M. Ylvisaker (Ed.), *Head injury rehabilitation: Children and adolescents* (pp. 361-382). San Diego: College Hill Press.

Bawden, H. N., Knights, R. M., & Winogron, H. W. (1985). Speeded performance following head injury in children. *Journal of Clinical & Experimental Neuropsychology, 7*(1), 30–54.

Begali, V. (1987). *Head injury in children and adolescents: A resource and review for school and allied professionals.* Brandon, VT: Clinical Psychology Publishing.

Black, P., Blumer, D., Wellner, A. M., & Walker, A. E. (1971). The head injured child: Time course of recovery, with implications for rehabilitation [Summary]. *Proceedings of The International Symposium on Head Injuries* (pp. 131–137). Edinburgh, Scotland: Churchill Livingstone.

Blosser, J. L., & DePompei, R. (1989). The head-injured student returns to school: Recognizing and treating deficits. *Topics in Language Disorders, 9*(2), 67–77.

Boll, T. J. (1983). Minor head injury in children—Out of sight but not out of mind. *Journal of Clinical Child Psychology, 12*, 74–80.

Brink, J. D., Garrett, A. L., Hale, W. R., Woo-Sam, J., & Nickel, V. L. (1970). Recovery of motor and intellectual function in children sustaining severe head injuries. *Developmental Medicine & Child Neurology, 12*(5), 565–571.

Brink, J. D., Imbus, C., & Woo-Sam, J. (1980). Physical recovery after severe closed head trauma in children and adolescents. *Journal of Pediatrics, 97*(5), 721–727.

Brown, G., Chadwick, O., Shaffer, D., Rutter, M., & Traub, M. (1981). A prospective study of children with head injuries and psychiatric sequelae. *Psychological Medicine, 11*(1), 63–78.

Chadwick, O., Rutter, M., Brown, G., Shaffer, D., & Traub, M. (1981). A prospective study of children with head injuries: II. Cognitive sequelae. *Psychological Medicine, 11*(1), 49–61.

DePompei, R., & Blosser, J. (1987). Strategies for helping head injured children successfully return to school. *Language, Speech & Hearing Services in Schools, 18*, 292–300.

Ewing-Cobbs, L., Fletcher, J. M., & Levin, H.S. (1985). Neuropsychological sequelae following pediatric head injury. In M. Ylvisaker (Ed.), *Head injury rehabilitation: Children and adolescents* (pp. 71–89). San Diego: College Hill Press.

Fay, G., & Janesheski, J. (1986). Neuropsychological assessment of head injured children. *Journal of Head Trauma Rehabilitation, 1*(4), 16–21.

Haarbauer-Krupa, J., Moser, L., Smith, G. J., Sullivan, D. M., & Szekeres, S. F. (1985). Cognitive rehabilitation therapy: Middle stages of recovery. In M. Ylvisaker (Ed.), *Head injury rehabilitation: Children and adolescents* (pp. 287–310). San Diego: College Hill Press.

Hauser, W. A. (1983). Post-traumatic epilepsy in children. In K. Shapiro (Ed.), *Pediatric head trauma* (pp. 223–240). Mount Kisco, NY: Futura.

Individuals with Disabilities Education Act. (1990, October 30). 20 USC. Sec. 1400–1485 as amended by PL 101-476, Title I, Sec. 101, Title IX, Sec. 1901(b) (10)-(20), 104 Stat. 1103–1142.

Jacobs, M. P. (1989). Head injured students in the public schools: A model program. *The Forum, 14*(4), 9–11.

Jaffe, K. M., & Hays, R. M. (1986). Pediatric head injury: Rehabilitative medical management. *Journal of Head Trauma Rehabilitation, 1*(4), 30–40.

Kalsbeek, W. D., McLauren, R. L., Harris, B. S. H., & Miller, J. D. (1980). The national head and spinal cord injury survey: Major findings. *Journal of Neurosurgery, 53*, 19–31.

Klonoff, H., Low, M. D., & Clark, C. (1977). Head injuries in children: A prospective five year follow-up. *Journal of Neurology, Neurosurgery, & Psychiatry, 40*, 1211–1219.

Klonoff, H., & Paris, R. (1974). Immediate short-term and residual effects of acute head injuries in children: Neuropsychological and neurological correlates. In R. M. Reitan & L. A. Davison (Eds.), *Clinical neuropsychology: Current status and applications* (pp. 179–210). New York: John Wiley & Sons.

Kraus, J. F., Fife, D., Cox, P., Ramstein, C., & Conroy, C. (1986). Incidence, severity, and external causes of pediatric brain injury. *American Journal of Diseases of Children, 140*(7), 687–693.

Levin, H. S., & Benton, A. L. (1986). Developmental and acquired dyscalculia in children. In I. Flemhig & L. Sterns (Eds.), *Child development and learning behavior* (pp. 317–322). Stuttgart, West Germany: Gustav Fisher.

Levin, H. S., & Eisenberg, H. M. (1979). Neurospychological impairment after closed head injury in children and adolescents. *Journal of Pediatric Psychology, 4*, 389–402.

Lezak, M. D. (1978). Subtle sequelae of brain damage: Perplexity, distractability and fatigue. *American Journal of Physical Medicine, 57*, 9–15.

Marquardt, T. P., Stoll, J., & Sussman, H. (1988). Disorders of communication in acquired cerebral trauma. *Journal of Learning Disabilities, 21*(6), 340–351.

Martin, R. (1988). Legal challenges in educating traumatic brain injured students. *Journal of Learning Disabilities, 21*(8), 471–485.

Mira, M. (1989, April). *Educational impact of traumatic head injury in school aged children.* Paper presented at 67th Annual Meeting of Council for Exceptional Children, San Francisco.

Mira, M. P., Meck, N. E., & Tyler, J. S. (1988). School psychologists' knowledge of traumatic head injury: Implications for training. *Diagnostique, 13,* 174–180.

Mira, M. P., Tucker, B. F., & Tyler, J. S. (1992). *Traumatic brain injury in children and adolescents: A sourcebook for teachers and other school personnel.* Austin, TX: PRO-ED.

National Head Injury Foundation Task Force (1988). *An educator's manual: What educators need to know about students with traumatic brain injuries.* Framingham, MA: National Head Injury Foundation.

Prigatano, G. P. (1987, December). *Neuropsychological rehabilitation: An integrated approach to cognitive, personality, and social issues.* Paper presented at National Head Injury Foundation Symposium, San Diego.

Public Law 101-476. Individuals with Disabilities Education Act of 1990.

Rosen, C. D., & Gerring, J. P. (1986). *Head trauma: Educational reintegration.* Boston: College-Hill Press.

Rourke, B. P., Fisk, J. L., & Strang, J. D. (1986). *Neuropsychological assessment of children: A treatment-oriented approach.* New York: Guilford Press.

Rutter, M. (1981). Psychological sequelae of brain damage in children. *American Journal of Psychiatry, 138,* 1533–1542.

Savage, R. C. (1987). Educational issues for the head-injured adolescent and young adult. *Journal of Head Trauma Rehabilitation, 2*(1), 1–10.

Savage, R. C., & Carter, R. (1984). Re-entry: The head injured student returns to school. *Cognitive Rehabilitation, 2*(6), 28–33.

Scott, M. B. (1984). *Educational consequences of closed head injury in children.* Doctoral dissertation, University of Pittsburgh.

Shaffer, D., Bijur, P., & Rutter, M. L. (1980). Head injury and later reading disability. *Journal of the American Academy of Child Psychiatry, 19,* 592–610.

Slater, E. J., & Rubenstein, E. (1987). Family coping with trauma in adolescents. *Psychiatric Annals, 17*(12), 786–794.

Telzrow, C. F. (1991). The school psychologist's perspective on testing students with traumatic brain injury. *Journal of Head Trauma Rehabilitation, 6*(1), 23–34.

Tyler, J. S. (1990). *Traumatic head injury in school-aged children: A training manual for educational personnel.* Kansas City, KS: University of Kansas Medical Center, Children's Rehabilitation Unit.

Tyler, J., & Mira, M. (1989). *Children and youth with traumatic head injuries: Are principals being informed about these students?* Unpublished manuscript, University of Kansas Medical Center, Kansas City, KS.

Walker, N., Luckhard, M., Owen, H., Easley-Bowman, J., & Scott, S. (1987, December). *Factors which predict successful school re-integration in traumatically brain injured children and adolescents.* Paper presented at National Head Injury Foundation Symposium, San Diego.

Ylvisaker, M. (1986). Language and communication disorders following pediatric head injury. *Journal of Head Trauma Rehabilitation, 1*(4), 48–56.

Ylvisaker, M., Hartwick, P., & Stevens, M. (1991). School reentry following head injury: Managing the transition from hospital to school. *Journal of Head Trauma Rehabilitation, 6*(1), 10–22.

The information presented in this article was funded in part by the following grants: Kansas State Department of Education Title VI-B Grant Project Number 8805-FY90 and Federal Government Grant Number MCJ-000944.

Mary Mira is an associate professor of pediatrics and Janet Tyler is the training coordinator for the Head Injury Project, Children's Rehabilitation Unit, at the University of Kansas Medical Center.

○ 14 ○

The authors contend that students with severe disabilities should be educated in local neighborhood schools in general education classrooms. They describe a program model employed in Vermont and offer a number of suggestions to assist systems in moving toward total inclusion. Their suggestions include proposed changes in teacher education that may facilitate inclusion.

Strategies for Educating Learners with Severe Disabilities Within Their Local Home Schools and Communities

Jacqueline S. Thousand and Richard A. Villa

In a number of schools in North America, we now can walk into elementary and secondary classrooms and observe students who could be labeled severely or multiply handicapped receiving their education together with similar-aged classmates who have no identified special education needs (Biklen, 1988; Blackman & Peterson, 1989; Brown et al., 1989; Forest, 1988; Nevin, Thousand, Paolucci-Whitcomb, & Villa, 1990; Porter, 1988; Schattman, 1988; Villa & Thousand, 1988; York & Vandercook, 1989). Inclusionary educational practices for learners with intensive educational needs have evolved over the last decade in Vermont. A number of administrative, organizational, instructional, and teacher preparation strategies support the education of intensively challenged or challenging learners in general education environments, and we call for national policy changes to support inclusive schooling for all students.

WHO ARE LEARNERS WITH SEVERE HANDICAPS?

Whether a student is considered as having severe handicaps often depends upon the idiosyncratic definition adopted by the state and community in which the student resides. A U.S. federal definition identifies students with severe handicaps as those who:

1) may possess severe language and/or perceptual-cognitive deprivations, and evidence abnormal behaviors such as: i) failure to respond to pronounced social stimuli, ii) self-mutilation, iii) self-stimulation, iv) manifestation of intense and prolonged temper tantrums, and v) the absence of rudimentary forms of verbal control, and 2) may also have extremely fragile physiological conditions. (20 U.S.C. 1401(7); Former 45 CFR 121.1)

Brown et al. (1983, p. 77) offered an alternative definition of "severely handicapped" students as school-aged students who function intellectually within the lowest 1% of their particular age groups. This 1% includes learners who may have labels such as physically handicapped; multiply handicapped; dual sensory impaired (i.e., deaf-blind); autistic or psychotic; trainably mentally retarded; or moderately, severely, or profoundly retarded.

At the local school level, formal definitions such as the two just presented have little functional meaning or use. What is considered a "severe handicap" varies from one school to the next and is contingent upon each school community's beliefs about and experience with students whose educational needs go beyond the school's standard curriculum or instructional practices. For example, a school community with little experience accommodating for individual students may think of a new student with Down syndrome as "severely handicapped." A second school, with extensive experience educating students who have a broad range of needs, may view much more challenged student as "just another student" with unique needs that must be met. Given this phenomenon of "relativity," terms such as *students with intensive educational needs, students who present intensive challenges to school personnel,* and *challenged* or *challenging students* are used here to represent students with "severe handicapping" characteristics described in the previous paragraph, as well as other students who, for whatever reason, are perceived by school personnel as "most challenging" to the current school culture or ecosystem.

WHO BELONGS IN GENERAL EDUCATION CLASSROOMS?

Currently there is an emerging recognition of the benefits of educating students with intensive educational needs in their local communities and schools (Brown et al., 1989; Sailor, 1989). There is, however, disagreement within the field as to whether students with intensive educational needs belong in general education classrooms; "the major placement issue of the day is whether students with severe intellectual disabilities should be based in regular or special education classrooms in home schools" (Brown et al., p. 12).

Writing for school principals, Burrello and Tourgee (1990) sorted out "students with severe disabilities" as the sub-population of students with handicaps for whom "maintaining a self-contained setting in a centrally located place in the building with socialization opportunities was the most realistic program" (p. 3). Jenkins, Pious, and Jewell (1990) determined that, although the regular education initiative (Will, 1986) should apply to most students with handicaps, students with intensive educational needs should be excluded, because their needs extend beyond the normal developmental curriculum that the classroom teacher is responsible for delivering and adapting for individual learners.

Others have devoted entire texts to describing strategies for including *all* students, regardless of perceived exceptionalities, within general education and community environments (Lipsky & Gartner, 1989; S. Stainback, & W. Stainback, in press; S. Stainback, W. Stainback & Forest, 1989; W. Stainback & S. Stainback, 1990a). Williams, Villa, Thousand, and Fox (1990) go so far as to suggest that the special versus regular class placement issue really is a non-issue for a number of reasons. The successful placement and education of students with intensive educational challenges in regular classes has been occurring for a number of years in schools throughout North America (Thousand et al., 1986). Furthermore, Public Law 94-142, the Education for All Handicapped Children Act, clearly specifies that placement of any student must be based upon the student's identified needs, not the student's handicapping condition or categorical label.

To even raise the question of whether regular class placement is appropriate for a category of learners (i.e., students with intensive educational needs) "assumes that placement can be made based upon handicapping condition without documentation of an individual student's needs and examination of whether the needs could be met in a regular class-based placement" (Williams et al., 1990, p. 333). Finally, learning and social benefits for students with and without identified handicaps have been documented (S. Stainback & W. Stainback, 1990a; Thousand & Villa, 1989), as have benefits for teachers, when educators collaborate to invent individualized, responsive educational programs (Nevin et al., 1990; Thousand et al., 1986; Thousand & Villa, 1990; Villa & Thousand, 1992).

The special/regular class placement question may be a non-issue. Yet, the norm within most North American schools is still for intensively challenged students to be educated in schools or classrooms other than those of their neighbors' children. Why? First, systems change takes time. Second, people thinking about change are more likely to "take the plunge" if they have models to observe, visit, and imitate. These are now available, and teachers, parents, students, and school board members can now share their stories about how to create schools in which students with intensive needs are welcome and successful.

A CASE STUDY IN VERMONT

Background and a Demonstration of Success

Vermont is a small, sparsely populated state, notorious for its strong small-town community spirit and interest in local community control in decision making. It is one of the few places where the populace of each small town turns out for a day-long annual town meeting to debate and decide upon issues large and small. Vermont is also a state with a long history of educating students who have mild handicaps in their local school general education classroom, with resource room and consulting teacher support to the classroom teacher (Christie, McKenzie, & Burdett, 1972; Idol, Paolucci-Whitcomb, & Nevin, 1986; Knight, Meyers, Paolucci-Whitcomb, Hasazi, & Nevin, 1981, McKenzie, 1972; McKenzie et al., 1970).

In the latter half of the 1970s, special classes for students with intensive education needs were established in public schools. Up to this time most of these children were not in public school and had not been offered educational services at home or in the institution in which they resided. To provide training and technical assistance to special class teachers in the new role of educating these "most challenging" students, an interdisciplinary support team—the I-Team— was jointly created with state and federal funding by the Vermont Department of Education and the University of Vermont (McKenzie, Hill, Sousie, York, & Baker, 1977). As members of this team traveled throughout Vermont, providing training and technical assistance, they noticed that some schools chose not to send their intensively challenged students to the newly formed special classes but instead chose to educate them along with their agemates in their local schools. This observation led to development of a pilot project demonstrating the successful transition of two students with intensive needs back to their home schools from a regional special class program.

The Homecoming Model Project

Encouraged by these results, funding was sought and secured from the federal Office of Special Education Programs to expand the effort with 26 schools in four school districts (Williams et al., 1986). The project's objectives were to develop, field-test, and evaluate a "model to bring 'home' students [with intensive challenges] from regional special education programs and prevent other students from ever being placed in them" (Thousand et al., 1986, p. 6). The project, known as *Homecoming*, achieved its objectives by its end, in the fall of 1986.

> A total of 77 students, ranging in age from 5 to 17 years, benefited from the Homecoming model. Of these students, 58 have been transitioned from regional special educational programs to regular classrooms in their local schools. An additional 19 students who were at risk of being placed in self-contained special classes or out-of-district programs continue to be maintained within regular education environments of their local schools. (Thousand et al., 1986 p. 6)

Of the original 58 students who transitioned to their home schools in the mid-1980s, all avoided re-referral to out-of-school placements. And, four years following the project's end, hundreds of additional Vermont students with various handicapping conditions have been returned from former regional and special class programs to dozens more local schools (O'Connor, 1990).

What has all this change taught us? What are the critical elements for a school district to successfully transition and maintain challenging students in local educational settings? An important outcome of the Homecoming project was the identification of conditions considered essential for intensively challenged students to be transitioned to and maintained within home school classrooms. Six critical ingredients, described in detail in *The Homecoming Model* (Thousand et al., 1986), are briefly presented in Table 1.

TABLE 1   Critical Elements for Transitioning and Educating Students in Their Home School

Elements	Indicators
1. Administrative commitment	The superintendent of schools, the special education administrator, and the building principals demonstrate, through their actions, support for the concept of educating all students within regular education environments in local schools. District administrators initiate review of current policies and procedures to determine barriers to age-appropriate regular class placement of all learners and make needed modification.
2. Instructional staff commitment	Despite varying levels of commitment, instructional staff are expected to demonstrate behaviors that support implementation of a model to serve all students in regular education environments. A variety of strategies are employed to develop staff commitment.
3. A means for accessing expertise	A collaborative relationship is established for expertise to be shared through the development of local planning teams, which include members of the school and greater community.
4. A process allowing for cooperation	Staff members receive training in collaborative teaming processes and skills so that members of local planning teams may effectively share expertise and accomplish team objectives.
5. A process for developing transition and maintenance plans	A structured (15-step) planning process designed for the transition and maintenance of students within regular education environments is used by local planning teams.
6. Access to consultative support	Members of local planning teams have access to professional(s) who have background and experience in developing integrated educational programs for intensively challenging students. The professional(s) provide consultation, training, and technical assistance.

Best Educational Practices for Educating Intensively Challenged Students

Along with the introduction of an increasing number of students with intensive educational needs into general education settings of Vermont schools was a pressing need to provide instructional staff with guidelines for delivering special education and related services to optimize student participation in integrated school and community settings. With Vermont Department of Education leadership and University of Vermont support, guidelines representing current *best educational practices* were generated, resulting in a document of 55 quality indicators in the nine best practice areas described in Table 2. These statements of best practice were validated by general and special education educators, administrators, and parents (Williams, Fox, Thousand, & Fox, 1990) and adopted by the Vermont Department of Education as guidelines for local education agencies. In 1987 they were made widely available for use by school personnel, parents, school board members, and community members.

TABLE 2   Best Practices Areas

1. *Age-appropriate placement in local public schools*
   The placement of choice for all students (with and without handicaps) should be within chronologically age-appropriate regular classrooms in the students' local public schools.

2. *Integrated delivery of services*
   IEP's and instructional programs should indicate the integration of instruction on education and related service goals into every-day school, home, and community activities. Related service providers should offer consultation and assistance to special and regular educators, parents, and others in developing, implementing, and integrating instruction on related service goals.

3. *Social integration*
   Students with handicaps should have access to the same environments as nonhandicapped peers of similar chronological age. Primary goals of social integration should be to increase the number of integrated community and school environments and to improve the quality of interactions in those environments.

4. *Transition planning*
   Transition planning should occur well in advance of major moves (e.g., early education, special education to elementary school, elementary to high school, high school to adult services). Transition objectives should be included in IEPs and reflect the input of significant parties affected by the transition.

5. *Community-based training*
   Students should have the opportunity to acquire and demonstrate specific skills within appropriate community settings. Conditions and criteria of IEP goals and objectives should include performance in natural environments.

6. *Curricular expectations*
   Curricula or curriculum guidelines should progress from no skills to adult functioning in all areas of integrated community life, with a system for longitudinal monitoring of student progress.

7. *Systematic data-based instruction*
   There should be written schedules of daily activities, clearly defined objectives, reliably implemented instructional programs, and systematic data collection and analysis. Instructional decisions should be based upon documentation of student's progress.

8. *Home-school partnership*
   Parents should have ongoing opportunities to participate in the development of their child's IEP and the delivery of educational and related services. There should be a clearly delineated system for regularly communicating with parents and providing parents with information. Parental concerns should be reflected in IEP goals and objectives.

9. *Systematic program evaluation*
   Educational and related services should be evaluated on a regular basis. Evaluations should actively involve the entire program staff and provide administrators and staff with information regarding the achievement of program goals; student progress; discrepancies requiring remediation; directions for future program change; and program impact upon students, their families, and the community.

Best Practices for Meeting the Needs of All Students

As educational personnel became more experienced and skilled in integrating intensively challenged students into the routine and culture of their local schools, additional exemplary educational practices (e.g., team teaching, cooperative group learning models, peer tutoring programs, peer support networks) and "critical ingredients" (e.g., expansion of the curriculum to include social skills development and community service, a new instructional role of employment specialist to expand vocational education to include job development and training) emerged, which benefited many students. With the practice of more and more generic inclusionary educational strategies, the original best practices clearly were too "special education" in nature and in the language (see Table 2). They communicated an inappropriate and unwanted message that educational practices effective for students with intensive educational needs were very different from the practices effective for the rest of the school population.

This led to revision of the best practice categories and indicators to reflect exemplary practices from both general and special education. As the items in Table 3 illustrate, the new best practice document is intended for use with *all* school-aged students (Fox & Williams, 1990). The categorical labels and the language used to define the items in Table 3 versus the original best practice items reveal a shift toward the conceptualization of best educational practices as supporting a single system of education responsive to all children versus a dual system of general and special education (W. Stainback & S. Stainback, 1984; Wang, Reynolds, & Walberg, 1988).

State-Level Support for Inclusionary Educational Practices

The shift of educational services for more challenging students from regionalized self-contained special classes to local schools, coupled with a dramatic rise in special education costs and the national interest in restructuring schools, created a need to examine the state's system for funding special education and to establish state board of education and department of education policies to support services in local school generated education classrooms. The "old" funding formula for special education services was founded upon the notion of "placement" rather than "services needed." It provided fiscal incentives for serving children in more restrictive environments; the more restrictive the placement (e.g., residential, special class), the greater the state's share of funding for that placement.

A 3-year collaborative and consensus-building effort among the Vermont State Board of Education, the Vermont State Department of Education, key state legislators, and the Vermont Education Coalition (representing the Vermont Headmasters Association, the Vermont Superintendents Association, the Vermont chapter of the National Educational Association, the Vermont Parent Teacher Organization, and the Vermont Coalition for Disability Rights) resulted in new educational goals, new legislation, and a new funding mechanism. The new education goals articulate the need to restructure schools to support very high performance for all students. They forward the vision that "there is no special education as we used to know it. Children are different from one another in lots of ways, and the schools [must] accommodate everyone with an inventive array of special services" (Vermont Department of Education, 1990, p. 2).

TABLE 3   Selected Best Practices from Regular and Special Education Sample Indicators

School Climate and Structure

Indicator #1

The school's philosophy statement and objectives should be developed by administrators, staff, students, parents, and community members and should reflect the school's commitment to meeting the individual needs of all students in age-appropriate integrated school and community settings.

Indicator #7

The school's instructional support system (e.g., classroom-based model for delivering support services, teacher assistance team, individual student planning teams, special education pre-referral process, volunteer system) should be developed by administrators, staff, students, parents, and community members and should be available to all students and staff.

Collaborative Planning

Indicator #9

The school should provide time during school hours for instructional support teams (e.g., individual student planning teams, teacher assistance teams, teaching teams) to meet and for individual team members to monitor services, and to provide timely consultation, support, and technical assistance to families and staff.

Social Responsibility

Indicator #13

The school should provide opportunities for students to develop a sense of responsibility and self-reliance through age-appropriate activities such as peer tutoring/mentoring, student government, participation in decision making about important school issues, and school and community jobs.

Curriculum Planning

Indicator #18

The school's curricula should be developed by administrators, staff, students, parents, and community members, and should identify age-appropriate content (e.g., reading, math, history, social/emotional, arts, health) and process-oriented (problem-solving and collaboration skills, study skills) goals and objectives that set a high standard of excellence and address the needs of all students.

Indicator #24

The system for monitoring the progress of students with intensive needs in basic skill and/or social areas should include: (a) indications of level of independence on identified skills/activities; (b) indications of environ-

ments in which those skills/activities have been demonstrated; (c) an annual summary; and (d) post-school follow-ups of employment, self-esteem, and socialization for purposes of program improvement.

Delivery of Instructional Support Services

Indicator #25

Instructional support services and staff (e.g., Chapter I, special education, speech and language, guidance, peer tutoring) should be incorporated into ongoing school and community activities.

Individualized Instruction

Indicator #30

The school should provide opportunities for all staff to become proficient in using a variety of instructional methods (e.g., cooperative learning, whole language, peer tutoring, drill and practice, incidental teaching, computer-assisted instruction), matching methods to individual student needs, and incorporating methods into ongoing activities.

Indicator #32

A variety of instructors (e.g., teachers, teacher assistants, same-age peer tutors, cross-age peer tutors, peer mentors, volunteers) should be available to students and matched to individual student needs.

Transition Planning

Indicator #41

There should be procedures for facilitating the smooth transition of all students from one educational setting to another, and from school to post-school life.

Family-School Collaboration

Indicator #44

The school should provide families with frequent opportunities to visit the school and to regularly communicate with school staff on topics important to both the family and the school.

Planning for Continued Best Practice Improvement

Indicator #49

A plan for improving best practice-based services within the school should be developed every three to five years by a school planning team consisting of administrators, staff, students, parents, and community members.

Note: Indicators were selected from a total of 58 indicators included in a July 3, 1990 draft of *Selected Best Practices From Regular and Special Education* (Fox & Williams, 1990).

Legislation in 1988 defined the state's share of special education costs at 50% and created a mechanism to fund educational services for students regardless of the place in which they were delivered. A 1990 modification of this legislation declared the following.

> It is the policy of the state that each local school district design and implement, in consultation with parents, a comprehensive system of education services that will result, to the maximum extent possible, in all students succeeding in the regular classroom. (Vermont Act 230, 1990, p.1)

This legislation also dedicates 1% of the total state special education budget to training teachers and administrators in strategies for providing in-class supports to students and requires each public school to establish a prereferral system—an "instructional support team"—to problem solve regarding any child who might need additional classroom support.

Change at the "micro" level (i.e., demonstrations of educating intensively challenged students in general education classrooms) and change at the "macro" level (e.g., promulgation of a funding formula and training dollars to support inclusive schooling) are always inextricably intertwined, continually interacting to alter the beliefs and practices of the time. Collaboration and advocacy on the part of parents, educators, and policy makers can result, and have resulted, in dramatic changes in the educational scene, as the Vermont history illustrates.

WHAT SCHOOL LEADERSHIP CAN DO

The formal leadership personnel of a school district are the ones charged with publicly representing the district's vision or mission and coordinating the actions of school personnel and students to be consistent with this vision. The educational leadership, then, is in the position of shaping the organizational structure of the schools within the district and the beliefs of the school community. These structures and beliefs can work to support or to inhibit a school's capacity to support the education of intensively challenged students in general education settings. The recommendations offered in this section are derived from research findings, model demonstration outcomes, and surveys of teachers and general and special education administrators in the United States and Canada who are concerned with educating *all* students in heterogeneous local school and community environments (Villa & Thousand, 1990; Villa, Thousand, Stainback, & Stainback, 1992).

Promoting an Inclusive Vision

Administrators involved in including intensively challenged students in their local schools stress the importance of clarifying for themselves, school staff, and the community a vision based upon at least the following assumptions: (a) all children are capable of learning; (b) all children deserve the opportunity to receive educational services with similar-aged peers in heterogeneous local school classrooms; and (c) the school district is charged with meeting the unique educational and psychological needs of all of its community's children. To articulate such an inclusive vision is necessary but not sufficient for school staff to adopt the desired school mission. Efforts have to be taken to foster understanding and consensus regarding the vision.

One strategy for building consensus is through education of the school staff. Smith (in press) has noted that how teachers interact with students depends, at least in part, upon the conceptual framework and the language they use to think and talk about students. Therefore, the district leadership must (a) develop and deliver a comprehensive inservice training agenda exposing the school community to information regarding the theoretical, ethical, and data-based rationale for inclusionary education, and (b) offer them opportunities to acquire a common knowledge base, language, and set of technical skills for communicating about and implementing exemplary educational practices.

A second powerful strategy for securing support for an inclusive vision is to involve representatives of school and community stakeholder groups in formulating the school district's mission and objectives for supporting students with intensive educational needs in regular education. People who participate as decision-makers more likely develop a sense of ownership for their decisions and act to promote agreed-upon outcomes than if decisions are imposed upon them (Thousand et al., 1986; Thousand, Nevin, & Fox, 1987; Thousand, Villa, Paolucci-Whitcomb, & Nevin, 1992).

Schools that are successful in realizing a vision (e.g., the education of all intensively challenged students in integrated environments) are ones that attend to the development of a spirit of enthusiasm and devotion to the common goal by creating rewards and incentives and publicly recognizing staff and students who model or actively promote the district mission of inclusion. In structuring rewards, administrators are advised to reward *groups* as well as individuals, as this highlights the district's valuing of collaborative team efforts. Staff and students should be asked what *they* consider rewarding. Any person holding any job (e.g., bus driver, secretary, cafeteria worker, community volunteer) within the school district can forward or thwart the inclusionary mission.

All members of the school community, then, need to be viewed as candidates for acknowledgement. Short notes of praise, posting of "thank you" notes from visitors, retreats for collaborative planning efforts, opportunities for conference attendance or presentations are just a few examples of recognition methods that administrators have successfully structured.

Strategies for building understanding and consensus will always be unique to the history, characteristics, and values of each school community. Although systemwide support for an educational mission is the ideal, not *all* members of the school community will or need to believe in that vision in order for the formal leadership to take actions to increase the district's capacity to provide quality support to intensively challenged students and quality instructional services to all students in heterogeneous learning environments.

Expanding the Curriculum

Those who have worked in both the historically separate general and special education systems know that the curriculum and effective instructional strategies employed in the two systems are fundamentally the same. Students eligible for special services are simply at a different place in the curricular sequence than their agemates. For students with intensive educational needs, the curriculum, with its focus upon work, social life, and recreation skills and use of the community as a learning environment, may seem to be notably different. A closer look, however, reveals that the general education curriculum clearly addresses vocational instruction, social skills (e.g., cocurricular activities and clubs, speaking and listening competencies), life skills (e.g., technology education, family living), and recreation needs (e.g., physical education, music, art). Furthermore, general education has always employed the community as an instructional setting (e.g., field trips, vocational placements, behind-the-wheel driving).

District leadership has to lead the school community in discovering the sameness of the curriculum for learners with and without intensive challenges and to work with them to reorganize content, instructional staff, and instructional settings so that a generic set of services may be made available to any student. The content of all courses has to be examined closely. Duplicate content should be eliminated (e.g., a special education basic skills class in math addresses much of the same content as the general education consumer math class), and responsibility for teaching common content has to be distributed across the instructional staff members who formerly worked exclusively in general or special education.

New curricular domains, such as social competence and responsibility, may have to be developed; and new job roles (e.g., integration or support facilitator, school-based employment specialist) may have to be developed to deliver the expanded curriculum in integrated school and community settings (W. Stainback & S. Stainback, 1990b). Community training sites should be examined for potential use by a broader range of students. An IBM plant may offer an intensively challenged student an assembly line job experience, an advanced computer science student programming experience, and the opportunity to acquire the social behaviors expected in a workplace.

Developing Partnerships for Change

More often than not, no one school district possesses all of the diverse human and material resources it may need to successfully initiate a change process (i.e., attempting the inclusion of intensively challenged and challenging students in a school system for the first time). The development of professional partnership relationships with State Department of Education personnel, faculty of institutions of higher education, consultants, and other school districts with similar interest in creating more responsive schools in a recommended administrative practice for gaining access to much needed human and fiscal resources.

State Department of Education personnel may be able to provide fiscal incentives or regulatory relief so that innovative model demonstration projects may be initiated. They also may provide valuable support in the public relations area—articulating in publications, circulars, and public presentations the need for school restructuring and the value of creating schools that welcome and exemplify excellence for all children.

People with specific expertise not yet available within the district (e.g., nonverbal communication specialists, experts in approaches for establishing constructive and positive school conduct, teachers with experience adapting curriculum for intensively challenged students, experts in cooperative group learning models) may be hired to provide needed technical assistance and training. Staff, students, parents, and administrators from school districts with experience in educating students with intensive educational needs in general education can provide training and should be tapped as trainers regarding the "how to's" of inclusion. They also are likely to have valuable insights to help forward the change process, insights based upon their own real life experiences with being in the middle of change.

School districts attempting to accommodate students with intensive challenges are advised to collaborate with institutions of higher education for the mutual benefit of both organizations. Together the two organizations might design and solicit state or federal support for model demonstration projects in the school district, arrange for valuable internship opportunities for graduate students in integrated educational settings, conduct research to document the impact (e.g., student achievement, social development, post-graduation employment, teacher competence and morale) of inclusive educational practices and local placement of all students, co-design and deliver a district's inservice training program, or co-develop and deliver preservice teacher preparation course content for new or emerging roles (e.g., integration or support facilitator) necessary for supporting a more diverse group of students, their teachers, and their families.

Finally, school districts that share a common vision of inclusive education should form partnerships with one another and exchange personnel (e.g., reciprocal inservice presenters) and resources, jointly problem solve the barriers to change, form a coalition to advocate for changes in teacher preparation programs and state-level policy or funding, and celebrate the positive outcomes of structuring heterogeneous learning opportunities for children.

Restructuring to Create a Climate of Equality and Equity

We cannot ask students to do what we, as adults and educators, are not willing to do ourselves. More specifically, we cannot expect children to support and respect one another in heterogeneous educational groupings if we are not willing to also create heterogeneous collaborative planning and teaching teams, actively involve families in decision making regarding their children's educational programs, and empower students to join in as instructors, advocates for themselves and others, and decision-makers regarding school-wide issues.

Redefining the Role of the Teacher and the Expert As Members of a Collaborative Team

Schools attempting to educate a diverse group of students have taken various steps to merge the instructional resources of general and special education to meet the needs of a heterogeneous student body. Some schools have dropped professional labels and distributed job functions across a number of school personnel (Villa & Thousand, 1988). The Winooski (Vermont) School District has created a single job description for all professional educators (classroom teachers, consulting teachers, speech and language pathologists, guidance personnel), which emphasizes collaboration and shared responsibility for educating all of the community's children.

Some schools have formed long-term team teaching arrangements among faculty (e.g., Bauwens, Hourcade, & Friend, 1989). Thousand and Villa (1990) describe the *teaching team*—"an organizational and instructional arrangement of two or more members of the school and greater community who distribute among themselves planning, instructional, and evaluation responsibilities for the same students on a regular basis for an extended period of time" (p. 152). By looking to the entire adult and student community as potential team members, teaching teams result in better instructor/learner ratios and ongoing exchange of knowledge and skill among team members—outcomes that benefit more students than just those requiring intensive support.

Personnel in schools that have been most successful in responding to the needs of intensively challenging students consistently identify as the cornerstone to their success a strong *collaborative team*, which engages in problem-solving and decision-making processes referred to as "collaborative teaming" (Thousand et al., 1986). Any adult or student interested in supporting the education of an intensively challenged student is a potential member of the student's team. In collaborative planning and teaching teams, members agree to coordinate their work to achieve common, publicly agreed-upon goals. Collaborative processes employed by the team are based upon the principles of cooperative group learning (Johnson & Johnson, 1987a), which prescribe five elements for effective team functioning (Thousand & Villa, 1990):

1. Face-to-face team interaction on a frequent basis.
2. An "all for one, one for all" feeling of positive interdependence.
3. A focus on the development of small-group interpersonal skills in trust building, communication, leadership, creative problem solving, decision making, and conflict management.
4. Regular assessment of the team's functioning and goal setting for improving relationships and task achievement.
5. Methods for holding one another accountable for personal responsibilities and commitments.

Instructional support teams, or teaching assistance teams, have long been available to teachers as a support in problem solving regarding students who present educational or behavioral challenges (Chalfant, Pysh, & Moultrie, 1979). The power of these teams and the individual student support teams that employ collaborative teaming processes lies in their capacity to merge the unique skills of talented adults and students, enfranchise team members through the participatory decision-making process, and distribute leadership authority beyond the administration to the broader school community (Thousand & Villa, 1990).

True collaborative teams also promote a climate of equality and equity in a number of ways. Effective collaborative teams have no single leader; leadership roles are distributed and rotated among all members. Specialists or experts have no extra authority; they are "just another member" of the team. Everyone in the group engages in collaborative consultation, alternately playing the consultant/expert and the consultee/recipient role and modeling learning as well as teaching (Thousand et al., 1992).

Family-Focused Education Goal Setting

Families of children with identified handicaps are guaranteed, through PL 94-142, certain rights of participation in the development of their children's education program. Family members of a child with intensive educational needs sometimes find themselves in a struggle with school personnel over what they and their child view as "the good life" and the role of the school in this life, and what professional educators and support personnel (e.g., physical therapist, occupational therapist, speech and language therapist) have been trained to believe are necessary educational goals and experiences for the child (Giangreco, Cloninger, Mueller, Yuan, & Ashworth, 1991).

The *C.O.A.C.H.* (Giangreco, Cloninger, & Iverson, 1990) assessment and planning instrument for learners with intensive educational needs has been designed expressly for the purpose of assisting family members and the educators of their child to jointly develop educational objectives and integrated school and community experiences considered relevant to the family. The tool is based upon six assumptions regarding families of children with intensive needs:

1. Families know aspects of their children better than anyone.
2. Families have the greatest vested interest in their children's learning.
3. Families likely are the only adults involved in their child's entire schooling.
4. Families have unique access to information about their children in the home and community.
5. Families can positively influence the quality of community services.
6. Families must live with the outcomes of educational decisions every day of the year.

C.O.A.C.H. is unique in that it puts the family in the position of driving the educational goal-setting process and requires family members and professionals to behave as equal members of a collaborative team. The respect for family members' knowledge and wishes structured into the assessment process is illustrated by Part 1 of the instrument. Included in this section are questions regarding five "quality of life indicators" identified by parents of children with multiple handicaps as parameters of a "good life" (Giangreco, Cloninger, & Iverson, 1990, p. 19). The family's answers to these questions are meant to offer team members a mutual understanding of the child's current status and issues important to the family.

Empowering Students to be Instructors, Advocates, and Decision Makers

The term *collaboration* usually conjures up the image of adults, usually *professional* educators, working together. Schools attempting to educate a diverse student population have expanded the list of potential collaborators to include students and other adults (e.g., parents, support personnel, instructional assistants, community volunteers). Villa and Thousand (1990) offer a rationale for placing students in the collaborative role.

First, given the diverse educational and psychological needs of an increasingly heterogeneous student population, school personnel have to take advantage of any and all available human resources. Students provide a rich pool of expertise, refreshing creativity, and enthusiasm at no cost to the school district.

Second, futurists suggest "a new collaborative role for teachers and students in which students accept an active senior partnership role in the learning enterprise" (Benjamin, 1989, p. 9). Educational reform recommendations also call for more active student participation in their learning and more opportunities for students to develop and use higher-level thinking skills (Boyer, 1983; Costa, 1985; Glasser, 1986; Hunter, 1982). This means involving students in planning, instruction, problem solving, and evaluation activities.

Third, futurists advise schools to offer opportunities for students to practice being contributing and caring members of society and to develop empathy for others (Benjamin, 1989; Falvey, Coots, & Bishop, 1990). By encouraging students to advocate for the educational interests and needs of a fellow student (e.g., a student with intensive educational needs), schools create opportunities such as these.

Fourth, given the current information explosion and the increasingly complex nature of a diverse global society, which will require people to pool their knowledge and skills through collaborative efforts, collaborative skills emerge as a core curriculum area for today's schools.

School personnel, then, have a responsibility to model collaboration by sharing their decision-making power with students, in a climate of mutual respect. Among the collaborative arrangements or strategies recommended for schools attempting to create a heterogeneous learning community that includes students with intensive educational challenges are:

- Students as instructors in partner learning, cooperative group learning and adult-student teaching team arrangements.
- Students as members of collaborative planning teams, determining accommodations for classmates with intensive challenges.
- Students functioning as advocates for a peer in transition or individualized education plan (IEP) planning meetings.
- Students supporting a challenged classmate in a "peer buddy" system or a Circle of Friends (Forest & Lusthaus, 1989).
- Students as coaches for their teachers, offering feedback regarding the effectiveness and consistency of their instructional and discipline procedures.
- Students as members of curriculum, inservice, and other school governance committees (e.g., school board).

We contend that collaborative arrangements such as these promote the desired outcomes of a quality integrated schooling experience for intensively challenged students, active participation and problem solving on the part of the student body, equity and parity among students and adults, and a spirit of community within the school (Villa & Thousand, 1992).

ADAPTING CURRICULUM AND INSTRUCTION: SELECTED STRATEGIES

Recently reviews have proliferated regarding methods for "individualizing" curriculum and providing "individualized" instruction (e.g., Glatthorn, 1987; Nevin et al., 1990; Villa & Thousand, 1988; Slavin, 1987; W. Stainback & S. Stainback, 1989; Wang, 1989). Several strategies considered appropriate and effective for responding to the individual needs of intensively challenged or challenging students are discussed in this section.

Data-Based Strategies For Adapting Curriculum and Instruction

In Glatthorn's (1987) summary of research on methods for adapting curriculum and instruction to respond to individual student differences, three specific sets of approaches were offered as having the strong support of quality research: mastery learning, computer-assisted instruction, and cooperative group learning.

Mastery Learning Models
Common to all of these mastery learning or outcome-based instructional models are the following teacher behaviors (Block & Anderson, 1975; Brookover et al., 1982; Vicker, 1988):

1. Frequent, brief diagnostic assessment of each student.
2. Individualization of learning objectives with clear preset mastery criteria.
3. Frequent specific provision of feedback regarding student performance.
4. Adjustment or supplementation of instruction or practice time, for students who do not meet their mastery criteria.

An underlying assumption of mastery learning models is that all children can learn, given time and the appropriate resources. This assumption, combined with the extensive effectiveness data that make mastery learning models so compelling for use in classrooms, includes intensively challenging students.

Computer-Assisted Instruction (CAI)
As Glatthorn (1987) notes, CAI is particularly useful in three areas of instruction:

1. *Tutorial*, in which new information is presented.
2. *Drill and practice*, in which old information is reviewed for the purpose of remediation or accelerating rate or level of mastery.
3. *Simulations*, in which concept learning or more complex problem solving is the focus.

For students who are physically challenged, nonverbal, or verbally unintelligible to the general public, computers frequently are used as an alternative or augmentative mode of communication as well as a learning tool.

THAT ALL MAY WORSHIP:
BUILDING BRIDGES TOGETHER

An interfaith conference promoting the inclusion of people with disabilities in congregations.

Our Programs represent a philosophical approach to human development and learning that guides all inst. endeavors.

Humanistic position
　　　　　　　　　Developmental = Interaction
Adult as a learner - continuing development - throughout life -

D-I A provides a basic framework for ed. of all children -

1) TEACHER - DIRECTED INSTRUCTION
　　　ENGLERT 1983, 1984

2) CONSULTANT TEACHER MODEL
　　Fuchs, Fuchs, and Bahr (1990)
　　Idol - Maestas (1983)

3) INCLUSION MODELS
　　Fuchs, Fuchs, - Fernstrom (1993)
　　Forness - Kavale (1987)
　　Johnson - Johnson (1975, 1983, 1991)

Harmarville
REHABILITATION CENTERS

Comprehensive Rehabilitation
Guys Run Road • Pittsburgh, PA 15238-0460
1-800-624-4673 • 412/781-5700

Cooperative Group Learning

As with effective collaborative teams, cooperative learning models (Johnson & Johnson, 1987b; Slavin, 1983) share five common elements:

1. Face-to-face interaction among a heterogeneous group of students.
2. Positive interdependence (structured through common goals or products, joint rewards, division of labor and roles, division of materials or information).
3. Teaching small-group interpersonal skills.
4. Regular assessment and goal setting regarding the appropriate use of small-group and interpersonal skills.
5. Individual accountability for achieving individualized academic and social objectives.

In Vermont, more than 20 integration facilitators (teachers with the job function of arranging supports for students with intensive educational needs) regularly work with classroom teachers to structure heterogeneous cooperative group lessons that meaningfully include intensively challenged students. How are lessons adapted to integrate a low-achieving student or a student identified as handicapped? Johnson and Johnson (1987b) describe several proven strategies, but sample lessons designed by classroom teachers with the assistance of an integration facilitator best illustrate how adaptations can be made (Villa & Thousand, 1992).

Example #1: A cooperative group lesson adapted for a young student with multiple handicaps. When this lesson occurred, John was 8 years old. He had recently transitioned from a special class for students with multiple handicaps to a combined first/second grade classroom in his local school. John occasionally vocalized loudly but did not yet use vocal behavior to communicate. One of the IEP goals for John was to develop his use of various switches as a first step in developing an augmentative communication system. Other IEP goals were for John to remain with a group throughout an activity, to keep his hands off others' materials, and to refrain from making loud vocalizations in a group.

In this lesson students were assigned to groups of five each. All group members, John included, were expected to sit in a circle, stay with their group, and use an "indoor" voice level. These social and behavioral expectations, by the way, directly addressed two of John's IEP goals.

Groups first were assigned the task of listening to a "talking book" story tape and following along with the illustrations from the story book. Each group had a copy of the story tape, a tape recorder, and the illustrated book. Each child in a group was assigned a specific job or role to perform during the lesson. One job was to turn the pages of the story book to correspond with the tape recording; another was to operate the tape recorder. John was assigned the role of tape recorder operator. His tape recorder was adapted so that he could activate it by pushing on a panel switch.

Being assigned the role of tape recorder operator gave John a valuable and needed role in his group, and it also addressed two of his IEP goals. First, it allowed for assessing the switch's potential for use in a meaningful real-life situation. Second, it inhibited John's grabbing behavior; during the lesson at least one of his hands was engaged in a behavior (pushing the switch to turn on the tape recorder) incompatible with grabbing. Tape recorders also are a popular leisure-time device for children and adults, so are appropriate for John to learn to use.

After listening to the story, groups generated and agreed upon answers to questions concerning the story. They then met as a large group and shared their responses. John's objectives for this part of the lesson continued to be behavioral in nature—to stay with the group and to refrain from making loud noises or grabbing other's materials.

Example #2: A cooperative group lesson adapted for an adolescent with multiple handicaps. Bob, a young man with multiple handicaps, attended his local junior high school. At the time of the biology lesson presented here, Bob was 13 years old and in seventh-grade classes. For this lesson students were arranged in groups of three or four students to dissect a frog for the purpose of identifying body parts. Bob was assigned to a group of four. Whereas other groups used lab tables to do their dissection work, Bob's group used, as their work space, the lap tray attached to his wheelchair.

Bob's objectives for this lesson were different from those of his classmates. He was engaged in a structured communication program (a two-choice discrimination task between real objects randomly placed on either side of his lap tray), which was simple to deliver and which his peers could, and did, easily implement along with their dissection activities at points throughout the class period.

Another of Bob's objectives was to increase the frequency of his vocalizations. Bob's teammates were instructed to regularly use his name as they worked, which they frequently did. The classroom teacher and her collaborating integration facilitator had instructed Bob's fellow group members regarding the two programs. During the activity no adult was directly involved in guiding the peers' interactions with Bob, although a teacher assistant sat near Bob's group, collecting data for the structured programs.

Partner Learning and Peer Tutoring Systems

Another powerful approach for adapting instruction is partner learning or peer tutoring. As Gartner and Lipsky (1990, p. 84), noted, "evidence of the instructional, social, and cost effectiveness of tutoring is mounting." The many benefits for the tutor and the tutee have been summarized in research reviews and a meta-analysis of research (Cohen, Kulik, & Kulik, 1982; Madden & Slavin, 1987; Pierce, Stahlbrand, & Armstrong, 1984). The documented benefits to students receiving instruction (learning gains, the development of positive social interaction skills with another student, and heightened self-esteem) are typical areas of concern for educators and families of intensively challenged students. As with other instructional and peer support strategies that utilize *peer power* (Villa & Thousand, 1988), "peer-tutoring partnerships are a cost-effective way for teachers to increase the amount of individualized instructional attention available to their students (Armstrong, Stahlbrand, Conlon, & Pierson, 1979)" (Villa & Thousand, 1988, p.146). Good and Brophy (1987) suggest that peers trained as tutors may be more effective than adults. They use more age-appropriate and meaningful vocabulary and examples; as recent learners of material being taught, they are familiar with the tutee's potential frustrations and problems; and they tend to be more direct than adults.

Same-age and cross-age partner learning systems can be established within a single classroom (Maheady, Sacca, & Harper, 1988), across more than one classroom, or across an entire school. Clearly, formalized school-wide peer tutoring systems cannot and do not arise overnight. The readers are referred to Villa and Thousand (1992; Villa, Thousand, & Nevin, in press) for an example of how a school-wide partner learning system can evolve over a 2- to 3-year period. The following two individual student examples from Villa and Thousand (1992) illustrate the power of partner learning for behaviorally challenging students.

Example #1: Andrew as a second-grade tutor. Serving as a tutor may have a powerfully positive impact on students identified as seriously emotionally disturbed (SED). Consider, for example, Andrew. During his sixth-grade year, Andrew served as a cross-age tutor the last 45 minutes of each school day in a second-grade classroom. This privilege was contingent upon daily demonstration of appropriate behavior as outlined in his behavioral contract. Although this young man still presented intensive behavioral challenges to his own teachers and agemates, the second-grade teacher considered him a model of appropriate behavior and a valued instructional asset. His second-grade tutoring time was one or two times during the day when an instructional assistant was *not* assigned to be available in case of disruptions. Andrew demonstrated the importance of his tutoring role the week before the Christmas holiday vacation, when he chose to forego his own class party to present individual gifts to the entire second-grade class and its teacher.

Example #2: Rebecca's role as a tutor. The tutoring role was intended to help Rebecca, a fourth grader identified as SED, to identify and moderate her own antisocial behavior. Following each tutoring session with second-grade students, she was asked to analyze her effectiveness in teaching and managing the students' behaviors. Her tutees' behaviors that interfered with teaching and management were highlighted, and analogies were drawn to her own behaviors and their effects upon learning. Strategies then were discussed for effectively moderating her own social behaviors.

Creative Problem Solving by Peers

A number of Vermont teachers who have students with dual sensory impairments (i.e., deaf-blind) use an elegantly simple method for determining meaningful curricular and instructional modifications for intensively challenged students as regular class members (Giangreco, 1990). As a routine part of the introduction of a lesson, these teachers ask, "How can we make sure (student's name) is included in this lesson?" or "How can we make (student's name) a meaningful part of this activity?" Teachers report that students are highly creative problem solvers and that they generate a great many realistic modification strategies from which to select.

In a more formal application of creative problem solving, students are taught a five-step problem-solving method (Parnes, 1981, 1988). In a Vermont second-grade classroom, students were guided through the five-step process in order to address the general issue of inclusion for their classmate with dual sensory impairments and multiple disabilities. During the initial 10-minute brainstorming stage of the 45-minute activity, the class generated more than 70 ideas for integrating the classmate into the daily routines of the school. When the ideas were assessed for feasibility in the next step of the process, most ideas were found to be usable. More important, the collaborating integration facilitator reported that in the weeks that followed, initiations directed by peers and staff toward the target student increased in both type and frequency.

Curriculum-Based Assessment

"Curriculum-based assessment" (CBA) refers to a set of criterion-referenced assessment methods for identifying a student's instructional needs by examining the student's ongoing performance within the selected curriculum the school uses with the student. Unlike norm-referenced assessment, CBA is not concerned with comparing students with one another but instead with examining a student's performance in comparison with a preset criterion or standard. CBA gives teachers information about what to teach, closely linking assessment with instruction. Of course, to use CBA, teachers have to identify and select or create a curriculum sequence that is both appropriate and specific enough to give teachers information for designing instructional programs. For in-depth descriptions of CBA methodologies, readers are referred to Deno and Mirkin (1977); Howell and Morehead (1987); Idol, Nevin, and Paolucci-Whitcomb (1986); Shapiro (1987); and Shriner, Ysseldyke, and Christenson (1989).

User-Friendly Measurement Systems

Meyer and Janney (1989) have pointed out that the measurement systems we use in general education settings with intensively challenging students must be "user-friendly" (p. 265)—capable of documenting desired outcomes and assisting teams to make decisions about instruction while at the same time being unintrusive. A user-friendly measurement system is one "which does not interrupt the flow of instruction or intervention in the classroom, requires minimal time to complete, and allows professionals and paraprofessionals to share both their objective and subjective observations" (p. 265). Meyer and Janney describe a variety of measurement systems that meet these criteria and that teachers in general education settings are more likely to use and find meaningful than trial-by-trial data collection practices, which once were viewed as "good" research methodology or best practice in handicapped-only classrooms.

A Decision-Making Process

Tools are now available to assist teams to creatively design an integrated daily schedule for students with intensive challenges (Giangreco, Cloninger, & Iverson, 1990; Iverson & Cloninger, 1990). One of these is known as the IEP-General Education Matrix. Figure 1 presents a sample completed matrix for a third grader. Notice that the student's team has listed, across the top of the matrix, normally scheduled general class activities, including major transition times (e.g., arrival, departure). (For older students these activities would be replaced with class offerings from the school's master schedule.) Along

Name: Tommy Smith
Grade: 3

Regular Class Schedule

		Arrival	Current Events	Reading	Math	Lang. Arts	Lunch	Recess	Science	Social Studies	P.E.	Art	Music
IEP GOALS	Summons Others	ML		CO	CO	ML	CO	CO	CO	CO	CO	CO	CO
	Makes Choices		ML	CO	CO	ML	CO	CO	CO	CO	CO	CO	CO
	Initiates Interactions	S		CO	CO	CO	ML		CO	CO	CO	CO	CO
	Imitates Skills	ML	CO	CO	CO	CO	CO		CO	CO	CO	CO	CO
	Leisure with Others	ML			CO		ML	ML					S
GENERAL CURRICULUM	Physical Education										ML		
	Music											S	S
	Art											S	S
	Socialization	ML	CO	CO	CO	CO	ML	ML	CO	CO	CO	CO	CO
	Communication	ML	ML	CO	CO	ML	S	ML	CO	CO	CO	CO	CO
	Personal Management	ML			ALT	ALT	CO/ALT/ML		ALT	ALT			
	Recreation/Leisure	ML				CO		ML					
	School	ML	CO	CO	CO	CO	CO		CO				
	Vocational (class)(jobs)	CO	CO	CO	CO	CO	CO	CO	CO				CO
MGMT NEEDS	Teach Others Commun.	CO	CO			CO	CO		CO	CO			
	Provider Personal Care	ML			ALT	ALT	ML	ML	ALT	CO	CO	CO	CO
	Positioning	ML	CO	→	→	→	→	→	→	→	→	→	→
	Access Modifications (use of)	CO	CO					CO			CO		

S=Some   ML=Multi-Level   CO=Curriculum Overlapping   A=Alternative

Source: From *C.O.A.C.H.—Cayuga-Onodaga Assessment for Children with Handicaps* (6th ed., p. 41) by M. Giangreco, C. Cloninger, and V. Iverson, 1990, Stillwater: Oklahoma State University, National Clearinghouse of Rehabilitative Training Materials. Copyright 1990 by National Clearinghouse of Rehabilitative Training Materials. Reprinted by permission.

FIGURE 1   Sample IEP—General Education Matrix

the left column the team has listed abbreviations for the student's IEP goals, general curriculum areas in which the student has learning outcomes, and any management needs (e.g., regular repositioning, personal care needs such as toileting, administration of medication, hearing aid battery checks).

The matrix offers a visual representation of when and where IEP and other learning goals *might possibly* be met. It is intended to assist a student's planning team in choosing when and where learning goals will be addressed in general education activities.

Options for the Delivery of Support Services

The matrix also may help the team to identify the types of curriculum modifications and instructional supports the student may need for educational objectives to be adequately addressed. Special services and supports may be delivered in general education settings in four broad ways, identified in Table 4 (Giangreco, Cloninger, & Iverson, 1990; Giangreco & Meyer, 1988). When initially exploring potential possibilities for inclusion, the team is advised to consider and decide which of these four options for delivering support is best suited or most likely to occur for each of the activities included in the matrix. As illustrated in Figure 1, codes may be entered on the matrix to represent the most likely adaptation option for each activity. When coding the matrix, however, these notations do not designate how the student actually is included in classroom activities when the daily schedule is finalized. At this point, the matrix is simply meant to offer a visual representation of how learning and management needs *might* be addressed in general education environments. It also is used to highlight when IEP objectives or management needs do not easily mesh with general education activities.

Problems in Meshing Learning Objectives and General Education Activities

At times it appears that no, or very few, general education opportunities are available to address a learning objective. This meshing challenge shows up on the matrix as an entire row or column of blank spaces. When an entire row is blank, the team must question whether the learning objective for that row is appropriate—whether it is both *functional* (likely to lead to more independent adult functioning or an enhanced social support network) and of *high priority*.

If the answer is "yes" to both of these criteria questions, the team should engage in creative problem solving to avoid the loss of an integration opportunity. Iverson and Cloninger (1990) offer specific strategies and examples for meeting various "match-up" 'challenges. Peers may be enlisted to help problem solve or to serve as peer tutors or buddies. If other students need alternative instruction, small groups can be arranged within a classroom. In cases where the objective is considered either nonfunctional or of low priority, the team may wish to review the IEP and assess whether the objective should be rewritten so that it is more functional, "put on hold," or dropped altogether.

Sometimes the IEP-General Education Matrix may reveal one or more general educational activities or classes during which few, if any, learning objectives or management needs seem to fit. These blocks of the school day may be used to focus upon objectives that have to be addressed outside of the classroom (e.g., community-based instruction, job

TABLE 4 Student Participation Options in General Education Classroom Activities

Same:

Students who pose intensive challenges can participate in regular class activities by doing what all the other students are doing. Suppose a class is scheduled for Music and students are practicing songs for the annual holiday concert. All the students, including the student with special educational needs, pursue the *same* objectives within the same activities.

Multi-Level:

Multi-level curriculum/instruction occurs when students are all involved in a lesson within the same curriculum area but are pursuing different objectives at multiple levels based on their individual needs (Campbell, Campbell, Collicott, Perner, & Stone, 1988). For example, all the students may be in a reading lesson. The student with special needs is learning to identify (read) representations on a communication board (e.g., photos, line drawings, symbols) while others are learning to read orally with appropriate pauses to match punctuation. Multi-Level Curriculum/Instruction merely suggests an extension to include students with a wider range of abilities than is typically pursued within regular education. For example, in a math lesson one student is applying computational skills to a word problem and another is learning to count with correspondence. Both students are pursuing math learning outcomes but at different levels within the same activity or lesson.

Curriculum Overlapping:

Curriculum overlapping occurs when a group of students is involved in the same lesson, but pursuing goals/objectives from different curricular areas (Giangreco & Meyer, 1988, p. 257; Giangreco & Putnam, 1991). Suppose students are in science lab learning about properties of electricity. A student with special needs may be involved in these activities for the primary purpose of pursuing objectives from other curriculum areas (e.g., communication, socialization) such as following directions, accepting assistance from others, or engaging in a school job with a nonhandicapped peer. When curriculum overlapping takes place, the regular class activity is primarily a vehicle used to attain other goals. This approach opens many opportunities for students to participate in classes previously considered "inappropriate." These settings are selected because they offer opportunities to address identified needs.

Alternative:

Occasionally students may need to pursue *alternative* activities if the regular class does not offer reasonable opportunities to address relevant learning outcomes through multi-level curriculum/instruction or curriculum overlapping. For example, during a time when general education students are taking a half-hour paper-and-pencil test, it may be appropriate to work on community-based activities such as pedestrian skills, because activities such as this may not be addressed adequately within the regular class schedule. Similarly, certain management needs are appropriately met in private (e.g., catheterization or postural drainage may be carried out in the health office). Caution should be exercised when selecting alternative activities, because most student needs can be met in regular class situations given creative planning, a commitment to inclusion, and collaboration among professionals and families.

Source: From *C.O.A.C.H.—Cayuga-Onondaga Assessment for Children with Handicaps* (6th ed., pp. 38–39) by M. Giangreco, C. Cloninger, and V. Iverson, 1990, Stillwater: Oklahoma State University. Copyright 1990 by National Clearinghouse of Rehabilitative Training Materials. Adapted by permission.

experiences, toileting). Consideration should be given, however, to *including* the student in activities or classes that do not specifically address learning objectives, particularly when they offer incidental learning opportunities in areas that have not yet been targeted as objectives or opportunities for social interaction and friendship building.

Designing an Integrated Daily Schedule

The culmination of the matrixing process is in designing a daily schedule for the student. In the elementary grades, where classroom routines remain relatively stable, teams have found the information represented on the matrix to be particularly helpful in identifying when additional peer or adult support is needed and when adaptations in materials, instructional strategies, or curriculum are needed. In the middle and secondary grades, where students move from class to class and have individual schedules, the matrix has been used to select classes.

Even though a student with intensive needs will have scheduled "regular education" experiences, the schedule must remain flexible so that the student's team may arrange for alternative instruction (e.g., individual instruction, vocational education) when particular units or topics fail to match the student's needs. Even at the high school level, meshing challenges have been overcome and have resulted in intensively challenged students receiving *more* services in integrated versus separate activities (Giangreco, Cloninger, & Iverson, 1990).

EDUCATIONAL ROLES FOR DELIVERING THE CURRICULUM

As already mentioned, one of the responsibilities of school district leadership is to guide the school community through a process of curriculum examination in order to discover the "sameness" of general and special education curricula, merge duplicate content taught in separate programs (e.g., general versus special versus compensatory education) and distribute instruction of this content across instructional staff of formerly separate programs, and develop new curricular domains (e.g., social skills and responsibility). An associated responsibility of school leadership is to examine the need for new job roles or job functions so that the expanded curriculum may be delivered in integrated school and community settings. The *school-based employment specialist* and the *integration* or *support facilitator* are two specific job roles that have emerged in the last several years to enable an expanded curriculum to be delivered to a broader range of students in heterogeneous school and community settings.

School-Based Employment Specialists

Recent follow-up studies indicate high dropout and low employment rates for students with handicaps who have exited school (Hasazi & Clark, 1988; Hasazi, Gordon, & Roe, 1985; Mithaug, Horiuchi, & Fanning, 1985). In their examination of young adults labeled moderately, severely, and profoundly retarded, Wehman, Kregel, and Seyfarth (1985) found only 12% employed either part-time or full-time. In addition, their wages were extremely low. These data clearly attest to the need for additional vocational options to enhance challenged students' employability.

The school-based employment specialist (SBES) is a secondary educator who works with a school district's guidance and vocational education department and community employers to expand the work experience and job skill training options so that students with intensive challenges and other students have needed work experiences before graduation. Cobb, Hasazi, Collins, and Salembier (1988) have provided a detailed description of the job functions of the SBES and have outlined the graduate-level program at the University of Vermont that prepares educators to serve as an SBES.

Integration/Support Facilitators

The integration facilitator or support facilitator is a second educational role that now is in place in a number of North American schools striving to educate intensively challenged students in local general education environments. An integration/support facilitator (ISF) may work at the elementary and/or secondary level in one or more school buildings or school districts. Job functions of the ISF include (W. Stainback & S. Stainback, 1990b):

- Fostering professional peer collaboration by team teaching and organizing and serving on teacher and student support teams.
- Locating material, equipment, and specialized technical human resources.
- Adapting curriculum and instructional methods.
- Organizing students into peer tutoring, peer buddy, and other peer support systems.
- Facilitating home-school partnership and communication.
- Lobbying for necessary support (e.g., an instructional assistant for a classroom, state or federal grant support).
- Facilitating community "ownership" for integration activities and removal of traditional special education labels assigned to students, classrooms, teachers and programs.

Since 1986 the University of Vermont has offered a graduate training concentration that "retools" educators to serve as ISFs in inclusionary public schools (Thousand & Fox, 1989). Students in the program work four days a week in the school districts in which they are or will be functioning as an ISF. On the fifth day they attend courses on the university campus. Central to their training are competencies in collaborative teaming and consultation (Thousand et al., 1986; Nevin et al., 1990; Thousand et al., 1992) as well as the other competency areas described in Table 5. As of this writing more than one third of Vermont's school districts employ at least one trained ISF in one or more of their schools.

Pitfalls to Avoid

S. Stainback and W. Stainback (1990b) have identified several potential pitfalls of creating an integration/support facilitator role within a school. These same potential pitfalls apply equally to the employment specialist role and any other educational role that emerges in response to the needs of a subgroup of the total school population.

One potential pitfall is that the ISF may be expected to work exclusively with intensively challenged students. This expectation is in conflict with the intended focus of the

TABLE 5   Competency Clusters for Integration/Support Facilitators

1.0 *Training others.* Trainees will demonstrate their ability to train others (members of collaborative teams, general and special educators, teacher assistants, students with and without handicaps, parents and other family members, other school and community members) to implement effective instructional programs for learners who pose intensive challenges, demonstrate collaborative teaming skills, and articulate an understanding of best educational practices.

2.0 *Technical assistance.* Trainees will demonstrate their ability to provide technical assistance to general and special educators, administrators, and community agency personnel to implement best educational practices and improve the education of learners who are challenged within their local schools and communities.

3.0 *Best educational practices.* Trainees will identify, provide a rationale for, and be able to clearly articulate the benefits of "best educational practices" for all learners that address the issues of school climate and structure, collaborative planning, social responsibility, curriculum planning, delivery of instructional support services, individualized instruction, transition planning, family-school collaboration, and planning for continued best practice improvement.

4.0 *Consultation, communication, and small-group skills.* Trainees will demonstrate knowledge of and the ability to implement techniques for building trust, effectively communicating, giving and receiving positive and negative feedback, and exhibiting appropriate leadership and conflict resolution styles with building-based support team members and other individuals concerned with the education of challenged learners.

5.0 *Collaborative teaming and cooperative group learning.* Trainees will collaborate with building-based support teams of parents, general and special educators, students, and administrators to plan, implement, and evaluate strategies for educating all learners within their local public schools. Trainees will develop and implement cooperative learning lessons that accommodate learners with intensive challenges and their typical peers.

6.0 *Supervision and peer coaching.* Trainees will provide direct feedback to teacher assistants, volunteers, peer tutors, peer buddies, and general and special educators, regarding the effectiveness of their instruction with learners who have intensive challenges, through clinical supervision and peer coaching conferences.

7.0 *Strategies from general education and theory of instruction for adapting curriculum and instruction to promote the inclusion of learners with intensive challenges.* Trainees will identify and be able to clearly articulate characteristics of "effective schools" and strategies in general education for adapting curriculum and instruction promoting the inclusion of learners with challenges in general education learning environments. These strategies include peer tutoring, cooperative group learning, outcomes-based instruction, computer-assisted instruction, multi-aged groupings, and theory of instruction regarding cognitive learning.

8.0 *Organizational skills (self and others).* Trainees will demonstrate the ability to manage their time and plan, schedule, and document their professional activities so they may evaluate their efficiency and effectiveness in achieving their goals and objectives.

9.0 *Establishment, implementation, and evaluation of a service delivery model for serving all learners in local school general education settings.* Trainees will establish, implement, and evaluate their role as a specialist who supports local school general education placement for students with moderate and severe challenges within their respective school districts and assigned schools.

ISF role, which is to "serve as a resource to the teacher, family, principal, and the class as a whole in building support networks" (p. 34). Restricting the range of students with whom the ISF may work has many potential negative consequences. For one, it denies other students and staff access to valuable expertise. In addition, exclusive association of the ISF with certain students may set those students apart from their peers and interfere with their forming natural peer support networks and friendships.

A second pitfall has to do with the ISF being perceived as the new "expert" in the system. Contrary to the desired role of the ISF as a model and coach in effective collaborative teaming and joint decisionmaking, many educators in the new ISF role find themselves being looked to as the expert responsible for solving the problems regarding certain students. Educators new to the role of ISF must be careful to demonstrate, through their behaviors, their belief in collaborative processes; they must model and expect others to demonstrate equity and parity (equal responsibility and power) in decisionmaking.

The Winooski (Vermont) School District dealt with this potential pitfall by initially training all support personnel (consulting teachers, speech and language pathologists, resource teachers) in core ISF competencies. Training in these same competency areas then was made available to all teachers, instructional assistants, and administrators. This training not only ensured that all support personnel and many other staff had enhanced skills for collaborating in heterogeneous classrooms; it also prevented perceptions that one person or one group of people were the "super special educators."

Finally, the ISF must be vigilant in *not* "oversupporting" a student. For a challenged student to increase independence and have access to natural peer support, adults (teaching assistants, the ISF, other support personnel) sometimes must step back a bit and observe what the student and the natural school ecosystem can do on its own to facilitate learning and relationship building.

The Role of Instructional Assistants And Common Concerns

As noted by Lindeman and Beegle (1988), employment of instructional assistants or paraprofessionals has increased dramatically since enactment of PL 94–142 in 1975. For many students with intensive educational challenges, particularly physically challenged students who will need personal attendants throughout their lives, the instructional assistant (IA) plays a vital support role. As a member of the classroom teaching team, the IA can provide a broad range of supports. These include assisting the teacher with clerical work, record keeping, and developing and preparing materials. IAs may provide students with physical assistance; and they may instruct, thereby bettering the adult/student ratio in the classroom and enhancing possibilities for individualized instruction. Studies suggest that IAs do spend most (60% to 70%) of their day instructing students, often in one-to-one arrangement (Harrington & Mitchelson, 1987; Mintzes, 1985; Vasa, Steckelberg, & Ronning, 1983).

While recognizing the tremendous potential of the IA as a support option for students with intensive educational needs, we must point out five commonly expressed concerns regarding the role of IAs in facilitating the inclusion of intensively challenged students:

1. The classroom teacher may not accept "ownership" for a student who comes with an IA, delegating responsibility for the child's instruction primarily to the IA.
2. The IA may become overprotective, overinvolved, or "attached at the hip" to the student.
3. The physical presence of the IA may impede interactions with peers.
4. IAs often are not included as members of student planning teams, even though the decisions of these teams usually have a great impact upon what the IA does on a day-to-day basis (most often expressed as a concern by IAs themselves). In addition, although IAs often are the least trained member of the team, they frequently are asked to engage in the most complex work (adapting, designing and implementing instruction) without adequate supervision or evaluation.
5. An administrative concern is the cost associated with hiring a full-time IA for each intensively challenged student or every student with a particularly "frightening" label.

Clearly, all of these concerns are valid. Administrators and teachers in Vermont schools, who are experienced with educating intensively challenged students in regular education, have wrestled with all of these issues and offer some strong advice:

1. Spend adequate time discussing and clarifying with the school community that the purpose of support is to enable a student to gain independence and form natural relationships with peers.
2. Clearly delineate the IA's job as a support to the teacher and the classroom as well as the challenged student.
3. Use collaborative teaming processes in planning, delivering, and evaluating instruction, and expect IAs to join the team as equally valued and vocal members.
4. Do not presume that all or certain intensively challenged students require full-time or part-time IA support. Instead, establish procedures for documenting the need for an IA. The documentation should require a description of the other types of accommodations and support already attempted.
5. Develop and regularly reexamine a plan for fading out the direct instructional and personal support the IA provides to the student. Many other adults and students can provide the same support, and an IA can in many ways share the responsibility with the challenged student's classmates for enhancing the quality of education.

PERSONNEL PREPARATION

Recommended Changes for Teacher Preparation Programs

School personnel are graduates of our colleges and universities. It is there that they learn there are at least two types of human beings and if you choose to work with one of them you render yourself legally and conceptually incompetent to work with the others. (Sarason, 1982, p. 258)

Sarason goes on to say that public schools are simply mirror images of today's colleges and universities. Sarason's words provide a powerful illustration of how the current division of teacher preparation programs into separate, distinct, and categorical special education programs (e.g., severe handicaps, learning disabilities, emotional disturbance, English as a second language) and general education concentrations hampers the ability of professionally prepared educators to either visualize or structure heterogeneous learning experiences that include students who, because of their *dis*abilities or their exceptional *capabilities* and talents, are considered a challenge to educate. Graduates of personnel preparation programs have few models of adults collaborating across their disciplines or areas of expertise. Is it any wonder that general and special education have evolved as separate systems (Wang et al., 1988) or that Sarason and colleagues long ago called teaching the "lonely profession" (Sarason, Levine, Godenberg, Cherlin, & Bennet, 1966, p. 74)?

S. Stainback and W. Stainback (1989) have offered a rationale and steps for facilitating merger of personnel preparation programs. They recommend that general and special education faculty sit down and analyze their curricula and identify agreed-upon knowledge and skills concerning philosophies and processes of instruction and learning that they considered critical. A core set of courses, such as that recommended in Table 6, then could be developed and required of all education majors. In addition to this core, each student would take courses in one or more areas in which they wish to develop special competence (e.g., reading, behavior management, history, alternative communication systems, employment, individualized and adaptive learning strategies).

Integration/support facilitators simply would be school personnel with expertise in competency areas such as collaborative teaming and consultation, curriculum and instructional modification, and partner and cooperative learning structures. By restructuring professional preparation programs in this manner, graduates no longer would get the message that they have to perpetuate a dual system of education. Instead they would have the cognitive set and the preparation to instruct a diverse student body in their respective selected specialty areas.

A Recommended School District Inservice Training Agenda

Staff of schools committed to educating all of their students in the mainstream of regular education need to acquire a common conceptual framework, language, and set of technical skills in order to communicate about and implement practices which research and theory suggest will enable them to better respond to a diverse student body. If personnel employed within the school have not received this training through their teacher preparation program, it becomes the job of those responsible for planning inservice for the local education agency to facilitate the formulation and ratification of a comprehensive inservice training agenda. This agenda may need to extend across several years to ensure that instructional personnel have the opportunity to progress from acquisition to mastery. (Villa, 1989, p. 173)

This statement acknowledges what many teachers have reported (Lyon, Vaassen, & Toomey, 1989), that neither their professional preparation nor their relatively isolated

TABLE 6 *Common Professional Core of Courses For All Educators*

Courses	Credit Hours
1. Historical/Philosophical Foundations of Education	3
2. Child and Adolescent Development	3
3. Human Relations and Sensitivity to Human Differences	3
4. Classroom Organization, Management, and Motivational Strategies	3
5. Curriculum Design and Adaptations	3
6. Educational Measurement and Curricular-Based Assessment	3
7. Adapting Instruction to Individual Differences	3
8. Utilization of Audiovisual/Media/Computer Technology	3
9. Home, School, and Community Relations	3
10. Issues and Trends in Education	3
Total	30

Source: From "Facilitating Merger Through Personnel Preparation" by S. Stainback and W. Stainback, 1989, in *Educating All Students in the Mainstream of Regular Education*, S. Stainback, W. Stainback, and M. Forest (Eds.), Baltimore, Paul H. Brookes Publishing Company. Reprinted by permission.

teaching experiences have adequately prepared them to meet the needs of a heterogeneous student population, including students who present intensive challenges. Fortunately, as Villa (1989) points out, schools do not have to wait for higher education to "get its act together" (p. 175) to empower staff to collaborate in the education of all children. He prescribes a four-tiered long-range inservice training agenda for school districts (see Table 7), which targets the entire community as the audience for the first tier of training. Training format options and incentives for encouraging participation also are suggested.

Higher Education, State Department of Education and School District Collaboration

In Vermont, collaboration between the State Department of Education and the state higher education institutions has been a critical factor in forwarding inclusionary education practices since the 1960s. In 1968, for example, this unique partnership created the *consulting teacher* special education professional preparation program (Christie et al., 1972; McKenzie et al., 1970), which enabled students with mild handicaps to receive special education support within regular classrooms. This mutually beneficial collaboration, envied throughout the United States, quickly expanded to include local school personnel as trainers of other adults. Classroom teachers and their consulting teacher partners provided practicum experiences for "consulting teachers-in-training" and coursework for local personnel to develop curriculum-based assessments, increase their behavior management and instructional adaptation skills, and keep abreast of current educational innovations.

TABLE 7   A Recommended Public School Inservice Training Agenda

Tier I   *Generic content relevant for all members of the school and greater community*

- General education research regarding the characteristics of "effective schools" (Brookover et al., 1982) and current exemplary "best educational practices" from general and special education (Williams & Fox, 1990).
- Models for adult collaboration and teaming and the development of small-group social skills Johnson & Johnson (1987a, 1987b); Thousand et al. (1986); Thousand et al. (1992; Thousand & Villa, 1992).

Tier II   *Selected content to respond to self-identified training needs of parents and community members;* for example:

- Legal rights and safeguards
- IEPs
- Behavior management
- Community-based training
- Transition between school environments
- Transition to adult services
- Post high-school follow-up

Tier III   *Training in assessment, behavior management, and instructional strategies for instructional personnel*

- Outcome-based instructional models (Block & Anderson, 1975; Guskey, 1985; Hunter, 1982), assessment models (Blankenship, 1985; Brown et al., 1989; Giangreco, Cloninger, & Iverson, 1990; Deno, 1985; Idol, Paolucci-Whitcomb, & Nevin, 1985; 1986; Ysseldyke & Christenson, 1987), and curriculum adaptation approaches (Campbell et al., 1988; Giangreco & Meyer, 1988) that enable teachers to discuss learner characteristics and make decisions about their own instructional behavior.
- Cooperative group learning models (Johnson, Johnson, Holubec, & Roy, 1984; Slavin, 1984).
- Computer-assisted instruction (Heerman, 1988).
- Classroom and school-wide behavior management and discipline approaches (Becker, 1986; Glasser, 1986; Curwin & Mendler, 1988).
- Methods for teaching and reinforcing students' use of positive social skills (Hazel, Schumaker, Sherman, & Sheldon-Wildgen, 1981).
- The use of student peers as tutors in partner learning, buddies in nonacademic situations, and members of individual student IEP planning teams (Good & Brophy, 1987; Pierce, Stahlbrand, & Armstrong, 1984; Villa & Thousand, 1988; Villa, Thousand, & Nevin, in press).

Tier IV   *Training in peer coaching and clinical supervision for supervisory personnel*

- (Cummings, 1985; Joyce & Showers, 1980; 1988).

Source: From "Model Public School Inservice Programs: Do They Exist?" by Richard A. Villa, 1989, *Teacher Education & Special Education, 12,* 173–176. Copyright 1989 by Special Press, San Antonio, TX. Adapted by permission.

In 1987, the Vermont Department of Education, integration/support facilitators from Vermont school districts, and University of Vermont faculty embarked upon yet another collaborative effort to jointly plan and deliver intensive week-long Summer Leadership Institutes to provide local school teams with critical knowledge and skills to educate students with intensive needs in regular education.

For a school team to attend the institute, two criteria must be met. First, the team must be *heterogeneous*, with representation from as many constituency groups as possible (e.g., the administration, general and special educators, parents, students, teaching assistants, guidance personnel, health personnel, speech and language pathologists). Second, the team must select at least one target student who is transitioning to the local school or for whom the team wishes to develop a more integrated daily schedule.

Training focuses upon four of the 10 competency core clusters in the integration/support facilitator training program (see Table 6), best educational practices (refer to Tables 2 and 3); consultation, communication, and small-group skills; collaborative teaming; and strategies for adapting curriculum and instruction to promote the inclusion of learners with intensive challenges. The instructional format alternates between team work sessions and formal presentations by parents, administrators, teachers, related service personnel (e.g., occupational therapists, physical therapists, speech and language pathologists), instructional assistants, and students with and without handicaps. Each team has an assigned "facilitator" (a university faculty member, State Education Department technical assistant, or a trained integration/support facilitator) who is available to answer technical questions, guide team work, and observe and process with group members their effectiveness in collaborating and managing conflict. By the week's end, each team has developed a 16-step "action plan" for delivering support to their target student and enhancing collaboration among the adults and students of their school.

The primary objective of the institute is to create a sense of group cohesion and a common conceptual framework and language among team members so they are able to support one another in transferring their newly acquired knowledge and skills to colleagues in their "home school" in the fall. As of this writing, nine Summer Leadership Institutes have been attended by over 500 Vermont educators, parents, and community members from the majority of the state's 60 superintendencies. Teams from several U.S. states and Canadian provinces also have attended and replicated the institute in their own communities. In Vermont, local school teams, regional groups of integration/support facilitators, and the state I-Team (which supports students with multiple handicaps) have replicated the summer training or extended the training as a one- or two-semester course offering within local school districts.

SUMMARY

Skrtic (1987; 1988) has described schooling in North America as a professional bureaucracy and argues that this paradigm diminishes teachers' ability to individualize for a great many students, including students with intensive educational needs. Skrtic explains:

The biggest problem is that schools are organized as professional bureaucracies . . . a contradiction in terms: Professionalization is intended to permit personalization; bureaucratization is intended to assure standardization. To blame the inability to individualize instruction totally on the capacity or will of professionals is misguided in that it blames the teacher for the inadequacies and contradictions of the organizational structure. This is the same kind of distortion of reality we make when we blame particular students for not learning from the existing standardized programs of the school organization. These students are the ones we call "handicapped," which is what I mean when I say that school organizations create "handicapped students." In both cases our tendency is to blame the victims—teachers who fail to individualize and students who fail to learn—for the inadequacies of the system. (Thousand, 1990, p. 31)

To enhance the capacity of schools to individualize for students, a "paradigm shift" is recommended: Educators should consider organizing into ad hoc teams (Patterson, Purkey, & Parker, 1986) or an *adhocracy* (Skrtic, 1987) so that educators may "mutually adjust their collective skills and knowledge to invent unique, personalized programs for each student" (Thousand, 1990, p. 32). In this new paradigm, the teacher is an inventor who has an implicit understanding that educational programs will have to be:

. . . continuously invented and reinvented by teachers in actual practice with students who have unique and changing needs. . . . The value of the adhocracy is that it is configured for diversity whereas the professional bureaucracy is configured for homogeneity, and so must remove diversity from the system through means like special education and other pull-out programs. (Thousand, 1990, p. 32)

What is suggested here is the need for organizational restructuring of schools. This restructuring already has begun. Ad hoc collaborative problem-solving and teaching teams composed of adults and students currently are emerging across North America in inclusion-oriented schools (see Nevin et al., 1990; Thousand & Villa, 1989; 1990; Villa & Thousand, 1992; Villa, Thousand, Stainback, & Stainback, 1992). These schools are right in the *middle* of a paradigm shift toward an "ideal" school structure of multiple ad hoc groups, which form and dissolve as needed to address the instructional and organizational barriers to the invention of personalized learning opportunities. Thousand et al. (1992) offer a detailed description of this ideal school for the 21st century and a scenario of how a school in the middle of a paradigm shift might transfer to the adhocratic structure.

We encourage an end to discussions of *where* students labeled severely or multiply handicapped can or should be educated. Instead, we propose that the discussion go another way, that it focus upon how to document, further refine, and disseminate the instructional, organizational, and technological innovations that allow neighborhood schools to respond to the diverse educational and psychological needs of any learner (Williams, Villa, Thousand, & Fox, 1990). Furthermore, teachers and administrators of each school building need to discuss how they will reorganize so that educators, students, and community members may form planning and teaching teams empowered to invent the future in the adhocratic fashion Skrtic prescribes.

"Student diversity is only a problem because of the kind of school organization we have" (Holmes Group, 1990). But that organization can and is now changing. We, therefore, propose a united advocacy effort to promulgate national policy prohibiting segregated education for any youngster entering school in the 21st century. This gives us this entire last decade of the 20th century to further research and refine strategies for inclusion and personalized instruction, not only for students with intensive educational needs, but for all students.

REFERENCES

Armstrong, S. B., Stahlbrand, K., Conlon, M. F., & Pierson, P. M. (1979, April). *The cost effectiveness of peer and cross-age tutoring.* Paper presented at international convention of Council for Exceptional Children. (ERIC Document Reproduction Service No. ED 171 058)

Bauwens, J., Hourcade, J. J., & Friend, M. (1989). Cooperative teaching: A model for general and special education integration. *Remedial & Special Education, 10*(2), 17–22.

Becker, W. (1986). *Applied psychology for teachers: A behavioral cognitive approach.* Chicago: Science Research Associates.

Benjamin, S. (1989). An ideascape for education: What futurists recommend. *Educational Leadership, 47*(1), 8–14.

Biklen, D. (Producer). (1988). *Regular lives* [Videotape]. Washington, DC: State of the Art.

Blackman, H., & Peterson, D. (Eds.). (1989). *Totally integrated neighborhood schools.* LaGrange, IL: Department of Special Education.

Blankenship, C. (1985). Using curriculum-based assessment data to make instructional decisions. *Exceptional Children, 54*, 233–238.

Block, J., & Anderson, L. (1975). *Mastery learning in classroom instruction.* New York: Macmillan.

Boyer, E. L. (1983). *High School.* New York: Harper & Row.

Brookover, W., Beamer, L., Efthim, H., Hathaway, D., Lezzotte, L., Miller, S., Passalacqua, J., & Tornatzky, L. (1982). *Creating effective schools: An inservice program for enhancing school learning climate and achievement.* Holmes Beach, FL: Learning Publications.

Brown, L., Long, E., Udvari-Solner, A., Schwarz, P., Van-Deventer, P., Ahlgren, S., Johnson, F., Gruenewald, L., & Jorgensen, J. (1989). Should students with severe intellectual disabilities be based in regular or in special education classrooms in home schools? *Journal of The Association for Persons with Severe Handicaps, 14*, 8–12.

Brown, L., Nisbet, J., Ford, A., Sweet, M., Shiraga, B., York, J., & Loomis, R. (1983). The critical need for non-school instruction in educational programs for severely handicapped students. *The Journal of The Association for the Severely Handicapped. 8*(3), 71–77.

Burrello, L., & Tourgee, B. (Eds.). (1990, June). *Principal letters: Practices for inclusion.* Bloomington: Indiana University, National Academy/CASE.

Campbell, S., Campbell, S., Collicott, J., Perner, D., & Stone, J. (1988). Individualizing instruction. *Education New Brunswick—Journal of Education*, pp. 17-20.

Chalfant, J., Pysh, M., & Moultrie, R. (1979). Teacher assistance teams: A model for within building problem solving. *Learning Disability Quarterly, 2*, 85–96.

Christie, L., McKenzie, H., & Burdett, C. (1972). The consulting teacher approach to special education: Inservice training for my classroom teachers. *Focus on Exceptional Children, 4*(5), 1–10.

Cobb, B., Hasazi, S., Collins, M., & Salembier, G. (1988). Preparing school-based employment specialists. *Teacher Education & Special Education, 11*, 64–71.

Cohen, P. A., Kulik, J. A., & Kulik, C. C. (1982). Educational outcomes of tutoring. *American Educational Research Journal, 19*, 237–248.

Costa, A. (1985). Developing minds: *A research book for teaching thinking.* Alexandria, VA: Association for Supervision & Curriculum Development.

Cummings, C. (1985). *Peering in on peers.* Edmonds, WA: Snohomish Publishing Co.

Curwin, R., & Mendler, A. (1988). *Discipline with dignity.* Alexandria, VA: Association for Supervision & Curriculum Development.

Deno, S. L. (1985). Curriculum-based measurement: The emerging alternative. *Exceptional Children, 52*, 219–232.

Deno, S. L., & Mirkin, P. K. (1977). *Data-based program modification: A manual*. Reston, VA: Council for Exceptional Children.

Falvey, M., Coots, J., & Bishop, K. (1990). Developing a caring community to support volunteer programs. In W. Stainback & S. Stainback (Eds.), *Support networks for inclusive schooling: Interdependent integrated education*. Baltimore: Paul H. Brookes Publishing Co.

Forest, M. (1988). Full inclusion is possible. *IMPACT, 1*, 3–4.

Forest, M., & Lusthaus, E. (1989). Promoting educational equality for all students: Circles and maps. In S. Stainback, W. Stainback, & M. Forest (Eds.), *Educating all students in the mainstream of regular education* (pp. 43–57). Baltimore: Paul H. Brookes Publishing Co.

Fox, T., & Williams, W. (1990, October). *Quarterly progress report. State-wide systems change: Vermont model for statewide delivery of quality comprehensive special education and related services to severely handicapped children*. Burlington: University of Vermont, Center for Developmental Disabilities.

Gartner, A., & Lipsky, D. (1990). Students as instructional agents. In W. Stainback & S. Stainback (Eds.), *Support networks for inclusive schooling: Interdependent integrated education* (pp. 81–93). Baltimore: Paul H. Brookes Publishing Co.

Giangreco, M. F. (1990, June). Including students with disabilities in regular classes through creative problem-solving. *I-Team News*. (Available from Center for Development Disabilities, University of Vermont, Burlington, VT)

Giangreco, M. F., Cloninger, C. J., & Iverson, V. S. (1990). *C.O.A.C.H.—Caguga-Onondaga assessment for children with handicaps* (6th ed.) Stillwater: Oklahoma State University, National Clearing House of Rehabilitative Training Materials.

Giangreco, M. F., Cloninger, C. J., Mueller, P., Yuan, S., & Ashworth, S. (1991). Perspectives of parents whose children have dual sensory impairments. *The Journal of the Association for Persons with Severe Handicaps, 16*(2), 14–24.

Giangreco, M. F., & Meyer, L. H. (1988). Expanding service delivery options in regular schools and classes for students with disabilities. In J. L. Graden, J. E. Zins, & M. J. Curtis (Eds.), *Alternative educational delivery systems: Enhancing instructional options for all students* (pp. 241–267). Washington, DC: National Association of School Psychologists.

Giangreco, M. F., & Putnam, J. (1991). Supporting the education of students with severe disabilities in regular education environments. In L. H. Meyer, C. Peck, & L. Brown (Eds.), *Critical issues in the lives of persons with severe disabilities* (pp. 245-270). Baltimore: Paul H. Brookes Publishing Co.

Glasser, W. (1986). *Control theory in the classroom*. New York: Harper and Row.

Glatthorn, A. (1987). How do you adapt the curriculum to respond to individual differences? In A. Glatthorn, *Curriculum renewal* (pp. 99–109). Alexandria, VA: Association for Supervision & Curriculum Development.

Good, T. L., & Brophy, J. E. (1987). *Looking into classrooms* (4th ed.). New York: Harper and Row.

Guskey, T. (1985). *Implementing mastery learning*. Belmont, CA: Wadsworth Publishing Co.

Harrington, R. G., & Mitchelson, D. (1987, Winter). Special education paraprofessionals: How effective are they? *New Directions*, 3–4.

Hasazi, S. B., & Clark, G. M. (1988). Vocational preparation for high school students labeled mentally retarded: Employment as a graduation goal. *Mental Retardation, 26*, 343–349.

Hasazi, S., Gordon, L., & Roe, C. (1985). Factors associated with the employment status of handicapped youth exiting high school from 1979 to 1983. *Exceptional Children, 51*, 455–469.

Hazel, J., Schumaker, J., Sherman, J., & Sheldon-Wildgen, J. (1981). *Asset: A social skills program for adolescents*. Champaign, IL: Research Press.

Heerman, B. (1988). *Teaching and learning with computers*. San Francisco: Jossey-Bass Publishers.

Holmes Group, The. (1990). *Tomorrow's schools: Principles for the design of professional development schools*. East Lansing, MI: Author.

Howell, K. W., & Morehead, M. K. (1987). *Curriculum-based evaluation for special and remedial education*. Columbus, OH: Charles E. Merrill.

Hunter, M. (1982). *Mastery teaching*. El Segundo, CA: TIP Publications.

Idol, L., Nevin, A., & Paolucci-Whitcomb, P. (1986). *Models of curriculum-based assessment*. Rockville, MD: Aspen Publishers.

Idol, L., Paolucci-Whitcomb, P., & Nevin, A. (1986). *Collaborative consultation*. Austin, TX: Pro-Ed.

Iverson, V. S., & Cloninger, C. J. (1990). *Vermont integration planning process—V.I.P.P.*, Burlington: University of Vermont, Center for Developmental Disabilities.

Jenkins, J., Pious, C., & Jewell, M. (1990). Special education and the regular education initiative: Basic assumptions. *Exceptional Children, 56*, 479–491.

Johnson, D. W., & Johnson, R. T. (1987a). *Learning together and alone: Cooperation, competition, and individualization* (2d ed.). Englewood Cliffs, NJ: Prentice-Hall.

Johnson, D. W., & Johnson, R. T. (1987b). *A meta-analysis of cooperative, competitive and individualistic goal structures.* Hillsdale, NJ: Lawrence Erlbaum.

Johnson, D. W., Johnson, R. T., Holubec, E., & Roy, P. (1984). *Circles of learning.* Arlington, VA: Association for Supervision & Curriculum Development.

Joyce, B., & Showers, B. (1980). Improving inservice training: The messages of research. *Educational Leadership, 37*, 379–385.

Joyce, B., & Showers, B. (1988). *Student achievement through staff development.* New York: Longman Publishing Co.

Knight, M. F., Meyers, H. W., Paolucci-Whitcomb, P., Hasazi, S. E., & Nevin, A. (1981). A four year evaluation of consulting teacher services. *Behavior Disorders, 6*, (2), 92–100.

Lindeman, D., & Beegle, G. (1988) Preservice teacher training and use of the classroom paraprofessional—A national survey. *Teacher Education & Special Education, 11*, 183–186.

Lipsky, D. K., & Gartner, A. (1989). *Beyond separate education—Quality education for all.* Baltimore: Paul H. Brookes Publishing Co.

Lyon, G. R., Vaassen, M., & Toomey, F. (1989). Teachers' perceptions of their undergraduate and graduate preparation. *Teacher Education & Special Education, 12*, 164–169.

Madden, N. A., & Slavin, R. E. (1987). *Effective pull-out programs for students at risk.* Baltimore: Johns Hopkins University, Center for Research on Elementary and Middle Schools.

Maheady, L., Sacca, M. K., & Harper, G. F. (1988). Classwide peer tutoring with mildly handicapped high school students. *Exceptional Children, 55*, 52–59.

McKenzie, H. S. (1972). Special education and consulting teachers. In F. Clark, D. Evans, & L. Hammerlynk (Eds.), *Implementing behavioral programs for schools* (pp. 103–125). Champaign, IL: Research Press.

McKenzie, H., Egner, A., Knight, M., Perelman, P., Schneider, B., & Garvin, J. (1970). Training consulting teachers to assist elementary teachers in the management and education of handicapped children. *Exceptional Children, 37*, 137–143.

McKenzie, H., Hill, M., Sousie, S., York, R., & Baker, K. (1977). Special education training to facilitate rural, community-based programs for the severely handicapped. In E. Sontag (Ed.), *Educational programming for the severely and profoundly handicapped* (pp. 96–108). Reston, VA: Division on Mental Retardation, Council for Exceptional Children.

Meyer, L., & Janney, R. (1989). User-friendly measures of meaningful outcomes: Evaluating behaviors interventions. *The Journal of The Association for Persons with Severe Handicaps, 14*, 263–270.

Mintzes, S. S. (1985). Education's stepchildren: The role of paraprofessionals in special education. *New Directions, 6*, pp. 1–2.

Mithaug, D. E., Horiuchi, C. N., & Fanning, P. N. (1985). A report of the Colorado statewide follow-up survey of special education students. *Exceptional Children, 51*, 397–404.

Nevin, A., Thousand, J., Paolucci-Whitcomb, P., & Villa, R. (1990). Collaborative consultation: Empowering public school personnel to provide heterogeneous schooling for all. *Journal of Educational & Psychological Consultation, 1*(1), 41–67.

O'Connor, K. (1990, June 29). Special kids joining peers in the classroom. *Rutland Herald, 34*(156), 1,4.

Parnes, S. J. (1981). *The magic of your mind.* Buffalo, NY: Creative Education Foundation, Inc. in association with Bearly Limited.

Parnes, S. J. (1988). *Visioning: State-of-the-art processes for encouraging innovative excellence.* East Aurora, NY: D. O. K. Publishers.

Patterson, J., Purkey, S., & Parker, J. (1986). *Productive school systems for a nonrational world.* Alexandria, VA: Association for Supervision & Curriculum Development.

Pierce, M. M., Stahlbrand, K., & Armstrong, S. B. (1984). *Increasing student productivity through peer tutoring programs.* Austin, TX: Pro-Ed.

Porter, G. (Producer). (1988). *A chance to belong* [Videotape]. Downsview, Ontario: Canadian Association for Community Living.

Sailor, W. (1989). The education, social vocation integration of students with the most severe disabilities. In D. Lipsky & Gartner (Eds.), *Beyond separate education: Quality education for all* (pp. 53–75). Baltimore: Paul H. Brookes Publishing Co.

Sarason, S. (1982). *The culture of the school and the problem of change.* Boston: Allyn and Bacon.

Sarason, S., Levine, M., Godenberg, I. I., Cherlin, D., & Bennet, E. (1966). *Psychology in community settings: Clinical, educational, vocational and social aspects.* New York: John Wiley & Sons.

Schattman, R. (1988). Integrated education and organizational change. *IMPACT, 1,* 8–9.

Shapiro, E. S. (1987). *Behavioral assessment in school psychology.* Hillsdale, NJ: Lawrence Erlbaum Associates.

Shriner, J., Ysseldyke, J., & Christenson, S. (1989). Assessment procedures for use in heterogeneous classrooms. In S. Stainback, W. Stainback, & M. Forest (Eds.), *Educating all students in the mainstream of regular education* (pp. 159–181). Baltimore: Paul H. Brookes Publishing Co.

Skrtic, T. (1987). The national inquiry into the future of education for students with special needs. *Counterpoint, 4*(7), 6.

Skrtic, T. (1988). The crisis in special education knowledge. In E. Meyen & T. Skrtic (Eds.), *Exceptional children and youth: An introduction* (3d ed.) (pp. 415–448). Denver: Love.

Slavin, R. E. (1983). *Cooperative learning.* New York: Longman.

Slavin, R. E. (1984). Review of cooperative learning research. *Review of Educational Research, 50,* 315–342.

Slavin, R. E. (1987). Ability grouping and student achievement in elementary school: A best-evidence synthesis. *Review of Educational Research, 57,* 293–336.

Smith, C. (in press). What's in a word? *Teacher Education and Special Education.*

Stainback, S., & Stainback, W. (1989). Facilitating merger through personnel preparation. In S. Stainback, W. Stainback, & M. Forest (Eds.), *Educating all students in the mainstream of regular education* (pp. 139–150). Baltimore: Paul H. Brookes Publishing Co.

Stainback, S., & Stainback, W. (1990a). Inclusive schooling. In W. Stainback & S. Stainback (Eds.), *Support networks for inclusive schooling: interdependent integrated education* (pp. 3–24). Baltimore: Paul H. Brookes Publishing Co.

Stainback, S., & Stainback, W. (1990b). Inclusive schooling. In W. Stainback & S. Stainback (Eds.), *Support networks for inclusive schooling: Interdependent integrated education* (pp. 25–36). Baltimore: Paul H. Brookes Publishing Co.

Stainback, S., & Stainback, W. (in press). *Teaching in the inclusive classroom: Curriculum design, adaptation, and delivery.* Baltimore: Paul H. Brookes Publishing Co.

Stainback, S., Stainback, W., & Forest, M. (1989). *Educating all students in the mainstream of regular education.* Baltimore: Paul H. Brookes Publishing Co.

Stainback, W., & Stainback, S. (1984). A rationale for the merger of special and regular education. *Exceptional Children, 51,* 102–111.

Stainback, W., & Stainback, S. (1989). Practical organizational strategies. In S. Stainback, W. Stainback, & M. Forest (Eds.), *Educating all students in the mainstream of regular education.* Baltimore: Paul H. Brookes Publishing Co.

Stainback, W., & Stainback, S. (1990a). *Support networks for inclusive schooling: Interdependent integrated education.* Baltimore: Paul H. Brookes Publishing Co.

Stainback, W., & Stainback, S. (1990b). The support facilitator at work. In W. Stainback & S. Stainback (Eds.), *Support networks for inclusive schooling: Interdependent integrated education* (pp. 37–48). Baltimore: Paul H. Brookes Publishing Co.

Thousand, J. (1990). Organizational perspectives on teacher education and renewal: A conversation with Tom Skrtic. *Teacher Education & Special Education, 13,* 30–35.

Thousand, J., Fox, T., Reid, R., Godek, J., Williams, W., & Fox, W. (1986). *The homecoming model: Educating students who present intensive educational challenges within regular education environments* (Monograph No. 7–1). Burlington: University of Vermont, Center for Developmental Disabilities.

Thousand, J., & Fox, W. (1989). *Certificate of advanced study program: Preparing post-masters level specialists to support local school placement for students with moderate and severe handicaps within rural Vermont.* (Available from Jacqueline Thousand, Center for Developmental Disabilities, 499C Waterman Bldg. University of Vermont, Burlington, VT 05452)

Thousand, J., Nevin, A., & Fox, W. (1987). Inservice training to support the education of learners with severe handicaps in their local public schools. *Teacher Education & Special Education, 10*(1), 4–13.

Thousand, J., & Villa, R. (1989). Enhancing success in heterogeneous schools. In S. Stainback, W. Stainback, & M. Forest (Eds.), *Educating all students in the mainstream* (pp. 89–103). Baltimore: Paul H. Brookes Publishing Co.

Thousand, J., & Villa, R. (1990). Sharing expertise and responsibilities through teaching teams. In W. Stainback & S. Stainback (Eds.), *Support networks for inclusive schooling: Integrated and interdependent education* (pp. 151–166). Baltimore: Paul H. Brookes Publishing Co.

Thousand, J., & Villa, R. (1992). Collaborative teams: A powerful tool in school restructuring. In R. Villa, J. Thousand, W. Stainback, & S. Stainback (Eds.), *Restructuring for caring and effective education* (pp. 73–108). Baltimore: Paul H. Brookes Publishing Co.

Thousand, J., Villa, R., & Nevin, A. (in press). *Creativity and collaborative learning: A practical guide to empowering students and teachers.* Baltimore: Paul H. Brookes Publishing Co.

Thousand, J., Villa, R., Paolucci-Whitcomb, P., & Nevin, A. (1992). A rationale for collaborative consultation. In S. Stainback & W. Stainback (Eds.), *Divergent perspectives in special education* (pp. 223–232). Boston: Allyn and Bacon.

Vasa, S. F., Steckelberg, A. L., & Ronning, L. U. (1983). *Guide for effective utilization of paraprofessionals in special education.* Lincoln: University of Nebraska-Lincoln, Department of Education.

Vermont Act 230 (1990). Vermont Department of Education, 120 State Street, Montpelier, VT 05602.

Vermont Department of Education (1990). *Vermont Education Goals.* Vermont Department of Education, 120 State Street, Montpelier, VT 05602.

Vicker, T. R. (1988). Learning from an outcomes-driven school district. *Educational Leadership, 45*(5), 52–55.

Villa, R. (1989). Model public school inservice programs: Do they exist? *Teacher Education & Special Education, 12*, 173–176.

Villa, R. & Thousand, J. (1988). Enhancing success in heterogeneous classrooms and schools: The powers of partnership. *Teacher Education & Special Education, 11*, 144–154.

Villa, R., & Thousand, J. (1990). Administrative supports to promote inclusive schooling. In W. Stainback & S. Stainback (Eds.), *Support networks for inclusive schooling: Integrated interdependent education* (pp. 201–218). Baltimore: Paul H. Brookes Publishing Co.

Villa, R., & Thousand, J. (1992). Student collaboration: The essential curriculum for the 21st century. In S. Stainback & W. Stainback (Eds.) *Adapting the regular class curriculum: Enhancing student success in inclusive classrooms.* Boston: Allyn and Bacon.

Villa, R., Thousand, J., Stainback, W., & Stainback, S. (1992). *Restructuring for caring and effective education: An administrator's guide to creating heterogeneous schools.* Baltimore: Paul H. Brookes Publishing Co.

Wang, M. (1989). Accommodating student diversity through adaptive instruction. In S. Stainback, W. Stainback, & M. Forest (Eds.), *Educating all students in the mainstream of regular education* (pp. 183–197). Baltimore: Paul H. Brookes Publishing Co.

Wang, M. C., Reynolds, M. C., & Walberg, H. J. (1988). Integrating children of the second system. *Phi Delta Kappan, 70*, 248–251.

Wehman, P., Kregel, J., & Seyfarth, J. (1985). Transition from school to work for individuals with severe handicaps: A follow-up study. *Journal of the Association for Persons with Severe Disabilities, 10*, 132–139.

Will, M. (1986). *Educating students with learning problems, a shared responsibility: A report to the Secretary.* Washington, DC: U.S. Department of Education. Office of Special Education and Rehabilitative Services.

Williams, W., Fox, T., Thousand, J., & Fox, W. (1990). Levels of acceptance and implementation of best practices in the education of students with severe handicaps. *Education & Treatment in Mental Retardation, 25*, 120–131.

Williams, W., Fox, W., Christie, L., Thousand, J., Conn-Powers, M., Carmichael, L. Vogelsberg, T., & Hull, M. (1986). Community integration in Vermont: Evolution and revolution. *Journal of the Association for the Severely Handicapped, 11*, 294–299.

Williams, W., Villa, R., Thousand, J., & Fox, W. (1990). Is regular class placement really the issue? A response to Brown, Long, Udvari-Solner, Schwartz, Van Denventer, Ahlgren, Johnson, Grunewald, & Jorgensen. *Journal of the Association for Persons with Severe Handicaps, 14*, 333–334.

York, J., & Vandercook, T. (1989). *Strategies for achieving an integrated education for middle school aged learners with severe disabilities.* Minneapolis: Institution on Community Integration.

Ysseldyke, J. E., & Christenson, S. L. (1987). *The instructional environment scale.* Austin: Pro-Ed.

Jacqueline Thousand is an assistant professor at the Center for Developmental Disabilities of the University of Vermont, Burlington. Richard Villa is the director of Instructional Services and Staff Development for the Winooski (Vermont) School District.

15

One of the topics of hottest interest in the 1990s will be schools' responses to children with complex health needs. Although these students have not been defined systematically, all schools recognize they are receiving more children whose education goes beyond instruction alone. They include children with HIV and those who need special feeding or medical support. Lehr gives suggestions for providing an appropriate education for these students.

Providing Education to Students with Complex Health Care Needs

Donna H. Lehr

Ever since enactment of the Education for All Handicapped Children Act (PL 94-142) in 1975, school districts have been opening their doors to students who pose greater and greater challenges to their teachers and administrators. The newest challenge is that of providing education to students with complex health care needs (Sirvis, 1988; Viadero, 1987). There has been a long tradition of providing education to students with chronic illnesses such as diabetes, asthma, spina bifida, sickle cell anemia, hemophilia, cystic fibrosis, and muscular dystrophy (cf. Hobbs, Perrin & Ireys, 1985; Kleinberg, 1982). But typically when those students' conditions progressed to the point that they needed health care services such as catheterization, respiratory therapy, tube feeding ventilation or oxygen, they were hospitalized or remained at home and did not attend school. The school(s) usually made adjustments for their absences or provided home or hospital instruction until their condition improved.

Now students are not automatically removed from schools for prolonged periods when they need complex health care services. After their medical conditions stabilize, students with chronic illnesses or other complex health care needs requiring specialized, skilled care, and possibly medical technology to support them, are coming to today's schools. Schools may have to take measures to ensure that serious communicable diseases are not spread within the school. The special needs student may require apnea monitoring, tube feeding, mechanical or machine suctioning, mechanical ventilation, oxygen, or other health care that is different, and often much more complex, than the schools typically have provided in the past.

Kathy, an 8-year-old student, is an example of such a child currently attending a public school. She was a healthy, normally developing child until age 2, when she wandered out of the family's summer cottage and found her way to the lake, where she nearly drowned. Kathy was in a coma for 4 weeks. Upon discharge from the hospital after regaining consciousness, Kathy was no longer able to walk, talk, or eat by herself.

Kathy has difficulty swallowing and coughing—processes necessary to deal with food and saliva present in her mouth and throat. Consequently, Kathy cannot eat food by mouth, but instead is fed through a tube that enters directly into her stomach. Because she is unable to deal with the build-up of saliva and mucus in her mouth and throat, especially when she gets a cold, those fluids must be removed frequently by use of a suctioning machine. The machine has a long tube that is inserted into her mouth, and into her throat, when necessary, to remove the excessive fluid.

EMERGENCE OF THE NEW POPULATION OF STUDENTS

Students like Kathy are present in increasing numbers in our schools. Why weren't they in the schools before? Among the reasons are technological advances in medicine, greater acceptance of the principle of normalization, an increase in programs for young children and those with severe handicaps (Lehr & Noonan, 1989), and increased group care of children with communicable diseases in schools.

Medical Technology

Improvements in medical technology have had two major consequences for students who have complex health care needs. First, children with serious health conditions are living longer than previously was possible. In the past, many children born prematurely with low birth weight, with congenital birth defects, or who acquired injuries after birth did not survive long enough to become students as they are doing now (Lehr & Noonan, 1989). Now, although they may survive, it is often with continued disabilities, sometimes very severe. The effort to save all children in distress has resulted in more students with severe handicapping conditions.

Improvements in medical technology also have resulted in the development of equipment to monitor and support these children's lives. Much of that equipment is now smaller than in the past, portable, and, in some cases, battery-operated. This enables children to be much more mobile than before. Children previously confined to places with electrical outlets can now move much more freely in their communities—attend picnics, participate in playground activities, and be transported in family cars and school buses, making attendance at school possible.

The Principle of Normalization

Changes in people's attitudes toward the care of individuals with disabilities also accounts for the increased numbers of individuals with complex health care needs in the schools. In the past, the usual practice was to segregate such individuals from the mainstream of society. Wolfensberger's (1972) principle of normalization called for the most normal environmental routines for all individuals, to obtain the most normal behaviors from the individuals. The philosophy was put into action through the deinstitutionalization movement and through the movement to place individuals with disabilities in the least restrictive placements appropriate to meet their needs. In the field of education, the principle of the least restrictive environment , set forth in PL 94–142, represents an embodiment of this philosophy. The result of all of this is that, now, efforts are being made to place all students, including those with complex health care needs, in the least restrictive, most like normal placement appropriate for each individual student.

Programs for Young Children and Those with Severe Handicaps

The third reason for the increase in numbers of students with complex health care needs in the schools is the increase in programs for very young students. PL 94–142 mandated programs for students to age 5, with incentives for students down to age 3. The 1986 amendment to that law, PL 99–457, mandates programs to age 3 in all states receiving federal funds, and further incentives for providing services to birth. Consequently, we have seen a steady increase in the number of programs serving young children with handicapping conditions. This young population of children has been the beneficiary of the improved medical technology, and consequently the children who survive with their birth defects but not without continued disabilities or complex health care needs.

PL 94–142 also requires school districts to serve all students including those with the most severe handicaps. This is the population of students that we see in the greatest number of those with accompanying medical needs (Hotte, Monroe, Philbrook, & Scarlata, 1984).

Group Care of Children with Communicable Diseases

Among children with severe handicaps are many who do not have control of body functions and require care such as feeding and toileting or diaper changing. Group care of children who do not control their body functions and who, as all young children do, explore their environment by mouthing things, increases the risks of transmitting contagious diseases unless careful attention is paid to hygienic care of students. Among the diseases of concern are the common cold, as well as more serious diseases such as cytomegalovirus, hepatitis, herpes, and a new concern, HIV infection.

Human immunodeficiency virus (HIV) was simply not known prior to 1982. Now, it is estimated that by 1992 it will be the leading cause of mental retardation and the fifth leading cause of death in children in this country. Although the disease is not transmitted through casual contact, public concern over the presence of infected students in the schools and the deadly consequences of infection require careful attention to matters regarding their inclusion in schools.

DEFINITIONS

"Students with complex health care needs" is a term I use to describe a specific, yet heterogeneous population of students. This term may include students who are labeled in the literature as (a) having chronic illnesses, (b) being technology-dependent, or (c) being medically fragile. The term goes beyond that, however, to encompass students whose needs require delivery of education and related services in new ways, different from those traditionally provided in the schools. Use of the term is, I hope, temporary, as service delivery, after a time, is expected to become more usual and not as complex. This is not to say that meeting these students' needs will become easy but, instead, that the issues and practices will become less complex to those involved.

Definitions exist for each of the subgroups comprising this population. Children with chronic illnesses may have "conditions such as burns; trauma from physical injuries that are long standing, such as spinal cord injuries or closed head trauma; and conditions more classically defined as chronic illnesses, such as asthma, diabetes, cystic fibrosis and cancer" (Kleinberg, 1982, p. 4). They may have "a set of conditions that affects one or more body organs and represents an active disease process. It may last many months or a lifetime" (p. 4).

These students have serious illnesses that may require special health care at some times and not at other times. This can be contrasted with the following definitions of technology-dependent and medically fragile children who require special health care continuously.

The U.S. Congress, Office of Technology Assessment (1987) defines a child who is technology-dependent as:

> . . . one who needs both a medical device to compensate for the loss of a vital body function and substantial and ongoing nursing care to avert death or further disability. (p. 3)

The Office of Technology Assessment report continues its explanation by identifying four populations within this group: (a) children dependent on mechanical ventilators, (b) children requiring nutrition or drugs intravenously, (c) children with the need for daily mechanical respiratory or nutritional support, and (d) children with long-term dependence on mechanical devices such as apnea monitors, renal dialysis and urinary catheters, or colostomy bags.

The Task Force on Technology Dependent Children (1988) has defined a technology-dependent child as one who:

> is a person from birth through 21 years of age; has a chronic disability; requires the routine use of a specific medical device to compensate for the loss of use of a life sustaining body function; and requires daily, ongoing care or monitoring by trained personnel. (p. vii)

The Council for Exceptional Children uses the term "medically fragile" to identify a population of students who "require specialized technological health care procedures for life support and/or health support during the school day" (1988, p. 1).

The last group of students included in this population termed "students with complex health care needs" are those students attending today's schools with serious communicable diseases. Among the diseases referred to are HIV (AIDS), herpes, and hepatitis. Although many other contagious diseases exist, these stand out because of their severe disabling consequences.

CHARACTERISTICS OF STUDENTS WITH COMPLEX HEALTH CARE NEEDS

Students with complex health care needs do not demonstrate a common set of learner characteristics. The group includes students with average or above-average intellectual abilities; but others have accompanying handicapping conditions such as mental retardation or significant neuromotor disabilities (Lehr & Noonan, 1989).

Although students with complex health care needs demonstrate tremendous variability in characteristics, they do share the following needs:

- the need to be provided with a free public educational program
- the need to be provided with an education in the least restrictive environment
- the need to have as a part of their educational program a health care plan
- the need to be treated as a child first, then a student, and not as a patient
- the need to interact with other children with and without similar health care needs.

ISSUES IN PROVIDING EDUCATION TO STUDENTS WITH COMPLEX HEALTH CARE NEEDS

Because the presence of students with complex health care needs in schools is new, many questions arise for which there are no clear answers. No federal guidelines exist, nor are there comprehensive models demonstrating the best practices. Consequently, program administrators are making difficult case-by-case decisions regarding how to serve such children (Lehr & Noonan, 1989). Issues being addressed include:

- health care procedures to be performed in schools
- responsibility for administering the procedures
- preparation for personnel to perform the procedures
- the relationship between educational and health care service provision
- student transportation.

Health Care Procedures Performed in Schools

In the past, students requiring procedures such as tube feeding or suctioning were routinely excluded from school. The zero exclusion principle and the least restrictive principle of PL 94-142 did much to change this automatic placement decision. But considerable variation continues to exist in these decisions. Children with complex health care needs are not automatically excluded from educational programs; however, their placement might be in a hospital, at home, in a segregated school, or in regular school. Some districts' policies are to serve all students with any health care needs necessary, others exclude students who require oxygen or those with communicable diseases such as HIV (AIDS), hepatitis, or herpes.

Responsibility for Administration of Procedures

Another issue is that of who has the responsibility to provide the health care procedures. Does the responsibility belong to the school district or the family, or other health agencies? If the schools have that responsibility, who in the school should perform the procedures? Issues revolve around the question of what is related service and what is a medical service, as defined in PL 94-142.

PL 94–142 specifies that a school district must provide related services including ". . . transportation, and such developmental, corrective, and other supportive services . . . as may be required to assist a handicapped child to benefit from special education" (Section 1401(a)(17)). Medical services are defined as "services provided by a licensed physician to determine a child's medically related handicapping conditions which results in the child's need for special education and related services" (34 CFR Reg 330.13(b)(4).

In *Tatro v. Texas* (1983), the U.S. Supreme Court determined that clean intermittent catheterization procedures were the responsibility of the school district as a related service necessary for the student to benefit from special education. In three other court cases revolving around the provision of health care to students, one led to a decision that the necessary procedures were related services and therefore school district responsibility (*Department of Education, State of Hawaii v. Dorr* 1983). In the other two cases, the health care procedures were considered to be more complex than those typically provided in schools and therefore not the school districts' responsibility (*Detsel* v. *Ambach*, 1986; *Bevin, H.*, 1986). Clearly, the courts are demonstrating differences of legal opinion regarding what constitutes related versus medical services in their decision making. Consequently, with the exception on the provision of clean intermittent catheterization, responsibility for other procedures is being decided by each school district.

When a decision is made that the school district is responsible for implementing procedures, the next question becomes: Who in the district is responsible? Tremendous variability exists. A student in one school district may be having his or her needs met by a school nurse, while another student, in a neighboring district, may be cared for by an instructional aide. The primary responsibility for providing school health services to students traditionally has rested on the school nurse. Nurses have the responsibility for establishing policy and procedures, with school administration, for emergency procedures, medication administration protocols, safety measures and programs, student/personnel health services, and health education (American Nurses Association, 1983). Although many health procedures have been carried out by school nurses, some of the students attending today's schools require procedures that are different and sometimes more complex than those routinely provided. One study indicates that school nurses do not believe they are adequately trained to implement many procedures required by students now attending public schools (Hester, Goodwin, & Igoe, 1980).

Further, nurses are not always available to provide the needed health care services. In many elementary schools a school nurse is assigned for as little as one half day per week. Obviously, this is an inadequate amount of time to meet the needs of a student who has to be tube-fed daily or one who requires suctioning hourly. Consequently, classroom teachers are routinely performing such procedures in their classrooms (Mulligan Ault, Guess, Struth, Thompson, 1988). Sirvis (1988) has pointed out, however, that in most cases even the most skilled special education teacher may be hesitant to provide for students with special health care needs.

Personnel Preparation for Service Provision

Even though they often do not feel adequately prepared to implement some of the procedures students require, school nurses, teachers, or aides may be responsible for implementing the procedures. Careful attention is being given to training those involved in the care of this population of students. What training should be provided? Who should provide it? Who should receive the training?

Several organizations are now emphasizing in their recommendations the need for policies regarding training to serve students with special health care needs. For example, the Task Force on Children with Special Health Care Needs in Iowa (1988) makes specific recommendations for both preservice and inservice training of all personnel involved with these children, including teachers, support staff, and even bus drivers.

Student Transportation

Transportation of students to school becomes another difficult decision for program administrators. Some students with special health care needs must come to school attached to their portable life-supporting or sustaining equipment. Some must receive immediate attention in case of medical emergency. The range encompasses students who are transported by family members, students transported by ambulance, and students transported on regular buses. Students are being transported with only the bus driver present or, at the other extreme, with a nurse present. In one case reported, a bus driver, who is alone in accompanying a student to and from school, has been trained to perform mechanical suctioning in the event it becomes necessary (Lehr & Haubrich, 1988).

Combining Education with Care

How the health care procedure will relate to education is another issue of concern. The teacher should view the child as first a child and second as a student, but not as a patient. These are *children* with health care needs. But concern about the child's health care can overshadow educational emphases.

Some students' education may relate specifically to their care needs. It may include instructional priorities related to less resistance or increased participation in their own care. Or it may relate to increased communication regarding care needs. At the same time, the students will have educational needs like those of their peers who do not have health care needs: the need to learn basic skills and knowledge; the need to learn to function as independently as possible, the need to learn to read, write, and do arithmetic. The presence of students with complex health care needs in the schools is causing educators to rethink the definition and purposes of education.

Students with communicable diseases pose some additional questions regarding the combination of education and care. Educational institutions are not accustomed to providing hygienic care for students. Until recently, self-care (toilet training) and self-feeding were prerequisites for admission into schools. Now students who lack control over their body functions are in schools, and teachers must pay careful attention to all students, but particularly to those with communicable diseases. Hygienic care procedures must become routine and unobtrusive to assure that they do not become the emphasis of, but rather a support to, the educational program.

Staff concern regarding the presence of a student with a communicable disease also may interfere with the delivery of education. The staff must be given information regarding disease transmission, methods for preventing and controlling the spread of diseases when caring for all students. In addition, maintaining confidentiality of information and proper education is essential to assure that the child's rights as a citizen are not violated.

Because no definitive federal or state rules are available regarding educational service provision to students with special health care needs (Task Force on Technology Dependent Children, 1988), services provided to those students are variable and inconsistent (Hobbs et al., 1985). Although variations in services are necessary to meet students' individual needs, these differences must be based on the needs of students, not on differences in district administrative resources or interest.

POLICIES FOR SERVING STUDENTS WITH COMPLEX HEALTH CARE NEEDS

The first step in developing consistency of services may be to develop policies. Several groups and organizations have begun to develop recommendations, guidelines, or policies to guide administrators in providing educational services to students with complex health care needs. These policies address children with special health care needs in general and communicable diseases specifically.

Children with Special Health Care Needs

The Council for Exceptional Children's Task Force on Medically Fragile Students (1988) has developed specific recommendations focused on nine basic issues:

1. Determining eligibility for special education services.
2. Providing related and noneducational services.

3. Assuring equal access to appropriate educational settings in the least restrictive environment.
4. Promoting a safe learning environment for all students and professionals.
5. Assuring that health care services are delivered by appropriately trained personnel.
6. Establishing support systems for staff, students, and families.
7. Including appropriate information about students' specialized health care needs in preservice, inservice, and continuing education programs.
8. Providing appropriate and safe transportation.
9. Promoting research that assesses current and future service delivery models.

For each of these points, suggestions are made as to how they can be addressed to assure that each student with specialized health care needs receives an appropriate education program.

A second task force coordinated by the Council for Exceptional Children has developed a document with guidelines to assist districts in determining whose responsibility it is to implement specific health care procedures in the schools (Joint Task Force for the Management of Children with Special Health Care Needs, 1990). While the document was intended to serve as a guideline, concern has been expressed by some (Lehr & Macurdy, in press; Sobsey & Cox, 1991) that the guidelines are being used as standards of practice that are based on the name of the procedure and not on the needs of the students. For example, they indicate that teachers should not feed a child with a feeding tube but could feed a student orally, despite the fact that oral feeding of some children requires more sophisticated skills than does tube feeding.

Iowa became the first state in the country to adopt a series of policy recommendations for dealing with children with special health care needs in the schools (Task Force on Children with Special Health Care Needs, 1988). These recommendations address the following needs:

1. To resolve issues relative to fiscal responsibility.
2. To involve health care professionals in IEP planning.
3. For statements by the Department of Education regarding evaluation and assessment practices and transportation needs.
4. For position papers on placement decision procedures, and service delivery issues including reevaluation, timelines, and care management responsibilities.
5. For the development of technical assistance and training for school personnel involved in the delivery of specialized health care for students.
6. The securement of model protocols and instructional materials for use by school nurses and staff responsible for providing health care to students.

Children with Communicable Diseases

Of the 59% of the 50 states and the District of Columbia responding to a 1988 survey, 70% had policies or guidelines regarding communicable disease in the schools (Lehr &

Peppey, 1988). Considerable differences, however, were observed regarding thoroughness of the guidelines or policies regarding placement, exclusion, care-providing procedures, confidentiality, and case management.

The American Academy of Pediatrics (1988) has developed policies regarding infection control of HIV (AIDS) in schools. Changes in the guidelines reflect changes in our knowledge base regarding the spread of this infectious disease. The 1986 guidelines suggested excluding from preschool settings children infected with AIDS, which has great care-providing demands. The 1988 guidelines reflect a modification of those recommendations; these cite the risk of transmission as being so remote that there is no reason for exclusion.

The Council for Exceptional Children (1989) has developed a policy statement on managing communicable and contagious diseases in the schools. The policy emphasizes the need for case-by-case decision making, education of students and staff, protection for staff, and collaboration across agencies in policy development. The CEC policy statement also emphasizes the dynamic data base, which requires frequent review and revision of any established policies. The full text is given at the end of this article.

PROGRAM PRACTICES

Although this area of educational service delivery is relatively new, a number of recommendations regarding programs practices have been developed by those currently working with this population of students. Some of these will be discussed in the following sections. Emphasis is placed on recommendations relating to program planning, the development of communication systems, the training of involved personnel, and family-centered care management.

Program Planning

All students with needs for special education programs must have individualized education programs (IEPs) under the law. The same is true for students with special education needs who have complex health care needs. For those students, however, careful attention must be paid to developing plans that include all of the following (Caldwell, Todaro & Gates, 1989):

- Methods for assuring communication between and among family, school personnel, and medical providers.
- Provisions for transition from hospital or home to school.
- Identification of resources for technical assistance.
- Health care and emergency plans.
- Provision of training and monitoring of education personnel.

An additional emphasis is that of including IEP objectives that specifically relate to students' health care needs. Objectives designed to increase students' tolerance of, participation in, or implementation of the procedures are critical. Examples of these are given at the end of this article.

The development of health care plans is also an important part of comprehensive planning. Health care plans should include information such as what is to be done, the purpose of the service, the frequency with which the procedures should be implemented, under what conditions the physician should be contacted, personnel who should be involved and the training they should receive, how the procedures should be implemented, and the equipment needed (Ferguson, 1988). Procedures to be followed in the case of an emergency must be included.

Increasing Communication

Students with complex health care needs usually receive services from a number of professionals, representing a number of disciplines, usually located at different geographical locations. For example, a student might attend school in his or her home community but be under the primary care of a pediatrician located in the nearest large city, 90 miles away. The student may be receiving physical therapy from the school district, and speech therapy from a private clinic in the home community. The students also may be receiving 6 hours of home health nursing services daily, by a nurse employed by a private home health care agency.

In this scenario, the student, in addition to being involved with care providers (natural or foster family or residential home staff), the teacher, physical therapist, and two paraprofessional aides in the school, is receiving direct services from three other professionals. With this many individuals involved, communication and coordination becomes a major concern. How can consistent approaches be developed? How can all be informed of critical information?

One person should be identified as the coordinator for information flow to and from the schools. Often this person is the parent or the school nurse or the teacher. Caldwell, Todaro, and Gates (1989) have pointed out that the parent is most often the person responsible for coordinating information between schools and medical professionals. Those authors also pointed out problems with this model when the parent's role as primary liaison is only assumed and not specifically established, which results in a lack of routine reporting and selective reporting and the parent making assumptions regarding what is important. The same problem may occur, of course, when the teacher's or nurse's role is not made explicit.

A second set of important factors leading to effective coordination relates to communication attitudes and specific skills; communication attitudes such as self-acceptance, acceptance of others, and empathy have a powerful impact on the ways in which information is exchanged (Holvoet & Helmstetter, 1989). Parents who feel that a professional is not accepting of them or their child are not likely to be open in their discussions with that individual. The consequence may be a significant barrier to the necessary exchange of information.

Specific communication skills related to listening, nonverbal communication and verbal responding are also essential to assure coordinated care (Holvoet & Helmstetter, 1989). Among the skills necessary in these areas are careful, attentive, active listening; careful interpretation of nonverbal messages; verbal responding such as paraphrasing, summarizing, and clarifying. Development and use of these skills results in increased accuracy of the information exchanged.

Whoever is responsible for communication coordination and those who participate in the communication process have the tremendous task of collecting and transmitting accurate information to assure coordinated, consistent care of children. Without this, quality care can not be realized.

Training

Personnel involved in providing educational and specialized health care services to students with complex health care needs must be properly prepared. This is essential in providing the best possible services to students and also in reducing the risks for liability. The Iowa State Department of Education (Task Force on Children with Special Health Care Needs, 1988) has recommended that preservice training programs for special education teachers include information and training related to:

- Certification in first aid and CPR.
- Physical care, general health and nutrition information, infection control, skin care, elimination and oral hygiene, common childhood diseases.
- Community resources and how to access them.
- The team approach to service provision, confidentiality, and dealing with sensitive information.
- Effective IEP writing for children with special health care needs. (p. 7).

The Iowa Department of Education also recognized the need for ongoing training for teachers currently in the field and made recommendations for periodic inservice training on topics similar to those listed.

Additional emphasis must be placed on training staff in the hygienic care of all students to prevent spread of infection and contagious diseases. Proper handwashing has been identified as the single most important procedure for preventing the spread of infections (Silkworth, 1988). Other essential procedures to learn include the cleaning of diapering surfaces, instructional materials, and eating/feeding equipment.

The need for training regarding HIV infection is critical to assure that school professionals are informed about transmission modes. Knowledge that transmission does not occur through casual contact, or through contact with saliva or feces and urine, will contribute to the acceptance of students who test positive for HIV. This knowledge also will result in school personnel using Universal Precautions in caring for all students in the school setting. Recommendations by the American Academy of Pediatrics (1988) regarding care for students with HIV infection in the schools are:

1. HIV-infected children who are old enough to attend school can be admitted freely to all activities, to the extent that their own health permits. The child's physician should have access to consultative expertise to assist in decision making.

2. As all infected children will not necessarily be known to school officials in high-prevalence areas, and because blood is a potential source of contagion, policies and procedures should be developed in advance to handle instances of bleeding. Such policies and procedures should be based upon the understanding that even within an area of high prevalence, the risk of HIV-infection resulting from a single cutaneous exposure to blood from a school-aged child or adolescent with unknown serologic status is minute. Considering such minimal risk, the only mandatory precautionary action should be washing exposed skin with soap and water. Lacerations and other bleeding lesions should be managed in a manner which minimizes direct contact of the caregiver with blood. Schools in high-prevalence areas should provide access to gloves so that individuals who would wish to further reduce a minute risk may opt for their use. Under no circumstance should the urgent care of a bleeding child be delayed because gloves are not immediately available.

Family-Centered Care

Former Surgeon General C. Everett Koop has been a significant leader in calling for community-based (as contrasted with hospital-based) systems of services for students with special health care needs and their families (Gittler, 1988). Strong in his message is the importance of the family as central in each child's life: "The family is the constant whereas the public and private agencies, organizations, institutions and individuals that provided health and other needed services for the child are transitory" (p. 5). The campaign calls for development of supports to assist families in their natural role as the primary providers for their children. It calls for the development of systems in which partnerships are formed between professionals and families in all aspects of planning and service provision (Gittler, 1988).

Throughout the country, many projects are emerging to develop the necessary supports for family-centered, community-based care. Programs are incorporating the following elements (Shelton, Jeppson, & Johnson, 1987, p. 1):

- Recognition that the family is the constant in the child's life while the service systems and personnel within those systems fluctuate.
- Facilitation of parent/professional collaboration at levels of health care.
- Sharing of unbiased and complete information with parents about their child's care on an ongoing basis in an appropriate and supportive manner.
- Implementation of appropriate policies and programs that are comprehensive and provide emotional and financial support to meet the needs of families.
- Recognition of family strengths and individuality and respect for different methods of coping.
- Understanding of and incorporating the developmental needs of infants, children, and adolescents and their families into health care delivery systems.
- Encouragement and facilitation of parent-to-parent support.
- Assurance that the design of health care delivery system is flexible, accessible, and responsive to family needs.

Only through this orientation of the child as part of a family can educators working with families and other professionals from a variety of fields develop comprehensive, effective programs of education and care for children with special health care needs.

SUMMARY

Providing educational programs in least restrictive environments to students with complex health care needs is a new challenge to public schools. Many questions about the best ways to meet these students' educational and health care needs are still unanswered. Although attention to this group of students is increasing, much additional work is necessary. Solutions to these questions and issues are not simple and cannot be solved by the schools alone. Collaborative efforts among educational and medical fields and with families are essential.

Dissemination of information and preservice and inservice training of personnel are necessary to quality programs that combine education and care. It is also necessary to prevent discrimination against students and spread of communicable diseases.

REFERENCES

American Academy of Pediatrics. (1986). School attendance of children and adolescents with Human T Lymphotropic Virus III/Lymphadenopathy—Associated Virus Infection. *Pediatrics, 77*(3), 430-432.

American Academy of Pediatrics (1988). Pediatric guidelines for infection control of HIV (AIDS) virus in hospitals, medical offices, schools, and other settings. *Pediatrics, 82*(5), 801–807.

American Nurses Association. (1983). *Standards of school nursing practice.* Kansas City, MO: American Nurses Association.

Bevin, H. In re. EHLR 508: 134, 1986.

Caldwell, T.H. (1988). *Children with special health care needs in schools.* Presentation at Conference Blue Print for Change, Council for Exceptional Children, Orlando, Florida.

Caldwell, T.H., Todaro, A.W., & Gates, A.J. (1989). Special health care needs. In J.L. Bigge, *Teaching individuals with physical and multiple disabilities.* Columbus, OH: Charles E. Merrill.

Council for Exceptional Children. (1988). *Report of the Council for Exceptional Children's ad hoc committee on medically fragile students.* Reston, VA: Council for Exceptional Children.

Council for Exceptional Children. (1989). *Policies Manual.* Reston, VA: Council for Exceptional Children.

Department of Education, State of Hawaii v. Katherine D. Dorr, 727, F. 2d 809 (9th Cir. 1983).

Detsel v. Ambach (ND NY 1986, 1985–86 EHCR D EC, 557:335).

Ferguson, H. (1988). *Getting school health services together.* Paper presented at TASH Conference, Washington, DC.

Gittler, J. (1988). *Community based service systems for children with special health care needs and their families.* Iowa City: National Maternal and Child Health Resource Center.

Hester, H.K., Goodwin, L.D., & Igoe, J.B. (1980). *The SNAP School Nurse Survey: Summary of procedures and results.* Project #1846002597A1. Washington, DC: U.S. Department of Maternal and Child Health.

Hobbs, N., Perrin, J.M., & Ireys, H.T. (1985). *Chronically ill children and their families.* San Francisco: Jossey-Bass Publishers.

Holvoet, J.F., & Helmstetter, E. (1989). *Medical problems of students with special needs: A guide for educators.* Boston: Little, Brown.

Hotte, E.A., Monroe, H.S., Philbrook, D.L. & Scarlata, R.W. (1984). Programming for persons with profound retardation: A three year retrospective study. *Mental Retardation, 22*(2), 75–78.

Joint Task Force for the Management of Children with Special Health Care Needs. (1990). *Guidelines for the delineation of roles and responsibilities for the safe delivery of specialized health care in the educational setting.* Reston, VA: Council for Exceptional Children.

Kleinberg, S.B. (1982). *Educating the chronically ill child.* Baltimore: Aspen Publications.

Lehr, D.H., & Haubrich, P. (1988). [Service Delivery Models for Students with Special Health Care Needs.] Unpublished raw data. University of Wisconsin–Milwaukee.

Lehr, D. H. & Macurdy, S. (in press). Special health care needs. In M. Agran, N. Marchand-Martella, & R. Martella (Eds.), *Health and safety for persons with disabilities: Applications across community settings.* Baltimore: Paul H. Brookes.

Lehr, D.H., & Noonan, M.J. (1989). Issues in the education of students with complex health care needs. In F. Brown & D.H. Lehr (Eds.), *Persons with profound disabilities: Issues and practices.* Baltimore: Paul H. Brookes Publishing.

Lehr, D.H., & Peppey, K. (1988). [Review of Communicable Disease Policies of State Departments of Education]. Unpublished raw data. University of Wisconsin–Milwaukee.

Mulligan Ault, M., Guess, D., Struth, L. & Thompson, B. (1988). The implementation of health related procedures for classrooms for students with severe multiple impairments. *TASH, 13*(2), 100–109.

Shelton, T.L., Jeppson, E.S., & Johnson, B.H. (1987). *Family-centered care for children with special health care needs.* Washington, DC: Association for the Care of Children's Health.

Silkworth, C.S. (1988). Handwashing techniques. In G. Larson (Ed.), *Managing the school-age child with a chronic health condition* (pp. 141-145). Wayzata, MN: DCI Publishing.

Sirvis, B. (1988). Students with special health care needs. *Teaching Exceptional Children, 20*(4), 40–44.

Sobsey, D., & Cox, A. W. (1991). Integrating health care and educational programs. In F. P. Orelove & D. Sobsey (Eds.), *Educating children with multiple disabilities* (pp. 155–186). Baltimore: Paul H. Brookes.

Task Force on Children with Special Health Care Needs. (1988). *Recommendations: Services for children with special health care needs.* Des Moines: Iowa Department of Education.

Task Force on Technology Dependent Children. (1988). *Fostering home and community-based care for technology dependent children.* Washington, DC: U.S. Department of Health and Human Services.

Tatro v. Texas, 625 F. 2d 557 (5th Cir. 1980), 703 F. 2d 823 (5th cir. 1983).

Tolsma, D. (1988). Activities of Centers for Disease Control in AIDS education. *Journal of School Health, 58*(4), 133–136.

U.S. Congress, Office of Technology Assessment. (1987). *Technology dependent children: Hospital vs. home care—A technical memorandum.* (TA-TM-H-38). Washington, DC: U.S. Government Printing Office.

Viadero, D. (1987). Medically fragile students pose dilemma for school officials. *Education Week, 1,* 14.

Wolfensberger, W. (1972). *Normalization: The principle of normalization in human services.* Toronto: Canada: National Institute on Mental Retardation.

TRAINING AND RESOURCE MATERIAL

Larson, G. (Ed.). (1988). *Managing the school age child with a chronic health condition.* Wayzata, MN: DCI Publishing. A book designed for all personnel in the schools who work with students with chronic health conditions; includes practical how-to-do information on planning and implementing health care procedures.

California State Department of Education. (1980). *Guidelines and procedures for meeting the specialized physical health care needs of students.* Sacramento: author. A manual including specific information on how to implement specialized health care procedures in the schools.

Graff, J., Mulligan Ault, M., Guess, D., Taylor, M., & Thompson, B. (1990). *Health Care for Students with Disabilities.* Baltimore: Paul Brookes. A manual to provide teachers with relevant information regarding health-related procedures their students receive.

Haynie, M., Porter, S., & Palfrey, J. (1989) *Children assisted by medical technology in educational setttings: Guidelines for care.* Boston: Children's Hospital.

VIDEO TRAINING TAPES*

CPR and Emergency Choking Procedures for Infants or Young Children. Introduces and reviews procedures to prevent and provide emergency treatment. 37 mins.

Clean Intermittent Catheterization. Includes information regarding benefits of, and procedures for performing, CIC, as well as how to instruct others. 25 mins.

Home Oxygen for Infants and Young Children. Demonstrates use of three commonly used home oxygen systems emphasizing precautions for use. 30 mins.

Home Tracheostomy Care for Infants and Young Children. Reviews physiology of infant airways and procedure for caring for the child with a trach tube. 40 mins.

Infection Control in Child Care Settings. Addresses necessary concerns regarding prevention of spread of contagious diseases in group care settings and provides instruction on effective control techniques. 30 mins.

*Available from Learner Managed Designs, 2201 K West 25th St., Lawrence, KS 66046.

Donna Lehr is an associate professor in the Department of Special Education at Boston University. This article is an adaptation of D.H. Lehr (1990), "Students with Complex Health Care Needs in Today's Schools," in E.L. Meyen (Ed.), Exceptional Children in Today's Schools, *Denver: Love Publishing.*

The Council for Exceptional Children's
Policy Statement on *Managing Communicable and Contagious Deseases*

Controlling the spread of communicable and contagious diseases within the schools has always been a problem faced by educators, the medical profession, and the public. Effective policies and procedures for managing such diseases in the schools have historically been developed by health agencies and implemented by the schools. These policies and procedures were primarily designed to manage acute, temporary conditions rather than chronic conditions which require continuous monitoring and remove children from interaction with other children while the condition is contagious or communicable.

The increased prevalence of chronic communicable diseases such as hepatitis B, cytomegalovirus, herpes simplex virus, and acquired immune deficiency syndrome have raised public and professional concern, necessitating the reassessment of existing school policies and procedures. The Council believes that having a communicable/contagious disease does not in itself result in a need for special education. Further, the Council believes that in developing appropriate policies for managing communicable diseases, schools and public health agencies should assure that any such policies and procedures:

a. Do not exclude the affected child from the receipt of an appropriate education even when circumstances require the temporary removal of the child from contact with other children.

b. Provide that determination of a nontemporary alteration of a child's educational placement should be done on an individual basis, utilizing an interdisciplinary/interagency approach including the child's physician, public health personnel, the child's parents, and appropriate educational personnel.

c. Provide that decision involving exceptional children's nontemporary alterations of educational placements or services constitute a change in the child's Individualized Education Program and should thus follow the procedures and protections required.

d. Recognize that children vary in the degree and manner in which they come into contact with other children and school staff.

e. Provide education staff with the necessary information, training, and hygienic resources to provide for a safe environment for students and educational staff.

f. Provide students with appropriate education about communicable diseases and hygienic measures to prevent the spread of such diseases.

g. Provide, where appropriate, carrier children with education about the additional control measures that they can practice to prevent the transmission of the disease.

h. Enable educational personnel who are medically at high risk in regard to certain diseases to work in environments which minimize such risk.

i. Provide educational personnel with adequate protections for such personnel and their families if they are exposed to such diseases through their employment.

The Council believes that special education personnel preparation programs should:

a. Educate students about communicable and contagious diseases and appropriate methods for their management.

b. Counsel students as to how to determine their level of medical risk in relation to certain diseases and the implications of such risk to career choice.

The Council believes that the manner in which policies for managing communicable and contagious diseases are developed and disseminated is critically important to their effective implementation. Therefore, the following must be considered integral to any such process:

a. That they be developed through the collaborative efforts of health and education agencies at the state, provincial, and local levels, reflecting state, provincial, and local educational, health, and legal requirements.

b. That provision is made for frequent review and revision to reflect the ever-increasing knowledge being produced through research, case data reports, and experience.

c. That policies developed be based on reliable identified sources of information and principles endorsed by the medical and educational professions.

d. That such policies be written in content and format to be understandable to a variety of consumers including students, professionals, and the public.

e. That policy development and dissemination be a continual process and disassociated from pressure associated with precipitating events.

Source: Council for Exceptional Children, 1989, Policies Manual, Reston, VA: Council for Exceptional Children. Reprinted by permission.

Catheterization: Individual Education Plan (IEP) Recommendations

Level 1 - Total Dependence

Goal: (Self-Help) Maintain healthy urinary status by tolerating catheterization in a cooperative manner.

Objectives:
- The student's family will provide, on a daily basis, the equipment necessary for catheterization, 100% of time.
- The student will remain still in a lying position while the assistant performs catheterization in school at 8:00 a.m. and 12:00 noon, 100% of the time.
- The student will assist in assuming the correct position for catheterization when the assistant indicates it is time for the procedure, 90% of the time.

Level 2 - Direction of Care

Goal: (Self-Help) Maintain healthy urinary status and obtain maximum level of independence by learning how to direct care.

Objectives:
- The student's family will provide, on a daily basis, the equipment necessary for catheterization, 100% of time.
- The student will identify equipment needed for catheterization 4 out of 5 trials.
- The student will be able to verbalize "What comes next?" 4 out of 5 trials.
- The student will be able to independently (verbally) direct the step-by-step prescribed procedure to include the collection of materials, cleaning, catheterization, and then clean-up, 4 out of 5 trials.
- The student will be able to state warning signs and symptoms of problems related to catheterization and answer related, "What if?" questions, 4 out of 5 trials.

Level 3 - Independent Completion of Catheterization

Goal: (Self-Help) Maintain healthy urinary status through the independent completion of catheterization.

Objectives:
- The student's family will provide, on a daily basis, the equipment necessary for catheterization, 100% of time.
- The student will identify equipment needed for catheterization 4 out of 5 trials.

- The student will be able to answer questions about the procedure (i.e., "What comes next?") 4 out of 5 trials.
- The student will be able to independently (verbally) direct the step-by-step prescribed procedure for the collection of materials, cleaning, catheterization, and then clean-up, 4 out of 5 trials.
- The student will be able to independently gather equipment for the procedure, 4 out of 5 trials.
- The student will be able to demonstrate on a doll the step-by-step procedure for cleaning hands and genital area, 4 out of 5 trials. Note: This may be accomplished through the purchase of an inexpensive doll with a hole cut in the genital area.
- The student will be able to answer question, "Why are you cleaning your hands? . . . your genital area?", 4 out of 5 trials.
- The student will be able to demonstrate placement of catheter in the doll, 4 out of 5 trials.
- The student will be able to set up for self-catheterization and clean self following the prescribed step-by-step procedure, 4 out of 5 trials.

Male
- The student will be able to hold his penis in the correct position, clean himself and identify opening, insert the catheter, and follow the prescribed step-by-step procedure, 4 out of 5 trials.

Female
- The student will be able to open her labia, clean herself, and identify the urethra, insert the catheter, and follow the prescribed step-by-step procedure, 4 out of 5 trials.
- The student will be able to independently complete self-catheterization according to the prescribed step-by-step procedure, 10 out of 10 trials.
- The student will be able to state warning signs and symptoms of problems related to catheterization and answer related "What if?" questions, 4 out of 5 trials.
- The student will be able to independently complete self-catheterization according to the prescribed step-by-step procedure during monthly observation.

Source: T. Caldwell, 1988, *Children with Special Health Care Needs in School* (presentation at Conference Blue Print for Change, Council for Exceptional Children, Orlando, Florida). Reprinted by permission.

16

Depression in children and adolescents has become a phenomenon that school personnel must face. Maag and Forness outline the process for identifying, assessing, and treating this condition in children. Their position is that educators not only must be informed, but they also must be willing to take action. The authors describe the research regarding the effectiveness of social skill training and cognitive-behavioral programs that educators can employ with students with depression.

Depression in Children and Adolescents: Identification, Assessment, and Treatment

John W. Maag and Steven R. Forness

Depression in children and adolescents is a mood (affective) disorder whose magnitude and clinical importance has only recently permeated the concern of educators. Once considered exclusively the domain of psychiatrists, depression can and should be considered by school personnel in identification, assessment, and treatment (Reynolds, 1984). Unfortunately, professionals in special education have been slow to recognize that depression affects a wide range of school-related functioning (Maag & Rutherford, 1987, 1988). A survey by 47 nationally recognized experts in education of the behaviorally disordered, for instance, did not even mention depression as an important research issue in the field (Epstein & Cullinan, 1984). Youngsters with behavioral disorders are not the only handicapped group at risk for developing depression. Depression has been identified in children and adolescents with mild mental retardation, learning disabilities, and speech and language disorders (e.g., Cantwell & Baker, 1982; Reynolds & Miller, 1985; Stevenson & Romney, 1984).

Depression may be overlooked as a potentially important area of concern in special education, in part, because of its colloquial presence and associated ambiguity (Kendall, Hollon, Beck, Hammen, & Ingram, 1987). At one end of the spectrum, depression is a commonly used term to denote "feeling a little bummed out." At the other end of the spectrum, depression refers to a clinical syndrome or disorder. Kazdin (1990) provides the following distinction:

> As a *symptom*, depression refers to sad affect and as such is a common experience of every-day life. As a *syndrome* or *disorder*, depression refers to a group of symptoms that go together. Sadness may be part of a larger set of problems that include the loss of interest in activities, feelings of worthlessness, sleep disturbances, changes in appetite and others. (p. 121)

These distinctions are more than a matter of semantics—different definitions and uses of the label "depression" have important implications (Kendall et al., 1987). The syndrome of depression can be present, in secondary ways, in other disorders. For example, a schizophrenic individual may manifest depressive symptomatology without meeting diagnostic criteria for major mood disorder (American Psychiatric Association, 1987).

In this article we are providing only a brief overview of the current status of knowledge in the area of child and adolescent depression. For in-depth reviews, see Dolgan (1990), Kazdin (1990), and Reynolds (1985). We describe diagnostic criteria and identification procedures as well as assessment methodology and intervention strategies. The focus is on depression in handicapped populations in school settings and the implications for special educators.

CURRENT PERSPECTIVES

For many years, controversy has surrounded the nature of depression in children and adolescents (Kaslow & Rehm, 1991). For example, conventional psychoanalytic doctrine postulates that depression cannot exist until the onset of adolescence and the development of the superego (Rie, 1966; Rochlin, 1959). A popular view during the 1970s reflected the belief that depression in children was "masked" and must be inferred from underlying behaviors such as hyperactivity, aggression, irritability, delinquency, and poor school performance, to name a few (e.g., Cytryn & McKnew, 1974; Malmquist, 1977). Lefkowitz and Burton (1978) suggested that depression represents a transitory developmental phenomenon which abates spontaneously without intervention; and Seifer, Nurcombe, Scioli, and Grapentine (1989) currently suggest that depression is but one symptom usually found in a pattern of other symptoms that seem to cluster together in children.

The current consensus among researchers and clinicians, however, is that depression in children and adolescents parallels that found in adults. Consequently, the diagnostic criteria for diagnosis of depression in adults also is appropriate and applicable to children and adolescents (Carlson & Cantwell, 1980; Chambers et al., 1985; Chiles, Miller, & Cox, 1980; Kashani, Barbero, & Bolander, 1981; Mitchell, McCauley, Burke, & Moss, 1988).

Diagnostic Criteria

The primary diagnostic system that researchers and clinicians currently use is the *Diagnostic and Statistical Manual for Mental Disorders–Revised* (DSM-III-R) (American

Psychiatric Association, 1987). The DSM-III-R criteria for all mood disorders in adulthood, including depression, are applied to children as well. Although depression is a clinical condition that can be diagnosed in children, adolescents, and adults, its specific symptoms, associated features, and clinical course can vary as a function of development (Kazdin, 1990). DSM-III-R provides a standardized nomenclature, but this system does not help to identify developmental differences. Cicchetti and Schneider-Rosen (1986) have suggested that depression becomes a problem when it interferes with social, cognitive, or emotional competencies necessary for the successful resolution of developmental tasks. A developmental perspective complements DSM-III-R criteria by providing a broader framework for understanding the nature of depression in children and adolescents (Carlson & Garber, 1986).

Depressive symptoms may be included in other types of disorders. Separation anxiety disorder, adjustment disorder with depressed mood, and uncomplicated bereavement are conditions associated with depressive symptoms such as sadness and loss of interest in usual activities. Severity, duration, and precipitants of the symptoms are major determinants of the type of depressive disorders diagnosed (Kazdin, 1990). A scheme depicting a continuum of mood disorders and selected differential problems is presented in Table 1.

Distinctions should be made between depression and dysthymia. The latter is seen as relatively less severe but recurring over a longer period, often punctuated by periods of normal mood that may last for days or even weeks. Another important distinction is between unipolar and bipolar depressive disorders. Unipolar depressive disorders consist of continuous or intermittent periods of dysphoric mood or anhedonia (inability to have fun), whereas bipolar disorders involve alternating episodes of depression and inappropriate euphoria, excessive energy, grandiosity, impulsivity, and poor judgment (Rizzo &

DSM-III-R *Criteria for Major Depressive Disorder*

At least five of the following symptoms must be present during the same 2-week period; at least one of the symptoms is either (1) depressed mood, or (2) loss of interest or pleasure.

- Depressed mood most of the day, nearly every day (either by subjective account; e.g., feels "down" or "low" or is observed by others to look sad or depressed)
- Loss of interest or pleasure in all or almost all activities nearly every day (either by subjective account or is observed by others to be apathetic)
- Significant weight loss or weight gain (when not dieting or binge-eating) (e.g., more than 5% of body weight in a month) or decrease or increase in appetite nearly every day (in children consider failure to make expected weight gains)
- Insomnia or hypersomnia nearly every day
- Psychomotor agitation or retardation nearly every day (observable by others, not merely subjective feelings of restlessness or being slowed down) (in children under 6, hypoactivity)
- Fatigue or loss of energy nearly every day
- Feelings of worthlessness or excessive or inappropriate guilt (either may be delusional) nearly every day (not merely self-reproach or guilt about being sick)
- Diminished ability to think or concentrate, or indecisiveness nearly every day (either by subjective account or observed by others)
- Thoughts that he or she would be better off dead or suicidal ideation, nearly every day; or suicide attempt

TABLE 1   Classification Scheme for Mood Disturbances

Pathology	Unipolar	Bipolar

Severe	Major depression:
	  Single episode*
	  Recurrent**
		Bipolar disorder:
		  Manic
		  Depressed
		  Mixed

Moderate	Dysthymia***	Cyclothymia***
Mild	Atypical depression	Atypical bipolar disorder

	Adjustment disorder:
	  Depressed mood
	  Withdrawal
		Adjustment disorder
		with anxious mood

Differential	Schizophrenia Schizoaffective disorder Separation anxiety	Paranoia Schizoaffective disorder
Nonpathological	Demoralization Bereavement	(no equivalent)

*Estimates are that more than 50% of individuals having a first single episode will eventually have recurrent episodes.
**Major depression, recurrent, may predispose to development of bipolar disorder.
***Dysthymia and cyclothymia may predispose to development of a major mood disorder.

Zabel, 1988). Common conditions of both differential pathological and nonpathological origin are noted in Table 1 as well; the former are those of similar severity but different pathological nature, and the latter are within the range of normal emotional responses.

Little is known about manic conditions in children, as they are believed to be rare and difficult to diagnosis in this age group (Kovacs, 1989). Criteria for major depressive disorder and dysthymia generally are necessary in the diagnosis of bipolar disorder and cyclothymia, respectively, along with specific criteria for alternating manic features. It is interesting to speculate whether the episodic nature of a bipolar disorder could render an afflicted child ineligible for special education in that he or she would fail to meet consistently the criterion of a "pervasive mood of sadness or depression" even though bipolar disorder is possibly more debilitating than depression per se (Forness, 1988).

Subtypes of Childhood and Adolescent Depression

The classification scheme illustrated in Table 1 represents a continuum of mood disorders, from the DSM-III-R, that may be present in children and adolescents. Childhood depression can further be classified into several distinct subtypes, each positing a slightly different etiological base and, therefore, having implications for identification, assessment, and treatment (Maag & Rutherford, 1988). Different subtypes of depression are presented in Table 2.

TABLE 2   Subtypes of Childhood and Adolescent Depression

Subtype	Characteristics
Anaclitic Depression	Loss of caregiver with no provision for a substitute; period of misery followed by loss of interest in environment.
Reactive Depression	Trauma or loss frequently accompanied by feelings of guilt for past failures; poor parent-child relationship is important factor.
Acute Depression	Onset occurs after some traumatic event; prognosis for recovery is good if relationship with caregiver is healthy.
Chronic Depression	Repeated separations from caregiver beginning in infancy; presence of depression in mother; no immediate precipitating event; periodic recurring emotional-depriving experiences; suicidal ideation early in childhood.
Endogenous Depression	Genetically or biochemically determined; no identifiable stressors; believed to exist, to some degree, throughout life of child; may reach psychotic or suicidal proportions.

Several important distinctions exist between each subtype. *Anaclitic depression*, also termed the "deprivation syndrome" (Spitz & Wolf, 1946), develops in an infant after loss of a caregiver and no provision of a substitute. *Reactive depression* differs from anaclitic depression in that loss of the caregiver does not invariably lead to anaclitic depression; poor parent-child relationships have the most impact on development of reactive depression (Abrahams & Whitlock, 1969). *Acute depression* develops in response to some traumatic event, such as the loss of a loved one, and the prognosis for recovery is good (Cytryn & McKnew, 1972). *Chronic depression*, in contrast, is more extreme and has no immediate precipitating events but is punctuated by repeated separations from the caregiver during early infancy. Finally, *endogenous depression* is thought to be genetic or biochemical in nature, and possibly related to learning disabilities in some children (Brumback & Stanton, 1983).

IDENTIFICATION AND ASSESSMENT

Upon examining prevalence figures of depression in children and adolescents, the importance for educators to identify this disorder becomes alarmingly apparent. The extent to which children and adolescents experience depressive symptomatology has been studied in school-based and clinical populations. Prevalence estimates usually are determined either through DSM-III diagnostic criteria or rating scales in which a score is translated into levels ranging from nondepressed to severely depressed (Reynolds, 1985). Because DSM-III focuses on clinical syndromes or symptom-clusters, prevalence estimates using this approach tend to be more conservative than those obtained for rating scales that provide only global indicators of symptom-severity. In fact, children obtaining rating scale scores in the severe range occasionally fail to meet DSM-III diagnostic criteria for depressive disorders (Kazdin, Colbus, & Rodgers, 1986).

Prevalence Estimates

Using DSM-III criteria, about 2% of school-based children (Kashani et al., 1983; Kashani & Simonds, 1979) and 10% to 20% of clinic-based children (Puig-Antich & Gittelman, 1982) have been diagnosed as depressed. When depression is identified using extreme scores on self report scales, between 2% and 17% of students attending general education school classes manifested moderate to severe levels of depressive symptomatology (Friedrich, Jacobs, & Reams, 1982; Kaplan, Hong, & Weinhold, 1984; Lefkowitz & Tesiny, 1985; Reynolds, 1983; Smucker, Craighead, Craighead, & Green, 1986; Teri, 1982a). Special education populations tend to have a much higher prevalence: Between 14% and 54% of learning disabled (LD) and seriously emotionally disturbed (SED) students manifested severe depressive symptomatology (Maag & Behrens, 1989a; Mattison et al., 1986; Stevenson & Romney, 1984).

A summary of selected prevalence studies is presented in Table 3. Only fairly recent studies employing large samples are included because they tend to be more accurate; however, considerable variability is evident, often depending on choice of diagnostic criteria and instrumentation.

TABLE 3   Selected Prevalence Findings in Childhood and Adolescent Depression

Study	Sample Type	Percent Depressed
School-Based General Education Samples		
Lefkowitz & Tesiny (1985)	3,020 3rd-, 4th-, & 5th-grade children, mean age 9.8	5.2%
Reynolds (1983)	2,874 adolescents, ages 13–18	7%
School-Based Special Education Samples		
Maag & Behrens (1989a)	465 LD and SED adolescents ages 12–18 attending resource programs	21%
Mattison et al. (1986)	109 students ages 6–18 referred for SED placement	18% (ages 6-12) 51% (ages 13-18)
Stevenson & Romney (1984)	103 LD students ages 8–13 attending resource programs	14%
Clinic-Based Samples		
Cantwell & Baker (1982)	600 children and adolescents ages 2–16 presented to a community clinic for speech and language evaluation	4%
Carlson & Cantwell (1980)	102 children and adolescents ages 7–17 presented for psychiatric evaluation to an outpatient department	58%
Colbert, Newman, Ney, & Young (1982)	282 children and adolescents ages 6–14 admitted to a child and family practice unit	54%

Another reason prevalence estimates tend to be somewhat inchoate stems in part from the failure of researchers to consider variables such as gender and age. Gender differences in prevalence of depression usually do not surface until adolescence, when more females than males experience severe symptomatology (Angold, Weissman, John, Wickramaratne, Drusoff, 1991; Kashani et al., 1983; Lefkowitz & Tesiny, 1985; Lobovits & Handal, 1985; Mezzich & Mezzich, 1979; Reinherz et al., 1989; Reynolds, 1985). Similar results have been obtained with LD and SED adolescents; females are three times more likely to report severe depressive symptomatology than their male counterparts (Maag & Behrens, 1989b).

In regard to age, except for very young children (aged 1-6), who have low rates of depression (Kashani, Cantwell, Shekim, & Reid, 1982; Kashani, Ray, & Carlson, 1984), age differences in both handicapped and nonhandicapped populations tend to be mediated by gender (e.g., Fleming & Offord, 1990; Maag & Behrens, 1989a; Rutter, 1986). Adolescents in general, however, seem to experience higher rates of depression than children do (Forness, 1988; Kazdin, 1990).

Educators' Perspectives on Depression

Given the unsettling prevalence of depression in school-based populations, educators clearly should play a strategic role in early identification. Youngsters spend more time in school than in most other structured settings outside the home, and their most consistent and extensive contact is with educators (Grob, Klein, & Eisen, 1983). Consequently, school personnel may be the first professionals to notice developing problems (Powers, 1979). To facilitate the identification process, school personnel must be knowledgeable of depression and sensitive to students who might exhibit it. Although school personnel possess some general knowledge of depression, they cleave to several misconceptions.

Maag, Rutherford, and Parks (1988) had a sample of regular education teachers, special education teachers, and school counselors complete a questionnaire assessing their ability to identify characteristics of depression. Their answers were coded into similar response categories and compared to information about depression drawn from empirical research. School counselors possessed the greatest knowledge of depression, whereas general and special educators identified only global characteristics. Of particular note, special educators tended to identify characteristics related to externalizing problems (e.g., disobedience, agression) more frequently than internalizing problems (e.g., sadness, loneliness, crying). Externalizing behaviors tend to correlate more highly to depression scores for males, and internalizing problems and negative view of self correlate more highly with depression scores for females (Smucker et al., 1986). More males than females typically receive special education services, so the belief in masked depression should not be resurrected.

In a similar study, Clarizio and Payette (1990) surveyed school psychologists. Although the school psychologists in the study possessed considerable knowledge of depression, their responses diverged relative to the literature in two important areas. *First*, a substantial number of school psychologists believed that childhood depression was substantively different from adult depression. They almost unanimously agreed that masked depression exists, even though this conceptualization has been discounted for several years (Kaslow & Rehm, 1991). *Second*, projective techniques (e.g., TAT, sentence completion) were one of the most frequently named methods for assessing depression. This finding contradicts evidence that projective tests are not sensitive enough to identify specific psychiatric conditions in childhood, including depression (Gittelman, 1980).

More alarmingly, some evidence suggests that educators may respond more negatively to depressed students than to their nondepressed peers. Peterson, Wonderlich, Reaven, and Mullins (1987) had teachers rate their feelings in response to four films in which a child was portrayed as either depressed or nondepressed and as having experienced either high or low life stress. The children who were both depressed and stressed received the most negative reactions from educators; the children who were either depressed or stressed were viewed less negatively; and the children who were neither depressed nor stressed received the most positive reactions. Depression clearly influenced educators' responses in ways that could serve to maintain a child's depression. Educators who communicate less positive and more negative behavior to a depressed child may enhance feelings of low self-esteem, dysphoria, inadequacy, and helplessness.

Because the risk of suicide also is greatly heightened with depression (Myers et al., 1991), educators have a particular need to be sensitive to this disorder. Guetzloe (1989) discusses issues of suicidality in school settings.

Early Identification

Early identification of depressed children and adolescents in school settings is desirable, but Reynolds (1986a) recognized several factors that make this goal problematic:

1. Prevalence figures may be somewhat misleading as depressive symptomatology tends to be overendorsed on the first administration of a self-report measure of depression. A second administration of the same measure shortly thereafter may not show depressive symptomatology. What happens is that a specific event or stressor may trigger a depressive episode, which may account for many cases of depression identified in prevalence surveys.
2. School personnel often have difficulty identifying specific symptom clusters associated with depression. To complicate matters, secondary teachers have limited contact with students.
3. Depressed students rarely refer themselves for help.
4. Some parents deny that their child may be suffering from a mood disorder.

On the basis of findings from prevalence studies of depression in children and adolescents and the lack of self-referral, teacher referral, or parent referral, Reynolds (1986a) developed a three-stage screening program to identify depressed children and adolescents in school settings: (a) conducting large-group screening with self-report depression measures; (b) 3 to 6 weeks later retesting children who, on the basis of the large-group screening in Stage 1, meet cutoff score criteria for depression; and (c) conducting individual clinical interviews with children who manifest clinical levels of depression at both Stage 1 and Stage 2 evaluations.

Classroom teachers can conduct group assessment of students, utilizing a self-report depression measure appropriate for children or adolescents. Self-report is particularly important in assessing depression because primary symptoms such as sadness, feelings of worthlessness, and loss of interest in activities reflect subjective feelings and self-perceptions (Kazdin, 1990). Common self-report measures for children and adolescents are given in Table 4.

TABLE 4   Commonly Used Measures for Childhood and Adolescent Depression

Measure	Response Format	Description
Self-Report (Child)		
Children's Depression Inventory (Kovacs, 1985)	27 items, each rated on a 0-2 point scale	Derived from Beck Depression Inventory (Beck, Ward, Mendelson, Mock, & Erbaugh, 1961). Items reflect affective, cognitive, and behavioral symptoms.
Reynolds Child Depression Scale (Reynolds, 1986b)	30 items, each rated on a 1-5 point scale	Items selected to measure depression in school characteristics (e.g., suicide) are replaced by less severe behavior (e.g., hurting oneself).
Self-Report (Adolescent)		
Beck Depression Inventory (modified for adolescents) (Chiles et al., 1980)	33 items, each on a scale varying from 0 to 2, 3, or 4 points	Changes in language, not content of Beck Depression Inventory (Beck et al., 1961).
Reynolds Adolescent Depression Scale (Reynolds, 1986c)	30 items, each rated on a 4-point scale	Items derived from symptoms included in major, minor, and unipolar depression.
Clinical Interviews (Child)		
Bellevue Index of Depression (Petti, 1978)	40 items, each rated on a 4-point scale of severity and 3-point scale for duration	Administered separately to child, parents, and others; helpful to combine scores from different sources.
Children's Depression Rating Scale (Poznanski, Cook, & Carroll, 1979)	16 items scored after interview; symptoms rated on a 6-point scale for severity	Derived from Hamilton Depression Rating Scale (Hamilton, 1967) for adults. Administered also to parents and others to combine different sources.
Schedule for Affective Disorders for School-Age Children (Chambers et al., 1985)	Multiple items for mood disorders; depressive symptoms rated for degree of severity for scales varying in point values	Patterned after adult Schedule for Affective-Disorders (Endicott & Spitzer, 1978) based on Research Diagnostic Criteria (Spitzer, Endicott, & Robins, 1978). Parent and child are interviewed.
Clinical Interviews (Adolescent)		
Hamilton Depression Rating Scale (Hamilton, 1967)	17-item semi-structured interview with probes	Measures severity of depression and probes for psychotic symptoms; translates well for use with adolescents.
Research Diagnostic Criteria (Spitzer et al., 1978)	11 depression subtypes (e.g., simple, recurrent, unipolar, agitated)	Provides greater specificity than DSM classification; primarily used in research.

Note. For an in-depth review of the characteristics of individual assessment techniques, see Kazdin (1988).

Reynolds (1986a) has suggested that teachers avoid telling students they are being tested for depression because this information may induce lower levels of mood awareness. Instead, students can be informed that the school is interested in how they are feeling about themselves. This information can be restated to students involved in a second screening. The second screening serves to weed out students who experienced a transient depressed mood during the initial screening or exaggerated their depressive symptomatology. During the last stage, individual clinical interviews are conducted with students who met depression criteria at both previous stages. Common interview schedules also are presented in Table 4. Obtaining measures other than self-reports is important as some students consistently overestimate or underestimate depressive symptomatology or misinterpret items or response format.

To screen initially for only a single disorder may be neither desirable nor efficient sometimes, especially given limited resources in some school psychology or consulting services budgets. As an alternative to screening only for depression, Walker and Severson (1990) have developed a multi-stage procedure to screen for both internalizing and externalizing disorders. In this process, teachers are asked to nominate and rank order pupils who demonstrate characteristics of these broad-band disorders in their classroom (Stage 1) but then also rate only the top three pupils in each category on brief measures of adaptive and maladaptive behavior as well as on critical events or symptoms (Stage 2). A school psychologist then conducts brief observations of classroom attention and playground social interaction on two different occasions (Stage 3) for any pupils who exceed critical cutoff scores in the first two stages. Although this procedure is not specific to depression, it may identify children with a potential diagnosis of this disorder, which then can be verified using the techniques described above.

Depression-Related Characteristics

Depression influences a wide range of behavioral, cognitive, and affective functioning (Maag & Rutherford, 1987). Many depression-related characteristics vary as a function of developmental level (Kazdin, 1987). For example, infants have not acquired the ability to verbalize and have not experienced the world and therefore express depression through eating and sleeping disorders (Evans, Reinhart, & Succop, 1980). Because preschoolers are motor-oriented, much of their mood is expressed through behavior such as night terrors, enuresis, and encopresis. Older school-age children may become more outwardly aggressive, anxious, and antisocial (Kazdin, French, & Unis, 1983). Depression becomes more overt in adolescents as their better-developed conscience exacerbates feelings of guilt and low self-esteem (Teri, 1982b).

A number of salient characteristics correlate with, if not contribute directly to, depression. Although the range of domains is quite large, several key characteristics occur quite frequently with depression. For example, low self-esteem is likely to be part of the symptom picture of depression. Hopelessness, or negative expectations toward the future, correlates with depression, suicidal ideation and behavior, and low self-esteem (DiGangi, Behrens, & Maag, 1989; Kazdin, Rodgers, & Colbus, 1986).

In addition to cognitive disturbances, social skill deficits often are associated with depression (Helsel & Matson, 1984). Environmental events that induce stress can contribute to the development and maintenance of depression as well (Compas, 1987). These depression-related characteristics often reflect specific theoretical models of depression including social skill deficits, cognitive theory, learned helplessness theory, self-control deficits, and deficits in problem solving.

Descriptions of the relevant models are presented in Table 5. A number of measures focus on key areas related to depressive symptoms based on these theoretical models. Table 6 lists common measures that are used to assess areas central to current conceptual views of depression and convey areas reflecting specific theoretical models.

Categorizing Problems Associated with Depression

Based on current theoretical models, depression may result from social skill deficits, self-control deficits, learned helplessness attributions, or cognitive distortions or deficits. Interpersonal problem-solving skills contribute to both cognitive and behavioral conceptualizations (Braswell & Kendall, 1988; Nezu, Nezu, & Perri, 1989). Systematically approaching and evaluating problem situations represents a general orientation common to most intervention approaches. In addition, environmental factors, such as inappropriate or absent reinforcement contingencies, inhibit expression of healthy and positive functioning or promote depression and related characteristics.

TABLE 5   *Theoretical Models Accounting for Depression*

Model	Description
Social Skill Deficits	Depression results from a lack of social skills necessary to obtain reinforcement from the environment (Lewinsohn, 1974). Low rates of response-contingent positive reinforcement results in reduced activity levels. Punishing and aversive consequences (unpleasant outcomes) may result from person-environment interactions and lead to symptoms of depression.
Self-Control Model	Maladaptive or deficient self-regulatory processes in coping with stress cause depression (Rehm, 1977). Self-regulatory processes include self-monitoring, self-evaluation, and self-reinforcement. Individuals with self-regulatory deficits focus on negative events, set overly stringent criteria for evaluating their performance, and administer little reinforcement to themselves.
Learned Helplessness	Depression results from individuals' experiences and expectations that their responses do not influence events in their lives. Perfidious attributional style filters experiences in such a way as to produce deficits in affect, motivation, and self-esteem associated with depression (Abramson, Seligman, & Teasdale, 1978).
Cognitive Triad of Depression	Depressed individuals have a systematically negative bias in their thinking, which leads them to have a negative view of themselves, the world, and the future (Beck, 1967). Negative cognitions are considered to affect the individual's judgment about the world and interpersonal interactions, and to account for affective, motivational, and behavioral symptoms of depression.
Interpersonal Problem-Solving Deficits	Inability to generate alternative solutions to social problems, engage in means-end thinking, and make decisions exacerbate effects of negative events (Nezu, Nezu, & Perri, 1989). Depression emerges in response to problems of daily living.

TABLE 6   Common Measures for Assessing Depression-Related Characteristics

Measure	Description
Social Skills	
Matson Evaluation of Social Skills with Children (Matson, Rotatori, & Helsel, 1983)	Items pertain to social skills, assertiveness, jealousy, and impulsiveness as related to interpersonal interaction. Self-report and teacher-report forms rated on 5-point scale.
Walker-McConnell Scale of Social Competence and School Adjustment (Walker & McConnell, 1988)	Teacher-rated scale consisting of 43 descriptions of peer-related interpersonal social skills and adaptive behavior required for success within classroom instructional settings.
Cognition	
Children's Attributional Style Questionnaire (Seligman & Peterson, 1986)	Self-report measure consisting of 48 forced-choice items that permit assessment of three attributional dimensions considered important in a learned helplessness model of depression: internal-external characteristics, stable-unstable characteristics, and good-bad outcomes.
Children's Negative Cognitive Error Questionnaire (Leitenberg, Yost, & Carroll-Wilson, 1986)	Self-report measure consisting of 24 items presenting hypothetical situations or events followed by a statement about the event that reflects cognitive errors (catastrophizing, overgeneralizing, personalizing, and selective abstraction). Children rate degree of similarity to their own thoughts. This measure is based on Beck's cognitive therapy of depression.
Problem Solving	
Problem Solving Measure for Conflict (Lochman & Lampron, 1986)	Six means-end stories with each stem describing a problematic situation and a conclusion in which the problem was no longer occurring. Children provide the middle. Scores are based on children's responses on three content areas: verbal assertion, direct action, and physical aggression. This measure is based on Shure and Spivack's (1972) means-ends problem-solving test.
Simulated Problem Situations (Gesten et al., 1982)	Measures of children's natural problem-solving behavior when confronted with a simulated problem situation. Interactions between confederates and target children are observed. Scoring is based on number of alternative solutions generated, number of solution variants offered, number of irrelevant solutions generated, total number of solutions generated excluding irrelevant solutions, and effectiveness of solutions.
Stressful Events	
Life Events Checklist (Johnson & McCutcheon, 1980)	Self-report measure consisting of 46 items that list stressful events. Children indicate whether the event occurred in the past year, whether it was bad or good, and degree of impact on their lives.

(Continued next page)

TABLE 6   Continued

Measure	Description
Stressful Events	
Life Events Record (Coddington, 1972)	Stressful events varying as a function of age whose occurrence is rated according to life change units. Parents complete the form for young children; older children complete the scale themselves.
Activities and Reinforcers	
Pleasure Scale for Children (Kazdin, 1989)	Children report on a 3-point scale the extent to which 39 items would make them happy. The instrument measures degree of anhedonia.
Adolescent Activities (Carey, Kelley, Buss, & Scott, 1986)	Adolescents rate the frequency of occurrence of 100 activities for degree of pleasantness and unpleasantness experienced during the last 2 weeks. The measure is based on Lewinsohn's work.
Children's Reinforcement Schedules (Cautela, Cautela, & Esonis, 1983)	Children identify events that can be used as reinforcers. Helpful as a method to assess pleasure children report in response to a variety of events.
Adolescent Reinforcement Survey Schedule (Cautela, 1981)	Parallels Children's Reinforcement Schedules.

*Although many problem-solving measures have been reported in the literature, none are ideally suited for either research or practice (Butler & Meichenbaum, 1981).

Figure 1 illustrates a four-category conceptualization of problems associated with depression. According to this model, depression can be conceptualized as resulting from social skill deficits, self-control deficits, cognitive distortions or deficits, and learned helplessness attributions. The presence of interpersonal problem-solving skills and environmental factors allows the categorization of depression for the basis of developing appropriate interventions. For example, poor social skills may result from erroneous problem solving or environmental factors. A child who is encouraged by his or her peers to participate in a game and is capable of performing the requisite behaviors but is unable to strategically select them probably indicates erroneous problem solving. Conversely, if the child lacks the behavioral requisites to participate in the game, social skill deficits may be targeted for intervention. Similarly, cognitive disturbances and misattributions may result from the child's inability to evaluate situations appropriately or perform the requisite behaviors.

TREATMENT OF CHILDHOOD AND ADOLESCENT DEPRESSION

The model depicting problems associated with depression presented in Figure 1 can be used to develop intervention programs for depressed youth. When developing a treatment program, the first consideration is whether depressive symptomatology represents a primary condition, (e.g., mood disorder) or is a byproduct of other behavior problems (Kaslow & Rehm, 1991). For example, youngsters who are hyperactive, aggressive,

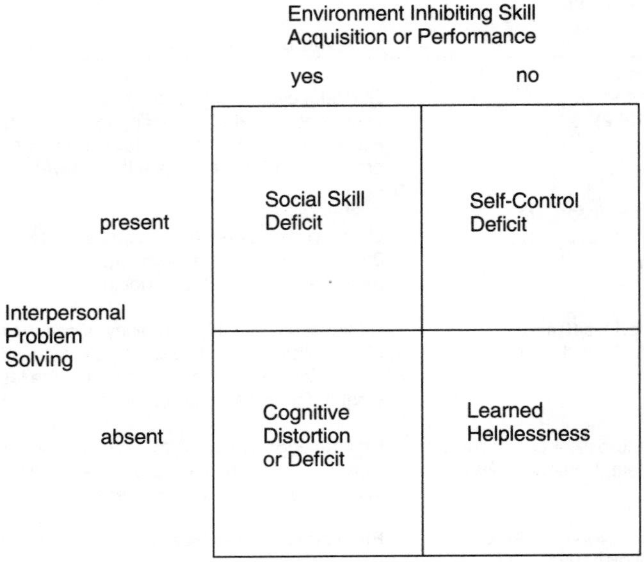

Environment Inhibiting Skill
Acquisition or Performance

	yes	no
present	Social Skill Deficit	Self-Control Deficit

Interpersonal
Problem
Solving

| absent | Cognitive Distortion or Deficit | Learned Helplessness |

FIGURE 1   Model for Determining the Nature of Depression Deficits

school phobic, or socially incompetent may experience depressive symptomatology and related dysfunctional cognitions as a result of these problems (Maag, Behrens, & Di-Gangi, 1992). If conventional treatments for these behavior problems are ineffective for ameliorating the primary problem and related depressive symptomatology, specific treatment strategies for depression should be employed.

Table 7 presents a summary of treatment approaches relative to theoretical models of depression. Intervention strategies generally reflect either behavioral or cognitive-behavioral orientations. Although techniques based on these models seem promising, only a few studies have investigated their efficacy with children and adolescents (see Maag, 1988a; Stark, 1990). In addition, Kazdin (1990) raises the issue of comorbidity (the individual meets criteria for more than one disorder). Several researchers have found that depression coexists with attention deficit disorders, conduct disorders, anxiety disorders, autism, and mental retardation (e.g, Anderson, Williams, McGhee, & Silva, 1987; Bernstein, 1991; Bernstein & Garfinkel, 1986; Bird et al., 1988; Fendrich, Weissman, & Warner, 1991; Forness & Kavale, in press; McClellan, Rupert, Reichler, & Sylvester, 1990; Strauss, Last, Hersen, & Kazdin, 1988).

Ironically, the phenomenon of comorbidity has led some researchers to suggest that it may be more meaningful to conceptualize depression in terms of the broader classification of internalizing symptoms rather than the more specific symptomatology of depression, which is more difficult to distinguish (Wolfe et al., 1987). This finding is particularly germane to special educators, as problems of an internalizing nature tend to be frequent in children with learning problems (Thompson, 1986).

TABLE 7   Treatment Strategies Following Theoretical Models of Depression

Model	Description
Social Skill Strategies	Main strategies include shaping procedures that use adult reinforcement, modeling or combined modeling and reinforcement procedures, and direct training procedures to make use of the child's cognitive and verbal skills. Specific training techniques include instructions, modeling, role playing, rehearsal, feedback, and self-management techniques. Verbal-cognitive approaches emphasize teaching specific social skills and general problem-solving techniques.
Self-Control Strategies	Self-management strategies including self-monitoring, self-evaluation, self-reinforcement, and self-instruction would be appropriate for remediating self-control deficits. Intervention should take into account children's cognitive developmental capacities and require the practitioner to play an active role in effecting the desired change by utilizing action-oriented techniques and concrete tasks.
Helplessness Strategies	Strategies follow an attribution retraining conceptualization in which children are taught to take responsibility for their failure and to attribute success or failure to effort. Adaptive coping responses are substituted for attributions of helplessness.
Cognitive Strategies	Treatment focuses on determining the meaning of the child's nonverbal and verbal communication. Any distorted cognitions the child expresses must be challenged. Bestowing acceptance and affection are important, as is assigning tasks that ensure success experiences. Techniques are designed to help the child identify, reality-test, and modify distorted conceptualizations and dysfunctional attitudes and beliefs.

Determining Choice of Strategies

Given the range of deficits associated with depression, and their implications for treatment, it is important to determine which factor(s) seem most responsible for the development and maintenance of this disorder (Kaslow & Rehm, 1991). Attempting to assess youngters' relative skills in each area is a tedious and exacting process. Nevertheless, to enhance treatment efficacy, intervention techniques should be matched to identified, specific problems (Maag, 1989).

In this regard, Kaslow and Rehm (1991) suggest sequencing potential intervention strategies and then making decisions on which ones to use in which order, depending on the results of assessment information. For example, if depression is secondary to a conduct or oppositional disorder, social skills training may be essential for the child to obtain an adequate level of response-contingent positive reinforcement in the environment. If the student's social skills are adequate, however, a more appropriate initial technique would be to modify the child's activity level.

Kaslow and Rehm (1991) also stressed the importance of eliciting overt behavior change prior to targeting cognitive factors, because overt behavior is easier to assess than self-reports of children's cognitions. In addition, obtaining an accurate sampling of the child's self-reported cognitions is easier once behavior has been modified. Figure 2 presents a modified version of the flowchart developed by Kaslow and Rehm (1991) for determining choice of intervention strategies. This figure is based on the need to accurately identify and define the problem using assessment measures previously described. Targets for intervention reflect three general areas: behavior, cognitive, and cognitive-behavioral. As with any aspect of depression in children and adolescents, care must be taken to modify intervention strategies based on the child's developmental level and level of cognitive, affective, and behavioral functioning (Cole & Kaslow, 1988).

Developing a Conceptual Model for Intervention

Although the treatment literature for childhood and adolescent depression is relatively sparse compared to other areas such as conduct disorders or attention deficit disorders, several new studies have investigated a variety of training techniques. Table 8 provides a summary of recent treatment studies for childhood and adolescent depression. One of the difficulties encountered when treating depression is organizing and integrating the various techniques into a structured training format (Maag, 1988a). Attempting to implement all available techniques would be cumbersome and time-consuming. Yet, many depressed youths exhibit a variety of deficits, and employing a single intervention technique may not be sufficient.

A comprehensive training format would provide a structured system for employing various techniques systematically. One conceptual format is offered in the stress inoculation training (SIT) paradigm. SIT is a multi-component intervention format that combines elements of didactic teaching, Socratic discussion, cognitive restructuring, problem solving, relaxation training, behavioral and imaginal rehearsal, self-monitoring, self-instruction, self-reinforcement, and environmental manipulation (Meichenbaum, 1985). SIT should not be viewed as a loose compendium of unrelated methods, but, rather, a set of interconnected techniques that can be combined in a systematic way.

SIT is implemented in three phases: (a) *conceptualization*; (b) *skills acquisition and rehearsal*; and (c) *application and follow-through*. In Phase I, youngsters are educated about the causes, consequences, and alternative methods of handling depression. Phase II involves training youngsters in relevant skills for coping with depression. In Phase III, youngsters practice applying coping skills *in vitro* and *in vivo* during exposure to regulated doses of stressors that arouse but do not overwhelm their coping skills. SIT has been used to treat depression (Maag, 1988b) and for aggression and anger management (Feindler & Fremouw, 1983; Maag, Parks, & Rutherford, 1988) (see Maag, 1988a for an in-depth description of using stress inoculation training for treating depressed youths).

Pharmacological Treatment

Pharmacotherapy is an essential adjunct to behavioral and cognitive-behavioral interventions, particularly in cases with vegative symptomatology and family history of mood disorders (Cantwell & Carlson, 1983; Gadow, 1986; Klein, Gittelman, Quitkin, & Rifkin, 1980). Five classes of psychotropics are used in depression; these are depicted in Table 9 in terms of their uses, side effects, and related considerations (see Gadow, 1986; Greist

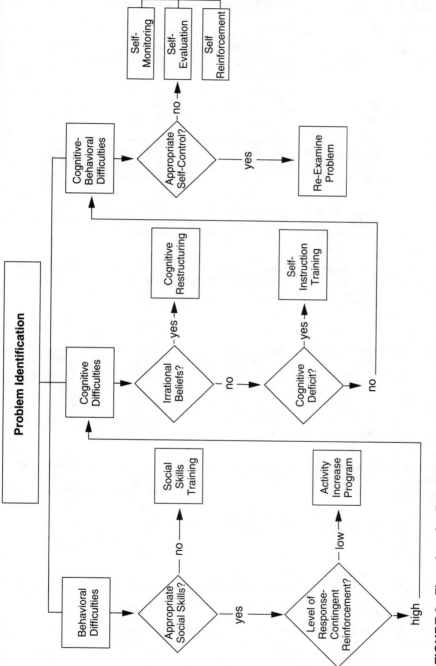

FIGURE 2 Flowchart for Determining Choice of Intervention Strategy

TABLE 8   Treatment Studies with Depressed Children and Adolescents

Treatment	Study	Sample	Findings
Social Skills Training	Calpin & Cincirpini (1978)	Two depressed inpatients (10-year-old girl, 11-year-old boy)	Improvement for both children on specific social skills (e.g., eye contact)
	Calpin & Kornblith (1977)	Four inpatient boys with aggressive behavior	Improvement of all boys on specific social skills (e.g., requests for new behaviors)
	Fine, Forth, Gilbert, & Haley (1991)	Five groups of 30 adolescent outpatients	Improvement to "nonclinical" levels on depression scales, but to a lesser degree than subjects receiving group therapy
	Frame, Matson, Sonis, Fialkov, & Kazdin (1982)	Borderline mentally retarded 10-year-old depressed male inpatient	Improvement on all target behaviors (e.g., inappropriate body position, lack of eye contact, poor speech quality)
	Petti, Bornstein, Delamater, & Conners (1980)	Chronically depressed 10½-year-old inpatient girl	Improvement on all target behaviors (e.g., eye contact, smiles, duration of speech)
	Matson et al. (1980)	Four depressed emotionally disturbed boys	Increased positive social responses on role-play scenarios for target behaviors (e.g., giving compliments)
	Schloss, Schloss, & Harris (1984)	Three depressed inpatient males	Improvement on five target behaviors (e.g., greets adult, maintains conversation, says goodbye)
Cognitive-Behavioral Interventions	Butler, Miezitis, Friedman, & Cole (1980)	56 fifth- and sixth-grade students	Decreases in depression for role-play and cognitive restructuring conditions; most improvement for role-play
	Maag (1988b)	56 adolescent inpatients	Decreases in depression and negative self-statement for subjects receiving stress inoculation training
	Reynolds & Coats (1986)	30 moderately depressed high school students	Decreases in depression and anxiety for subjects receiving either cognitive restructuring or relaxation training
	Stark, Kaslow, & Reynolds (1987)	29 fourth-, fifth-, and sixth-grade students	Decreases in depression for subjects receiving either self-control or problem-solving training

TABLE 9 Common Psychopharmacologic Medication Used with Depressed Children or Adolescents

Type (Trade name)	Indication	Dosage*	Therapeutic Effects	Side Effects	Other Considerations
Tricyclics:					
Imipramine (Tofranil)	Unipolar in children	10-175 mg	Improvement in vegetative symptoms at first, followed by improvement in mood some 3 or 4 weeks later	Dry mouth, drowsiness (especially Elavil), blurred vision, constipation, cardiac arrythmias (EKG monitoring is essential and overdose in suicidal patients becomes a concern)	After offset of 1 month, discontinue gradually over 3 or more months (withdrawal symptoms mimic depression). Has been used to treat separation anxiety, hyperactivity, enuresis.
	Unipolar in adolescents	75-225 mg			
Amytriptyline (Elavil)	Unipolar in adolescents (little research with children)	45-110 mg			
Lithium Carbonate (Lithonate)	Bipolar in adolescents and occasionally in multiple episodes of unipolar	450-1800 mg	Improvement in symptoms in 4-10 days, with most of effect within first 2 weeks; "smooths" rather than eliminates symptoms, but early treatment may suppress recurrences	Nausea, drowsiness, thirst, frequent urination, hand tremor, possible cardiac or kidney problems	Small dose added to tricyclic medication during withdrawal as long-term prophylaxis against recurrence. Has been used to treat aggression.
Monoamine Oxidase Inhibitors (Nardil)	Atypical depression in adolescents	30-60 mg	Gradual improvement over 1- to 3-week period	Nausea, dizziness, fainting, sleep disturbance and possible fatal reactions upon ingestion of certain cheese or yeast products	Used primarily in intractable conditions refractory to other drugs.
Carbamazepine (Tegretol)	Bipolar in adolescents, especially rapid-cycling	30-60 mg	Relatively more rapid onset of improvement	Nausea, drowsiness, weight loss, ataxia in instances, and possible toxic reactions with lithium	Primarily a seizure medication but has been used in lithium-resistant depression.
Fluoxetine Hydrochloride (Prozac)	Unipolar depression in adolescents	20-80 mg	Gradual improvement over 5-6 weeks (long-term effects have not been systematically studied)	Anxiety, nervousness, insomnia, weight loss, hypomania or mania, and seizures	Prozac has not been systematically studied for its potential for abuse, tolerance, or physical dependence

*These are doses in what have generally been considered as optimum levels and, in most cases, are determined on a mg/kg ratio based on body weight. Dosage levels vary widely, so these ranges should be considered with caution.

& Greist, 1979; Kazdin, 1990; and Petti, 1983 for reviews of pharmacological interventions). Imipramine seems to be the drug of choice for children and adolescents alike (Esman, 1981; Kashani, Shekim, & Reid, 1984; Petti & Law, 1982; Preskorn, Weller, & Weller, 1982; Puig-Antich, 1982); but other drugs, such as lithium and tegretol, are widely used for adolescents who have variant forms of mood disorders (Campbell, Schulman, & Rapoport, 1978; Kishimoto, Ogura, Hazama, & Inoue, 1983).

Although pharmacotherapy is prescribed by psychiatrists, school personnel should be aware of the types of drugs used and their potentially serious side effects. A classroom observation study documenting single-subject classroom effects of imipramine and lithium suggests important considerations for teachers (Forness, Akiyama, & Campana, 1984). Educators need to become much more involved in evaluating effects of such medication on classroom-based measures of treatment outcome (Forness & Kavale, 1988).

Integrating Treatment

Even as treatment of childhood and adolescent depression seems promising, factors external to the child should be considered. Because of parents' influence over their children, Kazdin (1990) suggests that family-based interventions should be incorporated into treatment programs. In this regard, teachers can play a pivotal role by cultivating positive relationships with parents. Positive parent-teacher relationships promote parental feedback to practitioners, enhance treatment outcomes, and extend positive effects of school programming into the home (Heward, Dardig, & Rossett, 1979).

In addition, parents can become trainers of their children by structuring activities and managing behavioral contingencies that promote participation in activities and social interaction (Kazdin, 1990). Parents have effectively implemented reinforcement and punishment techniques and taught prosocial behaviors to their children with externalizing behaviors (e.g., Kazdin, 1985; Patterson, 1982). Parent programs have resulted in decreases in maternal depression and increases in family cohesion (e.g., Eyberg & Robinson, 1982; Forehand, Wells, & Griest, 1980; Karoly & Rosenthal, 1977; Patterson & Fleischman, 1979).

School-based intervention adds several other dimensions as well. Many special educators already conduct social skills training and utilize other cognitive-behavioral techniques for working with aggressive and socially incompetent youngsters (Maag, 1990). Treating depression represents a natural extension of these responsibilities. Furthermore, peers can be recruited for the intervention process as they represent a resource for promoting entrapment (McConnell, 1987) of behaviors that may combat depression. Special educators, therefore, can play a vital role in the early identification, assessment, and treatment of depression.

SUMMARY AND CONCLUSION

Depression represents one of the most significant mental health problems facing children and adolescents. An emerging body of research addresses the nature and characteristics of this disorder in school-aged populations, but educators just recently have begun to address this problem. Part of the difficulty has been educators' lack of knowledge of this disorder and its impact on youngsters' functioning.

Early identification is considered essential, and schools should play an important role in this process. Assessment should focus not only on depressive symptomatology but also on related characteristics, such as social skills. Perhaps most important in treating depression from a school standpoint is that many special educators currently employ many of the intervention strategies that are effective for ameliorating depression for a variety of other conditions such as conduct and attentional disorders. Treatment can be enhanced by sequencing intervention techniques systematically and employing a structured training format.

No one intervention approach will be optimally effective with each youngster. Youngsters who have similar depressive symptomatology may vary greatly with respect to etiological factors, related characteristics, and environmental circumstances. For this reason, depression must be viewed from a holistic framework. This model should guide the development and implementation of treatment decisions. In sum, decisions regarding depression should be made on the basis of empirically based knowledge and the youngster's specific characteristics.

REFERENCES

Abrahams, M. J., & Whitlock, F. A. (1969). Childhood experience and depression. *British Journal of Psychiatry, 115*, 883–888.

Abramson, L. Y., Seligman, M. E. P., & Teasdale, J. D. (1978). Learned helplessness in humans: Critique and reformulation. *Journal of Abnormal Psychology, 87*, 49–74.

American Psychiatric Association. (1987). *Diagnostic and statistical manual of mental disorders–Revised* (3rd ed.). Washington, DC: American Psychiatric Association.

Anderson, J. C., Williams, S., McGhee, R., & Silva, P. A. (1987). The prevalence of DSM-III disorders in preadolescent children: Prevalence in a large sample from the general population. *Archives of General Psychiatry, 44*, 69–76.

Angold, A., Weissman, M. M., John, K., Wickramaratne, P., & Drusoff, B. (1991). The effects of age and sex on depression ratings in children and adolescents. *Journal of the American Academy of Child and Adolescent Psychiatry, 30*, 67–74.

Beck, A. T. (1967). *Cognitive therapy and the emotional disorders.* New York: International Universities Press.

Beck, A. T., Ward, C. H., Mendelson, M., Mock, J., & Erbaugh, J. (1961). An inventory for measuring depression. *Archives of General Psychiatry, 4*, 53–63.

Bernstein, G. A. (1991). Comorbidity and severity of anxiety and depressive disorders in a clinic sample. *Journal of the American Academy of Child and Adolescent Psychiatry, 30*, 43–50.

Bernstein, G. A., & Garfinkel, D. B. (1986). School phobia: The overlap of affective and anxiety disorders. *Journal of the American Academy of Child Psychiatry, 25*, 235–241.

Bird, H. R., Canino, G., Rubio-Stipec, M., Gould, M. S., Ribera, J., Sesman, M., Woodbury, M., Huertas-Goldman, S., Pagan, A., Sanchez-Lacay, A., & Moscoso, M. (1988). Estimates of the prevalence of childhood maladjustment in a community survey of Puerto Rico: The use of combined measures. *Archives of General Psychiatry, 45*, 1120–1126.

Braswell, L., & Kendall, P. C. (1988). Cognitive-behavioral methods with children. In K. S. Dobson (Ed.), *Handbook of cognitive-behavioral therapies* (pp. 167–213). New York: Guilford.

Brumback, R. A., & Stanton, R. D. (1983). Learning disability and childhood depression. *American Journal of Orthopsychiatry, 53*, 269–281.

Butler, L., & Meichenbaum, D. (1981). The assessment of interpersonal problem-solving skills. In P. C. Kendall & S. D. Hollon (Eds.), *Assessment strategies for cognitive-behavioral interventions* (pp. 197–225). New York: Academic Press.

Butler, L., Miezitis, S., Friedman, R., & Cole, E. (1980). The effect of two school-based intervention programs on depressive symptoms in preadolescents. *American Education Research Journal, 17,* 111–119.

Calpin, J. P., & Cincirpini, P. M. (1978, May). *A multiple baseline analysis of social skills training in children.* Paper presented at Midwestern Association for Behavior Analysis, Chicago.

Calpin, J. P., & Kornblith, S. J. (1977). *Training of aggressive children in conflict resolution skills.* Paper presented at meeting of Association for the Advancement of Behavior Therapy, Chicago.

Campbell, M., Schulman, D., & Rapoport, J. L. (1978). The current status of lithium therapy in child and adolescent psychiatry. *Journal of Child Psychiatry, 17,* 717–720.

Cantwell, D. P., & Baker, L. (1982). Depression in children with speech, language, and learning disorders. *Journal of Children in Contemporary Society, 15,* 51–59.

Cantwell, D. P., & Carlson, G. A. (Eds.). (1983). *Affective disorders in childhood and adolescence: An update.* New York: Spectrum.

Carey, M. P., Kelley, M. L., Buss, R. R., & Scott, W. O. N. (1986). Relationship of activity of depression in adolescents: Development of the Adolescent Activities Checklist. *Journal of Consulting & Clinical Psychology, 54,* 320–322.

Carlson, G. A., & Cantwell, D. P. (1980). Unmasking depression in children and adolescents. *American Journal of Psychiatry, 137,* 445–449.

Carlson, G. A., & Garber, J. (1986). Developmental issues in the classification of depression in children. In M. Rutter, C. E. Izard, & P. B. Read (Eds.), *Depression in young people: Developmental and clinical perspectives* (pp. 399–435). New York: Guilford.

Cautela, J. R. (1981). *Behavior analysis forms for clinical intervention* (Vol. 2). Champaign, IL: Research Press.

Cautela, J. R., Cautela, J., & Esonis, S. (1983). *Forms for behavior analysis with children.* Champaign, IL: Research Press.

Chambers, W. J., Puig-Antich, J., Hirsch, M., Paez, P., Ambrosini, P. J., Tabrizi, M. A., & Davies, M. (1985). The assessment of affective disorders in children and adolescents by semistructured interview: Test-retest reliability. *Archives of General Psychiatry, 43,* 696–702.

Chiles, J. A., Miller, M. L., & Cox, G. B. (1980). Depression in an adolescent delinquent population. *Archives of General Psychiatry, 37,* 1179–1184.

Cicchetti, D., & Schneider-Rosen, K. (1986). An organizational approach to childhood depression. In M. Rutter, C. E. Izard, & P. B. Read (Eds.), *Depression in young people: Developmental and clinical perspectives* (pp. 71–134). New York: Guilford.

Clarizio, H. F., & Payette, K. (1990). A survey of school psychologists' perspectives and practices with childhood depression. *Psychology in the Schools, 79,* 57–63.

Coddington, R. D. (1972). The significance of life events as etiological factors in the diseases of children: A study of normal population. *Journal of Psychosomatic Research, 16,* 205–213.

Colbert, P., Newman, B., Ney, P., & Young, J. (1982). Learning disabilities as a symptom of depression in children. *Journal of Learning Disabilities, 15,* 333–336.

Cole, P. M., & Kaslow, N. J. (1988). Interactional and cognitive strategies for affect regulation: A developmental perspective on childhood depression. In L. B. Alloy (Ed.), *Cognitive processes in depression* (pp. 310–343). New York: Guilford.

Compas, B. E. (1987). Stress and life events during childhood and adolescence. *Clinical Psychology Review, 7,* 275–302.

Cytryn, L., & McKnew, D. H. (1972). Proposed classification of childhood depression. *American Journal of Psychiatry, 129,* 149–155.

Cytryn, L., & McKnew, D. H. (1974). Factors influencing the changing clinical expression of the depressive process in children. *American Journal of Psychiatry, 131,* 879–881.

DiGangi, S. A., Behrens, J. T., & Maag, J. W. (1989). Dimensions of depression: Factors associated with hopelessness and suicidal intent among special populations. In R. B. Rutherford, Jr., & S. A. DiGangi (Eds.), *Severe behavior disorders of children and youth* (Vol. 12, pp. 47–53). Reston, VA: Council for Children with Behavioral Disorders.

Dolgan, J. I. (1990). Depression in children. *Pediatric Annals, 19,* 45–50.

Endicott, J., & Spitzer, R. L. (1978). A diagnostic interview: The Schedule for Affective Disorders and Schizophrenia. *Archives of General Psychiatry, 35,* 837–844.

Epstein, M. H., & Cullinan, D. (1984). Research issues in behavior disorders: A national survey. *Behavioral Disorders, 10,* 56–59.

Esman, A. H. (1981). Appropriate use of psychotropics in adolescents. *Hospital, 12,* 49–60.

Evans, S., Reinhart, J., & Succop, R. (1980). Failure to thrive: A study of 45 children and their families. In S. Harrison & J. McDermott (Eds.), *New directions in childhood psychopathology*. New York: International Universities Press.

Eyberg, S. M., & Robinson, E. A. (1982). Parent-child interaction training: Effects of family functioning. *Journal of Clinical Child Psychology, 11*, 130–137.

Feindler, E. L., & Fremouw, W. (1983). Stress inoculation training for adolescent anger problems. In D. Meichenbaum & M. Jaremko (Eds.), *Stress reduction and prevention* (pp. 451–485). New York: Plenum.

Fendrich, M., Weissman, M. M., & Warner, V. (1991). Longitudinal assessment of major depression and anxiety disorders in children. *Journal of the American Academy of Child and Adolescent Psychiatry, 30*, 38–42.

Fine, S., Forth, A., Gilbert, M., & Haley, G. (1991). Group therapy for adolescent depressive disorder: A comparison of social skills and therapeutic support. *Journal of the American Academy of Child and Adolescent Psychiatry, 30*, 79–85.

Fleming, J. E., & Offord, D. R. (1990). Epidemiology of childhood depressive disorders: A critical review. *Journal of the American Academy of Child and Adolescent Psychiatry, 29*, 571–580.

Forehand, R., Wells, K. C., & Griest, D. L. (1980). An examination of the social validity of a parent training program. *Behavior Therapy, 11*, 488–502.

Forness, S. R. (1988). School characteristics of children and adolescents with depression. In R. B. Rutherford, Jr., C. M. Nelson, & S. R. Forness (Eds.), *Bases of severe behavioral disorders in children and youth* (pp. 177–203). San Diego: College-Hill Press.

Forness, S. R., Akiyama, K., & Campana, K. (1984, November). *Problems in antidepressant medication and classroom performance*. Paper presented at Annual Conference on Severe Behavioral Disorders of Children and Youth, Tempe, AZ.

Forness, S. R., & Kavale, K. A. (1988). Psychopharmacologic treatment: A note on classroom effects. *Journal of Learning Disabilities, 21*, 144–147.

Forness, S. R., & Kavale, K. A. (in press). School identification and response to conduct disorders. In A. Duchnowski & R. Friedman (Eds.), *Conduct disorders: Research, practice, and issues*. Tampa: Florida Mental Health Research Institute.

Frame, C., Matson, J. L., Sonis, W. A., Fialkov, M. J., & Kazdin, A. E. (1982). Behavioral treatment of depression in a prepubertal child. *Journal of Behavior Therapy & Experimental Psychiatry, 13*, 239–243.

Friedrich, W., Jacobs, J., & Reams, R. (1982). Depression and suicidal ideation in early adolescents. *Journal of Youth and Adolescence, 11*, 403–407.

Gadow, K. D. (1986). *Children on medication: Volume 2. Epilepsy, emotional disturbance, and adolescent disorders*. San Diego: College-Hill Press.

Gesten, E. L., Rains, M. H., Rapkin, B. D., Weissberg, R. P., Flores de Apodaca, R., Cowen, E. L., & Bowen, R. (1982). Training children in social problem-solving competencies: A first and second look. *American Journal of Community Psychology, 10*, 95–115.

Gittelman, R. (1980). The role of psychological tests for differential diagnosis in child psychiatry. *Journal of the American Academy of Child Psychiatry, 19*, 413-438.

Greist, J. H., & Greist, T. H. (1979). *Antidepressant treatment: The essentials*. Baltimore: Williams and Wilkins.

Grob, M. C., Klein, A. A., & Eisen, S. V. (1983). The role of the high school professional in identifying and managing adolescent suicidal behavior. *Journal of Youth & Adolescence, 12*, 163–173.

Guetzloe, E. C. (1989). *Youth suicide: What the educator should know*. Reston, VA: Council for Exceptional Children.

Hamilton, M. (1967). Development of a rating scale for primary depressive illness. *British Journal of Social & Clinical Psychology, 6*, 278–296.

Helsel, W. J., & Matson, J. L. (1984). Assessment of depression in children: The internal structure of the Child Depression Inventory (CDI). *Behaviour Research and Therapy, 22*, 289–298.

Heward, W. L., Dardig, J. C., & Rossett, A. (1979). *Working with parents of handicapped children*. Columbus, OH: Charles E. Merrill.

Johnson, J. H., & McCutcheon, S. M. (1980). Assessing life stress in older children and adolescents: Preliminary findings with the Life Events Checklist. In I. G. Sarason & C. D. Spielberger (Eds.), *Stress and anxiety* (Vol. 7, pp. 111–125). Washington, DC: Hemisphere.

Kaplan, S. L., Hong, G. K., & Weinhold, C. (1984). Epidemiology of depressive symptomatology in adolescents. *Journal of the American Academy of Child Psychiatry, 23*, 91–98.

Karoly, P., & Rosenthal, M. (1977). Training parents in behavior modification: Effects on perceptions of family interaction and deviant child behavior. *Behavior Therapy, 8*, 406–410.

Kashani, J. H., Barbero, G. J., & Bolander, F. D. (1981). Depression in hospitalized pediatric patients. *Journal of the American Academy of Child Psychiatry, 20,* 123–134.

Kashani, J. H., Cantwell, D. P., Shekim, W. O., & Reid, J. C. (1982). Major depressive disorder in children admitted to an inpatient community mental health center. *American Journal of Psychiatry, 139,* 671–672.

Kashani, J. H., McGee, R. O., Clarkson, S. E., Anderson, J. C., Walton, L. A., Williams, S., Silva, P. A., Robins, A. J., Cytryn, L., & McKnew, D. H. (1983). Depression in a sample of 9-year old children. *Archives of General Psychiatry, 40,* 1217–1223.

Kashani, J. H., Ray, J. S., & Carlson, G. A. (1984). Depression and depression-like states in preschool-age children in a child development unit. *American Journal of Psychiatry, 141,* 1397–1402.

Kashani, J. H., Shekim, W. O., & Reid, J. C. (1984). Amitriptyline in children with major depressive disorder: A double-blind crossover pilot study. *Journal of Child Psychiatry, 23,* 248–251.

Kashani, J. H., & Simonds, J. F. (1979). The incidence of depression in children. *American Journal of Psychiatry, 136,* 1203–1205.

Kaslow, N. J., & Rehm, L. P. (1991). Childhood depression. In R. J. Morris & T. R. Kratochwill (Eds.), *The practice of child therapy* (2nd ed., pp. 27–51). New York: Pergamon.

Kazdin, A. E. (1985). *Treatment of antisocial behavior in children and adolescents.* Homewood, IL: Dorsey.

Kazdin, A. E. (1987). Assessment of childhood depression: Current issues and strategies. *Behavioral Assessment, 9,* 291–319.

Kazdin, A. E. (1988). Childhood depression. In E. J. Mash & L. G. Terdal (Eds.), *Behavioral assessment of childhood disorders* (2nd ed., pp. 157–195). New York: Guilford.

Kazdin, A. E. (1989). Evaluation of the pleasure scale in the assessment of anhedonia in children. *Journal of the American Academy of Child and Adolescent Psychiatry, 28,* 364–372.

Kazdin, A. E. (1990). Childhood depression. *Journal of Child Psychology & Psychiatry, 31,* 121–160.

Kazdin, A. E., Colbus, D., & Rodgers, A. (1986). Assessment of depressive disorder among psychiatrically disturbed children. *Journal of Abnormal Child Psychology, 14,* 499–515.

Kazdin, A. E., French, A., & Unis, A. (1983). Child, mother, and father evaluations of depression in psychiatric inpatient children. *Journal of Abnormal Child Psychology, 11,* 167–180.

Kazdin, A. E., Rodgers, A., & Colbus, D. (1986). The Hopelessness Scale for Children: Psychometric characteristics and concurrent validity. *Journal of Consulting & Clinical Psychology, 54,* 241–245.

Kendall, P. C., Hollon, S. D., Beck, A. T., Hammen, C. L., & Ingram, R. E. (1987). Issues and recommendations regarding use of the Beck Depression Inventory. *Cognitive Therapy & Research, 11,* 289–299.

Kishimoto, A., Ogura, C., Hazama, H., & Inoue, H. (1983). Long-term prophylactic effects of carbamazopine in affective disorder. *British Journal of Psychiatry, 143,* 327–331.

Klein, D. F., Gittelman, R., Quitkin, F., & Rifkin, A. (1980). *Diagnosis and drug treatment of psychiatric disorders in adults and children* (2nd ed.). Baltimore: Williams and Wilkins.

Kovacs, M. (1985). The Children's Depression Inventory. *Psychopharmacology Bulletin, 21,* 995–998.

Kovacs, M. (1989). Affective disorder in children and adolescents. *American Psychologist, 44,* 209–215.

Lefkowitz, M. M., & Burton, N. (1978). Childhood depression: A critique of the concept. *Psychological Bulletin, 85,* 716–726.

Lefkowitz, M. M., & Tesiny, E. P. (1985). Depression in children: Prevalence and correlates. *Journal of Consulting & Clinical Psychology, 53,* 647–656.

Leitenberg, H., Yost, L. W., & Carroll-Wilson, M. (1986). Negative cognitive errors in children: Questionnaire development, normative data, and comparisons between children with and without self-reported symptoms of depression, low self-esteem, and evaluation anxiety. *Journal of Consulting & Clinical Psychology, 54,* 528–536.

Lewinsohn, P. N. (1974). Clinical and theoretical aspects of depression. In K. S. Calhoun, H. E. Adams, & K. M. Mitchell (Eds.), *Innovative treatment methods of psychopathology* (pp. 63–120). New York: Wiley.

Lobovits, D. A., & Handal, P. J. (1985). Childhood depression: Prevalence using DSM-III criteria and validity of parent and child depression scales. *Journal of Pediatric Psychology, 10,* 45–54.

Lochman, J. W., & Lampron, L. B. (1986). Situational Social problem-solving skills and self-esteem of aggressive and nonaggressive boys. *Journal of Abnormal Child Psychology, 13,* 527–538.

Maag, J. W. (1988a). Treatment of childhood and adolescent depression: Review and recommendations. In R. B. Rutherford, Jr., & J. W. Maag (Eds.), *Severe behavior disorders of children and youth* (Vol. 11, pp. 49–63). Reston, VA: Council for Children with Behavioral Disorders.

Maag, J. W. (1988b). *Treatment of adolescent depression with stress inoculation training.* Unpublished doctoral dissertation, Arizona State University, Tempe.

Maag, J. W. (1989). Assessment in social skills training: Methodological and conceptual issues for research and practice. *Remedial & Special Education, 10*(4), 6–17.

Maag, J. W. (1990). Social skills training in schools. *Special Services in the Schools, 6*, 1–19.

Maag, J. W., & Behrens, J. T. (1989a). Depression and cognitive self-statements of learning disabled and seriously emotionally disturbed adolescents. *Journal of Special Education, 23*, 17–27.

Maag, J. W., & Behrens, J. T. (1989b). Epidemiologic data on seriously emotionally disturbed and learning disabled adolescents reporting extreme depressive symptomatology. *Behavioral Disorders, 15*, 21–27.

Maag, J. W., Behrens, S. T., & DiGangi, S. A. (1992). Dysfunctional cognitions associated with adolescent depression: Findings across special populations. *Exceptionality, 3*, 31–47.

Maag, J. W., Parks, B. T., & Rutherford, R. B., Jr. (1988). Generalization and behavior covariation of aggression in children receiving stress inoculation therapy. *Child & Family Behavior Therapy, 10*, 29–47.

Maag, J. W., & Rutherford, R. B., Jr. (1987). Behavioral and learning characteristics of childhood and adolescent depression: Implications for special educators. In S. Braaten, R. B. Rutherford, Jr., & J. W. Maag (Eds.), *Programming for adolescents with behavioral disorders* (Vol. 3, pp. 55–70). Reston, VA: Council for Children with Behavioral Disorders.

Maag, J. W., & Rutherford, R. B., Jr. (1988). Review and synthesis of three components for identifying depressed students. In R. B. Rutherford, Jr., C. M. Nelson, & S. R. Forness (Eds.), *Bases of severe behavioral disorders in children and youth* (pp. 205-230). San Diego, CA: College-Hill Press.

Maag, J. W., Rutherford, R. B., Jr., & Parks, B. T. (1988). Secondary school professionals; ability to identify depression in adolescents. *Adolescence, 23*, 73–82.

Malmquist, C. P. (1977). Childhood depression: A clinical and behavioral perspective. In J. G. Schulterbrandt & A. Raskin (Eds.), *Depression in children: Diagnosis, treatment and conceptual models* (pp. 33–59). New York: Raven.

Matson, J. L., Esveldt-Dawson, K., Andraski, F., Ollendick, T. H., Petti, T. A., & Hersen, M. (1980). Observation and generalization effects of social skills training with emotionally disturbed children. *Behavior Therapy, 11*, 522–531.

Matson, J. L., Rotatori, A. F., & Helsel, W. J. (1983). Development of a rating scale to measure social skills in children: The Matson Evaluation of Social Skills with Youngsters (MESSY). *Behaviour Research and Therapy, 21*, 335–340.

Mattison, R. E., Humphrey, F. J., Kales, S. N., Handford, H. A., Finkenbinder, R. L., & Hernit, R. C. (1986). Psychiatric background and diagnoses of children evaluated for special class placement. *Journal of the American Academy of Child Psychiatry, 25*, 514–520.

McClellan, J. M., Rupert, M. P. M., Reichler, R. J., & Sylvester, C. E. (1990). Attention deficit disorder in children at risk for anxiety and depression. *Journal of the American Academy of Child and Adolescent Psychiatry, 29*, 534–539.

McConnell, S. R. (1987). Entrapment effects and the generalization and maintenance of social skills training for elementary school students with behavioral disorders. *Behavioral Disorders, 12*, 252–263.

Meichenbaum, D. (1985). *Stress inoculation training.* New York: Pergamon.

Mezzich, A. C., & Mezzich, J. E. (1979). Symptomatology of depression in adolescence. *Journal of Personality Assessment, 43*, 267–275.

Mitchell, J., McCauley, E., Burke, P. M., & Moss, S. J. (1988). Phenomenology of depression in children and adolescents. *Journal of the American Academy of Child and Adolescent Psychiatry, 27*, 12–20.

Myers, K., McCauley, E., Calderon, R., Mitchell, J., Burke, P., & Schloredt, K. (1991). Risks for suicidality in major depressive disorders. *Journal of the American Academy of Child and Adolescent Psychiatry, 30*, 86–94.

Nezu, A. M., Nezu, C. M., & Perri, M. G. (1989). *Problem-solving therapy for depression: Theory, research and clinical guidelines.* New York: Wiley.

Patterson, G. R. (1982). *Coercive family process.* Eugene, OR: Castalia.

Patterson, G. R., & Fleischman, M. J. (1979). Maintenance of treatment effects: Some considerations concerning family systems and follow-up data. *Behavior Therapy, 10*, 168–185.

Peterson, L., Wonderlich, S. A., Reaven, N. M., & Mullins, L. L. (1987). Adult educators' response to depression and stress in children. *Journal of Social & Clinical Psychology, 5*, 51–58.

Petti, T. A. (1978). Depression in hospitalized child psychiatry patients: Approaches to measuring depression. *Journal of the American Academy of Child Psychiatry, 22*, 11–21.

Petti, T. A. (1983). Imipramine in the treatment of depressed children. In D. P. Cantwell & G. A. Carlson (Eds.), *Affective disorders in childhood and adolescence: An update* (pp. 375–415). New York: Spectrum.

Petti, T. A., Bornstein, M., Delamater, A., & Conners, C. K. (1980). Evaluation and multimodal treatment of a depressed prepubertal girl. *Journal of the American Academy of Child Psychiatry, 19*, 690–702.

Petti, T. A., & Law, W. (1982). Imipramine treatment of depressed children: A double-blind pilot study. *Journal of Clinical Psychopharmacology, 2*, 107–110.

Powers, D. (1979). The teacher and the adolescent suicide threat. *Journal of School Health, 49*, 561–563.

Poznanski, E. O., Cook, S. C., & Carroll, B. J. (1979). A depression rating scale for children. *Pediatrics, 64*, 442–450.

Preskorn, S. H., Weller, E. B., & Weller, R. A. (1982). Depression in children: Relationship between plasma imipramine levels and response. *Journal of Clinical Psychiatry, 43*, 450–453.

Puig-Antich, J. (1982). Major depression and conduct disorder in prepuberty. *Journal of Child Psychiatry, 21*, 118–128.

Puig-Antich, J., & Gittelman, R. (1982). Depression in childhood and adolescence. In E. S. Paykel (Ed.), *Handbook of affective disorders* (pp. 379–392). New York: Guilford.

Rehm, L. P. (1977). A self-control model of depression. *Behavior Therapy, 8*, 787–804.

Reinherz, H. Z., Stewart-Berghauer, G., Pakiz, B., Frost, A. K., Moeykens, B. A., & Holmes, W. M. (1989). The relationship of early risk and current mediators to depressive symptomatology in adolescence. *Journal of the American Academy of Child and Adolescent Psychiatry, 28*, 942–947.

Reynolds, W. M. (1983, March). *Depression in adolescents: Measurement, epidemiology, and correlates.* Paper presented at annual meeting of National Association of School Psychologists, Detroit.

Reynolds, W. M. (1984). Depression in children and adolescents: Phenomenology, evaluation and treatment. *School Psychology Review, 13*, 171–182.

Reynolds, W. M. (1985). Depression in childhood and adolescence: Diagnosis, assessment, intervention strategies and research. In T. R. Kratochwill (Ed.), *Advances in school psychology* (Vol. 4, pp. 133–189). Hillsdale, NJ: Lawrence Erlbaum.

Reynolds, W. M. (1986a). A model for the screening and identification of depressed children and adolescents in school settings. *Professional School Psychology, 1*, 117–129.

Reynolds, W. M. (1986b). *Reynolds child depression scale.* Odessa, FL: Psychological Assessment Resources.

Reynolds, W. M. (1986c). *Reynolds adolescent depression scale.* Odessa, FL: Psychological Assessment Resources.

Reynolds, W. M., & Coats, K. I. (1986). A comparison of cognitive-behavioral therapy and relaxation training for the treatment of depression in adolescents. *Journal of Consulting & Clinical Psychology, 54*, 653–660.

Reynolds, W. M. & Miller, K. L. (1985). Depression and learned helplessness in mentally retarded and nonmentally retarded adolescents: An initial investigation. *Applied Research in Mental Retardation, 6*, 295–306.

Rie, H. E. (1966). Depression in childhood: A survey of some pertinent contributions. *Journal of the Academy of Child Psychiatry, 5*, 635–685.

Rizzo, J. V., & Zabel, R. H. (1988). *Educating children and adolescents with behavioral disorders: An integrative approach.* Boston: Allyn & Bacon.

Rochlin, G. (1959). The loss complex. *Journal of the American Psychoanalytic Association, 7*, 299–316.

Rutter, M. R. (1986). The developmental psychopathology of depression: Issues and perspectives. In M. R. Rutter, C. E. Izard, & P. B. Read (Eds.), *Depression in young people: Developmental and clinical perspectives* (pp. 3–30). New York: Guilford.

Schloss, P. J., Schloss, C. N., & Harris, L. (1984). A multiple baseline analysis of an interpersonal skills training program for depressed youth. *Behavioral Disorders, 9*, 182–188.

Seifer, R., Nurcombe, B., Scioli, A., & Grapentine, W. L. (1989). Is major depressive disorder in childhood a distinct diagnostic entity? *Journal of the American Academy of Child and Adolescent Psychiatry, 28*, 935–941.

Seligman, M. E. P., & Peterson, C. (1986). A learned helplessness perspective on childhood depression: Theory and research. In M. Rutter, C. E. Izard, & P. B. Read (Eds.), *Depression in young people: Developmental and clinical perspectives* (pp. 223-249). New York: Guilford.

Shure, M. B., & Spivack, G. (1972). Means-ends thinking, adjustment and social class among elementary school-age children. *Journal of Consulting & Clinical Psychology, 38*, 348–353.

Smucker, M. R., Craighead, W. E., Craighead, L. W., & Green, B. J. (1986). Normative and reliability data for the Children's Depression Inventory. *Journal of Abnormal Child Psychology, 14*, 25–39.

Spitz, R. A., & Wolf, K. M. (1946). Anaclitic depression: An inquiry into the genesis of psychiatric conditions in early childhood. *Psychoanalytic Study of the Child, 2*, 313–341.

Spitzer, R. L., Endicott, J., & Robins, E. (1978). Research diagnostic criteria: Rationale and reliability. *Archives of General Psychiatry, 35*, 773–782.

Stark, K. D. (1990). *Childhood depression: School-based intervention.* New York: Guilford.

Stark, K. D., Kaslow, N. J., & Reynolds, W. M. (1987). A comparison of the relative efficacy of self-control therapy and a behavioral problem-solving therapy for depression in children. *Journal of Abnormal Child Psychology, 15*, 91-113.

Stevenson, D. T., & Romney, D. M. (1984). Depression in learning disabled children. *Journal of Learning Disabilities, 17,* 579–582.

Strauss, C. C., Last, C. G., Hersen, M., & Kazdin, A. E. (1988). Association between anxiety and depression in children and adolescents. *Journal of Abnormal Child Psychology, 16,* 57–68.

Teri, L. (1982a). The use of the Beck Depression Inventory with adolescents. *Journal of Abnormal Child Psychology, 10,* 277–282.

Teri, L. (1982b). Depression in adolescence: Its relationship to assertion and various aspects of self-image. *Journal of Clinical Child Psychology, 11,* 101–106.

Thompson, R. J. (1986). Behavior problems in children with developmental and learning disabilities. *International Academy of Research in Learning Disabilities Monograph Series, 3,* 1–125.

Walker, H. M., & McConnell, S. R. (1988). *Walker-McConnell Scale of Social Competence and School Adjustment.* Austin, TX: Pro-Ed.

Walker, H. M., & Severson, H. H. (1990). *Systematic screening for behavior disorders,* Longmont, CO: Sopris West.

Wolfe, V. V., Finch, A. J., Jr., Saylor, CA. F., Blount, R. L., Pallymeyer, T. P., & Carek, D. J. (1987). Negative affectivity in children: A multitrait-multimethod investigation. *Journal of Consulting & Clinical Psychology, 55,* 245–250.

John Maag is an assistant professor at the University of Nebraska, Lincoln. Steven Forness is affiliated with the UCLA Neuropsychiatric Institute.

○ 17 ○

The authors examine the underrepresentation of low-income students and minorities in programs for the gifted and the problems in trying to identify more of them for inclusion. They review the literature and conduct a survey of the states. Although most states voice support for programs for at-risk gifted students, very few special programs tailored to their needs have been developed. A recent federal funding initiative under the Javits Act has resulted in the creation of national models of such programs.

Disadvantaged Gifted Learners: At Risk for Educational Attention

Joyce VanTassel-Baska, James Patton, and Doug Prillaman

Two of the most neglected populations within the rubric of gifted education are (a) individuals whose talents may not be actualized because they are culturally different from the mainstream culture and (b) socially and economically disadvantaged individuals. These populations of students frequently are overlooked for special programs by school districts whose identification procedures fail to find them or whose standards for program entry are above the tested levels that many of these students achieve.

Furthermore, even when these students are found and placed in programs, little attention is given to the background cultural and socioeconomic factors that may seriously affect their performance in special programs and their future achievements beyond these programs. Consequently, the following questions warrant attention:

1. Who are these disadvantaged gifted students, and how do we find them?
2. What common and differential provisions should be made for them in schools?
3. What types of additional facilitation of talent development would be most useful to them?

These questions are fundamental to examining the problems and issues associated with this population.

WHY THE NEED TO FOCUS ON THESE NEGLECTED GIFTED?

Many educators and politicians would question the wisdom of targeting resources for such small-incidence populations within the larger segment of gifted students. Studies have shown, for example, that most gifted learners come from higher socioeconomic backgrounds (Sears & Sears, 1980; VanTassel-Baska & Willis, 1988). Thus, we are looking for a minority within the already limited population of gifted learners. But there are important reasons to pursue this issue:

1. Our sense of a low-incidence rate is not substantiated, for the most part, by data. It is limited by the restrictions we place on the meaning of the term *gifted*. Historically, more students who came from mainstream culture and advantaged home and school backgrounds have been identified as part of the gifted population. Yet, even when we look within restricted definitions according to standardized testing protocols, we find sizable numbers of students, such as 15.5% in an eight-state regional talent search, or some 2,800 students in seventh and eighth grades (VanTassel-Baska & Chepko-Sade, 1986) meeting a criterion for economic disadvantagement. Thus, the incidence rate of disadvantaged gifted learners may be far greater than we have assumed.
2. There is a clear underrepresentation of minority students, particularly blacks, in gifted programs at the K–12 level of schooling (Baldwin, 1985). The disparity between minority representation in the general population and in gifted programs is an issue that must be addressed in a pluralistic society.
3. Colleges and universities, as well as selected professions, are still experiencing an underrepresentation of minorities capable of meeting entry standards.
4. The gap between low socioeconomic status (SES) and higher SES level is widening and, contrary to popular opinion, the upward mobility rate of lower SES individuals is less than 3% (Sennett & Cobb, 1972).
5. The plight of the underclass black family, which is experiencing an increasing rate of single parentage, teenage pregnancy, and high unemployment, points to a need for increased interventions for the children in such situations who constitute the new poor and a sizable segment of tomorrow's adult population.
6. Gifted education has been seen as "elitist," addressing the concerns of a group of learners that many perceive as not being in need of special services, based on their advantaged socioeconomic status. Although such charges clearly do not reflect an appreciation of the need to attend to individual differences in schooling, regardless of the nature or type of difference, gifted educators need to be cognizant of this charge. As a field, we need to focus attention and resources on finding talented learners whose needs may be understood more readily and then clarify the importance of providing a needs-based education to all who show exceptional promise.

It is precisely these neglected gifted learners who do not have the support structures necessary to make it on their own. It is this population of learners that is in the greatest need of programs and services to help optimize their human potential. And it is this population that is at greatest risk of being forgotten in the context of both gifted and general education.

REVIEW OF THE LITERATURE ON DISADVANTAGED GIFTED LEARNERS

A recent 3-year study of key demographic features of "disadvantaged" gifted learners in the Midwest defined *disadvantaged* in purely economic terms (VanTassel-Baska & Willis, 1988). Large-scale sociological studies have focused on consideration of a father's education and occupational status as the key variables (Jencks, 1972). Other recent efforts, within the field of gifted education focused on minority status and cultural difference as important variables in defining the term (Baldwin, 1985; Frasier, 1980).

No one definition appears to be clearly accepted by the field, for these variables can occur singly or in combination (Baldwin, 1985). The result of such variance can be seen in the state of California's omnibus definition of disadvantaged gifted that considers all of the following diverse factors: environmental, economic, cultural, language, and social.

Studies that have been done on disadvantaged gifted populations based on the "culturally different" definition have focused on four needs:

1. The need to use nontraditional measures to identify the disadvantaged student (Bernal & Reyna; 1974, Bruch, 1978; Frasier, 1979; Torrance, 1971).
2. The need to recognize cultural attributes and factors in deciding identification procedures (Baldwin, 1985; Gay, 1978; Samuda, 1975; Miller, 1974; Witty, 1978).
3. The need to focus on strengths in nonacademic areas, particularly in creativity and psychomotor domains (Bruch, 1975; Hilliard, 1976; Torrance, 1977).
4. The need to create programs that address noncognitive skills and that enhance motivation (McLelland, 1978; Moore, 1978).

A recent study commissioned by the Secretary of Education cited the following statistical conditions in our schools as indicative of the need to address the issue of disadvantaged gifted learners more specifically (U.S. Department of Education, 1989):

- Minority students are underrepresented in programs designed to serve gifted and talented students. Although minorities comprise 30% of public school enrollment, they represent less than 20% of the students selected for gifted and talented programs.
- Whereas students from low-income backgrounds comprise 20% of the student population, they make up only 4% of students who perform at the highest levels on standardized tests (those who score at the 95th percentile or above).
- High school seniors from disadvantaged families (in which the mother did not complete high school) are less than half as likely to have participated in gifted and talented programs as are more advantaged seniors.

- Disadvantaged students are far less likely to be enrolled in academic programs that can prepare them for college and are about half as likely to take coursework in advanced math and science than are more advantaged students. Only 2% of high school seniors from poor families take calculus, whereas approximately 7% of those from more advantaged backgrounds do.

Table 1 coalesces the research findings on successful interventions with disadvantaged learners across several study areas. By synthesizing these findings across types of studies, we emerge with a clearer picture of some generic interventions that appear to work well, given the nature of the population. These interventions include:

1. Early and systematic addressing of the needs of these children.
2. Parental involvement in the educational program model.
3. Effective schools' strategies (e.g., time on task, school leadership).
4. Use of experiential and "hands-on" learning approaches.
5. Use of activities that allow for student self-expression.
6. Use of mentors and role models.
7. Involvement of the community.
8. Counseling efforts that address the issue of "cultural values" in facilitating talent development.

Based on these findings, it seems apparent that some general directions have been identified for intervention with disadvantaged gifted learners. It remains for the field of gifted education to translate these areas into systematic program development efforts.

A NATIONAL STUDY

Concern for the culturally different and socioeconomically disadvantaged learner prompted us to explore the nature and extent of programs and services for these populations of gifted students throughout the United States. The study was organized around three basic areas of inquiry:

1. Determining the philosophical and definitional considerations used to address these special populations of gifted learners.
2. Ascertaining the major approaches the states utilized to identify and provide program interventions for these populations.
3. Determining the level and extent of state funding patterns, policies, procedures, and program standards for these learners.

The study was organized in three phases. Phase 1 consisted of a survey of all 50 states and territories seeking answers to the areas of inquiry outlined previously. Phase 2 involved a survey of all local school districts nominated by their states for having active programs for disadvantaged gifted learners. Phase 3 included the development of a series of 12 case studies probing the nature of exemplary programs across the United States for

TABLE 1   *The Disadvantaged Student: Research Topics and Successful Interventions*

Research Topics	Successful Interventions
Early Intervention	Preschool programs Small adult-child ratio Parent participation Service to families
School and Classroom Environment	Motivated leadership/principal expectations Supervision of teachers Teacher morale Emphasis on reading instruction Communication with parents/parental involvement Structured learning environments Staff development Matching of instruction to learning style/diagnostic-prescriptive teaching
Effective Teachers	Use of student ideas Praise and encouragement Verbal recognition of student feelings Time on task More activities per period
Language Development	Teaching the English language Acting out what is read Using ethnic literature Employing creative writing
Mathematics and Science	Using familiar concrete objects as teaching tools and hands-on learning techniques Using minority role models Educating and involving parents Focusing on the *value* of math and science Extending time through out-of-school programs Providing accelerated study through universities and special schools Providing career awareness programs
Counseling	Teaching problem-solving strategies Using cognitive therapy techniques Using mentors/role models Respecting minority culture and related issues Exploring cultural identity issue Focusing on future career roles Early intervention Community involvement
Gifted Disadvantaged	Using mentors Community involvement Early counseling Providing hands-on learning experiences

these learners. This article focuses on highlights from Phases 1 and 2 of the study. A more complete review of the study may be found in a recent monograph (VanTassel-Baska, Patton, & Prillaman, 1991).

PHILOSOPHICAL AND DEFINITIONAL CONSIDERATIONS

Just as the concern for, or interest in, increasing the representation of minorities and low socioeconomic learners in programs for the gifted has been espoused recently by researchers (Baldwin, 1985; Frasier, 1989; Richert, 1987; VanTassel-Baska & Willis, 1988), data from the responding states indicate a general moderate to high level of philosophical orientation in this regard. Yet, as can be gleaned from the subsequent discussions regarding definitional structure, few states actually are operationalizing that philosophical orientation.

Although the literature has consistently supported the definitional structure of low SES as a major variable that should be accounted for in assessment and identification techniques designed to find gifted students (Baldwin, 1985; VanTassel-Baska & Willis, 1988), a limited number of states include low SES as a frequently used factor in identifying students for gifted programs.

The states report race as being a slightly more frequently used factor than SES or an amalgam of race and SES in the process of identifying students for gifted programs. Interestingly, however, 21.2% (18) of the states responding to the survey indicated that they did not include the variable of race at all in the process of identifying students for gifted programs. This last finding is significant in that this variable, rooted in historical and environmental precursers, is generally understood to be a significant factor to consider in developing assessment and identification techniques necessary to uncover the hidden talents of "disadvantaged" learners (Baldwin, 1985)

Because only a minority of states utilize factors of "disadvantagement" in defining students who are eligible for gifted programs, it is not surprising that the majority of responses to questions relating to inclusion of variables such as environmental factors, socioeconomic factors, linguistic factors, cultural factors, and ethnicity in state definitions for gifted students were in the negative direction (see Table 2).

Although cultural differences were reported by the largest percentage of states (32.7%) as the most often used factor of "disadvantagement" used in state definitions for gifted students, the largest percentage of the responding states (38.5%) had no provision for considering "disadvantagement" in the state definitions. Further, although states reported race as the most frequently used factor in the process of identifying students for gifted programs, only eight states included this factor in their public definitions of gifted students.

Generally, the findings indicate that although states have been consistent in their philosophical support of cultural and racial diversity, they have lagged in incorporating these concerns for equity and pluralism into the definitional structures of their gifted programs. Given the present and projected increase of culturally and racially diverse student populations and students from low socioeconomic backgrounds in public schools, implications of the lack of congruence between states' philosophies regarding policies and these demographic factors cause concern.

TABLE 2   Factors of Disadvantagement Used in State Definitions for Gifted Students

N = 52

Types of Factors Used	Frequency of Use By States	Percent*
No inclusion of disadvantaged considerations in state definitions	20	38.5
Consideration of cultural differences	17	32.7
Consideration of ethnicity status	9	17.3
Socioeconomic considerations	14	26.9
Linguistic considerations	13	25.0
Consideration of environmental factors	11	21.2

*Percentages over 100% are caused by overlapping responses to categories.

Who disadvantaged gifted learners are and the size of the pool from which they might be identified require systematic definition at state and local levels. Minority status and low income status are variables that any local district might examine in relationship to students within each group who show promise on standardized measures, and therefore should be considered for special programming at early stages of development.

IDENTIFICATION AND INTERVENTION ISSUES

Several perspectives are associated with examining the identification and intervention approaches states and local districts use in focusing on disadvantaged gifted learners. One of these perspectives is *equality of treatment*. Many states reported no difference in either identification or intervention for the disadvantaged gifted when compared to other gifted learners, based on a conception that equal treatment was legally and politically the most appropriate strategy. This mode of thinking has several strands. One strand argues that the goal of gifted programs is to educate leaders for American society; thus, mainstream culture and values must be assimilated in order to participate in realizing that goal. Another strand argues that gifted programs should educate for "giftedness" regardless of other factors; thus, other kinds of differences should be minimized in favor of best practices for a population of learners based on discernible advanced development. A third strand of this position holds that differentiating identification or program standards based on low SES or race is an insult to those youngsters and ultimately serves them poorly in an educational sense.

A second perspective is that of equity or *affirmative action*. This concept holds that minority students should be included in special programs, such as gifted education, at a level commensurate with their representation in the general population. Because traditional approaches to identification have not found minority students in these numbers, both nontraditional instruments and selection processes should be tried to meet the affirmative action goal. Some states and several local school districts ascribe to this idea in principle and may even meet established quotas; yet support mechanisms for retention and success in gifted programs usually is not assured in such contexts; and data are scanty regarding this issue.

A third perspective worthy of citing is the principle of *individualization*, deeply ingrained in the philosophy of gifted education. Differentiation in identification and intervention would occur most naturally at the level of an individual child, not at the level of an ethnic group or SES category. Consequently, some states could not begin to comment effectively on the survey questions that inferred group treatment based on characteristics beyond aptitude.

The majority of state directors of gifted programs hold to the first and third perspectives as ways of interpreting the seemingly limited provisions for disadvantaged gifted learners at the state level. These perspectives also affect the interpretation of this section of the study. Except for a few states that responded affirmatively to the question of differential services, results regarding identification and intervention practices are duplicative with other populations of gifted learners.

The state questionnaire revealed that directors of state programs perceived their states as embracing a moderate stance toward a broadened conception of giftedness in terms of identification issues, with a mean rating of 3.3 on a 5.0 scale. Nevertheless, the full range of responses to this item reflected a great deal of individual state variation on the issue. Only 22 states responded that use of a broadened conception was extensive.

The data also reveal a generally moderate view toward operationalizing a new conception of giftedness. Even though the field of gifted education has officially embraced an expanded view of who the gifted are in respect to categories (Marland, 1972), the lack of movement in that direction on the part of states 16 years later is surprising. New theoretical and research work published in the late 1970s and early 1980s has also lent additional credibility to an expanded vision of giftedness (Feldman, 1983; Gardner, 1983; Renzulli, 1978; Sternberg, 1985). Yet clearly the states do not reflect these views in standards for funding programs and services.

In the area of nonbiased assessment techniques, all of the states responding to the question indicated some use. But when queried further regarding specific aspects of a nonbiased assessment protocol that might be employed, extent of use dropped dramatically. One component of many nonbiased assessment protocols, for example, is the use of nontraditional tests or use of different norming standards for an existing test. Yet 48.1% of the states indicated little or no use of such testing measures, as contrasted to the 19.2% who indicated only a little use of nonbiased assessment techniques.

This discrepancy may be interpreted in several ways. One interpretation may be that the respondents are not familiar with the specific components of a nonbiased assessment protocol, even though they react affirmatively to the terminology. Another interpretation may be that respondents view techniques such as observation by teachers and parents as more indicative of what is meant by nonbiased assessment. A third interpretation, however, is that reported use of nonbiased assessment techniques is greater than actual use when one examines individual components of an identification system.

The data also reflect strong use of traditional approaches to identifying the disadvantaged gifted, with 88.5% of the respondents indicating the use of norm-referenced tests and 90.4% using teacher nominations. No other techniques were so extensively used in the identification process. The mean response to this item was 4.4, and all states who responded to the item reported some use. Twelve states reported using additional procedures, which vary considerably from one another. No clear pattern of use emerged.

Although one might see merit in not differentiating basic programs and services for the disadvantaged gifted, lest they be denied the best quality program available, there is little basis for the support of not building beyond that basic delivery system to include more specialized services from which they might uniquely profit. Academic self-competence usually is not an issue for advantaged gifted learners, but it may be for disadvantaged ones (VanTassel-Baska et al., 1991). Thus, the need for additional opportunities for counseling, mentorships, and special tutorials seems warranted. We also have ample evidence that these students, even those who perform well on typical in-grade standardized tests, do not score as well as their advantaged counterparts on more powerful test measures (VanTassel-Baska & Willis, 1988). Thus, intervention opportunities that can assist these students with accessing advanced skills also seem warranted.

Currently, support for early intervention programs in general is viewed as the best policy initiative that might be enacted (National Committee for Economic Development, 1988). Not coincidentally, this is the area in which research evidence of long-term effects is the strongest (Brandt, 1986; Lazar, 1982; Schweinhart, 1985). Yet, with our most promising learners among the disadvantaged, this intervention approach is still underutilized.

Clearly, demographic trends reflect the need for greater, rather than less, attention to at-risk populations. As the vehicle in schools for enhancing talent development, gifted education is in a unique position to make a significant impact on this population. But the field must unify around a common understanding of who the disadvantaged are, how they can be found, and what interventions may be the most important for them to receive.

As the data in this study suggest, however, a focus on the disadvantaged gifted is not a major priority area within the state department framework, with a few notable exceptions. Consequently, if we are interested in enhancing efforts in this area, policymakers at the state level must become more cognizant of the issues and find ways to incorporate solutions to them into state standards and funding formulas.

PROGRAM STANDARDS ISSUES

None of the states said they had separate state-developed program standards for disadvantaged gifted students. In fact, when asked this question, 53.1% of the states (n=26) responded "no." The largest percentage of respondents, 44.9% (n=22), indicated that their state program standards were the same for the disadvantaged gifted and gifted students who are not identified as disadvantaged.

The data indicate that 82.7% of the states (n=43) employ no state initiatives to monitor LEA implementation of programs for disadvantaged gifted students. But 17.3% (n=9) of the states indicated their state had initiatives to monitor local programs for including disadvantaged gifted students in the gifted program.

When asked if special materials, handbooks, guidelines had been developed by their state, 69.2% of the respondents (n=36) stated "no." Similarly, six states, representing 11.5% of the total survey, gave no response to this question. But 19.2% (n=10) indicated that these materials either exist or are in the process of being developed.

The final question on the survey asked whether data were available on the number of disadvantaged gifted students being served in each state. Forty-six (88.5%) of the respondents replied that these data were not available. Six (11.5%) states responded affirmatively.

In its 1983 report, *A Nation at Risk*, the National Commission on Excellence in Education stated, "The Federal Government, in cooperation with states and localities, should help meet the needs of key groups of students such as the gifted and talented" (p. 32). Four years later Congress passed the first federal initiative to aid education for gifted and talented students. This meager bill, a $20 million authorization, is included in the larger Omnibus Education Bill and provides funds for research, personnel preparation, and innovative projects. Since approval of the bill in 1988, $8 million currently has been appropriated, with a large percentage being applied to model programs for these populations throughout the country.

States vary widely in terms of interest or ability to assist localities in developing and maintaining gifted programs. Figure 1 depicts the level of support by states (Mitchell, 1984). Consequently, it was not surprising to find no set-asides for special populations, except in one state.

The majority of states have developed standards for services to gifted and talented students. Those available for review provide ample information for localities to use in developing comprehensive programs. Maker (1986, p. 233) suggested that programs should adhere to seven components:

1. Provide a variety of options.
2. Be coordinated and articulated.
3. Have clearly defined policies and procedures.
4. Be well planned.
5. Demonstrate success through well designed, responsive evaluations.
6. Have a sound theoretical base.
7. Respond to the needs of the community.

Kaplan (1988) describes eight program standards as benchmarks of quality control:

1. Goals and objectives.
2. Decision making.
3. Monitoring.
4. Limitations.
5. Expenditures.
6. Perceptions.
7. Training.
8. Philosophy.

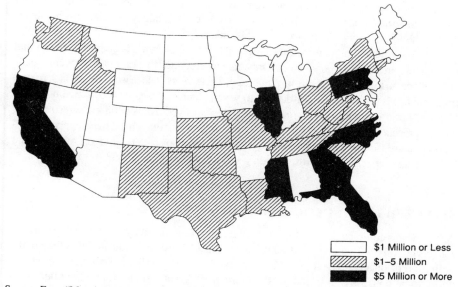

	$1 Million or Less
	$1–5 Million
	$5 Million or More

Source: From "Mapping a State Advocacy Plan for the Gifted" by P. B. Mitchell, 1984, *Journal for the Education of the Gifted, 7*(4), pp. 252–269. Adapted with permission.

FIGURE 1   *State Appropriations for Education of Gifted Students*

Several states do refer to the disadvantaged gifted in their state plans. In Mississippi, state programs are not mandated; however, local education agencies may design programs for four distinct populations—intellectually gifted, talented, gifted handicapped, and disadvantaged gifted. The State Department of Education (SDE) provides a specific definition of the gifted disadvantaged population. The regulations for approved programs and criteria for classification of gifted and talented students and culturally and educationally deprived students in Nebraska cite program criteria and selection procedures as two areas in which specific guidelines are to be followed. Within the program criteria, LEAs must provide evidence of planning to "assure access to programs by members of minority or educationally disadvantaged groups" (p. 4).

The selection procedures section of the Nebraska regulations specify that "instruments and criteria shall be chosen to reflect the emphasis of the differentiated curriculum to be provided and to protect members of minority or educationally disadvantaged groups from test bias discrimination" (p. 6). Likewise, the Minnesota Standards require that all instruments and procedures must be examined for cultural bias and "efforts must be employed to insure that representation and participation of all student populations in gifted and talented educational programs include individuals of all races, creeds, national origins, genders, physical handicaps, or economic status" (p. 6).

Although most states do not have data on the number of disadvantaged gifted students served, several states report some estimates by racial or ethnic categories. In Florida, 5,202 culturally diverse students (Black Non-Hispanic, Hispanic, Asian, and American

Indian) are receiving services in programs for the gifted and talented. Approximately 35% of the gifted students in California are members of minority populations; however, the number of low-income disadvantaged is unknown.

Data from the 52 states and territories reveal that little attention is given to proportional funding for various gifted populations. Only one state reported that funds (20%) were specifically allocated to programs for disadvantaged gifted learners. The reasons for the lack of proportional funds probably are attributable to several factors. One, the total state budget for all gifted programs is relatively small. Two, states have yet to devote time and resources to underrepresented populations (gifted women, underachievers, gifted handicapped). Program standards for the gifted disadvantaged population also are very limited. Only one state has developed specific standards regarding services to this population.

SELECTED LOCAL PROGRAM ISSUES

A survey was completed by 57 local school districts nominated by their state departments for serving on disadvantaged gifted learners. Only 12 districts indicated that they had a definition of disadvantaged gifted learners, and of those, only nine districts reported a definitional construct. Four included culturally different, minority, and the poor. Two sample definitions from these local districts are:

1. . . . those children regardless of race or ethnic group who may have language patterns and experiences, cultural backgrounds, economic disadvantages and/or educational disadvantages or differences which make it difficult for them to demonstrate their potential using traditional identification procedures.
2. Intellectually gifted children and youth are those who have potential for outstanding performance by virtue of superior intellectual abilities. Intellectually gifted means outstanding performance or potential for outstanding performance by virtue of superior intellectual abilities (K.A.R. 91-12-22 [q]). Both those with demonstrated achievement and those with minimal or low performance who give evidence of high potential in general intellectual ability, specific academic aptitudes, and/or creative thinking abilities are included in this definition.

Most frequently cited nontraditional identification measures used by responding districts were the Ravens Progressive Matrices (n=5) and the Kaufman-ABC (n=3). In the area of observation of children by adults, the most frequently used scales were locally developed (n=9). Some districts used the Renzulli scales or portions thereof (n=3). For creativity indices, the majority of districts reporting indicated use of the Torrance Test of Creative Thinking in some way (n=7). The most frequently used norm-referenced tests were traditional, in-grade standardized achievement tests (n=10). Additionally, a few districts used the Cognitive Abilities Test (n=3).

Very few of the local school districts responding to the survey showed congruence in their perspective about successes or problems in working with disadvantaged gifted students. The only perspectives indicated by at least two respondents were the following: Successes were perceived to be (a) achieving in the face of adversity, (b) strength of creative skills for personal and academic coping, (c) overcoming language difficulties, and (d) being identified for special programs. Problems were perceived to be in the following areas: (a) peer pressure, (b) a familial pattern that lacked resources to foster academic learning, (c) lack of self-esteem, (d) lack of funding for programs, (e) language deficiencies, and (f) transiency.

Even given the problems, respondents reported a hopeful note regarding the future education for these students:

"Getting this program in place has been a very slow process. I have received total support from staff and administration. The main problem is that the Mexican population comes and goes, and, therefore, ongoing instructional time is minimal. Our program goals usually go unrealized because of the transiency of our students during the implementation phase." (Coordinator A)

"Progress in improving the academic situation for gifted Native American students is very slow. However, we are gradually making progress. Our most important success has been the growth of acceptance, among Indian and white students, teachers, and parents, of there being gifted Indian students." (Coordinator B)

"Our programs are designed as supplemental, so we lack true program continuity. What we do find, though, is that teachers will send us students who don't "qualify" for traditional gifted/talented programs because these kids display a special talent. In our courses they shine because their strengths are being recognized and enhanced. They can only be successful. Many teachers have reported that even short-term exposure to our program enhances other kinds of in-school performance." (Coordinator J)

"Small rural schools with great family stability (in terms of location—families stay in one town for generations) develop expectations for certain kids because 'that's how the family is.' Many kids never are expected to achieve until they attend our special courses." (Coordinator K)

Based on the survey results from local school districts that were nominated by their state directors of gifted education for running special programs for disadvantaged gifted learners, we can discern key issues for this population at the local level. These issues tend to revolve around the dimensions of definition, identification, intervention, delivery, and evaluation approaches used in programs for this population.

Definition

Just as was found at the state level of analysis, only a limited definitional structure is in place for disadvantaged gifted learners. Most districts do not define the term and tend to operationalize it within the demands of the local context. For example, if a local district has a 90% minority population, the definition of disadvantaged tilts toward that minority group. If, on the other hand, the district is primarily low socioeconomic, made up of many ethnic groups, the focus tilts toward the issue of low SES. Although such a stance appears to be practical at the local level, it does limit the conception of who may need to be served under the rubric of the disadvantaged gifted.

A clear definition that recognizes different types and levels of disadvantagement is needed at the policy level in local school districts. Only through such an approach can low-SES students or minority students have a chance of service, particularly in districts in which their numbers do not dominate.

Identification

Several of the identification practices that these local school districts use appear promising, yet do not represent a stringent interpretation of the recommended practices from the literature. The most promising practices appear to be the most personalized—when a sensitive adult nominates or promotes a child in the school context. In these districts this has been a favored technique, and it has been found to be successful. The main danger inherent in its use, however, is in missing children who would do well in programs but were not discovered based on individual observations. All of the districts reported using multiple measures, however. This increases the likelihood that a child would be included through another approach.

A second promising practice appeared to be the "tryout" system, in which all students were given "gifted" activities to perform and then judged on the basis of their capacity to perform these activities in a classroom setting. Such an approach equalizes opportunity to demonstrate readiness without using tests as an arbitrary screening device. Its disadvantage, however, lies in the administrative arena of assuring all students access to tryouts in the regular classroom and training all teachers in a given context to provide the key activities. Nevertheless, it significantly strengthens the relationship between program expectations and student identification practices.

Intervention

Program intervention approaches used in these local districts mirror the state data regarding this issue. Traditional gifted program approaches are the norm, and more tailored or personalized program approaches are the exception. This finding is particularly surprising at the local level, where advertised programs for disadvantaged learners are provided. One might expect greater diversity in programming models and greater experimentation with differential program prototypes.

Of special note is the lack of systematic intervention at early ages, and the lack of counseling programs—two areas in which current studies and demonstration programs for these learners are consistent in regard to importance and efficacy. The need to provide more tailored and personalized interventions for disadvantaged gifted learners appears to be great, even in districts that are most responsive to their needs.

Delivery

These local districts did appear to be providing some differentiation for disadvantaged gifted learners at the level of classroom delivery, particularly as it related to keying in on individual characteristics of the students in the area of affective needs. Evidence of responsiveness to ethnic diversity also was prevalent through classroom techniques. The district data provide interesting portraits of perceived differences between advantaged and disadvantaged learners, with the greatest congruence among district respondents coming in the areas of (a) preference for oral over written work, (b) need for confirmation of ability, and (c) erratic performance. These perceived differences point toward a need for recognition of these factors and tailoring of curriculum and instruction to respond to them in deliberate ways.

Evaluation

Evaluation approaches that these districts utilize are, for the most part, standard ones used in the assessment of efficacy in all gifted programs. Thus, these programs experience the same problems in evaluation that are apparent in the field as a whole—an overreliance on attitudinal perceptions of various groups about the program and a lack of student impact data. In fact, only a few of these programs were able to produce valid student impact data, even though the majority of them have been in place for several years. If we are to learn and advance as a field on this issue, there will have to be well designed evaluation studies of existing programs. Little current evidence indicates that such data exist or can be utilized effectively to advance our knowledge.

Conclusion

The local district questionnaire has provided interesting insights into several dimensions of working with disadvantaged gifted learners. It further substantiates the general picture provided by the state survey that concrete policies at all levels are lacking regarding service to this population. Yet, it yielded some promising identification practices and classroom delivery approaches. It corroborated findings from the state questionnaire also regarding lack of differentiated programs and limited evaluation data.

OVERALL RECOMMENDATIONS

The recommendations of this national study emerge out of a careful consideration of the data available and the noticeable lack of data in several key areas of the questionnaire probes. An attempt was made to recommend policy based on three central aspects of the study: definitional issues, identification and intervention, and program standards and funding. The policy recommendations have been generated for consideration at state and local levels, although they carry implications for national policy as well. The major recommendations of the study are:

1. *We should eliminate the use of the term "disadvantaged."*

In describing culturally diverse populations, for example, the term *disadvantaged* carries a negative connotation. Cultures differ from each other; inherently, no one culture or class is superior to another. Accordingly, "cultural diversity" merely acknowledges the condition of such status without placing a value judgment on such a condition.

In an attempt to create awareness of inequities in our educational system, we have resorted to negative terminology. Like the word "handicapped," "disadvantaged" carries both a negative connotation and a generic notion of deficit or deficiency. This generic notion is problematic because individuals can be both disadvantaged and resilient, handicapped and gifted. And because the term is so generic, it frequently creates its own meaning in a particular local context.

To identify children who may be at risk for educational opportunities commensurate with their abilities because of a variety of factors, such as "disadvantaged," is to diffuse the issue in a way that blocks appropriate interventions. It is much more appropriate to consider the leading factors contributing to at-risk status—low socioeconomic status, member of an ethnic minority, handicapped in a specific way, a child of an unstable home environment (e.g., alcoholism, abuse), or language deficiency. These factors should be seen as the basis for special identification and intervention approaches whether they are present in 1% of a given school district population or 80% of that population. And in contexts where "at-risk" and "at-promise" conditions both prevail, gifted educators are obligated to intervene.

The terminology of "unserved" and "underserved" also have been used frequently to describe this population. Unfortunately, because of the stage of development of the field of gifted education, these terms only further confuse the issue because many other sub-populations of gifted learners—the highly gifted, gifted girls, the young primary gifted child, and certain categories of giftedness such as leadership—remain un- or underserved. Consequently, the "at-risk" factors that focus our attention on sociological issues of context are more useful for formulating policy.

2. We need to translate expressed philosophical concerns for "at-risk" learners into definitional structures of giftedness.

All levels of data collection have a strong orientation toward wanting these learners to be included in gifted programs. Yet, at the point of entry into the structure of the program—namely, the operational definition—few states and local districts focus on an inclusionary statement. Until educational institutions explicitly define who they mean by "at-risk" gifted learners and seek to identify and program for them, the current status of service will show little change.

A suggested example of a definitional structure that focuses on the specific factor of disadvantagement is:

a. Students who come from low-income families in which the parents' educational and occupational status is also commensurately low.
b. Students who come from different cultural backgrounds that require an understanding of the cultural perspective in order to find and serve them appropriately.
c. Students who possess limited English proficiency because of recency of immigration or community norms.

d. Students who possess physical or learning handicaps that may mask their potential.

e. Students who come from dysfunctional family backgrounds (e.g., single parent, abuse, alcoholism).

f. Students who possess a combination of these characteristics.

3. *We must recognize that "at-risk" gifted learners share many commonalities with all gifted learners and yet vary in significant ways.*

This knowledge requires educators to combine unique elements used in defining, identifying, and developing programs for these learners, with qualitatively different approaches needed for all gifted learners. Just as the gifted share common characteristics with all learners, so too does the "at-risk" gifted learner share many characteristics with both typical learners and other gifted learners.

Nevertheless, it is in the area of deviance that our efforts to program must focus. Special characteristics create special educational needs that should be addressed differentially if we are to enhance the capacities of at-risk children. Thus, a recognition of deviance and a willingness to address it are required in charting a qualitatively distinctive program for these learners. Special characteristics also imply a need for seeing these students in different ways. Thus, an identification protocol that is cognizant of background factor differences is necessary.

4. *We need to initiate the use of multiple measures, among them assessment measures perceived to be nonbiased, for the identification and selection of at-risk students into gifted programs.*

Based on our questionnaire studies on identification, districts should have little reason not to employ a combinational model for identification that places some validity on nonbiased assessment procedures. The protocol may vary as long as an effort is made to include in the context instrumentation that may be less biased.

A selection committee process or selection that considers child-centered issues beyond the numbers added on the identification form also appears prudent. If our goal is to find promising at-risk learners, we must find ways to establish a pool of such students within each of the risk factor categories, a task calling for nontraditional approaches.

5. *We should encourage the use of a "try-out' program for all students nominated to the gifted program in which responsiveness to differentiated classroom curriculum becomes a part of the selection paradigm.*

Too much emphasis on gifted program development has been placed on the identification process in a vacuum, devoid of significant interaction to the actual curriculum provided to students. This situation is especially problematic when we consider at-risk students who are being overlooked in our quest to find the traditionally gifted learner. Consequently, if we reverse the order of program development, so that enriched opportunities in the classroom become one level of identification, we will have established an important, yet frequently missing, link between identification and curriculum intervention.

6. *We need to develop program prototypes for use with atypical gifted learners.*

The study points up a real need for prototypical models for intervention with at-risk gifted learners. Although the recommendations in Table 1 are useful in that they reflect the current literature, it is equally important that our programs begin to generate successful models that work in the local context. At present there is a real need in this area. Most of the interventions used with these learners are the standard for all gifted programs.

Providing equal treatment programs has merit, but greater merit is inherent in providing additional levels of programming to at-risk learners—programming that addresses some of their unique needs. This value-added concept of programming might occur in the context of the regular gifted program through an IEP model, individual contract, or more personalized delivery of services. Special groupings of such learners based on the particular risk factor might have merit in some contexts.

7. *We need to develop individual services such as tutoring, mentoring, and counseling for at-risk gifted learners.*

Insight into what works for at-risk learners suggests the importance of personalized services, delivered by a caring individual who understands the nature of the child's status and has ideas for helping him or her negotiate education successfully. This individual represents an important link for at-risk learners in the schools.

Because volunteer personnel likely would have to be utilized for such a service, two key groups should be considered: (a) community groups containing large numbers of highly skilled retirees and unemployed individuals, and (b) student groups, of college age and even high school students, who could work in such a program as their community service contribution. If businesses want to assist schools, organizing a community support network for these learners would be a wonderful way to contribute to the individual lives of such children.

8. *We should consider a "matching funds" model to encourage program development for at-risk gifted students.*

Just as volunteer assistance may be necessary to activate the level of personalized service these learners require, so, too, funding models will have to go beyond the gifted budget in order to make inroads into viable programs and services. Linkages to programs focusing on each "at-risk" factor would seem to be the best strategy, coupled with the funding initiatives in a local context that frequently may focus on this type of child if the incidence rate is perceived substantial enough. This type of shared funding must be systematically explored so that we have the flexibility to try new practices and prototypes with these learners. Without additional incentive funding, our current level of limited programming is apt to prevail.

9. *We need to collect systematic data on at-risk students being served in gifted programs.*

As the study has revealed, few local school districts and states are capable of providing incidence data regarding at-risk gifted populations. Moreover, even those capable of this level of reporting are not systematically collecting evaluation data on classroom/program effectiveness with this kind of learner. Consequently, some funding and energy should be targeted at data collection efforts on this population. Because the evaluation problem is endemic of the gifted education field in general, accomplishing this needed program measure may be difficult. Yet the success of future work with disadvantaged gifted learners depends heavily on our having access to good data about program practices.

REFERENCES

Baldwin, A. (1985). I'm Black but Look at Me, I am also Gifted. *Gifted Child Quarterly, 31,* 180–185.

Bernal, E.M., & Reyna, J. (1974). Analysis and identification of giftedness in Mexican American children: A pilot study. In B.O. Boxton (Ed.), *A resource manual of information on educating the gifted and talented.* Reston, VA: Council for Exceptional Children.

Brandt, R. (1986). On long-term effects of early education: A conversation with Lawrence Schweinhart. *Educational Leadership, 44*(3), 14–18.

Bruch, C.B. (1975). Assessment of creativity in culturally different gifted children. *Gifted Child Quarterly, 19*(2), 164–174.

Bruch, C.B. (1978). Recent insights on the culturally different gifted. *Gifted Child Quarterly, 22*(3), 374–393.

Feldman, D. (Ed.). (1983). *Developmental conceptions of giftedness.* San Francisco: Jossey-Bass.

Frasier, M.M. (1979). Rethinking the issue regarding the culturally disadvantaged gifted. *Exceptional Children, 45*(7), 538–542.

Frasier, M.M. (1980). Programming for the culturally diverse, in J. Jordan & J. Grossi, *An Administrator's Handbook on Designing Programs for the Gifted and Talented,* Reston, VA: Council for Exceptional Children.

Frasier, M. (1989). A perspective on identifying black students for gifted programs. In Maker, J. (Ed.), *Critical issues in gifted education* (Vol. 2). Rockville, MD: Aspen Publications.

Gardner, H. (1983). *Frames of mind.* New York: Basic Books.

Gay, J. (1978). A proposed plan for identifying black gifted children. *Gifted Child Quarterly, 22*(3), 353–360.

Hilliard, A. (1976). *Alternatives to IQ testing: An approach to the identification of the gifted in minority children* (Rep. No. 75175). San Francisco: San Francisco State University.

Jencks, C. (1972). *Inequality.* New York: Basic Books.

Kaplan, S.N. (1988, October). Maintaining a gifted program. *Roeper Review, 11*(1). October 1988.

Lazar, I. (1988). Measuring the effects of early childhood programs. *Community Education Journal, 15*(2), 8–11.

Maker, C.J. (Ed.). (1986). *Critical Issues in Gifted Education: Defensible Programs For the Gifted.* Austin, TX: Pro Ed.

Marland, S. (1972). *U.S. Report to Congress on the Gifted and Talented.* Washington, DC: Government Printing Office.

McClelland, D.C. (1978). Managing motivation to expand human freedom. *American Psychologist, 33,* 201–210.

Miller, L. (1974). *The testing of black students: A symposium.* Englewood Cliffs, NJ: Prentice-Hall.

Mitchell, P.B. (1984). Mapping a state advocacy plan for the gifted. *Journal for the Education of the Gifted, 7*(4), 252–69.

Moore, B. (1978). Career education for disadvantaged gifted high school students. *Gifted Child Quarterly, 22*(3), 332–337.

National Commission on Excellence in Education. (1983). *A Nation At Risk: The Imperative For Educational Reform.* Washington, DC: United States Department of Education.

National Committee for Economic Development. (1988). *Children In Need.* Washington, DC.

Olszewski, P., Kulreke, M., Willis, G., & Krasney, N. (1987). A study of the predictors of success in fast paced classes and the validity of entrance scores, Evanston, IL: Northwestern University, Center for Talent Development.

Renzulli, J. (1978). What makes giftedness: Re-examining a definition. *Phi Delta Kappan, 60,* 180–184.

Richert, S. (1987). Rampant problems and promising practices in the identification of disadvantaged gifted students. *Gifted Child Quarterly, 31,* 149–154.

Samuda, R.J. (1975). *Psychological testing of American minorities: Issues and consequences.* New York: Dodd, Mead.

Schweinhart, L.J. (1985). The Preschool Challenge. High/Scope Early Childhood Policy Papers, no. 4. Ypsilanti, MI: High/Scope Education Research Foundation.

Sears, P., & Sears, R. (1980). 1528 little geniuses and how they grew, *Psychology Today*, February, 28–43.

Sennett, R., & Cobb, J. (1972). *The Hidden Injuries of Class.* New York: Random House.

Sternberg, R. (1985). *Beyond IQ.* Cambridge, MA: Cambridge University Press.

Torrance, E.P. (1971). Are the Torrance Tests of Creative Thinking biased against or in favor of disadvantaged groups? *Gifted Child Quarterly, 15,* 75–80.

Torrance, E.P. (1977). *Discovery and nurturance of giftedness in the culturally different.* Reston, VA: Council for Exceptional Children.

United States Department of Education. (1989). *No gifted wasted: Effective strategies for educating highly able, disadvantaged students in mathematics and science.* Washington, DC: Government Printing Office.

VanTassel-Baska, J., & Chepko-Sade, D. (1986). *An incidence study of disadvantaged gifted students in the Midwest,* Evanston, IL: Northwestern University, Center for Talent Development.

VanTassel-Baska, J., Olszewski, P., & Kulieke, M. (1991). Differences between advantaged and disadvantaged populations on personality measures. Paper presented at the American Education Research Association Annual Meeting, Chicago.

VanTassel-Baska, J., Patton, J., & Prillaman, D. (1991). *Gifted youth at risk.* Reston, VA: Council for Exceptional Children.

VanTassel-Baska, J., & Willis, G. (1988). A three year study of the effects of low income on SAT scores among the academically able. *Gifted Child Quarterly, 31,* 169–173.

Witty, E.P. (1978). Equal educational opportunity for gifted minority children. *Gifted Child Quarterly, 22*(3), 344–352.

Joyce VanTassel-Baska is the Jody and Layton Smith Professor of Education and director of the Center for Gifted Education. James Patton is the associate dean of the School of Education, and Doug Prillaman is a retired professor of special education. All three authors are at the College of William and Mary in Virginia.

Author Index

Subject Index

A

Academic achievement
  of children with attention deficit disorders, 254
  effect sizes related to, 217-220
  effects of videodisc program on, 154
  factors effecting, 111
  of learning disabled students, 110-111
  of traumatic brain injured students, 280-281
Acute depression, 345. *See also* Depression
Administrator attitudes, 101
Adolescents
  developmental characteristics of attention deficit disorder in, 261
  learning disabilities among, 105-106. *See also* Learning disabled students
  prevalence of depression in, 347. *See also* Depression
  prevalence of head injury in, 268
  reading proficiency of, 113
Adults, attention deficit disorder in, 261
African-American students, 370
AIDS. *See* Human immuno-deficiency virus (HIV)
American Academy of Pediatrics, 332, 334-335
Anaclitic depression, 345. *See also* Depression
Anhedonia, 343
Anxiety disorders
  in children with attention deficit disorder, 249
  depression and, 354
Aptitude by Treatment Interaction (ATI), 234-235

Assessment. *See also* Curriculum-based assessment; Curriculum-based measurement; Functional assessment
  of attention deficit disorder, 252-254
  cost and benefits of traditional, 228-230
  to determine developmental delays, 35-36
  of home environment, 12
  of infants and children for transitions, 20-22
  as measure of program effectiveness, 70-71
  under Part H, 37-38
  of traumatic brain injured students, 277-278
  treatment implications for traditional, 233-235
  use of nonbiased, 385
At risk, 35, 36
Attention deficit disorder (ADD)
  assessment of, 252-254
  and associated conditions, 249, 251-252
  cross-generational finding regarding, 262
  depression in children with, 249, 261, 354
  developmental characteristics of, 260-261
  education legislation and, 242-246
  educational treatment of, 256-258
  family counseling and parent training for, 258-260
  gender issues in, 260
  history of, 246-249
  medical treatment of, 254-256
  overview of, 241-242
  social deficits associated with, 261-262
  with and without hyperactivity, 247-249, 261

Attention deficit hyperactivity disorder (ADHD). *See also* Attention deficit disorder
  behavior disorders and, 252
  explanation of, 247, 249
  peer relations among children with, 261
Autism, 354

B

Basic skills, instruction for learning disabled students in, 108, 112-119
Behavior assessment, 232
Behavior control, 119-121
Behavior disorders
  attention deficit disorders and, 251-252, 257, 262
  classification of, 228, 231, 233, 234
  depression and, 354
Behavior problems, in traumatic brain injured students, 280-281
Bevin, H., 328
Bipolar depressive disorders, 343-344
Brain damage syndrome, 246, 247. *See also* Attention deficit disorder (ADD)
Brain injury. *See* Traumatic brain injury
Buros Mental Measurement Yearbook, 236-237

C

Catherization, 340
Child Service Demonstration Centers (CSDCs), 106-108
Children. *See also* Adolescents; Infants; Preschool-age children
  developmental characteristics of attention deficit disorder in elementary school age, 261